THE PAPERS OF
WOODROW WILSON
VOLUME 59
MAY 10–31, 1919

SPONSORED BY THE WOODROW WILSON
FOUNDATION
AND PRINCETON UNIVERSITY

THE PAPERS OF

WOODROW WILSON

ARTHUR S. LINK, *EDITOR*

DAVID W. HIRST, *SENIOR ASSOCIATE EDITOR*

JOHN E. LITTLE, *ASSOCIATE EDITOR*

MANFRED F. BOEMEKE, *ASSOCIATE EDITOR*

DENISE THOMPSON, *ASSISTANT EDITOR*

MARGARET D. LINK, *EDITORIAL ASSISTANT*

PHYLLIS MARCHAND, *INDEXER*

Volume 59
May 10–31, 1919

PRINCETON, NEW JERSEY
PRINCETON UNIVERSITY PRESS
1988

Printed in the United States of America
by Princeton University Press
Princeton, New Jersey

INTRODUCTION

THIS volume begins only three days after the presentation by Clemenceau of the Preliminary Conditions of Peace to the German delegates at the Trianon Palace at Versailles on May 7, 1919. Now commences what might be called the unknown two-month period of the Paris Peace Conference, during which the Big Four negotiate with a German delegation determined to achieve a settlement that will not for long prevent Germany's recovery to the status of a world power. The Germans' most powerful ideological weapon, which they use with consummate skill, are the Fourteen Points. By the time this volume ends, the Germans have presented objections and counterproposals to all the major provisions of the preliminary peace treaty, except for those providing for the virtual disarmament of their country. These the Germans accept on the understanding that the first order of business of the League of Nations will be to set under way a worldwide reduction of armaments. As the documents in this volume reveal, the Big Four consider the German case with high seriousness and a deep concern to achieve, according to their perceptions, a just and lasting peace. These negotiations are still in progress as this volume ends.

During all this give and take, the Big Four labor under constraints that make it almost inevitable that they will have to soften the terms of the preliminary peace treaty. The constraint that operates with the most powerful force during the period covered by this volume is the almost certain likelihood that no German government can be found that will sign a harsh and patently unjust peace treaty. To the Four, the threat of a German refusal to sign raises the specter of the necessity of occupying and administering Germany for an indefinite period at a huge cost in manpower and money, and this at the very time when the Allied governments are near bankruptcy and the demobilization of the British and American armies is proceeding rapidly.

Before May 7, the Big Four have concentrated upon the preliminary peace treaty with Germany. But once that document is completed, the Four are compelled to confront directly the numerous problems of a Europe-wide settlement, decisions concerning which they have heretofore been able to postpone. The major task facing Wilson, Lloyd George, and Clemenceau is that of thwarting Italian ambitions in the region of the Adriatic and, now, also of thwarting Italy's determination to acquire territory in the former Ottoman Empire and to become a major near eastern power. The wrangling with the Italians over an Adriatic settlement intensifies, and all efforts at compromise founder upon Italy's implacable determination to stay in Fiume. The controversy over Italy's imperial pretentions in Asia Minor is also complicated by rival British and French ambitions and Greek claims in the area. At the same time, the Big Four have to come to terms with one of the major results of the Allied victory— the dissolution of the Austro-Hungarian Empire and the fact of the territorial imperialism of two of the so-called successor states, Poland and Rumania. The Big Four talk for many weary hours about how to get the Poles out of Galicia and how to restrain Rumanian troops from rampaging through Hungarian Transylvania. In addition, the Four want to protect Jews and other minorities in the two historically anti-Semitic states of Poland and Rumania. But the more the Big Four try to achieve these objectives, the more evident it becomes that their power to impose their own settlements on eastern Europe is problematic.

Another matter that consumes the time and debilitates the energies of the Big Four is the question, discussed since the first days of the peace conference, of the possibility of doing anything to influence the outcome of the civil war in Russia. When Lenin returns what the Big Four regard as an unsatisfactory reply to the Nansen proposals, the Big Four open negotiations with Kolchak, who seems on the verge of triumph, with the aim of assuring the creation of a new democratic Russia. These futile efforts only illustrate once again the powerlessness of the Big Four to control the fate of most of Europe.

Meanwhile, Wilson achieves a fairly good recovery from his viral and neurologic illnesses of April and plays an active and important role in these discussions and events. However, he is no longer the commanding actor on the grand stage; Lloyd George is beginning to emerge as the most important force in the Supreme Council.

"VERBATIM ET LITERATIM"

In earlier volumes of this series, we have said the following: "All documents are produced *verbatim et literatim*, with typographical and spelling errors corrected in square brackets only when necessary for clarity and ease of reading." The following essay explains our textual methods and review procedures.

We have never printed and do not intend to print critical, or corrected, versions of documents. We print them exactly as they are, with a few exceptions which we always note.

We never use the word *sic* except to denote the repetition of words in a document; in fact, we think that a succession of *sics* defaces a page. We usually repair words in square brackets when letters are missing. As we have said, we also repair words in square brackets for clarity and ease of reading. Our general rule is to do this when we, ourselves, cannot read the word without having to stop to puzzle out its meaning. Jumbled words and names misspelled beyond recognition of course have to be repaired. We correct the misspelling of names in documents in the footnotes identifying those persons.

However, when an old man writes to Wilson saying that he is glad to hear that Wilson is "comming" to Newark, or a semiliterate farmer from Texas writes phonetically, we see no reason to correct spellings in square brackets when the words are perfectly understandable. We do not correct Wilson's misspellings unless they are unreadable, except to supply in square brackets letters missing in words. For example, he consistently spelled "belligerent" as "belligerant." Nothing would be gained by correcting "belligerant" in square brackets.

We think that it is very important for several reasons to follow the rule of *verbatim et literatim*. Most important, a document has its own integrity and power, particularly when it is not written in perfect literary form. There is something very moving in seeing a Texas dirt farmer struggling to express his feelings in words, or a semiliterate former slave doing the same thing. Second, in Wilson's case it is essential to reproduce his errors in letters which he typed himself, since he usually typed badly when he was in an agitated state. Third, since style is the essence of the person, we would never correct grammar or make tenses consistent, as one correspondent has urged us to do. Fourth, we think it is very important that we print exact transcripts of Charles L. Swem's copies of Wilson's letters. Swem made many mistakes (we correct them in footnotes from a reading of his shorthand books), and Wilson let them pass. We thus have to assume that Wilson often did not read his letters before signing them, and this, we think, is a significant fact.

We think that our series would be worthless if we produced unreliable texts, and we go to considerable effort to make certain that the texts are authentic.

Our typists are highly skilled and proofread their transcripts carefully as soon as they have typed them. The Editor sight proofreads documents once he has assembled a volume and is setting its annotation. The Editors who write the notes read through documents several times and are careful to check any anomalies. Then, once the manuscript volume has been completed and all notes checked, the Editor and Senior Associate Editor orally proofread the documents against the copy. They read every comma, dash, and character. They note every absence of punctuation. They study every nearly illegible word in written documents.

Once this process of "establishing the text" is completed, the manuscript volume goes to our editor at Princeton University Press, who checks the volume carefully and sends it to the printing plant. The galley proofs are read against copy by the Press' proofreaders. We ourselves read the galley proofs three times. Our copyeditor gives them a sight reading against the manuscript copy to look for remaining typographical errors and to make sure that no line has been dropped. The Editor and Senior Associate Editor also sight read them against documents and copy. We then get the page proofs, which have been corrected at the Press. We check all the changes three times. In addition, we get *revised* pages and check them twice.

This is not the end. The Editor, Senior Associate Editor, and Dr. Boemeke give a final reading to headings, description-location lines, and notes. Finally, our indexer of course reads the pages word by word. Before we return the pages to the Press, she brings in a list of queries, all of which are answered by reference to the documents.

Our rule in the Wilson Papers is that our tolerance of error is zero. No system and no person can be perfect. There may be errors in our volumes. However, we believe that we have done everything humanly possible to avoid error; the chance is remote that what looks at first glance like a typographical error is indeed an error.

N.B. Our readers will please note that the family name of Whitney Hart Shepardson is misspelled as "Shephardson" in Volumes 56 and 57. Readers are also advised that place names mentioned in documents in this volume, that is, Volume 59, are indexed under those names. If changes in name or nationality have occurred since 1919, the new place name and nationality are given.

We continue to be indebted to John Milton Cooper, Jr., William H. Harbaugh, Richard W. Leopold, and Betty Miller Unterberger for reading the manuscript of this volume and being helpful critics. As in the case of earlier peace conference volumes, Philippe-Roger Mantoux carefully reviewed our translations of his father's notes of the conversations of the Big Four. Alice Calaprice was editor of this volume for Princeton University Press.

We hereby take note of the retirement of our colleague, Fredrick Aandahl. Dr. Aandahl joined the Papers of Woodrow Wilson as Associate Editor in October 1979, worked full-time from that date until the summer of 1984, and has worked part-time since then. We thank him for significant contributions to Volumes 38-41, 51, and 53-58, and we are happy that he continues to work on special projects on a volunteer basis.

The Editors note the death on March 7, 1988, of Katharine Edith Brand, a member of the Editorial Advisory Committee since its constitution in 1959. We have already given a sketch of her career in the Introduction to Volume 40, and we here only note with much sadness the death of a friend, adviser, and collaborator to the Editors and at least two generations of Wilsonian scholars.

THE EDITORS

Princeton, New Jersey
April 6, 1988

CONTENTS

Memoranda, reports, aide-memoire, and position papers

Diaries

News reports

General Diplomatic and Military Affairs

Wilson correspondence
  From Wilson to

Domestic Affairs

Personal Affairs

ILLUSTRATIONS

Following page 326

Entering Suresnes Cemetery, May 30, 1919
National Archives

Speaking at Suresnes Cemetery
National Archives

A French woman lays flowers on the graves of American soldiers
National Archives

Peace Conference Diarists

Cary Travers Grayson
Princeton University Library

Ray Stannard Baker at his desk in Paris with Arthur Sweetser
National Archives

Vance Criswell McCormick
National Archives

David Hunter Miller
National Archives

Edith Benham and Charles Seymour
National Archives and Princeton University Library

ABBREVIATIONS

A.C.N.P.	American Commission to Negotiate peace
A.E.F.	American Expeditionary Force
ALS	autograph letter signed
BMB	Bernard Mannes Baruch
CC	carbon copy
CCL	carbon copy of letter
EAW	Ellen Axson Wilson
EMH	Edward Mandell House
FLP	Frank Lyon Polk
FR	*Papers Relating to the Foreign Relations of the United States*
FR 1919, Russia	*Papers Relating to the Foreign Relations of the United States, 1919, Russia*
GFC	Gilbert Fairchild Close
HCH	Herbert Clark Hoover
Hw, hw	Handwriting, handwritten
HwI	handwritten initialed
JPT	Joseph Patrick Tumulty
MS, MSS	manuscript, manuscripts
PPC	*Papers Relating to the Foreign Relations of the United States, The Paris Peace Conference, 1919*
RG	record group
RL	Robert Lansing
T	typed
TC	typed copy
TCL	typed copy of letter
THB	Tasker Howard Bliss
TI	typed initialed
TL	typed letter
TLI	typed letter initialed
TLS	typed letter signed
TS	typed signed
WBW	William Bauchop Wilson
WCR	William Cox Redfield
WJB	William Jennings Bryan
WW	Woodrow Wilson
WWhw	Woodrow Wilson handwriting, handwritten
WWsh	Woodrow Wilson shorthand
WWT	Woodrow Wilson typed
WWTLI	Woodrow Wilson typed letter initialed
WWTLS	Woodrow Wilson typed letter signed

ABBREVIATIONS FOR COLLECTIONS AND REPOSITORIES

Following the National Union Catalog of the Library of Congress

CSt-H	Hoover Institution on War, Revolution and Peace
CtY	Yale University
DLC	Library of Congress
DNA	National Archives

MH-BA	Harvard University Graduate School of Business Administration
NHC	Colgate University
NjP	Princeton University
OO	Oberlin College
PRO	Public Record Office
RSB Coll., DLC	Ray Stannard Baker Collection of Wilsoniana, Library of Congress
SDR	State Department Records
WC, NjP	Woodrow Wilson Collection, Princeton University
WP, DLC	Woodrow Wilson Papers, Library of Congress

SYMBOLS

[May 20, 1919]	publication date of published writing; also date of document when date is not part of text
[May 28, 1919]	composition date when publication date differs
[[May 17, 1919]]	delivery date of speech when publication date differs
* * * * * * *	text deleted by author of document

THE PAPERS OF

WOODROW WILSON

VOLUME 59

MAY 10-31, 1919

THE PAPERS OF

WOODROW WILSON

From the Diary of Dr. Grayson[1]

Saturday, May 10, 1919.

The President went to his study immediately after breakfast. He had before him the text of the first two protests which had been presented by the German delegates against certain sections of the treaty. They dealt with what the Germans claim was discriminating against Germany in not allowing her to become an immediate member of the League of Nations, and they also asked for the privilege of discussing the terms orally. Clemenceau and Lloyd-George had passed the notes on to the President with the request that he dictate the replies. The President prepared these and they were submitted to the Big Four at its morning session at 11:00 o'clock and unanimously approved, after which they were sent on to the German delegates at Versailles. The text of the German notes and the President's reply are as follows: . . .

The President handed his replies to me to give out to the newspapers through the publicity department.

After luncheon the President sat in as a member of the French Institute. He was elected to membership in it shortly after he came here last December and a gold medal had been stricken to commemorate his election. However, the Institute is more or less of a practical body and it is a necessity that any person chosen to membership shall quality for such membership by being present for at least one hour at one of its stated meetings. The meeting had been arranged to meet this qualification and the President was welcomed by some of the biggest minds in France. The President delivered an address at the meeting of the Institute, which was commented upon very freely by the French and British newspapers as having been a remarkable statement of fact.

The President and Mrs. Wilson spent a quiet evening together, the President playing Canfield the greater part of the evening, while Mrs. Wilson crocheted and read aloud to him.

T MS (in the possession of James Gordon Grayson and Cary T. Grayson, Jr.).
[1] About this diary, see n . 1 to the extract from it printed at Dec. 3, 1918, Vol. 53.

An Address to the Academy of Moral and Political Science[1]

Paris, May 10, 1919

Mr. President: It is with the keenest sense of gratification and pleasure that I find myself in this company. You have not only said that I was at home here, but you have made me feel at home, Sir, by the whole tone and tenor of your cordial welcome. I should in one sense in any case have felt at home, because I am more or less familiar with the works of the members of this Institute. I have worked in the same field. I have felt that quick comradeship of letters which is a very real comradeship, because it is a comradeship of thought and of principle. Therefore, I was prepared to feel at home in the company of men who have worked as I have in a common field.

Fortunately, Sir, there is one thing which does not excite the jealously of nations against one another. That is the distinction of thought, the distinction of literature, the achievement of the mind. Nations have always cheered one another in these accomplishments rather than envied one another. Their rivalry has been a generous rivalry, and never an antagonistic rivalry. They have cooperated in the fields of thought as they have not cooperated in other fields. Therefore, this is an old association of sentiment and of principle into which you have permitted me to enter. I would have liked very much sooner to take my actual seat in this company, except that I wanted to deserve your confidence by preferring my duty to my privilege. I wanted to be certain that I was not neglecting the things that you, as well as my fellow–countrymen, would wish me to do in order to have the pleasure of being here in your presence and receiving a greeting, as well as giving to you my own very cordial greeting and adherence.

I have had in recent months one very deep sense of privilege. I have been keenly aware that there have been times when the peoples of Europe have not understood the people of the United States. We have been too often supposed to be a people devoted chiefly, if not entirely, to material enterprises. We have been supposed, in the common phrase, to worship the almighty dollar. We have accumulated wealth, Sir, we have devoted ourselves to material enterprises with extraordinary success, but there has underlain all of that all the time a common sense of humanity and a common sympathy with the high principles of justice, which have never grown dim in the field even of enterprise. And it has been my very great joy in these recent months to interpret the people of the United States to the people of the world. I have not done more, Sir. I have not uttered in my public capacity my own private thoughts. I have uttered what I knew to be the thoughts of the great people whom I represent. I have uttered the things that have been stored up in their heart and purpose from the time of our birth as a nation. We came into the world consecrated to liberty, and, whenever we see the cause of liberty imperiled, we are ready to cast in our lot in common with the lot of those whose liberty is threatened. This is the spirit of the people of the United States, and they have been privileged to send two million men over here to tell you so. It has been their great privilege, not merely to tell you so in words, but to tell you so in men and material—the pouring out of their wealth and the offering of their blood.

So may I not take to myself the pleasant thought that, in joining this company, I am joining it in some sense as a representative of the people of the United States? Because my studies in the field of political science, Sir, have been hardly more than my efforts as a public man. They have constituted an attempt to put into the words of learning the thoughts of a nation, the attitude of a people towards public affairs. A great many of my colleagues in American university life got their training even in political science, as so many men in the civil sciences did, in German universities. I have been obliged at various times to read a great deal of bad German, difficult German, awkward German. And I have been aware that the thought was as awkward as the phrase, that the thought was rooted in a fundamental misconception of the state and of the political life of people. And it has been a portion of my effort to disengage the thought of American university teachers from this misguided instruction which they have received on this side of the sea. Their American spirit emancipated most of them as a matter of course, but the form of the thought sometimes misled them. They spoke too often of the state as a thing which could ignore the individual, as a thing which was privileged to dominate the fortune of men by a sort of inherent and sacred authority. Now, as an utter democrat, I have never been able to accept that view of the state.[2] My view of the state is that it must stop and listen to what I have to say, no matter how humble I am, and that each man has the right to have his voice heard and his counsel heeded, insofar as it is worthy of heed.

I have always been among those who believed that the greatest freedom of speech was the greatest safety, because if a man is a fool, the best thing to do is to encourage him to advertise the fact by speaking. It cannot be so easily discovered if you allow him to remain silent and look wise, but if you let him speak, the secret is out and the world knows that he is a fool. So it is by the exposure of folly that it is defeated—not by the seclusion of folly—and in this free air of free speech men get into that sort of communication with one another which constitutes the basis of all common achievement.

France, through many vicissitudes and through many bitter experiences, found the way to this sort of freedom, and now she stands
at the front of the world as the representative of constitutional liberty.[3]

T MS (WP, DLC).
   [1] Wilson was introduced by Charles Morizot-Thibault, Counselor to the Court of Appeal
of Paris and President of the Academy of Moral and Political Science. After his address,
Wilson was presented with the Academy's medal by Charles Léon Lyon-Caen, Doyen of
the Faculty of Law of the University of Paris and permanent secretary of the Academy.
Le Temps, May 11, 1919.
   [2] These are curious comments in light of Wilson's deep indebtedness to German scholars in the fields of public law, public administration, and other social sciences.
   [3] Another curious statement. Wilson had never believed that France stood at the front
of the world as the representative of constitutional liberty.

Hankey's and Mantoux's Notes of a Meeting of the Council of Four[1]

President Wilson's House,
C.F.5.   Paris, May 10, 1919, 11 a.m.
   §Mantoux's notes:
   Clemenceau (to President Wilson). The note from the German
delegation[2] must be answered; I propose to do it in five lines.
   Wilson. The terms of that note are so general that I do not see exactly how it should be answered. The Germans are complaining that
we do not provide for their admission into the League of Nations: we
can only refer them to the article of the Covenant which deals precisely with that question and where it is said that the league is open
to all nations which govern themselves truly according to a democratic regime. We are obliged to wait and see what the real character
of the German government is, and other articles of the Covenant of
the League of Nations leave no doubt as to the conditions under
which a new member can be admitted.
   Clemenceau. They must be told that it is the good conduct of a
people which is the essential condition of their admission.
   Wilson. The Covenant says it expressly.

   [1] The complete text of Hankey's minutes is printed in PPC, V, 537-40.
   [2] U. K. C. von Brockdorff-Rantzau to G. Clemenceau, May 9, 1919, PPC, V, 563. Brockdorff enclosed a lengthy German plan, or program, of a league of nations (printed in
ibid., VI, 765-78). However, he also asked one question in regard to the Covenant of the
League included in the peace treaty presented to Germany: "In the meantime it [the German peace delegation] begs to call attention to the discrepancy lying in the fact, that Germany is called upon to sign the statute of the League of Nations, as an inherent part of
the Treaty-draft handed over to us, on the other hand, however, is not mentioned among
the states which are invited to join the League of Nations. The German Peace Delegation
begs to inquire whether, and if so under what circumstances, such invitation is intended."

Clemenceau. Do you want to draft this response?

Wilson. I will take care of it.

Clemenceau. We have a decision to take on the evacuation of Corfu, which the Greeks call for. We are ready to withdraw the French troops; the British government asks nothing better than to withdraw its troops. But it is necessary that the Italians do as much. I will ask M. Orlando this question presently.

Wilson. Have you learned anything new about the mood of the Germans?

Clemenceau. I think that the negotiation will have its ups and downs, but that, in the end, they will sign.

Foch. When they will have made their counterproposals, in two weeks, and you will have answered, they are capable of stating that it is impossible for them to take a decision without referring to their government.

Wilson. The impression of the Germans is that I am ready to favor a compromise. What shall I do to persuade them that I consider as just the peace conditions that we have worked out among ourselves, and that I have no intention of favoring them?

Clemenceau. You could do it by an interview.

(Mr. Lloyd George enters.)§

(Marshal Foch and General Weygand were introduced.)

I. M. CLEMENCEAU explained to Marshal Foch that the Council had under consideration the possibility, though not probability, that Germany might refuse to sign the Terms of Peace. They wanted Marshal Foch's views as to the means available and the action to be taken in such an eventuality.

MARSHAL FOCH said that on April 24th last, he had held a meeting with the Commanders-in-Chief of the Belgian, British, French and United States Armies[3] and they had made a sum of their total forces. It had been established that, for the whole of the month of May, at least 40 divisions with 5 cavalry divisions would be available to operate on the front of the Rhine. He required 8 days' [a week's] warning to put them in a state to march. The reason for this was that many men were on furlough and many officers were away on commissions or leave. Everything was prepared, and, at the end of 8 days, the army would be ready to march. If and when the moment came to intervene the action to be taken would be organised according to the objects aimed at. If it was a case of a regular Government refusing to sign, it would be necessary to strike at the centre of that Government. For example, Weimar and Berlin. It might be, however, that the situation would be less clear and that the German Gov-

---

[3] Lt. Gen. Baron Augustin Michel Du Faing d'Aigremont, Gen. Sir William Robert Robertson, Gen. Henri Philippe Pétain, and Gen. John Joseph Pershing.

ernment might say that it could not decide or that it required a plebiscite. Still, if the resistance was that of a regular Government at
Berlin or Weimar, this resistance must be broken. The shorter roads
should be followed with the maximum possible forces. The army
would start from its bases at Cologne and Mayence [Mainz]. Advancing from this base line towards Weimar and Berlin, the army
would penetrate a zone very favourable to its advance, as its flanks
would rest to the north on the River Lippe and to the South on the
River Main. This zone was so advantageous for the advance that the
enemy might be expected to capitulate before the armies reached
their objective. Further, by advancing from the Rhine along the valley of the Ruhr, the result would be achieved of considerably reducing the enemy's financial resources. Advancing from the Rhine by
the valley of the Main, the armies of the Allied and Associated Powers would cut Germany off from Bavaria, and, in addition, would be
in a position to join hands with the Czecho-Slovaks. This was a perfectly feasible and not dangerous operation, and might achieve results without bringing the operations to a conclusion. These lines of
advance would take the Allied Armies into the heart of the German
Government. In reply to M. Clemenceau, he said that he envisaged
action by the Czechs, which would be combined.

GENERAL WEYGAND, in reply to Mr. Lloyd George, said that the
Czechs had 3 complete divisions formed, but these were now disposed along the Hungarian frontier. They had also several brigades,
but a good deal of organisation would be required.

MARSHAL FOCH said that information on this point had been asked
for. He then explained his plan by reference to a large map. He
added one advantage to those he had already given, namely, that if,
for any reason, the march had to be stopped, a line could be established on the River Weser parallel to the Rhine where the armies
could rest in conditions very similar to those prevailing on the
Rhine. In reply to President Wilson, he said there were no fortified
places on the way and that neither Weimar nor Berlin were seriously
fortified. In reply to Mr. Lloyd George he said that he certainly contemplated action by Polish troops which were already in occupation
of Posen. In reply to President Wilson, he said that the nominal
strength of the German forces was 450,000 men, but they were dis-
armed and dispersed and practically Germany could offer no resistance at all. In reply to Mr. Lloyd George, he added that he did not
contemplate action by sea, as this was not feasible with modern artillery. He summed up by saying that, with 8 days' warning, he was
prepared and was in accord with the various Commanders-in-Chief
for an advance with incontestable superiority of forces and with his
flanks secured. He would undertake to cut off Bavaria from Germany.

M. CLEMENCEAU asked whether he anticipated any danger from the mass of the working population [in the Ruhr].

MARSHAL FOCH said mainly in regard to their feeding.

§ Mantoux's notes:

Foch. We will have enough machine guns so that that population will not stir.

Weygand. Perhaps the most difficult problem will be the victualing of that population, of which we will perforce have to take charge. §

M. CLEMENCEAU alluded to Marshal Foch's request for 8 days' warning. This might be difficult for the Governments to give. He asked if Marshal Foch could reduce it, so that if the Governments saw the storm coming they could give an order which would be followed by action in less than 8 days.

MARSHAL FOCH said that this was practicable by stopping leave in the Armies.

MR. LLOYD GEORGE pointed out that if leave was stopped and the men came back, the Germans would at once know it.

M. CLEMENCEAU said that this would not be a bad thing.

MR. LLOYD GEORGE suggested that it might be done in such a way that Cologne and Mayence should see what was happening.

MARSHAL FOCH said that he had prepared a series of measures with the object of impressing the German people. Next week, for example, he proposed to go to the Rhineland and inspect the troops.

GENERAL WEYGAND said that the great difficulty was that, if the Germans were given warning, they would denude the railways both of material and personnel, which would make the advance very difficult. Consequently, under Marshal Foch's directions, he had prepared a surprise operation with motor cars and cavalry, in order to leap forward at a moment's notice and seize certain junctions and important places. This could be done in a few hours.

MARSHAL FOCH said that he contemplated a surprise operation of great range, which involved very few troops and which would produce a surprise and considerable effect. He was now studying the execution of this measure, but it involved having 2 or 3 divisions in each army ready to march at a moment's notice and this could only be done by cancelling leave.

M. CLEMENCEAU asked when the plan could be ready.

GENERAL WEYGAND said it could be ready to-morrow.

M. CLEMENCEAU said there was no need for it for 10 or 12 days but it ought to be got ready.

MARSHAL FOCH said he could stop leave in, say, 2 divisions of each army, which would be enough to carry out this part of his plan.

MR. LLOYD GEORGE suggested that it might be an advantage to have some demonstration at an early stage. The Germans were now making up their minds. Possibly they thought that the Allied and Associated Powers would not march.

M. CLEMENCEAU said that that was exactly what the Germans were saying. They believed the French Army incapable of marching and that the United States Army was going home.

MR. LLOYD GEORGE said that it might be too late 10 days hence and he thought some action ought to be taken now to show that the Allied and Associated Powers had made their minds up. He would like a demonstration made within a day or two. The most impressive form of demonstration would be to bring the cavalry to the front.

MARSHAL FOCH said that his cavalry were too few for a great demonstration, but he proposed himself to make an immediate visit to the Commanders-in-Chief of the various armies in such a way that while apparently secret, it would be known to everyone and all Germany would be puzzling to know what he was up to.

PRESIDENT WILSON suggested a secret journey with careful leakage.

MARSHAL FOCH said that this was what he intended.

MR. LLOYD GEORGE asked what he proposed to do about cancelling leave.

MARSHAL FOCH said that during his trip he proposed to ask each Commander-in-Chief to stop leave in 2 divisions of his army and to get these divisions ready to march. In reply to Mr. Lloyd George, he said that he could start any day next week.

M. CLEMENCEAU said the sooner the better.

PRESIDENT WILSON agreed in this.

M. CLEMENCEAU said he had received two documents, one of which stated that Scheidemann and Ebert would sign and the other that they would not sign.

MR. LLOYD GEORGE said that the demonstration should be immediate, in order that Germany might know that we meant business. Monday would be too late. The Germans were making up their minds and it was important to influence them before they settled down in an attitude of refusal.

MARSHAL FOCH pointed out that nothing could happen before the 22nd, when the Germans might refuse the peace terms, so that if he commenced his visit on the 12th that would be soon enough. He would be back by the 18th.

M. CLEMENCEAU said that he was already receiving papers from the Germans. He suggested that Marshal Foch should support his tour by troop movements.

MARSHAL FOCH agreed, and added also movements of munitions.

MR. LLOYD GEORGE pointed out that it would take some time for the Germans to know that Marshal Foch was there. The German mind was not a quick one. Consequently, Monday was, in his view, too late for Marshal Foch's start.

M. CLEMENCEAU agreed with Mr. Lloyd George that it was important to press the Germans as soon as possible.

PRESIDENT WILSON and M. ORLANDO also agreed.

MARSHAL FOCH undertook to leave at the earliest possible moment.

(Marshal Foch, accompanied by General Weygand, withdrew.)

T MS (SDR, RG 256, 180.03401/5, DNA); Paul Mantoux, *Les Délibérations du Conseil des Quatre (24 mars-28 juin 1919)* (2 vols., Paris, 1955), II, 21-22, 24; used with the approval of the late Mme. Paul Mantoux and of Philippe-Roger Mantoux and Jacques Mantoux.

Hankey's Notes of a Meeting of the Council of Four[1]

President Wilson's House,
C.F.6.   Paris, May 10, 1919, 11:45 a.m.

(1) With reference to C.F.4, Minute 8,[2] M. ORLANDO said that he accepted the draft which had been submitted by Sir Maurice Hankey on the previous afternoon on the subject of the recognition of the various States formed out of the former Austro-Hungarian Empire and contiguous States. (Appendix I.)

(2) M. CLEMENCEAU said that M. Venizelos had asked that the Allied Powers should evacuate Corfu.

M. ORLANDO, MR. LLOYD GEORGE and PRESIDENT WILSON agreed.

(It was agreed that the Allied forces should withdraw from Corfu.)

(3) M. ORLANDO reminded President Wilson of a request he had made to him on the previous day that he should prepare a text of a reference to the Committee dealing with Reparation in regard to Austria and Hungary.

PRESIDENT WILSON said that he had not had time up to the present, but that he would take it in hand as soon as possible.

(4) With reference to C.F.2,[3] Sir Maurice Hankey handed to M. Orlando a revised draft of Article 430 of the Treaty of Peace presented to the German Delegates, which had been prepared by the Drafting Committee, as well as an English translation of the Drafting Committee's Note. (The following text submitted by the Drafting Committee was approved:

"In case either during the occupation or after the expiration of the fifteen years referred to above the Reparation Commission finds that Germany refuses to observe the whole or part of her obligations under Part VIII (Reparation) of the present Treaty the whole or part of the areas specified in Article 429 will be re-occupied immediately by the Allied and Associated Forces.")

(The words underlined show the alteration in the original draft.)[4]

M. CLEMENCEAU undertook to transmit this to the Germans through Colonel Henri, to be substituted for the original Article.

(5) M. CLEMENCEAU handed round a communication he had received from the German Delegation, making some preliminary comments on the Treaty of Peace.[5]

(The Secretary was out of the room when this document was read, and was unable to obtain a copy.)

PRESIDENT WILSON suggested the following reply:

"In reply to the general objections which the German plenipotentiaries present to the provisions of the Treaty, it is only necessary to remind the German plenipotentiaries that we have formulated the terms of the Treaty with constant thought of the principles upon which the armistice and the negotiations for peace were proposed. We can admit no discussion of our right to insist upon the terms of the peace substantially as stated. We can consider only such practical suggestions as the German plenipotentiaries may have to present." (Further consideration of the matter was postponed until the afternoon Meeting.)

(6) M. CLEMENCEAU read the following note from the Japanese Delegation:

"La Délégation Japonaise présente ses compliments les plus empressés à Son Excellence Monsieur Georges Clemenceau, Président de la Conférence de la Paix, et a l'honneur de lui exprimer son désir de se faire représenter aux Comités qui viennent d'être constitués pour examiner les observations que les plénipotentiaires Allemands pourraient avoir à présenter relativement aux Conditions de Paix."

(It was agreed that the Japanese request should be granted.)

(7) SIR MAURICE HANKEY reported that the Secretary of the Japanese Delegation, M. Saburi,[6] had called on him that morning and had presented a verbal request from Baron Makino that a representative of the Japanese Delegation should be invited to attend the meeting of the Supreme Council when any question relating to the disposal of German warships or submarines was under consideration.

(It was agreed that this request should be granted.)

(8) PRESIDENT WILSON said that Mr. Lansing knew the Austrian Delegate, Professor Lammasch,[7] very intimately, and knew him to be a very reliable man. Professor Lammasch was not well, and had asked that his wife and daughter[8] might be allowed to accompany him to St. Germain.

M. CLEMENCEAU said he had already received a similar request, and had taken on himself to grant it. He said that the Austrian Delegates were expected on Wednesday.

(9) MR. LLOYD GEORGE handed to M. Orlando a copy of the document signed by M. Clemenceau, President Wilson and himself, in regard to the proportions in which receipts from Germany should be divided between the Allied and Associated Governments in accordance with Article 7 of the Reparation chapter of the draft Treaty with Germany. (I.C.178.D., Appendix 3.)[9]

M. ORLANDO undertook to give it his careful consideration.

APPENDIX I TO C.F.6.

It is agreed:

That the Treaties of Peace with Austria and with Hungary shall each contain Articles binding Austria and Hungary as well as the other High Contracting Parties to recognise the frontiers of the various States formed out of the former Austro-Hungarian Empire and of all contiguous States. Wherever possible the complete boundaries of all these States are to be fixed in the said Treaties of Peace with Austria and with Hungary. In cases, however, where it is not found practicable to fix the whole of these boundaries before the signature of these Treaties Austria and Hungary as well as the other High Contracting Parties shall agree to recognise these States within such boundaries as may be subsequently determined by the Principal Allied and Associated Powers. This will, of course, not apply to Austrian-Hungarian territory, the boundaries of which will be fixed by the respective Treaties of Peace.

T MS (SDR, RG 256, 180.03401/6, DNA).

[1] The complete minutes of this meeting are printed in *PPC*, V, 541-43.

[2] See the minutes of the Council of Four printed at May 9, 1919, 4 p.m., Vol. 58.

[3] See the minutes of the Council of Four printed at May 9, 1919, 11:25 a.m., *ibid.*

[4] Mantoux, II, 26-27, adds at this point:

"Clemenceau. Is this a new version?

"Wilson. No, it is a return to our original text, or, to be more exact, a precise draft of the decision taken here among ourselves.

"Clemenceau. Permit me to compare the two texts carefully, and I will give you the answer."

[5] U. K. C. von Brockdorff-Rantzau to G. Clemenceau, May 9, 1919, *PPC*, V, 564. It reads as follows:

"The German Peace Delegation has finished the first perusal of the Peace Conditions which have been handed over to them. They have had to realise that on essential points the basis of the Peace of Right, agreed upon between the belligerents, has been abandoned. They were not prepared to find that the promise, explicitly given to the German People and the whole of mankind, is in this way to be rendered illusory.

"The draft of the treaty contains demands which no nation could endure, moreover, our experts hold that many of them could not possibly be carried out.

"The German Peace Delegation will substantiate these statements in detail and transmit to the Allied and Associated Governments their observations and their material continuously."

[6] That is, Sadao Saburi.

[7] That is, Heinrich Lammasch.

[8] Nora Gemeiner Lammasch and Marga Lammasch.

[9] See the minutes of the Council of Four printed at May 1, 1919, 11 a.m., Vol. 58.

Hankey's Notes of a Meeting of the Council of Four[1]

President Wilson's House,
C.F.7.   Paris, May 10, 1919, 12 noon.
(M. Tchaykowsky[2] was introduced.)[3]

1. M. TCHAYKOWSKY said that he had spent 28 years of his life in England and 4 years in the United States of America, so that half his life had been spent in English speaking countries.

PRESIDENT WILSON said that the Council was very anxious to have his views as to the best policy to be pursued towards Russia. All those present were friends of Russia and anxious to help her, and would be glad of any suggestions M. Tchaykowsky might have to offer.

M. TCHAYKOWSKY remarked that this was a large order.

PRESIDENT WILSON said that perhaps it would guide M. Tchaykowsky if he was to state the difficulties. The principal feature in the situation was the growing strength of Koltchak and his rapid advance westwards, which might presently enable him to get in touch with forces to the north and perhaps those to the south. He and his colleagues, however, were not entirely satisfied that the leadership of Koltchak was calculated to preserve what ought to be preserved of the new order of things in Russia. They had some fear that it would result in a policy of reaction and military power.

M. TCHAYKOWSKY said that he had already had the pleasure of presenting assurances on this point, both from Koltchak[4] and from Denekin. Yesterday, a further definition of his policy had been received from Denekin, who had made his suggestion at the instigation of the various Attachés. This had appeared in the newspapers.

---

[1] The complete text of these minutes is printed in *PPC*, V, 544-52.
[2] That is, Nikolai Vasil'evich Chaikovskii.
[3] Mantoux, II, 27, here reads as follows:
"Lloyd George. We have summoned M. Tchaikovsky. Before we hear him, I would like to share with you a report forwarded to me by the Russian Red Cross. It indicates that the strength of the Bolsheviks is declining rapidly. A new bourgeoisie was born out of the revolution, and, like the purchasers of national property in France, it now wishes to return to a stable order."
[4] Chaikovskii probably here refers to the letter which he, Prince Georgii Evgen'evich L'vov, Vasilii Alekseevich Maklakov, and Sergei Dmitrievich Sazonov had addressed to Clemenceau on April 15, 1919 (printed in *FR 1919, Russia*, pp. 332-33). They wrote on behalf of the "Unified Governments," that is, the anti-Bolshevik regimes headed by Admiral Kolchak, General Denikin, and Chaikovskii, which all nominally recognized the leadership of Kolchak. The Unified Governments, they wrote, had no intention of restoring the monarchy or of taking land away from the peasants. The purposes of the "national movement" of these governments were to reestablish national unity and to "found the regeneration of Russia upon the solid basis of a democratic organization." "It is for the Russian people themselves," they declared, "to decide their destiny by means of a Constituent Assembly elected freely and under legal conditions. As soon as the Bolshevist tyranny is crushed and the Russian people can freely express their will, we will proceed with the elections and the present governments will turn over their power into the hands of the National Assembly." They appealed for "aid" from the Allies to secure these ends.

He then handed in the original which had been received on May 8th.[5]

M. CLEMENCEAU said that he had not seen this before.

MR. LLOYD GEORGE and PRESIDENT WILSON were in the same position.

M. TCHAYKOWSKY said that it was a despatch from M. Neratoff to M. Sazonoff, dated the 5th May, 1919, and had emanated from Constantinople. (The document was then read by President Wilson.) (A copy of the original telegram is attached. Appendix.) On the initiative of the Allied and Associated Governments, the Commander-in-Chief (General Denekin) has communicated to the Head of the United States' Mission, as well as to the Heads of the other Missions, the following decisions suggested by the said representatives, and he asked them to bring to the notice of their respective Governments the aims pursued by the Commander-in-Chief in South Russia in his struggle against the Soviet. His programme was as follows:

1. The suppression of Bolshevist anarchy and the restoration of order in Russia.
2. The re-construction of the Russian Army and of a united Russia.
3. Convocation of the Russian National Assembly, elected on universal suffrage.
4. Decentralisation of administration. Local autonomy subject to a Central Government.
5. Religious liberty.
6. Land Reform.
7. Labour legislation, protecting the labouring classes against oppression either by the Government or by capitalists.

This bore the signature of the Commander-in-Chief and had been published locally. This, continued M. Tchaykowsky, was the fullest declaration that had yet been made. He explained that M. Sazonoff was the head of General Denekin's foreign department, but, during his absence in Paris, M. Neratoff was acting for him.

PRESIDENT WILSON suggested that probably the military representatives of the Allied and Associated Powers had only suggested that the programme should be communicated to Paris.

M. TCHAYKOWSKY said that this was Denekin's programme. Koltchak's declarations were clear enough as to his aims.

PRESIDENT WILSON said that Koltchak's proclamation had been in very general terms, particularly in regard to land reform. He did not obtain a distinct impression from it.

[5] Anatolii Anatolievich Neratov to S. D. Sazonov, May 5, 1919, T telegram (SDR, RG 256, 180.03401/7, DNA). An English translation is printed in *PPC*, V, 551-52. Chaikovskii repeats the substance of the telegram below. Neratov, Deputy Foreign Minister of Russia from 1910 to 1917, was at this time a foreign-policy adviser to General Denikin.

M. TCHAYKOWSKY said that in Siberia the land question was not nearly so acute as it was in European Russia. In the first place, the population was thin and there was plenty of land. In the second place, communal management of the land was in force. Hence, the land question was not so vital or so epochmaking there as in European Russia. In the Northern regions also, there was the land problem. All they could do at present, until a Constituent Assembly had settled the fundamental principles, was to satisfy themselves that land temporarily taken should not be returned unless the interests of the State demanded it. For example, in Archangel, there was a very important cattle breeding ground on which a considerable part of the population was dependent for its living. To deprive them of their forage and hay would be very detrimental to the public interest. In case of the appropriation of such land, the State would step in and see that the public interest did not suffer. The same applied to timber. There was an old law by which any peasant could obtain from the Government a plot of forest land for gradual cutting. In 40 years, this land became communal. Some peasants had spent a good deal of money and labour on such land during the revolution, and both would be lost if the plot be seized. Here again, the State had to protect the rights of the worker who contracted with the State. The policy they pursued generally was to allow the occupied land to be kept until a Constituent Assembly finally decided the principles. The provisional government was the guardian of the common interest. It allowed renting of land but did not allow its sale, since purchase was the foundation of ownership. It was quite clear to him that Koltchak was acting on the same principle and leaving the final dispositions to a Constituent Assembly.

MR. LLOYD GEORGE suggested that two things were essential. First, the summoning of a Constituent Assembly, which should be a *bona fide* Assembly and not jerrymandered. The suffrage should not be twisted about to suit particular interests, as had been the case in Germany,[6] where the suffrage had been divided into three classes. The first thing, therefore, was to see that the Assembly was on a *bona fide* basis, and then the land question could be safely entrusted to it. The second essential was to define the attitude of the Central Government towards the small States, such as Finland, Esthonia, Estland,[7] Livonia, Lithuania, etc.

M. TCHAYKOWSKY said that in regard to Mr. Lloyd George's first

[6] Actually, in Prussia. See n. 13 to the Enclosure printed with RL to WW, Nov. 12, 1917, Vol. 45, and C. W. Ackerman to EMH, May 4, 1918, n. 1, Vol. 47. Significant suffrage reform did not take place in Prussia until the revolution in November 1918. See Arthur Rosenberg, *The Birth of the German Republic, 1871-1918*, trans. Ian F. D. Morrow (New York, 1962), pp. 223-25.
[7] The German word for Estonia.

point, he understood that the doubts and apprehensions that were felt arose from the fear of a military dictatorship menacing the functions of the Constituent Assembly. Once it was spread over political matters, military power might refuse to sign away its authority. There might be Mexican arguments at work. This, he understood, to be the foundation of the doubts that were felt. As for Koltchak, in a speech to the Zemstvos, he had promised to resign his position immediately there was a chance of getting a Constituent Assembly. No one could ask more of him that that. Siberia, he pointed out, was more democratic than other parts of Russia. There had been no class of nobles or of large landowners, although there had been a few millionaires, but they did not now exercise former authority. There was only a small middle class and the bulk of the population consisted of peasant proprietors. There was practically no reactionary class. The only reactionaries in Siberia were the military element and had only come temporarily. It was on this population that Koltchak was dependent in his government and for his military success. This was why Koltchak, although a dictator, both in a military and political sense, was constantly announcing democratic measures. This, indeed, was essential to his position. Denekin's position was quite different. In his part of Russia, there were large numbers of landowners, from which class his military officers were largely drawn. This made General Denekin's declaration all the more significant. In reply to President Wilson, he said that Koltchak was much stronger than Denekin, who had largely exhausted his recruiting resources and could only be strengthened from outside. Koltchak, on the other hand, was entering a populous district and region from which he would be able to draw his recruits.

Referring to Mr. Lloyd George's second point, M. Tchaykowsky said that the question of the relations between the Central Government and the smaller States was a most delicate and unsatisfactory one in Russia. One result of the over-centralisation of Czardom and the treatment of those States by the Bolshevist population had been that all the national groupings that had sprung up had been seized by a fashion of independence. But when they looked at the question coolly and viewed their economic position, they were far from suggesting any such solution. Economically, these small States were weak and they must inevitably fall into dependence on someone else. The Lithuanians, for example, he understood, had already received large sums from the Germans. The same would apply to Esthonia and Latvia. He had had several conversations with Esthonian representatives in Paris and they admitted the truth of this. They at first said that since Germany had overrun Esthonia, they must consider themselves free of any ties with Russia and start afresh. He had replied that he understood their standpoint but could not admit such a *tabula rasa* argument since Reval[8] stood as the gate of the Finnish Gulf and since it had been built by Russian energy. Eventually, they had promised that, if when the day came for the final reckoning, Russia would treat them as equal to equal and not as obligatory members of the Russian State, they would be prepared to deal. They had sent a telegram in this sense to the head of their Government, but, owing to the serious situation there and the elections, the reply had been delayed. In reply to Mr. Lloyd George, he said that Esthonia had two representatives in Paris.[9] He believed, also, that Lithuania had representatives.[10] These representatives had no authority to decide questions, but could negotiate.

MR. LLOYD GEORGE asked if Koltchak had a representative in Paris.

M. TCHAYKOWSKY said that all four Russian delegates[11] have been confirmed by Koltchak, but Prince Lvov had been particularly delegated from Siberia. M. Sazonoff in the similar way represented General Denekin. The constitution of Denekin's Government at the present time was rather complicated. He himself had written several letters to members of Denekin's Council, and had tried to persuade them to adopt the following principles:

(i)   To devote the energy of the Commander-in-Chief, principally to meeting the enemy;

(ii)   To organise the right system of power, the essential element of which was a clear demarcation between their military and their political functions.

The full power belonged to the Commander-in-Chief, but he ought to use all his energies for military operations, and not to interfere in policy nor to allow his subordinates to do so. The political Government, however, ought to have a military department to deal with such matters as the recruiting, training, and supply of the army. He knew this well, because they had had great difficulties in the Archangel region in this respect. Now, however, their system was functioning perfectly.

MR. LLOYD GEORGE read the following quotation from a Memorandum from the Foreign Office, dated May 1st, 1919:

"The most recent telegrams refer to the fact that over 90% of the

    [8] The German name for Tallinn.
    [9] The chief representatives of the provisional government of Estonia in Paris were Jaan Poska, the Foreign Minister, and Ants, or Antoine, Piip.
    [10] The leader of the Lithuanian delegation in Paris was Augustinas Voldemaras, the Minister of Foreign Affairs in the Lithuanian nationalist government. For other members of the delegation, see Alfred Erich Senn, *The Emergence of Modern Lithuania* (Westport, Conn., 1975), pp. 89-91, 239.
    [11] That is, Chaikovskii, L'vov, Maklakov, and Sazonov, the leading figures in the Russian Political Conference, about which see R. H. Lord to J. C. Grew, April 8, 1919, n. 1, Vol. 57.

burgher population and 80% of Russian peasants are co-operators loosely associated with the right wing of the Socialist Revolutionary party, who greatly resent the indifference to public support shown by Koltchak's Government, and more particularly condemn the Rinov[12] policy of attack on all representative institutions, which is doing the greatest harm."

He asked who Rinov was.

M. TCHAYKOWSKY said Rinov was not a Minister, and he did not know who he was. It was very difficult to judge of matters of this kind from a distance of thousands of miles.

MR. LLOYD GEORGE then continued to read:

"They are, however, represented as in no way objecting to recognition of Koltchak's Government by us, as long as it is conditional on his taking a broader public basis."

M. TCHAYKOWSKY said that he was a co-operator himself, and was indeed president of several Co-operative organizations. As far as he knew, however, the above information was contrary to the facts. He had personal friends in Siberia, who were high up in the Co-operative movement, and these were supporting Koltchak actually from the head offices of the Co-operative Societies. They would not dare do this if Koltchak were unpopular, as the Co-operative Societies were democratic in their organisation.

MR. LLOYD GEORGE again quoted from the same document:

"Koltchak's recent brilliant successes on his front are neutralised to a certain extent by the growing unrest in his rear."

M. TCHAYKOWSKY said he had a question to ask. Did this information come direct from Siberia, and, if so, what was the date of the report?

MR. LLOYD GEORGE read the following note by Lord Curzon explaining the position of the memorandum from which he had quoted:

"As on many previous occasions I circulate this note by an able writer in the Foreign Office, not as committing the Foreign Office or the Secretary of State, but as representing the views of an expert authority."

M. TCHAYKOWSKY said that this kind of report was often heard. Some facts took place, and were then exaggerated. For example, Koltchak himself was treated as the man who had carried out the coup d'état. This was not correct. Others had carried out the coup d'état, and had then forced the position of dictator on Koltchak by urging that if he would not accept it, his country would go to pieces.

[12] That is, Gen. Pavel Pavlovich Ivanov-Rinov. The remark about his "policy" presumably refers to his generally harsh and often brutal tactics in suppressing all opposition in the area of his military operations in eastern Siberia.

Koltchak had not pushed himself into it. In reply to Mr. Lloyd George, he said that Koltchak was an Admiral who had during the war commanded with distinction at Sebastopol. He did not know exactly from what class he was drawn. Most of his Ministers were former Socialists.

PRESIDENT WILSON asked whether the people who carried out the coup d'état were now Koltchak's guides and counsellors.

M. TCHAYKOWSKY said they were, and he mentioned as an instance one of the Ministers who had been a well-known Social Revolutionary. His own position, he said, was very delicate in this matter. He stood between the two parties, and he did not want to be in the position of an arbitrator saying which was right and which was wrong. He stood only for the State, and his position was mid-way between the parties.

MR. LLOYD GEORGE said that as President Wilson had explained, the Allied and Associated Powers did not want to associate themselves in the establishment of a militarist regime in Russia. He asked if M. Tchaykowsky had any information about General Judenitch.[13]

M. TCHAYKOWSKY said he had been a very successful General in the Army of the Caucasus. He was a man who could be thoroughly trusted in military matters, and he was a man who was not prepared to be guided by reactionaries, of whom there were some in Finland.

MR. LLOYD GEORGE asked whether, if General Judenitch were given the means to take Petrograd, he could be trusted to maintain the democracy there.

M. TCHAYKOWSKY thought he could, and said that in any case he and his friends would look after that.

M. ORLANDO asked whether M. Tchaykowsky had considered the constitution in Russia of a Federated State comparable to the United States of America. Was this possible, he asked, in this vast country?

M. TCHAYKOWSKY said that absolutism in Russia had proved itself impossible. It meant an absolute faith in the Head of State, as though he were a god on earth. This had died out. No one ever spoke of it now. It was essential, however, to eradicate the most anarchic feelings in Russia, and some thought that this could only be done by having a Constitutional Monarchy.

MR. LLOYD GEORGE asked whom they would choose for the throne.

M. TCHAYKOWSKY said there was no candidate. It was a mere abstract proposition. He himself did not wish it. Whether this temporary event should take place or not, he was convinced that Russia

[13] Gen. Nikolai Nikolaevich Yudenich, or Iudenich, commander of the Russian Army of the Caucasus from 1915 to 1917, at this time commander of the anti-Bolshevik Northern Corps, operating in the Baltic region.

would eventually become not only a Republic, but a Federated Republic. He had made a speech twelve years ago in Chicago, where he had said that in ten years Russia would become a Republic. This had come true.

(General Wilson entered at this point.)

GENERAL WILSON explained on a map the military situation.

(The following addition was kindly furnished by M. Tchaykowsky with his corrections):

In the course of this conversation M. Tchaykowsky said, in reply to Mr. Lloyd George's question, that it was very essential for the Russian interest now that Petrograd should be taken by an anti-Bolshevik force.

MR. LLOYD GEORGE suggested that this could be done by a Finnish force.

M. TCHAYKOWSKY said that if the appearance of Finns in Petrograd be inevitable, then Russian forces should also be there; otherwise a very delicate and complicated situation would arise seeing that the Finns are now claiming Russian territories.

GENERAL WILSON here produced a map on which he pointed out the line showing the present extent of the Finnish claims. It included not only the whole of Carelia[14] but the whole Murman Coast and the Kola Peninsula, also cutting the White Sea from the Kem Town to the Gorge[15] of the Sea.

Other approaches to the Petrograd being mentioned, M. TCHAYKOWSKY answered some detailed questions as the number of Russian forces available among the Russian prisoners of war now in Germany and also among Russian troops in Esthonia.

T MS (SDR, RG 256, 180.03401/7, DNA).

---

[14] That is, Karelia.
[15] Apparently a reference to the Russian word *gorlo*, meaning strait or neck; in this case, the strait connecting the White Sea to the Barents Sea.

Hankey's Notes of a Meeting of the Council of Four[1]

                                    Mr. Lloyd George's Residence,
                                    23, Rue Nitot, Paris,
C.F.-7A.   May 10, 1919, 3 p.m.
              The Landing of Greek Troops at Smyrna.

MR. LLOYD GEORGE suggested it would be best to begin by obtaining full information as to the present situation.

---

[1] The complete text of these minutes is printed in *PPC*, V, 553-58.

CAPTAIN FULLER[2] said that the following warships were at present at Smyrna:

British: One light cruiser, two destroyers, two sloops: One light
cruiser, one leader, four destroyers ordered to Aegean:

French: One battleship, one cruiser:
One battleship is due to arrive on May 12th.

Greek: One battleship, one cruiser, one destroyer.

Italian: One battleship, six small vessels.

Admiral Kakoulides[3] in KILKIS is proceeding to Constantinople from Black Sea to confer with Commander-in-Chief.

Transports for from 12,000 to 14,000 men were assembling at Kavalla. They had left Athens, but their arrival at Kavalla had not yet been reported. More transports were being sent from Athens to convey the material, but the date of their departure had not yet been reported.

M. VENEZELOS said that 14,000 Greek troops were available at Kavalla. He hoped that the whole of the transports would arrive at Kavalla this evening. They would then commence to embark.

CAPTAIN FULLER said that their embarkation should occupy from 24 to 36 hours. He agreed with Mr. Lloyd George that the whole force should be embarked by Monday evening.

MR LLOYD GEORGE asked how long the material would take to embark? There was no time to lose.

GENERAL BLISS thought that 48 hours would be enough for the embarkation of the material, if, as he understood, there were no horses.

M. VENEZELOS suggested that if the matter was urgent the troops could be embarked and the transports could sail without waiting for the impediments. This was only a case of the occupation of a town and not of big military movements.

GENERAL WILSON thought that sufficient transport could be requisitioned in Smyrna for the purpose of distributing the food.

CAPTAIN FULLER said that the forts were on the hills outside the town.

M. VENEZELOS, in reply to President Wilson, said that not more than 24 hours would be required for the voyage from Kavalla to Smyrna.

MR LLOYD GEORGE asked if, when the Turks were told that Smyrna would be occupied, they would be told that the forts were to be handed over? He believed that the French had a considerable land-

---

[2] Capt. Cyril Thomas Moulden Fuller, R.N., technical expert on naval questions in the British delegation to the peace conference.

[3] The name is also transliterated as Kakoulidis. The Editors have been unable to learn his given name.

ing party of blue-jackets or marines on board their ships. The Turks would probably raise less objection to the surrender of the forts to the French or the British than to the Greeks.

M. CLEMENCEAU said he did not mind whether it was the French or the British.

MR LLOYD GEORGE said he did not either.

PRESIDENT WILSON asked if there was not a danger from the lack of unity of command?

CAPTAIN FULLER said that the whole of the transport and escort and landing operations would be under the supreme command of Admiral Calthorpe,[4] who was the Allied Commander-in-Chief in that part of the Mediterranean.

M. CLEMENCEAU said that the Greek troops were under their own command.

MR LLOYD GEORGE said that orders should be given for the forts to be handed over to the Greek troops when they had arrived.

PRESIDENT WILSON said he understood it had been agreed that both the Turks and Italians were to be informed just before the landing. The Allied representatives should be instructed to inform both by Monday night.

MR LLOYD GEORGE said that the Italians ought to be told in Paris.

GENERAL WILSON suggested that Admiral Calthorpe should be instructed to inform the Turks that the forts were to be handed over under the terms of the armistice. They should be told that the forts were to be handed over to allied troops, for, if they were not told they would have a legitimate right to resist.

GENERAL BLISS asked what objection there was to warning both the Turks and the Italians in time to ascertain their attitude? The chance of a conflict was much greater if they had no warning. Not to warn them was to invite disaster.

MR. LLOYD GEORGE said that there was no fear of resistance by the Italians. The danger was that the Italians would egg the Turks on to fight. He asked M. Venezelos' view.

M. VENEZELOS said he disagreed with General Bliss. If the Italians were told beforehand they would tell the Turks. He advised that the Turks should be told only 12 hours before the landing. Admiral Calthorpe would direct the movements of the transports, and he would know at what moment to make the communication.

GENERAL WILSON suggested that the Italians would probably insist on joining in the landing as allies.

GENERAL BLISS pointed out that the Italians could not put many men ashore.

[4] Adm. Sir Somerset Arthur Gough-Calthorpe, R.N., commander in chief of Allied forces in the eastern Mediterranean and British High Commissioner at Constantinople.

GENERAL WILSON pointed out they could bring up plenty of troops from Rhodes.

PRESIDENT WILSON said he foreshadowed a difficulty if the British Admiral went to Smyrna, having reached an understanding only with the Greek Commander. If the Italian Commander had no instructions to cooperate, an awkward situation would arise. The Italian Commander would have received no instructions to take orders from Admiral Calthorpe.

CAPTAIN FULLER pointed out that Admiral Calthorpe was Commander-in-Chief of the Allied forces in the Eastern Mediterranean. Before giving any order to the Italians he would, of course, have to consult the Italian commander.

PRESIDENT WILSON said that we did not want the Italians to land their troops.

GENERAL WILSON said it would be very awkward if the Italians had a battalion on the spot and wanted to land. Was our Admiral to be instructed to forbid it?

CAPTAIN FULLER pointed out that Admiral Calthorpe would very likely remain at Constantinople and delegate the command to the French Admiral.

MR LLOYD GEORGE said in that case the French Admiral would have command over the Italians as well as the other allied forces.

PRESIDENT WILSON pointed out that, in that event, the Italians would ask why they were not to cooperate. They would also ask why the forts were to be handed to the Greeks.

GENERAL BLISS anticipated that, in the absence of any definite instructions, the Italian Admiral would say to himself that he did not want to lose the trick, and he would anticipate trouble with his own government if he did not take part in the landing. If, however, he knew beforehand, there would be no friction. Without instructions he felt sure the Italian Admiral would insist on participating in the landing.

PRESIDENT WILSON said that in his place he would certainly do so.

MR LLOYD GEORGE remarked that if the Italians were informed on Monday their Admiral would know before Tuesday, and with the greatest expedition a landing could not take place before that day.

M. VENEZELOS urged the importance of Admiral Calthorpe going specially to Smyrna as Commander-in-Chief of the Allies in the Aegean. The Commander of the Italian ships would then never think of opposing him unless he had instructions from his own government. He believed that if the Italians were notified only some hours before-hand all would go well, on condition that the French occupied the forts.

PRESIDENT WILSON agreed that Admiral Calthorpe's personal authority would not be questionable, but if he deputed his authority to someone else, it was more doubtful.

MR LLOYD GEORGE said that Admiral Calthorpe, in that case, ought to be told to go to Smyrna.

CAPTAIN FULLER undertook to do this.

MR LLOYD GEORGE recalled, however, that it was also important that Admiral Calthorpe should inform the Turks of what was taking place. Should he, he asked, do this by deputy?

M. VENEZELOS said he had received a despatch from the Greek representative at Constantinople,[5] who had discussed the whole matter with Admiral Calthorpe, who had told him that he wanted to go to Smyrna, but that this was difficult owing to the absence of Admiral Seymour[6] in the Black Sea, which prevented him from leaving.

CAPTAIN FULLER said that it had not been possible to release the British ships from the Black Sea to go to Smyrna, consequently Admiral Seymour was detained. In reply to Mr. Lloyd George he said that perhaps Admiral Seymour could be brought down to Constantinople, but it would take three days for him to come from the Crimea.

MR LLOYD GEORGE considered there was a great deal to be said for Admiral Calthorpe being at Smyrna. He agreed with M. Venezelos that in that case the Italians were much less likely to make difficulties.

M. VENEZELOS and M. CLEMENCEAU agreed.

GENERAL WILSON expressed doubts as to whether 12 hours was a long enough warning to the Turkish Government. They did not function very rapidly and the Commanders of the forts might not have received warning to hand over. In this case they would be justified in resisting. The difficulty might be got over by an order issued locally.

GENERAL BLISS was inclined to favour this.

MR LLOYD GEORGE asked whether they would obey an order given locally under the armistice?

M. VENEZELOS suggested that the Turks should be asked to surrender the forts to the allied forces under the terms of the armistice 36 hours before the operation took place. 24 hours later they should be informed that allied troops were about to arrive.

CAPTAIN FULLER said that the landing party would be a French one. In reply to President Wilson he said he believed there were two forts.

---

[5] Efthymios Kanellopoulos.
[6] Rear Adm. Michael Culme-Seymour, R.N., commander of the Black Sea and Caspian Squadron of the Royal Navy.

GENERAL WILSON expressed doubts as to whether the size of the landing party was sufficient to deal with two forts.

CAPTAIN FULLER said there was little information about the forts.

(*At this point there was considerable discussion about the forts.*)

CAPTAIN FULLER read a draft of the instructions which he understood he was to send to the Admiralty for transmission to Admiral Calthorpe.

(*These instructions were slightly modified during the discussion, but in their final form are recorded at the end of these Notes.*)

(PRESIDENT WILSON *withdrew, and shortly after* ADMIRAL DE BON, *who had been summoned by telephone, arrived.*)

PROFESSOR MANTOUX, at M. Clemenceau's request, explained the situation to Admiral de Bon.

M. CLEMENCEAU asked if the Turks could be warned without warning the Italians also?

MR LLOYD GEORGE said that if the Italians were informed on Monday they would communicate it to the Turks.

M. VENEZELOS suggested that the Turks ought to be informed in regard to the forts on Monday afternoon.

ADMIRAL DE BON pointed out that Admiral Amet[7] was at Constantinople.

MR LLOYD GEORGE said that in this case it would be unnecessary to recall Admiral Seymour from the Crimea. He asked what was the strength of the French landing party available.

ADMIRAL DE BON said it was from 300 to 400 men.

MR LLOYD GEORGE suggested that this was enough unless the Turks intended to fight. If they should fight then a much larger number would not be sufficient.

GENERAL WILSON asked whether the Italians in Paris would be informed that no Italian troops were to be landed?

MR LLOYD GEORGE said that this difficulty should be surmounted by telling Admiral Calthorpe that the landing party was to consist entirely of French forces so as to avoid mixing up nationalities.

The following is a summary of the decisions reached:

(1) At the Meeting of the Supreme Council of the Allied and Associated Powers on Monday afternoon the Italian representatives should be informed of the action to be taken, and should be asked to issue instructions to place their Senior Naval Officer at Smyrna under Admiral Calthorpe's orders:

(2) Captain Fuller should make a communication on the following points to the British Admiralty, in order that instructions might be given to Admiral Calthorpe:

---

[7] Vice Adm. Jean François Charles Amet, at this time French High Commissioner at Constantinople.

(a) That, in view of the presence of Italian ships at Smyrna, it was very desirable that Admiral Calthorpe should be at Smyrna just prior to and during the operations;

(b) That it was presumed that the Greek troops would arrive at Smyrna not before Wednesday morning, May 14th;

(c) That the Italian representatives would be informed on Monday afternoon, as stated above;

(d) That Admiral Calthorpe should arrange with Admiral Amet at Constantinople to make the following communications to the Turks:

   (i) Thirty-six hours before the Greek troops are due to land at Smyrna, the Turks at Constantinople to be informed that the forts at Smyrna are to be handed over to allied detachments:

   (ii) Twelve hours before the Greek troops are due to land at Smyrna, the Turks at Constantinople should be informed that allied troops will be landed at Smyrna in accordance with the armistice terms, and that these movements have been decided on in view of reported disorders in the neighbourhood of Smyrna:

Admiral Calthorpe should also be informed that the forts will eventually be turned over to the Greek troops;

(e) Admiral Calthorpe should be instructed to arrange that no men are to be landed from Italian ships, nor should any British parties be landed. The landing parties for taking over the forts should be entirely French, thus avoiding the mixing up of nationalities:

(f) Admiral Calthorpe should, as soon as possible, report the date and time at which transports would leave Kavalla, and the date and time of their expected arrival at Smyrna, so that, if they are due at Smyrna later than Wednesday morning, the Supreme Council can adjust the time for informing the Italians in Paris to correspond.

   (NOTE: *A communication in the above sense has been sent to the Admiralty, London, and Admiral de Bon is instructing Admiral Amet to follow Admiral Calthorpe's directions in this operation.*)

T MS (WP, DLC).

Hankey's and Mantoux's Notes of a Meeting of the Council of Four[1]

President Wilson's House,

C.F.8.   Paris, May 10, 1919, 4:00 p.m.

(1) M. CLEMENCEAU handed round two notes on the Peace Terms which had been forwarded by the German Delegation.[2]

PRESIDENT WILSON produced the draft replies which he had prepared.

(It was agreed:

(i) To approve the replies prepared by President Wilson;[3]

(ii) That both the Notes and the Replies should be published at once.)

(The two Notes with the Replies are reproduced in the Appendix.)

(2) M. CLEMENCEAU produced a report that had been sent to him by the Ministry of Marine, signed by Admiral Benson, Admiral de Bon, and Admiral Hope in regard to the measures to be taken to maintain order in Slesvig during the operation of the plebiscite. The Admirals had come to the conclusion that it was not their function to decide which nation should have the command of the Allied force. The report had been called for by a Meeting of the Council of Foreign Ministers on April 30th.

MR LLOYD GEORGE suggested that as the matter was not urgent, it should be postponed.

(This was agreed to.)

(3) M. CLEMENCEAU produced a report containing the results of consideration given by the Council of Foreign Ministers to the boundaries of Austria and Hungary.

MR LLOYD GEORGE and PRESIDENT WILSON asked that before the report was discussed, it might be circulated.

---

[1] The complete text of Hankey's notes is printed in *PPC*, V, 559-64.

[2] For these notes, see n. 2 to the minutes of the Council of Four printed at May 10, 1919, 11 a.m., and n. 5 to the minutes of the Council of Four printed at May 10, 1919, 11:45 a.m.

[3] Wilson's replies (printed in *PPC*, V, 563-64) read as follows:

"The receipt of the German programme of a League of Nations is acknowledged. The programme will be referred to the appropriate Committee of the Allied and Associated Powers. The German plenipotentiaries will find upon a reexamination of the Covenant of the League of Nations that the matter of the admission of additional Member States has not been overlooked but is explicitly provided for in the second paragraph of Article I."

"The Representatives of the Allied and Associated Powers have received the statement of objections of the German plenipotentiaries to the Draft Conditions of Peace.

"In reply they wish to remind the German Delegation that they have formed the Terms of the Treaty with constant thought of the principles upon which the Armistice and the negotiations for peace were proposed. They can admit no discussion of their right to insist upon the Terms of the Peace substantially as drafted. They can consider only such practical suggestions as the German plenipotentiaries may have to submit."

There is a WWhw draft of the reply in regard to the League of Nations in WP, DLC.

(Sir Maurice Hankey was instructed to reproduce and circulate the report.)

(4) MR LLOYD GEORGE asked what impression M. Tchaikowsky had made.

PRESIDENT WILSON said that he had not been as definite as he himself would wish. He had received the impression that Koltchak's advisers had inclined to the Right as soon as they had got power. This very often happened.

MR LLOYD GEORGE said he got the impression that M. Tchaikowsky did not quite trust Denekin. He did evidently like Koltchak, though he himself had not got a very clear impression of Koltchak's "entourage." He did not think public opinion would allow us to abandon Koltchak even if he should establish a reactionary Government, because the world would say that the establishment of order was so important. It would be awkward to be placed in the position of supporting a Government that we did not believe in.

PRESIDENT WILSON said he thought a fresh view ought to be obtained of Koltchak. He did not like being entirely dependent upon the views of British and French military men.

MR LLOYD GEORGE pointed out that Colonel John Ward, who commanded the Middlesex Battalion, was a Labour Member of Parliament.

(After some discussion President Wilson undertook to ask an American gentleman named Mr Morris (?),[4] who was at present at Tokio, to proceed as rapidly as possible to Omsk in order to gather as much information as he could about Admiral Koltchak's political intentions.

He undertook to instruct him to consult Colonel Ward and Colonel Johnson,[5] Commanding the 5th Hants. Battalion, as to their view of the political situation.)

PRESIDENT WILSON said that Koltchak's programme was all right viewed in the background of M. Tchaikowsky's mind. What, however, did it look like, he asked, viewed in the background of Admiral Koltchak's mind?

§Mantoux's notes:

Lloyd George. What is your impression of M. Tchaikovsky?

Wilson. It is good. But he did not answer our questions as clearly as I would have liked.

I see in all these governments, once constituted, a general tend-

[4] That is, Roland Sletor Morris.
[5] Lt. Col. Robert Arthur Johnson, commander of a battalion of the Hampshire Regiment of the British army which had been sent to Siberia from India to assist in the training of anti-Bolshevik troops.

ency toward the right. That is rather human. From what M. Tchaikovsky said I did not get a very clear impression of Denikin nor of his entourage.

If we decide to support Kolchak and Denikin, the opinion of the entire world would not be able to understand if we were to abandon them afterward, even if they were later behaving as reactionaries. This is what I am afraid of and what causes me to hesitate to commit myself.

Lloyd George. On the other hand, we cannot lose contact with the Russians: the consequences of that would be serious. We must inform ourselves at all costs. There is an English officer with Kolchak; he is a member of the English Parliament, a member of the Labour Party, John Ward. He is very hostile to the Bolsheviks.

Wilson. I have a very intelligent representative in Tokyo; he is our Ambassador, Mr. Morris, who was once my student.

Lloyd George. I do not believe that it would be worth the trouble to ask General Knox's opinion; he is an excellent soldier, but he is only a soldier.

Wilson. I have confidence in Morris. He was born in Philadelphia, which might be considered as the center of the least advanced opinion in the United States. There is a kind of very conservative aristocracy there, and Morris, who grew up in the middle of it, has fought against these tendencies all his life.

Lloyd George. The man who matters to us is Kolchak; we must know if we can or cannot count on him. A practical question arises immediately: that of knowing if we should march to meet him near Kotlas. We must know who he is at all costs.

Clemenceau. Do you have the means to do it in due time?

Wilson. I can get information from Morris within a week.

Lloyd George. I believe that it is necessary to telegraph him, and we could ask him to get in touch with John Ward, who must be in Vladivostok.

Hankey. We also have an officer in Siberia, Johnson, who is a former editor of the *Westminster Gazette*.

Lloyd George. It might be worthwhile to consult him. It is useless to apply to Knox, except on military questions.

Wilson. And on the subject of Denikin, how do we inform ourselves?

Clemenceau. It is not easy.

Lloyd George. General Milne[6] has seen Denikin; but he also could only give us a soldier's opinion.

---

[6] That is, Lt. Gen. George Francis Milne.

Wilson. If Kolchak's intentions are those M. Tchaikovsky describes to us, all is well; but I am not certain of it.

Lloyd George. In any case, you may be certain that it will be a general who will prevail and make himself master of Russia. If it is not Kolchak, it will be a leader of the Bolshevik troops.

Wilson. The Russian Bonaparte would find himself in a very different situation from that of Napoleon, who had behind him an organized country, with stable elements, despite the revolution. In Russia there is only an amorphous and anarchic mass of peasants. §

MR LLOYD GEORGE said he felt sure that a soldier was bound to get to the top in Russia. Even if the Bolsheviks ultimately prevailed, it would probably be by military action.

(5) With reference to C.F.4, Minute 6,[7] Sir Maurice Hankey again brought forward Lord Cunliffe's letter asking for a decision as to whether new States such as Poland, were to bear any portion of the costs of the war. He was informed that a decision on this point was essential before the experts on Reparation by Austria and Hungary could proceed with their enquiry, and he was also informed that this was the most backward part of the Austrian and Hungarian Treaties.

PRESIDENT WILSON said that his first and sentimental idea was that Poland ought to be let off altogether. Poland had been caught, as it were, in three nets—the Austrian, the German, and the Russian, and had in consequence suffered dreadfully. It seemed only common justice to leave her out from any share of costs of the war or reparation. The same did not apply to other parts of Austria-Hungary, but he did not know on what basis their share of reparation was to be reckoned. He asked whether they were to take a share of the national debt or only of reparation?

MR LLOYD GEORGE said that their share of the national debt should be regarded as cancelled, as the Allied and Associated Powers were not concerned in this.

PRESIDENT WILSON suggested that reparation should be worked out on the same principles as for Germany, by categories of damage.

MR LLOYD GEORGE said that if put in the same categories as for Germany, the Austrian reparation would become merely collateral to Germany, and to that extent they would relieve Germany of her debt.

PRESIDENT WILSON said that one of the elements in his mind was that in fairness to Italy, to make Austria collateral, would increase the possibility of adequate reparation to Italy.

[7] See the minutes of the Council of Four printed at May 9, 1919, 4 p.m., Vol. 58.

MR LLOYD GEORGE said that Italy was in exactly the same position as Great Britain.

M. ORLANDO agreed.

PRESIDENT WILSON said the difficulty was that there would not be enough to go round, and this was the argument for making Austria collateral.

MR LLOYD GEORGE said that if Germany's capacity to pay were adequate, all would agree that to make Austria collateral would be a relief. Even if Germany's resources were inadequate, this would provide some relief. He suggested that the claim for Austria and Hungary ought to be on a different basis. It ought to be assumed that Austria could not pay the whole of the damages, and it would be better to lay down definitely how much Austria and Hungary were to pay.

PRESIDENT WILSON hoped that a moderate sum would be named.

M. CLEMENCEAU asked who was to estimate the amount.

PRESIDENT WILSON said theoretically this could be done, but he did not know whether the sources of information were sufficient to enable the sum to be estimated and allotted.

MR LLOYD GEORGE said it would be very dangerous to impose an unknown liability on these new countries.

PRESIDENT WILSON asked whether the Reparation scheme for Germany could not be applied in some way, so as to make Austria's share collateral but independent.

MR LLOYD GEORGE proposed, without prejudicing the decision, that the experts should be asked to report as to how much the whole group of countries in the former Austro-Hungarian Empire could pay.

PRESIDENT WILSON suggested that the experts should be asked to report whether it would be feasible to form a conclusion as to how much the whole group, omitting Poland, could pay, and, in the event of this not being feasible, to add to the suggestion an outline of the proportion to be paid by each component part.

MR LLOYD GEORGE and M. CLEMENCEAU agreed.

M. ORLANDO said that it was a very complex question, which would have to be referred to experts. For example, considering the case of war debts only, it would be very difficult to ascertain the precise situation of the several States formed out of the old Austro-Hungarian Empire. It would be found that some had a war debt, and others had not, and the situation would be very confusing. The best plan was to put the matter in the hands of experts, who should be asked to take as the basis of their work that all the States except Poland should pay: on this basis the experts should estimate the capacity of the whole group to pay. Then they should examine the distribution of liability, as well as of means of payment. The Germans might have the right to complain if they did not know how much their former allies were to pay. This was an additional reason for dealing with the problem reasonably.

MR LLOYD GEORGE said there was another reason. All the Allied Powers had incurred heavy debts for the emancipation of these races. They had been freed not by their own efforts, but by those of the Allies. Their only share in the war had been to fight against us. Without taking a final decision to the case of Poland, he thought the enquiry should be extended to Poland.

PRESIDENT WILSON said that Poland had been prostrated by the war almost as much as Belgium. He did not think that she ought to bear any part of the Austro-Hungarian war debt. He did not think that any of the new countries should bear a part of the Austro-Hungarian war debt, but only a part of reparation.

(Sir Maurice Hankey was instructed to draft a decision on this matter for consideration.)

(6) Sir Maurice Hankey said he had been asked by the British representatives on the Committee which was preparing the Financial Clauses for the Austrian and Hungarian Treaties to obtain authority to consult the Czecho-Slovaks and other States concerned.

(It was agreed that the Committee considering the Financial Clauses should have authority to consult the Czecho-Slovaks or delegates of any other State represented at the Peace Conference.)

T MS (SDR, RG 256, 180.03401/8, DNA); Mantoux, II, 36-37.

From Thomas Nelson Page

Personal.

My dear Mr. President: [Paris] May 10 1919.

The situation in Italy has become so serious that I have come up to tell you of it personally. I am at the Crillon and hold myself at your convenience; but I think the matter of much urgency, and if you can see me today I would be glad to come at any hour you find suitable— as indeed, I shall always be.

I called yesterday afternoon to ask for an appointment.

Always with highest regard

                    Yours most sincerely   Thos Nelson Page

P.S. A telephone message to the Embassy will reach me between one and half past two today. TNP

ALS (WP, DLC).

From the Diary of Colonel House

May 10, 1919.

I have been so rushed in one way and another that I have not been able to dictate the diary on the 8th and 9th. I will therefore merely give a general summary of what has happened.

Friday night I received a letter from Lloyd George concerning the Irish American delegation, Messrs Walsh, Dunne and Ryan.[1] His letter and my reply,[2] and his letter of today[3] are attached and need no explanation further than that they show George up in his usual character. He makes two misstatements in his letter, and of course this is done in order to give himself a strong case with the British public. The English press pretty generally have abused him unstintedly because he permitted these Irish-Americans to go to Ireland, and he evidently conceived this way of getting out of it. Up to now he has not published the letter and I doubt whether he will since he knows that I will deny some of his statements. The suggestion that the Irish-Americans call on him was entirely his own.

Sonnino called yesterday by appointment. My letter to the President of that date[4] will give the purport of his visit. He was in a very conciliatory mood. Speaking of Sonnino reminds me to say that the President is still stubborn on the Adriatric question. Our Experts, who at one time were irreconcilable to anything being done with Fiume except to give it to the Jugo-Slavs, have now a plan[5] by which it is to be placed in the hands of the League of Nations for a period of years, and at such time as the League shall indicate, a plebi[s]cite shall be held to determine whether it shall become Jugo-Slav or Italian. If it goes Italian, then the Italians are to build a port for the Jugo-Slavs below Fiume.

Trumbitch has been seen and approved the plan for the Jugo-Slavs, and yet the President will not listen to it. In other words, he is willing to concede less to Italy than the Jugo-Slavs. If this question is not settled amicably it may easily lead not only to the disruption of the Peace Conference, but to another war. If the Italians are not satisfied, they will insist upon the Treaty of London, and France and England have already notified us that they will keep their faith. In this event, unless we accede to it, the Peace Conference will be shattered.

One of the great defects of the President's character is his prejudice and self-will. He gives way when sufficient pressure is borught [brought], but the trouble is that he is always running the risk of getting into an inextricable situation. The manner in which the [he] has antagonized the Republicans in Congress is an instance of this. He has steadily built up a fire there which is now beginning to scortch [scorch] him and it will become worse and worse as his term wanes. It was all so useless and it has hampered him in the exercise of his public work and will probably hamper him in the exercise of the Treaty provisions.

T MS (E. M. House Papers, CtY).
    [1] See D. Lloyd George to EMH, May 9, 1919, printed as an Enclosure with EMH to WW, May 9, 1919, Vol. 58.
    [2] See EMH to D. Lloyd George, May 9, 1919, *ibid.*
    [3] Printed as an Enclosure with WW to EMH, May 13, 1919 (first letter of that date).
    [4] See EMH to WW, May 8, 1919, Vol. 58.
    [5] See D. W. Johnson to WW, May 9, 1919, *ibid.*

From the Diary of Edith Benham

May 10, 1919

Things seem to be dark on the Italian front. Mrs. W. tells me the Italian fleet is mobilizing, and the French, English and Americans are doing likewise—secretly. Whenever there is a conference here of Clemenceau, L.G. and the P., Orlando always comes, too, as he seems to get wind of it in some mysterious way, or he may telephone. Anyway, he is always here. So yesterday as the P. wished to arrange details with L.G. and C. for mobilization of fleets, and naturally they didn't want Orlando snooping around, he went officially to L.G.'s to call, but really stayed here. There certainly would seem no doubt that the Japanese held a pistol at the head of the conference and so got Shantung. Thomas Nelson Page, after writing that the excitement about Fiume was mostly cooked up, has now come on here to see the P. and plead with him to give Fiume to the Italians. I fear the gentleman had a bad quarter of an hour with the P. It would be so terrible if all this ghastly war business should begin again. The P. seemed quite depressed by the situation I suppose.

T MS (Edith Benham Helm Papers, DLC).

Pleasant Alexander Stovall to the American Commissioners

Berne, May 10, 1919.

592. STUTTGARTER NEUES TAGBLATT 8th reports numerous murders of Government soldiers by Spartikistes in Munich who hiding in groups all parts of city and attacking from behind small troops patrols. Number officers shot in this manner. Same paper reports Joffe[1] former Bolshevic Ambassador to Berlin killed by Poles.

Discussing peace conditions Ludwig Bauer writes in NATIONAL ZEITUNG Basel 8th that while Germany destroyed ruthlessly and absolutely inexcusably Belgian and French provinces the peace as formulated in conditions just published will destroy Germany for all eternity. Not only this but it will destroy also every hope for justice and friendship among human beings. The world now faces an infinitely magnified Brest Litovsk. All that is in this treaty is incomprehensible to everyone not immersed in war psychology but the most incomprehensible is fact that Woodrow Wilson sat beside Clemenceau and listened quietly to that mockery of his ideals. The world has been defeated of a great hope. If it were conceivable that this treaty not only be signed but become permanent reality then a great people would be smothered from humanity, the greatest injustice in international relations perpetuated and slavery again instituted. There is no hope that this treaty can be improved for in its every word it is immoral, dictated by revenge and rapacity and an open injury of an obligation assumed before the whole world to conclude a peace of right and justice. May be conceivable that it will be signed but inconceivable that it will ever be carried out for the simple and excellent reason that it cannot be carried out. The great problem after its signature will be as to whether modern technique of arms will permit permanent imprisonment of Central Europe or whether the moral rascality is developed to such an extent that free great and old civilized peoples will undertake the role of perpetual dungeon keepers. Neither disarmament genuine true peace nor justice will come but only hatred revenge war and tumults. A terrifying disaster has befallen entire humanity.

Same paper reports from Berlin at session Prussian Diet Minister President Hirsch[2] stated no trace of reconciliation or justice found in peace conditions and if treaty accepted will mean slavery for Germany now facing question to be or not to be. Everything must be done to have planned peace of oppression changed into real peace of justice. Adolf Hoffmann[3] also condemned bitterly peace of oppression in name of Independents and also appealed to proletarians of all countries to destroy Entente peace through social revolution.

Same paper 9th reports from Berlin that interviews with parliamentarians reflect fact that all parties from extreme right to extreme left unanimously agreed that Entente peace treaty absolutely impossible for Germany and that no German Government can sign it. Independent Socialists look only for revision through world's revolution. German delegates also dumbfounded by conditions and of opinion that no German Government can subscribe to treaty as they would thus become slaveholders of own people. German delegates will not make unfruitful protests nor attempt barter with Entente but will formulate counter proposals on basis Wilson's fourteen points and present them to conference.

Same paper reports from Stuttgart at session Wuerttemberg Diet President Keil[4] states peace conditions absolutely incompatible with Wilson's principles. Intended that German people be humiliated to people of slaves who in future must do slave work for capitalists and imperialists of Entente states. Not slightest trace of right self-determination of peoples which was cornerstone of Wilson's peace principles. Same paper quotes FRANKFURTER GENERAL ANZEIGER statement that no other way to be seen than rejection and that no other consolidation than that new generation will grow to be strong enough to break the chains with which limbs of German people are being bound. This not peace of permanence for its natural consequences will be coming wars.

NEUE ZUERCHER ZEITUNG 9th reports from Berlin at session of peace committee of National Assembly President Fehrenbach[5] stated acceptance of peace treaty would signify perpetual enslavement of German people. Incomprehensible how Wilson who promised world peace of justice upon which honest League Nations would be established was able to remain and witness presentation of this treaty saturated with hatred. Scheidemann in long speech attempted show incompatibility between actual terms and Wilson's 14 points and in conclusion stated Government must consider quietly this document of hatred and has absolute duty not to allow itself to be overcome by sentimental feelings which it naturally shares all Germans. Government hopes to reach an agreement through negotiations but will not attempt to barter with Entente. It has instructed delegates at Versailles to present counter proposals to enemy Governments and to request oral negotiations. Government desires quiet and peace as country and people in such desperate condition as ours cannot afford to assume heroic pose.

Stovall.

T telegram (WP, DLC).
[1] Adolf Abrahamovich Joffe (Ioffe). The report of his death was erroneous. At this time, he was engaged in Communist party work in the Ukraine. He lived until 1927.
[2] Paul Hirsch, Social Democratic party leader, Minister President of the Prussian constituent assembly.
[3] Adolf Hoffmann, Socialist member of the Prussian constituent assembly.
[4] Wilhelm Keil, President of the constituent assembly of Württemberg.
[5] Konstantin Fehrenbach, President of the National Assembly in Weimar.

Two Telegrams from Joseph Patrick Tumulty

[The White House, May 10, 1919]

No. 113 The work of the Industrial Board is at an end because of the failure of Mr. Hines' committee to agree on a price for steel. Mr Redfield has been making statement after statement in the public press which in my opinion have embarrassed Hines and those who were sincerely striving to arrive at a settlement.[1] I hope if Mr. Redfield cables you, you will suggest advisability of ending the matter without further public discussion.   Tumulty.

[1] About the Industrial Board of the Department of Commerce and the controversy over the price of steel rails, see the index references in Vols. 56-58. The Editors have found only two public statements in the press for which Redfield was clearly responsible, although he undoubtedly approved a third statement made by George N. Peek on April 10, which was printed in the *New York Times*, April 11, 1919. On April 11, Redfield issued a brief statement in which he reviewed the controversy up to that point. *Ibid.*, April 12, 1919.

On the occasion of accepting the resignation of the members of the Industrial Board, a dénouement which was the direct result of the controversy, Redfield issued the following statement on May 9:

"At my desire the members of the Industrial Board have retained their official positions until the outcome of the conference between the Railroad Administration and the steel industry, which took place on the 8th instant, should be known. That conference was arranged at my suggestion by the Industrial Board with the approval of the Director General of Railroads. It appears from the statement issued by the Railroad Administration that the conference has failed to bring an agreement and the further assistance of the Industrial Board is not desired. In view of the announcement made by the Railroad Administration I have regretfully concluded that it is not proper longer to detain from their respective affairs the gentlemen who comprise the Industrial Board.

"That board was conceived in the spirit of unselfish public service and has so acted from the beginning. I repeat what was said yesterday: That there has been no change in its viewpoint, policy or attitude from the beginning. No statement nor inference to the contrary has a basis of fact. It has had the widespread support of industry and commerce throughout the country. It has sought merely to serve and has been ready to consider all figures, to respect all facts, and to reconsider any statement or conclusion in the light of further knowledge.

"Its mind has been open and its purpose was directed not to winning a controversy but solely and simply to serving the country. I believe it has developed standards of public cooperation which will be of permanent value."

In speaking to reporters, Redfield also commented upon the ruling of Attorney General A. Mitchell Palmer that the board's attempt to come to agreement with the steel industry violated the antitrust laws. "But the point is," Redfield said, "that the board has known that it has had no authority in law. It never expressed the desire for any such authority—never sought it. I do not understand that by his ruling the Attorney General held that any action taken by the board was illegal." *Ibid.*, May 10, 1919.

[The White House, May 10, 1919]

No. 114 In the beer proclamation[1] time is of the essence. Great demonstration of 250,000 labor men scheduled for next week. If you wait until after demonstration, you will seem to be whipped into action. Election of Republican Mayor of Baltimore last week by 10,000, first Republican Mayor in forty years, significant.[2] Analysis shows many votes lost to Democrats by reason of your proclamation.

If you set us right in this matter, we will carry New Jersey, New York, Massachusetts and Kentucky this fall, otherwise danger. Cummings, who has been in many states of the West, agrees with me as to political effect. Tumulty.

T telegrams (WP, DLC).
¹ See HCH to WW, Sept. 13, 1918, Vol. 49, and JPT to WW, May 9, 1919 (third telegram of that date), Vol. 58.
² In the election held on May 6, William Frederick Broening, a Republican and the Attorney for Baltimore of the State of Maryland, defeated the Democratic candidate, George Weems Williams, by a plurality of approximately 9,000 votes. The brief report in the *New York Times*, May 7, 1919, commented that many independents had voted for Broening because of their dismay at the defeat of the incumbent Democratic mayor, James Harry Preston, in the primary election held a month earlier, and that "home rule" had been an issue in the campaign, since Williams had been supported by the state Democratic party organization in the primary. The report in the *New York Herald*, May 7, 1919, said that Broening's victory was "believed to mean a protest against prohibition, the democratic party being held responsible for the 'dry' spell to come."

From the Diary of Dr. Grayson

Sunday, May 11, 1919.

The President arose about 10:00 o'clock. He did not go to church as Mr. Clemenceau called up early in the morning asking for a conference with the President. Clemenceau stated that it was extremely important and urgent. It was a rather remarkable coincidence that about the time Clemenceau called up I learned that the French newspapers this morning were very loud in their praises of the "magnificent manner" in which Clemenceau had disposed of the German claims. As usual, the French were doing their best to steal the credit for the work that the President was doing. All along this has been in evidence. Whenever something especially good is handed out they try to make it appear—and the British do the same for Lloyd-George—that it was the product of either of the French or the British Premiers. In this respect, however, they differ very little from some of the American delegates who also try to take credit for what the President has done or is doing.

The President accordingly arranged to see Clemenceau at about 11:30. In addition to Clemenceau, he had Balfour and Mr. Venizelos of Greece at the meeting. They discussed the Italian effort to seize certain of the Greek Islands under the pretense that they had been ceded to them by the Pact of London. The Greek Government feels very strongly over this question, and Mr. Venizelos made it extremely plain that Greece expected that her rights to these Islands would be protected.

In the afternoon, after luncheon, the President and Mrs. Wilson went for a long motor ride. They returned in time for dinner, and after dinner the three of us spent a quiet evening here at the temporary White House. The President told me that information had reached him today that the Italians had changed the name of Via Wilson to Via Fiume. He simply laughed and said: "They are a big lot of babies." He said that it was so amusing that he told Mr. Balfour and Mr. Venizelos this morning and they both laughed very heartily. Mr. Venizelos understands English quite well and has an excellent sense of humor. Mr. Balfour always enjoys a good joke.

The President during the evening reminisced about his student days. He told a story about Dr. James McCosh, who was President of Princeton University when the President was a student there. He was an old Scotchman and very serious. They had services every morning in the Chapel. The President said that it was always the custom for the boys to applaud their class number. The President was in the class of '79. One morning the old man got up and announced: "We will now sing Hymn No. 79." And the boys all applauded. He became very indignant, closed the hymnal, laid it down, and lectured them on their disrespect. He then picked up the hymnal, opened it, and said: "We will now sing, let me see, Hymn No. 80—No, No, No, we won't sing that—you will make noise—we will turn to a higher number." Whereupon they all applauded. But the old man could not see the point.

The President told another story that when he was a student at Princeton he was entirely out of money and did not even have a stamp with which to write home for funds. He remembered that a short while before a penny had rolled under his bureau, so he got down on his knees looking for it but he was unable to find it. He removed the bureau and finally located the penny back in the corner. With it he bought a postal card and wrote home for money.

Mantoux's Notes of a Meeting of the Council of Four

May 11, 1919, 12 noon.

Balfour. I see that there has been an indiscretion in Constantinople and that the Turks have been informed—from what it appears, by our own representatives—of our intentions regarding Smyrna. I am very angry about it.

Clemenceau. I come to ask you to delay our action for forty-eight hours: we must, indeed, be careful about our position vis-à-vis the Italians. We will tell them that we were obliged to take a decision in their absence, but that we wish to talk to them about it before it has taken effect.

I took the time to review the Treaty of London and the accord of Saint-Jean de Maurienne.[1] Mr. Lloyd George said the other day that the promise to give Smyrna to Italy was contingent on Italian participation in England's military action in the East; now, I do not find one word about that in the convention of Saint-Jean de Maurienne. Mr. Lloyd George's memory has betrayed him. I know well that, by the Treaty of London, the Italians committed themselves to declaring war immediately against our enemies and that they only declared war against Germany after thirteen months and against Turkey after eighteen months.

Balfour. The Treaty of London provided compensations for Italy in case we ourselves made acquisitions in the East.

Clemenceau. The Italians should not be given the opportunity to say that, after having refused them Fiume, which had not been promised to them, we are refusing them Smyrna after having promised it to them.

Mr. Balfour re-reads the Treaty of London (summary):

In case of acquisitions by the Powers in the eastern Mediterranean, Italy will receive compensation in the province of Adalia, where her interests are already recognized by the Allied Powers, and, if the Ottoman Empire should be divided, Italy would have the right to occupy certain specified territories.

Balfour. I have had many conversations on this subject in London, with the Marquis Imperiali, M. Paul Cambon, and the Russian Chargé d'Affaires.[2] It was a question of defining that obligation more precisely. Such was the situation when I left for America. In my absence, the Italians demanded a solution instantly. I had shown my opposition to their pretentions toward Smyrna: at Saint-Jean de Maurienne, Mr. Lloyd George, no doubt for valid reasons, promised it to them. Indeed, the other day he said that it was in exchange for a promise of cooperation in Asia; but, as M. Clemenceau has said, his memory deceived him.

What we can say is that that promise does not bind us, because it depended upon the consent of Russia, and that this consent was never given.

Wilson. Whatever our position might be from a purely legal point of view, I do not see how we can morally justify the cession of Smyrna to Italy.

Hankey. The document issuing from the negotiation at Saint-Jean de Maurienne is rather obscure; but there is no doubt that it was signed under the condition of the consent of Russia.

[1] About which, see n. 13 to the minutes of the Council of Four printed at May 6, 1919, 11 a.m., Vol. 58.
[2] Konstantin Dmitrievich Nabokov.

Clemenceau. That is what we can say to the Italians.

Wilson. I am not disposed to let the Italians do what they will in that part of the world. I distrust their intentions. If I published in America all that we know about their activity and their intrigues, that would cause their infernal machine to hang fire for a long time.

Clemenceau. In any case, I ask that you delay our action in Smyrna. I insist, furthermore, that our troops land together. I agree with you about not letting the Italians occupy the forts; but if they should not land with us and with you, we would put ourselves in a bad case. I propose that the French, English and Italians land at the same time, promising each other to reembark when the Greeks come to take their place.

Wilson. It is on this point that the Italians can resist us.

Clemenceau. We must expect resistance on their part. It is better that it take place now, when we will be speaking to them about it.

Wilson. Are you firmly of the opinion that Smyrna must go to the Greeks?

Clemenceau. Yes; I only ask that you delay our operation in Smyrna for at least twenty-four hours. We will tell the Italians that we were obliged to take this decision in their absence. If they ask us why we did it, we will tell them that we were given disturbing information about the danger run by the Greek populations and that we could not wait for their return.

Balfour. That will not get us out of our difficulty, for they will ask the question: "Will you leave Smyrna to the Greeks?"

Clemenceau. For my part, I am ready to give it to them; but there is no reason to say so before the time when we will be taking general decisions about the fate of the Ottoman territories.

Vénisélos. I have just received a dispatch from the commander of the warship that we have at Smyrna. He reports that the Italian battleship *Regina Elena* has landed workmen at Scala Nuova[3] who have fitted the jetties and landing-stages in anticipation of a landing. Three hundred sailors, along with officers, landed next; but two days later, they reembarked, after a kind of inspection of the coast. Landings of this type seem to indicate designs upon Smyrna. The Treaty of London, as far as I can tell, promised the Italians Adalia.[4] But when we speak of Adalia, we exclude Smyrna; otherwise all of the south of Asia Minor would go to the Italians.

As for the conference of Saint-Jean de Maurienne, M. Ribot[5] explained to me what took place there: the heads of the Allied governments were assembled there in order to discuss the letter from the

3 Now known by its Turkish name of Kusadasi.
4 Now usually known as Antalya.
5 That is, Alexandre Félix Ribot, who was Prime Minister of France at the time.

Austrian Emperor to Prince Sixtus of Bourbon[6] and not to discuss Asiatic questions. Mr. Lloyd George suddenly revealed to M. Ribot that he had decided to offer Smyrna to Italy, in order to turn the Italian government toward the idea of a separate peace with Austria. Thus that offer of Smyrna to Italy was not the result of negotiations; it was made by English initiative to Baron Sonnino, who naturally accepted it, and who, moreover, made his objections to the idea of a separate peace with Austria.

The Italians have already made landings not only at Adalia, but at Marmaris; they seem to be preparing to make them near Smyrna.

A commission, as you will recall, attempted to settle the Greek question in Asia Minor by determining the ethnographic boundaries. In the calculation of ethnic majorities, I had proposed to include the population of the islands with that of the peninsula. But that proposal was rejected. As a result, the Greek majority has diminished or disappeared in certain regions; this is why the country to the south of Smyrna was not assigned to us in the report of the commission. But if that region should be placed under a European mandate, we will ask that this mandate be entrusted to us, at least for a period of ten years. It must not be given to Italy: she would have still another very long stretch of coast to the south of Anatolia, along with large territories in the interior, including the *vilayet* of Konia.

Wilson. But if Italy should keep the Dodecanese, would it not be better that the neighboring continental region were placed under the same government? It is not, for my part, what I wish.

Vénisélos. I really hope that the Dodecanese will not be left to Italy. There is not even there, as in Dalmatia, 4 percent of Italian population. These islands are entirely Greek and have always been for three thousand years. I must say that, in a conversation which I had some time ago with M. Orlando, he told me: "The Dodecanese and Smyrna will return to you, but when we have settled our own affairs in the Adriatic."

To come back to the planned landing, I have had information from two telegrams from the English naval attaché in Athens,[7] which indicates that Admiral Calthorpe will take over the forts with English and French contingents. The landing of the Greeks will only take place later, after understanding with Italy.

Wilson. The Italians will not fail to ask why they should not land also.

Vénisélos. I think that, if Admiral Calthorpe is present in person, all will go well.

Clemenceau. I will call to your attention that we are not dealing

[6] About which, see RL to WW, May 10, 1918 (first letter of that date), n. 1, Vol. 47.
[7] Acting-Commander Gerald Talbot.

with a purely military affair. It would be a great error to proceed to an act of sheer force without having first spoken to the Italians about it.

Vénisélos. It is not an act of war: it is only a police operation.

Clemenceau. You do not dispose of the forces of the Entente. You have the right to give your opinion, and I have the right to give mine. My responsibility is too great in this affair for me to accept the least unnecessary risk.

Vénisélos. Would not the best way to proceed be to tell Admiral Calthorpe to summon the Turks to surrender the forts, and to warn you immediately if the Turks refuse?

Clemenceau. Impossible: that would be the worst of all. Do you see us asking the Turks for permission to occupy the forts and exposing ourselves to their refusal?

Balfour. What had been proposed on the subject of the Italians was that they land at the same time as the French and the English, but that they occupy the docks and customs, while the French and the English occupied the forts.

Wilson. If necessary, we could say that the Italians made a landing without warning us and that we have the right to do the same.

Clemenceau. That can be a good argument in the conversation which we will have with them; but that conversation must take place.

Balfour. I should recall that this question touches on two considerable problems: the one of the mandates in Asia Minor and the one of the Italian situation, which gives me much anxiety. The Italians, without any doubt, are behaving very badly. But unless we wish to break with them, it will be necessary to accommodate ourselves to some of their methods.

Their state of mind is very singular. Yesterday, at the Quai d'Orsay, we were discussing the southern frontier of Austria. Baron Sonnino, at a moment when a proposal was being made which was in no way contrary to Italian interests, cried out: "The atmosphere here appears completely hostile to Italy!" Believe me: regarding them, we are like a man who walks on very thin ice. It is possible that it might end in conflict, but we must do nothing to precipitate it. That affair over Smyrna, in the mind of the Italians, will be tied to the Adriatic affair, like that which we were discussing yesterday, about the railroad from Trieste to Villach. We can be forced into a conflict; but unless you mean to provoke it yourselves, do what M. Clemenceau asks, speak first to the Italians. We shall see if that conversation produces an explosion.

Wilson. I myself am ready to burst; I will soon be forced to speak. Everywhere, the Italians are creating dangers for peace by the injustice of their claims. If their case were publicly exposed in its crudity, the entire world would abandon them. I have always said that I reserved my right to appeal to my country.

Balfour. A policy of conciliation is necessary, at least until the signing of the peace treaty with Germany.

Wilson. The Germans have already anticipated our break with Italy.

Balfour. That would create the most painful situation.

Wilson. They must be spoken to tomorrow.

Balfour. What was the origin of our decision? Was it the Greeks who were the first to speak to us about their fears of massacres in Asia Minor?

Vénisélos. No, I was consulted when the discussion had already begun. Like you, I had received disturbing information about the situation in Asia Minor; I said that it was inconceivable that Greek troops remain inactive in Macedonia while the Turks were massacring Greek populations in Asia.

Balfour. Do you not fear that, if we land at Smyrna, that would only provoke massacres in other parts of the country?

Vénisélos. No; the Turks respect force.

Balfour. I am not going back on the decision taken; the question is how we must carry it out.

Wilson. Is not the best thing to send Admiral Calthorpe to Smyrna, telling him to observe and to await orders?

Balfour. What change in our earlier decision does M. Clemenceau propose?

Clemenceau. I ask that we wait twenty-four hours.

Wilson. I suggest that we to send Admiral Calthorpe there without delay, while delaying the execution by twenty-four hours.

Clemenceau. I see no objection to that.

Vénisélos. Meanwhile, the fleet could stop at Chios.

Clemenceau. Why stop it half way? I would prefer that it wait twenty-four hours in the harbor of Smyrna.

Mr. Balfour reads aloud an outline of a telegram drawn up in the sense indicated, addressed to Admiral Calthorpe.

Balfour. There are other questions to settle. M. Clemenceau has informed us that he sees a difficulty in the French occupying the forts alone, and that for diplomatic reasons. Do the heads of government wish to modify their resolution in this sense?

This modification is adopted.

Clemenceau. I believe that we will not be able to land more than two hundred men.

Balfour. Is it very certain that the Turks will not fire?

Clemenceau. I fear nothing on that score.

Vénisélos. Care should be taken to indicate that the Italians must not land troops in numbers greater than your own; otherwise they will seize the opportunity to play the dominant role and to put themselves in command.

Balfour. As a matter of fact, they must be in a position to land more men than we, and they will do it, in the absence of an express agreement.

Mantoux, II, 39-44.

From the Diary of Colonel House

May 11, 1919.

Thos. Nelson Page and André Tardieu were the only interesting callers. Page told me he had put in his letter of resignation to the President to take effect at the end of June. He is disturbed at the Italian situation, although his resignation has nothing to do with it. He has contemplated it for some time. He feels, as I do, that the President, Clemenceau and George are trifling with a dangerous situation. The President has not set a time for seeing Page although he has written him two notes and I have telephoned him. I told the President if he did not see Page he would probably resign immediately and that, I thought, would make the situation even more difficult than now. The President disagreed with this, saying it would make no difference whether Page resigned now or later.

I had an interesting talk with Tardieu upon the Italian question. He says he cannot make Clemenceau look upon it seriously; that the old man seems delighted that the Italians came back without being invited, and that no attention has been paid to them. He does not seem to realize where the lack of appreciation of this very delicate and dangerous situation may lead. Tardieu says that Lloyd George is even more indifferent than Clemenceau. I told him the President was but little better. He wondered how they could be brought to a proper realization, and we discussed different methods. Tardieu discusses matters with me with the utmost frankness. Everything that goes on in French Cabinet circles that he knows about, he imparts to me.

He says Foch has lost much prestige by having declared to the Ministry that he would resign unless he had his way in the peace terms and then failing to do so when he was defied. Tardieu was interested to hear me say that the French Ambassador to Rome[1] was turned back at the Swiss frontier in the middle of the night. Pichon had given him permission to come to Paris. Clemenceau heard of it and immediately countermanded Pichon's permission and had imperative orders given to the Ambassador to return to Rome. Clemenceau considers that the Ambassador has made as much mischief as he well can at Rome and he did not intend that he should come to Paris to continue it. Page tells me he was on the same train with Barere (?) and said goodnight at ten o'clock and made arrangements to see him in the morning. When Page asked for him the next morning he was startled to find that at two o'clock he had disembarked.

¹ That is, (Pierre Eugène) Camille Barrère.

From Joseph Patrick Tumulty

[The White House, May 11, 1919]

No. 115 In view of the opening session next week, quick action highly desirable to block probable Republican action on the following matters:

First, opening American shipyards to foreign contracts;

Second, statement that telegraph lines and telephones and railroads (if Hines thinks this wise) will be returned to owners July first and remedial action to reimburse sought afterwards. Leffingwell agrees with me as to telegraph lines and telephones.

Third, lifting prohibition bans;

Fourth, statement from you that Harris has agreed to vote for suffrage and therefore amendment will be adopted.¹

Republican conference to take action on these matters in a few days here, which makes it necessary to act immediately to forestall them.

Tumulty.

T telegram (WP, DLC)
¹ See WW to JPT, May 13, 1919.

From the Diary of Dr. Grayson

Monday, May 12, 1919.

The President arose early and worked in his study until 11:00 o'clock when the Big Four resumed its session, taking up for consideration the two notes sent by Brockdorff-Rantzau, and which referred to the question of German prisoners of war and the international labor situation. The German note regarding the prisoners of war dealt with conditions of repatriation and requested that conditions be relieved among the German prisoners held in France and Great Britain. It was also asked that these prisoners before repatriation should be allowed to obtain in France articles of wearing apparel, especially boots and shoes, which were not now obtainable in Germany. The note dealing with the labor situation criticised the labor program prepared by the Allies and asked that another labor conference be held at which the German government and especially the German labor experts should be allowed to be present. Both of the notes were referred by the Big Four to committees of the Peace Conference to prepare replies.

The President and Mrs. Wilson lunched together. I was suffering from a boil on my neck, and I asked them to excuse me from coming to the table, as I did not think my boil a good dinner companion. They both were very sweet in insisting that I should come to the table.

In the afternoon the Council of Ten reconvened for the first time in several weeks, taking up for discussion the boundary clauses which were to be inserted in the treaty of peace with Austria. This was a very necessary matter inasmuch as it is now obligatory upon the Peace Council to define the boundaries of the states into which the former Austro-Hungarian Empire has been separated.

After dinner I went down and sat with the President and Mrs. Wilson for a few hours. They played Canfield and I sat by and talked with them.

Hankey's Notes of a Meeting of the Council of Four[1]

President Wilson's House,

C.F.9.   Paris, May 12, 1919, 11 a.m.

1. M. CLEMENCEAU read a letter he had had from Brockdorff-Rantzau on the subject of Labour Legislation (Appendix I),[2] together with a draft reply (Appendix II).[3]

[1] The complete text of these notes is printed in *PPC*, V, 565-75.

[2] U. K. C. von Brockdorff-Rantzau to G. Clemenceau, May 10, 1919, TCL (SDR, RG 256, 180.03401/9, DNA), printed in *ibid.*, pp. 571-72.
  Brockdorff enclosed a draft of an international agreement on labor law (not included with this document but printed in *ibid.*, VI, 774-78). He made three general comments on the labor provisions of Section XIII of the draft peace treaty. First, he noted that Section XIII "only partly realized in principle" the "demands for social justice repeatedly raised . . . by the working classes of all nations." Second, he declared that the German delegation deemed it necessary that all nations should participate in the labor agreement, even if they did not belong to the League of Nations. Third, he suggested that representatives of the national trade union organizations of all the contracting powers "should be summoned to a conference at Versailles to discuss and take decisions on international Labour Law" before the conclusion of the peace conference. The proceedings of this labor conference should be based upon the resolutions adopted by the International Trade Unions Conference held in Bern, February 5-9, 1919.

[3] "PRELIMINARY DRAFT OF A REPLY TO HERR BROCKDORFF-RANTZAU," May 12, 1919, T MS (SDR, RG 256, 180.03401/9, DNA), printed in *ibid.*, V, 573.
  The draft responded in turn to the points raised by Brockdorff in the letter summarized in n. 2 above. First, it noted that Article 427 of the draft peace treaty indicated clearly that the enu-

MR. LLOYD GEORGE said that the reply was a matter of some importance and should be carefully studied. It would be a serious matter for France and for Great Britain if the Germans were to work 10 hours while we were limited by law to 8 hours.[4]

PRESIDENT WILSON said that as an 8 hours man he did not share this view. The United States' experience had been that men could produce more in 8 hours than in 10.

MR. LLOYD GEORGE agreed generally, but said that in some forms of labour, for example, cotton, he did not think the principle applied. In regard to coal, for example, the British experience had been that the adoption of shorter hours had lessened output.

PRESIDENT WILSON agreed in regard to unskilled labour but not in regard to cotton. He thought the real argument was that it would be disadvantageous to the Allied and Associated Powers to have the sympathy of their working classes excited in favour of the German working classes, thus setting up a sympathetic connection between the two.

MR. LLOYD GEORGE suggested the question should be referred for a reply to the Labour Advisers of principal Allied and Associated Powers.

(It was agreed that the letter from the German Delegation should be referred to a Committee of Labour Experts which should in-

---

meration of principles in Section XIII was not inclusive. "The purpose of the organisation set up by that part of the Treaty," it continued, "is that it should pursue the constant development of the International Labour Regime. All the necessary improvements will be brought about through that organisation."

In response to Brockdorff's second point, the draft responded as follows: "The Labour Convention has been inserted in the Treaty of Peace and Germany will therefore be called on to sign it. In the future, the right of your country to participate in the organisation created by Article 387 will be determined by the situation of Germany in respect of the League of Nations, that situation being defined by Article I of the Treaty and by the reply sent on May 10th by the Allied and Associated Governments to your letter dated 9th of the same month."

On the third point, the draft said that it had "not been thought necessary" to summon a labor conference at Versailles. The conclusions of the "Syndical Conference at Berne" had been studied "with the closest attention," and representatives of the "Syndicates" had participated in the preparation of the articles of the peace treaty relating to labor. Moreover, the proposed program of the first session of the International Labor Conference, to be held at Washington as soon as the peace treaty came into force, already comprised "the majority of the questions raised at the Syndical Conference at Berne."

[4] The discussion in this and the ensuing three paragraphs seems to be based upon a careless reading, at least by Lloyd George, of the documents sent by Brockdorff. The German draft of an international agreement on labor law (cited in n. 2 above) and the resolutions of the International Trade Unions Conference at Bern in February 1919 (for the text of which see *Conditions of Peace With Germany*, 66th Cong., 1st sess., Sen. Doc. No. 149, pp. 36-39) both provided for the eight-hour day for workers in all nations signing such an agreement. However, Brockdorff also enclosed two other sets of resolutions adopted by international labor conferences held in Leeds in July 1916 and in Bern on October 4, 1917 (both are printed in *ibid.*, pp. 39-47). Both of these documents included a provision permitting a ten-hour workday. Moreover, German delegates were present at the conference at Bern in 1917. It was presumably the ten-hour-day provision accepted by the latter conference that Lloyd George had in mind in the above comments. He simply ignored, or failed to note, the fact that the plan presented by Brockdorff called for an eight-hour day.

clude M. Colliard,[5] of the French Delegation, Mr. Barnes of the British Delegation and Mr. Robinson of the United States Delegation.)

M. Orlando undertook to nominate an Italian representative.

Sir Maurice Hankey was instructed to communicate this decision to the Secretary-General.

2. M. CLEMENCEAU read a letter he had received from the German Delegation on the subject of prisoners of war (Appendix III), but the question of the reply was postponed until the afternoon.

3. With reference to C.F.8. Minute V,[6] Sir Maurice Hankey handed round the draft of a letter to Lord Cunliffe on these subjects.

(The letter was approved, signed by M. Clemenceau and dispatched to Lord Cunliffe.)[7]

4. M. ORLANDO said he had a question of special interest to Italy to raise in connection with reparation by Austria and by Hungary, namely, the question of the tonnage in the Adriatic. In his view, the same distribution of the enemy tonnage could not be applied in the Adriatic as in the case of the German tonnage. The reason of this was that in the Adriatic whether the ships served Italian interests or Jugo-Slav interests, there was this common bond between them that if they were taken away from the Adriatic, it would deal a death blow to Italian ports and to Jugo-Slav ports. Hence, the portion of the Austrian-Hungarian tonnage in the Adriatic must not be dealt with on the same principles as the German tonnage. In reply to M. Clemenceau, he stated that these ships had been sequestrated by the Allies and used in the Mediterranean for the benefit of the Allies. The question now arose as to whom they should belong in the future. It would mean ruin to all the ports in the Adriatic if they were taken away from that sea.

M. CLEMENCEAU said he did not quite understand what was proposed.

MR. LLOYD GEORGE said that surely M. Orlando did not suggest that Italy, while obtaining a share of the German ships, should also appropriate all the Austrian ships remaining in the Adriatic. If this were done, the Northern Powers being excluded from any share in

[5] That is, Pierre Colliard.

[6] See the minutes of the Council of Four printed at May 10, 1919, 4 p.m.

[7] It is missing in the minutes of this meeting. However, an abstract, dated May 12, 1919, appears in Philip Mason Burnett, *Reparation at the Paris Peace Conference, From the Standpoint of the American Delegation* (2 vols., New York, 1940), I, 275-76. It reads as follows: "Says Cunliffe's letter of May 8, asking whether Succession States should bear part of costs of war, was considered by Supreme Council on May 10. Agreed that these should bear no part of Austro-Hungarian war debt, but that experts should take as basis of discussion that they should pay share of reparation. Experts to estimate what Succession States as whole capable of paying; then recommend apportionment, taking prewar liabilities as well as capacity into account. This investigation without prejudice to final decision on whether Poland should participate."

the Austrian ships, while the Italians were receiving not only the whole of the Austrian ships but their share of German ships also, would not be fairly treated.

M. ORLANDO said that the question of the Austrian ships would not make an addition to the Italian tonnage, since they had a special economic use which was quite distinct from the Italian mercantile developments. To say to Italy that the acquisition of these ships would compensate her losses was not fair because, in fact, Italy would be acquiring certain ports that had essential shipping needs of their own. These ships would have to be appropriated as they had been in the past for the services of these ports.

MR. LLOYD GEORGE said he did not mind if Italy would stand out of the German claim altogether and take her chance of recouping herself from the Austrian-Hungarian Mercantile Marine. Most of the fighting with Germany had been done by Great Britain and France but, nevertheless, it had been decided to give Italy a share of the shipping. If Italy was to have a share of the ships of the nation she had not fought and in addition to have all the merchant ships of the nation she had fought, he really could not understand what logical basis was being acted on.

PRESIDENT WILSON said that what M. Orlando was claiming was that the Adriatic fleet should not be removed from that sea.

MR. LLOYD GEORGE said it would be equally fair and right to say that North Sea ships were not to be removed from the North Sea. The German ships plying in the North Sea were just as essential there as the Austrian shipping was in the Adriatic. Nevertheless, the British Government had never thought of making such a demand.

M. ORLANDO wished to put the question in another aspect. He greatly regretted the effect of his proposal on Mr. Lloyd George as he was firmly convinced of its justice. Italy was now to have Trieste which was a great commercial sea port. If, however, Trieste was to be handed to Italy but its mercantile fleet was to be taken away, Italy would receive a ruined city. It had been rightly decided that Alsace-Lorraine was not to contribute towards reparation. Alsace-Lorraine was not a maritime country but was a riverside country and in that case it had been decided that the river craft should not be included in the German craft ceded for reparation, but should be left to Alsace. All he asked was the application of the same principles to Trieste since without these ships Trieste would be a ruined city.

M. CLEMENCEAU pointed out that Great Britain had lost a very formidable tonnage.

M. ORLANDO said Italy had also.

M. CLEMENCEAU said that the Italian losses were not comparable to the British.

MR. LLOYD GEORGE thought that the British losses were larger in proportion even than the Italian.

M. CLEMENCEAU said he entirely agreed with the views expressed by Mr. Lloyd George.

PRESIDENT WILSON asked what exactly M. Orlando intended by the Trieste mercantile fleet.

M. ORLANDO said the merchant ships registered at the port of Trieste.

MR. LLOYD GEORGE said he was not familiar with what had been decided about river craft on the Rhine, but he would point out that these could not be used anywhere else, whereas the ships registered at Trieste could for the most part be used in any part of the world. If Italy gave notice of this proposal, he would object to Italy having any share of the German ships. During M. Orlando's absence it had been agreed to share the Italian ships equally. Now Italy said that she was quite prepared to share equally in the German ships, but must have also all the Austrian and Hungarian ships. He must enter a strong protest against this proposal.

M. ORLANDO said that he regretted that his ideas of justice did not correspond with those of Mr. Lloyd George and M. Clemenceau. He then read the following extract from Annex III of the Reparation Clauses in the Treaty with Germany (Part VIII, Annex III, Clause 3, Page 108):

"The ships and boats mentioned in paragraph 1, including all ships and boats which (a) fly, or may be entitled to fly, the German Flag; or (b) are owned by any German national, Company or Corporation, or by any Company or Corporation belonging to a country other than an Allied or Associated country, and under the control or direction of German nationals; or (c) or which are now under construction (i) in Germany; (ii) in other than Allied or Associated countries for the account of any German national, Company or Corporation."

All he asked was that the the same basis should be applied to the Austro-Hungarian nationals, but it should not apply to any citizen of Trieste, since these were becoming Italians.

MR. LLOYD GEORGE said that what M. Orlando meant was that, as in the German treaty only ships belonging to German nationals were being taken, the ships registered at Trieste must not be taken, since the inhabitants of Trieste became Italian citizens.

PRESIDENT WILSON pointed out that they would not be Italian citizens until the Treaty was signed.

MR. LLOYD GEORGE said he was quite unable to understand how this proposal could be made. Hundreds of thousands of tons of Allied shipping had been sunk in carrying wheat and coal and munitions to Italy, and yet the Allies were not to participate in the tonnage received from Austria. Under this scheme Trieste and Pola were to be ruled out, because they were to become Italian, and the only ships to be taken were those in Sebenico and Spalato and other Jugo-Slav ports. In fact, as the Jugo-Slavs had now become Serbs and were Allies, the principal Allied and Associated Powers would be ruled out altogether.

M. CLEMENCEAU agreed that if this principle was adopted they would never touch a penny.

MR. LLOYD GEORGE said he hoped it would never be necessary to tell this story in Parliament, in order to explain why Great Britain could get no part of the Adriatic Fleet.

M. ORLANDO said that it would be impossible for Italy to deprive Trieste of her Fleet so that the result would be that the rest of Italy would get no reparation for the ships lost.

MR. LLOYD GEORGE said that the most dangerous voyage during the war had been that to Italy, and the British mercantile marine had lost very heavily in these narrow seas. He entirely disputed that Trieste would be ruined any more than any other port. If there was a chance of trade and business being done, ships of all flags would go there.

PRESIDENT WILSON pointed out that Austria by this treaty was likely to be deprived of all access to the sea, so were the Czechs and other parts of the old Austro-Hungarian Empire. Consequently, by the application of M. Orlando's principle all the ships belonging to Czechs and Hungarians would be divested of their nationality.

M. ORLANDO asked if he would be free, as Mr. Lloyd George suggested, to abandon the Italian share of the German commercial fleet and accept instead the whole of the fleet registered at Trieste and Pola.

M. LLOYD GEORGE said there were two principles of reparation. Either (1) that Italy should put in a claim against the Germans for damage inflicted on her by Germany and another claim against the Austrians and Hungarians for damage inflicted by Austria and Hungary; or (2) to share in the total amount for reparation. Possibly there might be a third principle, namely, that Italy should look to Austria for the whole of her reparation, while Great Britain and France looked to Germany. He knew of no other principle except those three.

M. ORLANDO said that the least he could ask was that Italy's share of the ships should include the ships at Trieste.

PRESIDENT WILSON asked if he made this demand whether the amounts were in the proper proportion or not.

M. ORLANDO replied yes.

MR. LLOYD GEORGE said that M. Orlando's intention was, supposing Italy received 100 ships, that these ships should be picked out from the Trieste ships. This was a question which might be discussed.

5. M. CLEMENCEAU said that there only remained the Greek affair, on which some explanation should be given. During the absence of the Italian delegates from Paris, the Greeks had asked us to agree to a disembarkation at Smyrna, which we conceded. As a consequence, a concentration of ships had taken place, he believed at Kavalla. There was no question of making a repartition affecting Smyrna, but we desired that the Greeks should be able to land to protect their co-nationals from massacres; many such had lately taken place. We considered it convenient that British, French and Italian detachments should take part in the landing. So far as we know there were at Smyrna many Italian warships, 6 or 7.

M. ORLANDO said there were only 2.

M. CLEMENCEAU said that we should not wish that the British, French and Italian disembarkation should be made in a different manner. France had there only a small force, and we should not like the Italians to land a much larger detachment. We could not do that without warning M. Orlando in order to ask him to make appropriate dispositions.

M. ORLANDO asked if it was a question of Greek, French, British, and Italian landing.

M. CLEMENCEAU said that the Greeks would occupy Smyrna, but, he repeated, we did not pretend to give an indication of any repartition of territory.

MR. LLOYD GEORGE said we proposed that the occupation should be a Greek occupation, to suppress massacres lately perpetrated against Greek subjects.

M. CLEMENCEAU repeated that the Greeks had asked permission to make this landing.

PRESIDENT WILSON, interrupting, said that the original suggestion had not come from the Greeks. The Council had suggested to the Greeks that they should land their troops to prevent massacres.

M. CLEMENCEAU said: Yes, that is right. In these circumstances, and in order to prevent a conflict, and to keep the best possible order, Admiral Calthorpe had been asked that he should go from Constantinople to Smyrna. According to his information, the Italians had already disembarked some time back some sailors at Smyrna, and then they had been withdrawn.

M. ORLANDO said he had no information to this effect.

M. CLEMENCEAU said that what was intended was that simultaneously with the Greek occupation there should be a disembarkation of Italians, French and English, leaving the custody of the city to the Greeks.

MR. LLOYD GEORGE said that the Allied disembarkation was solely for the occupation of the forts, and that they would be replaced by Greeks, when they would embark again. It was natural that there should not be more commands in a single place. The command at Smyrna would be Greek.

(Turning to Colonel Hankey, he asked if Turkey had been warned.)

SIR MAURICE HANKEY said it had not.

MR. LLOYD GEORGE said that Sir George Riddell[8] had received a letter from a British inhabitant of Smyrna, a thoroughly reliable man whom he himself knew quite well, giving a very bad account of Turkish atrocities on the Greeks, which included massacres and tortures.

M. ORLANDO said he was not well up in this question, and would like to postpone his answer in the afternoon when he had talked it over with M. Sonnino.

MR. LLOYD GEORGE said that according to his information, three Italian landings had taken place without any notice to their Allies, namely, at Makri, Marmaris, Budrum and at Scala Nuova. He asked if that was true and what was the reason for them.

M. CLEMENCEAU said that there was also a landing in Adalia.

MR. LLOYD GEORGE said we knew all about that.

M. ORLANDO said it was on this question that he wished to consult M. Sonnino, who knew all about the matter.

PRESIDENT WILSON asked that he would take particular note of the landings mentioned by Mr. Lloyd George.

6. PRESIDENT WILSON asked Sir Maurice Hankey how matters stood as regards the preparation of the Austrian and Hungarian Treaties.

SIR MAURICE HANKEY replied that he had, in accordance with instructions, circulated the report of the Foreign Ministers on the subject of boundaries, and that this was ready for consideration.

(It was agreed to meet on the same afternoon with the Foreign Ministers at the Quai d'Orsay and consider the boundaries of Austria and Hungary.)

[8] That is, Sir George (Allardice) Riddell.

Letter from Herr Brockdorff-Rantzau to M. Clemenceau on the Subject of Prisoners of War

(Translation.)

German Peace Delegation,
Versailles, 10th May, 1919.

Sir,

The German Delegation has noted with satisfaction that the Draft Treaty handed to it recognises the principle that the Repatriation of German Prisoners of War and German Interned Civilians is to be effected with the greatest possible rapidity.

It is in accordance with the opinion of the German Peace Delegation that the task of settling the details of execution of that Repatriation should be entrusted to a Special Commission. Direct conversations between the Commissions pretty well of all the Bellligerent States in regard to Prisoners have been shown to be the best means of solving the difficulties, and it ought to be all the easier at the present moment to clear up by early discussion in a Commission any divergencies of view or doubts in regard to certain points. The German Peace Delegation, bearing in mind the difference of jurisdiction in the various countries concerned, is of opinion, for instance, that it is indispensable for Prisoners of War and Interned Civilians, who have been detained for offences other than those against discipline, to be repatriated unconditionally. Germany has recognised this same principle as regards the Prisoners of War and Interned Civilians of the Allied and Associated Powers detained in Germany. In the view of the German Peace Delegation, certain alleviations should, as a matter of course and for reasons of equity, be agreed in favour of Prisoners of War and Interned Civilians for the period which will elapse until their final departure.

The German Peace Delegation has, moreover, been compelled to note that the arrangements contemplated are favourable only to the Allied and Associated Governments, for instance, so far as concerns the restoration of private property, the search for persons who have disappeared and the care to be taken of graves. The German Peace Delegation presumes that, for questions such as these, complete reciprocity may be required for general reasons of humanity.

Because of the great technical difficulty of repatriating Prisoners of War and Interned Civilians, especially in view of the shortage of tonnage and the lack of coal, the greatest importance should be attached to finding a solution of all preliminary questions before the despatch of the repatriated Prisoners and Interned Civilians actually begins. For that reason, the German Peace Delegation proposes that the Commission should start its deliberation forthwith, separately from all other questions. The explanation of this proposal lies, firstly in the fact that there are thousands of German Prisoners of War and Interned Civilians in oversea countries, but the German Delegation is likewise thinking of the Germans who are in Siberia, and whose despatch seems to be a question not only of special urgency, but of extraordinary difficulty.

The German Delegation, for reasons of internal policy, regards it of the utmost importance that the German Prisoners of War and Interned Civilians should be returned to their homes in as normal conditions as possible, in order that they may there be brought back as rapidly as possible into the economic life of the country. That only appears possible—the precise settlement of transport problems apart—if everything possible is done to improve the mental and physical state of those who are returning home.

Having regard to the present situation in respect of economic existence in Germany, it must be admitted that Germany is unable to do with her own resources everything required in order to secure that end. This refers especially to food and clothing; therefore the German Delegation thinks it desirable that the deliberations of the Commission should likewise include an examination of the question of the manner in which the Allies and Associated Governments might assist Germany in the solution of these problems. The question arises, for instance, of supplying against repayment complete sets of clothing (underclothing and civilian clothing), and footwear for the prisoners before their despatch.

I avail, etc., etc.,   (Signed)   BROCKDORFF-RANTZAU.

T MS (SDR, RG 256, 180.03401/9, DNA).

Hankey's Notes of a Meeting of the Council of Four[1]

President Wilson's House,
C.F.10   Paris, May 12, 3:30 p.m.

1. M. LOUCHEUR was introduced.

With reference to C.F.6, Minute 4,[2] M. LOUCHEUR drew attention to the revised edition of Article 430 of the German Treaty as approved by the Supreme Council of the principal Allied and Associated Powers on May 10th, which reads as follows:

"In case either during the occupation or after the the expiration of

the fifteen years referred to above, the Reparation Commission
finds that Germany refuses to observe the whole or part of her obligations under Part VIII (Reparation) of the present Treaty, the
whole or part of the areas specified in Article 429 will be re-occupied immediately by the Allied and Associated Forces."

He pointed out that some portions of the Reparation Clauses were
scattered through the Treaty, and not included in Part VIII. He
therefore asked for the omission of the words "under Part VIII."

(It was agreed that the words "under Part VIII (Reparation) of the
present Treaty" should be omitted, and that the following should
be substituted: "For reparation as provided in the present Treaty."
Article 430 of the Treaty should therefore read as follows:
"In case either during the occupation or after the expiration of the
fifteen years referred to above, the Reparation Commission finds
that Germany refuses to observe the whole or part of her obligations for reparation as provided in the present Treaty, the whole or
part of the areas specified in Article 429 will be re-occupied immediately by the Allied and Associated Forces."
(The words underlined show the alteration in the last draft.)

2. MR. LLOYD GEORGE said that there was a demand from the British Parliament for the Treaty of Peace to be laid on the Table of the
House. He had replied that he must consult his colleagues before he
could possibly consent. Mr. Bonar Law had given his view that as a
summary had been published,[3] the inference would be drawn if the
Treaty was not published that the summary was inaccurate.

M. CLEMENCEAU said he had already refused to lay the Treaty,
both to the Senate and the House of Representatives [Chamber of
Deputies].

M. ORLANDO said he did not like publication, as it made it so much
more difficult to make changes.

M. SONNINO agreed with this view.

PRESIDENT WILSON said that he could not lay the Treaty before
the Senate until he returned to the United States.

(It was agreed that the text of the Treaty of Peace as handed to the
Germans should not be laid before the legislatures of the Allied &
Associated Powers.)

(M. Loucheur withdrew.)

3. PRESIDENT WILSON asked what was the decision of his Italian
colleagues in regard to the questions put to them that morning.

M. ORLANDO said he accepted in principle. He thought it might be
preferable to leave the troops of the Principal Powers on shore, and
not to withdraw the British, French and Italian detachments, pending the final decision as to the disposal of Smyrna. That was the only
alteration he asked for.

PRESIDENT WILSON said that the landing parties from the British and French ships would not exceed 200.

MR. LLOYD GEORGE said that the British detachment would not exceed 50.

M. SONNINO said that their retention on shore would give the expedition an international character.

M. CLEMENCEAU asked who would have the command?[4]

MR. LLOYD GEORGE said the Greeks.

PRESIDENT WILSON agreed that the command must be Greek, since Greece disposed of by far the largest force.

M. CLEMENCEAU thought it unsuitable to place the troops of the Principal Allied Powers under Greek command. Nothing could be more to the point than the decision taken today that the landing was without prejudice to the ultimate disposal of Smyrna in the Treaty of Peace.

PRESIDENT WILSON thought it undesirable to leave handfuls of men on shore.

MR. LLOYD GEORGE said that Sir George Riddell's correspondent, of whom he had spoken in the morning, had himself seen Turkish troops firing at Greeks, and had seen two quite harmless people shot. There had been no rebellion or provocation.

PRESIDENT WILSON considered a continued joint occupation unwise.

M. ORLANDO said he would not insist.

MR. LLOYD GEORGE asked whether the Turks would now be told?

PRESIDENT WILSON said they would be told 12 hours before the movement took place.

MR. LLOYD GEORGE asked if the Greeks could leave at once?

PRESIDENT WILSON said he understood that they could. Kavalla was only 24 hours distant.

M. SONNINO asked if the ships were already assembled?

MR. LLOYD GEORGE said that this was the case. The decision had been taken more than a week ago.

(It was agreed:

That the Greek force should start from Kavalla as soon as ready, and that an Italian detachment should take part in the landing of Allied forces.

Sir Maurice Hankey was instructed to communicate this decision to the British naval authorities for the information of Admiral Calthorpe, and to M. Venizelos.)

T MS (SDR, RG 256, 180.03401/10, DNA).

[1] The complete text of these notes is printed in *PPC*, V, 576-78.

[2] See the minutes of the Council of Four printed at May 10, 1919, 11:45 a.m.

[3] About which, see JPT to WW, May 7, 1919 (second telegram of that date), n. 1, Vol. 58.

[4] Mantoux, II, 51, here reads as follows:
"Clemenceau. We say to you: today Smyrna belongs to no one; it is not a question of determining the fate of that city, but of carrying out a temporary operation, with a well-defined objective. I would see great difficulties in leaving French, English, and Italian troops under the command of a Greek general."

Hankey's Notes of a Meeting of the Council of Ten[1]

BC-61.   Quai d'Orsay, May 12, 1919, 4:00 p.m.

Frontiers of Austria and Hungary.
A. Frontier between Jugo-Slavia and Austria.

M. CLEMENCEAU asked M. Tardieu to explain the finding of the Committee on Jugo-Slav affairs.

M. TARDIEU gave an explanation of the finding of the Committee substantially identical to that given in I.C.182 and in I.C.184.[2]

MR. BALFOUR asked whether any method of obtaining a plebiscite in the Klagenfurt Basin[3] had been thought out.

M. TARDIEU replied that no methods had been suggested, as the Committee had not thought it necessary to propose any, until the plebiscite had been accepted in principle.

M. CLEMENCEAU enquired whether the principle of the plebiscite was accepted.

PRESIDENT WILSON replied in the affirmative.

MR. LLOYD GEORGE also agreed.

BARON SONNINO expressed the view that if a plebiscite were resorted to in this area, there should be one in Marburg[4] and in other doubtful corners along the proposed frontier.

MR. BALFOUR said that it was true there were other regions with mixed populations, but if the Conference were satisfied that it possessed sufficient knowledge to solve these problems without a ref-

[1] The full text of these minutes is printed in *PPC*, IV, 501-507.
[2] I.C.182 and I.C.184 are identical with FM-12 and FM-14, that is, the notes of the meetings of the Council of Foreign Ministers held on May 8 and May 10, 1919, printed in *PPC*, IV, 670-77, and 696-703, respectively. In the meeting of May 8, the Foreign Ministers and the experts present discussed the reports of the several territorial committees on the boundaries of Hungary. The explanations centered on the necessity to leave sizable ethnic minorities outside their natural homelands if the boundaries were to be drawn in any logical fashion and with regard to geographic, economic, and other considerations. The Foreign Ministers also considered the question of whether the existing boundary between Austria and Hungary should be modified. At the meeting on May 10, they discussed the report of the Committee on Yugoslav Affairs on the proposed boundary between Austria and Yugoslavia. Again the problem of ethnic minorities was stressed.
[3] Often referred to also as the "Klagenfurt area." It covered roughly the area of the Drau (or Drave) River Valley between the towns of Villach, Völkermarkt, and Lavamünd on the west, north, and east, respectively, and the Karawanken Mountains to the south. The center of the Klagenfurt Basin was the industrial and rail city of Klagenfurt. For a precise definition of the boundaries of the Klagenfurt Basin ultimately included in the plebiscite, see Article 49 of the Treaty of St. Germain, as printed in Nina Almond and Ralph Haswell Lutz, eds., *The Treaty of St. Germain: A Documentary History of Its Territorial and Political Clauses* (Stanford, Calif., and London, 1935), pp. 138-39.
[4] Now Maribor, Yugoslavia.

erendum, he could see no reason why a plebiscite should not be resorted to in the isolated case of the Klagenfurt Basin if the Conference did not think itself sufficiently well-informed to decide its fate without one.

M. TARDIEU pointed out that the Commission had been unanimous not only regarding the rest of the frontier, but in recommending a plebiscite in this area.

PRESIDENT WILSON pointed out that the most urgent business before the meeting was to frame a clause for the Treaty. Some definite stipulation should be put down. He read the draft prepared by the Committee on Roumania and Jugo-Slavia, given as Article 5 on page 31 of Report No. 2, (W.C.P. 646):

"In the whole of the basin of Klagenfurt, as defined below, an Inter-Allied Commission will be charged by the five Allied and Associated Powers with the duty of ascertaining on the spot the wishes expressed by the inhabitants as to the attachment of their territory to that of the Jugo-Slav State.

If the conclusions of this Commission establish the formal desire of the population to be attached to the Jugo-Slav State, the five Allied and Associated Powers reserve the right to give satisfaction to such desire."

MR. BALFOUR agreed that all Austria need know was that the people in the area in question would be consulted.

M. ORLANDO said that if he understood the clause aright, it meant that the fate of this territory was reserved until the conclusion of the labours of the Commission set up by it. On these terms he would accept the draft Article.

The draft Article regarding the consultation of the population in the Klagenfurt Basin by an Inter-Allied Commission was accepted.

M. TARDIEU then proceeded to explain the difficulty regarding the triangle south-east of Tarvis.[5] (See I.C. 184 and Annexure.)[6]

[5] Now Tarvisio, Italy.
[6] Tardieu referred to the so-called "Assling Triangle," a territory whose center was the rail junction town of Assling (now Jesenice, Yugoslavia). At the meeting of the Council of Foreign Ministers on May 10 (discussed in n. 2 above), Sonnino had argued vigorously that both this triangle and the Tarvis area itself should be assigned to Austria rather than Yugoslavia, so that the two vital railroad lines connecting Trieste with Austria would not cross territory held by what he regarded as an unfriendly third power, Yugoslavia. The report of the Committee on Yugoslav Affairs had recommended that the boundary line between Austria and Yugoslavia be drawn north of the Tarvis and Assling areas and that the disputed territory be ceded by Austria to the Allied and Associated Powers, which would determine its ultimate disposition. Sonnino, in the interest of a speedy settlement with Austria, agreed to this proposal, with the proviso that the boundary line should be so drawn as to include the more westerly of the two rail lines, that from Trieste to Villach via Udine and Tarvis, within the area permanently held by Austria. In addition to the minutes of the Council of Foreign Ministers cited in n. 2 above, see the map of the area printed in René Albrecht-Carrié, *Italy at the Paris Peace Conference* (New York, 1938), p. 165, and H. W. V. Temperley, ed., *A History of the Peace Conference of Paris* (6 vols., London, 1920-1924), IV, 368-69.

BARON SONNINO asked at what date the final attribution would be made. He expressed the opinion that the occasion of making a Treaty with Austria was the best moment for settling this.

MR. BALFOUR explained that the result obtained at the last meeting of the Foreign Ministers (see I.C.184) a compromise had been reached solely in order to obtain means of settling speedily with Austria. He agreed with Baron Sonnino that the final attribution of this territory must be made at some date. He suggested that if it were not settled immediately, it might be considered when the Conference came to decide on the boundaries of Jugo-Slavia.

M. CLEMENCEAU suggested that this course should be adopted.

BARON SONNINO adhered to the view that the matter should be settled immediately; not only was it an Italian interest, but it was also a first rate Austrian interest. It concerned the Austrians to know by what means they would communicate with the sea. The territory in question was a small mountainous wedge with a very small population. It was quite separate from the question of Fiume, and it could readily be decided in connection with the forthcoming Treaty with Austria.

PRESIDENT WILSON pointed out that two questions were involved. One was that of the ultimate sovereignty to be acknowledged by the population of the district. As this population was predominantly Jugo-Slav, the natural answer would be that the sovereignity should be Jugo-Slav. The second question was that of direct railway communication between Austria and Italy. In a similar instance the Conference had found no great difficulty in settling an almost identical problem. Arrangements had been made to ensure unimpeded transit between Eastern and Western Prussia.

BARON SONNINO pointed out that in order to give Czecho-Slovakia some 60 kilometres of railway, about 60,000 Magyars were to be subjected to Czecho-Slovak sovereignty. This had been done in order to ensure unimpeded railway communication between Czecho-Slovakia and Roumania. Similarly, no less than 280,000 Magyars had been handed over to Roumania, and in Poland, together with 100 kilometres of railway, some 100,000 Germans had been made Polish subjects.

(Considerable dissent was expressed from this statement. Such solutions might have been proposed by Committees, but had not yet been accepted by the Council.)

M. CLEMENCEAU said that the proposal which he asked the Council to accept or reject was, that the limits of Austria should be fixed provisionally, and that the final attribution of the triangle in question be reserved until the frontiers of Jugo-Slavia were determined. This would be in accordance with the decision of the Foreign Secretaries of the previous Saturday. (I.C.184.)

(This was finally agreed to and the frontier of Austria as proposed by the Committee on Jugo-Slavia in the report and in the annexure to I.C.184 was accepted.)

(The southern frontier of Hungary as set forth in the document annexed to these Minutes (Annexure A) was also accepted.)

B. Frontier between Czecho-Slovakia and Austria.

M. CAMBON made a statement explaining the findings of the Committee on Czecho-Slovak affairs. He pointed out that the administrative boundary between Austria and Bohemia had been followed almost throughout. There were two small deviations. Firstly, at Gmund, the railway junction of which was to be left within Czecho-Slovakia. This junction was situated at some 4 kilometres from the town and was the junction of the two main lines serving Bohemia. The second deviation was near Feldsberg, at the join of the rivers Thaya and Morava. These two streams were the main arteries of Moravia and gave access to the Danube. The line had therefore been drawn in such a way as to give the stream to Czecho-Slovakia, while the railway parallel with the stream which was necessary to Vienna, was left within Austria.

M. CLEMENCEAU asked whether any objections were raised to the solution proposed by the Committee.

(No objections were raised, and the frontier proposed by the Committee was adopted.)

C. Frontier between Austria and Hungary.

PRESIDENT WILSON pointed out that it would be necessary to specify the frontier between Austria and Hungary in the Treaty with the former. He reminded the Meeting that it had been decided to set up a Commission to investigate this matter in order to prepare the Conference for the raising of the question by either of the parties interested. He was informed that the Austrians would raise the question, and that the Allied and Associated Powers would be called upon to decide it. He read the decision recorded in I.C.182 Para. 1D,[7] and asked whether any nominations had been made.

(No nominations had been made.)

BARON SONNINO asked whether it would not be enough to require Austria to recognise the independence of Hungary, and Hungary that of Austria, without raising the frontier question at all.

PRESIDENT WILSON said that he was informed the Austrians would raise the question.

---

[7] The decision was as follows: "It was decided that a Commission be appointed to collect information regarding any possible rectification of frontier between Austria and Hungary which might be proposed by either of the parties concerned. The object of the investigation was to be to place the Council [of Foreign Ministers] in a position to settle rapidly any trouble that might arise between Austria and Hungary on this subject. No action would be taken unless the question were to be raised by Austria or Hungary." *PPC*, IV, 675.

(After some discussion it was decided that Austria would be required to recognise the frontier of 1867 between Austria and Hungary, and that if any difficulty arose regarding this frontier, the Allied and Associated Powers might if necessary arbitrate.)

D. Remaining Frontiers of Hungary.

After a short statement by M. Tardieu the frontiers of Hungary, as laid down in Annexure A,[8] were accepted.

(The Meeting then adjourned.)

T MS (SDR, RG 256, 180.03101/68, DNA).
  [8] Printed in *PPC*, IV, 505-507.

Two Letters from William Shepherd Benson

My dear Mr. President: Paris, May 12, 1919.

I beg to quote for your information the following letter from Rear Admiral Andrews,[1] dated May 18, 1919, relative to conditions in and about Fiume and Trieste:

"1. In regard to the number of Italian troops around Fiume and Trieste, and to the northward and eastward respectively of each, I find the figures given in the fourth paragraph of my personal letter of 6 May[2] to be practically correct. The Duke d'Aosta's[3] Third Army comprises about 100,000 men. The Italian General here[4] informs me that his own force in this district has been very little increased, and that no more increases will be made. I have had very frank talks with him, and have asked him absolutely direct questions, and have gotten satisfactory and good natured answers. He says that the defenses that he has made are of the most elementary character, and erected only for the purpose of guarding against rush on the part of the Serbians. I personally went around the Gulf of Bakar this morning and up through the Serb and Jugo-Slav territory to the railroad station at Bakar, and returned by the upper road to Fiume. I saw no barbed wire entanglements, no trenches and no defenses of any kind. At the same time, I know that they have been prepared. I stopped at a railroad crossing which has Serb sentries on one side and Italian sentries on the other, and interviewed them. They said that they each was friendly with the other and that they crossed the lines and mixed all the time, that they had had no trouble, and that they liked each other. At this point the Italians have only a small outpost which looks at the passports of people going into Fiume on the railroad line. They walk half a mile to the railroad station of Bakar, which is within the Serb lines, examine the passports of the people on the trains, and walk back to their little camp. After seeing for myself the entire lack of danger in this particular point, I doubt very much if there is any more danger at any other point, and it seems to me that the chance of accidental collision between the Serbs and the Italians is exceedingly small. General Grazzioli said to me this morning that if this happened it would be on account of some drunken soldier, and I told him if such a thing did happen it should be treated by both sides as a local incident of no moment.

"The matter of the establishment of a neutral zone which I suggested to the French General[5] and the Italian General is in abeyance this moment. The French General thought it an excellent idea, but when he had time to think about it concluded that the Serbians could not possibly withdraw any distance from the Bakar railroad station, and I find a similar reluctance on the part of General Grazzioli to withdraw any further at that particular point. After seeing this particular locality, however, and noting the narrow winding roads, and the excessively hilly country, I don't think it makes much difference, certainly at that point, whether they move back from each other or not.

"General Savey, the French General, and Major Furlong,[6] U. S. Army, are out now, in accordance with my request, looking around the Armistice lines. They were to return last night, but had an accident to their automobile and have not yet returned. General Grazzioli has given additional urgent instructions to his front line soldiers to avoid trouble of any kind, and not to edge forward in the slightest degree. His desire to avoid trouble and his preparation of defenses of various kinds, I believe is not due to any orders that he has from Italy, but to his keen desire to preserve his professional reputation intact. It is a personal anxiety about his reputation, and his fear that some attack might possibly be made that leads him to take these unusual precautions. He claims now that he has received authentic news of the concentration of Serb troops at Ogolin [Ogulin].

"The MAURY is alongside of the dock nearest the town. The people from the town, Italian soldiers and sailors come down to the dock; some come on board to visit the MAURY, and many stop and talk back and forth to the men. Thirty men are going on liberty from the MAURY each day, and the number will be increased to fifty, which is the usual number going. Liberty is also being given by the ISRAEL at Venice, and the men belonging to the Port Office in Trieste move back and forth and around the city as usual. Nowhere is there even a glance of disapproval or distrust. The Italian officials are very polite, and in all places I have been, have been particularly friendly to me. My coming here has been welcomed by the French and British Commanders, and by the Slav people. They say it makes them feel safer. I believe, too, that the Italian General is glad to have me here.

"The men-of-war present are as follows:
Italian Armored Cruiser PISA
Italian Battleship EMANUEL[E] FILIBERTO.

Italian Battleship SAN GIORGIO.

2 Italian Destroyers.

British Cruiser CARDIFF.

British Destroyer CERES.

French FOUDRE (repair ship)

1 French destroyer.

"In conclusion: The situation here is not menacing nor even alarming. I consider the chance of any trouble here to be exceedingly small. I am awaiting the return of the French General to again take up the question of the neutral zone between the Serbs and Italians. I have not given up the question. If it cannot be accomplished at all points on the line where they touch, will try to get it agreed to at as many points as possible.   /s/   PHILIP ANDREWS."

The following Addenda to the above quoted letter was attached on a separate sheet:

"At my request, the French General here and Major Charles W. Furlong, U.S.A., American Military Observer, made an observation trip yesterday outside the armistice lines into Croatia. The[y] travelled about two hundred and twenty-five kilometers in a large triangle and saw only about twenty or thirty Serbian or Jugo-Slav soldiers in all. At Ogulin, where the Italian General had positive information there was a heavy concentration of Serbian troops, they saw no troops whatever and no soldiers at all of any kind. The whole country they passed over looked as if it had never heard of war and as if it had no desire to engage in it.

"Regular occupations were going on. There was plenty of cattle and the whole country looked entirely peaceful. No barbed wire was seen. No defenses were seen.

"Major Furlong has just returned, 4:00 p.m., 8 May, and reported the results of the trip. I told him to see General Grazzioli and let him know the results of the trip, and of the fact that there are no Serbian troops to the eastward in this vicinity."

Sincerely yours,   W. S. Benson.

¹ That is, Philip Andrews.
² It is missing in the W. S. Benson Papers, DLC.
³ Emanuele Filiberto di Savoia, Duke of Aosta, cousin of King Vittorio Emanuele III and former heir to the throne, commander of the Third Army, stationed on the eastern frontier of Italy.
⁴ That is, Gen. Francesco Saverio Grazioli.
⁵ Gen. Joseph Jean Michel Savy, commander of the French supply base of the Army of the Orient at Fiume.
⁶ Maj. Charles Wellington Furlong.

My dear Mr. President: [Paris] 12 May 1919.

The following despatch was received May 11th from Rear Admiral Bristol,¹ Senior U. S. Naval Officer Present in Turkish waters:

"Date, May 9th, 10:30 a.m. Smyrna, Turkey, quiet. Great Grecian demonstration for battleship LEMNOS. British destroyer arrived with Commodore Earl.[2] British Tankship WAR RAJAH for American ships."   Sincerely yours,   W. S. Benson.

TLS (WP, DLC).
  [1] That is, Mark Lambert Bristol.
  [2] Unidentified.

From Thomas Nelson Page

VERY CONFIDENTIAL

My dear Mr. President,   Paris, May 12th, 1919.

The information about the Italian situation is so disturbing that I feel that unless the situation be relieved I must return to Rome without delay and make due arrangements for eventualities. I came hoping for the opportunity to lay before you personally the information which I have received and which I hoped might tend towards a solution.[1] If I appear at all urgent it is because the matter is growing steadily more urgent. I have not seen any of the Italian representatives here, having purposely kept away from them until I could see you. I learn, however, this morning that they are making arrangements to return to Italy to-morrow, unless the Fiume matter is got out of the way before the Austrian Delegation is received, as any other course adopted by them would inevitably lead to their complete overthrow in Italy and possibly to such violent agitation there as would require all the efforts of the Government to prevent serious excesses. I hear on the other hand that French influences are working very effectively to create a situation touching America which will throw on us the entire blame for all trouble whatsoever and will present France as Italy's sole friend whose good offices have been prevented by America from enabling Italy to attain her expectations. Fiume still appears the one thing around which Italian expectation has been centered. Italy I believe appreciates fully the motives of France, I mean the Italian Government does, and yet they are ready to accept France at her word to escape from a situation which contains more immediate perils for them. The present situation is so crucial that I feel that you will pardon my seeming urgency in requesting a chance to place all the information in my possession at your disposal.

Always my dear Mr. President,
                    Yours very sincerely,   Thos. Nelson Page

TLS (WP, DLC).
  [1] In her diary entry for May 10, 1919, Miss Benham notes that Wilson saw Page for fifteen minutes on that same day. Obviously, Wilson did not give Page an opportunity to say very much.

From the Diary of Colonel House

May 12, 1919.

Today has been busy. It might well be called Italian Day. Sonnino and di Cellere lunched with us, Orlando called immediately after lunch and the President arrived around six o'clock to discuss the Italian question. The other guests at luncheon were, Lady Curzon, Lady Paget and Mrs. Leeds, Col. Mott[1] was also present. Sonnino had just left when Orlando arrived. He apologized for not having called in person sooner, but said he did not wish to embarrass me. We exchanged terms of friendship and admiration. He asked if he might come tomorrow at 9.30 for a real conference. I am looking forward to seeing him always hoping that we may strike a successful formula.

I have asked David Miller to see di Cellere tonight and tell him what I have in mind and urge him to get the Italians to accept it. He is to let me know in advance of Orlando's coming. . . .

The President's visit to the Crillon was wholly devoted to Italy, and I took the occasion to tell him how serious I considered it. Henry White was also present and sustained me, though weakly. I likened the present Conference to the Balkan Conference at London which broke up in a way which caused the second Balkan War, and really precipitated the World War. I deprecated the fact that he, Lloyd George and Clemenceau were not conscious of the fact that Italy had gone mad, as mad, indeed, as Germany had been just before and after the beginning of the World War. The remedy I proposed was the placing of Fiume and Dalmatia wholly under the League of Nations for such a period as was deemed necessary to allow good sense and calm judgment to prevail. He seemed for the first time impressed with the seriousness of the situation and I am more hopeful of a successful outcome. I told him of Orlando's visit today and of his proposed visit tomorrow in which he was deeply interested.

I took occasion, too, to tell him of his friend Prof. George D. Herron. He looked somewhat embarrassed and said with some asperity, "I am through with him." . . .[2]

The Associated Press gave me a copy of President Ebert's tirade against the President and his fourteen points.[3] I asked the President if he desired to answer it. He said no, and did not even want to read it, for the American people were satisfied with the peace and he did not care whether Germany was or not.

[1] That is, Grace Elvina Trillia Hinds Duggan Curzon, Mary Fiske Stevens Paget, and Thomas Bentley Mott. Mrs. Leeds cannot be identified.
[2] There is nothing in either the E. M. House Papers, CtY, or in WP, DLC, which reveals what House told Wilson about Herron. However, it probably concerned Herron's strong pro-Italian bias in the Adriatic controversy. There can be little doubt that Wilson's embarrassment and "asperity" grew out of Herron's attitude on this subject.

Herron himself had provided the evidence which led to Wilson's decision to have nothing further to do with him in G. D. Herron to Ante Trumbić, May 1, 1919, TCL, enclosed in G. D. Herron to WW, May 1, 1919, TLS, both in WP, DLC.

In his letter to the Serbian Foreign Minister, Herron was defending himself for his opinions as reported in a recent newspaper article which, he claimed, gave a very inaccurate summary of an interview he had granted to the author of the article. He denied, as he had repeatedly denied before, that he was a "delegate" to the peace conference or that he in any way spoke for Wilson or the American government. It was true that he had "upheld" Wilson in the European press and elsewhere for the past three years and that he had, from time to time, expressed to Wilson his own opinions on one or another phase of the European situation. However, he declared, he had "no reason whatever" for supposing that any opinion of his had ever had "the slightest influence" upon Wilson, or upon the American delegation at Paris. "In fact," he continued, "there is scarcely anything I know of in which the decision of the American Peace Commission has not been different from what I hoped such decision would be." He then reminded Trumbić that he had previously told him that he believed no "ethnographical solution" of the Yugoslav-Italian territorial dispute was possible: "I could see only a solution that was geographical." His solution was that Italy should have the geographical frontier of the Julian Alps, together with Trieste, Gorizia, and Istria; that Yugoslavia should have Dalmatia; and that "Fiume should be made an international free port for the whole of South-Eastern Europe, and for Italy as well."

Then Herron came to the nub of the dispute: "If Europe had consented to the making of peace on the actual basis of the Fourteen Principles, to which all countries were pledged by the signing of the armistice, then the ethnographical solution might be proposed. . . . But, as you yourself are perfectly aware, dear Dr. Trumbić, not a single one of those Fourteen Principles has actually been applied in one single instance in the settlement of territorial questions, or, so far as I can see, in any other questions. . . . *Peace has not been made on the basis of the Fourteen Principles, but on a basis of compromise. And the peace being actually what it is, and being made on the basis of compromise by all other nationalities, I feel that Italy is receiving the greatest injustice. Why should Italy's claims be settled by one law and the claims of all the other nations settled by another law? Why should Italy not be treated as the equal at least of Yougoslavia? If Yougoslavia is entitled to include alien populations in her frontiers, if France is so entitled, if Tchekoslovakia is so entitled, and in each case on the ground of security, why should Italy be put outside of the considerations which other nations are receiving at Paris?"*

Finally, Herron declared that Italy was being unfairly criticized for its alleged intransigence on the Adriatic question. He said that he himself had been asked by the Italian government to mediate the issue. Furthermore, he claimed that, on a second occasion, he had been asked by Wilson himself to talk to the two sides and that Orlando and Sonnino had shown a willingness to cooperate.

It should be noted here that there is no other evidence in the Wilson Papers to support this claim. The only response to Herron's letter to Wilson and its enclosure was GFC to G. D. Herron, May 6, 1919, CCL (WP, DLC), saying that he was bringing them to the President's attention.

From Wilson's standpoint, it was undoubtedly bad enough that Herron had expressed such opinions in a private letter to the Serbian Foreign Minister. However, Herron immediately compounded his error by publishing similar opinions in a Rome newspaper. The *New York Times*, May 4, 1919, summarized Herron's communication as follows:

"ROME, May 2.—The *Epoca* prints a letter today from Professor George D. Herron declaring that grave injustice is being done to Italy, and that the people of the various countries do not know what is happening behind the scenes in Paris.

"Professor Herron affirms positively that a settlement of the Adriatic question was about to be effected on two occasions, and that it only failed as a result of the intrigues of a few international financiers, diplomatically privileged, who, he declares, are the real cause of the existing crisis and 'all the political and moral failures of the Peace Conference,' and on whom 'will fall the responsibility for the ruin threatening the world.'

"This group, Professor Herron declares, seeks concessions for the development of Fiume and the Dalmatian ports, so as to monopolize shipping on the Adriatic. The scheme, he says, is one which contemplates the exploitation of the Serbian people and entailing [entails] complete commercial ruin on Italy by driving her flag off the seas and destroying her commercial and political relations with Rumania and the Balkans."

If all this were not enough to alienate Wilson, G. D. Herron to WW, May 7, 1919, TLS (WP, DLC), enclosed Ing. A. Coppo to G. D. Herron, May 5, 1919, TCL (WP, DLC). Coppo, whom Herron identifies as an Italian architect, asserted that French, English, and American bankers were primarily responsible for the Adriatic crisis. Herron's covering letter stated that the "facts" set forth by Coppo "about certain financial transactions" were "true." GFC to G. D. Herron, May 13, 1919, CCL (WP, DLC), stated that Wilson had read Herron's letter of May 7 and its enclosure "with interest." GFC to G. D. Herron, May 23, 1919, CCL (WP, DLC), acknowledging a Herron letter of May 20, which is missing, was the last direct or indirect communication from Wilson to Herron or from Herron to Wilson.

[3] The Associated Press seems only to have released to American newspapers a brief characterization, with a few brief quotations, of Friedrich Ebert's interview with, or statement to, an A.P. reporter on May 11. At any rate, the same brief report appears in the American newspapers examined by the Editors. *The New York Times*, May 13, 1919, quoted Ebert as saying that his statement was "a moral declaration of war upon all that remains of the old system of international politics." He called the treaty, as presented to Germany, a "monstrous document." He was also quoted as follows: "Germany has seized and unfurled a new banner on which are inscribed President Wilson's Fourteen Points, which the President apparently has deserted." The report then added that Ebert "discussed with outspoken frankness the peace situation, the state of the German people and the prospect of the immediate future."

The London *Times*, May 14, 1919, had a similar characterization of Ebert's statement but did quote two paragraphs as follows:

"Where is there to be found in the peace draft which Wilson jointly signed the slightest trace of the exalted ideals that he proclaimed? In his reply to the Note from the Pope, President Wilson said, on August 27, 1917, that peace would not be secured if based on political and economic restrictions calculated to benefit a few nations and paralyse others. When was there ever a peace offered to a defeated people which so completely contemplated its physical, moral, and intellectual paralysis as do the terms now enunciated at Versailles?

"The German people hope the world will not countenance such an avenging aspiration. It is already expectantly catching the first voices from the ranks of the French and English working men, and it pins its hope upon these harbingers of a new and better world. I and my colleagues hope and pray that the German people who staked all on Wilson and the United States will not find themselves deceived. If, however, American democracy actually accepts the present peace terms it becomes the accomplice and abettor of political blackmailers and surrenders the traditional American principle of fair play and sportsmanship."

Klaus Schwabe, *Woodrow Wilson, Revolutionary Germany, and Peacemaking, 1918-1919: Missionary Diplomacy and the Realities of Power*, trans. Rita and Robert Kimber (Chapel Hill, N. C., and London, 1985), p. 334, translates another passage from Ebert's statement from the version in the *Deutsche Allgemeine Zeitung*, May 13, 1919, as follows: "In our view, President Wilson should have refused to sign the treaty if he was forced to abandon his Fourteen Points altogether. * * * American democracy as a whole will become a party to this document of shame if Wilson's name remains on it. * * * We are depending on America to hold to its word despite all the objections the perpetrators of this policy of brazen thievery may raise. How this should be done is not our concern. That is the concern of those who proposed the Fourteen Points. If this sacred promise is broken, then the American people will be approving the fact that their name was misused to deceive a great nation that had fought bravely into laying down its arms."

From the Diary of David Hunter Miller

Monday, May 12th [1919]

After the meeting I stopped in to see Colonel House. In the first place he saw me with Sweetser[1] and arranged that Mr. William Allen White was to see me the next morning and I was to give him information and pass him on to other people. White is going to write articles or a book in favor of the President.

Colonel House then asked me about various matters: first, whether the President could appoint him as the representative of the United States on the Council without confirmation by the Senate. I told him I preferred to look up this question before giving my opinion; that in any event the Attorney General should be asked for an opinion; and in answer to his further question I said that I thought the President should follow out the Attorney General's opinion whether Congress thought so or not. I also told Colonel House that in view of the technical situation about the Treaty the President had the matter of its ratification in his own hands. He asked me to write him a memorandum on this point as well as an opinion on the former point.

He then talked about the Italian situation. He told me that he had seen Sonnino and Orlando at lunch and that he had spoken of me to them in very high terms so as to facilitate my negotiations. He said that he wanted me to see di Cellere and said to see if some suggestion could not be made for leaving the question of Fiume and Dalmatia for solution by the League of Nations later. He spoke of the necessity of giving time to permit American and Italian relations to improve. Mr. Auchincloss said that the Italians have had a cable saying that they are being delayed in their financial arrangements with the United States; that the Treasury is only doing what it must, and that the Guaranty Trust Company has turned suddenly very cold on the proposition for a $25,000,000.00 credit, and that they believe that this is due to the action of our Government, which, of course it is, as Davis sent a cable a few days ago directing it, or at least suggesting it.[2]

I then called up di Cellere and got him at the Meurice and went to see him. I told him that there were difficulties in the situation which I had alluded to but had never mentioned and could not discuss in detail. I suggested to him that the Italians should propose that Fiume and the mainland of Dalmatia should be left to the League of Nations for subsequent decision. He asked about the islands and I told him I thought that some of the islands could be assigned now to Italy as Colonel House had indicated this in response to my question, and that the remaining islands could be, perhaps, left under the same control as the Dalmatian hinterland. He spoke about the two ports of Zara and Spalato and I was not very precise as to these but I told him that when I spoke of the Dalmatian hinterland I meant that involved in the Pact of London, and said also that the other frontiers of Italy should be definitely determined now. He asked me what view I thought Colonel House would take and I told him I felt authorized to say that Colonel House would do what he could in the matter. He then spoke of his feeling of hopelessness since his interview with the President.[3] I simply mentioned in reply that the President, I understood, had been at the Crillon that afternoon and I had not seen him. At this he got up and said that he would immediately try to see Orlando and arrange for me to meet him at the Meurice at 11:15 tonight. He understood, of course, perfectly from my remark that Colonel House had talked with the President before giving me my instructions.

In the course of the conversation I suggested to him and told him that it was my own idea that possibly a formula might be drawn up regarding the subsequent disposition of these territories, something to the following effect: that in making their disposition the League of Nations should take into account the aspirations of the population[s], the necessities of the populations of the hinterland for access to the sea, and the interests and security of Italy upon the Adriatic.

He pressed me upon the question of the administration of Fiume and of Dalmatia. I told him that these were in my opinion, different questions and that I would suggest in each case, particularly in the case of Fiume, an administration somewhat similar to that provided for the Basin of the Saar, to which France had consented.

David Hunter Miller, *My Diary at the Conference of Paris, with Documents* (21 vols., New York, 1924), I, 300-302.
    [1] That is, Arthur Sweetser.
    [2] About this matter, see N. H. Davis to WW, April 18, 1919, and WW to N. H. Davis, April 19, 1919, both in Vol. 57, and N. H. Davis to WW, April 23, 1919, Vol. 58.
    [3] See the extract from the Grayson Diary printed at May 3, 1919, Vol. 58.

Frank Lyon Polk to the American Commissioners

Washington. May 12th, 1919.

1946. Referring my 1920, May 9th, 8 p.m.,[1] and Poole's 106, May 7th, to Mission, from Archangel,[2] following extracts from various cables furnished Department from time to time by Russian Embassy may prove of interest.

Kolchak's oath of office January 29th 1919 contains following passage: "I vow and swear to administer the supreme power vested in me by the Council of Ministers in accordance with the laws of the country until the establishment of a form of government by the freely expressed will of the people."

On his return from a tour of the front in March 1919 Kolchak addressed an assembly of the members of the municipalities, the zemstvos and the social organizations. His speech contained the following passage: "During this tour I have frequently met representatives of the zemstvos, municipalities and social organizations. I can affirm with great satisfaction that there is no divergency between the governments and my own opinions and those expressed by the people in the country. The time has passed, never to return, when state authority places itself in opposition to public opinion as a force to which it was distant and even hostile. New free Russia must repose on the principles of a union between the government and the people. I consider that in free Russia there can only be a democratic rule. The principal aims pursued by the government are universal suffrage, and in questions of local autonomy the expansion of this autonomy on broad democratic lines; social legislation regarding the labor and land questions the government bases its reform on the principles of state necessity and of social impartiality. As to international relations, the government is endeavoring to continue the relations established at the moment of Russia's entry into the war and to strengthen the old ties of friendship. The government, penetrated by the idea of the regeneration of our country, considers the sanc[t]ity [Russian people]3 the sole masters of their destiny and when the people, freed from the oppressing yoke of Bolshevism, will have expressed through representatives freely elected to the national constituent assembly their free will concerning the principles upon which shall be based the political, economic and social structure of the state, then my government and myself will esteem it as our duty to transfer to the government chosen by the national constituent assembly the full power now lodged in our hands."

The following concluding passage is taken from the declaration of the Omsk Government published February 10 in regard to the land question: "Laws governing the questions of land and property, its utilization, the temporary possession of seized lands, the equitable repartition of the land as well as indemnities to the former proprietors will be enacted in the near future. These laws will tend to transfer the land which formerly was cultivated by third persons (?) [remunerated] by the proprietors to the population which cultivates it and to contribute to the development of small rural properties which [whether they] belong to individuals or to communities. In arranging for the transfer of the land to the tilling peasants, the government will endeavor to give them the possibility of acquiring the land in entire ownership. The government assumes the responsibility of this act of historical importance fully convinced that such decisive measures will alone lead to re-establishment and will secure and guarantee the prosperity of the Russian rural population numbering tens of millions, this prosperity acting as a strong and solid foundation on which will be built a free regenerated and prosperous Russia."

The Embassy has furnished me with statements showing that during March and April declarations of allegiance to the Omsk Government were presented by municipalities, political and social organizations, and union of co-operative credit societies and the council of the co-operative societies of all Siberia; also numerous zemstvos organizations and the Cossacks of the Amur.

I bring this to your attention because of my belief that adequate

assurances which will require prompt observance in (?) [practice]
will be furnished by the Omsk authorities as soon as the allies indicate that we are prepared to give them definite support.

Polk, Acting.

T telegram (WP, DLC).
  [1] Printed as an Enclosure with V. C. McCormick to WW, May 17, 1919.
  [2] D. C. Poole, Jr., to the American Commissioners, May 7, 1919, T telegram (WP, DLC).
A copy of this telegram, addressed to Polk, is printed in *FR 1919, Russia*, pp. 342-44.
Poole reported that the anti-Bolshevik government at Archangel was "incomparably
stronger" than it had been as recently as February. However, the bulk of Poole's telegram
was devoted to a fervent plea that the Allies in general, and the United States in particular, should end their procrastination and take a strong, public stand against the Bolshevik
government in Moscow.
  [3] Corrections from the copy printed in *ibid.*, pp. 347-48.

Joseph Clark Grew to Gilbert Fairchild Close

Dear Mr. Close: Paris, May 12, 1919.

The accompanying communication[1] has been received from the
Secretary General of the Peace Conference under date of May 11,
1919, and is transmitted to you in accordance with a request by the
Secretary General that it be sent immediately to the President.

Very sincerely yours,   J. C. Grew.

TLS (WP, DLC).
  [1] N. P. Pašić to G. Clemenceau, May 9, 1919, TCL (WP, DLC). Pašić asserted that the
German and Austro-Hungarian armies had carried off from Serbia during the course of
the war virtually all of its cattle, agricultural implements, and other tools and had also
destroyed the country's railroads. Hence, Serbia was absolutely unable to take up her economic life. The Yugoslav delegates to the Commission on Reparation had strongly
pressed the need for adequate compensation for these losses, but the commission had
been unresponsive. Pašić urged that the Council of Four should allocate to Yugoslavia
two of the twenty billion marks to be turned over by Germany to the Allies in the immediate future.

From the Diary of Edith Benham

May 12, 1919

Nothing much to record yesterday, save dining with Mr. and Mrs.
Morgenthau last night. Col. and Mrs. Strong[1] were there. I think he
is or has been an Army Dr., for she spoke of having been in Manila
for twelve years and thought she knew you.[2] Mr. M. is a very interesting man, and asked if I wouldn't write a book with him about the
Peace Congress and the P.

He really meant it seriously, but I wouldn't take it so, for it would
be more glory for Morgenthau, whose reputation is already made,
and none for E.B. He voiced in another way something which I have
always felt might be the case—that the P. may run again. I have al-

ways felt, though the P. talks of the joy he will have when he is free and how nothing would induce him to run, that subconsciously he has that in his mind. I base this principally on the fact that every candidate mentioned for the Democrats while commending some of their qualities, he always gives conclusive reasons why they shouldn't run, and if they did why they couldn't be elected. Of course, none of this did I mention to Mr. M. when he said the P. had not come out for any candidate and probably he couldn't till next year. He said he would be under a fearful storm of criticism about the conduct of the war, the expense, and he will have the fight of his life this year, and the fate of his party rests on him and to save himself and his party he would have to declare himself a candidate and see if he could get a vote of confidence from the country by being elected.

[1] Richard Pearson Strong, M.D., and Agnes Leas Freer Strong. Strong had been Professor of Tropical Medicine at the Harvard Medical School since 1913 and director of the Government Biological Laboratory in Manila from 1901 to 1913. He had served with the A.E.F. as head of the Division of Infectious Diseases and was at this time general medical director of the League of Red Cross Societies.
[2] That is, Rear Adm. James Meredith Helm, to whom Miss Benham wrote the letters that were later typed up in diary form.

To Joseph Patrick Tumulty

Paris, 12 May, 1919.

Please ask the Attorney General to advise me what action I can take with regard to removing the ban from the manufacture of drink and as to the form the action should take. Please give the Secretary of the Treasury my heartiest congratulations on the success of the loan.[1]

Woodrow Wilson.

T telegram (WP, DLC).
[1] Carter Glass had decided early in 1919 that a fifth Liberty Loan would be necessary in the spring in order partially to fund the still increasing federal deficit. Congress provided for the so-called Victory Loan in an Act approved on March 3, 1919. The Treasury Department announced on March 12 that the loan campaign would begin on April 21 and end on May 10. On April 14, the Department further announced that the loan would be for a total of $4,500,000,000 in the form of $4\frac{3}{4}$ per cent three- or four-year convertible gold notes of the United States, exempt from state and local taxes, except estate and inheritance taxes, and from normal federal income taxes. On May 10, Glass issued a statement which predicted that the issue would be oversubscribed by midnight of that date. The prediction proved to be accurate. See the *Annual Report of the Secretary of the Treasury on the State of the Finances, for the Fiscal Year Ended June 30, 1919* (Washington, 1919), pp. 32-54, and the *New York Times*, May 11, 1919.

To Frank William Taussig

My dear Taussig: Paris, 12 May, 1919.

I am about to cable a message to Congress, which is to convene next Monday, and I would very much value a suggestion from you as to any recommendations that you think ought to be incorporated with regard to revenue legislation, particularly as affecting tariff duties. In fact, I would appreciate any advice you would be kind enough to give me in this connection.

Cordially and sincerely yours,   [Woodrow Wilson]

CCL (WP, DLC).

Three Telegrams from Joseph Patrick Tumulty

[The White House, May 12, 1919]

No. 116 There is a case involving the constitutionality of Act making country dry July first before Judge Hand, which may be decided any moment.[1] Think you ought to allow it to be announced at the White House here that you intend to raise the ban immediately. The form of the proclamation can be settled later. If you agree to this, please send me form of announcement.   Tumulty.

[1] Tumulty was a bit confused. The case did not involve the constitutionality of the so-called War Prohibition Act of November 21, 1918, about which see JPT to WW, Sept. 7, 1918, n. 1, Vol. 49, and WJB to WW, Nov. 20, 1918, n. 1, Vol. 53. Actually, the case involved enforcement of that Act. Augustus Noble Hand, judge of the United States District Court for the Southern District of New York, ruled on May 17, 1919, in a suit brought by the Jacob Hoffman Brewing Company for an injunction to restrain United States District Attorney Francis Gordon Caffey and the Acting Collector of Internal Revenue for the Third District, Richard J. McElligott, from attempting to interfere with the manufacture and sale of beer containing not more than 2.75 per cent of alcohol. Judge Hand ruled that the suit should come to trial. Hand denied Caffey's plea to have the suit dismissed and declared that the district court would have to decide whether or not 2.75 per cent beer was intoxicating under the terms of the War Prohibition Act. *New York Times*, May 18, 1919.

On May 23, Julius Marshall Mayer, another judge of the United States District Court for the Southern District of New York, after hearing a case combining the Hoffman suit with three similar ones, granted a preliminary injunction restraining Caffey and McElligott from interfering with the manufacture and sale of 2.75 per cent beer on the ground that it was not intoxicating within the meaning of the law. *Ibid.*, May 24, 1919. On June 26, 1919, the United States Circuit Court of Appeals for the Second Circuit upheld the contention that 2.75 per cent beer was not intoxicating and that McElligott had to issue the excise stamps for such beer, but ruled that the district court had been in error in enjoining the District Attorney from instituting criminal proceedings. *Ibid.*, June 27, 1919. Over the next few months, federal courts in various parts of the country ruled in opposite ways on the question of 2.75 per cent beer. The Supreme Court, on October 13, agreed to hear an appeal on the issue. *Ibid.*, October 14, 1919. On January 5, 1920, the high court ruled that the government could prohibit the manufacture of 2.75 per cent beer under the provisions of the Act of November 21, 1918. *Ibid.*, Jan. 6, 1920; 251 U.S. 264. By that time, of course, with the Eighteenth Amendment and the Volstead Act due to take effect on January 17, 1920, the issue had become moot.

[The White House, May 12, 1919]

No. 117 Have consulted the Attorney General with regard to removing ban upon manufacture of alcoholic liquors. Am in receipt of a letter from him in which he says, "The only action you can take until demobilization may be determined and proclaimed, will be to issue a public statement or send a message to Congress declaring that since the purpose of the Act has been entirely satisfied, nothing prevents your lifting the ban on the manufacture and sale of beer, wine or other intoxicating malt or vinous liquors except the limitations imposed by the Act which maintains it in force until demobilization is terminated after the conclusion of the war." My own opinion is that you should send a statement to be given out at the White House saying that the purpose of the Act of November 21, 1918, having been served, you intend to lift the ban and that you intend to consult the Attorney General to see if this is possible. If he advised you that owing to the terms of the Act this was not possible without further legislation, you would recommend that Congress repeal the Act.   Tumulty.

T telegrams (WP, DLC).

The White House, 12 May, 1919.

Issue of high cost of living most acute. It is felt here that the efforts of the Wheat Administration to avoid deficit has caused it to maintain price of wheat by artificial measures. Wheat is keystone in arch of high prices. Congress appropriated one billion dollars to make good guarantee to farmer. In trying to save this money for the Government, the whole cost of living is maintained at present high level. Opinion everywhere is that Government should take its hands off. You cannot understand how acute situation is brought about by rising prices of every necessity of life.   Tumulty.

T telegram (J. P. Tumulty Papers, DLC).

From William McAdoo[1]

My dear Mr President,   New York May 12th 1919.

To come out of so many complexities and such a whirlpool of national ambitions, passions and prejudices, the Treaty is, in my judgement, as nearly perfect, as such a document could be made.

At a time of doubt, I ventured to express to you the opinion, that it was your imperative duty to go to Europe.

If you had not gone, by this time, the whole world would have gone whirling into universal confusion, until the reactionary forces in every country would have clamored for the adoption of the pagan and brutal practices of the Prus[s]ian State.

The gentle, loving Jesus having overthrown the cruel, heartless, blood and iron Moloch of Bismarck and William II, you were consecrated and appointed to secure the harvest of a peace founded in justice, for suffering and sinning, but repentant and regenerated humanity. It was a Heavenly call that cried to you that your place was at Paris, and there you must stay until your work is finished.

I am taking advantage of confinement to my home, as the result of a painful, but happily not serious accident, (knocked down, bruised, and foot run over by an automobile) to impose this screed upon you.

In spite of Senator Lodge, Lenine, and Judge Cohalan the Fourteen Points prevail!

"Judgement also will I lay to the line, and righteousness to the plummet; and the hail shall sweep away the refuge of lies, and the waters shall overflow the hiding place." Isa. 28.17

That your bodily strength may equal the tremendous and unequaled burdens you bear, and that as the apostle of Justice and Righteousness, you may accomplish all you desire, is the heartfelt prayer of Mrs McAdoo, my daughter,[2] and myself.

Very sincerely yours,   William McAdoo

ALS (WP, DLC).
[1] Former Democratic congressman from New Jersey (1883-1891); at this time, Chief City Magistrate of the Magistrates' Courts of New York.
[2] Eva Lee Tardy McAdoo and Eva T. McAdoo.

From the Diary of Dr. Grayson

Tuesday, May 13, 1919.

The President arose early and spent the morning in his study going over various matters pertaining to the Peace Treaty. Because the committees to which the German labor and prisoner of war notes had been referred were not ready to report, there was no work for the Council of Four in the morning, and the President took advantage of it to clean up a good deal of business matters that had been hanging fire.

The President devoted a part of the morning to writing out headings for his forthcoming Message to Congress on his own typewriter and afterwards went unaccompanied for a short ride.

My boil was still troubling me so I remained in my room and I did not lunch with the President and Mrs. Wilson. Immediately after lunch the President came to my room to inquire how I was feeling. He sat down by the bed and discussed the future of the medical profession. He said: "I feel shy at the doctors who specialize too much. They only become acquainted with one area of the body— perhaps a very small area, and they do not know what is going on in the other regions. As I have heard you say, when a patient goes to see an up-to-date physician he is sent to one assistant or colleague to examine his blood, another his urine, another to an eye specialist, and so on, each making an examination without knowing what is going on in the other regions. I think it has a tendency to narrow the individual physician. I want for mine a general practitioner, who does not depend so much for other assistance and machinery to make his diagnosis. I think the old time general practitioner is the best medical man, and I believe that the medical profession will have to react back to that. I hope you will continue to practice in general and not localize too much." The President said that one winter[1] he, Mrs. Wilson and their three daughters had thirteen specialists during the winter, and he added with a smile: "And it wasn't such a very ill family at that after all. Fortunately, thirteen is my lucky number and we came out all right."

The President talked with me until time for his conference with Thomas Nelson Page, United States Ambassador to Italy. He gave the President at first-hand his impressions of what should be done to solve the controversy with Orlando and Sonnino.

In the afternoon the Council of Four conferred again, taking up the terms of peace with Austria. They referred to the drafting committee a number of problems upon which an agreement had been reached. These dealt especially with the eastern Austrian boundary question.

After dinner the President brought in his little Hammond typewriter in its case and put it on the table and resumed the work of framing his message to Congress. Before beginning he said: "I can change this key-board and can make it French, Italian or almost any other language. I do this by changing a bar of the type. However, all but English is barred." He said: "This message must of necessity be very short because I am leaving my real message until my return home so that I can deliver it in person."

The President and Mrs. Wilson were very solicitous about my neck, and Mrs. Wilson offered to open the abscess for me saying that she had done it a number of times for her father, who had been affected with the same trouble. I gladly accepted her generous offer. Their sweetness and kindness to me is indeed touching. They are so human and genuine.

[1] Of 1904-1905.

From the Diary of Colonel House

May 13, 1919.

Orlando was my most important caller. He arrived at 9.30 and remained until 10. We discussed the Adriatic question from every angle. I advised that the disputed territory be turned over to the League of Nations for a period until calmer judgment prevailed. I also suggested that I send David Miller to his apartment and that they together discuss the legal means by which a settlement could be brought about through the League of Nations or otherwise. Orlando named 11.30 for the appointment with Miller.

Miller was with him for an hour and a half. They did not reach an agreement but made some progress. They are to meet again tomorrow at nine. I advised the President of what I was doing and he expressed alarm for fear Orlando would take what I was saying as a direct offer from him, because of our close relations. I calmed his mind about this and assured him that Orlando understood just how matters were. However, I asked the President how a settlement could ever be reached if we did not discuss it in some such way as I was doing. I let him see that I thought he was being misled by the English and the French. They are constantly telling him of Italian misdeeds in the Near East, but they fail to speak of the misconduct of their own troops elsewhere.

From the Diary of David Hunter Miller

Tuesday, May 13th [1919]

I stopped in at Colonel House's and told him of my talk with di Cellere. I also handed him a copy of the American note which I delivered to Clemenceau a few days ago.[1]

Coming out of his office I met Orlando and Prince di Scordia[2] coming in.

Soon after reaching the office I had a telephone message to go over to see Colonel House. He told me that he had seen Orlando and had a satisfactory talk with him; that he had talked with the President over the telephone and that the President was aware of my conversation with Orlando; that the President had said that he would consider any solution which was reached by Orlando and myself. Colonel House said that I was to meet Orlando at the Edouard VII at 11:30 and that I was to tell him that I was not authorized by the President to reach an agreement but that any agreement reached between Orlando and myself would be supported by Colonel House, who would endeavor to put it through.

I went to see Orlando at the Edouard VII at 11:30. I was received by Count di Cellere who said Orlando would be a little late as he was talking with Lloyd George.

While waiting for Orlando I told di Cellere my powers and also showed him a map which I had brought with me.

At about 11:40 Orlando came in and commenced our conversation. No one else was present but di Cellere, who said very little, and the conversation was entirely between Orlando and myself and was carried on in French.

Orlando commenced by thanking me for my interest in the matter and my friendship for Italy and asked me if I would state in detail the idea which I had expressed through Count di Cellere.

He said that the Treaty of London was his last line of defense; if no solution was possible, if no delay were obtained, he would be compelled to fall back upon the Treaty of London for he would have nothing else, although he would not like it and did not believe it was in accordance with the principles of the President. He said that the question of Fiume was one of sentiment for Italy and not of interest; it was one of great importance.

I said to him that I had no authority to bind the President; that the President knew of the conversations which I had had with Count di Cellere and knew of the conversation which Signor Orlando had had with Colonel House that morning, and knew also that I was seeing Orlando; that the President had said that any solution which Signor Orlando might accept and which I would recommend he would consider. I added that Colonel House had stated that any such solution he would endeavor to have accepted; in other words, I said somewhat jokingly, "I have not full powers from President Wilson but I have full powers from Colonel House." To this Signor Orlando replied "C'est beaucoup."

I then said to Orlando that there was one question that seemed to me at least of as much importance as any that he had mentioned, and that was the continuance of the friendship which had so long existed between Italy and America; that there were persons and States represented in Paris, which it was unnecessary for me to name, who would be glad to see an interruption of that friendship, and that nothing in the interest of Italy could be so important as its continuance.

I then said that the solution which I proposed was the adoption of the frontier line of Italy in Istria west of the railroad which ran from Fiume to Vienna; the placing of Fiume and the entire Dalmatian coast under the administration of the League of Nations, including certain islands off the coast, the rest of the islands to be assigned to Italy; that the administration of Fiume should be somewhat like that of the Saar Basin, and likewise the administration of Dalmatia; that I would see no objection to granting to Italy a mandate for Zara and Sebenico, and that the League of Nations should be empowered to determine the future of these territories at any time or say after a period of five years, and that Italy would bind herself to accept the solution laid down by the members of the Council of the League of Nations other than the Italian representative. I added that Valona would go to Italy.

Orlando replied that he wished to talk with me with the utmost frankness and in the deepest confidence. He said, "I wish to show the weakness of my position. The feeling in Italy, particularly in the Army, is very strong. A month ago, not knowing what the Jugo Slavs would do, I ordered the stoppage of the demobilization despite the wishes of the men to go home, and to my surprise there has been no complaint of that order. Even men who served in the war with Turkey and who have been practically eight years under the colors were content not to go home but to continue under arms. I do not know whether, if I gave the order for the evacuation of Fiume, it would be obeyed."

Looking at the map showing the railroad from Fiume to Vienna, he replied that in a similar case before the Council of Ten he had advocated giving the railroad to Austria. I told him that I had seen the reports of that conversation and that I had simply adopted an Italian idea in suggesting that the railroad be given to Jugo-Slavia. He said that they would not particularly object to that solution although it would mean the loss of contact with Fiume if they were to have an interest in Fiume.

Then speaking of Fiume he said that it was of no value to Italy except as a matter of sentiment; that they had no interest in it in reality but that it was nevertheless a question of the utmost importance.

Speaking of my solution, he said that he was really thinking it out and that he was not making any proposition but simply discussing frankly the situation. "Would it not," he said, "be just as well to make Fiume an independent and free city in a political sense as to postpone its solution under the administration of the League of Nations, and in the meantime to assign a mandate to Jugo-Slavia for the Dalmatian coast except for the two towns I had mentioned?"

Speaking further of my proposition, he said it occurred to him that there was perhaps no [another] solution which was in principle the same as mine, namely, that it offered an opportunity for delay; namely, the continuance of the *status quo* and of the occupation by Italy with an agreement for a solution of the question after two or three years of such occupation. I told him that I saw enormous difficulties in the way of a continued occupation of Fiume by the Italians.

Orlando then spoke of the difficulties under which Italy was laboring. He said "France gets her news of the Peace all at once, whereas we get it little by little. How can we say to our people we lose Fiume when they do not know what we get?" I had no answer to this question.

At the end he said that he would like to continue the conversation; that in the meantime he would think over what I had said, and I could consider his observations; and after suggesting tomorrow evening as the time of meeting, he changed his suggestion to tomorrow morning at 9 o'clock, to which I agreed.

Coming out with di Cellere I asked him what he thought of our conversation, and he said he was somewhat encouraged. It was then after one o'clock. . . .

I saw Colonel House at 6:30 and told him of my talk with Orlando. He suggested sending a memorandum to the President on it but I told him that I thought it was best that the negotiation should go on until something more definite could be said to the President to which he agreed. In the meantime I had drawn up what I called a "Definitive Solution,"[3] which I proposed to submit to Orlando in the morning. Colonel House approved of it and said he would accept it in a minute and seemed hopeful as to the result of the negotiations. Indeed, he said that if the Three would keep their hands off and let me go on with Orlando it could be ended.

The maps which I had with me at the meeting with Orlando are in the files. I had also a copy of the Treaty of London. The map which I particularly showed to Orlando is the fourth map, and I explained to him jokingly that these were Jugo-Slav maps and it was better to adjust the question in using them than in using Italian maps.

I explained to Colonel House the difficulties in the situation. I told him that if I could think of anything which belonged to the British or the French which I could offer to the Italians I would be very glad to do it. Colonel House suggested that the definitive solution which I had drawn up be submitted to the President so that we could know what he thought of it. I objected to this. I said I would be very glad to know what he thought of it before it were necessary to go a little farther, but if the President agreed with this we would then have the difficulty of having to go farther with him, and Colonel House concluded that it would be unwise to interrupt the negotiations that way.

Mr. Auchincloss who was present suggested the possibility of a vote in Fiume, which Colonel House and I both thought was too late.

I am convinced from my talk today that the Italians realize perfectly that they cannot and will not have Fiume and that no negotiation is possible which does not admit this. I believe that Orlando would prefer a definite solution if it is one that it is possible for him to support at home. It is with this purpose that I intend to propose a definite solution in the morning.

Miller, *My Diary at the Conference of Paris*, I, 303-308.
    [1] Printed as Appendix II to the minutes of the Council of Four, May 6, 1919, 5:30 p.m., Vol. 58.
    [2] Prince G. di Scordia was a member of the Italian diplomatic service and one of Orlando's secretaries. The Editors have been unable to determine his given name.
    [3] It reads as follows:
    "1. Fiume will become an independent city and free port under the protection of the League of Nations.
    "2. The frontier of Italy in Istria shall exclude the railroad running from Fiume to Vienna.
    "3. The Dalmatian coast is assigned to the Jugo-Slav State except the Italian towns of Zara and Sebenico which are to be under the sovereignty of Italy as free ports.
    "4. The whole Dalmatian coast is neutralized, including Zara and Sebenico. No fortifications shall be erected, no bases established, and no military, naval, or air operations shall be conducted. The inhabitants shall not be subject to military service except for the purposes of local order.
    "5. Pago shall be considered as part of the Dalmatian coast assigned to Jugo-Slavia. The other islands in the Adriatic claimed by Italy are assigned to her.
    "6. Valona shall be Italian and any mandate of the League of Nations in respect of Albania shall run to Italy."
    Printed in Miller, *My Diary at the Conference of Paris*, IX, 314.

Hankey's Notes of a Meeting of the Council of Four[1]

President Wilson's House,
C.F.10.A.   Paris, May 13, 1919, 4 p.m.

1. M. CLEMENCEAU said that three of the German Plenipotentiaries had left for Berlin, saying that they would not sign, but Herr Brockdorff-Rantzau, according to his information, said there was no way of avoiding it.

MR. LLOYD GEORGE drew attention to the speech by Scheidemann,[2] reported in the French newspapers, from which, however,

    [1] The complete text of these minutes is printed in *PPC*, V, 579-88.
    [2] Philipp Scheidemann had made an impassioned attack on the proposed peace treaty in a speech before the German National Assembly on May 12. "This treaty," he said, "is, in the view of the Imperial German Government, unacceptable, so unacceptable that I am unable to believe that this earth could bear such a document without a cry issuing from millions and millions of throats in all lands, without distinction to party. Away with this murderous scheme!" He appealed for national unity in the face of the threat to Germany's existence occasioned by the treaty. "Let me speak without tactical considerations," he continued. "The thing which is at the basis of our discussion is this thick volume in which 100 sentences begin 'Germany renounces.' This dreadful and murderous volume by which confession of our own unworthiness, our consent to pitiless disruption, our agreement to helotry and slavery, are to be extorted—this book must not become the future code of law."
    Scheidemann also attacked Wilson by name. "The world," he declared, "has once again lost an illusion. The nations have in this period, which is so poor in ideals, again lost a belief. What name on thousands of bloody battlefields, in thousands of trenches, in orphan families, and among the despairing and abandoned has been mentioned during these four years with more devotion and belief than the name of Wilson? Today the picture of the peace bringer as the world pictured him is paling beside the dark forms of our jailors." Continuing with this metaphor, he asserted that, if the treaty was accepted, Ger-

he said it was difficult to draw a conclusion as to whether he intended to sign or not.

2. PRESIDENT WILSON said that he had invited his experts to make a further study of the Italian claims. A proposal had been put before him, which he thought would, at any rate, be acceptable to the Jugo-Slavs, and which was based on the idea of a plebiscite all down the Dalmatian Coast. He then produced some suggestions for the solution of Adriatic problems, which, he understood, emanated from the British Delegation. It so happened that their line, drawn quite independently, corresponded very closely to the line drawn by the United States experts. He then explained on a map the line proposed by the United States experts, the principal features of which (so far as could be gathered) were a departure from the Treaty of London in favour of the Italians in the region of the Sexten Valley; the proposal being to straighten the line and avoid a curve, thus closing up the only open valley through the Alps; the allocation of the railway junction of Villach to Austria, of Tarvis to the Italians, and of Assling to the Jugo-Slavs. The line continued thence along the crest of the mountains across the Istrian Peninsula, differing from the Italian claim, which took in the southern slope of the mountains. The Treaty of London, President Wilson continued, had laid down that the line should be drawn along the point where the rivers flow eastward. As a matter of fact, they flowed underground in this region, and the Italians drew the line at where the rivers emerged from underground. For this area between the line of the crest and the line of the outflow of the rivers, the United States experts proposed a plebiscite. In order to surmount the objection that the island

many would become a prison camp, with her sixty million inhabitants at hard labor for the benefit of the Allies. The treaty would destroy Germany's international commerce and her domestic economy. Without her mercantile fleet and without the raw materials formerly obtained from such territories as Upper Silesia, Alsace-Lorraine, and the Saar Valley, Germany could not hope to meet the monetary demands of the Allies. "What," he asked, "is a people to do which is confronted by the command that it is responsible for all losses and all damages that its enemies suffered in the war? What is a people to do which is to have no voice in fixing its obligations?"

In contrast to this angry rhetoric, Scheidemann expressed one hopeful note. "We have made counter-proposals," he said, "and shall make still more. With your consent we regard it as our sacred task to come to negotiations. Here and there insight and the common obligations of humanity are beginning to make themselves felt in neutral countries; in Italy and in Great Britain, above all, too. This is a comfort for us in this last fearful flaming up of the policy of the mailed fist—and in socialist France voices are being heard whereby historians one day will measure the state of humanity after four years of murder."

The above summary and quotations are taken from the extensive extracts, in English, in the Associated Press dispatch printed in the *New York Times*, May 14, 1919. The full text is printed in Germany. Nationalversammlung. *Verhandlungen der Verfassunggebenden Deutschen Nationalversammlung, Stenographische Berichte*, Vol. 327 (Berlin, 1920), pp. 1082-84. This is part of a subset, Vols. 326-43, covering the period of the National Assembly in Weimar, of the lengthy series: Germany. Reichstag. *Verhandlungen . . . Stenographische Berichte* (440 vols. in 437, Berlin, 1871-1938), covering the period 1871 to 1938, with all volumes numbered consecutively.

of Cherso in Italian hands would strangle the Port of Fiume, the United States experts proposed that this island should be Jugo-Slav, but that a group of islands south of it, which they stated were ethnologically Italian should go to the Italians. In the portion of Dalmatia claimed by Italy, they proposed that a plebiscite should be held on the understanding that any part should be Italian that declared in favour of Italy. They proposed further, that a plebiscite should be held at Fiume, the population of Fiume being told that they would only assume Italian nationality after Italy had constructed an efficient port in Buccari, which was a good port a few miles to the southward of Fiume, rather enclosed by mountains.

MR. LLOYD GEORGE said that would settle the question of Fiume, as they would never create a rival port so close.

PRESIDENT WILSON, continuing, said there was some reason to believe that the capitalists who controlled shipping, wanted to kill Fiume as a port. He did not see how the Italians could decline so favourable a plebiscite as one in which parts could elect to become Italian. His object was to find a formula by which a decision could be postponed and put into another process than the present Peace Conference.

M. CLEMENCEAU said he would like to find a formula also, but he was not sure of this plan. He thought the Italians would agree to accept Zara and Sebenico without the islands, but the Jugo-Slavs wanted the islands above all.

PRESIDENT WILSON said that the decision from which he could not depart was that the Conference had no right to hand over people to a sovereignty they did not wish. If, by hook or by crook, the Italians obtained Fiume, how were the British and French then bound to give them Dalmatia?

MR. LLOYD GEORGE said that if the Italians obtained Fiume, the British and French were entitled definitely to say that they must give up Dalmatia.

PRESIDENT WILSON said the difficulty was that public opinion in Italy was far more inflamed about Fiume than about Dalmatia. He read an interesting document, giving both the Jugo-Slav and the Italian version of the declaration made at Fiume in favour of annexation to Italy.[3] From both accounts, it was clear that it was no general popular demand, but merely a declaration formed by a group of private persons, who, according to the Italian account, did get some kind of a meeting to endorse it. His view was that if Fiume was allowed to become Italian after the creation by Italy of an efficient Croatian port at Buccari, the Treaty of London would no longer be binding.

[3] The Editors have been unable to find this document.

MR. LLOYD GEORGE described a conversation he had had with the Aga Khan,[4] the head of an Indian Mohammedan sect, a man of immense wealth and vast knowledge. In the course of the conversation, the Aga Khan had said that the mistake made in the Treaty of Peace with Germany was in the handing over of so many Germans to the Poles, whom they regarded as an inferior race. He had also said that he knew Fiume well, and that it was in all respects an Italian town.

PRESIDENT WILSON said he had been informed by an American officer, who was thoroughly sympathetic to the Italians, that if he were in the place of the Italian Government and secured Fiume, the first thing he would do would be to clear out the so-called Italians and replace them with real Italians. They were like citizens of other countries, who had long resided abroad and had lost the real qualities of their nationality.

MR. LLOYD GEORGE said he wished to explain the conception he had formed of the Italian case, which, he thought, had never been quite understood. Italy had a good deal of national pride. The feelings they had, sprang not merely from their treatment in regard to Fiume, but over the whole field of the Treaty of Peace. They were not being treated quite as a great first class power. In fact, not quite as equals of the other great Powers. They realised that there were a certain number of backward people to be taken in hand by more efficient nations. They knew the question had arisen, for example, as to whether the United States could take in hand certain parts of Turkey, an onerous and difficult task. No one, however, was asking Italy to undertake this burden. Consequently, their pride of race was hurt. They knew that the Japanese were being allowed to accept a mandate in the Pacific, but no one was saying to Italy "will you not take this backward people in hand." It would be much better to settle the question of Fiume in this sort of atmosphere. The principal Allied and Associated Powers were the real trustees of the League of Nations looking after the backward races, and for a long time, they would remain the trustees of the League of Nations.

(President Wilson agreed.)

We were saying to Turkey "we cannot leave you to run alone any longer; you have got into a rut; and you will remain in it until some big country comes along and pulls you out." Gaul and Britain would have remained in such a rut if Rome had not come along and pulled them out. Asia Minor was now in exactly the same situation. The question now arose as to whether Italy should not be asked to take charge. The Italians, he pointed out, were an extremely gifted race. It was curious in this war, how they had developed some of the qual-

[4] Aga Sultan Sir Mohammed Shah, Aga Khan III.

ities for which the Romans had been famous. For example, they were amazingly good engineers and had created the most wonderful roads.

PRESIDENT WILSON agreed that it was marvellous how they had maintained the war in the mountains.

MR. LLOYD GEORGE, continuing, said that this showed what gifts the Italian people had. Italy was a very poor country. It contained no coal and no iron. Yet it had produced a vigorous and manly race.

M. CLEMENCEAU referred to the remarkable emigration from Italy to the two Americas.

MR. LLOYD GEORGE said he had been trying to give his colleagues a picture of what was in his mind. Why should we not say frankly to the Italians "we have not quite worked you into the picture yet." He thought that the Italians had been underrated. Consider, for example, the question of police. The Greeks had asked the British Government to organise the police forces for them in the towns, and he believed that they were right, because the British were very good police. In the mountains, however, the Greeks had not gone to the British Government, but to the Italians for police. In Asia Minor, the Italian police would be working under conditions similar to those that had once prevailed in Italy, which had been infested with bandits. He was not proposing that Italy should be offered a mandate for the whole of Anatolia, but why, he asked, should they not be invited to police, and develop a part of Anatolia, where they would find a country not dissimilar from their own. He understood that inland, there were great patches of desert but they contained lakes, and, as in Mesopotamia, there were possibilities of irrigation. He was told that before the war, Italian emigration had been as great as 800,000 to 900,000 a year. Why should these not be diverted to Turkey, which had not the population to develop Anatolia. He felt that the whole frame of mind of the Italian representatives would change if the questions could be discussed as a whole. There was Somaliland. He knew there were difficulties in regard to this. Directly the question was raised, the French said they could not live without Djibouti, and the British said much the same.

Turning to M. Clemenceau, he said that if France could not give up something here, neither could we. He thought, however, something might be done here. The British experts claimed that there were coal and oil, but Great Britain had plenty of coal and oil elsewhere. Moreover, there was a difficulty about Aden, which was dependent on Somaliland for its supplies of fresh vegetables and food. To this he had replied, that the Italians would probably produce far more food than anyone else.

PRESIDENT WILSON agreed that Mr. Lloyd George had stated the case on right principles. He would like, however, to set out the plan in parts. Considering first the part of Anatolia which needed supervision, he would like Smyrna and the adjacent district, as proposed in the report of the Greek Commission, to be united to Greece, in complete sovereignty. The same would apply to the Dodecanese. In addition, he would like to give Greece a mandate for the remainder of the territory claimed by M. Venizelos.

(Mr. Lloyd George at this point left the room to fetch a map.)

President Wilson explained his proposals on the map.

MR. LLOYD GEORGE then made a suggestion on the following lines. The United States should take a mandate for Armenia; France should take a mandate for Northern Anatolia; Italy for Southern Anatolia; and Greece should be dealt with as proposed by President Wilson. The United States, he earnestly hoped, would also take a mandate for Constantinople.

PRESIDENT WILSON said he could not settle this question until he had returned to the United States and definitely ascertained whether the United States would accept a mandate. He reminded his colleagues that it had been represented to him that certain influential and important elements in Turkey were very anxious that Turkey should not be divided, but that it must be subjected to guidance. There should be a single mandate for the whole. The principle was the same as that which he had contended in the case of the Arabs, namely, that the mandate should not be divided. He felt there was much to be said for this proposal.

MR. LLOYD GEORGE said that he did not think this could be done in practice.

PRESIDENT WILSON said that his idea was that the southern parts of Anatolia should be economically developed, involving a question of administration. In northern Anatolia, however, the mandate should be limited to advice and guidance.

M. CLEMENCEAU said that to be frank it was not so easy to distinguish between a mandate for development and administration, and a mandate for mere guidance.

PRESIDENT WILSON thought there was a great difference between guidance and administration.

MR. LLOYD GEORGE then turned to the map of Anatolia attached to the report of the Greek Commission. He pointed out that there was no very convenient port in the Italian sphere, and he urged it would be necessary to give them part of Makri.

PRESIDENT WILSON said it would be easy to draw the line so as to leave Makri to the Italians. He again repeated that he thought the Greeks ought to have a mandate outside the purely Greek zone. He felt that the whole district included in the western slope of the mountains should be treated as one geographical unit, and ought not to be divided.

MR. LLOYD GEORGE said he understood the Italians attached importance to including Scala Nuova.

SIR MAURICE HANKEY, in reply to a question by Mr. Lloyd George, said he had visited Ephesus, which was a short distance inland from Scala Nuova, and had also anchored in the Bay of Scala Nuova in a battleship. His recollection of it was a flat, alluvial plain, where the sea had receded, low-lying, with slight undulations, surrounded by hills. There was a railway, as well as a road, running from Ephesus to Smyrna, but he could recall no road across the plain, which was only traversed by mules. The population was scanty, and so far as he could remember, the villages were miserable collections of hovels, inhabited by Turks, although the hotels and better class people were Greek.

PRESIDENT WILSON said that the Greeks had hitherto never been taken, as it were, into the family of nations. He thought that if they were given what Venizelos had claimed—which he stated very frankly, and with great ability—he felt that a new spirit would be put into the Greek nation. He felt that under leaders such as Venizelos, they might make a success. It was, he thought, true of nations as of men, that when given a big job, they would rise to the occasion.

MR. LLOYD GEORGE pointed out that they were very good traders in all parts of the world.

PRESIDENT WILSON said it would add a good deal if some cession could be made to the Italians in Somaliland.

MR. LLOYD GEORGE said that he personally would like to add Cyprus to Greece, although there were considerable difficulties. He thought that such an act would deprive the whole transaction of any atmosphere of "grab."

PRESIDENT WILSON said it would be a great thing if Mr. Lloyd George could accomplish that.

MR. LLOYD GEORGE said that of course the Turks had a right to be in Turkey, but they had no right to make it a wilderness.

PRESIDENT WILSON said that people who knew the Turks well said that the body of the population were really docile people. They were all right so long as they were not put in authority. Under the guidance of a friendly power, they might prove a docile people.

M. CLEMENCEAU agreed, but said he was very anxious not to cheat anyone out of what belonged to him.

PRESIDENT WILSON said that his conception of a mandatory for Turkey was a guide, but a guide who must be obeyed. If advice was rejected, it might be necessary to exercise pressure. Normally, the position should be one of guiding.

M. CLEMENCEAU said that the United States would not have an easy task in Armenia.

PRESIDENT WILSON said he had at the present moment before him reports on affairs in Armenia of such an appalling nature that he found it difficult to read them.

M. CLEMENCEAU said that the first thing to be done was to decide what was to be allotted to Italy.

MR. LLOYD GEORGE asked whether the Turks would stand the Italians as mandatories. The Italians, he thought, were a more efficient executive race than the Greeks, and always had been in history. The Greeks had had more ideas, but the Romans had been the superior executive nation.

PRESIDENT WILSON said that he was rather anxious about putting a superior executive race as mandatory round the Greeks at Smyrna. The effect might be ruinous.

M. CLEMENCEAU said a decision ought to be taken about Scala Nuova.

MR. LLOYD GEORGE undertook to make enquiries about the possibilities of creating a port at Makri. He asked M. Clemenceau to make enquiries also. If no port could be constructed at Makri, it might be necessary to give the Italians Mersina. What the Italians wanted was Heraclea, where there were some coal mines. Italy had no coal and no fuel. He understood that the Italians would be satisfied if, as part of their reparation from Germany, they could receive the German shares in the mines of Heraclea and Zonguldak.[5] He asked M. Clemenceau to consider this.

M. CLEMENCEAU undertook to do so.

PRESIDENT WILSON asked if Mr. Lloyd George could draw up a complete picture of the settlement.

MR. LLOYD GEORGE agreed that this would be the best plan. If President Wilson would draw up a scheme for Dalmatia, he would draw up a scheme for Asia Minor.

PRESIDENT WILSON said his idea was that if the Italians should get Fiume under the plebiscite he had proposed that they should surrender all claims to Dalmatia and the islands, except one group of islands inhabited by Italians South of Cherso, and the island of Lissa. The getting of Fiume could depend upon the Italians consenting to restrict the boundary to the crest of the mountains on the Istrian Peninsula. He asked if his proposal for a Greek mandate over the territory in the hinterland of the Smyrna region to be assigned to the Greeks, was acceptable.

[5] That is, Heraclea Pontica, the ancient name of Eregli, a port on the Black Sea some 120 miles from the Bosporus. It is located in Zonguldak Province, an important coal-mining region. Zonguldak is the capital of that province and is another Black Sea port near Eregli.

MR. LLOYD GEORGE said his only fear was that the Mohammedan population was a very fierce one, and he doubted if the Greeks could handle it.

M. CLEMENCEAU said that in Crete a very strange thing had happened. Although there could be seen in Crete any number of Greek villages which had been destroyed by the Turks, and of Turkish villages destroyed by the Greeks in the past, when he had visited Candia he had been received by a Turkish mayor who was on the best of terms with the Greeks, and the two populations seemed to live in accord.

(Mr. H. Nicolson[6] was introduced.)

MR. LLOYD GEORGE told Mr. Nicolson he had been invited in to hear the general lines of the proposals that had been made, in order that he might draft a proposition in regard to them.

PRESIDENT WILSON explained that his proposal was to unite to Greece in full sovereignty Smyrna and the surrounding district, as proposed in the report of the Greek Commission (as subsequently modified by agreement between the British and American experts so as to exclude the valley of the Meander and the country South of it), and in addition to give Greece a mandate over the larger area claimed by M. Venizelos. Mr. Lloyd George, however, had suggested that in order to give the Italians a harbour, the line should be drawn so as to leave Makri to them. The Dodecanese should be united to Greece in full sovereignty. Italy should have a mandate for the remainder of the Southern part of Anatolia, for which the Council would be glad if Mr. Nicolson could draw a line on an economic basis.

MR. NICOLSON, referring to a line drawn on the map which Mr. Lloyd George had produced, said that this had only been very hastily drawn, and he could no doubt find a more logical basis if given a little more time. This line had been drawn so as to exclude the Baghdad railway from the Italian zone.

MR. LLOYD GEORGE said there was no reason to exclude the railway, because in any event the railway would have to pass through the territory included in several mandates, and arrangements would have to be made for it to become an international line.

(Mr. Nicolson withdrew.)

PRESIDENT WILSON said that the Italians had always asked for a comprehensive proposal. He hoped, therefore, that the result of the present meeting would be to produce one. It would be a great advantage if something could also be said about Somaliland. He proposed

---

[6] The Hon. Harold George Nicolson, a staff member of the British Foreign Office and a technical adviser on political and diplomatic questions in the British delegation to the peace conference.

that M. Clemenceau should see M. Simon,[7] and that the French should take the initiative in some proposal.

M. CLEMENCEAU undertook to see M. Simon on the subject.

MR. LLOYD GEORGE repeated the objections which the British Colonial experts had to the cession of Somaliland.

3. It was agreed that the Council of Foreign Ministers should be asked to consider and make recommendations in regard to the territorial boundaries of Bulgaria. They should be authorised to consult the representatives in Paris of the various nations concerned in this settlement.

4. M. CLEMENCEAU handed round a letter from Count Brockdorff-Rantzau on the subject of Prisoners of War,[8] together with a draft reply.[9]

5. (It was agreed that the Indian Delegation should be heard in regard to Constantinople at the end of the present week.)

MR. LLOYD GEORGE undertook to endeavour to find someone who could state the Mohammedan case in regard to Constantinople in addition to the statement by the Maharajah of Bikaner and Lord Sinha.[10] He thought possibly some Mohammedan expert might be attached to the Indian Delegation.

6. SIR MAURICE HANKEY handed to M. Clemenceau a communication from the Secretary-General of the Peace Conference, enclosing a copy of a letter addressed by M. Pachitch to M. Clemenceau, requesting that two milliards of francs out of the 20 milliards required from Germany as an instalment in respect of reparation for damage should be allotted to Serbia.

MR. LLOYD GEORGE pointed out that Serbia was acquiring very large new territories.

(It was agreed that the question should be referred in the first instance to the Committee considering the question of Reparation in the Austrian and Hungarian Treaties.)

7. (It was agreed that on the following day the Council should meet the principal Members of the Commission on Ports, Waterways and Railways, in order to discuss the clauses prepared by them for the Austrian and Hungarian Treaties.)

8. MR. LLOYD GEORGE asked whether the Turks were to be invited to Paris, or whether they should be met somewhere else.

PRESIDENT WILSON said that as only some of the Allied and Asso-

[7] That is, Henry Simon.
[8] Printed as Appendix III to the minutes of the Council of Four printed at May 12, 1919, 11 a.m.
[9] Printed as Appendix I (B) to the minutes of the Council of Four printed at May 14, 1919, 12:15 p.m.
[10] Maharaja Shri Sir Ganga Singh Bahadur, Maharaja of Bikaner, and Satyendra Prasanno Sinha, first Baron Sinha of Raipur, Parliamentary Under Secretary of State for India. Both were Indian delegates to the peace conference.

ciated Powers had been at war with Turkey, it might be better to agree on terms and then send a Commission to meet the Turks. His own position in the matter was that as a member of the League of Nations, the United States would have to guarantee the arrangement.

MR. LLOYD GEORGE said that their position was a good deal more than that, since he hoped the United States would accept the Mandate.

> (It was agreed that in view of the pressure of work on the Drafting Committee, the Treaty with Turkey should not be put in hand just yet.)

T MS (SDR, RG 256, 180.03401/10½, DNA).

Mantoux's Notes of a Meeting of the Council of Four

May 13, 1919, 4 p.m.

Lloyd George. Have you read Scheidemann's speech to the German National Assembly? It can serve as a preface to the signing of the treaty as well as to a refusal to sign. In it I notice attacks on President Wilson, which will help to make him popular in other countries of Europe.

Scheidemann, like all those who until now have expressed German opinion, protests above all against the economic losses imposed on Germany, against the cession of coal mines and potash deposits; he gets all worked up about the regime anticipated for the Saar Basin and above all about the cession of Upper Silesia to Poland.

There is no doubt that it is above all the modification of their eastern frontier which touches the Germans: they shudder at the thought of seeing their compatriots placed under the domination of a people whom they consider as inferior. With the French, they at least feel that they are among equals; but they do not hide their contempt for the Poles.

Wilson. We are assembled today to study the Italian questions together and to seek the solution. I have a proposal to make, which I know will be accepted by the Yugolslavs: it amounts to instituting a plebiscite along all the coast of the Adriatic.

If we take the Italian frontier starting from the north, I would propose first to give Italy the valley of Sexten, which, it is true, contains three or four thousand Germans, but whose possession by Italy would close off one of the last open passages for invasion across the Alps.

The question of the tunnels of Tarvis was raised in the Council of

Foreign Ministers. The proposed solution would give one of the tunnels, with the town of Tarvis, to the Italians; the station of Assling would go to the Yugoslavs and Villach would remain with the Austrians. Thus the branches of the railroad would be fairly equitably divided.

In Istria, the frontier would follow the crest of the mountains; it would be considerably to the west of the line indicated by the Treaty of London. This, moreover, is drawn by the Italians according to a broad interpretation of the treaty. The treaty says, in effect, that the frontier must follow the line where the waters divide; but since, in this region, many rivers flow eastward by an underground course, the Italians have determined the frontier line not according to the point of origin of each watercourse, but according to the point where it appears on the surface.

Since the island of Cherso blocks the harbor of Fiume absolutely, I am of the opinion to leave it to the Yugoslavs, but to give Italy a group of islands farther south, the majority of whose population is Italian.

In Dalmatia, on the islands as well as on the mainland, there would be a plebiscite, and Italy could claim every part of this territory, small or large, whose population would vote for her.

As for the city of Fiume, the Italians have often spoken of the possibility of replacing its port, for the Yugoslavs, with an equivalent port, that of Buccari, which is a very good natural port, although too closely bounded by mountains. I would propose to put to the population of Fiume the following question: "Does the city of Fiume wish to attach itself to Italy, when Italy has built an equivalent port at Buccari for the use of the Yugoslavs?"

Lloyd George. That would be telling the inhabitants of Fiume: "As soon as you become Italians, you will cease to exist, and your commerce will pass to a neighboring city."

Wilson. It is Italy herself who offered to create a port at Buccari.

Clemenceau. Yes, but with the idea of acquiring Dalmatia. I may be mistaken, but that is how I understand her intention.

Lloyd George. I do not know exactly what they are looking for in Fiume.

Clemenceau. They want above all to save face; they do not know how to get out of the situation into which they have placed themselves.

Wilson. It is also possible that the capitalists of Trieste want Fiume to be Italian in order to ruin its competition at will.

Lloyd George. It is the policy of Landru:[1] possess in order to kill.

[1] Henri Désiré Landru, formerly known to French police as a petty criminal convicted

Wilson. The Italians tell us: "These lands are Italian." In that case, they cannot refuse to ask them to express, themselves, their will by a plebiscite. If it was possible, by the way, to delay that solution—not to settle it by the procedure of the peace treaty—perhaps that would be better.

Clemenceau. I am afraid that is impossible. The monster must be confronted resolutely. We must oblige the Italians to study a reasonable solution of the question of Fiume. We must know what they want in Dalmatia; it seems that Zara, Sebenico, and the islands are what interest them most.

Wilson. I cannot depart from the principle of free choice: it is impossible for me to hand over a population to Italy without its consent.

Clemenceau. As for us, the Treaty of London binds us.

Wilson. If you give Fiume to the Italians, how can you give them Dalmatia?

Lloyd George. That would obviously be impossible; if they want Fiume, which is outside the Treaty of London, they must abandon Dalmatia.

In a conversation which I had with M. Pašić, it seemed to me that he did not particularly care about Fiume and that he would in the end leave it to the Italians, if they would renounce Dalmatia.

Wilson. That is not M. Trumbić's attitude.

Lloyd George. It's possible: M. Pašić is a Serb and M. Trumbić a Croat.

Clemenceau. What would be most dangerous would be for the Italians to renounce Fiume and claim Dalmatia.

Wilson. I do not believe that you would run this risk, because Italian opinion has become especially excited over the question of Fiume. I have been informed about the supposedly popular vote of Fiume in favor of union with Italy: it is the result of the action of a small group of people. I have information on the subject from two sources, Italian and Yugoslav: both clearly reveal action taken by a group of individuals seizing power on their own authority. Here is what the Yugoslavs say: the proclamation of the independence of Fiume, at the time of the Armistice, was the act of about ten people,

---

several times of forgery and fraud, had been arrested in Paris on April 12, 1919, and charged with the murder of several women. The lengthy investigation which ensued suggested that Landru had murdered by unknown means at least ten women and the adolescent son of one of them and had probably disposed of their bodies by dismembering and burning them. His lure was to hold out to them the prospect of marriage, and his motive was to secure their money and valuable possessions. Despite the fact that none of the bodies was ever found whole or in part, Landru was ultimately convicted on the basis of circumstantial evidence and was guillotined on February 25, 1922. By May 1919, the case had already become a cause célèbre, as successive revelations appeared in the newspapers. For a detailed study of Landru's career, see Dennis Bardens, *The Ladykiller: The Life of Landru, the French Bluebeard* (London, 1972).

who proclaimed themselves "the Italian Council of the City of Fiume." On October 29, the Austrians having left the city, the National Croatian Council, in session at Agram, declared that Fiume was an integral part of Croatia. But at the same time the "Italian Council of Fiume" proclaimed the Italian character of the city. This council had no representative character. The Italian occupation followed on November 17, and, since then, no opportunity has been offered to popular opinion to express itself freely. Admiral Buller,[2] the American admiral who first visited that region, confirms for us that the Council of Fiume was formed solely by the Italian fraction of the population, and all witnesses agree on this point. This council worked in the most arbitrary fashion to italianize the city, imposing the Italian language in the schools, on signs, arresting and deporting inhabitants of Croatian nationality, etc.

I propose nevertheless to act as if we did not contest the Italian sympathy of Fiume, and to say to the Italians: "As soon as you have constructed the port at Buccari, you may take possession of the city of Fiume if it solemnly renews by plebiscite the expression of its will to be united to Italy." As for you, gentlemen, that solution will liberate you from the Treaty of London.

Lloyd George. Yesterday I had an interesting conversation with the Agha Khan, an extraordinary character, whom I can only compare to Monte Cristo. He is a man of rare intelligence, without peer among the Muslims of India; he possesses an immense fortune, acquired by selling advance tickets to places in Paradise. He knows all languages and all countries, discusses competently French and English political questions, criticizes certain articles of the treaty, particularly those concerning the eastern frontier of Germany. He also spoke to me about Fiume, which he knows, and told me: "Whatever the exact proportion is of the different elements of the population in Fiume, the city is certainly Italian, not only in its appearance, but in its commerce and in all its ruling forces." This same personage naturally spoke to me about eastern questions, and he advises us to listen to the Muslims of his country before settling the Turkish question. We do not realize enough all that Turkey represents for the Muslims of India.

Wilson. I recently glanced at an article in the *Contemporary Review*[3] which shows that there is some agitation in India, because the Muslims are worried about the fate of Turkey.

Lloyd George. We are now having difficulties with Afghanistan;

[2] That is, Rear Adm. William Hannum Grubb Bullard, not Buller, at this time director of naval communications.

[3] "The Political Situation in India," *The Fortnightly* (not *Contemporary*) *Review*, CXI (May 1919), 742-51.

they are not very dangerous, because the Afghans are lost if they leave their mountains. But we have intercepted messages between them and the Bolsheviks. I believe that it is necessary to take account of this danger and to hear the Muslims.

Wilson. Returning to Fiume, I can tell you that one of our officers, whose report I have recently received, thinks, like the Agha Khan, that Fiume is rather an Italian city. But he adds: "If I were the Italian government and I seized Fiume, I would begin by making the Italians there leave in order to replace them with real Italians."

Lloyd George. There is something to be said in favor of Italy. For her, the great question is the question of national pride. It seems to the Italians that they are not quite being treated as equals.

Take the question of mandates in particular. We concur in thinking that certain backward nations should, in their own best interest, be administered by those which have attained the highest degree of culture and administrative experience. When it is a question of certain parts of Turkey, the United States is asked, despite its natural repugnance to leave its own domain, to assume the mandate. The Japanese must have territories in the Pacific. No one is turning to Italy; it is necessary to make offers to her, and to create thereby an atmosphere which would help us to settle the question of Fiume.

Being today the true representatives of the League of Nations, we are considering the situation of backward countries, and we think that we must do for them what Rome did for us: without the Romans, we would have remained half-savages for centuries longer. Can we not ask Italy to participate in this common effort? If the Italians have not always shown themselves superior in the arts of war, I believe them very well qualified for the arts of peace. Consider what their engineers accomplished in the construction of the most difficult routes across mountainous terrain; visualize to yourselves how Italy supports, on relatively infertile land, a population of nearly 40 million inhabitants, who are strong and of a superior type.

Can we not say to the Italians: "You are right, your role has not yet been what it should be"? I believe Italy capable of doing great things in Asia. Her administration is good, and the Greeks themselves recognize that the Italians are superior to themselves in policing mountainous regions. Asia Minor is infested with brigandage; the Italians will know how to eradicate it. If we cannot offer them all of Anatolia, we can at least propose that they establish order and undertake the development of a part of this country. Where the Turks created a vacuum, the Italians can build roads, railways, irrigate the soil, and cultivate it. They can even populate these territories; it should not be forgotten that their emigration before the war was several hundred thousand men each year.

In speaking to them of these questions as soon as we meet them face to face again, we will put them in a better state of mind. We have, moreover, to keep the promise made, in signing the Treaty of London, to grant them colonial compensation to balance our own acquisitions. They expect to receive British Somaliland from us. It is true that our colonists are resisting and saying that Berbera is indispensable to us. The French colonials undoubtedly say as much about Djibouti. It is up to us to play our part by acting in common accord. It would seem that there is coal and petroleum in Somaliland; this is precisely what Italy lacks, and as for ourselves, we have enough.

These are the questions which I would like to settle before taking up the difficult problem of Fiume.

Wilson. It seems to me that this starts on the right foot. We would give a mandate to Italy in southern Anatolia. Greece would receive complete ownership of Smyrna and the territory upon which our experts agree, along with the Dodecanese, and I propose to institute a mandate of the League of Nations, which would be entrusted to Greece, for the remainder of the *vilayet* of Aidin.[4]

Lloyd George. Northern Anatolia remains. If the United States accepts the mandate for Armenia, I would propose to give the mandate for northern Anatolia to France. If the American Congress rejects the idea of the mandate in Armenia, then I would give all of Anatolia to Italy, with France having the Armenian mandate.

Clemenceau. Is it possible to predict what the American Senate will do?

Wilson. I believe that it will accept the venture. I will remind you furthermore that from different sides we are told that, what the Turks wish above all, is not to have their territory divided; they will accept a superior authority on the condition that it be a single one.

Clemenceau. You will not find anyone who is in a position to give this large country the development it needs.

Wilson. My opinion is that we can govern and develop fairly completely the southern part and limit ourselves, in the rest of the country, to playing the role of counselors.

Clemenceau. It is very difficult to establish a boundary between these two roles.

I consider it as given that the Americans will accept the mandate over Constantinople.

Lloyd George. I hope so, whatever the solution to the other questions may be. If the Italians are established in southern Anatolia, they would have to be given the port of Makri, if they cannot have

[4] Now Aydin.

the one of Mersina. Greek administration would extend south of the region of Smyrna but would stop before the harbor of Makri.

Clemenceau. The Greeks do not have much administrative capacity. I covered the entire Peloponnese without seeing a single road. I do not wish to say anything against them; but these are the facts.

Wilson. The Greeks have not yet been treated as a modern nation. By showing them our confidence, we will give them the ambition to do well.

Clemenceau. Greece is still a country where the women till the soil while the men smoke their pipes. I believe, however, that there is something to be done for these people.

Wilson. Can we not say of races, as of men, that when one sets them to great tasks, one elevates them?

Clemenceau. Their men, with a very few rare exceptions, are mediocre and do not know a word of their ancient history; I remember that they asked me to explain it to them!

Wilson. If you were able, in the offers which could be made to Italy in the name of the League of Nations, to add that of Somaliland, that would help in the solutions that we desire.

Lloyd George. My intention is also to give Greece the island of Cyprus.

Clemenceau. Do not forget that, according to the Treaty of Berlin, you need my authorization for that.

Lloyd George. I hope you will give it to me.

Wilson. if you can make this gift to Greece, it will be a great thing.

Lloyd George. That would dispel the atmosphere of covetousness and greed the impression of which is to be feared. Regarding the Turks, I do not have any scruples toward them; they have no rights over a country which they have only been able to turn into a desert.

Wilson. All that we owe the Turkish population is the right to live and the guarantee of a good administration. I do not know the Turks directly. But all witnesses agree in representing them as a docile people, against whom no reproach can be made as long as they are not granted the fatal gift of command. It is often repeated that the Turk is a gentleman;[5] he will obey without difficulty the power which will serve him as a guide.

Lloyd George. According to the plans that have been made, Armenia will be very extended.

Clemenceau. Its administration will be an arduous task for the Americans; unfortunately, it is a country where massacre is a chronic disease.

_____
[5] "Gentleman" in English in the original.

Wilson. At this very moment, the Turks are interning a great number of Armenians, many of whom are dying of hunger. I have been given some horrible details.

Lloyd George. It would be good to publish them in America: that would help your public opinion to understand why the United States must assume the responsibility of the mandate. The Turk, when he has the slightest degree of power, is a brute. Whatever the difficulties which we may encounter from the Muslims of India, we must put an end to the Turkish regime.

Clemenceau. The most pressing matter is for us to agree on what shall be reserved to Italy.

Wilson. I would consent to put Makri in the zone of the Italian mandate; but as for the rest of the *vilayet* of Aidin, I persist in believing that the mandate must be given to Greece.

Lloyd George. The question is knowing which administration the Turks will best tolerate.

Clemenceau. On that score, there is no doubt: it is the Italian administration.

Wilson. What I fear is putting in immediate contact with the Greek zone a power of superior administrative capability. I would like the entire zone of southwest Anatolia to be treated as a geographical entity. If the Turks feel that they have before them not the Greeks alone, but a great international system of which the Greeks are the mandatories, they will not resist them.

Hankey. I can testify that around Salonika, the environs of which were very dangerous under the Turkish regime, the Greeks have perfectly reestablished order.

Lloyd George. Could the port of Makri be easily connected to an existing railway? According to the map, that appears to be rather difficult. Furthermore, these coasts do not offer any natural port all the way to Mersina. Adalia cost not a little money and is worthless from the maritime point of view.

Clemenceau. Could we not give Scala Nuova to the Italians?

Wilson. In this case, a large part of the *vilayet* of Aidin would be taken away from Greece. Even Makri must not be given to the Italians.

Lloyd George. They must have Makri if they do not have Mersina, and they need a port for their warships. Marmaris, from this perspective, would be excellent. What interests the Italians most is Heraclea, on the other side of the peninsula; they have neither coal nor any other combustible and they would like to have the mines of Heraclea.

Clemenceau. But those mines are French.

Lloyd George. The Italians say that they are in part Italian and in part German, and that if the German share was transferred to them, they would occupy a preponderant position. I do not know if there is any great harm in giving them these German shares; they could thus make use of these mines, which would not prevent France from having the mandate for northern Anatolia. The output of the mines of Heraclea is not, by the way, very substantial: 600,000 tons, and the quality of the coal is mediocre.

Wilson. Regarding the Adriatic, you already know my proposals.

Lloyd George. Do you wish to assume the task of speaking to them about the Adriatic, while we make them our offers in Asia?

Wilson. Do we all agree about the mandate to entrust to Greece?

Lloyd George. I fear that the Greeks do not have well in hand these Muslim populations of the *vilayet* of Aidin, who are reputed to be rather intractable.

Clemenceau. In Crete, most of the Turkish population has remained there since the island became Greek, and the two populations live side by side, without reciprocal complaints; I do not believe that there is anything to fear there.

Mr. Nicolson is introduced and receives the necessary instructions to prepare a map of the mandates in Asia Minor.

Wilson. The important thing is for us to agree about the proposals to make to Italy—and on the proposals which will relieve us of the Treaty of London.

Lloyd George. The best thing is to treat the problem as a whole. I will study the question of Somaliland; I had a conversation this morning with Lord Milner on this subject. I must say that he is making strong objections.

Wilson. If France should take the initiative to offer the part of Somaliland which she owns, on the condition that England do as much there, that could undoubtedly help you overcome Lord Milner's resistance.

Clemenceau. What is Lord Milner's argument?

Lloyd George. He says: "We are in Aden. If the Italians are across from us on the African coast, Aden loses its value." He adds that the garrison of Aden is fed by what comes from Berbera. I answered him that the Italians are at least as good gardeners as we, and that they will send us their vegetables.

Clemenceau. Can we not settle the Bulgarian questions tomorrow? Everything seems ready.

Wilson. The United States is not at war with Bulgaria, but I will attend your discussion. Concerning the Turks, are we going to receive them, or take a decision here and communicate it to them by a commission?

Lloyd George. That remains to be seen. When will you hear the

Muslims from India? I can have an important Muslim personality come here, who lives in London. I will also summon the Maharaja of Bikener and the counselors who surround him. The Maharaja himself is not Muslim, but he represents the sixty million Muslims who live in India, and the effect, in India, will be excellent, if they learn that the Four heard the men charged to speak in their name.

Clemenceau. When can you have them come here?

Lloyd George. Thursday or Friday.

Wilson. What will the program be tomorrow?

Hankey. You will have to study the military agreements relating to the occupied territories on the left bank of the Rhine, the report of the commission on ports, waterways, and railways concerning Austria, and the questions relative to Bulgaria.

Lloyd George. Can we not refer the Bulgarian questions to the Ministers of Foreign Affairs? If they reach agreement, we will only have to approve.

This proposal is adopted.

Hankey. There is also a Serbian memorandum, in which Serbia asks to participate in the reparations for a sum of two billion francs.

Lloyd George. She is not as demanding as Belgium, but I do not know if she has a right to anything at all, given her territorial acquisitions.

Clemenceau. Indeed, Serbia is acquiring large territories free of debt.

Wilson. You will recall that that question has already been posed, but that we concluded that it was a question of debit and credit; it is an account to be established.

Lloyd George. It must then be referred to our financial experts.

This proposal is adopted.

Mantoux, II, 53-63.

To Avetis Aharonian

My dear Sir,   Paris, 13 May, 1919.

In common with all thoughtful and humane persons, I have learned of the sufferings of the Armenian people with the most poignant distress, and beg to assure you that if any practicable means of assisting them in their distress presented themselves at the moment, I for one would rejoice to make use of them. It adds to the tragical distress of the whole situation that for the present there seems to be no way which is not already being as far as possible followed in which to relieve the suffering which is exciting the sympathy of the whole world. I can only hope that as the processes of peace are hastened and a settlement is arrived at which can be insisted upon, that an opportunity may then promptly arise for taking effective steps to better the conditions and eventually assure the security of the people of Armenia.

May I not say with what deep distress I feel obliged to make this reply to your letter of the tenth of May?[1]

Cordially and sincerely yours,   [Woodrow Wilson]

CCL (WP, DLC).
  [1] A. Aharonian to WW, May 10, 1919, TLS (WP, DLC).

To Edward Mandell House, with Enclosure

Dear House: Paris, 13 May, 1919.

I think you ought to have this letter in your own files.[1] We have already orally compared views about it.

In haste,   Affectionately yours,   Woodrow Wilson

TLS (E. M. House Papers, CtY).
  [1] About this letter, see ns. 1, 2, and 3 to the entry from the House Diary printed at May 10, 1919.

ENCLOSURE

David Lloyd George to Edward Mandell House

Dear Colonel House,   Paris. 10th May 1919.

I greatly regret that there should be any misunderstanding as to the origin of my promise to see the Irish American Representatives. I was certainly under the impression that it was your wish that I should see them—an impression which I derived, first from Sir William Wiseman, and later from you personally. My only object in writing to you in regard to their proceedings in Ireland was that having promised to receive them I did not wish to cancel the interview without fully explaining my reasons for doing so.

As, however, you now assure me that these gentlemen do not wish to see me, and that you also do not wish it, I propose to cancel the interview.

As regards the second paragraph of your letter may I point out that in his official statement on arrival in Dublin, Mr. Walsh himself declares that he asked the American Representatives to obtain facilities for him to go over to Ireland in order that he and his associates "might accept the invitation conveyed by President de Valera for a

Conference, as well as to make a first hand study of actual conditions in Ireland for use at the Peace Conference in Paris."

I gather from the fact that you do not take any notice of the quotations from the speeches which have been made by the Irish American representatives in Ireland that you disinterest yourself in their conduct. I am, therefore, giving instructions to the Viceroy[1] to take such action in regard to them as he may think necessary in the interests of peace and order.

Yours sincerely,   D Lloyd George

TLS (E. M. House Papers, CtY).
   [1] That is, Field Marshal John Denton Pinkstone French, Viscount French of Ypres and of High Lake, at this time Lord Lieutenant of Ireland. "Viceroy" was obviously a typographical error.

To Edward Mandell House, with Enclosure

Dear House,   [Paris, c. May 13, 1919]

This is what our Irish "friends" said in Ireland—and what they said about their passports involves our Government by implication. What do you suggest?   Aff'y,   W.W.

TCL (E. M. House Papers, CtY).

E N C L O S U R E

From Philip Henry Kerr

Dear Mr. President: Paris. May 12, 1919

I enclose copies of the documents Mr. Lloyd George promised you this morning.

Yours sincerely   P. H. Kerr.

THE FREEMAN'S JOURNAL, Monday May 5th 1919.

THE MANDATE.

"Clearly expressed in application for passports."

Mr. Walsh, on behalf of the Commission, was pleased to indicate in an interview with our representative the origin and objects of the mission which they had been deputed to carry out.

"We came to Paris," said Mr. Walsh, "with a mandate from the Irish Race Convention held at Philadelphia on the anniversary of George Washington's birthday. That mandate was to ask President Wilson and his confreres to see to it that Messrs de Valera, Griffith and Plunkett, the regularly elected representatives of the Irish people, were given a full opportunity to present the case of Ireland to the Peace Conference. In the event that this was not done we were to ask the same privilege for the American Commission on Irish Independence. The mandate was clearly expressed in the application for passports made to the American Government at Washington, and upon which the Commission proceeded to Paris, namely—

'To obtain for the delegates elected by the people of Ireland a hearing at the Peace Conference, and to place before the Conference, if that hearing be not given the case of Ireland, her insistence upon her right of self-determination, and to international recognition of the Republican form of Government established by her people.' "

THE LLOYD GEORGE CONFERENCE.

"The request for the safe-conduct from Dublin to Paris and the return of Messrs de Valera, Griffith and Plunkett," continued Mr. Walsh, "was presented to the President of the United States, who referred the matter to Colonel House. We have every assurance that this safe-conduct will be granted to the Irish representatives."

When the request was presented to Mr. Lloyd George by Colonel House he expressed the desire to have a Conference with Messrs Frank P. Walsh, Edward F. Dunne, and Michael J. Ryan, the American Commissioners, but owing to his close occupation with the general Peace articles and the presence of the German plenipotentiaries in Paris, he asked that the Conference be held over till next week.

"Having received an invitation from President de Valera and his associates to visit Ireland, the Commission, which did not have passports to England or Ireland, requested of the American Representatives that such credentials be obtained at once, so that in the interval the Commission might accept the invitation conveyed by President de Valera for a Conference as well as to make a first hand study of actual conditions in Ireland for use at the Peace Conference in Paris, as well as to embody [it] in a report to the American people."

"Present Irish Republic"

"We do not appear in Paris or in Ireland in any position except as that of advocates of the recognition of the present Irish republic, and we have no duty to perform, except to assist the representatives of Ireland in any steps which they may find suitable to carry on without interference the governmental functions necessary to the well-being and development of their own land in their own way."

"Next week we have an engagement with Mr. Lloyd George,

made through Sir William Wiseman, the liaison officer between the American and English Government in Paris."

Mr. Walsh was asked if the people of America recognised the existence of the present Irish Republic as referred to in his conversations. His reply was in the affirmative adding that they did so along the lines laid down in the declaration of the Entente Allies as to the purpose of the war, and expecially the declaration by the American Government as to its purpose in entering the war, namely, that all who submit to authority should have a compelling voice in their own Government.

Mr. Walsh proceeded: "The Commission is composed of native born Americans who owe no allegiance spiritual or otherwise to Ireland or any other nation in the world but who, in common with our fellow citizens, are devoted to the principles contained in the American Declaration of Independence, and carried into its constitution and practices as a nation for a century and a half. We believe that the form of government in America contains the absolute minimum of Independence which any people should be asked to live under."

FREEMAN'S JOURNAL. Tuesday May 6, 1919
SPEECH *made by* MR. DUNNE *in* BELFAST, *5th* MAY *1919.*

Mr. E. F. Dunne, who was most heartily received, said that his colleagues and himself would be less than human if they did not appreciate the significance of that splendid demonstration.

"We recognise," he proceeded, "that the tremendous outpouring of the people of that metropolitan city has not been occasioned by any desire to do honour to us personally but the desire to do honour to the mission upon which we are engaged. We come from a country in which men died and made tremendous sacrifices that they might be able to assert the right of self-determination, the establishment of a Republic. We and those before us have lived in the great Republic for some 140 years, and we appreciate the beneficent results of a Constitution, selected with the consent of the governed under a Republican form of government. Therefore, we are here simply to express our sympathy with you and for the other people of the world who are struggling for self-determination and a Republican form of Government."

T MS (E. M. House Papers, CtY).

To Robert Lansing

My dear Lansing: Paris, 13 May, 1919.

I would appreciate it very much if you would draw up such a statement as you here suggest.[1] You are more familiar with these various
cables from China than I am and will know best how to draft it. I
shall be very glad to sign it myself, if you desire, though I think it
would carry very great weight indeed as coming from yourself. I
shall be glad to confer with you about it, so soon as you have satisfied
yourself with the form.

Cordially and faithfully yours,   Woodrow Wilson

TLS (SDR, RG 256, 185.1158/121, DNA).
  [1] See RL to WW, May 8, 1919 (first letter of that date), Vol. 58.

To Ferdinand Foch

My dear Marshal Foch: Paris, 13 May, 1919.

I did not more promptly reply to your letter of the fifth of May,[1]
because I knew that you would at once be afforded an opportunity
to see the whole body of provisions of the Treaty of Peace. You may
be sure that I was as ready as any one of the others to accord you that
privilege, and that I with the others always value your advice.

Sincerely yours,   [Woodrow Wilson]

CCL (WP, DLC).
  [1] F. Foch to WW, May 5, 1919, TLS (WP, DLC).

To Felix Frankfurter

My dear Mr. Frankfurter: Paris, 13 May, 1919.

Just a line to acknowledge your important letter of May eighth,[1]
and to say how deeply I appreciate the importance and significance
of the whole matter.

Cordially and sincerely yours,   [Woodrow Wilson]

CCL (WP, DLC).
  [1] F. Frankfurter to WW, May 8, 1919, Vol. 58.

Gilbert Fairchild Close to Samuel Gompers

My dear Mr. Gompers: Paris, 13 May 1919.

The President has asked me to acknowledge receipt of your letter
of April 23rd[1] and to thank you for it. He does not feel, however, that

he will be in a position to judge about the matters which you present until after he gets home and becomes thoroughly conversant again with the situation as a whole.

The President asks me to express the hope that you are rapidly getting all right.   Sincerely yours,   [Woodrow Wilson]

CCL (WP, DLC).
  [1] S. Gompers to WW, April 23, 1919, Vol. 58.

From Vance Criswell McCormick

My dear Mr. President: Paris. May 13, 1919.

In accordance with my instructions from the Supreme Economic Council, I have sent to Sir Maurice Hankey, who is acting as Secretary of the Council of Four, a plan for a complete blockade to be used in the event of Germany's refusing to sign the Peace Treaty, provided that the Associated Governments decide upon this form of pressure.[1] The plan which we have submitted contemplates a blockade even more drastic than the old one, and, if carried out, will reduce Germany to a state of starvation, and will completely crush her economically. Believing as I do that Germany, in refusing to sign the Peace Treaty, will offer only passive resistance without military effort, it would therefore be a terrible mistake to resume such a strict blockade, because it can only lead to chaos, revolution, economic and social demoralization, not only for Germany but for the greater part of Europe, and throw away all chance of securing any reparation for our needy Allies.

In my opinion, the solution of the problem should be military occupation, along with the control of imports into Germany. Germany could thus receive food and raw materials sufficient for her social and economic life, and thereby enable her to produce as much as possible for reparation, and at the same time be prevented from receiving any commodities which might be utilized in resuming military activity. I discussed this matter with Lord Robert Cecil at yesterday's meeting of the Supreme Economic Council, and he advised me confidentially that the military authorities told him that military occupation was impossible due to the great expense incidental thereto, and for other good reasons. If this be true, we face a serious situation indeed, because the only alternative will then be a drastic blockade, which means chaos and revolution in Europe. I feel this situation so keenly that I wanted you, when considering this matter, to have before you a true picture, as I see it, after months of blockade experience, of what would take place in the event of the resumption of the Blockade.

Very sincerely yours,   Vance C. McCormick

TLS (WP, DLC).
    [1] There is an undated T MS of this document, entitled "REPORT OF SUPERIOR BLOCKADE COUNCIL TO THE COUNCIL OF FOUR," in WP, DLC; it is printed in *PPC*, V, 603-604.

From Norman Hezekiah Davis, with Enclosures

My dear Mr. President: Paris, 13th May, 1919.

For your information I am enclosing copy of a dispatch received by Signor Orlando from Signor Stringher, Minister of the Italian Treasury, which Signor Crespi handed me yesterday with the apparent expectation of evoking my sympathy and cooperation in relieving the situation. I am also enclosing copy of the cable which, at your suggestion, I sent to Secretary Glass, and his reply thereto.

I am, my dear Mr. President,

Faithfully yours,   Norman H. Davis

TLS (WP, DLC).

E N C L O S U R E   I

A Translation of a Letter from Bonaldo Stringher to Vittorio Emanuele Orlando

To Signor Orlando, President of the Council. Rome, May 7th, 1919.

Some days ago I had occasion to inform Your Excellency on the relations between the Federal Treasury and the Italian Treasury.

From information which I have received, and from communications to hand from the R. Embassy at Washington, it appears that whereas hitherto it seemed that the ability of the American Treasury to give us credits would cease on the conclusion of peace, to be determined by a Message from the President of the Republic, I have since been officially informed that no further credits would be granted us after June 1st.[1] I also mentioned to Your Excellency negotiations now going on in America with a view to the financing of our cotton purchases, and to ensure to an association of Italian Banks the means wherewith to make payments for our purchases in the United States; and on this head I expressed the hope that said negotiations would proceed in a manner satisfactory to ourselves.

Now however information sent me from our representative on the

Instituto dei Cambi at New York, and a further telegram from the Treasury Officer accredited to our Embassy at Washington, inform me that the recent political events have seriously affected the development of our financial activities in that country.

For instance, both the Federal Reserve Board and the Guaranty Trust Company, which was to have been at the head of the group of Banks undertaking the financing of 25 million dollars worth of cotton purchases, have completely changed their attitude towards us, so much so that they have openly declared that until the political situation is cleared up they will be unable to carry out the transactions already under way or concluded. Moreover, the information given me confirms the opinion I had already formed that the dilatory attitude which the representative of the Federal Reserve Board and of the American Treasury had taken with regard to us was due to instructions received from Paris.

I deem it my duty to call the attention of Your Excellency to this state of affairs, which if it were prolonged might become exceedingly dangerous for us.

Signed   Stringher.

CC MS (WP, DLC).
    [1] About Wilson's decision on this matter, see n. 2 to the extract from the Miller Diary printed at May 12, 1919.

E N C L O S U R E   I I

Norman Hezekiah Davis to Carter Glass

Paris, May 6, 1919.

D-281, for Glass. VERY URGENT.

1. The President has been informed from several sources that newspapers have, within last two days, announced additional credits or advances to Italy. Fearing that the publication of any such notice under present state of affairs will be misunderstood and have bad effect, the President was rather disturbed and asked me about it. I told him I had seen no such notices, but that I had received a cable from Rathbone[1] about ten days ago quoting letter written to Italian representative defining an arrangement and the establishment of conditional credits thereunder. I further explained that this arrangement was principally to cover commitments already made and was communicated to the Italians before you had received my cable stating that on account of present situation he had not yet approved the establishment of an additional credit of $50,000,000 in favor of Italy about which you had cabled me.

I also explained that advances under established credits are only made, as a rule, when, in your judgment, they should be made. The President then asked me to say to you that, for various reasons, just now he questions the advisability of establishing additional credits in favor of Italy, and that advances under credits already established should be limited to definite commitments and absolute necessities. While of course we must certainly comply with any commitments, I gather that the President wishes to satisfy himself that advances made cannot be employed even indirectly for any purposes for which they are not intended, and that meanwhile the Italians should realize that their requests cannot have the same sympathetic consideration as formerly.   Davis

[1] That is, Albert Rathbone.

ENCLOSURE III

Carter Glass to Norman Hezekiah Davis

Washington May 10, 1919.

1928. For Davis from Glass.

Your 281. Italian credit mentioned in the newspapers was of course not that for which I had recently asked you to obtain the President's approval, but was a portion of a credit for which President had previously given his approval. Establishment was unavoidable in order to carry out definite written commitment entered into before newspaper reports of Italian break or your warning cable reached me here. Credit was established several days before it was reported in newspapers and was necessary in order to enable Italian government to make payments to Americans under contracts approved by the Treasury long before present situation at peace conference arose. Failure to establish credit would have injured our own people rather than Italian Government. Since April 15th Italians have been required to make daily reports of expenditures. Advances to them are being made only to enable them to cover previous commitments made with approval of Treasury before present difficulty arose. Until President's decision on whole subject I shall not approve further new purchases or commitments by Italy. It will however be necessary to make further advances and perhaps establish further credits, within amount previously approved by the President, and I assume he would wish me to do so in so far as it may be necessary to meet existing commitments. If I should refuse, Italy would stop payment to Americans with whom it has made contracts previously approved by Treasury and would be able to state that its failure to make these payments was due to the refusal of American Treasury to carry out its written agreements and provide funds to meet contractual obligations to Americans which had been previously submitted to and approved by the American Treasury. That course would arouse sympathy for Italy and bitter resentment and criticism of the administration. The President need have no doubt that I am following in letter and spirit his instructions conveyed to me through you.   Polk   Acting

T telegrams (WP, DLC).

From David Hunter Miller, with Enclosure

13 May, 1919.

MEMORANDUM FOR THE PRESIDENT:

It is expected that a report of the Committee on New States will be presented to the Council of Four tomorrow, May 14th.[1]

This report will present clauses dealing with the rights of minorities in Poland and will, I think, be unanimous. It has been substantially agreed to by the British and French and I think will be agreed to by the Italian representative, who has attended only one meeting.

The text of the report,[2] subject to probable unimportant changes, is transmitted herewith.

There will be presented on behalf of the British a separate proposal to exempt the Jews from Sunday legislation, which was objected to by the other members of the Committee.

The attitude of the British representative, Mr. Headlam-Morley, has shown an extraordinary change from the time of my first discussions with him. He was then anti-Jewish and pro-Polish, but changed to the extent of being willing to go farther in favor of the Jews than I thought reasonable. In the meantime I learned that Sir Herbert Samuel[3] had lunch here with Mr. Lloyd George, and it was immediately after this that the change in Mr. Headlam-Morley's attitude appeared.

The Committee has not heard any representatives of Poland but will ask the Council of Four as to this. Neither has the Committee heard any representative of the Jews in Poland although the members of the Committee have discussed the Jewish question with American, British, and Roumanian Jews.

David Hunter Miller

TS MS (WP, DLC).
    [1] This report was presented to the Council of Four on May 17, 1919, 11:10 a.m., and is printed as an Enclosure with D. H. Miller to WW, May 15, 1919.
    [2] That is, in fact, the draft treaty printed as the Enclosure with this letter.
    [3] Herbert Louis Samuel, former M.P. and cabinet member.

ENCLOSURE

Draft of a Treaty between the United States of America, Great
Britain, France, Italy and Japan, described as the Principal Allied
and Associated Powers, on the one hand, and Poland on the other
hand, to carry out the provisions of Article 93 of the Treaty of Peace
with Germany.

WHEREAS the Allied and Associated Powers have by the successful conclusion of the late war restored to the Polish nation the independence of which it had been unjustly deprived, and

WHEREAS by the proclamation of March 30, 1917, the former Government of Russia assented to the re-establishment of an independent Polish State, and

WHEREAS the Polish State which now in fact exercises sovereignty over those portions of the former Russian Empire which are
predominantly occupied by Poles, has already been recognized as a
sovereign and independent State by the high contracting parties,
and

WHEREAS it has been determined by the Treaty of Peace signed on
even date with this between the Allied and Associated Powers on the
one hand and Germany on the other hand, a Treaty to which Poland
is a party, that certain portions of the former German Empire should
be incorporated in the territory of Poland, and

WHEREAS it has in the same Treaty been agreed and determined
that the boundaries of Poland not laid down in that Treaty shall be
subsequently determined by the Principal Allied and Associated
Powers,

The above mentioned Powers have agreed to the articles sub-
joined:

CHAPTER I.
Article 1.
(America, Great Britain, France, Italy, Japan) hereby confirm
their recognition of the Polish State within the boundaries above indicated as a sovereign and independent member of the family of nations.

CHAPTER II.
Article 1.
Poland being desirous to conform its institutions to the principles
of liberty and justice and to give a sure guarantee to all the inhabitants of the territories over which it has assumed sovereignty, of its
own free will agrees with the other parties hereto to the following
articles, and recognizes them to be obligations of international concern of which the League of Nations has jurisdiction:

Article 2.

Subject to the provisions of Article 90 of the Treaty of Peace with Germany, Poland admits and declares to be citizens of Poland of their own right and without any requirement of special proceedings,

(a) All persons who on the 1st August, 1914, were habitually resident within the frontiers of Poland as now or hereafter established and who were at that date nationals of Germany, Austria-Hungary or Russia.

(b) All persons heretofore born in the said territory except those who have been naturalised in a foreign country other than Germany, Austria-Hungary or Russia.

Article 3.

Within a period of two years from the coming into force of the present Treaty any such person may opt for citizenship in any other State which consents thereto.

Option by a husband will cover his wife and option by parents will cover their children under 18 years of age.

Persons who have exercised the above right to opt must before the expiration of three years from the coming into force of the present Treaty transfer their place of residence to the State for which they have opted.

Article 4.

The persons who have exercised the above right to opt will be entitled to retain their immovable property in the territory of Poland. They may carry with them their movable property of every description. No export duties or charges may be imposed upon them in connection with the removal of such property.

Article 5.

All persons hereafter born within the frontiers of Poland as now or hereafter established who are not born nationals of another state shall *ipso facto* be citizens of Poland.

Article 6.

Poland undertakes full and complete protection of the life and liberty of all inhabitants of Poland without distinction of birth, race, nationality, language or religion.

All inhabitants of Poland shall be entitled to the free exercise, whether public or private, of any creed, religion or belief, whose practices are not inconsistent with public order or public morals.

Article 7.

All citizens of Poland shall be equal before the law and shall enjoy the same civil and political rights without distinction as to race, language or religion.

Differences of religion, creed or confession shall not prejudice any citizen of Poland in matters relating to the enjoyment of civil or political rights, as for instance admission to public employments, functions and honours, or the exercise of professions and industries.

No restriction shall be imposed on the free use by any citizen of Poland of any language in private intercourse, in commerce, in religion, in the press or published works, or at public meetings.

Notwithstanding any establishment by the Polish Government of an official language, reasonable facilities shall be given to Polish citizens of non-Polish speech for the use of their language, either orally or in writing, before the courts.

Article 8.

Polish citizens who belong to racial, religious or linguistic minorities shall enjoy the same treatment and security in law and in fact as the other citizens of Poland and in particular shall have an equal right to establish, manage and control at their own expense charitable, religious and social institutions, schools and other educational establishments, with the free use in them of their own language and religion.

Article 9.

Poland will provide in the public educational establishments of towns and districts in which are resident a considerable proportion of Polish citizens of other than Polish speech, reasonable facilities to assure that instruction shall be given to the children of such Polish citizens through the medium of their own language.

In those towns and districts where there is a considerable proportion of Polish citizens belonging to racial, religious or linguistic minorities, these minorities shall be assured of an equitable share in the enjoyment and application of sums which may be provided for out of public funds by any State Department, municipal or other budget, for educational, religious or charitable purposes.

Article 10.

A Scholastic Committee, appointed by all the Jewish communities of Poland, shall assure, under the general control of the State, the distribution of the proportional part of the public funds assigned to the Jewish Schools and the organization and direction of these schools.

Article 11.

The foregoing provisions providing for education in languages other than Polish do not prevent the Polish Government from making obligatory the teaching of Polish.

Article 12.

Poland agrees that the foregoing obligations shall be deemed embodied in her fundamental law as a bill of rights with which no law, regulation or official action shall conflict or interfere, and as against which no law, regulation or official action shall have validity.

Article 13.

(Provisions regarding right of appeal or protection by the League of Nations and a time limit for expiration or revision. The language is not yet agreed upon)

T MS (WP, DLC).

From Jane Addams

[Zurich, c. May 13, 1919]

Following resolution moved by Mrs. Pethick Lawrence[1] England seconded by Madame Waern-Bugge[2] of Sweden and supported by Signora Genoni[3] Italy was unanimously adopted today by women representing fifteen countries majority from Entente[4] QUOTE This international congress of women regards the unemployment famine and pestilence extending throughout great tracts of central and eastern Europe and through parts of Asia as a profound disgrace to civilization. This congress urges the governments of all the powers assembled at the Peace Congress to develop the interallied organization formed for purposes of war into an international organization for purposes of peace and urges that the following immediate steps be taken: one that the blockade be immediately lifted, two that all resources of the world food, raw materials, finance, transport be organized immediately for the relief of the peoples from famine and pestilence; three that if there is an insufficiency either of food or of transport to supply all the demands luxuries shall not be given transport from one country to another until the necessaries of life are supplied to all and that the people of every country be rationed in order that all the starving shall be fed. We believe that only immediate international action of this kind can save humanity and bring about the permanent reconciliation and union of the peoples.

JANE ADDAMS,   President,
Glockenhof, Zurich.

T telegram (WP, DLC).
    [1] Emmeline (Mrs. Frederick William) Pethick-Lawrence, English social worker, suffrage leader, and peace advocate.
    [2] Gustava Elisabeth Waern-Bugge, Swedish suffrage and peace leader.
    [3] Rosa Genoni of Milan, active in many liberal causes, including woman suffrage and the peace movement.

⁴ This was the Women's International Conference for Permanent Peace, held in Zurich from May 12 to May 19, 1919. It was a sequel to the International Congress of Women, held at The Hague in 1915, about which see WW to Juliet B. Rublee, June 2, 1915, n. 2, Vol. 33. For the conference of 1919, see the *New York Times*, May 14-20, 1919, and Gertrude Bussey and Margaret Tims, *Women's International League for Peace and Freedom, 1915-1965: A Record of Fifty Years' Work* (London, 1965), pp. 29-33.

A Translation of a Letter from Pietro Cardinal Gasparri to Edward Mandell House

Sir: The Vatican, May 13, 1919.

As I do not wish to disturb President Wilson, of whose many occupations I am aware, and on the other hand as I know how much you are moved by humanitarian sentiments and the high esteem in which the President and all the members of the Peace Conference hold you, I address myself to you.

As soon as His Holiness learned that the Central Powers had just asked for an armistice, He wrote President Wilson through Cardinal Gibbons,¹ begging him for the good of humanity and appealing to his noble sentiments to take into consideration this request to secure moderate conditions of peace in keeping with the honor of the nations at war and conceived so as to avoid further misunderstandings and conflicts.

I can assure you, Colonel, that some allied Powers share the same feelings.

The bishops of Germany have just begged the Holy Father to intervene in order to have the conditions of peace mitigated, for, in their opinion, they cannot be carried out and they are so framed as to drive the German people to despair.

His Holiness cannot remain untouched by this appeal and through you He renews His request of the President. I can assure you that the Holy Father in again turning to the President is not moved by any special interests nor by any sort of sympathy: but is actuated only by a desire to see the world rendered and assured a truly durable peace.

In requesting you to be so good as to submit this request to the President's consideration, I am glad to seize the occasion to offer you, Colonel, the assurances of my very high and most distinguished consideration.   Signed: Pierre Cardinal Gasparri

Gasparri is as you know the Pope's Secretary. E.M.H.

T MS (WP, DLC).
¹ See Benedict XV to WW, Oct. 10, 1918, printed as an Enclosure with J. Bonzano to WW, Oct. 11, 1918, and J. Card. Gibbons to WW, Oct. 12, 1918, both in Vol. 51.

John Charles Frémont[1] to Cary Travers Grayson

Paris, 13 May, 1919.

MEMORANDUM for the Naval Aid to the President:

In the absence of Admiral Benson I transmit below the summary of a report dated May 10th, from Rear Admiral Andrews, Commander U. S. Naval Forces Eastern Mediterranean, on conditions in and about Fiume and Trieste, in order that the information contained therein may be placed before the President.

U.S. Naval officer attached to Port Office at Trieste,[2] while en route from Vienna to Trieste, in conversation with Austrian business man, an ex-Army officer, who had recently passed through Marbourg, was told that large numbers of men throughout that part of the country were hurrying to Marbourg for mobilization. They were all being armed and organized, and mobilization is on a five-year basis.

Major Furlong, U.S.A., investigated reports of deportations from Fiume and vicinity, and obtained information from apparently reliable source that six Jugo-Slavs have been actually deported since the Italians assumed the government. He believes that about two thousand Jugo-Slavs have been exiled or forced to leave Fiume through coercion either by Italian sympathizers or, as in some cases, a couple of military police would tell a Jugo-Slav family that they could no longer be protected and that it would be advisable for them to get out. It is understood that a large number have left on this account.

The so called Young Italian Party[3] has effaced a great number of signs of Jugo-Slav business men by means of black paint or big posters bearing the inscriptions "Vive Italia" and "Italia o Morte." The Italian police and military apparently make no effort to prevent this, nor to prevent intimidation of the Jugo-Slavs. The French and English Generals have called the attention of the Italian General[4] in command to matters of this kind, with result that the Italian General stirs around a great deal but does not seem to prevent similar occurrences. Admiral Andrews' efforts to obtain information and his urging Italian General to avert a clash with Serbs have had a very good effect. It has been represented to both the Italian and Serbian Generals[5] that it was a very disastrous time for both sides to have anything disagreeable happen. The Italian General is anxious to prevent anything of this kind, and has sent an invitation to the Serbian General to come to dinner in his quarters at Fiume.

Admiral Andrews has been making efforts to facilitate trade by exchange of commodities. The Italians are very much in need of wood, and Serbian Government will not permit wood to come out of Bosnia through Knin down into the Italian occupied zone. This is also the case in the American zone. Wood comes down from Bosnia for Spalato only for local consumption. The same condition exists at Fiume. This policy on the part of the Serbs is distinctly ridiculous, in opinion of Admiral Andrews, and he believes the folly of it should be represented to the Serbian Government.

At request of Admiral Andrews the Food Minister from Belgrade[6] telegraphed to the government at Belgrade, from Spalato, regarding exchange of commodities, and made a definite request that lumber be allowed to come out of Bosnia to be used as an exchange commodity. As a result the restriction was removed the next day, but the restriction on commodities going out of Jugo-Slav territory still remains and should be lifted to allow the Jugo-Slavs to sell their excess commodities, and to prevent the spread of Bolshevism.

The French General has said that, in case Fiume is given to the Italians, the Serbs will raise an economic wall between Fiume and Croatia. It appears quite likely that they will do this, but if they do they will be playing the Italians' game. The aim of the Italians is chiefly to get Fiume in order to control its trade is [in] such manner as not to interfere with development of Trieste.

The Italian Battleship DANTE ALIGHIERI was expected to arrive at Fiume on May 10th, making a total Italian force of three battleships, one armored cruiser, and a number of destroyers.

J. C. Frémont   by direction.

TS MS (WP, DLC).
    [1] Commander, U.S.N., grandson of the explorer, member of Admiral Benson's staff.
    [2] Unidentified.
    [3] He probably meant the *Giovine Fiume* ("Young Fiume") association, founded in 1905, organized to stress the ties of Italian Fiumans to Italy and still very active at this time. See Michael A. Ledeen, *The First Duce: D'Annunzio at Fiume* (Baltimore, 1977), pp. 23, 63, 68.
    [4] Gen. Joseph Jean Michel Savy, Brig. Gen. Herbert Gordon, and Gen. Francesco Saverio Grazioli, respectively.
    [5] The Serbian general cannot be identified.
    [6] Ljubomir Jovanović.

To Joseph Patrick Tumulty

Paris, 13 May, 1919.

Senator Harris has given out a statement that at my request he had agreed to vote for suffrage.[1]

Please announce unless advised to the contrary by the Shipping Board that American shipyards will be open to foreign contracts so far as they can be without interfering with building for American registry.

Please let me know what Burleson and Hines think ought to be the announcement about the telegraph and telephone lines and the railways respectively.

My present judgment inclines to the appointment of Edwin F. Gay[2] as member of the Shipping Board. I know much more about him than I know about Scott[3] and he has certainly proved out during the war. Do you know any reason why I should not choose him?

Woodrow Wilson.

T telegram (WP, DLC).
[1] See JPT to WW, April 30, 1919; JPT to WW, May 2, 1919 (third telegram of that date); the extract from the Grayson Diary printed at May 8, 1919; and JPT to C. T. Grayson, May 9, 1919, all in Vol. 58. The Editors have found no "statement" by Harris at this time. However, the New York Times, May 10, 1919, under the dateline Washington, May 9, reported as follows: "Information reached Washington today that William J. Harris . . . has told President Wilson that he will vote for the equal suffrage amendment resolution." The New York Evening Post, May 9, 1919, carried a similar report.
[2] That is, Edwin Francis Gay, dean of Harvard's Graduate School of Business Administration.
[3] Thomas Albertson Scott, president of T. A. Scott & Co., an engineering firm of New London, Conn.

Three Telegrams from Joseph Patrick Tumulty

[The White House, May 13, 1919]

No. 119 Republicans are promising revision of the tariff. Of course, it is ridiculous, but would it not be to our advantage to suggest changes where changes are obviously necessary, to protect us against dumping, etc? Would it not be wise for us to get in touch with Taussig and ask him if he has any suggestions, particularly with reference to dyestuffs and chemicals? It would be wise for us to make a test of the efficiency of the Tariff Commission and would put our party in the position of acting in matters of tariff upon facts scientifically ascertained.   Tumulty.

[The White House, May 13, 1919]

No. 120 Please do nothing about Gay appointment until I can cable you.   Tumulty.

[The White House, May 13, 1919]

No. 121 In answer to your inquiry, the Postmaster General requests me to send you the following:

"My cablegram of May fifth[1] set forth my views on the entire telephone and telegraph situation. It will not be necessary for you to make any announcement as to these companies other than what will be set forth in your message."   Tumulty.

T telegrams (WP, DLC).
  [1] Sent as ASB to WW, May 7 (not 5), 1919, Vol. 58.

From Walker Downer Hines

[The White House, May 13, 1919]

No. 122 In answer to your inquiry, Director General of Railroads requests me to send you the following:

"I think it is desirable to announce that it is the present intention of the President to relinquish the railroads from the existing federal control on December 31st, next. Mr. Burleson concurs in this view. I gave my reasons for this conclusion in my letter of April fourth,[1] which was delivered to you by Secretary Baker."   Tumulty.

T telegram (WP, DLC).
  [1] Printed at that date in Vol. 56.

From Newton Diehl Baker

My dear Mr. President: Washington. May 13, 1919.

In accordance with request received from the Governor of Porto Rico,[1] I beg to inclose herewith copy of a petition[2] which was presented by the Commissioner of Education of Porto Rico,[3] on behalf of the children of that island, to the delegation of congressmen who visited Porto Rico last month, and in which request is made that the United States assist Porto Rico in publicly educating its children, by making an annual appropriation of two million dollars for a period of twenty years for that purpose.

As pointed out in the petition, the people of Porto Rico are now citizens of the United States, and in view of the fact that the island's revenues are insufficient to meet the educational needs and requirements of its children, I am most heartily in favor of any assistance that Congress might see fit to extend to Porto Rico along that line.

The census of 1910 shows that the percentage of adult illiteracy of Porto Rico was 66.5%, while in the United States proper, for persons ten years of age and over, it was only 7.7%, and among the negroes, where of course the percentage of illiteracy was the greatest, it was only 30.4%. These figures as to the need of additional educational facilities in Porto Rico are convincing, and I trust that the inclosed petition will receive your careful consideration with a view to your recommending to Congress that an appropriation for educational purposes in Porto Rico be granted.

I might add that it is becoming more difficult every year to obtain competent teachers in the United States for the purpose of teaching in Porto Rico because of the low salaries that can be offered them and because of the fact that they have always had to pay their own traveling expenses to and from the island.

Copies of the inclosed petition are now being printed in Porto Rico and will soon be available for distribution to all members of Congress, and I hope that you may support this worthy request with a favorable recommendation on the subject to Congress during the forthcoming session.   Very sincerely,   Newton D. Baker

TLS (WP, DLC).
  [1] That is, Arthur Yager.
  [2] The enclosure is missing in WP, DLC.
  [3] Paul Gerard Miller.

From Frank William Taussig

My dear Mr. President: Paris, France, May 13, 1919.

I enclose some paragraphs which you may find useful in connection with the drafting of your message.[1]

Pray note particularly the paragraph on page 2a, and consider whether it is expedient to say *anything* of the kind. I have no question about the justice of what is there recommended. But I am inclined for myself to think it unwise to touch at all upon the question of general tariff revision. What I hear from the other side indicates that projects for general revision will be considered by the Ways and Means Committee, and that the whole tariff business will be brought up. But in view of the discussions upon the peace treaty it is hardly wise to arouse unn[e]cessarily any antagonism, and this might be the consequence of such a paragraph as is here drafted. Better ignore matters that would start partisan controversy.

You will observe that I have referred to the Tariff Commission itself in the closing paragraph. I hope you will endorse its recommendation as there summarized. This particular recommendation is not likely to raise partisan ire.

                        Very sincerely yours,   F. W. Taussig

TLS (WP, DLC).
  [1] "DRAFT PARAGRAPHS," T MS (WP, DLC).

From the Diary of Dr. Grayson

Wednesday, May 14, 1919.

The President had an early breakfast. The Council of Four this morning received three additional notes from the Germans. These notes dealt with a suggestion relative to the Saar Valley and Basin, with the demand on the part of the Germans that they be allowed to discuss orally the differences between the recommendations made by the Allied and Associated economic experts and the Germans, and also that they be accorded complete freedom of intercourse with the Austrian delegates. The Germans were working overtime preparing their objections to the treaty and had sent two of their political experts to Berlin to discuss with the government just what was to be done in the event as was considered certain that the Allied and Associated governments declined to moderate the peace terms.

The Big Four also heard the report of the Committee on Internationalization of Harbors and Waterways, and especially certain points in dispute which had arisen in that committee.[1] The British Government's policy of giving preferential treatment to British merchantmen at coaling stations scattered throughout the world had come in for severe criticism and certain of the members of the Waterways Committee recommended to the Big Four that in all cases where coaling stations were within territory over which a mandatory was exercised complete freedom be granted to all vessels and that they be coaled in the order of arrival, thus avoiding preferential discrimination.

The President had Senator Peter Gerry of Rhode Island and Mrs. Gerry[2] as luncheon guests. After lunch the President had a long talk with the Senator. Senator Gerry told me afterwards that he was delighted with the President's physical condition showing that my care was having results. I laughingly assured him that the President had been picking up ever since I insisted on his getting away from the cares of state for an afternoon and going out to the Longchamps Course to see the races there.

After conferring with Senator Gerry the President went for a ride, I accompanying him, and later returned to the White House in time for an afternoon conference with the Big Four, which had before it the report of the Foreign Ministers dealing with the Eastern frontiers of Austria.

Mrs. Wilson was indisposed and so the President had dinner with her in her room. After dinner I went in the President's room and sat with him a little while. He completed the initial draft of his Message to Congress.[3] The President as usual had done the job so well that when he came to read it over he only changed one word and that he wrote in with a pencil.[4] He discussed with me the matter of sending it by cable. He thought the message would cover between three and four thousand words.

[1] Hankey's notes of this meeting, not printed in this volume, are printed in *PPC*, V, 589-98.
[2] Mathilde Scott Townsend (Mrs. Peter Goelet) Gerry.
[3] There is a WWsh outline of this address in WP, DLC. The WWT MS is in the C. L. Swem Coll., NjP.
[4] The WWT draft is heavily emended by WWhw and WWT. Grayson was referring to the final draft, which is printed at May 20, 1919.

From the Diary of David Hunter Miller

Wednesday, May 14th [1919]

At 9 o'clock I went over with di Cellere to see Orlando. He said that it had occurred to him that there was a third way in this matter. Some time ago, before the events of the 21st of April there had been a meeting between two business men of Italy and two business men of the Jugo-Slavs.[1] He mentioned the name of one of the Italians, which I thought was "Querriti," and said all of them indeed were men "très sérieux," and that the Italians were men of very large affairs in Italy. These men, none of whom he further said had any official mandate, had discussed the question of the Adriatic and had arrived, so far as they were concerned, at an agreement which was this: Italy should have Fiume politically but the Jugo-Slavs were to have very great commercial rights there—ports, docks, etc. The Dalmatian Islands were to be divided; and as to the Dalmatian coast the solution was in the alternative: the Italians were to have Zara and a portion of the surrounding territory running to the Bay of Sebenico but not including Sebenico; or, Zara, Sebenico and Spalato were all three to be made free ports.

Orlando said that he had been begged to go on with this matter but at that time could not do it, but that while it represented the sacrifice of a great deal that Italy wished, if the Jugo-Slavs were willing now to come to an agreement on this basis he would be willing to do so. He said there were two questions to be determined, although not in any particular way: first, whether such a solution would be acceptable to the President even if it were a solution as it had been proposed which was contrary to the solution which the President himself would like; second, whether the Jugo-Slavs were willing to go on with the matter.

I told Orlando that I thought that the President would be willing that any agreement freely reached should be accepted and that I would endeavor to inquire specifically on the two points. I then told him that I had been thinking about the possibility of a definitive solution and I read to him in French the paper which I had drawn up the night before.[2] He did not make much comment. He spoke of the necessity of having the frontier of Italy run to Fiume, as otherwise sentimental ties would be entirely lost, and I told him that if that were the only question I personally would be willing to waive it. Orlando said, however, that a solution which would satisfy everybody would he thought be the best solution, and I agreed with this.

I then went to see Colonel House and told him of my talk with Orlando, and he tried to get the President on the telephone but was unsuccessful. Accordingly, I drew up the text of a letter from him to the President, and left it there for him to see as Colonel House went out.

Miller, *My Diary at the Conference of Paris*, I, 308-10.
    [1] One of the Italians was Ferdinando Quartieri, an industrialist of Milan and a technical expert on economic and financial questions in the Italian delegation to the peace conference. The other Italian was a man named Bensa. The Editors have been unable to learn his given name and his occupation. See Albrecht-Carrié, *Italy at the Paris Peace Conference*, p. 174.
    The identity of the two Yugoslav businessmen is less certain. However, they may have been two of the three technical advisers to the Yugoslav delegation on merchant marine questions, Božo Banać, Melko Čingrija, and Filip Wolf-Vuković, who had met unofficially with three unnamed Italian maritime experts several times in early April 1919 to discuss a division between Italy and Yugoslavia of the Austro-Hungarian merchant fleet then in Italian hands. During these meetings there had been some discussion of widening the talks to include the entire Adriatic question. The only direct result of these talks was an informal meeting between Ante Trumbić and Silvio Crespi on April 11, at which the negotiations broke down in total disagreement over the disposition of Fiume. See Ivo J. Lederer, *Yugoslavia at the Paris Peace Conference: A Study in Frontiermaking* (New Haven, Conn., and London, 1963), pp. 188-93. However, it is possible that some or all of the Yugoslav maritime experts continued their talks with the Italians into the week of April 14-21 mentioned by Albrecht-Carrié, cited above.
    [2] That is, the document quoted in n. 3 to the extract from the Miller Diary printed at May 13, 1919.

From the Diary of Colonel House

May 14, 1919.

The Adriatic settlement was again on the boards with me most of the day. I drew the President, Mezes, Beers [Beer] and Miller into it. See my letter to the President and his notation. Matters look more favorable. I have sent for Trumbitch to be here tomorrow at ten, and if he agrees, it is my purpose to have the Italians here in one room and the Jugo-Slavs in the other with my study between. In this way I hope to bring about an agreement.

I am delighted to have the matter coming back into my hands. I hope nothing will upset the plan. There has never been a time when I have felt that it could not have been settled if properly and constantly directed.

From Edward Mandell House

Dear Governor: Paris, 14 May, 1919.

This morning, in a conversation with David Miller, Signor Orlando has suggested the possibility of an agreement being reached between Italy and the Yugo-Slavs on the whole Adriatic question, including Fiume.

The two questions which Orlando asks are these: First, would the President approve an agreement freely reached between the Italian and Yugo-Slav Governments, assuming that they reached a solution different from that which he would lay down; second, if the President's answer to the first question is favorable, would the President be willing that conversations between the Italian and Yugo-Slav Governments be carried on through the friendly medium of a representative of the American Government.

Will you please advise me?

Affectionately yours,   E. M. House

Yes to both questions (note the words I have underscored)   W.W.

TLS (E. M. House Papers, CtY).

From the Diary of Vance Criswell McCormick

May 14 (Wednesday) [1919]

Was called to the President's house at 11.00 to submit to Big Four our plan for blockade in the event of Germany refusing to sign. While waiting for our turn I had a good talk with Lord Robert on many subjects, among them Russia. I was interested to see he agreed with me that the Omsk Government should be recognized as a de facto government and said he thought so long ago. When we started meeting I handed the President a letter I had just written him[1] strongly recommending the use of military occupation instead of blockade in the event of Germany not signing and told him of Lord Robert's opinion that for financial and other reasons he thought military occupation impossible. I told the President this could not be and that the alternative was starvation and revolution in Germany. Everything would be lost to the Allies while occupation would save something out of the wreck. President made this statement to the Big Four and urged occupation. Lloyd George at once said that it would only be a blockade of several weeks and did not say that military occupation was impossible. President also stated that in our blockade plan he thought we should adopt the formal (legal) blockade because to return to the old one might recognize England's blockade operations which we had always held as illegal. He joked with Lord Robert about it, who said nothing about legality but agreed with the President a formal blockade was now possible and should be adopted.

Lord Robert read the notice to Germany we had agreed upon yesterday at Supreme Economic Council in regard to removal of blockade if Germany signed and giving also our relaxations up to date.[2] This was approved.

Am always impressed with the cordiality and harmonious workings of the Four even with Orlando present. They are apparently frank with each other, differing frequently and earnestly but always in a most friendly spirit. Three big men trying to do the big thing in the proper spirit. They could not have gotten as far as they have if this spirit had not been present.

Printed copy (V. C. McCormick Papers, CtY).
  [1] That is, V. C. McCormick to WW, May 13, 1919.
  [2] Printed in *PPC*, V, 601-603.

Hankey's Notes of a Meeting of the Council of Four[1]

President Wilson's House,
C.F.12.   Paris, May 14, 1919, 11:45 a.m.

1. *Proposals with regard to the Blockade of Germany.*

Lord R. Cecil stated that there were two subjects for consideration: viz., (a) A Public announcement indicating the present position of the Blockade of Germany and stating that it would be raised in the event of signature of the Peace Treaty (Annex 1) (b) a plan of the measures to be taken in the event of its being decided to reimpose the blockade. (Annex 2.) In referring to this plan Lord Robert Cecil drew attention to the proposal in the last paragraph that the Governments of the neutral countries contiguous to Germany should now be invited to consent to prohibit trade with Germany if called upon to do so. This would make it possible to exercise a more immediate and more effective pressure on Germany, if such pressure should become necessary.

2. *Statement with regard to the present position of the blockade (Annex 1).*

Mr. Lloyd George drew attention to the words in the first sentence of the Statement "as soon as the German representatives have signed the Treaty of Peace." He suggested that after the signature of the treaty the German assembly might repudiate it.

M. Clemenceau asked whether it would be necessary to wait for the approval of the Treaty by the Allied Parliaments, before raising the blockade. It was agreed that this would be unnecessary.

President Wilson proposed that the words quoted above should be amended to read:

"as soon as Germany has formally accepted the Treaty of Peace."

It was agreed that the Statement should be published, subject to this amendment.

3. *Measures to be taken in the event of reimposition of the blockade.*

President Wilson stated that this was not the time to discuss whether we should or should not reimpose the blockade in the event of Germany refusing to sign the Peace Treaty. In his judgment the most suitable means of pressure would be some kind of military occupation rather than blockade measures which would tend to reduce her population to starvation and despair. To have our armies in an area thus starved would not be an edifying spectacle. Blockade would be more terrible than military occupation and presents many inhumane features; if it were reimposed it would presently become distasteful to the world. The President expressed grave doubts whether the blockade should be reimposed unless no other course were open.[2]

Mr. Lloyd George was of opinion that in any case the application of the blockade would only be necessary for a fortnight or three weeks. An excuse was wanted in Germany for signing the Peace Treaty. The fear of the reimposition of the blockade would provide such an excuse. Haase,[3] for example is afraid of the blockade. There is a pressure in Germany against signing the Treaty, which is a very painful Treaty to sign.

Mr. Lloyd George expressed himself as all in favour of a military occupation as a demonstration but not as the only means of pressure. Some parts of Germany would not mind a military occupation. After only a fortnight of the reimposed blockade there would be a general cry to Scheidemann of "Sign, Sign."

4. On the question of the declaration of a formal blockade, Lord R. Cecil drew attention to the statement of the British Admiralty as to objections to such a declaration; he understood that the Admiralty view was that the ships now in commission were insufficient for the maintenance of a strictly "effective" blockade.

President Wilson said that the United States had never admitted the legality of the existing form of blockade. The Admiralty caveat was thus a little inacceptable.

Lord R. Cecil said that whether the blockade was absolutely effective or not did not matter, what mattered was the general stoppage of trade.

President Wilson added that there was a difference between blockade breaking and blockade running. Under the conditions indicated by the Admiralty there might be cases of blockade running: but a definite breach of blockade, such as would render it legally ineffective, would require a naval force which Germany does not now possess.

It was agreed that if blockade measures have to be reimposed a formal blockade should be declared. No definite decision was arrived at as to whether blockade measures should or should not be taken in the event of Germany refusing to sign the Peace Treaty; but it was understood that such preparations would now be made as would render it possible to give effect to the blockade measures proposed, in the event of its being necessary to take such action.

In particular it was agreed that the Démarche to Neutral Governments referred to by Lord R. Cecil (see general note at end of Annex 2) should be made now.

5. Lord R. Cecil referred to the possibility of exercising economic pressure on countries, which were appealing to the Allies for assistance and supplies, and were at the same time fighting with their neighbours in defiance of the wishes of the Council.

He cited the case of Poland which is at present engaged in operations against the Ukraine. He referred also to the food supplies withheld by Serbia in the Banat.

He suggested that the Council might on occasion think it desirable to notify the Supreme Economic Council that economic pressure should be applied in such cases.[4]

It was agreed that this should be done and that the Supreme Economic Council should be free to take such action as seemed to them desirable in such cases.

T MS (SDR, RG 256, 180.03401/12, DNA).
    [1] The complete text of these minutes is printed in *PPC*, V, 599-604.
    [2] Mantoux, II, 69, adds at this point: "Clemenceau. I still prefer to use them [economic means] rather than to have our soldiers killed."
    [3] That is, Hugo Haase, leader of the Independent Social Democratic party.
    [4] Mantoux, II, 70, adds at this point: "Wilson. I am of the opinion to give a carte blanche on these matters to the Economic Council; but it is natural that we use the means at our disposal to cause our just decisions to be respected."

Hankey's Notes of a Meeting of the Council of Four[1]

President Wilson's House,
Paris, May 14, 1919, 12:15 p.m.

C.F.13.

I. M. ORLANDO said that two questions had been raised by the Drafting Committee in regard to the Austrian and Hungarian Treaties. One of these questions concerned responsibilities for the breaches of the laws of war. Naturally, the clause in the German Treaty applying to the Kaiser, was not applicable to the Austrian and

    [1] The complete text of these minutes is printed in *PPC*, V, 605-13.

Hungarian Treaties, and there was no equivalent Article. Where, however, some alteration was required was in the case where subjects of the old Austro-Hungarian Empire had committed crimes and had subsequently assumed some fresh nationality, such as Czecho-Slovak, or one of the other nationalities. Provision should be made that such persons should not escape trial.

PRESIDENT WILSON pointed out that no provision inserted in the Austrian and Hungarian Treaties could compel the Czech-Slovak Government to surrender people accused of crimes.[2]

MR. LLOYD GEORGE drew attention to a mistake in Article 227 of the German Treaty, where it was stated that the special tribunal "will be composed of four judges, one appointed by each of the following Powers; namely, United States of America, Great Britain, France, Italy and Japan." The number four should, apparently, be five.

Sir Maurice Hankey was instructed to call the attention of the Secretary-General to the above mistake, in order that the Germans might be notified.

2. M. ORLANDO said that there was a second point to which he wished to draw attention, namely, the language of the Austrian and Hungarian Treaties. He had consented to the German Treaty being drafted in the English and French languages, to the exclusion of Italian. In view, however, of Italy's special position towards Austria and Hungary, he asked that the Austrian and Hungarian Treaties might also be drafted in the Italian language.

M. CLEMENCEAU said he had no objection.

PRESIDENT WILSON said he had no objection, provided that the Italian representatives of the Drafting Committee were fully qualified to prepare the necessary drafts.

M. ORLANDO said that they were amply qualified. (It was agreed that the Austrian and Hungarian Treaties should be prepared in the Italian, as well as in the English and French languages.)

3. The Council had before it a letter from Herr Brockdorff-Rantzau, dated May 10th, on the subject of German Prisoners of War and Interned Civilians, together with a draft reply (Appendix I, (A)[3] & (B)).

MR. LLOYD GEORGE said that he had no objection to the substance of the draft reply, but thought it might be couched in more sympathetic language, particularly in regard to the portion relating to the graves of the fallen.

PRESIDENT WILSON said that was precisely his view.

[2] Mantoux, II, 70, here adds: "It is agreed that this question will be referred back to the commission."
[3] Printed as Appendix III to the minutes of the Council of Four printed at May 12, 1919, 11 a.m.

M. CLEMENCEAU asked if Mr. Lloyd George would prepare a revised draft.

MR. LLOYD GEORGE undertook to do this.

4. With reference to C.F.9, Minute 1, the Council had before it a letter from Herr Brockdorff-Rantzau, transmitting a draft International Agreement on Labour Law,[4] prepared by the German Government, together with a draft reply prepared by the Committee to which the question had been referred. (Appendix II.)[5]

MR. LLOYD GEORGE said it was worth considering whether it would not be desirable to admit the Germans to the Labour Organisation before they were admitted to the League of Nations.

(It was agreed that before the draft reply was approved, the Committee should be invited to express their views on this question.)

5. M. CLEMENCEAU read the attached résume of three German Notes which had arrived in the night of 13th/14th May, 1919 (Appendix III).[6]

(It was agreed that these notes should be referred to the appropriate Committees set up by the Peace Conference to consider such questions.)

(Sir Maurice Hankey was instructed to place himself in communication with the Secretary-General on the subject.)

6. PRESIDENT WILSON read the following letter which he had received from Mr. Lansing, relating to two pamphlets received from the Chinese Delegation:

"The Mission has received from the Chinese Delegation direct and also through the Secretariat-General two pamphlets,[7] one of which sets forth China's claim submitting for abrogation by the Peace Conference the Treaties and Note by and between China and Japan of May 25, 1915, and the other presents for readjustment by the Conference a number of important questions, among which may be mentioned 'the withdrawal from China of Foreign

[4] About which, see n. 2 to the minutes of the Council of Four printed at May 12, 1919, 11 a.m.

[5] G. N. B[arnes], "Copy of Draft Letter to the German Delegation," printed in *PPC*, V, 610-12. The first three sections of this draft are very similar to the three sections of the preliminary draft reply summarized in n. 3 to the minutes of the Council of Four printed at May 12, 1919, 11 a.m. However, the new draft included a fourth section which pointed out deficiencies in the draft agreement on labor law which Brockdorff-Rantzau had submitted (again, see n. 2 to *ibid.*) which were in fact covered in the labor clauses of the peace treaty.

[6] It is printed in *PPC*, V, 612-13. Clemenceau summarizes it well as recorded by Mantoux: "Clemenceau. I have received three new communications from the German delegation. The first declares that the economic losses imposed on Germany will not permit her to live. The second refuses to acknowledge the responsibility of Germany in the origins of the war. The third protests against our assertion of having applied the principles of the Armistice and dwells upon the violations of law which the treaty is preparing in Poland, in the Saar Basin, etc." Mantoux, II, 71.

[7] See V. K. W. Koo to WW, April 17, 1919, n. 1, Vol. 57, and J. C. Grew to GFC, April 25, 1919, n. 1, Vol. 58.

Troops and Police, the withdrawal of Foreign Post Offices and the Abolition of Consular Jurisdiction.'

The first pamphlet deals with a question growing out of the war, and one affecting not only American rights but those of other associated Governments, but it seems unlikely that the Claim can have consideration by the Conference.

The second pamphlet has to do with questions not directly related to the war and questions therefore still more unlikely to be considered by the Conference.

But in view of the present feeling in China in consequence of the decision in the Kiachow Question, I beg to suggest that the Council of Four send the Chinese Delegation a written statement pointing out that it will be impossible for the Peace Conference to consider these matters, whose importance is fully recognized, and suggesting that they be brought to the attention of the Council of the League of Nations as soon as that body is able to function."

(Mr. Lansing's proposal was agreed to, and Sir Maurice Hankey was instructed to draft a letter for the signature of the President of the Conference.)

7. MR. LLOYD GEORGE said that Mr. Arthur Henderson, as Chairman of the Berne Labour Conference, had approached him and asked if the Supreme Council of the Principal Allied and Associated Powers would receive a deputation from the Conference in regard to the Peace Terms.

He had replied to him that as Chairman of the Labour Conference he had already received a summary of the Peace Terms; that these Peace Terms had now been delivered to the Germans; and that consequently no useful purpose would be served by the deputation. He asked if an official reply might now be sent in the same sense.

(This was agreed to, and Sir Maurice Hankey was instructed to draft a letter, either from the President or from the Secretary-General of the Peace Conference.)

8. PRESIDENT WILSON said that since the communication which he had been asked to send to Luxembourg through the medium of an American Officer, no action had been taken in regard to the future status of Luxembourg. He then read a document,[8] the gist of which was that the people of Luxembourg wanted the Supreme Council of the Principal Allied and Associated Powers to receive a delegation, and did not wish to hold a plebiscite until after that.

M. CLEMENCEAU said it would be impossible to refuse.

MR. LLOYD GEORGE agreed.

PRESIDENT WILSON said the communication had no doubt been

[8] E. Reuter to WW, May 6, 1919, TLS (WP, DLC).

addressed to him, rather than to the President of the Conference, because he had been the medium for transmitting the previous communication from the Supreme Council.[9]

(It was agreed that President Wilson should reply that the Supreme Council of the Principal Allied and Associated Powers would be glad to receive a deputation from the people of Luxembourg.)

9. MR. LLOYD GEORGE said that he had received from the British Representatives in Siberia reports as to the risk of trouble between the United States forces in Siberia and the Russian troops. The view of the British Representatives, which of course he could not confirm, was that the Russian General Ivanoff had done his best to smooth matters, and that the trouble was largely due to General Graves.

PRESIDENT WILSON said that General Graves was a man of most unprovocative character, and wherever the fault might lie, he felt sure it was not with him. The British representatives were, he would not say partisans of, but at any rate friendly to, Koltchak.

MR. LLOYD GEORGE said they might fairly be termed partisans.

APPENDIX I (B) TO C.F. 13.

Mr. President,

I beg to acknowledge the receipt of your letter of May 10, relating to prisoners of war.

1. Prisoners of war and civilian prisoners who have been guilty of crimes or penal offences cannot be allowed to return to their native country. As such crimes have been committed on the soil of the Allies, the cases have been dealt with by the proper authorities in the various territories and punishment carried out accordingly. To say the least, it would seem strange that the perpetrator of a particular crime should receive punishment according to his nationality, i.e. that he should be set at liberty if he be German, whilst an Englishman, an American, a Frenchman or an Italian in a similar case would have to undergo the maximum penalty. This would imply the according of specially favoured treatment to the Germans, an idea which cannot be entertained.

How could we undertake to liberate such a malefactor as the German prisoner HOPPE who was sent to work on a farm in the Seine-

---

[9] Mantoux, II, 72, adds at this point: "Wilson. I have also received a telegram from Luxembourg indicating that the Chamber has decided to begin immediately the discussion on the question of the economic referendum. The Clerical majority seeks a decision soon, which would confront us with a fait accompli. At the same time, they are slowing down the negotiations with Belgium. If the French government does not declare that it does not want an economic union with Luxembourg, the vote will go in this sense; if France makes that declaration, the result will be the maintenance of the status quo, and probably the reestablishment of relations with Germany. Such appears to be the scheme of the Luxembergian Clerical party."

Inférieure? This prisoner at night broke into the farmer's house and murdered him and his wife in cold blood with a bill-hook.

For this double murder HOPPE was sentenced to death on June 11th 1918 by a regularly constituted Court-Martial. The Berne Conventions have suspended the execution of the sentence until peace has been signed. Would justice be satisfied if, as a consequence of the Peace Treaty, this murderer were reprieved. We cannot conceive that the terms relating to prisoners of war should guarantee immunity to those guilty of murder and other penal offences.

According to the terms of the Treaty of Peace all Germans who have committed actions contrary to the laws of the countries of the Allied and Associated Powers, are to be handed over to those Powers, wherever those action were committed.

How then is it possible to demand at the same time that those Germans in the Allies' territory who have committed crimes most severely punished by the Penal Code, should be released by those Powers?

For cogent reasons, it was prescribed in the Armistice terms of Nov. 11th 1918, that civil and military prisoners belonging to the Allied and Associated Powers should be returned unconditionally. Now the fate of the German criminals awaits decision. Justice cannot be robbed of her imprescriptible rights by the inclusion in the Peace Treaty of an Amnesty for crimes committed by prisoners.

2. There is no special point in the improvement of conditions asked for on behalf of prisoners of war. Unlike the Germans in their treatment of the subjects of Allied and Associated Powers, these latter to their honour have invariably assured to German prisoners of war treatment in keeping with the laws of humanity and international agreements.

3. The restitution of personal property constitutes a legal right. But as Germany has not fulfilled her undertakings and as she still withholds the personal property belonging to repatriated prisoners, the Allied and Associated Powers are under the necessity of calling upon Germany to respect her obligations. It is to this end that Art. 223 has been framed.

4. As regards search for the missing, the Allied and Associated Powers have invariably supplied the Germans with such information as was in their possession. Their attitude in this respect will not undergo any modification.

In Germany on the other hand a considerable number of the subjects of the Allied and Associated Powers have been deprived of the right of communicating with their relatives. This violation of international agreements has been the occasion of poignant anguish and uncertainty to many families. The measures enumerated in Art. 222 aim at putting an end to all such uncertainty.

5. As regards places of burial, Articles 225 and 226 of the Treaty have doubtless escaped your attention. Your demand is fully met by them.

6. The Allied and Associated Powers cannot in any way contemplate the cession of clothing and underwear.

The steps to be taken for repatriating prisoners will be determined immediately after the signing of Peace Preliminaries.

Believe me, Mr. President,   Your obedient Servant,

T MS (SDR, RG 256, 180.03401/13, DNA).

Hankey's and Mantoux's Notes of a Meeting of the Council of Four[1]

C.F.13A.

President Wilson's House,
Paris, May 14, 1919, 4 p.m.

§ Mantoux's notes:

M. Clemenceau reads aloud an intercepted telegram from Count Brockdorff-Rantzau to the German government: Count Brockdorff-Rantzau approves of the tone of the speeches of M. Scheidemann and of the President of the National Assembly[2]; protests against the treaty, in the Assembly and in the press, will second the efforts of the delegation, which seeks to induce the adversaries of Germany to grant her an acceptable peace.

Wilson. This shows that we are dealing with a bluff. Brockdorff writes to Scheidemann: "Continue to play your role, I will play mine." In my opinion, that is rather reassuring, for it does not indicate the will to refuse to sign.

Lloyd George. At the same time, one of the words of that dispatch indicates fear of the military occupation which would follow a refusal. §

1. The Council had before it two resolutions prepared for Mr. Lloyd George by Mr. Harold Nicolson of the British Delegation. (Appendix I and Appendix II.)

MR. LLOYD GEORGE explained that these proposals had been prepared as part of a comprehensive scheme to be presented to the Italian Delegation.

---

[1] The complete text of Hankey's minutes is printed in *PPC*, V, 614-23.

[2] That is, Konstantin Fehrenbach. He, too, had spoken against the terms of the peace treaty before the National Assembly at its session on May 12. About Scheidemann's speech on that occasion, see n. 2 to Hankey's minutes of the Council of Four printed at May 13, 1919, 4 p.m. For a summary of Fehrenbach's remarks, see Alma Luckau, *The German Delegation at the Paris Peace Conference* (New York, 1941), p. 100. The full text appears in Germany. Nationalversammlung. *Verhandlungen der Verfassunggebenden Deutschen Nationalversammlung*, Vol. 327, pp. 1110-11.

2. PRESIDENT WILSON said that he would accept the resolution contained in Appendix I in regard to the acceptance of a Mandate by the United States of America for Armenia and another for Constantinople and the Straits, subject to the assent of the Senate. The only alteration he wished to make was the inclusion in paragraph 2 of the Italian Delegation among the Powers to agree on the frontiers of the mandate in regard to the Straits.

M. CLEMENCEAU also accepted Appendix I with this alteration.

3. MR. LLOYD GEORGE produced a map which had been prepared by Mr. Nicolson of the British Delegation to accompany the resolutions in Appendix II.

PRESIDENT WILSON noted that, in this map, the valley of the Meander[3] was included in the territory to be united to Greece. He agreed that this was the best arrangement. When the United States' experts had proposed to cut this out of the Greek zone, they had done so in the Turkish interests and on the supposition that there would be an independent Turkish State. The present scheme, however, was not providing for a separate Turkey independent of mandate.

MR. LLOYD GEORGE said that the Italians would press very strongly for Scala Nuova.

PRESIDENT WILSON said that it would be inexpedient to have the Italians there in such close contact to the territory united to Greece.

MR. LLOYD GEORGE pointed out that the map did not give Mersina to the Italians. This raised the question of what port Italy was to have.

SIR MAURICE HANKEY read the following notes about the ports of Marmarice, Karaghatch and Makri,[4] which had been prepared in the Naval Section of the British Delegation:

"*Marmarice.*

This magnificent harbour is completely landlocked, and affords secure anchorage with good holding ground for a large number of deep draught vessels. It is well adapted for use as a Naval Base. There appears to be no reason why it should not also be equally suitable as a commercial port, provided the communications to the interior were developed.

Karaghatch.

This is also a fine harbour, but does not appear to be so suitable

---

[3] Actually, the Maeander River, now known as the Buyuk Menderes River or, simply, the Menderes River.

[4] Marmarice and Makri are now Marmaris (or Marmaras) and Fethiye, respectively. Karaghatch, or Karagach, if it still exists, is too small to appear in standard atlases and gazetteers. It was located approximately twelve miles east of Marmaris at the head of the next adjacent inlet from the sea. See Map P included with Miller, *My Diary at the Conference of Paris*, in the special box at the end of the Miller series.

as Marmarice for a commercial port, owing to the rugged nature of the surrounding land. Communication with the interior is quite undeveloped.
Makri.

This harbour though affording complete shelter is not so large as the two harbours mentioned above, and owing to neighbouring marshes, the town is exceedingly unhealthy. It would appear to afford better facilities for reclamation and wharfage than Marmarice and Karaghatch, and communication with the interior is more developed. An Italian Syndicate shortly before the war was considering the question of constructing railways from Makri to Mougla, etc."

He also read extracts from the "Mediterranean Pilot," Vol. 5,[5] and produced the charts.

PRESIDENT WILSON urged that the line should be drawn so as not to include the harbour of Marmarice, which he understood to have been the intention on the previous day.

(This was agreed to.)

(Mr. Harold Nicolson entered.)

PRESIDENT WILSON and MR. LLOYD GEORGE gave Mr. Nicolson the necessary instructions for re-drawing the map so as not to include Marmarice in the Italian zone. Mr. Nicolson was also instructed to revise Appendix II, Page 2, so as to substitute Makri for Marmarice.

(Mr. Nicolson withdrew.)

PRESIDENT WILSON then read Appendix II. In Resolution 3, the following sentence: "In view of the fact that the Turkish Government has not shown itself able to protect the interests of Christian populations under its sovereignty" was altered by the omission of the word "Christian" and the substitution of the word "the." The name "Makri" was substituted for "Marmarice."

MR. LLOYD GEORGE considered that the arrangement was now all right.

M. CLEMENCEAU also agreed.

PRESIDENT WILSON said it looked to him all right.

(The resolutions reproduced in Appendices I and II were approved, as the basis of part of an offer to be made to Italy.)

4. PRESIDENT WILSON pointed out that the boundaries of the Armenian Mandate had not yet been drawn. He suggested that the map in the ante-room, which had been drawn by American experts, provided suitable boundaries.

[5] England. Admiralty. Hydrographic Department, *Mediterranean Pilot*, Vol. V. *Comprising the Coasts of Tripoli (Libia), Egypt, Karamania, Cyprus and Syria* (London, 1915).

(The Council then adjourned to the ante-room and studied the map prepared by American experts.)

PRESIDENT WILSON pointed out that the Southern boundary was drawn so as to leave Alexandretta south of the Silesian [Cilician] boundary.

MR. LLOYD GEORGE pointed out that the Western boundary in the region of the Black Sea differed somewhat from the line prepared by British experts. He handed a map drawn by British experts to President Wilson, who undertook to consider it in consultation with his own experts.

(The Council returned to the Library.)

5. M. CLEMENCEAU said that, in order to make a clean job of it, some arrangement ought to be made between General Allenby and the Emir Feisal. The latter had behaved very well since his arrival in Syria.

MR. LLOYD GEORGE suggested that, at the moment, the best plan would be to draw a map of occupation, showing what territories would be occupied by the various Powers concerned. He suggested that there should be a small Committee to examine the question.

(M. CLEMENCEAU nominated M. Tardieu.

MR. LLOYD GEORGE nominated General Sir Henry Wilson.)

6. M. CLEMENCEAU said that the French experts in the Foreign Office would not hear of any arrangement with the Italians about Djibouti.

7. PRESIDENT WILSON said it had been brought to his notice that the clause intended to have been included in the Reparation Clauses of the Treaty of Peace with Germany, Part VIII, Annex 2, paragraph 2, had been omitted. He suggested, therefore, that the only thing to be done was to sign an agreement, of which he read a draft.

MR. LLOYD GEORGE thought it would be better to reinsert it in the Treaty of Peace.

PRESIDENT WILSON agreed that it might be put in an errata.

MR. LLOYD GEORGE proposed that it should be included when the final reply was given to the Germans. He did not like having too many documents on these subjects.

PRESIDENT WILSON agreed.

(The Agreement in Appendix III was initialled, and Sir Maurice Hankey was instructed, after obtaining M. Orlando's initials, to forward it to the Drafting Committee for incorporation in the final Treaty with Germany.)

(M. Orlando's initials were affixed the same evening. M.P.H.)

§ Mantoux's notes:

Wilson. We could now study the map of Asia Minor and agree definitively on the assignment of the mandates. The territory assigned definitively to Greece would be extended a bit to the south and would include the lower valley of the Meander. If we had wanted at first to leave the valley of the Meander to the Turks, it was to give them access to the Aegean Sea. But we no longer have that concern.

Lloyd George. Does not the projected boundary for the region of the Italian mandate give the port of Mersina to Italy?

Wilson. No, but it would give them Marmaras.

Examination of the documents on the ports of Asia Minor, furnished by Lieutenant-Colonel Sir Maurice Hankey.

Wilson. I see that Marmaras is an excellent port, especially for the navy, but with little communications with the interior. Makri, which we spoke about the other day, was already the site chosen by an Italian company as the starting point of a railroad. I ask myself if it would not be better to give the Italians Makri, without Marmaras. The position of Marmaras dominates the island of Rhodes too much.

Lloyd George. Our intention the other day was to assign to Italy Makri, and not Marmaras.

President Wilson rereads a series of proposals: (1) establishment of a mandate of the League of Nations over Constantinople and the Straits; (2) annexation to Greece of the region of Asia Minor around Smyrna, including the lower valley of the Meander; (3) division of the Turkish territory proper among three distinct mandates: (a) a Greek mandate in the vicinity of the region of Smyrna (*vilayet* of Aidin[6]); (b) an Italian mandate over southern Anatolia, up to the desert region; (c) a French mandate for northern and central Anatolia.

Another memorandum determines the boundaries of Armenia and gives more precise details on the mandate for Constantinople.

Lloyd George. There remains to be settled the question of the spheres of military occupation in Asia. We must come to an agreement directly on this subject; the French and English Foreign Ministers will never agree.

Clemenceau. I am always accused of making too many concessions to you.

Lloyd George. This question must be handled by two trustworthy persons.

Clemenceau. I suggest to you M. Tardieu.

Lloyd George. Do you wish him to confer with Sir Henry Wilson?

Clemenceau. That suits me perfectly. §

8. PRESIDENT WILSON informed Sir Maurice Hankey that it had

---

[6] Again, now Aydin.

been agreed during an informal conversation on the previous after-noon that the Drafting Committee should only take instructions from the Supreme Council of the Principal Allied and Associated Powers in regard to the material for Articles to be inserted in the Treaties of Peace, and that these instructions should be initialled by the Heads of State.

9. SIR MAURICE HANKEY read the following note from Mr. Hurst, on behalf of the Drafting Committee:

"The present intention of the Drafting Committee is to insert the Covenant of the League of Nations and the draft Labour Convention and Resolutions in the Treaty of Peace with Austria in exactly the same manner as has been done in the draft Treaty of Peace with Germany. If this is not in accordance with the wishes of the Council of Prime Ministers, we should be glad if you would let us know. I have ascertained from Lord Robert Cecil and Mr. Barnes that the above is in accordance with their views. Some of the Allied and Associated Powers represented at the Peace Conference were not at war with Austria, but we are making them all parties to the Treaties and modifying the language of the first clause, so as to bring in statements as to the termination of the war and the resumption of the relations being consistent with their being parties; consequently, it is quite feasible to insert the Covenant of the League of Nations without any alteration, as the signatories to the Austrian Treaty and to the German Treaty will be the same; no alteration, therefore, will be required in Article I and in the Annex to the Covenant."

(The above was approved and initialled. Sir Maurice Hankey was instructed to forward it to Mr. Hurst, after obtaining M. Orlando's initials.)

10. PRESIDENT WILSON expressed the hope that M. Clemenceau's proposal would be adopted and that Austria would be inserted in the list of Nations invited to adhere to the League of Nations. He, himself, was strongly in favour of this proposal. He doubted, however, whether the Supreme Council had the right to decide this without consulting a plenary meeting.

M. CLEMENCEAU said it ought not to decide in the absence of the Italian Representatives.

PRESIDENT WILSON agreed.

11. MR. LLOYD GEORGE asked what was the nature of the mandate contemplated for the Italians in Anatolia.[7]

---

[7] Mantoux, II, 75, adds at this point:
"Wilson. I thought that we were in agreement to establish mandates of a different character in the northern part and in the southern part.

PRESIDENT WILSON said he had in mind the Moslem feeling about not wiping out the Turkish race. His idea had been to set up a Turkish State in the north of Anatolia and to put it under the supervision of France. He pointed out that, under the scheme of mandates as originally devised, there were three classes, one class consisted of nations which were on the verge of being able to run themselves and only required a very loose mandate, a second class provided for less developed countries, and a third class provided for wholly dependent countries.

M. CLEMENCEAU asked what differences he contemplated in regard to the Turkish population in the Italian and French mandates in Anatolia.

PRESIDENT WILSON said he had understood that in the north the population was more purely Turkish.

MR. LLOYD GEORGE said that this was not the case outside the coastal districts.

PRESIDENT WILSON said that the awkward question to decide was that of sovereignty. If what Mr. Lloyd George said was correct, it would be better not to extend the sovereignty of Northern Anatolia over Southern Anatolia, otherwise both France and Italy would have advisers at the Turkish capital dealing with different parts of Turkish territory.

MR. LLOYD GEORGE said that that was the great argument against dividing Anatolia.

M. CLEMENCEAU asked what sort of mandate was contemplated in each case.

PRESIDENT WILSON said it was substantially the same.

MR. LLOYD GEORGE read a memorandum which had been prepared by Mr. Balfour in consultation with experts in the Foreign Office, in which some sort of a condominium was contemplated.[8]

M. CLEMENCEAU said that a condominium would never do. It was bound to give rise to difficulties and might even give rise to wars. He was reminded by Mr. Lloyd George that there had been great trouble between France and Great Britain in Egypt, which might have resulted in war between the two countries but for his personal intervention.

MR. LLOYD GEORGE continued to read Mr. Balfour's memorandum, in which some international body for finance was proposed.

PRESIDENT WILSON was altogether opposed to that. In regard to a

---

"Clemenceau. I thought I understood that the role which you wanted to give us was that of advisers and, as for myself, I have no desire to make of this country a French colony."

[8] It is missing, but a revised version of it is printed as an appendix to the minutes of the Council of Four printed at May, 17, 1919, 11 a.m.

proposal in the memorandum providing for prior claims in regard to concessions for the mandatory Power, he pointed out that this was contrary to the principle provided for in the League of Nations' Covenant for equal opportunity to all Nations in mandated territory. This did not mean that the United States of America would rush in everywhere. Direct American enterprise was certainly not to be expected in Anatolia. There would certainly be a natural priority to the Mandatory but there should not be a priority of claim.

MR. LLOYD GEORGE quite agreed and pointed out that it would be very unfair if the Italians had a priority of claim in Southern Anatolia when the British were compelled to give equal opportunity in German East Africa.

PRESIDENT WILSON said that his object all along had been to avoid even an appearance of grabbing. Those considerations brought us face to face with the problem as to the form of political unity which was to exist in Southern Anatolia. His idea would be to organise it as a self-governing unit, to elect its own Governor-General with Konia as its capital. Otherwise, there would be the difficulty of a single capital in which the representatives of both Mandatories would live.

MR. LLOYD GEORGE said that another scheme was that the Sultan should remain in Constantinople exercising supervision over the whole of Turkey. France would then overlook one part of Anatolia, Italy another part, Greece a third, while the United States overlooked the Sultan. If Bursa was in the French Mandate and the Sultan ruled over the whole of Anatolia, it would create a very awkward situation for the Italians.

PRESIDENT WILSON said that Southern Anatolia would have to be constituted as a separate unit.

M. CLEMENCEAU asked who would appoint the Governor?

MR. LLOYD GEORGE suggested the Sultan under advice.

PRESIDENT WILSON asked if the Turks could not elect a Governor.

MR. LLOYD GEORGE said this would make it a Republic.

PRESIDENT WILSON said he had no objection to this.

MR. LLOYD GEORGE thought that difficulties would arise in connection with the Khalifate in this case.

M. CLEMENCEAU said his objection to any scheme by which the Sultan nominated the Governor or to any scheme of election was that there would be a French and an Italian candidate and this would always give rise to friction and difficulty. He suggested that a Prince should be drawn from the Sultan's family and appointed to rule in Anatolia. In any other scheme, there would be trouble all the time.

PRESIDENT WILSON suggested that the Italians should be left to choose a member of the Sultan's family.

M. CLEMENCEAU said that Southern Anatolia would then be an independent State under an Italian Mandate.

(On President Wilson's suggestion, it was agreed in principle that Anatolia should be separated politically into two parts, the method of separation being left for further consideration. It was also agreed that, as President Wilson had some information to the effect that there was a prospect of the Italians and Yugo-Slavs coming to an understanding on the Adriatic question and as the proposals in regard to Asia Minor were only part of comprehensive proposals to be presented to the Italian Delegation, the resolutions agreed to should not be presented to the Italian Delegation for the moment.

M. Clemenceau undertook to speak to M. Orlando in this sense.)

12. With reference to C.F.6. Minute 1, and Appendix I to those Minutes,[9] SIR MAURICE HANKEY read the following letter from Mr. Hurst, the British Representative on the Drafting Committee:

"You will remember the instructions that went to the Drafting Committee about the frontiers of Austria and Hungary and of contiguous countries. It is a paper marked Appendix II to C.F.4.[10] The interpretation which we are putting on the second sentence is that the Big Four desire that the frontiers of a country like Roumania who [should], so far as possible, be set out in the Treaty with Hungary, not merely the frontier between Roumania and Hungary itself. That is to say, that the Northern frontier of Roumania where it joins Russia and the Southern frontier where it touches Bulgaria will both be set out when a decision has been come to as to what that frontier should be. The same would apply even though the State concerned had no common frontier whatever with the enemy before with whom the treaty was made. For instance, Roumania. Though Roumania will not touch Austria, the Roumanian frontiers would nevertheless be set out in the Treaty with Austria. This seems to follow from the second sentence of your paper, but I should like to make sure that we are right in this." (After a short discussion, it was agreed that Mr. Hurst's interpretation of the previous decision was correct, and Sir Maurice Hankey was authorised to inform him accordingly.)

13. With reference to C.F.13, Minute 6,[11] M. CLEMENCEAU signed the following letter to the Head of the Chinese Delegation:
"Your Excellency,   14th May, 1919,

On behalf of the Supreme Council of the Principal Allied and Associated Powers, I beg to acknowledge the receipt from the Chinese

---

[9] See the minutes of the Council of Four printed at May 10, 1919, 11:45 a.m.
[10] Actually, Appendix III to the minutes of the Council of Four printed at May 9, 1919, 4 p.m., Vol. 58.
[11] See the minutes of the Council of Four printed at May 14, 1919, 12:15 p.m.

Delegation of two pamphlets, one of which sets forth China's claim submitting for abrogation by the Peace Conference the Treaties and Notes by and between China and Japan of May 25th, 1915, and the other presents for readjustment by the Conference a number of important questions, among which may be mentioned the withdrawal from China of foreign troops and police, the withdrawal of foreign post offices and the abolition of consular jurisdiction.

In reply I am asked to state that while the Supreme Council of the Principal Allied and Associated Powers fully recognises the importance of the questions raised they do not consider that they fall within the province of the Peace Conference and they suggest that these matters should be brought to the attention of the Council of the League of Nations as soon as that body is able to function.

I am

Your Excellency's obedient Servant
(Signed)   G. CLEMENCEAU.

His Excellency
M. Lou Tseng-Tsiang,
Ministre des Affaires Etrangères."

14. With reference to C.F.13, Minute 7,[12] M. CLEMENCEAU signed the following letter to Mr. Arthur Henderson:
"Sir,   14th May, 1919.

I am asked by the Supreme Council of the Principal Allied and Associated Powers to inform you that they have considered your request, transmitted verbally through Mr. Lloyd George, that the Supreme Council shall receive a deputation from the International Trades Union Conference in Berne.

In reply I am asked to state that as the summary of the Peace Terms is already published and has been communicated to the German plenipotentiaries, it is felt that no useful object would now be served by the proposed deputation.

I am, Sir,

Your obedient Servant,
(Signed)   G. CLEMENCEAU.

The Rt. Hon. A. Henderson."

15. SIR MAURICE HANKEY reminded the Council that before the Meeting with the German Delegates the question had been raised as to the recognition of Montenegro, and that it had been agreed that a decision ought to be taken in regard to Montenegrin representation before the Austrian settlement was concluded (I.C.181.E., Minute 6).[13]

MR. LLOYD GEORGE said that according to his recollection early in

[12] Ibid.
[13] See the minutes of the Council of Four printed at May 7, 1919, 11 a.m., Vol. 58.

the Conference it had been agreed that the United States should send a Commissioner to investigate and report on matters in Montenegro.

(Sir Maurice Hankey was instructed to investigate this question.)

APPENDIX I, C.F.13A.[14]

RESOLUTION

(Agreed to by M. Clemenceau, President Wilson, and Mr. Lloyd George on 14th May, 1919, as part of a proposal to be made to the Italian Delegation.)

The President of the United States of America, on behalf of the United States, and subject to the consent of the Senate thereof,

ACCEPTS:

1. A mandate over the Province of Armenia as constituted within frontiers to be agreed upon between the United States, British, French and Italian Delegations, whose recommendations, if unanimous, shall be accepted without further reference to the Council.

2. A mandate over the City of Constantinople, the Straits of the Bosphorus and Dardanelles, the Sea of Marmora and a small contiguous territory, the frontiers of which shall be determined by agreement between the United States, British, French and Italian[15] Delegations, whose recommendations, if unanimous, shall be accepted without further reference to the Council.

N.B. The words underlined were added to the original draft in the course of discussion.

APPENDIX II TO C.F.13A.[16]

(Agreed to by M. Clemenceau, President Wilson, and Mr. Lloyd George, on 14th May, 1919, as part of a proposal to be made to the Italian Delegation.)

IT IS RESOLVED:

(1) That Turkish sovereignty shall cease over Constantinople, Turkey in Europe, the Straits and the Sea of Marmora.

(2) That the ports of Smyrna and Aivali[17] and the connected district as shown by the red line on the map, which embraces a predominantly Greek population, as well as the islands of the Dodecanese and the island of Castollorizo,[18] shall be ceded to Greece in complete sovereignty.

(3) That what remains of Anatolia east of the frontier suggested

---

[14] There is a T MS of this resolution in WP, DLC.
[15] WWhw in the T MS of this document.
[16] There is a T MS of the following resolution in WP, DLC.
[17] Usually spelled Ayvalik.
[18] Usually spelled Kastellorizo.

for Armenia shall constitute the future State of Turkey, and be treated as follows:

In view of the fact that the Turkish Government has not shown itself able to protect the interests of the populations under its sovereignty and is not now in a position to develop the natural resources of the country, it is realised that the future State of Turkey will stand in need of external guidance. Taking, however, into account the existence of numerous Greek minorities in Western Anatolia and the established interests of Italy in the regions bordering upon the province of Adalia, it is felt that the mandate to assist Turkey should preferably be entrusted to three Powers.

It is proposed therefore:

(1) That in the west Greece should be granted complete sovereignty over the region and Islands above mentioned together with a mandate over the contiguous region enclosed within the dotted red line as shown on the map.

(2) That Italy should be granted a mandate over the southern seaboard stretching from a point to the west of the port of Makri to the point where the suggested frontier for Armenia strikes the Mediterranean. The frontier of this Italian zone is shown in green upon the map and has been drawn in such a way as to provide a convenient geographical and administrative boundary, while affording full opportunity for economic development and irrigation in the province of Konia.

(3) The mandate for the remaining portion of the future Turkish State shall be entrusted to France.

(4) The rights of allied holders of Turkish stock shall be safeguarded by the maintenance of the Administration of the Ottoman Public Debt in a form to be determined upon by the Four Great Powers and Greece. An expert Committee shall be nominated to examine and report on the means necessary to give effect to this decision.

APPENDIX III TO C.F. 13A.

It appearing that the clause relative to right of withdrawal from representation on the Reparation Commission was by inadvertence omitted from the Conditions of Peace as presented to the German plenipotentiaries, we agree that the said clause shall be reinserted, unless the Germans object to such reinsertion. In any event the clause shall be deemed to establish the right of, and procedure for, withdrawal, in so far as concerns the several Allied and Associated Powers. The clause in question, which was designed to form a part of Annex II, Paragraph 2, Part VIII (Reparation clauses), reads as follows:

"Each Government represented on the Commission shall have the right to withdraw therefrom upon twelve months' notice filed with the Commission and confirmed in the course of the sixth month after the date of the original notice."

(Initialled)   G.C.
W.W.
D.Ll.G.

T MS (SDR, RG 256, 180.03401/13½, DNA); Mantoux, II, 73-74.

To Frank Lyon Polk

[Paris] 14 May, 1919.

For Acting Secretary Polk. Please instruct Morris at Tokio to proceed to Vladivostok and, after learning all that he cares to know from Graves, to proceed westward, if he can with safety, to the headquarters of the Kolchak government for the following purposes: to obtain from that government, official and definite assurances as to the objects that they have in view with regard to the future governmental regime in Russia and the methods by which they mean to set a new regime up, asking particular assurances with regard to the reform of land tenure, and the extension and security of the suffrage, and the choice and projected action of a constituent assembly, and also seeking to learn as definitely as possible the influences that Kolchak is under. My object is to satisfy myself as to whether the Kolchak government deserves the recognition, or at least the countenance, if not the support, of our government; and I beg that you will suggest to Morris that there are two persons whom it might be worth his while particularly to consult, both of them Englishmen, namely Colonel R. A. Johnson of the Fifth Hants, and Colonel John Ward, commanding a Middlesex unit. The latter was formerly a representative spokesman of Labor in Great Britain and, I have reason to think, has genuine popular principles and sympathies.

Woodrow Wilson[1]

T telegram (WP, DLC).
[1] This was transmitted to Polk in JPT to FLP, May 15, 1919, TLS (F. L. Polk Papers, CtY). Polk forwarded Wilson's instructions to Morris in FLP to R. S. Morris, May 15, 1919, *FR 1919, Russia*, p. 349.

From Vance Criswell McCormick

My dear Mr. President: Paris. May 14, 1919.

I thought that you might be interested in the following extract of a letter which I have just received from Mr. Wooley:[1]

"The President's announcement with respect to the Italian situation has consolidated American sentiment largely in his favor and judging from newspaper comments it would appear that he will establish a new procedure in the world of diplomacy, and further add to his laurels as the practical idealist in international politics—which to my mind simply means that he sees realities sooner than the average statesman, and has the courage and spirit to support his purpose unto successful realization.

"There are only a very few kickers these days in connection with the League of Nations idea, and those who were so perniciously partisan in the earlier stages of this controversy are now compelled to perform the unpleasant task of retracting.

"I have had many pleasant visits with Senator Hitchcock, and he has certainly been a loyal supporter of the Chief."

Very sincerely yours,   Vance C. McCormick

TLS (WP, DLC).
 [1] That is, Robert Wickliffe Woolley.

From Jan Christiaan Smuts

PERSONAL.

My dear Mr. President,   Paris. 14th May, 1919.

The more I have studied the Peace Treaty as a whole, the more I dislike it. The combined effect of the territorial and reparation clauses is to make it practically impossible for Germany to carry out the provisions of the Treaty. And then the occupation clauses come in to plant the French on the Rhine indefinitely, even beyond the already far too long period of fifteen years, under an undefined régime of martial law. East and West blocks of Germans are put under their historic enemies. Under this Treaty Europe will know no peace; and the undertaking to defend France against aggression may at any time bring the United States also into the fire.

I am grieved beyond words that such should be the result of our statesmanship. I admit it was hard to appear to fight for the German case with our other Allies, especially with devastated France. But now that the Germans can state their own case, I pray you will use your unrivalled power and influence to make the final Treaty a more moderate and reasonable document. I fear there may be a temptation to waive aside objections which will be urged by the Germans, but which will be supported by the good sense and conscience of most moderate people. I hope this temptation will be resisted and that drastic revision will be possible even at the eleventh hour.

Democracy is looking to you who have killed Prussianism—the silent masses who have suffered mutely appeal to you to save them from the fate to which Europe seems now to be lapsing.

Forgive my importunity; but I feel the dreadful burden resting on you, and write from motives of pure sympathy.

Yours very sincerely,   J C Smuts

TLS (WP, DLC).

From Felix Frankfurter

My dear Mr. President,   Paris May 14th. 1919.

You know how profoundly words, even familiar words, move people to-day—how their hopes and their faith are sustained or saddened, by what you say, or fail to say. Therefore, I know you will want me to inform you, in all candor, that your note of acknowledgement to my letter of May eighth has occasioned almost despair to the Jewish representatives now assembled in Paris, who speak not only for the Jews of Europe, but also for the American Jewish Congress, the democratic voice of three million American Jews. I do not fail to appreciate the forces which confront you here, and the circumspection which conditions impose upon you. On our side the task is to keep literally millions of Jews in check. Uncertainty, indefinite delay, seeming change of policy bring a feeling of hopelessness which only those in intimate contact with the people whose fate is at stake can fully gauge. We are bending every energy to avert the slow attrition of the spirit of such a people.

Therefore, you will forgive me for submitting to you the wisdom and justice of a reassuring word, written or spoken,—even though it be repetitive—that you are purposing to have the Balfour Declaration written into the Treaty of Peace, and that you are aiming to see that Declaration translated into action before you leave Paris.

Faithfully yours,   Felix Frankfurter.

TLS (WP, DLC).

From Aleksandr Feodorovich Kerenskii and Others

Mr. President,   [Paris, c. May 14, 1919]

At the present moment, when peace is being settled, when former international relations are crumbling, when through your initiative the foundation is laid for a new understanding among peoples, under the protection of the League of Nations, at this moment of grave responsibility, we, the undersigned Russian citizens, consider it our duty to lay the following before you.

We have no formal authority to speak in the name of the Russian people; neither have any people or institutions outside of Russia or in Russia itself such authority.

We have been identified with the Russian democracy for a long time; some of us occupied responsible positions in the State, and all of us are members of the First Pan-Russian Constituent Assembly; we know the views and frame of mind of our people well, we know the present conditions of life in Russia and what the democracy of the country thinks of them: we therefore consider that we can claim the right to be the interpreter of its opinion.

The League of Nations, created at your initiative does not include a representative of Russia. This absence of a Russian representative does not mean that Russia has lost the right of representation in spite of her rôle of a great power in the past and notwithstanding the immense sacrifices made for the sake of the victory of the Allies. This absence is explained solely by the fact that a united Russia does not exist at present, and there is no united body that could speak in Russia's name, as the country is passing through a difficult period of civil war and anarchy.

We feel confident that this absence of Russia from the League of Nations is felt at every step. Consequently, the sooner she comes out of her present condition, the sooner her voice is heard at the meeting of representatives of peoples, the better it will be for the work of the League of Nations and for the peace of the world.

The help of the democracies of Europe and the United States, as represented by their governments, can play a vital part in hastening this moment. But we can welcome this help only if it is prompted by but one aim, namely the regeneration of a democratic republican Russia with a united democratic Government; the adjustment of a united Russia, based upon a free federation of free nationalities.

The Powers have three patent means of action at their disposal. First, the recognition of the right of various peoples and nationalities of Russia to a separate and independent existence. Second, the recognition of one or another of the existing Governments as a legal or even as a Pan-Russian Government. Third, the aid given to one or another government in Russia while the civil war is in progress.

The policy of the powers, directed towards furthering the creation of small states, which formed parts of united Russia, states which are for the most part extremely artificial, which have not grown out of a manifestation of the will of the people, expressed by means of a regular suffrage, but which are prompted by private interests,— such a policy would be fatal, as it would only facilitate the unlawful seizure of the territories of Russia, creating incredible confusion in the future internal organisation of Russia and would not at all help the regeneration of the State by means of readjusting its separate parts.

The task can only be achieved, when the peoples of Russia are afforded the opportunity to solve freely the question of state organisation, and we are certain that they will solve it in the spirit proclaimed by our Revolution of March, 1917, as a free federation of peoples.

The policy of Powers should be directed towards this end in questions relating to the fate of the various nationalities of Russia.

The Russian democracy attaches much importance to the policy of the Powers in the question of recognition of one or another Government.

After all that is known about the Government of Soviet Russia and its system, we need not prove how worthless and harmful it is. For the Russian Democracy which firmly believes that Russia can be regenerated only by the principles of government by the people, the Bolshevik regime and its government, being the negation of every right and order, disregarding the will of the people, is only a stronghold of reaction and of further destruction of the foundations of social and state life.

Every positive act of the Powers in relation to the Bolshevik Government, particularly the recognition of this government, would be a blow to Russia, as it would increase the power of dictatorship of violence and would prolong the civil war.

Then there is the question of the attitude of the Powers towards other, non-bolshevik governments of Russia. A series of government organisations sprang up in the struggle against bolshevik violence. These form now three fundamental groups: the Siberian Government, with Admiral Koltchak as the supreme chief, the Kuban Government, with General Denikin as a military dictator, and the Archangel Government.

These Governments possess territories and armies, which were created in the course of the long and obstinate fight of small units of volunteers. The democratic elements that constituted, and now constitute the bulk of the rank and file of the forces fighting the Bolsheviks, have always been aiming at the creative work directed towards strengthening the front and the armies and establishing normal conditions of life in the rear. In the summer of 1918, the united democracy was able to work out a plan of state organisation in the territories of the Volga, the Urals and Siberia, and in September of the same year, it created, by means of an election, a united democratic authority, based on the principle of coalition.[1] This authority

---

[1] About the State Conference at Ufa, September 8-23, 1918, and the creation of the Ufa Directorate, see n. 1 to Enclosure II, printed with RL to WW, Sept. 24, 1918 (second letter of that date), Vol. 51.

was met by the universal sympathy of the population. But soon, by means of the Coup d'Etat of November 18 in Omsk,[2] this creative work was interrupted by violence by forces within the ranks of democracy that was fighting the Bolsheviks. Reactionary elements, supported by reactionary officers' circles and by certain army units, succeeded in taking by force the supreme power from the hands of the democracy and converting it into a personal dictatorship.

We cannot refrain from pointing out here, Honored President, that in the fight of the reactionary elements for power and in their triumph, the help of some responsible and irresponsible representatives of foreign powers played an important rôle. This help manifested itself in two ways, first, in a passive, often negative relation towards the fact of the existence of an All-Russian democratic government and some regional governments, and in the slowness of their diplomatic recognition; and secondly, in the help given to the reactionary enterprises of the Russian military circles by the foreign military missions and representatives of Allied Powers. This has occurred in Siberia, in the South and North of Russia; a similar policy is continued also at present.

The reactionary elements, having seized control of supreme power in one way or another are striving to retain it by means of violence and by methods identified with military dictatorship. White terror, arbitrary acts of vengeance thus become inevitable phenomena. The dictatorship, now heading the antibolshevik fronts, being a means of realisation of reactionary interests, cannot, of course, carry on creative work and guarantee the security of the rear and the ranks of the army against the bolshevik influence. And that in spite of the success of arms, reported recently on some fronts, particularly the Siberian front. The victories over the bolshevik armies that are gained here and there, do not represent a real victory over bolshevism in the sense of revulsion of feeling and sympathies of the people; as the policy of the reactionary governments cannot create in the territories freed from Bolsheviks the firm democratic order for which the population is longing.

The people, weakened by war, by civil strife and economic disintegration and therefore fallen under the force of the bolshevik dictatorship, can, of course, temporarily become the prey of reactionary violence. But Russia cannot be regenerated in this abnormal condition, upon this foundation. Thus cannot be called forth her creative forces. Under such circumstances the civil war and alternate dictatorship are prolonged. The Russian democracy, alive to the danger and endless chaos and disintegration of the country has to struggle

[2] That is, Admiral Kolchak's seizure of power, about which see *ibid.* and WW to RL, Nov. 20, 1918 (first letter of that date), n. 1, Vol. 53.

against the destructive tendencies of bolshevism from the left and of reaction from the right. And in this struggle it feels that it has the right to count upon the support of the Democracies of Europe and of America.

The question of recognition by the Powers of Admiral Koltchak, the military dictator and the "supreme ruler" of Siberia, as an All-Russian supreme Ruler, was recently discussed. We can only protest vigorously against such a step in connection with what we said about the threatening reaction from increasing growth of military dictatorships in Russia. The masses of the people that are fighting Bolshevism at present would willingly carry on this fight and, what is more important, would willingly work upon the organisation of a healthy state, if they are but guided by leaders and a Government in whom they have confidence, in whose democratic spirit they have faith,—a government created by agreement with social forces of democracy.

Therefore we cannot but protest against the decision of the Russian Political Conference, an institution existing in Paris and subject to Admiral Koltchak's authority, to further his recognition as an All-Russian Ruler.[3] We protest likewise against all attempts to call this opinion of the Russian Conference the opinion of the Russian Democracy.

If the Democracies of the United States and Europe are really desirous of helping the regeneration of Russia, they must oppose the methods of this help employed thus far. They were really supporting Russian military-reactionary circles and military dictatorships. They should begin to help the Russian Democracy and support it. They should formulate t[h]eir policy so as to strengthen the position of Russian Democracy at the antibolshevik fronts.

This help to the Democracy will only be realised when the League of Nations or the Alliance of free States will get from the various local Russian governments (whoever they may be) guarantees, and not on paper only, but in deed, that these governments will actually realise a democratic programme. Out of these considerations, we take the liberty, Mr. President, to bring to your notice the following points, which are, in our opinion, in accordance with the above conditions.

A body expressing the united will of democratic powers—the League of Nations, now being created, the Peace Conference or the Alliance of free States [s] ought to address itself *openly* and *officially*

---

3 Probably a reference to the advocacy of Kolchak's cause by N. V. Chaikovskii, a leading member of the Russian Political Conference, at his appearance before the Council of Four. See the minutes of that body printed at May 10, 1919, 12 noon.

to *all* the existing governments of Russia with the following proposal:

1. The Powers are prepared to give any help to those governments
in Russia which will accept the *fundamental* condition of building
up Russia upon a democratic basis, e.g. the calling of a Constituent
Assembly. Those Russian Governments, which will not accept this
condition, will be deprived of the support of the League of Nations,
as, by declining this, they will be the cause of continuation of civil
war and the ruin of Russian Democracy.

If all the governments of present day Russia will not accept these
proposals, and consequently the civil war will go on, then to bring
the war to a speedy end and in the interests of Democracy, help in
the form of munitions, food, and other supplies, should be given to
the governments that accept the conditions of the proposals.

2. But the free powers, to safeguard the interests of Democracy,
should not limit themselves to making this general declaration to
the local governments of Russia about the ultimate democratic
aims. To guarantee the strengthening of a democratic order, the
Powers should propose to the local Russian governments to introduce immediately a series of measures that will not only not be in
opposition to the plan, but, on the contrary, will further its realisation. Owing to a civil war, it is impossible to convoke a Constituent
Assembly at the present moment. Therefore the Powers should propose to immediately start the elections for regional legislative Assemblies on the basis of a general, direct, equal and secret franchise.
These legislative Assemblies must create an authority on a democratic basis. The Powers should propose to re-establish immediately,
by means of elections, the democratic local government boards and
to grant to the population all the civil liberties.

3. To represent the united body of free States, to explain to the
population and to the governments their object, a Delegation should
be sent to Russia, composed of representatives of these Powers. This
Delegation would give the assurance of their high aims and disinterestedness of the help given in the common interests of peoples of
Russia,—to the population and the governments of Russia, as well
as to the Democracies of the world at large.

These are the minimum demands that should be made by the
Powers as a condition for their help. To control the fulfilments of the
guarantees required, the Powers should have on the territories of
the governments their authoritative representatives acting according to a program agreed upon beforehand.

At the present moment there arises in the press as well as in official circles the question of help in the form of food to be given to Bol-

shevik Russia. Being wholly in sympathy with the wish of the Democracies of the United States of America and of Europe to help the
suffering population of Russia, we consider it necessary to state:

1. The question of help in the form of food can only be considered
from a humanitarian point of view. We consider all attempts to give
help to the hungry population, assuming the form of agreements
with the Bolshevik authority or appeals for cessation of the civil war
to be most harmful.

2. Therefore, assistance should pass through the institutions of
the Soviet authority, but must be organized without the help of the
Bolshevik Government, and absolute guarantees must be given that
the products will be distributed equally and correctly without regard
to the system of rationing according to classes. It must also be made
absolutely certain that these food-stuffs will not be used by the Red
Army.

3. At the same time, medical help is urgent and of the utmost importance, to combat the various epidemics that are threatening to
assume terrifying proportions during the Spring and Summer.

Such are the proposals we consider it our duty to bring to your notice, Honored President.   Respectfully yours,   A. Kerensky
                                          N. Avxentieff
                                            F. Minor
                                        A. Argounoff
                                        V. Zenzinoff
                                          M. Slonim
                                       G. Ragovsky.
                                        B. Sakaloff[4]

TLS (WP, DLC).

[4] Those signers not previously identified were Nikolai Dmitrievich Avksent'ev, a
leader of the right-wing faction of the Social Revolutionary party and a former member of
the Ufa Directorate; Andrei Aleksandrovich Argunov, also a leader of the right wing of the
Social Revolutionary party and a deputy to Avksent'ev in the Ufa Directorate; Vladimir
Mikhailovich Zenzinov, Social Revolutionary party leader; Mark L'vovich Slonim; and
Boris Fedorovich Sokolov, a physician. All had been members of the Constituent Assembly of 1917. F. Minor and G. Ragovsky cannot be identified.

A Memorandum by Ellis Loring Dresel

Confidentially communicated to
the President by H.W. May 14th 1919

MEMORANDUM FOR MR. WHITE.

With the approval of Mr. White and Colonel House, I saw Ambassador Dutasta[1] for a few minutes on Tuesday evening. I began by
saying that I presumed Mr. Dutasta knew of my stay in Berlin during the last two weeks, to which Mr. Dutasta replied that he did. I

then said that it had occurred to me that it might possibly be of benefit in inducing the Germans to sign if I could have the opportunity of continuing informally the conversations which I had in Berlin with Count Rantzau. I thought if I could assure Count Rantzau personally of the entirely united feeling in the United States that the peace was just and must be signed, it would have some effect. Mr. Dutasta made no comment other than to ask whether I came in the name of the Commission, to which I replied at once that I came on my own initiative. Mr. Dutasta asked whether a request would be made by the Commission that I should go to Versailles as suggested, to which I answered in no case would such a request be made and that the matter would be dropped at once if this were considered essential. Mr. Dutasta then said he would at once discuss the matter with Monsieur Clemenceau who would perhaps feel that he should talk it over personally with the President. I said that of course this would be entirely satisfactory. Mr. Dutasta's attitude throughout was interested and cordial, but non-committal.

I cannot help feeling considerable doubt about the advisability of another journey to Berlin at the present moment. Almost inevitably the following questions would be put to anyone going in:

1. Will it be possible to modify the peace terms in any respect?

2. Can any definite assurances of credits and facilities for raw materials and tonnage be given?

3. How can it be claimed that the present Treaty is in accordance with the President's Fourteen Points?

In the present extremely excited state of mind in Germany, it seems to me probable that anyone who went in without being able to answer these questions would have great difficulty in accomplishing anything. There is a further question whether such a journey would not be looked on with considerable suspicion by the British and French at the present moment.

I am, however, strongly of opinion that should it appear, either by informal conversations at Versailles or in any other way, that the present Government would accept the peace terms, I or someone better qualified should go to Berlin at once with the objects, first, of giving such moral support to the present Government as is possible, second, of gradually paving the way of taking up relations, and, third, of making recommendations as to economic assistance.

Should it nevertheless be thought that a journey on my part at the present moment would be of use, I am entirely ready to start.

I am quite sure that nothing was said to me on my recent trip as to how the German Government or people were to know when the President thought that the time had arrived for signing peace, and nothing of the kind appears in my telegrams. It is barely possible that an intimation of the kind was given me during my stay last January, but I cannot distinctly remember it. In any case the attitude towards America has changed since then. It was felt in Germany while I was there the last time, even before the peace terms came out, that they were not in accordance with the Fourteen Points, and the inclination to lean on the United States was far less noticeable in all circles, especially those of the Government.   ·E.L.D.

T MS (WP, DLC).
    [1] That is, Paul Eugène Dutasta.

Charles Seymour to His Family

Dear People: Paris, May 14, 1919.
    . . . Wilson looks tired, but has not lost his debonair manner or good humor in debate. As I have written there can be no real understanding between them, but they are enough men of the world to make it seem as if they were on the closest terms. Wilson was very genial to me, when I explained the various points of importance, and contrary to our fears raised no objections. The president is temperamental. At times, as you know, he works regardless of any advice; this has happened here, notably in the cases of Dantzig and the Saar. At other times he accepts absolutely the advice given him by the men whom he thinks are capable of giving it. That was true in the case of Fiume. Monday he was in the latter mood and took all our recommendations without question. "If anyone who knows about this will tell me what to do, I will do it," were his very words. As usual he was very quick to understand the points at issue. In this respect he stands head and should[e]rs ahead of anyone at the conference.
. . .
    Bowman went back yesterday with his wife.[1] We gave him a dinner Monday night where we discussed the history of the Inquiry and the way it had developed and the part it had played here. Bowman may justly be proud for he did much to avoid the various pitfalls and is largely responsible for the fact that the Inquiry has put through its programme in the main and done the big job here. There were fourteen of us, of whom nine had served on commissions in some form or other and had direct contact with the President. Of the fourteen only five called themselves Democrats and they were of the Mugwump variety. But it was interesting to notice that everyone, including the strongest Republicans were unanimous in the belief that Wilson was the only man in America who could have handled our foreign relations effectively since last summer. I think that all of us feel that his policy up to the beginning of the conference was prac-

tically flawless, with the possible exception of not allowing the war to continue a fortnight longer; but that responsibility, with the terrible loss of life that would have come, would have been heavy. All of us feel that no one living in America could have secured what Wilson has secured at the conference, although some of us feel that Roosevelt in his prime would have done better. Of course it was too much to expect that we could have preserved our prestige as it was last January, everywhere. It is now very high in central and southeastern Europe and, I think, in England. It has inevitably been lowered in France and Italy. I think the chief criticisms passed on the President were first that he has a one-track mind and that this fact slowed up the conference. Instead of making an immediate and very general peace, purely preliminary in character, once he got on a subject he would not leave it until some sort of a definite solution had been arrived at; this accounts for the amount of time lost at the start. The other Powers were not strong enough to insist upon an immediate general settlement. With the consequent delay the value of the cards which we held in January diminished. A second criticism is that, as at home, he kept himself isolated. He should have lived at the Crillon and kept in closer personal touch with his own commissioners and those of other Powers. Fortunately Col. House acted as intermediary and thus indirectly kept the president in touch with all the currents. There was some disagreement as to whether or not the time spent on the League of Nations had held up the conference. Personally I think not. . . .   Lots of love,   C.

TLI (C. Seymour Papers, CtY).
    [1] Cora Olive Goldthwait (Mrs. Isaiah) Bowman.

From the Diary of Edith Benham

May 14, 1919

Tonight the P. spoke of Foch with not a little disgust for he is now saying that but for the P. he would have carried the war into Germany and he stopped him in his career, etc., etc. The P. said, "The French were beaten, *beaten*; it was the Americans who saved them and Foch was in deadly fear that the Armistice terms were so severe that the Germans would not accept them." Senator and Mrs. Gerry came to luncheon today, for the P. wanted to see him and talk over affairs at home, and I imagine get some insight into the political situation to help him in his message. She is a very beautiful woman, a daughter, as you know, of Mrs. Townsend of Erie.[1] She spoke of the absurd prices over here now, and of the orgy of spending which seems to be going on, and said her mother gave her the address of a shoemaker of whom she had heard glowing reports. She inquired his prices and they are $200—not francs—for evening slippers, and he gets it, from rich Americans.

¹ Mary T. Scott (Mrs. Richard H.) Townsend. She had moved from Erie, Pa., to Washington in 1885 when her father, William Lawrence Scott, took office as a Democratic congressman from Pennsylvania.

From Joseph Patrick Tumulty

[The White House, May 14, 1919]

No. 123 Dean Gay unquestionably great statistician and rendered good service with War Trade Board during the war. He worked harmoniously with McCormick, but was frequently in friction with present members of Shipping Board and officials of Emergency Fleet Corporation, although acting as their representative. Am fearful that his appointment would provoke old antagonisms, and at this time it is highly advisable to have harmonious and sympathetic board. Would like to discuss matter with you when you return so that you may have whole situation before you. Scott would be impartial and Cummings would be grateful, and it would be reasonable Republican progressive for New England.   Tumulty.

T telegram (WP, DLC).

From the Diary of Dr. Grayson

Thursday, May 15, 1919.

The President had breakfast and went to his study before the meeting of the Big Four at 11:00 o'clock. They took up the consideration of the Adriatic and of the new territorial assignments and boundary changes which must be made to reconcile the Italian and Jugo-Slav claims which are extremely conflicting. No announcement of a decision was made.

Just before lunch I spoke to Lloyd George about sending Lord Derby to America as the British Ambassador. I told him that he was such a good mixer and such a fine all-around man. I predicted that he would be the most popular Ambassador Great Britain had ever had in America after he had spent a couple of years there and got to know our people and they got to know him. Lloyd George said: "I agree with you and if you can persuade him to take it, you can count on my backing. It is a fine suggestion. But candidly, I am afraid you cannot get him to go owing to his business affairs in Liverpool. You know, he has horses and likes sport and racing." I said: "We can sat-

isfy him to his heart's content on that line too. And we can guarantee
him a good time." Lloyd George replied: "Your arguments are un-
answerable. I am with you. I leave it to you. But I think you will have
to use some strong persuasion to get him to go to America."

The President lunched with Mrs. Wilson alone. I had lunch in my
room. After lunch the President called me up on the telephone in my
room and asked if I felt like taking a ride with him. He discovered
that Bernard M. Baruch was with me, and he asked him also to accompany him, which Mr. Baruch did. Mr. Baruch was seated on one
side of the President and I on the other. We motored for 2½ hours,
passing St. Germain, the headquarters of the Austrian delegation.
The President entertained us with light conversation. He told Baruch that he wished him to think over the matter of naming a member of the Reparation Board over here. It seems a man will have to
remain here for some time in this capacity. Baruch named him right
off: Eugene Meyer, of New York, who is now a member of the War
Finance Board in the Treasury at Washington. He also suggested
Judge Parker,[1] a lawyer, who is here now, but formerly resided in
Texas, as his second choice. Baruch praised Meyer as a business
man and as being thoroughly honorable and brilliant. He said: "To
be candid with you, he was a rival of mine in business in New York,
and I think he is the smartest man I ever bucked up against. Finally,
I went to him and said: 'Why fight each other, why not form a partnership?' And we did."

In response to an inquiry made by Mr. Baruch as to why a railroad
station was located apparently on an abandoned roadway with no
evidences of any railroad operation in the vicinity, the President
said: "Have you ever heard the story of an old negro who drove a bus
from a little town about two miles away from the railroad station?
The railroad station consisted only of a few buildings. There were
two afternoon trains—one from the north and one from the south,
and it was his habit to make one trip accommodate the passengers
on both trains. One afternoon the southbound train was on time and
a very quarrelsome drummer got off and got into the old colored
man's bus. The northbound train happened to be nearly an hour
late. The drummer became very much irritated at waiting, and finally said to the old colored driver in a very abrupt manner: 'Why did
they put this station here?' The old colored man replied: 'I don't exactly know, boss, except for the fact that it is alongside the railroad
track." By this time we were close to the structure and saw evidences
that tracks had been laid but had been removed probably due to the
war-time conditions.

The President was very entertaining, and he and Baruch discussed the individual merits of available material for Presidential

timber for the next election. He also entertained us by telling us his idea of how to educate a boy. He spoke of the disadvantages of the way many college courses are conducted.

I asked the President what teacher he got the best training from. He answered right away: "Why, my father." He said: "I got ten times more from my father than I did at college. He was a rare exception as a teacher."

There was no meeting of the Big Four in the afternoon owing to the fact that Lloyd George was anxious to spend Friday in Luxemburg saying good-bye to a Welsh Division that was being returned home to be mustered out of the British Army.

The President spent the evening with Mrs. Wilson, reading some private papers. He also prepared a cablegram to Secretary Tumulty.[2]

¹ That is, Edwin Brewington Parker.
² A draft of his special message to Congress (CC MS, [WP, DLC]), cabled to Tumulty under the date of May 16, 1919.

Hankey's Notes of a Meeting of the Council of Four[1]

President Wilson's House,
Paris, May 15, 1919, 11 a.m.

C.F.14.

(NOTE. This was not a regular meeting, but there was some delay in the assembly of the experts for the discussion of the Military, Naval and Air Clauses for the Austrian and Hungarian treaties, and advantage was taken of this interval to deal with the following questions.)

1. With reference to C.F.13, Minute 3,[2] MR. LLOYD GEORGE produced a re-draft of the reply to Herr Brockdorff-Rantzau's letter on the subject of Prisoners of War. (Appendix I.) Before the reply was sent, however, he wished to raise a question of principle, namely, as to whether supplies of clothing, including underclothing and boots, if available, ought not to be given to prisoners of war on release, as proposed by Brockdorff-Rantzau. He thought it possible that some stocks of German uniforms and clothing might have been captured in the advance of 1918, and he suggested that these, supplemented by any other stocks that might be available, might be used to provide some outfit to prisoners of war.

M. CLEMENCEAU doubted whether any stocks were available, but had no objection to inquiry being made.

PRESIDENT WILSON agreed that inquiry should be made.

(It was agreed:

That the reply in regard to Prisoners should be suspended pending inquiry by the Governments concerned as to whether any stocks of German uniforms and clothing, or other stocks, were available for the purpose of providing against repayment an outfit to German prisoners.)

2. With reference to C.F.13, Minute 4,[3] M. CLEMENCEAU said he had understood on the previous day that the intention was to send the reply drawn up by the expert Committee to which it had been referred. Consequently, he had despatched the letter to Herr Brock-dorff-Rantzau. If necessary, a supplementary letter could be sent on the subject, when the Committee reported on the question of whether the Germans should be admitted to the Labour Organisa-tion, before they were admitted to the League of Nations.

3. Sir Maurice Hankey was instructed to write a letter to Lord Cunliffe, informing him, for the information of the Committee on Reparation, that the Supreme Council would be glad to receive the draft clauses on Reparation for inclusion in the Austrian and Hun-garian Treaties not later than Saturday, May 17th.

4. SIR MAURICE HANKEY reported that, as requested on the pre-vious afternoon, he had made inquiries as to how the question stood of the representation of Montenegro. He found that on January 12th, 1919, it has been decided in principle that Montenegro should be represented at the Conference, but the decision had been left open as to how her Representatives should be chosen. On that oc-casion M. Sonnino had suggested that in the meantime the United States of America should send a representative to discover how things were in that country. M. Clemenceau had pointed out that if President Wilson wished to send someone to inquire, he would do so without any authority from the Powers associated with him. Presi-dent Wilson had then said he was willing to send someone, but not an official representative on behalf of this Conference, and Mr. Lloyd George had agreed. (See Procès-Verbal of March 12th, I.C.104, p. 6.)[4]

PRESIDENT WILSON undertook to inquire if any action had been taken in the matter by his Government.

5. M. ORLANDO approved and initialled the proposals of the Draft-ing Committee on this subject,[5] which had been approved and ini-tialled by his colleagues on the previous afternoon.

6. SIR MAURICE HANKEY handed copies of the Report of the Com-mittee on New States to M. Clemenceau, President Wilson, Mr. Lloyd George and M. Orlando.

APPENDIX TO C.F.14.

Sir,

The representatives of the Allied and Associated Powers have given consideration to the note of the German Peace Delegation dated 10th May 1919 in regard to the repatriation of the German prisoners of war. In reply they wish to state that they cannot agree that prisoners of war and civilian prisoners who have been guilty of crimes or penal offences should be released. Those crimes and penal offences have been committed on Allied soil and have been dealt with by the legally constituted authorities without reference to the fact that the wrongdoer was a German rather than an Allied citizen. For instance a certain German prisoner broke at night into the house of a farmer on whose estate he was set to work and murdered the farmer and his wife in cold blood with a bill-hook. For this double murder the said prisoner was sentenced to death on June 11th 1919 by a regularly constituted court martial. Under the Berne Convention, however, the execution of the sentence is suspended until peace has been signed. Justice would certainly not be satisfied if, as a consequence of the Treaty, this murderer were reprieved. For these reasons the Allied and Associated Powers cannot agree to alter the provisions of the Draft Treaty in respect of prisoners of war who have been guilty of crimes of penal offences.

In regard to the second question, the German Peace Delegation makes no specific suggestions as to the alleviation which they would propose for the prisoners of war and interned civilians between the date of the signing of peace and their repatriation. The Allied and Associated Powers are not aware of what alleviation it is possible to make seeing that they have scrupulously endeavoured to observe both the laws of war and the dictates of humanity in the treatment which they have given to prisoners of war, and that as provided in the last section of Article 218 it is essential that prisoners of war and interned civilians should remain subject to discipline and control pending their repatriation in the interests of all concerned. The German Peace Delegation may rest assured that it is the intention of the Allied and Associated Powers to treat their prisoners of war during the period between the signing of peace and repatriation with full consideration of their feelings and their needs.

The restitution of personal property to prisoners of war constitutes a legal right which the Allied and Associated Powers have every intention of respecting. As regards information about the missing, the Allied and Associated Powers have always endeavoured to supply the German Government with all information in their possession on this subject and they will certainly continue to do so after Peace is signed. Concerning the care of graves they would point out that Articles 225 and 226 would appear to assure to the German people that the graves of their fellow citizens shall be both respected and properly maintained and that so far as is practicable under Clause 225 the bodies of their soldiers and sailors may be transferred to their own country.

In regard to the German request for complete reciprocity the representatives of the Allied and Associated Powers have to state that they felt it necessary to include Article 222 in view of the treatment which their own nationals have received while interned in Germany during the war. As there was no parallel between the treatment which was accorded to prisoners of war by the German Government on the one side and the Allied and Associated Powers on the other no claim for reciprocity in this respect can arise.

In regard to the third question, the representatives of the Allied and Associated Powers are ready to do everything possible to repatriate German prisoners of war and interned civilians properly fed and properly cared for after the conclusion of peace. They regret, however, that the pressing demands upon them from territories recently liberated from the German yoke as well as from their own nationals will probably make it impossible for them to supply the prisoners of war with the clothing etc., for which the German Peace Delegation asks.

Finally, in regard to the appointment of a Commission to deal with the repatriation of prisoners of war, the representatives of the Allied and Associated Powers will be glad to set up such Commission immediately upon the signature of peace. They regret, however, that they do not see their way to appoint them until they are notified of the intention of the plenipotentiaries of the German Empire to sign peace.

T MS (SDR, RG 256, 180.03401/14, DNA).
  [1] The complete text of these minutes is printed in *PPC*, V, 624–26.
  [2] See the minutes of the Council of Four printed at May 14, 1919, 12:15 p.m.
  [3] *Ibid.*
  [4] See the minutes of the Council of Ten printed at January *not* March 12, 1919, Vol. 54.
  [5] A T marginal note at this point reads as follows: "League of Nations & Labour Convention in the Treaties of Peace with Austria & with Hungary."

Hankey's Notes of a Meeting of the Council of Four[1]

President Wilson's House,

C.F.15.   Paris, May 15, 1919, 11 a.m.

CONDITIONS OF PEACE—AUSTRIAN MILITARY, NAVAL AND AERIAL CLAUSES.

[The conferees discussed this subject at some length. The only part of the discussion in which Wilson played a significant role follows.]

MR. LLOYD GEORGE suggested that M. Orlando's proposal should be accepted. That is to say that the military representatives should

  [1] The complete text of these minutes, including the Annexures, is printed in *PPC*, V, 627-67.

be directed to examine the whole question on a broader basis and to report what forces should be allowed to Austria, Hungary and all the adjoining small States. The question was one of the greatest importance, and unless the matter were considered, as a whole, the Peace of Europe would again be disturbed in the near future. A decision to reduce the Austrian and Hungarian armies to 15,000 men each would not achieve the desired result if, at the same time, no limit were placed on the armaments to be maintained by Czecho-Slovakia, Jugo-Slavia, Roumania, Bulgaria and Greece. Unless restricted, each of the latter States would pass all their men through the army and in a short time would possess forces varying from one to two million men. He fully agreed with M. Clemenceau that Vienna had, in the past, been a centre of intrigue: but, in his opinion, what had created a warlike temper in Europe had been the constant succession of wars in the Balkan provinces. The military men in Europe had seen wars going on in those regions and those feats of arms had aroused in them a warlike spirit. Therefore, should Jugo-Slavia be permitted to raise an army of one million; Czecho-Slovakia an army of one million; Roumania an army of two millions; Greece an army of 600,000, the result would be appalling. Many pugnacious people still existed in Germany, and even in Russia, and should these large armies be permitted in the Balkan States, the Allied and Associated Powers would be bound to get mixed up in the troubles that would inevitably arise. He need not remind his colleagues that, in accordance with the laws of mankind, the oppressed of to-day become the oppressors of to-morrow. The State with a big army would inevitably start bullying the State with a small army, especially if the former had itself in the past been bullied. In that connection, Italy had no desire in the future to be compelled to maintain a large army, including millions of men, whether raised by a voluntary or a compulsory method of enlistment, in order to protect herself, but should her neighbours on the opposite side of the Adriatic be allowed to maintain large armaments, she would have no option in the matter. He urged his colleagues, therefore, to accept M. Orlando's proposal, namely, that the military representatives at Versailles should be instructed to consider what forces should be allowed to Austria, Hungary, Roumania, Czecho-Slovakia, Jugo-Slavia, including Serbia and Montenegro, Poland, Bulgaria and Greece, on the basis of maintaining the same proportionate standard as had been fixed in the case of Germany, bearing in mind local conditions and, in the case of Poland, the fact that she would have to defend herself against the possible attacks of Bolshevik forces in the East. He thought all these questions should be settled before the signature of the Treaty of Peace.

M. CLEMENCEAU said it should be clearly understood that the Military Representatives would examine the question merely from a military point of view.

PRESIDENT WILSON agreed. He thought it would be impossible for the Council to determine the size of the Austrian army until the sizes of the armies to be maintained by the adjoining States had been decided. In his opinion, all these questions hung together to form a single scheme. Naturally the calculation could not, as stated by M. Clemenceau, be carried out on a strictly mathematical basis: but the military regime applied to Germany should be taken as the standard, making an exception in the case of Poland.

M. CLEMENCEAU suggested that the military representatives should begin with a study of the Austrian question as it was very urgent. Moreover, several of the other questions mentioned were mixed up with the Russian question; that is to say, they involved an unknown factor. His remarks applied more particularly to Poland.

MR. LLOYD GEORGE thought that it would not be possible to consider the question for each State independently; otherwise the Council would be confronted with the answer of Austria, who would say that she did not mind accepting the figure of, say, 15,000 men; but before doing so she would be entitled to know what armies were to be maintained by the countries surrounding her.

(It was agreed that the Military Representatives, Supreme War Council, Versailles, should prepare and submit a report showing what forces should be allowed to Austria, Hungary, Czecho-Slovakia, Jugo-Slavia (including Montenegro), Roumania, Poland, Bulgaria and Greece, taking the German figures as a proportional standard. In the case of Poland due allowance shall be made for the existing situation on the Eastern frontier.)

(2) PRESIDENT WILSON drew attention to the following two reservations made by Admiral Benson, the American Naval Representative:

(i) The terms of the Treaty should require that surrendered vessels of war or war material be destroyed or broken up:

(ii) That Naval terms should contain no prohibition against the manufacture within the limits of States formerly a part of the Austro-Hungarian Empire of naval war material on foreign order.

His judgment agreed with Admiral Benson's first reservation, and the second reservation he thought was very reasonable indeed, and he strongly supported it.

M. CLEMENCEAU pointed out that in the German conditions of peace a similar clause had been inserted. He saw no reason why an exception should be made in the case of Austria, and he certainly did not wish to enable Germany to start factories for the manufacture of arms, ammunition and other naval war material in Austria.

PRESIDENT WILSON pointed out that in the matter of the manufacture of naval war material, Germany was differently situated to Austria. Germany had a seaboard, whereas the new state of Austria would have no seaboard.

ADMIRAL HOPE[2] explained that Austria could nevertheless manufacture mines and torpedoes and deliver them to the Germans. The particular article under discussion had, however, in reality been introduced into the Austrian conditions of peace in order to keep the latter in line with the German conditions.

ADMIRAL DE BON[3] explained that the object of the article in question was to prevent Austria from supporting other nations, who might enter into war, by supplying them with arms, ammunition and other naval war material. He wished to point out that Austria at the present moment possessed a very magnificent war material in the form of a heavy gun.

PRESIDENT WILSON invited attention to Article 16 of the draft Military Clauses, wherein it was clearly laid down that the manufacture of arms, munitions or any war material should only be carried out in one factory, which should be owned and controlled by the State. Furthermore, all the establishments in excess of the one authorised would have to be rendered useless or converted to a purely commercial use in accordance with the decision to be taken by the Inter-Allied Committee of Control. Under the circumstances, he thought that the danger contemplated by the naval experts would be extremely small.

M. ORLANDO thought that if Austria were given the opportunity of manufacturing war material for export to foreign countries, she could nominally pretend to work for, say, South America, whilst in reality manufacturing for Germany.

ADMIRAL DE BON made the suggestion that by the omission of this clause, very great complications might arise in the future, should some new war material be invented, since such article might very possibly be constructed in factories outside the one permitted, without openly contravening the Articles of the Conditions of Peace.

ADMIRAL THAON DI REVEL[4] observed that during the war, it had been shown how rapidly factories could be transformed to war uses. For that reason, he thought it would be far more effective to restrict the output, rather than to restrict the number of factories.

PRESIDENT WILSON said he was extremely anxious to make some

[2] That is, Rear Adm. George Price Webley Hope.
[3] That is, Vice Adm. Ferdinand Jean Jacques de Bon.
[4] That is, Adm. Paolo Thaon di Revel.

distinction in favour of Austria, in order to wean her away from her old Ally. Germany had been the chief archenemy of peace in Europe. He thought, therefore, it would be both to the advantage of the Allies and to the advantage of the whole group of nations in Europe, should the object he had in view be achieved.

MR. LLOYD GEORGE agreed that the question was not one of great importance in regard to Austria. He would, therefore, support President Wilson's proposal.

M. CLEMENCEAU said he had been greatly impressed by Admiral de Bon's point of view. He failed to see why any safeguard should be renounced. In his opinion, the Council were far too ready to assume that its decisions would be faithfully followed by the enemy. He wished to insist that his opinion should be carefully recorded on this point, namely, that the decisions of the Council would, in all probability, not be followed in their entirety. Germany, Austria, Hungary, Bulgaria, would take every opportunity to evade their part of the contract. American troops would then be far away. Nevertheless, the Council were inclined always to eliminate such precautions as it had decided to take, knowing full well that most of these precautions would disappear in the course of time. President Wilson had said that the question under reference constituted merely a small matter. In his opinion, it was not a small matter to take precautions to prevent future bloodshed and loss of life. Both Admiral de Bon and Admiral Revel had expressed the view that by omitting the condition under discussion, Austria would be in a position to manufacture war material for Germany. In conclusion, should his views not be accepted, he wished his dissent to be clearly understood and recorded.

PRESIDENT WILSON said that, owing to some misunderstanding, his naval advisers had not been apprised of the meeting. Consequently, he had not the advantage of their advice. On the other hand, steps had been taken to limit Germany's power of constructing war material, and, in addition, the manufacture of arms, munitions or any war material in Austria had been restricted to one factory. Under those conditions, he failed to see wherein the danger lay. That might be due to intellectual disability on his part, but he could only see visible things; he could not see invisible things. Furthermore, in drafting the Conditions of Peace with Austria, he was anxious not to go too much into details which were immaterial. He thought it would be in the best interests of the Allied and Associated Governments that they should assist in the future industrial development of Austria. At present, Austria had lost all her industries, which had now been absorbed by Czecho-Slovakia. He thought it would be highly desirable to bring about the industrial development of Austria. However, it would not be possible for him to reach a decision on the question under reference, without first consulting his naval adviser. He proposed, therefore, that further discussion should be adjourned. (It was agreed to adjourn the further consideration of President Wilson's proposal, namely, that the Naval terms of Peace should contain no prohibition against the manufacture within the limits of States formerly a part of the Austro-Hungarian Empire, of naval war material on foreign orders.)

3. (It was agreed to accept the Air Clauses, subject to a second reading.)

4. (It was agreed to accept the Clauses relating to Inter-Allied Commissions of Control, subject to a second reading.)

5. PRESIDENT WILSON invited attention to Article 50 which read as follows:

"So long as the present Treaty shall remain in force, the State of Austria undertakes to submit to any investigation that the League of Nations, by a majority of votes, may consider necessary."

He thought the words "to submit to an investigation" were too harsh, and he suggested that the words "to respond to any enquiry" should be substituted.

MR. LLOYD GEORGE pointed out that in the Conditions of Peace with Germany, the Clause had been made somewhat less harsh. It read as follows:

"So long as the present Treaty remains in force, Germany undertakes to give every facility for any investigation which the Council of the League of Nations, acting, if need be, by a majority vote, may consider necessary."

(It was agreed that Article 50 of the Draft Military, Naval and Aerial Clauses (General Clauses) should be amended to read as follows: "So long as the present Treaty shall remain in force, the State of Austria undertakes to respond to any enquiry that the League of Nations by a majority vote may consider necessary.")

6. MR. LLOYD GEORGE said that he had just heard with great regret that the Supreme Council would no longer have the benefit of the counsel of Admiral de Bon, who was about to take up another appointment. On behalf of the British Delegation, he wished to place on record how much the solidarity which had existed between the British and French Admiralties had been due to Admiral de Bon's tact, judgment, good sense and ability. He (Mr. Lloyd George) spoke with very great feeling.

PRESIDENT WILSON and M. ORLANDO very heartily endorsed Mr. Lloyd George's remarks.

ADMIRAL DE BON returned thanks for the kind words spoken by Mr. Lloyd George, President Wilson and M. Orlando.

(The Meeting then adjourned.)

T MS (SDR, RG 256, 180.03401/15, DNA).

From Clive Day

To: The President
From: Mr. C. Day
Re: Fiume.   May 15, 1919.

Substance of memorandum: The need of Fiume for invested capital to maintain and develop the port cannot be satisfied unless Jugo-Slavia is assured economic control.

Mr. Johnson informs me that he quoted Mr. Young and myself as economists in support of the above proposition. I beg leave to confirm his statement and to sketch the reasons for it.

Both Triest[e] and Fiume have in the past been treated as national interests, supported out of the public funds of Austria and of Hungary respectively. The future of Fiume as an independent outlet for Jugo-Slavia will be blocked not merely if the city goes to Italy but even if it is taken outside the Jugo-Slav economic system and constituted an independent port in competition with an Italian Triest.

(a) Fiume could not levy port charges sufficient to finance its development without driving trade to Triest where the Italian state would finance improvements, and keep charges low.

(b) Private investors would not put money into an enterprise in competition with a subsidized port like Triest.

(c) The Jugo-Slav State would be unwilling to spend the necessary sums if Fiume were not subject to its economic control.

If Jugo-Slavia be assured control of Fiume it will readily and properly find the funds to develop the port. Much of the trade which in the past appeared to come from Hungary really originated in Jugo-Slav districts and had been diverted to Hungarian railways for political reasons. Jugo-Slavia will get some of the richest export territory formerly included in Hungary (notably the Western Banat), and can hope to get for Fiume some of the northern trade, formerly kept in Austrian territory and directed to Triest for political reasons. All this trade will be added to that which in the past was recognized as coming from Jugo-Slav districts. The future of the power under Jugo-Slav control appears to be assured even if, (as appears unlikely), political influences reduce the trade coming from Hungary and Rumanian Transylvania.

                    Respectfully submitted,   [Clive Day]

CC MS (C. Day Papers, CtY).

A Memorandum by Gordon Auchincloss

MEMORANDUM RESPECTING PASSPORTS
OF IRISH-AMERICANS

May 15, 1919.

The following cable has been received from Acting Secretary
Polk:

"76, May 13, 11 am. Very urgent. Secret for Auchincloss only
from Polk. Your May 12, 5 pm. in regard to passports for Irish delegates.

Applications stated object of visit 'Irish race convention.' This
was stricken out and 'business reasons' written in in the Department. Each application however was accompanied by a letter
dated March 27th addressed to me as Acting Secretary of State
and signed by each applicant, as follows: 'Dear Sir: We respectfully request the issuance of passports to France to Frank P.
Walsh of New York; Michael J. Ryan of Philadelphia, Pa.; and Edward F. Dunne of Chicago, Illinois, who have been appointed by
the recent Irish race convention held in the city of Philadelphia,
Pa., on February 22nd and 23rd, 1919, and whose object in visiting France is to obtain for the delegates selected by the people of
Ireland a hearing at the Peace Conference and to place before the
conference, if that hearing be not given, the case of Ireland; her
insistence upon her right of self-determination; and to the recognition of republican form of government established by her people. Very respectfully.'

When the President was here I spoke to him of the probability
of Irish representatives asking for passports and asked for instructions. The President discussed the matter with Reading and
Reading I understand suggested that it would be a bad policy to
refuse passports, his reason being that it would cause more irritation here among the Irish and the delegates would do no particular harm in Paris. The President then instructed me if applications were made to grant passports. Applications were made the
end of March while I was in White Sulphur but I instructed Phillips to issue passports for France only as the applications only
asked for France there should be no difficulty on this point. I was
very careful to emphasize the fact that they should not be permitted to go to England or Ireland.

It seems to me that the British have brought all this trouble on
themselves by visaing their passports for England and Ireland. I
would be glad to know whether they visaed the passports without
having them amended in any way by our Embassy in Paris. I cannot see that we have any responsibility in the matter. Would it not

be sufficient if a statement were given out that the passports we gave were for France only and that they were guests of the British Government in their visit to Ireland and England. This will probably be unsatisfactory to the British officials but it will put the responsibility on them. POLK, Acting."

The sworn declaration of the holders of these passports on file at the Passport Department of the American Embassy, Paris, is as follows:

"I solemnly swear that it is necessary for me to visit the following countries: British Isles   not now included in my passport, for the purpose of   Unofficial Political Mission
In this connection I submit, in addition to my passport, the following documents:

    Amended at request of President Wilson and Lloyd George."
(Then follows the signature of these three gentlemen)

This explains itself—I would advise doing nothing as long as possible.   E.M.H.[1]

T MS (WP, DLC).
[1] EMHhw.

From the Diary of Vance Criswell McCormick

May 15 (Thursday) [1919]

At 2.00 went to President's house with Hoover, Davis and Baruch to discuss with the President the blockade policy as to food if Germany refused to sign. Hoover urging food should go to Germany in any event, he being worried because millions had been contracted for and if stopped suddenly Relief Committee would be broke. President told him of our conversation with Big Four yesterday and that he advocated military occupation rather than starvation methods. President discussed freely his difficulties with his colleagues in Council—called them mad men, particularly Clemenceau, whom he now understands better since he has read some of his earlier writing in which he advocated the "survival of the fittest."[1] He says he has a great pity for them. They have such fear of the Germans and such great self pity. He spoke feelingly of his struggles with Clemenceau and Lloyd George to hold them down to justice and reason and could not vouch for his being able to convince them that military occupation was better than the starvation method because the military occupation would cost more in money. He discussed certain proposals for the Fiume dispute, one is that plebiscite be held as to whether the people of Fiume would be willing to remove to a nearby port if built by the Italians. This was suggested by Jugo-Slavia. He says he will propose it but doubts if Italians will accept. When it was suggested that Sonnino had been the trouble, the President stated that he thought he had played fair as he had signed the London Pact which really gave Fiume to Croatians and he had never heard him claim Fiume. I gathered he rather blamed Orlando. As a matter of fact, I blame Lloyd George and Clemenceau for not supporting more strongly the President as I believe they could have called the bluff of Orlando and changed the tide before it had gone so far.

The President seemed rested and discussed some of the points of his message to Congress. We had an hour and a quarter's talk with him.

¹ Clemenceau had often expressed in his journalistic writings some version of the idea that, in both the natural and human realms, the struggle for existence was between the weak and the strong, and that the result was most often the survival of the fittest. The most extended exposition of his thoughts on this subject is the collection of his journalistic pieces published as *La Mêlée Sociale* (Paris, 1895), especially the lengthy introduction to that volume. This book was reprinted in 1919. See also David Robin Watson, *Georges Clemenceau: A Political Biography* (London, 1974), pp. 140-42.

From the Diary of Colonel House

May 15, 1919.

The better part of today, as have also previous days, [has] been taken up with the Adriatic question. Trumbitch was with me a large part of the morning. Thos. Nelson Page followed, and Orlando came in the afternoon. I do not know what progress I shall be able to make with these people but it would be a great triumph if I could bring about a settlement of this difficult, delicate, and dangerous problem.

There is no need to go into the arguments used by me or by them, but the situation is different from what it formerly was. The Italians are now talking sense for the first time.

From Herbert Clark Hoover

My dear Mr. President: [Paris] May 15th, 1919.

With regard to the proposed reduction of the credits to Serbia, Czecho-Slovakia, and Roumania, would you be so kind as to introduce into your approval of these reductions, the phrase to the effect that such reduction should not encroach upon the $25,000,000 credits set aside for foodstuffs for Roumania, the $45,000,000 credits set aside likewise for Czecho-Slovakia, and the $20,000,000 set aside for Serbia, without the approval of Mr. Hoover?

I fully realize the difficulties to the Treasury, but not only are these credits absolutely vital for the feeding of these people, but they have been agreed upon with the Treasury, and the food is actually purchased and a large part of it is in motion toward Europe.

I may mention that I have made such re-arrangements in Belgian finance as to enable a reduction of $20,000,000 credits for food previously established, for French account, and similarly a reduction of $5,000,000 in Serbian accounts.

Yours faithfully,   Herbert Hoover

TLS (WP, DLC).

From Thomas William Lamont, with Enclosure

Financial Conditions in Europe.

Dear Mr. President: [Paris] May 15, 1919.

Attached to this note is the brief report which, some little time ago, you suggested that we make to you. Mr. McCormick, Mr. Baruch and Mr. Hoover have gone over this and I believe them to be in substantial accord with Mr. Davis and myself in this presentation.

We have not attempted to lay out a complete financial plan; but rather to analyze the situation with sufficient clearness to make certain solutions fairly manifest. If, for instance, our British and French friends were to agree with this analysis of ours, we are inclined to believe that they might think it wise to make certain fresh proposals far more reasonable than the original Keynes' suggestion.[1] We should prefer to have the British and French make these new suggestions, as the matter is of even greater concern to them than to America.

You may not deem it wise to hand a copy of this report to Mr. Lloyd George or Mr. Clemenceau, for the reason that it is drawn up for your own private consideration and embodies certain suggestions with reference to possible Congressional action. We can, however, readily revise the text on these points.

If you were to find time before tomorrow to glance through this draft report, we should then be in a position, if you can see us tomorrow, to go over a few principal points in it upon which we desire to secure your personal views.

With great respect, I am, dear Mr. President,

Sincerely yours,   Thomas W. Lamont

TLS (WP, DLC).
[1] See the Enclosure printed with D. Lloyd George to WW, April 23, 1919, Vol. 58.

ENCLOSURE

MEMORANDUM RE FINANCIAL AND ECONOMIC

SITUATION IN EUROPE.

May 15, 1919.

Aside from food requirements for Europe up to the next crop, which have been substantially provided for:

There are certain situations which require immediate consideration, to-wit:

(1) Credits for the newly constituted, or lesser, nations, such as Poland, Czecho-Slovakia, Greater Serbia, Roumania and the Baltic States.

(2) Credits for raw materials for France, Belgium and Italy.

(3) Credits to France and possibly Belgium for reconstruction.

(4) Working capital for the enemy states.

AS TO:

(1) Credits for Poland, Czecho-Slovakia, Greater Serbia, Roumania and the Baltic States are essential for:

(a) The purchase of raw materials, railway stocks and agricultural implements required for the resumption of their industrial and agricultural productivity;

(b) The establishment of a reserve sufficient to enable these countries to establish a stable circulating medium. At present they have no gold reserve and it will be necessary either to obtain gold or to make special credit arrangements to take the place of gold as a reserve against notes to be issued.

Any credits established for (a) and (b) would, of course, be under special arrangements, fixing conditions as to the note issues and supervision regarding this and the purchases. It is estimated that $500,000,000 would be sufficient to meet the above requirements of those newly constituted or lesser nations.

AS TO:

(2) Raw materials for France, Belgium and Italy. $500,000,000 to $600,000,000 would be sufficient to purchase the raw materials necessary to restock the requirements of the factories in these countries. It is our opinion, however, that credits for this purpose can and should be obtained by the nationals of these respective countries through private channels in the United States and elsewhere, and that it is unnecessary and inadvisable to obtain such funds through governmental loans.

AS TO:

(3) Credits for reconstruction of France and possibly Belgium. There is considerable exaggeration as to the purchases to be made

outside of France and Belgium for this purpose. The greater portion of reconstruction will represent labor and materials to be supplied in France and Belgium. At any rate, it will take considerable time to get this work going, and France should have sufficient dollars available to cover all purchases to be made in the United States for reconstruction purposes during the next eight months.

AS TO:

(4) Working capital for Germany and enemy states.

Germany requires working capital; without it she will be unable to restart her industrial life, and thus to make any substantial progress in the way of reparation. But the provisions of the reparation clauses of the proposed Treaty demand that Germany shall deliver over at once all her working capital, being practically the total of her liquid assets. The only logical manner of meeting Germany's requirements for working capital is obviously to leave Germany with sufficient of her present working capital to enable her to restore her industries. It is for the Governments which expect to receive reparation to consider this situation with respect to the enemy's working capital. America has no further suggestion to make on this point.

GENERAL REMARKS.

Credits to Europe, especially for raw materials, should, so far as possible, be extended through the normal channels of private enterprise and commercial banking credits. For the moment, however, while the situation is still unsettled and while, therefore, private credits may not be available in sufficient amount, some further government aid on a limited scale may be necessary. So far as the United States Government is concerned, the War Finance Corporation, through recent legislation, may be able to give considerable immediate assistance.

Moreover, the extension of both private and public credits should, for the present, be conditioned upon the guaranty of the several governments in each instance where credit is granted. The situation in Europe financially is closely interwoven and should be considered as a whole, even though the action taken may be independent. Both governmental and private commercial and banking interests in Europe should understand the necessity for cooperation among themselves.

In the same way, so far as America is concerned, if it is able in the long run, to extend sufficient credits through private channels, then it is essential that American investment resources should be mobilized so as to obtain unity of action. Further, the European countries, in order to be justified in looking for outside credit, must at once address themselves to arrange their international situation as to currency, taxes, &c., in a way to command the confidence of the investing public. In the granting of credits, the active cooperation of the United States, England, France, and neutral countries as well, should be enlisted. In this connection, the countries furnishing raw materials should be prepared to extend the credits required to cover the sales of such materials.

CC MS (T. W. Lamont Papers, MH-BA).

From Henry White

Dear Mr. President: Paris, May 15, 1919.

With reference to your letter of May 2nd to Mr. Lansing and further correspondence regarding the Montenegrin situation,[1] I am enclosing herewith for your information a copy of a report prepared by Dr. Day, the Technical Expert, on this question,[2] who believes that the Agents of the King of Montenegro, now in Paris, do not represent the views of the majority of Montenegrins and who, furthermore, states that in his opinion the American Government should not support the claims of the King.

I am enclosing copies of certain communications setting forth the views of the opponents of the King,[3] which have been received from M. Radovitch,[4] representative of Montenegro in Paris, and suggest that in view of the variety of the claims presented, efforts be made to postpone a final settlement of the question until the return of the Miles-de Salis Mission of investigation, which has been sent to Montenegro.[5]   Faithfully yours,   Henry White

TLS (WP, DLC).
    [1] WW to RL, May 2, 1919, Vol. 58.
    [2] C. Day to RL, May 6, 1919, T MS (WP, DLC). Day suggested that there were only two conceivable political courses for Montenegro: independence or union with the new Yugoslav state. "Independence," he said, "under present conditions appears to be absolutely impracticable. The country is so small and so ill endowed that in an economic as well as in a political and military aspect it would be unable to stand alone." Those who advocated independence really argued on behalf of King Nicholas and were "really playing in the hand of Italy." Union with the Yugoslavs, Day believed, was sure to come, since the Montenegrins shared with them a common language, religion, and economic interests. Most Montenegrins were relatively indifferent politically and asked only to be left alone. Of the politically active groups, the Royalist party supported the claim of Nicholas and had the support of perhaps 10 per cent of the population. The largest and most influential group was the party for union with the Yugoslavs, who worked for union with Yugoslavia, but with considerable autonomy for Montenegro. This group included some advocates of a republic, but most would probably accept the Serbian monarchy, provided Montenegro was given "a dignified place in the Jugo-Slav State." The pro-Serb party, which controlled the provisional government of Montenegro but probably had even fewer adherents than the Royalist party, wanted "Serbian rule in any form" and intrigued actively with Serbian officers and agents to bring about a complete fusion between Montenegro and Serbia. Day stated the interests of the great powers in Montenegro concisely: "England and the United States are impartial; France has supported the movement toward fusion with Serbia; Italy aims to maintain a nominal independence under the former monarch [Nicholas], so that it may work through Montenegro to weaken the Jugo-Slav State."
    Day's recommendations for an American policy were equally concise: "I assume that

the use of American troops to occupy Montenegro, repress the fighting factions, and get a fair vote of the people regarding their future is impracticable. In that case it appears to me that the United States will do most for a fair and lasting settlement of the problem if it throws its influence in favor of a union of Montenegro with the other Jugo-Slavs, but act as a moderator in repressing the arbitrary and violent measures of the Serbs. . . . In every aspect it would seem to be most unfortunate if the American Government did anything to support the claims of King Nicholas who is thoroughly discredited in his own country and is used by the Italians only to further their own interest in the Balkans."

[3] Members of the National Executive Committee of Montenegro to G. Clemenceau, March 31, 1919, and National Executive Committee of Montenegro to the Government of the French Republic, March 25, 1919, both TCL (WP, DLC). The first letter urged Clemenceau, as President of the peace conference, to have that body grant a hearing to representatives of the National Executive Committee, especially since it had already heard a representative of "ex-King Nicholas." The second letter explained in some detail that the National Executive Committee had been charged by the "Great National Assembly," meeting at Podgoritza on November 26, 1918, to bring about the union of Montenegro and Serbia. It asserted that this union was "unanimously desired" by the people of Montenegro. The same "Great National Assembly" had deposed Nicholas. Now Nicholas, with the support of Italy, was attempting to overturn these decisions. The balance of the letter roundly condemned Nicholas, his Prime Minister, Jovan Plamenatz, and their Italian allies.

[4] That is, Adrija Radović.

[5] For the origins of this mission, see A. J. Balfour to EMH, March 28, 1919, and the extract from the House Diary printed at April 1, 1919, both in Vol. 56, and RL to WW, April 30, 1919, Vol. 58.

From David Hunter Miller, with Enclosure

Memorandum for the President: 15 May, 1919.

Herewith are transmitted two reports[1] by the Committee on new States.

The second report contains as Annex A, the draft of clauses for a Treaty with Poland for the protection of minorities. These clauses are not substantially different from those heretofore transmitted,[2] except that the text of Article 13 now appears.[3]

These clauses do not go as far as the American Jews desire, but in my judgment go further than any such Treaty has ever gone before and are sufficient.

Annex B[4] of this report is the British proposal which none of the other delegations accept. The first paragraph of Annex B would be contrary to the law of many of the States of the American Union. The second paragraph of Annex B would make by Treaty the Jewish Sabbath a more sacred day than Sunday.

David Hunter Miller

TS MS (WP, DLC).

[1] He must have also included a copy of the committee's first report, or the text of the draft treaty, which is printed as an Enclosure with D. H. Miller to WW, May 13, 1919.

[2] That is, in the report just cited.

[3] This new article reads as follows: "The provisions contained in the foregoing articles regarding the protection of racial, religious or linguistic minorities concluded between the High Contracting Parties shall be under the protection of the League of Nations, and the consent of the Council of the League of the Nations is required for any modifications thereof."

[4] It reads as follows: "Jews shall not be compelled to perform any act which constitutes

violation of their Sabbath nor shall they be placed under any disability by reason of their refusal to attend courts of law or to perform any legal business on their Sabbath.

"Poland hereby declares its intention to refrain from ordering or permitting elections, whether general or local, to be held on a Saturday, nor will registration for electoral or other purposes be compelled to be performed on a Saturday."

ENCLOSURE

THE COMMITTEE ON NEW STATES.

SECOND REPORT.

May 13, 1919.

The Committee have considered the question of the protection of minorities with special reference to Poland, and submit draft clauses for insertion in the new Treaty with Poland. (ANNEX A). If these are approved they will then be able to proceed to apply the same principles with such modifications in detail as may be necessary to the other States.

The draft articles have, with few exceptions, received the unanimous approval of the Committee.

They comprise:

1. Articles defining citizenship. In order [to] secure the necessary protection both to the Jews and to other minorities, very definite provisions on this point are necessary. The experience of the Jews in Rumania since 1879 has shown that for want of attention to this matter the guarantees inserted in the Treaty of Berlin for the purpose of securing equal rights to the Jews were rendered abortive. The Committee are therefore unanimously agreed that these clauses are essential.

2. Articles guaranteeing to all inhabitants of Poland protection of life and liberty and the enjoyment of religious freedom.

3. Articles guaranteeing to all citizens of Poland the free use of any language and the right to establish and control their own religious, charitable, social and educational institutions.

Articles under headings 2 and 3 have been so drafted as to avoid, as far as possible, the suggestion that any attempt is being made to interfere between the Polish Government and Polish citizens, except so far as may be necessary to protect minorities.

4. An article providing for the allocation of public funds in districts where there is a considerable linguistic minority for the establishment of schools in which instruction shall be given in the minority language. This clause is specially defined to insure that the Germans in those parts of the transferred district where they form a large portion of the population, and the Ruthenians and White Russians, should have schools in their own language.

5. Special articles dealing with the Jews.

In drafting the clauses dealing with minorities and the Jews, there was much discussion on the following points:

(*a*) Whether it was desirable to enumerate the minorities in question.

(*b*) Whether the Jews should be separately named or whether adequate protection could be given to them without separate clauses.

As regards the first point, so far as present information goes the minorities in question will be Germans, Ruthenians or Little Russians, White Russians or Lithuaniens. It was eventually unanimously decided that it would be wiser not to specify each of these by name; to some extent this decision was made owing to the present uncertainty as to the future boundaries of Poland and the numbers of the respective minorities who would be included in the territories of the Polish State. In this matter the Polish precedent will perhaps not be applicable to other States such as Czecho-Slovaquia or Rumania.

With regard to the second point an attempt was made to draft the clauses without specific mention of the Jews. It was however found that if this was done, it would not be possible to give them that protection which the information available as to the actual situation in Poland at this moment shows is clearly necessary. The following considerations carried special weight:

(i) The Jews are diffused over practically the whole of Poland. The facilities guaranteed to them cannot be confined to special areas but must be extended to Jews in Poland wherever they may be found. The other minorities differ from the Jews in that they are national minorities inhabiting in more or less compact bodies certain specified areas. It is therefore reasonable that the facilities accorded to these minorities should be confined to the limited areas predominantly inhabited by them.

(ii) The Jews are both a religious and a racial minority and special questions therefore arise in their case which do not arise in the case of other minorities.

(iii) It is necessary to take into account the existence of the strong anti-semitic feeling in Poland which is not denied even by the Poles themselves, and there is strong evidence of a deliberate purpose to submit them to a cruel and calculated moral and physical persecution; this throws upon the Allies an obligation to provide safeguards which it is hoped will not be necessary for the other minorities.

(iv) It was in particular felt that it would not be for instance to the German citizens in Poland safe or just to Poland to give those special rights which seem clearly necessary for the Jews.

The claims made by the Jews themselves through some of their spokesmen are very wide reaching. A demand, for instance, has been made that the Jewish body should be recognized as a definite nationality which would have separate electoral curias in the Diet and other electoral bodies. It was unanimously agreed that these claims could not be accepted for they would be setting up a State within a State and would very seriously undermine the authority of the Polish Government. Unofficial discussions by individual members of the Committee with those who are qualified to speak for the Jews seem to show that these more ambitious claims were not really necessary. The essential points to secure are first guarantee for the normal protection of life, liberty and property, and impartial administration of the law, and apart from this, the essential thing seemed to be that the Jews should have control of their own schools.

The whole scheme is therefore drafted with the object of securing these two points. The protection of life and liberty is provided by the general clauses coupled with the general right of protection by the League of Nations.[1]

As to education there is an essential difference between the terms suggested for other minorities and the Jews. For other minorities, all that is secured is an obligation on the part of the Polish State to give education to the children belonging to such minorities through the medium of their own language. It seemed however necessary that the Jews should be given control of their own schools. This, it is believed, can be done without incurring the danger of setting up a State within the State which would have been involved had the Committee accepted the proposals actually made by the Jews themselves.

The British Delegation further propose a special clause for the Jewish sabbath (ANNEX B). The fact that the Jewish observance of the Sabbath has been made in recent years a special instrument of persecution in Poland seems to them to render imperative the insertion of a special and specific guarantee in the Treaty. The American and Italian Delegations are opposed to the insertion of this clause believing that such legislation should not be adopted as it would be a constraint of Poland which would be rejected as legislation by all modern States. The French Delegation, while not raising definitive objections, are inclined to deprecate the adoption of it. The clause is therefore submitted for consideration as a separate recommendation by the British Delegation.

The Committee is inclined to think that a general clause for protection by the League of Nations of the provisions of the Treaty is sufficient and such a clause is inserted. The view that detailed provisions for appeal may be advisable, is one that the Committee may wish to consider further after examination of the condition in other States.[2]

Finally, the Committee have thought it best, especially in view of the short time at their disposal, not to give a formal hearing to either

Jews or Poles, though, individually and informally, they have taken the opportunity of ascertaining the views of persons interested on either side. They were, in particular, unwilling to communicate to the Poles the proposed articles until these articles had received the approval of the Council of Four. They venture to suggest that if the Council of Four approve these articles they should communicate them forthwith to the Polish Delegation with an intimation that they are approved in principle, but that the Committee are authorised to receive any observations which the Polish Delegation may desire to place before them on questions of detail. In the event of any important observations being put forward by the Polish Delegation, the Committee presume that it would also be incumbent on them to hear the Jewish representatives.

The Committee venture to draw attention to the fact that while Japan appears as one of the proposed signatories of the Treaty, there is no Japanese representative on the Committee. It is therefore presumed that steps will be taken to secure the assent of the Japanese Delegation to the proposals.

Insert on page 4 after the second line:

Much difficulty was experienced in drafting the clause dealing with this matter. On the whole the majority of the Committee was inclined to think that a general clause placing the provisions of this chapter under the protection of the League of Nations would be sufficient and such a clause is in fact attached (Article 13). On the other hand the view was expressed that it might be desirable to insert more detailed provisions giving to the representatives of the minorities themselves the right to approach the League of Nations directly; the question was discussed whether, if such a right were given, it should be confined to the Jews or given to the other minorities; if it were given to the other minorities the question then arose whether it should be confined to those who inhabit the transferred territories or extended to those Polish citizens, not Poles by origin, who inhabited the nucleus formed by the Old Congress Poland. It was eventually determined that more time was required to consider this matter as it is one which closely affects the League of Nations itself, and it was also felt that further light might be thrown upon the problem when the Committee examined the condition of other States. They therefore put forward Article 13 tentatively and would ask to be allowed, if it appears necessary, to make further suggestions as to this point at a later stage.

Omit the last paragraph but two of page 4.

Printed copy with T and Hw additions (WP, DLC).
[1] See the addition at the end of this document.
[2] This is the paragraph omitted.

Ray Stannard Baker to Gilbert Fairchild Close, with Enclosure

[Paris] May 15, 1919.

MEMORANDUM FOR: MR. CLOSE.

From: Mr. Ray Stannard Baker.

1. I spoke to the President in regard to the plans of President King, who was appointed to the Syrian Commission and he suggested that President King submit a memorandum on the subjects he wished to consider. I enclose the memorandum and would be pleased if you would see that the President gets it.   Ray Stannard Baker

TS MS (WP, DLC).

ENCLOSURE

A Memorandum by Henry Churchill King

[c. May 15, 1919]

MEMORANDUM OF POINTS
DESIRED TO BE TAKEN UP WITH THE PRESIDENT.

I THE POSITION OF THE COMMISSION:

 1. Is the Commission certainly going? If so, how soon can it go?
 2. Are its Official Instructions to be changed, for example, so as to include Turkey proper?
 3. Would it be well for the Commission to have an American ship at their disposal? (That might have the advantage of expediting travel, showing the American flag, and making the whole inquiry a little easier in taking the other members as guests.)
 4. If the Peace Conference dissolves in the meantime, to whom will the Commission report?

II THE PRESIDENT'S PERSONAL DESIRES AND PURPOSES AS TO THE COMMISSION:

 1. What points in the inquiry does he desire especially to emphasize?
 2. Can America be expected to accept a mandate for Armenia, or Syria, or Constantinople, or for the whole of Asia Minor, if that seems best?

III LIMITATIONS OF TIME AND TERRITORY:

 1. Are there definite limitations of time for the Commission? Is it desired that the Commission should confine itself to a certain time, and do what it can within that time, or should

it take such time as seems necessary for intelligent recommendation all around?
2. What is the intended territorial scope of the inquiry?
   (1) Do you wish it to include the visiting of all the Areas
        mentioned in the Official Instructions?
   (2) Are Adalia and Smyrna and the Peninsula of Arabia to be
        included?
   (3) Should the Commission make any reference to the dis-
        position of Turkey proper, as bearing on the possibility of
        a single mandatory for Turkey proper and Armenia?
   (4) Is it desired that the Commission visit Russian-Armenia
        and possibly other like regions, as bearing on possible
        recommendation of a federation of Armenian, Georgian
        and Kurdish States?

IV   EXISTING AGREEMENTS OR UNDERSTANDINGS:
   1. How far is the Zionist question closed?
   2. How far is the Mesopotamian question closed?
   3. How far is the question of Arabia closed?
   4. Is the Commission bound by any pre-Conference or other
       agreements? If so, what are they?
   5. Are there any Conference understandings that close any
       part of the question; or, is all open? Have any mandato-
       ries been agreed on?

T MS (WP, DLC).

From Edward Mandell House

Dear Governor: Paris, 15 May, 1919.
   I enclose a cable for you which I have just received.[1]
   Mr. Lamont has told me in strict confidence that before he left
New York last January he suggested to Gay the plan of taking entire
charge of the New York Evening Post, and his understanding is that
Gay is planning to do this as soon as he finishes his present work in
Washington.   Affectionately yours,   E. M. House

TLS (WP, DLC).
   [1] NDB to WW, May 14, 1919, T telegram (WP, DLC). It reads as follows: "Stevens of
the Shipping Board has asked me to say a word to you in regard to Dean Gay as a pro-
spective appointee for membership on the Board. I do not know whom else you are considering. My own experience with Gay is that he is highly efficient and able. His knowledge of shipping affairs is quite extensive."

From the Diary of Dr. Grayson

Friday, May 16, 1919.

The President had breakfast early. He had a busy day. Because there were no meetings in connection with the Peace Conference an effort was made to clear his appointment list, and he received a large number of callers commencing at 11:00 and winding up at 3:30. The complete list of the engagements is as follows:

11.00 A.M.- Prince Charron and the other members of the Siamese Delegation.[1]

11.45 A.M.- Mr. Olivier,[2] President of the National Union of Railwaymen of France. (Wishes to inform the President of the work, and the humanitarian and sanitary program of the National Union of French and Belgium Railwaymen.)

12.00 M.- Mr. J. Jacob,[3] President of the Celtic Circle of Paris. (To present "The Anthology of the National Bards and Poets.")[4]

12.15 P.M.- Dr. Juan Antonio Buero, Delegate from Uruguay, and brother-in-law of the President of Uruguay.[5]

12.30 P.M.- Turkhan Pasha, President of the Provisional Government of Albania. (To present the "just claims of Albania.")

2.15 P.M.- Dr. Edward Benes and Mr. Kramer.[6] (On the question of Silesia and Teschen.)

2.30 P.M.- M. Damour, French Deputy, Chairman of Committee.[7] (For the purpose of explaining the plans for the erection of a statue at the mouth of the Gironde River, to commemorate the arrival of the American troops in France.)

2.45 P.M.- The Delegation of the Parliament of Kouban (Northern Caucasians.)

3.00 P.M.- Chrysanthos (Archbishop of Trebizond.)

3.30 P.M.- Mr. Joseph Reinach.[8]

The President lunched as usual, and after his engagements were completed he and Mrs. Wilson and I motored out to St. Cloud; returning we motored through the Bois de Boulogne, down the Champs Elysée, directly across the City of Paris, and proceeded all through the ancient part at Vincennes, which is accepted as one of the most picturesque of the European parks. In many respects the Vincennes Park reminds one of Rock Creek Park in Washington. The vegetation is not so thick inasmuch as the French prune their trees and keep the undergrowth closely cut. On the cross-roads the

grassy plots are allowed to grow their own way, in this respect differing from any of the other French parks.

The trip through Paris was not designed to rest one's nerves. The
automobile traffic in the city is enormous now that the war is over
and pleasure cars have been released for private ownership. We
passed three or four wrecked cars that had been smashed in collision but fortunately we escaped any injury. The trip, however, in the
city kept all of our nerves on edge.

The President and Mrs. Wilson and I had dinner. It was the first
time I had dinner with them since last Sunday owing to the unpleasant associate on the back of my neck.

[1] Prince Charoon, not Charron, the Siamese Minister to France; Prince Traidos Pra-
bandhu, Under Secretary of State for Foreign Affairs; and Phya Bibadh Kosha, Minister
to Italy.
[2] He cannot be further identified.
[3] He cannot be further identified.
[4] Camille Le Mercier d'Erm, *Les Bardes et Poètes Nationaux de la Bretagne Armori-
caine: Anthologie Contemporaine des XIXe-XXe Siècles* (Rennes, n.d.).
[5] Baltasar Brum.
[6] That is, Karel Kramář.
[7] Maurice Joseph Damour, chairman of the committee to erect the statue mentioned
just below.
[8] Joseph Herman Reinach, author and journalist, best known for his *Histoire de l'Af-
faire Dreyfus* (7 vols., Paris, 1901-11), most recently a correspondent for *Le Figaro*. Colonel House characterized him in some detail in EMH to WW, April 20, 1915, Vol. 33.

To Jan Christiaan Smuts

My dear General Smuts: Paris, 16 May, 1919.

No apology was needed for your earnest letter of the fourteenth.
The Treaty is undoubtledly very severe indeed. I have of course had
an opportunity to go over each part of it, as it was adopted, and I
must say that though in many respects harsh, I do not think that it
is on the whole unjust in the circumstances, much as I should have
liked to have certain features altered. I am in entire agreement with
you that real consideration should be given to the objections that are
being raised against it by the Germans, and I think I find a growing
inclination to treat their representations fairly. As it happens, they
have so far addressed their criticisms only to points which are substantially sound.

I feel the terrible responsibility of this whole business, but inevitably my thought goes back to the very great offense against civilization which the German State committed, and the necessity for
making it evident once for all that such things can lead only to the
most severe punishment.

I am sure you know the spirit in which I say these things, and that

I need not assure you that I am just as anxious to be just to the Germans as to be just to any one else.

 With unaffected thanks for your letter.

     Cordially and sincerely yours, Woodrow Wilson

TLS (J. C. Smuts Papers, National Archives, Praetoria).

To Vance Criswell McCormick, with Enclosure

My dear McCormick: Paris, 16 May, 1919.

 I am quite willing that the enclosed should be sent to Polk but beg that you will ask him to consider it in the light of my recent instructions to Morris at Tokio.[1]

 In haste,   Faithfully yours, Woodrow Wilson

TLS (V. C. McCormick Papers, CtY).
 [1] WW to FLP, May 14, 1919.

E N C L O S U R E

 Department's 1877, May 6, 8 P.M.[1] The President approves of the communication to Koltchak, in such manner as the Department may think best, of a statement substantially as follows:

 The Government of the United States, animated by a desire to see established in Russia a government responsive to the will of the people which will maintain domestic tranquility and friendly and orderly relations with foreign states, has carefully and sympathetically noted the efforts of the organization headed by Admiral Koltchak to attain this result. The Government of the United States is not disposed to recognize any government in Russia which has assumed and is exercising power without the sanction of the Russian people freely given. The Government of the United States recognizes that conditions in Siberia may now be suitable for an expression of the will of the people and in the event of the securing of an expression of the popular will in favor of a government which satisfies the conditions above referred to, the Government of the United States would take under favorable and sympathetic consideration, in the light of the then situation, the question of recognizing such a government as a de facto government of such portions of Russia as might then or thereafter be under its actual control with the consent of the peoples governed.[2]

T MS (V. C. McCormick Papers, CtY).
 [1] FLP to the American Commissioners, May 6, 1919, Vol. 58.
 [2] For the telegram as sent, see V. C. McCormick to FLP, May 17, 1919.

To Joseph Patrick Tumulty

Paris, 16, May, 1919

Please ask Polk to add to the instructions to Morris at Tokio the request that he particularly inquire as to the kind of men and influences surrounding Koltchak and form an opinion as to whether Koltchak is strong enough and liberal enough to control them in the right direction.   Woodrow Wilson.[1]

T telegram (WP, DLC).
  [1] This was transmitted to Morris as FLP to R. S. Morris, May 16, 1919, *FR 1919, Russia*, p. 349.

To Felix Frankfurter

My dear Mr. Frankfurter: Paris, 16 May, 1919.

I have your letter of May 14th. I never dreamed that it was necessary to give you any renewed assurance of my adhesion to the Balfour declaration, and so far I have found no one who is seriously opposing the purpose which it embodies. I was very much taken by surprise that you should deem anything I wrote you discouraging. I see no ground for discouragement and every reason to hope that satisfactory guarantees can be secured.

In haste,   Sincerely yours,   [Woodrow Wilson]

CCL (WP, DLC).

To Jane Addams

Paris, 16 May, 1919.

Your message[1] appeals both to my head and to my heart and I hope most sincerely that means may be found, though the present outlook is extremely unpromising because of infinite practical difficulties.   Woodrow Wilson.

T telegram (WP, DLC).
  [1] J. Addams to WW, May 13, 1919.

To Frank William Taussig

My dear Taussig: Paris, 16 May, 1919.

I am warmly obliged to you for the paragraphs suggested for my message.[1] I have embodied practically the whole of what you wrote, and am your debtor.

            Cordially and sincerely yours,   [Woodrow Wilson]

CCL (WP, DLC).
  [1] See F. W. Taussig to WW, May 13, 1919, n. 1.

To James King Hewison[1]

My dear Mr. Hewison: Paris, 16 May, 1919.

It was with sincere pleasure that I received your kind and interesting letter of the twelfth of May,[2] and I thank you for it very warmly. It does not seem possible, alas, that I should visit Britain on my return home. My labors here have extended so much beyond the time that I expected to be away from home that when I am once free, I must take the shortest way back that is open to me, which means, I fear, that I must sail directly from Brest.

I am very much interested that you should have put Dr. Woodrow's discourse upon Peace in a volume worthy of it,[3] and it is very generous of you to intend the volume for me.

You kindly ask whether I have a picture of Dr. Woodrow. I am sorry to say I have not, and I do not think I have ever seen one. I should be very much interested in possessing a copy of any portrait of him that may exist.[4] But the chief thing I shall value is your own kindness and friendship.

            Cordially and sincerely yours,   [Woodrow Wilson]

CCL (WP, DLC).
  [1] Pastor of Rothesay Parish Church (Reformed) on the island of Bute, Scotland, and author of several works of local history and antiquarianism.
  [2] J. K. Hewison to WW, May 12, 1919, ALS (WP, DLC).
  [3] The letter cited in n. 2 above, together with J. K. Hewison to WW, May 31, 1919, ALS, and WW to J. K. Hewison, June 4, 1919, CCL, both in WP, DLC, reveal that Hewison had had Robert Wodrow's manuscript discourse, or sermon, on "Peace" bound into a handsome volume for presentation to Wilson. He sent it to Wilson at the end of May. Robert Wodrow (1679-1734), minister of the parish at Eastwood, near Glasgow, was best known as a church historian, chiefly for his *The History of the Sufferings of the Church of Scotland from the Restoration to the Revolution* (2 vols., Edinburgh, 1721-22). Several other volumes of his writings, including a life of his father, James Wodrow, Professor of Divinity at the University of Glasgow, were published posthumously. Both Wodrows were maternal ancestors of Woodrow Wilson.
  [4] Hewison sent to Wilson on June 7 two tear sheets from a magazine which contained an article about Wodrow and included a photograph of a portrait of him. He promised to try to obtain a large photograph of the painting for Wilson. J. K. Hewison to WW, June 7, 1919, ALS (WP, DLC).

Lewis Strauss to Gilbert Fairchild Close, with Enclosure

My dear Mr. Close: [Paris] May 16th, 1919.

The attached letter to the President was written by Mr. Hoover prior to the interview which you arranged for yesterday. I am sending it anyhow, because the President may desire it as a memorandum. Faithfully yours,   Lewis Strauss

E   N   C   L   O   S   U   R   E

From Herbert Clark Hoover

Dear Mr. President: Paris, 14 May 1919.

The principal objects for which I have been asking for an interview have been:

First, that I might express to you my strong view that we should not be led into joining with the Allies in a food blockade against Germany as a method of forcing peace. The margins on which the German people must live from now until next harvest are so small that any cessation of the stream of food, even for a short time, will bring the most wholesale loss of life. It might be that the imposition of a blockade would be effectual in securing the German signature to the peace. I seriously doubt whether when the world has recovered its moral equilibrium that it would consider a peace obtained upon such a device as the starving of women and children as being binding upon the German people. If the Germans did resist, it is my impression that it would throw Germany into complete chaos and military occupation would need to follow in order to save Europe.

My second point is that I am placed in a serious embarrassment by the threat of a blockade, because we have a constant stream of nearly one hundred million dollars worth of food in motion towards Germany. With all the effort they make, they are scarcely able to keep pace with their gold and security payments with the actual arrivals in Germany, so that the total risk of this vast current of foodstuffs is now falling on my shoulders. If the current were stopped, it would mean we would have to pile up large amounts of footstuffs in Europe, a large part of which is not of the type at present salable to the Allied countries. For instance, we are shipping rye, which the Allies do not eat, and types of fats of which the Allies have ample supply. We would have to face very great loss and seriously jeopardize the financial stability of the Food Administration. I have been willing to take the risk, in the feeling that without it peace and stability will not be secured, but I seriously doubt whether I have any right to involve you in the ensuing difficulties if I were to continue without your approval after I knew the gate to Germany would probably be closed.

My third point is that it is my belief that Germany cannot pay for her foodstuffs through until next harvest with any liquid resources she can secure. Under the new Wheat Act[1] I believe we could sell Germany breadstuffs on credit. This would probably involve acrimonious feeling in the United States for a time, of which I am prepared to stand my full share should it come to this issue. I would, however, like to have your advice in the matter. Any proposal of this kind should be contingent upon the Allies doing their share and securities being given in priority (except Belgium) to reparation.

Faithfully yours,   Herbert Hoover

TLS (WP, DLC).
  [1] 40 *Statutes at Large* 1348. Wilson had signed this Act on March 4. For a brief description of the purpose of the legislation, see C. Glass to WW, March 1, 1919, Vol. 55. The Act did in fact allow the export of wheat or flour for cash or on credit.

From Herbert Clark Hoover, with Enclosure

Dear Mr. President: Paris, 16 May 1919.

You will please find enclosed herewith copy of the reply of the Bolshevik Government to Doctor Nansen's proposal.[1] One has to read it with a certain sense of elimination. Approaching it from this point of view, they do not accept the conditions laid down by the four national Chiefs, but in turn propose that Doctor Nansen should go ahead with his food work and that on the political side they should open up peace negotiations direct with the Allied and Associated Governments.

For what it may be worth, I will be addressing you in the course of the day a memorandum as to my views on the whole Russian situation.[2]   Faithfully yours,   Herbert Hoover

TLS (WP, DLC).
  [1] See the Enclosure printed with F. Nansen to WW, April 17, 1919, Vol. 57.
  [2] This was probably the memorandum summarized in n. 8 to the minutes of the Council of Four, May 20, 1919, 11 a.m.

E N C L O S U R E

Copenhagen May 14, 1919

For Hoover

Following telegram was received by wireless through Swedish station to Mr. Fridtjof Nansen:

"Sir: Your very kind message of April 17th containing your exchange of letters with the Council of Four reached us only on May the 4th by way of the Nas Wireless Station and was at once given to the Peoples Commissariat of Social Welfare for thorough examination. Wish in the name of the Russian Soviet Government to convey to you our heartiest thanks for the warm interest you manifest in the well being of the Russian people. Great are indeed the suffering and privations inflicted upon the Russian people by the inhuman blockade of the Associated and so-called Neutral Powers and by the incessant wars forced upon it against its will. If left in peace and allowed free development Soviet Russia would soon be able to restore her national production, to regain her economic strength, to provide for her own needs and to be helpful to other countries. But in the present situation in which she has been put by the implacable policy of the Associated Powers help in foodstuffs from abroad would be most welcome to Russia, and the Russian Soviet Government appreciates most thankfully your human and heartfelt response to her sufferings, and considering the universal respect surrounding your person will be especially glad to enter into communication with you for the realization of your schemes of help which you emphasize as being purely humanitarian. On this basis of humanitarian work or help to suffering people we would be disposed to do everything in our power to further the realization of your project. Unfortunately your benevolent intentions which you indicate yourself as being based upon purely humanitarian grounds and which according to your letter must be realized by a commission of fully non-political character have been mixed up by others with political purposes. In the letter addressed to you by the four powers your scheme is represented as involving cessation of hostilities and of transfer of troops and war material. We regret very much that your original intentions have thus been fundamentally disfigured by the governments of the Associated Powers. We need not explain to you that military operations which obviously have in view to change external or internal conditions of the involved countries belong wholly to the domain of politics and that likewise cessation of hostilities which means preventing the belligerent who has every reason to expect successes from the obtaining them is also a purely political act. Thus your sincerely charitable intentions have been misused by others in order to

cover such purposes which are obviously political with the sem-
blance of an action originally humanitarian only. Being ready to lend
every assistance to your scheme so far as it bears the character you
have ascribed to it in your letter, we at the same time do not wish to
be the objects of foul play, and knowing that you like ourselves
mean business and wish really to attain the proposed, we would like
to ask whether this incantation of heterogeneous purposes has been
finally adopted by yourself. We expect that we will be able to make
it clear to you that in order to realize your intentions this interpretation must be carefully avoided. You are no doubt aware that the
cessation of the wars upon the Russian people is likewise the object
of our most warm desires and it must be known to you that we have
many times proposed to the Associated Governments to enter into
negotiations in order to put an end to the present bloodshed and that
we have even agreed to take part at the Conference at Prinkipo[1] notwithstanding the extremely unfavorable conditions proposed to us
and also that we were the only party to accept it. Responded in the
same peace loving sense to overtures made by one of the Great Powers.[2] The Prinkipo Conference was frustrated not by us, but by our
adversaries, the protegées of the Associated Powers, the counter-
revolutionary governments of Koltchak, Denikin and the others.
These are the Thislu [tools][3] with the help of which the Entente
Governments are making war upon us and are endeavoring to obtain our destruction and wherever they are victorious their victory
means the triumph of the most extreme barbarity and bestiality,
streams of blood and untold sufferings for the laboring masses
[dom]ination of the wildest reaction. Koltchak from the East, Denikin from the South, the Roumanian Feudris [feudals], the Polish
and Finnish most reactionary militarists, the German Barons and
Esthonian white guards from the West, and Russian white guard
bands from the north, these are the enemies whom the Entente
Governments mob against Soviet Russia and against whom as
against Entente troops, we are carrying on a desperate struggle with
ever growing success. The so-called governments of Koltchak and
Denikin are purely monarchical, all power belongs there to the wildest adherents of Tzarism, extreme Tzarist papers are in every way
imported by them. Tzarist hymns are constantly sung their cere-
monies. The so-called constitution of Koltchak is in reality monarchical; among their soldiers they distribute only Tzarist literature;
under the domination of Denikin the adherents of constitutional

[1] See n. 1 to the report of a press conference printed at Feb. 14, 1919, Vol. 55.
[2] A reference either to the Buckler-Litvinov negotiations in Stockholm or to the Bullitt
mission to Russia, about both of which see the index references in Vols. 54, 55, and 56.
[3] Corrections from the text printed in FR 1919, Russia, pp. 111-15.

government of the people are persecuted and under the domination
of Koltchak the adherents of the constituent assembly are imprisoned or shot. Program [Pogrom-] making literature is being widely
distributed by these so-called governments and whenever Jews
come under their domination they are the object of the most horrible
bestialities. In the West the Polish legionaries and the troops of the
Ukrainian counter revolutionary Pelliura [Petliura] who are both
supported and even directed by Entente officers, have perpetrated
such massacres of Jews which by far surpass the most horrible misdeeds of the black hundred of old Tzarism.[4] As the Russian Red
Cross in its appeal to the International Red Cross on April the 28
states, whole villages, whole towns, were turned the Russian [to
ruins]. Neither sex nor age was spared and in numerous places the
whole Jewish population was literally wiped out by these troops,
headed by Entente Generals and officers. The realm of Koltchak and
Denikin, everything that was gained by the peasants through the
revolution, is being taken back from them. Koltchak declares solemn manifestoes that peasants must not have possession land taken
by force from the nobility. He orders in his decrees that the seizure
of the land of the Gentry by the peasants should be prosecuted as a
serious crime and crushes the resistance of the peasants by wholesale massacres during which some parts of Siberia many thousand
of peasants were killed en masse. For the workers this domination
means every possible persecution, oppression, wholesale arrests,
and many cases wholesale shootings, so that in some towns the
workers are simply wiped out by the enraged extzarist officers, who
are the head of Koltchaks troops. The horrors perpetrated by these
Koltchak officers defy description and their victims are innumerable
including all that is progressive, all that is free thinking in Siberia.
Inebriated officers are torturing, flogging, tormenting in every way
the unfortunate laboring population under their domination and to
be a worker is to be predestined to be the object of their brutalities.
These are the adversaries owing to whom we are engaged in desperate struggle and whom the Associate Governments are in every
way supporting, providing them with war material, foodstuffs, financial help, military commanders, and political advisers, and on

[4] Black Hundred was the name given to various right-wing, protofascist groups in Russia, which, from 1900 on, attempted to combat what they considered to be dangerous liberal or radical and modernizing movements of the time by calling for a return to traditional values and unquestioning support of the Czar and the system which he
symbolized. The best known and most persistent of these groups was the Union of the
Russian People, founded in 1905. One of the most striking characteristics of these organizations was a new and especially virulent form of anti-Semitism, which sometimes took
the form, especially among their lower-class adherents, of violent pogroms against Jews.
See Hans Rogger and Eugen Weber, eds., *The European Right: A Historical Profile*,
(Berkeley and Los Angeles, 1965), pp. 475-98.

the north and east fronts sending their own troops to help them. In the hands of these barbarous bandits Entente rifles and Entente cannons are sending death to the Russian workers and peasants, struggling for their life and liberty. The same Entente Governments are the real source of the military supplies with the help of which our Polish, Roumanian, Finnish and other adversaries from the west are uninterrupted by [uninterruptedly] attacking us and it was officially declared in the French Chamber of Deputies and in the British House of Commons that the policy of the Entente is now to send against Soviet Russia the armies of these nationalities. An American radio of May 6th sent from Lyons says most emphatically that the Entente encourages the movement of the troops raised by the Russian counter-revolutionary General Youdenitch which presumably threatens Petrograd, that the Entente expects that the Bolsheviki will be forced to withdraw to Moscow, and that the Associated Governments intend connection herewith to bind [abandon] your plan of revictualling Russia. While declaring they have abandoned the idea of intervention the Associated Governments are in reality carrying on the most reckless intervention policy and even the American Government, despite all the statements to the contrary published in the American Press, seems at present to be wholly dominated by implacable hostility of the Clemenceau Ministry against Soviet Russia. This being the case we are [in a] position to discuss cessation of hostilities only if we discuss the whole problem of our relations to our adversaries, that is in the first place to the Associated Governments. That means to discuss peace and to open real negotiations bearing upon the true reasons of the war waged upon us and upon those conditions that can bring us lasting peace. We were always ready to enter into peace negotiations and we are ready to do it now as before and we will be glad to begin discussing these questions, but of course directly with the other belligerents, that is with the Associated Governments, or else with the persons empowered by the latter. But it is of course impossible for us to make any concessions referring to these fundamental problems of our existence under the disguise of a presumably humanitarian work. This latter must remain purely humanitarian and nonpolitical and we will welcome every proposal from your side made to us in the spirit of your letter sent by you to the Council of Four on April 3rd. [To] These wholly nonpolitical proposals we respond most gladly, we thank you most heartily for your good intentions, we are ready to give you every possibility of controlling the realization such humanitarian scheme, we will of course cover all the expenses of this work and the cost of the foodstuffs and we can pay if you desire by Russian goods. But seeing that your original plan has been so unfortu-

nately disfigured and considering that the most complete and difficult questions that have been created must first be thoroughly
elucidated, we would suggest that you take the necessary steps to
enable delegates of our government to meet you and your collabo-
rators abroad and discuss these questions and we ask you kindly to
indicate the time and the place for this conference between our delegates and the leaders of your commission and what guarantees can
be obtained for the free passage of our delegates through countries
influenced by the Entente. Signed Peoples Commissary for Foreign
Affaires, Tchitcherin."[5] Nansen adds "Please tell Hoover that I intend to meet Lenin's delegates perhaps Stockholm but shall be glad
to hear Hoover's opinion soon as possible."

T telegram (WP, DLC).

[5] That is, Georgii Vasil'evich Chicherin.

From William Shepherd Benson

MEMORANDUM FOR THE PRESIDENT.

16 May, 1919.

SUBJECT: Austrian Naval Terms.
            Reservations by Admiral Benson.
(1) "The terms of the Treaty should require that surrendered ves-
    sels of war or war material should be broken up."

COMMENT.

The views of the Naval Advisory Staff have been already fully presented to the President. All the Principal Powers, with the exception
of France, favour the destruction of these ships; but if provision for
destruction is not embodied in the Treaty, there will be no binding
agreement that the ships will not be ultimately distributed. Article
192 of the Treaty with Germany provides that surrendered arms and
war material will be destroyed or rendered useless. The same provision should be in the Austrian treaty.
(2) "That naval terms should contain no prohibition against the
    manufacture, within the limits of States formerly a part of the
    Austro-Hungarian Empire, of Naval war material on foreign or-
    der."

COMMENT.

The prohibition of the manufacture and export of arms, ammunition and other naval war material, denies to Austria the right in
time of peace to do what is freely permitted to other States. It is believed that measures of this kind can not be made permanently ef-

fective without the exercise of an espionage and repression that would be a constant source of irritation.

Admiral Benson has consistently opposed any measures that impose a limitation on the full exercise of sovereignty of the enemy States after the conclusion of peace, except in so far as such limitations are imposed by common agreement in the League of Nations.

It is believed that repressive measures make for war and not for peace. The present generation will be forced by circumstances to yield, but there is always the danger that a future generation may not be so submissive.

CC MS (W. S. Benson Papers, DLC).

From Jan Christiaan Smuts

My dear Mr. President,   Paris. 16th May, 1919.

There are some matters of considerable urgency which I should be glad to discuss with you, and I should be very grateful if you would be good enough to give me an appointment at an early date, so that I may have an opportunity of ascertaining your views. I know that you are extremely busy, and I should be prepared to hold myself at your convenience, and shall come at whatever time you fix.

   With kind regards,
      Believe me,   Yours sincerely,   J. C. Smuts.

TLS (WP, DLC).

From Louis Marshall and Julian William Mack

Dear Mr. President: Paris. May 16th, 1919

It is only because of the great importance of the subject and of your deep interest in our aims that we venture in these burdened days to direct your attention to a few salient points involved in the treaty with Poland which is to be laid before the Council of Four presently.

We have had an opportunity to examine a draft of the treaty as formulated by the Special Commission and find it in most respects admirable.[1] We have suggested a number of verbal changes which will doubtless receive due consideration. It is our purpose to advert to the following three points, vital in character and in our judgment essential to the attainment of what in your heartening Fiume note you aptly referred to as "the giving of international sanction to the equal and equitable treatment of all racial and national minorities."

1) Whilst the draft as prepared recognises the right of the Jews to maintain their own schools and other cultural institutions and to a certain extent contemplates that they shall share in public funds appropriated for such objects through State, departmental and Municipal budgets, the provision as made is inadequate and quite unworkable. It is indefinite as to the extent to which such funds shall be allotted to the racial, linguistic and religious minorities. It declares that the shares allocated shall be *equitable*. It should be proportionate to the numbers of the minority and of the entire population. What is or is not equitable would depend on the Chancellor's foot—a standard foreboding inequalities. It provides for the appointment of one of [or] more committees designated by the Jewish communities to distribute the public funds allocated for the Jewish schools. This is quite vague. It is the opinion of those whose interests are affected, as it is ours, that it should be provided in the first instance that the Jews of Poland (and for that matter any other minorities) shall have the right to organise themselves as distinct minority groups on a racial, religious, and linguistic basis. That would give recognition to the several groups as legal entities or public corporations. As fitting into this framework would come the right of these several minorities to designate such committees or agencies as would enable them to manage their schools and other educational establishments and in addition thereto (which is not made clear in the draft) their religious, charitable and social institutions. On such a basis the plan would become effective and the benefits sought to be conferred, enjoyed; otherwise confusion and grave abuses are likely to arise.

Without undertaking to provide details, it would be also desirable to give explicit recognition to the principle of proportional minority representation in all legislative and municipal bodies.

2) The Commission is divided in opinion as to whether or not the Treaty shall contain a clause relating to what is known as the Sabbath question. One phase only of the subject is dealt with in the annex to the Report to be submitted to the Council of Four. It omits however the most important aspect. Our proposal reads:

"Those who observe any other day than Sunday as their Sabbath shall not be require[d] to perform any acts on their Sabbath or holidays which by the tenets of their faith are regarded as a desecration, nor shall they be prohibited from pursuing their secular affairs on Sunday or other holidays."

The Jews constitute approximately 14% of the population of Poland. Those who observe Saturday in accordance with their ancient tradition and as a matter of conscience, if prevented from working peaceably on Sunday, would be deprived of one sixth of their economic power. That would place them at a cruel disadvantage in their struggle for existence. That they should not be compelled to dese-crate the day which they and their ancestors have treasured as holy for centuries requires no argument. Of course they must render such public service on that day as the welfare of the State requires, but otherwise they should not be agonized.

3) Recognizing in the League of Nations a Tribunal wherein relief may be obtained against a violation of any of the guarantees of the individual and collective rights specified in the treaties with Poland, Rumania and other East European States we trust that the racial, religious, and linguistic minorities may be enabled upon such con-ditions as the League of Nations may prescribe to lay their com-plaints regarding any violations of such guarantees before that tri-bunal. The grant of the right will in itself afford the highest sanction for the rights to be secured.

We take this opportunity of giving expression to the gratitude that the Jews of all the world owe to you for your mighty endeavours to obtain for them that measure of justice for which they have waited well-nigh 20 centuries.   Faithfully yours.   Louis Marshall
Julian W. Mack

TLS (WP, DLC).
¹ The second report of the Committee on New States, printed as an Enclosure with D. H. Miller to WW, May 15, 1919.

From the Diary of Colonel House

May 16, 1919.

It has been the Adriatic settlement again today. Trumbitch came in the morning and it was with difficulty I obtained his consent to a discussion with the Italians, with me acting as intermediary. This was finally accomplished and I had Trumbitch in the large reception room, Orlando and Count di Cellere in the salon, with my study be-tween. Miller and Beers [Beer] I placed with the Italians, and Fra-zier and Johnson with Trumbitch. I directed everything from my study for the first two hours, but later took up the discussion myself, going from one room to the other.

Again I used every argument on both sides that I could think of. I let them know that I felt the peace of the world was in the balance and that if they left without an understanding, no one could say what might happen in the future. I got them so nearly to an agree-ment that it was a matter of deep regret that I could not bring them all the way.

The Italians agreed that Fiume should be a free city. They agreed to give the Jugo-Slavs all of Dalmatia if certain islands could be Italians [Italian], and if the cities of Zara and Sebenico might become free cities under Italian sovereignty.

The Jugo-Slavs pratically agreed that Italy should recied [receive] (1) the Sexten Valley, (2) Tarvis District. It was agreed by both that (1) Fiume, including Susak was to be an independent city and a free port under the protection of the League of Nations. (2) Dalmatia to be neutralized under Jugo-Slav sovereignty. (3) Pago to go to the mainland.

The Jugo-Slavs agreed that Lussan and Pelogossa should go to Italy, but they dissented as to Lissa, although they said they would accept it if we insisted.

The Italians wanted the eastern part of Istria to be included in their boundaries. To this the Jugo-Slavs objected. I think, however, we could have reached a compromise upon this. The Italians wanted Zara and Sebenico to be free cities under Italian sovereignty. The Jugo-Slavs would not agree. Italy wanted the remaining islands within the line of the Treaty of London. To this also the Jugoslavs objected.

As a matter of fact, the difference between them is now very slight. Zara has only about 12000 people and Sebenico about 3000. Some of the islands the Italians desire are perfectly barren and have only a few hundred inhabitants. We started the conference a little after five o'clock and did not break up until nine at night. The Italians regarded it as a last effort to come to a direct agreement, but they are returning here tomorrow at 9.30 to see whether they cannot reach an understanding with me.

I saw the President in the afternoon and told him what I was doing in the matter of the Adriatic settlement. He thanked me but showed no inclination to be conciliatory to the Italians.

General Smuts called in the morning to tell me that he and Botha had almost decided not to sign the Treaty if the Entente refused to make such changes in it as the Germans suggested, and which the liberal world would approve. He thought the Germans would win a decided diplomatic victory by pointing out the many injustices which the Treaty contained. He also thought in the event the Entente refused these just demands, and should then undertake to blockade Germany and starve her people into submission, it would cause world-wide revolution. We agreed that while public opinion did sustain the Entente in its blockade of Germany when they were fighting for their lives, it would not sustain them when they were starving women and children for the purpose of trying to force the signing of a treaty.

It is a matter I have thought about a good deal recently and I sincerely trust that this ordeal will not have to be faced. I shall not be in favor of starving the people of Germany. At one time I thought perhaps this would be the only way out in the event Germany did not sign, but at that stage I did not know the real conditions in Germany and how much suffering there was. I have never been in favor of the blockade. I tried my best at the beginning, before we entered the war, to have some understanding reached by which food could go into Germany through neutral ports without question. My diary will show my activities in that direction. I have never been [in] favor of doing anything, even to win the war, that was in any way contrary to human principles. I have never permitted myself to get into an excited and unfair frame of mind. I have wanted to beat the Germans and have done my best in that direction, but I have never hated them as a people, and I have certainly never wished women and children to suffer.

Pichon was my first caller this morning. He wished to know whether I would agree to the publication of those parts of the Treaty which had already been published in Germany and which are now coming into France in German papers.[1] I spoke to the President and he at first agreed. Later he thought it was best not to do so while Lloyd George was absent. George is on one of his periodical jaunts. The President himself is not in favor of any publication and he was speaking more for himself I think than for Lloyd George.

I urged the contrary policy, and that the entire Treaty should be given to the public. There is no reason why it should not be. Pichon also asked me about placing Monnet[2] as a French representative on the Secretariat of the League of Nations. He wished to know when the League of Nations would sit in London, and how often it would be necessary for him to go over in the event he was called upon to represent the French Government.

The Secretary of State for India, E. S. Montagu, was another caller. He came to point out the danger of breaking up the Turkish Empire. He said the entire Mohamedan population of India and the East was in a highly nervous state in regard to it, and that he personally believed if this was done it would eventually lead to Great Britain having to abandon her Asiatic possessions. He thought it meant revolution throughout India and the East.

He was insistent that Italy should not be given a mandatory over Anatolia. He thought the Mohamedans would be willing to have the United States, England or even France, but they would revolt at Italy.

It has been one of my busiest days, for besides those I have mentioned there were many other callers, with our Experts who came in and out for consultation.

¹ Thus far, only an official summary of the treaty had been published in the United States and the Allied nations. See JPT to WW, May 7, 1919 (second telegram of that date), n. 1, Vol. 58. As the minutes of the meeting of the Council of Four printed at May 17, 1919, 11:10 a.m., reveal, the council, including Lloyd George, decided once again that the treaty, as presented to the German delegation, should not be published "at present."
² That is, Jean Omer Marie Gabriel Monnet.

Two Telegrams to Joseph Patrick Tumulty

Paris, 16 May, 1919.

Please send following message to Mrs. Minnie Fisher Cunningham, President of the Texas Woman Suffrage Association, 605 Littlefield Building, Austin, Texas QUOTE

I am looking forward with the greatest interest to the referendum of May 24th on Woman Suffrage and entertain the confident hope that the men of Texas will by very great majority render gallant justice to the women of the state. UNQUOTE   Woodrow Wilson[1]

¹ Wilson was responding to Carrie C. L. C. Catt to WW, embodied in JPT to WW, May 13, 1919, T telegram (WP, DLC). She urged Wilson to send a message supporting passage of the Texas suffrage amendment.

Paris, 16 May, 1919.

Please convey following to William G. Lee,[1] triannual convention Brotherhood of Railroad Trainmen QUOTE

Please express to the trainmen assembled in convention my warm appreciation of the message you have just sent me.[2] It has done my heart good and made me feel the fine spirit of such friends in a way to make the work here easier for me. My warmest best wishes for the success of the convention. UNQUOTE   Woodrow Wilson.

T telegrams (WP, DLC).
¹ That is, William Granville Lee, president of the Brotherhood of Railway Trainmen.
² Wilson was responding to W. G. Lee to JPT, May 14, 1919, T telegram (WP, DLC).

From Joseph Patrick Tumulty

[The White House, May 16, 1919]

No. 127   Mr. Gompers told an intimate friend of mine that he had been "sold out" in the matter of the labor programme. I understand he feels very bitter. Situation in this country with reference to League of Nations is such that should Gompers throw support of labor against it, it would have a most serious effect.

Tumulty.

T telegram (WP, DLC).

From Newton Diehl Baker

[Washington, May 16, 1919]

For Auchincloss only from Polk. Please deliver the following message confidentially to the President from Secretary Baker:

"Governor General Harrison of the Philippine Islands was divorced by the courts of California yesterday and immediately remarried.[1] His present wife is a very young woman whose parents[2] have vigorously *and in the public press* protested against the marriage. I am strongly of the belief that as the Philippines are a Catholic country and the regulations of the church on the subject of divorce are rigid, delicate situations would be created by Harrison's return to Manila. I understand he plans to leave the United States June 12th. I would like to have your approval of a request from me to him that he may defer his departure until after your return so that you can consider whether or not he ought to return."

                                        Polk,   Acting.

T telegram (WP, DLC).
[1] As early as April 4, Francis Burton Harrison had announced his engagement to Salena Elizabeth Wrentmore. A brief notice of the engagement in the *New York Times*, April 5, 1919, stated also that Miss Wrentmore's mother was reported to have said publicly that she opposed the marriage "on the ground of disparity of age between her daughter and Governor General Harrison."
The *New York Times*, May 16, 1919, reported that Harrison's former wife, Mabel Judson Cox Harrison, had obtained a decree of divorce at noon on May 15 in the Superior Court at San Diego, California, and that Harrison had married Miss Wrentmore at 5:30 p.m. that same day in Chicago. The bride was reported to be an eighteen-year-old student at the University of California at Berkeley who had met Harrison in Manila a year previously. She was given in marriage by her brother. It was further reported that her parents, who had objected to the match, had sent a wireless message to Chicago that afternoon.
[2] Clarence George Wrentmore and Margaret McFarland Wrentmore. He was a civil engineer who in 1912 organized and became the first Dean of the College of Engineering of the University of the Philippines.

Edward Wyllis Scripps[1] to Edward Mandell House

                          San Diego, Calif., May 16th, 1919.

I consider it a matter of desperate urgency that the President take the occasion of the signing of peace treaty to grant almost complete amnesty and pardon to all American citizens in prison or under arrest on account of their expression, in speech and in print, of their personal beliefs with regard to the Government's activities during the period of the war.

It was through the personal activities of my son James, who at present controls the Seattle Star as well as my other newspapers, that a serious catastrophe did not occur in Seattle.[2] There is great danger of other and more serious emergencies. I and many others holding positions of great influence, official and otherwise, who have been most faithful and loyal in their support of President Wilson, have been excessively grieved and alarmed because the President's preoccupations have prevented him giving full consideration to the dangers that threaten us. There is a vast public discontent, especially amongst the working class of our citizens, because of the suppression of free speech, free assembly and free press. This policy is continuing months after the time when there was any excuse at all for it. The persons who are mainly responsible for what we now consider to have become a policy of persecution are identically those who, by reason of personal interest and temperament, have always opposed and always will oppose those of the President's policies which we, the President's friends, most admire and love him for possessing. It is these persons who, through the press they control and other channels, are seeking to make use of conditions which arose during wartime to suppress a free discussion of reforms in the economic and industrial world. It is not only because of our friendship for the President, although that is great, or for reasons of expediency, that we are so greatly moved, but because of our love of justice and hence the welfare of our nation.

I have been urged to make this appeal by certain persons high in the President's esteem, whose positions are such as to make them feel that I should do so rather than they, and though I do not know you personally, I have been urged to make the appeal to you. I have spent a lifetime in journalism conducted in such a way as to win for me and my papers the respect and confidence of millions of my fellow countrymen. Yet, on account of the Seattle affair, I know that I am being regarded with suspicion, not only by my own peculiar constituency, but by men and women who have won the right to be considered leaders in progress and real democracy.

Please answer if you consent to speak to the President about this matter.   E. W. Scripps.

T telegram (E. M. House Papers, CtY).
    [1] Newspaper magnate, publisher of the largest chain of newspapers in the United States, controlling owner of the United Press and of the Newspaper Enterprise Association.
    [2] The Seattle *Star* had been in the forefront of voices calling upon Mayor Ole Hanson to suppress a general strike which had been precipitated by a strike of some 35,000 shipyard workers against the Emergency Fleet Corporation. The general strike, called by the Seattle Central Labor Council, began on February 6. At Hanson's request, federal troops moved into the city on the same day. Amid charges by Hanson and certain newspapers, including the Seattle *Star*, that the strike was being conducted by "Reds" and the I.W.W., the strike was broken on February 10, 1919. This incident is generally regarded as one of the earliest manifestations of the Red Scare that would soon engulf the country. See Robert K. Murray, *Red Scare: A Study in National Hysteria, 1919-1920* (Minneapolis, Minn., 1955), pp. 58-66, and Robert L. Friedheim, *The Seattle General Strike* (Seattle, Wash., 1964).

From the Montana Grain Growers

Great Falls, Mont., May 16, 1919.

Montana Grain Growers organization in state conference earnestly protest action of wheat administrator Barnes[1] in his agreement to reduce the price of wheat entered into in New York Tuesday, May 13, in conference of millers, bakers and grain traders to all of whom satisfactory profits were guaranteed. The millions of farmers who are growing the wheat were ignored and their profits from a world's demand are to be denied. Barnes action was not only in violation of anti-trust law but of sound public policy. This unlawful price fixing will cost American farmers hundreds of millions of dollars if permitted to stand. They must not be made the sole victims of price fixing. Congress made no provision for breaking down the wheat price but had in mind solely making good your minimum guarantee. If world conditions will fix higher prices for wheat American farmers are clearly entitled to the same. We therefore appeal to you to forbid Barnes and others from consummating this unlawful and terribly damaging program.   Montana Grain Growers.

T telegram (WP, DLC).

[1] Julius Howland Barnes had met, among others, with representatives of grain handlers, millers and jobbers, and bakers in New York on May 13 to discuss "the basic principles for making effective the Government's guaranteed price of $2.26 a bushel for the 1919 wheat crop." *New York Times*, May 14, 1919. On May 14, Barnes' office issued a statement on what transpired at the meeting. "The views of the various trades," it said, "on the effect of certain policies and methods of operation suggested for next year's Wheat Administration were requested by the Wheat Director. He explained that it was desirable that there should be the least disturbance to established business to make effective the guarantee to the producer, as intended by the national pledge, and, at the same time, make assured the reflection to the consumer of a proper price for flour, reflecting as nearly as possible the supply and demand situation in America and the world. There was a general agreement, in order that all of the wheat producers of the country over such a wide territory and in such great numbers could secure the benefit by contract, to see that wheat trading should be only on the guaranteed price level throughout the country. Then, if a lower basis was justified with the development of world factors as the season advanced, this lower basis could be made to reach the consumer by trade agreements with the millers and manufacturing facilities, the Wheat Director making the readjusting basis effective by payment of the difference, as allowed under the act of Congress." *Ibid.*, May 15, 1919.

It appears that, on the basis of Barnes' statement, the Montana grain growers assumed that he intended to hold the price of wheat paid to the producer down to the figure of $2.26 per bushel earlier agreed upon as the price to be guaranteed by the federal government. That this was not in fact the case is shown by statistics which reveal that the price of wheat per bushel remained consistently above the guaranteed level of $2.26 until October 1920. See Frank M. Surface, *The Grain Trade During the World War: Being a History of the Food Administration Grain Corporation and the United States Grain Corporation* (New York, 1928), pp. 146-60, and the tables on pp. 121-22.

From the Diary of Dr. Grayson

Saturday, May 17, 1919.

The President had an early breakfast, and at eleven o'clock a meeting of the Big Four was held here at the temporary White House. The reports of economic experts dealing with the Austrian reparations were considered at the morning session.

The President, Mrs. Wilson and I had lunch, and after lunch the President and I motored to St. Cloud. At 4:30 o'clock the Big Four met to consider the petition of the delegations representing British India.[1] This was a typical meeting, and I believe that the inclusion of the stenographic record will show just what the Big Four had to deal with in matters that were in no way collateral to the war itself. The record is as follows: . . .

After dinner the President, Mrs. Wilson, Dr. Axson, Miss Benham and myself went to one of the local theatres to see a performance given by the 88th Division theatrical troop.

[1] At this meeting of the Council of Four at President Wilson's house, E. S. Montagu presented the Aga Khan and other Indian leaders who, with Montagu, claimed to speak for the seventy million Mohammedans of India. They all pleaded strongly for at least an hour and a half for the maintenance of the integrity and independence of Turkey and warned that the destruction of Turkey would inflame the whole Moslem world and be a dire threat to international peace. At the end of their speeches, Wilson made the following three comments:

"I want to speak of one thing that has been mentioned, though it has not been dwelt upon, in order to avoid any possible misunderstanding. That is the suggestion that entrance into the League of Nations should be left open as freely to Mussulman Governments as to others. There is really no difficulty upon that point; but I want to call your attention to the fact that the covenant of the League limits membership to self-governing nations, and that Germany is not admitted at once because we are not sure that she is a self-governing nation. It was the opinion among all the conferees on this subject that we must wait until we had conclusive proof that Germany was no longer under the government of a single individual or a small group of individuals, but under the government of her own people, and that therefore her disposition to the rest of the world and her ambitions were altogether altered before she could be admitted into the League. I for my part do not anticipate any opposition to the admission of any government that displays those changes. So that it is not a question of present political relationship.

"MR. LLOYD GEORGE: There will certainly be no religious question.

"THE PRESIDENT: Certainly not. It is merely a question of political form of government.

"There is another matter that I would like to make clear in that connection: The whole theory of mandates is not the theory of permanent subordination. It is the theory of development, of putting upon the mandatory the duty of assisting in the development of the country under mandate, in order that it may be brought to a capacity for self-government and self-dependence which for the time being it has not reached, and that therefore the countries under mandate are candidates, so to say, for full membership in the family of nations. I think that is a very important fundamental idea of the whole mandatory conception. . . ."

"Of course, I think we all recognize that the trouble in Asia Minor has been the rivalry and clash of nationalities and religions, and that the problem is complex because the mixture is so complex and the competition so sharp." T MS (SDR, RG 256, 180.03401/18, DNA). The complete minutes of this meeting are printed in in PPC, V, 690-701.

Hankey's Notes of a Meeting of the Council of Four[1]

President Wilson's House,
C.F.15A.   Paris, May 17, 1919, 11:00 a.m.

1. Attention was drawn to the draft notes circulated by Sir Maurice Hankey on the subject of the proposed mandates in Asia Minor. (C.F.13A. Minute 3, Minute 11, and Appendices 1 and 2.)[2] Sir Maurice Hankey was instructed to make it clear in the revise of the Minutes that the decision had only been intended as provisional, and as part of a proposal that it was contemplated to make to the Italian Delegates.

2. MR. LLOYD GEORGE said he had received information from M. Venizelos sent by the Governor General of Samos,[3] to the effect that the Italians had landed 500 men at Scala Nuova and occupied the Customs House. Consequently, they were now in possession of the whole coast of Asia Minor from Scala Nuova to Adalia. He felt that some immediate representation ought to be made to M. Orlando on the subject.

PRESIDENT WILSON suggested that a joint memorandum should be signed by Mr. Lloyd George, M. Clemenceau and himself, addressed to M. Orlando. This would give him an opportunity to look into the matter. He should be told that the independent action on Italy's part was a matter of serious concern to the Allied and Associated Powers. If his explanations were not satisfactory, he should be told that Italian claims could not be discussed. A joint communication of this kind would be more formal and more impressive than a verbal remonstrance.

MR. LLOYD GEORGE handed round a memorandum from Mr. Balfour (Appendix), which he described as a powerful one, in regard to provisional decisions taken on the subject of Anatolia. He felt considerable doubt as to whether this provisional conclusion was a correct one. In any case, if the Italians continued on their present lines, it might be better to have only one mandate for Anatolia.

M. CLEMENCEAU said for his part he did not want it.

PRESIDENT WILSON produced an ethnographical map of Anatolia, and pointed out how much more mixed the population was in the southern half of Anatolia than in the north, where it was almost wholly Turkish.

MR. LLOYD GEORGE said it had to be borne in mind that the whole Mohammedan world would be aroused by this partition of Turkey, and this affected France just as much as it did Great Britain.

---

[1] The complete text of these minutes is printed in *PPC*, V, 668-72.
[2] See the minutes of the Council of Four printed at May 14, 1919, 4 p.m.
[3] Unidentified.

(It was agreed that Mr. Lloyd George should prepare the draft of the memorandum for consideration, and possibly for subsequent presentation to M. Orlando, on the subject of the Italian landings on the Coast of Asia Minor.)

APPENDIX TO C.F.15.A.[4]

THE PROBLEM OF ITALY AND TURKEY IN ANATOLIA.

May 16th, 1919.

The scheme provisionally accepted on Wednesday last at a meeting of the "Three,"[5] contemplates the final destruction of the Turkish State. This is already condemned, and I think rightly, to the loss of its European possessions, its Arab-speaking population, and Armenia. It is therefore in any case reduced, so far as the area of its Empire is concerned, to a mere fraction of its former self; this fraction, however, we originally proposed to preserve, thus leaving to the Sultan[6] that great block of Anatolia lying west of the meridian of Constantinople, which is not merely inhabited by a population the vast majority of whom are Turks, but which contains within its boundaries most of the Turkish race. For this scheme has now been substituted one which cuts this region into two separate states, with different capitals, different sovereigns and different mandatories.

I look with much misgiving at this proposal. It will not only deeply shock large sections of Mohammedan opinion, but I think it will also be made the subject of a great deal of very unfavourable Christian commentary. We are all most anxious to avoid as far as possible placing reluctant populations under alien rule; but ought we not to be quite as careful to avoid the opposite fault? Is it a greater crime to join together those who wish to be separated than to divide those who wish to be united? And if the Anatolian Turks say they desire to remain a single people under a single sovereign, to what principle are we going to make appeal when we refuse to grant their request?

I think we must admit that no such scheme would ever have been thought of, if it had not been necessary to find some method of satisfying Italian ambitions. Unfortunately, this necessity haunts and hampers every step in our diplomacy. The Italians, armed with the Treaty of London, and supported by a passionate public opinion, will never be content with fragments of Tyrolese and Jugo-Slav territory in Europe; with French and British Colonial concessions in Africa, and with the Caucasus in the Middle East. We have also to find something for them out of the Turkish Empire in Asia Minor. Now I believe there are only two kinds of schemes possible by which the

[4] There is a CC MS of this memorandum in WP, DLC.
[5] Again, see the minutes cited in n. 2 above.
[6] Mehmed VI.

latter operation can be accomplished;—the scheme of partition advocated by the "Three," and the scheme which I ventured to lay before them. This last has not, perhaps, in all respects, been very clearly understood; which is not surprising, for it was very hastily written, and not very fully explained. But the matter is so important that I may be permitted to return to it.

Under my scheme Turkey remained an undivided State without a Mandatory. Its status was substantially that of the historic Turkish Empire. Its territories were, indeed much diminished; it could no longer count as a Great Power; but in other respects the Sultan would reign at Brussa or Konia as his predecessors had formerly reigned at Constantinople.

Now it must be remembered that even at Constantinpole representatives of the Western Powers had special positions in his administration, justified, and, indeed, rendered necessary for various well-known reasons. The public debt, the customs, and in some cases the police, were under the control or supervision of foreign advisors. This system I do not propose to alter, but rather to perfect. The Turks are familiar with it, up to a certain point they welcome it, and they do not deem it inconsistent with their unity or their independence.

The alternative scheme, which found favour on Wednesday, destroys both; for it cuts Turkey into two halves; and puts each half under a separate Mandatory. What are its compensating advantages? It is said, in the first place, that it avoids the evils of a Condominium. A Condominium, we are told, is never a success; it is slow moving, ineffectual and the occasion of endless friction between the controlling Powers;—a friction so acute as even to endanger the peace of the world.

But the plan I propose is not a Condominium. A Condominium, as I understand it, is the joint Government of a single State by many Powers acting collectively. Under such a system, the Powers first agree upon a policy, and then impose it upon the subordinate State. They control, actually or potentially, the whole administration. If they differ, the administrative machinery stands still. If their differences are due to their being moved by inconsistent interests, they may become acute and even dangerous. The subordinate Government is perpetually tempted to play one off against the other, and the whole country becomes the theatre of rival intrigues. Everybody quarrels, and nothing is done.

Now nobody will pretend that the Constantinople Government was a good one, but it was not as bad as all this. There were, of course, endless intrigues, political and financial. There was a per-

petual struggle to obtain influence with the Sultan and his Ministers. There was much corruption; there was much mal-administra-
tion. But it was never a Condominium. The Sultan appointed his
ministers; he appointed the Governors of his Provinces; he raised
and commanded the Army; he directed the foreign policy of his
country, and was in these and all other important respects, an independent sovereign. Certain branches of his administration were
no doubt controlled, not by a foreign Condominium, but by foreigners. He remained, nevertheless, in quite a different position from
that which he would have held either under a Condominium or under a Mandatory.

Another objection raised against my scheme is that it gives special
privileges to Italy in the southern part of the Turkish state. This is
quite true, and of course I should greatly prefer that it were otherwise. But inasmuch as the whole plan is primarily devised in order
to do something to satisfy Italian appetites, that is, I am afraid, inevitable. From an administrative point of view, the scheme would no
doubt be much better if the Italians played no part in it. I freely admit it—but I submit that the argument is irrelevant. The Italians
must somehow be mollified, and the only question is how to mollify
them at the smallest cost to mankind.

Then it is said that to give the Italians a first claim to concessions
in any district is to violate the principle of equal opportunities for all
nations. Again, I am not prepared to deny the charge. My whole object is to give the Italians something which they will really like, and
it seems that they have a great liking for concessions. I remember,
when the Marquis Imperiali was comparing the advantages which
the French would get out of Cilicia with the advantages which Italy
was likely to get out of her share of Asia Minor, he was wont to dwell
upon the wonders of a certain copper mine, which he said, I am sure
quite truly, was to be found somewhere in the French zone. In the
same way, I observe that Baron Sonnino's eyes are lovingly fixed
upon a very indifferent coal mine on the Southern shores of the
Black Sea. Personally, I regard these hopes and expectations with
considerable scepticism. I doubt the existence of these hidden
riches in Southern Anatolia. Even if they exist, I doubt whether
their exploitation is going to make Italy rich; and I have a strong suspicion that even if these industrial enterprises are started under Italian patronage, they will be found after no great lapse of time to be
under German management. But all this does not seem to me to be
to the point. The object is to find some privileged position for the
Italians in Southern Anatolia; and I particularly beg the "Three" to
remember that she has already got the germs of such a position by a

pre-war arrangement which she made with the Turks, in respect of the region neighbouring on Adalia. My suggestion only extends and emphasises her privileges. It does not create them.

In any case, as Italy is not, under my plan, intended to occupy the position of a Mandatory in these regions, the general principle—that no Mandatory has a right to exceptional trade advantages in the country which it controls—is not violated. The only difference that I can see between what would happen under my plan, and what would happen if nothing were done for the Italians in Asia Minor, is that in the first case Italy would without question or controversy have the refusal of all concessions within a certain area: in the second case these concessions will be scrambled for at Brussa by the rival company-mongers of every country under Heaven, supported, no doubt, by their respective Ministers. The first plan may be an infringement upon the liberty and equality, nominally at least, secured by the second; but I do not know that these most excellent things are seen to the best advantage when they are enjoyed by corrupt administrators and greedy speculators.

But once again, this is relatively unimportant compared with the main objects of the scheme I am endeavouring to support. This is designed to do two things; to maintain something resembling an independent Turkish Government, ruling over a homogeneous Turkish population; the other is to find a position for the Italians within this Turkish state which will make a sufficient appeal to the ambitions of the Italian Government. From every other point of view the plan is, I admit, a bad one; but from this point of view—which is the one at the moment chiefly occupying our thoughts—I still think it worthy of serious consideration.   (Intd)   A.J.B.

T MS (SDR, RG 256, 180.03401/15½, DNA).

Hankey's Notes of a Meeting of the Council of Four[1]

President Wilson's House,
C.F.16.   Paris, May 17, 1919, 11:10 a.m.

I. M. CLEMENCEAU reported that there was a very strong demand for the publication of the Treaty of Peace with Germany. He was informed that the Germans themselves had published certain portions, so that the text of these portions would soon be in the hands of the Press. Consequently, he had yesterday spoken to President Wilson and Mr. Balfour on the subject, and had gathered that they were favourable to publication.

PRESIDENT WILSON said that he had only expressed himself fa-

[1] The complete text of these minutes is printed in PPC, V, 673-85.

vourable to the publication of those parts which the Germans had already published, and even so, he had insisted that the decision must be reserved until Mr. Lloyd George returned.

MR. LLOYD GEORGE recalled that only a few days before, he had raised this very question in consequence of a telephone message from Mr. Bonar Law, and as a result of their discussion, an emphatic reply had been given that the Treaty would not be published. His objection was, then when the Treaty was once published, it was very difficult to alter it, and there might be some details which we ought to concede to the Germans, if it would make it more acceptable to them.

(At this point M. Orlando and Count Aldrovandi entered.)

PRESIDENT WILSON said there was a great difference between what was published by the Germans and what we gave officially to our own people. Once we had published them to our own people, the Clauses assumed an official form, and made it very difficult to change.

MR. LLOYD GEORGE pointed out that the original Treaty had been somewhat defective and yet it was rather difficult to publish a different document to what the Germans had received. He was informed by Sir Maurice Hankey that it was physically impossible to publish the Treaty before Tuesday or Wednesday, as it could not be printed in London before then. By Wednesday, however, the German reply was due, and he thought the matter might be postponed until then. He did not like going back on a previous decision.

M. CLEMENCEAU said he would do whatever Mr. Lloyd George wished.

(It was agreed that the Treaty of Peace as handed to the Germans, should not be published at present.)

2. MR. LLOYD GEORGE said that on the previous day, he had addressed some British troops, and had pointed out to them how disastrous it would be to throw away the results of five years warfare, by not seeing the matter through. He had told them that in certain eventualities, it mighty be necessary to go to Berlin, and they had shown themselves to a man, quite ready to do so, if necessary. This was a division that had lost nearly 9,000 men in the advances of last year.

3. M. CLEMENCEAU handed in a list of material which could be supplied by the French Government, if it were so decided, in order to provide outfits for German Prisoners of War. (Appendix I.)[2] He

---

[2] Gen. H. M. C. E. Alby to G. Clemenceau, May 16, 1919, TCL (SDR, RG 256, 180.03401/16, DNA), printed in *ibid.*, pp. 682-83. Alby, the chief of the French General Staff, reported that the total supply of clothing available for German prisoners consisted of 2,000 pairs of trousers, 7,200 sweaters, 800 cloaks, 500 "Horse buckets [biankets?]," and "a wagon load of boots, half boots, and lace boots."

said that the remainder of the captured material had already been used to supply the German prisoners.

MR. LLOYD GEORGE said he was informed that the quantities that the British Government could supply were very small, but he had no details up to the present.

PRESIDENT WILSON said he had not received his list.

4. M. CLEMENCEAU handed to Sir Maurice Hankey for translation and circulation a draft prepared by the appropriate Committee of the Conference, to Herr Brockdorff-Rantzau's letter on the subject of the Saar Valley.

5. M. CLEMENCEAU handed to Sir Maurice Hankey for translation and circulation a copy of a draft reply, prepared by the appropriate Committee of the Peace Conference to Herr Brockdorff-Rantzau's letter on the subject of reparation.

6. M. CLEMENCEAU drew attention to a Memorandum prepared by Mr. W. T. Layton,[3] of the British Delegation, and circulated at the request of Lord Robert Cecil, on the subject of the supply of Armaments to the new States of Central and Eastern Europe (Appendix II).[4]

MR. LLOYD GEORGE recalled that during the war the Ministers of Munitions used to confer together on such matters.

M. CLEMENCEAU suggested that the first step was to find out what was being done.

---

[3] Walter Thomas Layton, formerly a lecturer in economics at Cambridge University, more recently an official of the British Ministry of Munitions.

[4] W. T. Layton, "NOTE ON THE SUPPLY OF ARMAMENTS TO THE NEW STATES OF CENTRAL AND EASTERN EUROPE," T MS (SDR, RG 256, 180.03401/16, DNA), printed in *ibid.*, pp. 683-84. Layton declared that it was "extremely important" that a general policy be laid down on this subject. At present, "certain quantities" of munitions were being allocated to various nations by France on the instructions of General Foch. Beyond that, however, the various new states were applying to the Allies individually to be allowed to purchase their surplus munitions, and there was nothing except "the financial difficulty" to prevent the Allied governments from selling these surpluses while the market was "brisk." Thus far, the British War Office had supplied no arms to Europe except for "certain munitions to Russia in accordance with Allied military policy." The War Office had refused even to entertain applications for small arms in view of negotiations among the Allies for the signature of an arms convention forbidding the sale of surplus stocks of small arms. However, the convention had not yet been ratified, and it was doubtful whether any of the Allies had hitherto regarded it as limiting their dealings with European countries. The results of the current unregulated situation were likely to be that some of the new states would become militarily much stronger than others and that many of them would dissipate their financial credits in the competitive purchase of munitions at the expense of the raw materials needed to reestablish their industries. Presumably, in time, the League of Nations would deal with the question of "rationing the Armaments allowed to the various States of Europe." Meanwhile, Layton made the following recommendations:

"(a) That the Heads of States should be asked to formulate an interim policy to govern both the scale of equipment and the means by which armament is to be provided for the new States of Europe—having regard to the disarmament terms to be imposed on enemy powers and—

"(b) That the Allied and Associated Governments should undertake not to make any sales or allocations of munitions except on the authorisation of an Inter-Allied Commission to be set up with the duty of seeing that the policy laid down in (1) [a] is adhered to."

MR. LLOYD GEORGE suggested that M. Loucheur and Mr. Layton should confer on the subject.

M. CLEMENCEAU agreed.

M. ORLANDO said he would nominate a representative.

PRESIDENT WILSON said that the United States of America had not supplied any armaments, except a few to General Koltchak.

M. ORLANDO asked what the states affected were.

MR. LLOYD GEORGE suggested the Poles, Czecho-Slovaks, Roumanians, Serbo-Croats, and he added that the various nationalities formed out of Old Russia and Siberia should also be considered.

(It was agreed that M. Loucheur, Mr. W. T. Layton, and an Italian representative to be nominated by M. Orlando should report on the facts as to what supplies of armaments or munitions have been or are being sent to Poland, Czecho-Slovakia, Roumania, Serbo-Croatia, Montenegro, Greece, and the various States formed or forming out of the former Russian Empire, including Siberia.)

7. MR. LLOYD GEORGE pointed out that the reference to this Committee was closely connected with the reference to the Military Representatives at Versailles to consider the size of the military forces of the new States in connection with the Military Peace Terms of Austria and Hungary.

M. CLEMENCEAU said that this was a very difficult question, and it would be necessary in his view to secure the intervention of the League of Nations.

PRESIDENT WILSON thought it would not be very difficult to get an agreement if all the nations were included in the group.

8. Arising out of the above discussion, attention was drawn by MR. LLOYD GEORGE to reports he had received to the effect that the supplies promised to Serbia were not reaching the Serbian Army.

(At. M. Clemenceau's request, he undertook to give M. Clemenceau a memorandum on the subject.)

9. PRESIDENT WILSON said that he had seen a report in the newspapers to the effect that the Polish Diet refused the view of M. Paderewski in favour of stopping operations on the Ukraine front, as desired by the Allied and Associated Powers. M. Paderewski had refused to accept the view of the Diet, and threatened to resign. If Poland continued fighting, he thought that the representatives of Poland ought to be asked to withdraw from the Peace Conference. His information, however, was entirely derived from the newspapers.

M. CLEMENCEAU doubted if this impression was correct. He had information to the effect that the Polish orders to continue fighting had been recalled.

MR. LLOYD GEORGE read extracts from a telegram received from

General Carton de Wiart to the effect that the military preparations were too far advanced, and public opinion was too firmly set for the operations to be stopped from Poland, and that hostilities could only be brought to an end by the direct intervention of the Peace Conference.

He then read a comment by Lord Robert Cecil, suggesting that the Supreme Economic Council should on Monday inform M. Dmowski that no further supplies would be sent unless hostilities ceased.

PRESIDENT WILSON said that M. Paderewski had a letter in his possession from Mr. Hoover, informing him that aid would only be extended to Poland so long as he was in charge.[5]

MR. LLOYD GEORGE then read extracts from a letter by General Botha, Chairman of the Polish-Ukrainian Armistice Commission, who pointed out that the Supreme Council was being brought into contempt by the neglect of its decisions by the Poles, and that the League of Nations would become nugatory unless the present Conference could enforce its decisions. He pointed out that the Ukraine was the only state formed out of the old Russian Empire to whom no armaments had been supplied, though they were fighting the Bolsheviks.

M. CLEMENCEAU said that the Ukrainians were more than half Bolshevik themselves.

PRESIDENT WILSON agreed with General Botha, and pointed out the difficulty that there were no means of obtaining exact information.

---

[5] If Hoover actually wrote a letter to Paderewski containing such a warning, several scholars have failed to find it. No such letter appears in the comprehensive edition of Paderewski's political correspondence: Halina Janowska *et al.*, eds., *Archiwum Polityczne Ignacego Paderewskiego* (4 vols., Warsaw, 1973-74). However, this collection does include H. C. Hoover to I. J. Paderewski, May 6, 1919. The significant portion of its text reads as follows:

"I beg to report that, as the result of the financial negotiations initiated by you, I am able to give you the following assurances:

"1. That the finance has now been provided for imported food supplies to Poland until the next harvest.

"2. That additional finance has been provided, which enables us to make a substantial start in the shipment of cotton in order that the Polish mills may be brought into early employment.

"3. Through exchange arrangements set up, we are confident we shall be able to afford to Poland some substantial assistance for other purposes." *Ibid.*, II, 141.

Kay Lundgreen-Nielsen, *The Polish Problem at the Paris Peace Conference: A Study of the Policies of the Great Powers and the Poles, 1918-1919* (Odense, 1979), pp. 311, 545 n. 261, suggests that the above letter may have been the one that inspired Wilson's comment. That this is the case is further suggested by the reply to Hoover's letter of May 6. The significant portion of I. J. Paderewski to H. C. Hoover, May 9, 1919, reads as follows:

"I beg to thank you from the bottom of my heart for your most generous letter.

"It contains assurances of relief both for the people and their government and will but strengthen the elements of peace and order in my country.

"I could not dream of a better and more substantial assistance at this critical moment.

"The Polish people are not forgetful, their sense of gratitude is very strong and you may be certain that your thoughtfulness and generosity will always be remembered." Janowska *et al.*, *op. cit.*, II, 148.

MR. LLOYD GEORGE said that the Council of the Principal Allied and Associated Powers was carrying on temporarily, pending the formation of the League of Nations. Its orders could not be defied without weakening the League of Nations itself.

PRESIDENT WILSON said it was the Conference, rather than the League of Nations, that would be discredited. The Conference was engaged in a final settlement, rather than on these temporary disputes. The fixing of the frontier between the Ukraine and Poland was a very difficult matter.

MR. LLOYD GEORGE said that the Ukraine was willing to stop fighting, and that it was the Poles who were making the difficulty.

PRESIDENT WILSON asked if General Haller's Army was still being transported to Poland? Could the transport of the remainder be stopped? His own opinion was that if 2 Divisions had gone, that was enough for the present.

MR. LLOYD GEORGE said that M. Paderewski ought to be supported, as he was a very honest and loyal man. He should be given an intimation that if the orders of this Council were not carried out, no further support would be given. He would do this through the Foreign Ministers.

PRESIDENT WILSON said it was important not to give even a superficial idea that M. Paderewski was not being supported. He had played the game straight throughout. The message ought to be sent, not to M. Paderewski, but to General Pilsudski, the Head of the Polish State.

MR. LLOYD GEORGE asked if it was possible to address the Head of the State.

PRESIDENT WILSON said that it was.

M. CLEMENCEAU asked President Wilson to draft a despatch.

(It was agreed that President Wilson should draft for consideration a draft addressed by the Council of the Allied and Associated Powers to General Pilsudski.)

10. During the above discussion the question arose as to what was the proper designation of the Council of Four.

SIR MAURICE HANKEY reported that he had been using the term "Supreme Council of the Principal Allied and Associated Powers."

PRESIDENT WILSON demurred to the use of the word "Supreme," which some of the smaller States disliked.

(It was agreed that in any future communications the nomenclature to be adopted should be "Council of the Principal Allied and Associated Powers," but that no announcement should be made.)

11. There was a short conversation on the subject of Teschen.

PRESIDENT WILSON said that on the previous day he had seen M. Benes and M. Kramar: M. Benes had given a very intelligent and unbiassed description of the Teschen question. He had explained that the question of coal was only one part of the subject. In any case, most of the coal basin, of which the Teschen coal mines formed a part, must form part of Poland. There was an important question, however, owing to the fact that the only lines of railway running east and west in the north of Czecho-Slovakia, ran through Teschen territory.

MR. LLOYD GEORGE asked what the population was.

PRESIDENT WILSON said they had not gone into this question. M. Benes had told him it was impossible for the Poles to agree with the Czecho-Slovaks, as they had been asked to do. The reason was that in Poland it was a party question and no party could afford to give way. This was not the case in Czecho-Slovakia.

MR. LLOYD GEORGE asked if everyone there was agreed to grab all they could.

PRESIDENT WILSON said that one of the strongest arguments in favour of the Czecho-Slovaks was that this part of Teschen had been the acknowledged boundary of Bohemia in the days of the Austro-Hungarian Empire. He had received a letter from Mr. Hoover to the effect that the coal output of Teschen had been reduced owing to the uncertainties of the situation to 25% of the normal. Mr. Hoover was urging him to suggest that some temporary international management should be adopted, in order to bring the output of coal up to the normal.

12. The Council had before them Report No. 2 of the Committee on New States.[6]

PRESIDENT WILSON said that the only controversial part of the report arose in connection with Annex B, dealing with the subject of the Jewish Sabbath.[7]

(After a short discussion, the first paragraph of Annex B. was agreed to.)

(Mr. Headlam-Morley entered.)

PRESIDENT WILSON asked Mr. Headlam-Morley to give his views

[6] The Enclosure printed with D. H. Miller to WW, May 15, 1919.

[7] Mantoux, II, 92-93, adds at this point, "Wilson. . . . Another question which we have to settle is that of the rights of minorities in Poland. You recall that the point upon which our experts did not agree concerned the Sabbath. The article not yet settled would stipulate that Jews could not be forced to do anything contrary to the observance of the Sabbath and that elections could not be held on a Saturday.

"Lloyd George. The Jews form an important minority in Poland, but I would not want an article which could seem to give them a preferential right. The first part of the article raises no objection; as for the second, it could be said that, by adopting it, we would be giving Saturday rest an inviolable character which would not be given even to Sunday.

"Orlando. In Italy, as in France, elections take place on Sunday so that workers and employees can vote.

"Lloyd George. It should be recognized that there is a great deal of anti-Semitism in Poland, and that one must fear obvious maneuvers which would tend practically to exclude the Jews from the electorate."

on Annex B. He understood that he had been the supporter of this clause, and had stood alone on the Committee.

MR. HEADLAM-MORLEY said that he had conferred with representatives of the Jews on this matter. M. Lucien Wolff,[8] whom he had found to be the most moderate representative, was against the extreme claims of the Zionists, and was supported by M. Neymer[9] of the British Foreign Office. They all insisted, however, that the provisions in Annex B were of extreme importance.

PRESIDENT WILSON said that he and his colleagues were quite agreed as to the first paragraph.

MR. HEADLAM-MORLEY said the second paragraph had been suggested by Sir Esme Howard, who was himself a Roman Catholic.

PRESIDENT WILSON asked whether the object of this paragraph, which suggested that elections should not take place on a Saturday, was put in to prevent action by the Poles, which otherwise would amount to a virtual disenfranchisement of the Jews.

MR. HEADLAM-MORLEY replied that this was the case. He added that his colleagues had felt that this was rather a small matter to insert in a Treaty, and might be provided for by an exchange of Notes. In view of the great importance attached to it by the Jews, however, he, himself, had felt that he would not be doing his duty if he did not bring it before the Council.

PRESIDENT WILSON said that Mr. Miller, the American representative on the Committee, had suggested that in view of the Continental practice of holding elections on a Sunday, it would make Saturday rather more sacred than Sunday.

MR. LLOYD GEORGE suggested that arrangements might be made for the Jews to record their votes separately on another day.

MR. HEADLAM-MORLEY said he presumed an opportunity would be given to the Poles to make their comments on this matter, which was of great importance to them. He suggested that they should be given an opportunity to send a formal note on the subject, in order to place their views on record. If their note was of a favourable character, this might meet the case.

PRESIDENT WILSON thought it would not. All sorts of technical difficulties would be raised about carrying out this decision. For example, in Roumania, by a quibble over the use of the word "citizen," the Jews had, in effect, been deprived of their rights. He feared that

[8] Lucien Wolf, not Wolff, English writer, editor, and historian of Jewish subjects, an authority on anti-Semitism, president of the National Union for Jewish Rights.

[9] Actually, Lewis Bernstein Namier, Polish-born naturalized British subject, the renowned historian, at this time a member of the Political Intelligence Department of the Foreign Office.

any sanction less formal than a Treaty would be read in such a way as to render it useless. It would be said that the assurances were informal and would be got round somehow.

MR. HEADLAM-MORLEY said that the Committee had left out one clause, which the Jews had suggested, namely, that not only should they not have to work on their Sabbath, but that they should be allowed to work on the Christian Sabbath.

MR. LLOYD GEORGE thought the Committee was right in this. To allow the Jews to work on Sunday would be regarded as an unfair advantage against the Christians. Such, at any rate, was the feeling in England, as regards the opening of Jewish shops.

PRESIDENT WILSON asked whether the last word of the first paragraph should not be "Saturday" instead of "Sabbath."

MR. HEADLAM-MORLEY said that Sabbath was the correct word, but that the word before—"the"—was a misprint for "their." The report was being reprinted, as it contained several inaccuracies.

PRESIDENT WILSON said that he, personally, was converted to the inclusion of Annex B.

MR. LLOYD GEORGE said it should be submitted to the views of the Poles.

PRESIDENT WILSON said he not only had a friendly feeling towards the Jews, but he thought it was perfectly clear that one of the most dangerous elements of ferment arose from the treatment of the Jews. The fact that the Bolshevist movement had been led by the Jews was partly due to the fact that they had been treated largely as outlaws. They had no affection for a country where they were only permitted to live on tolerance, with every man's hand against them. He therefore felt it was necessary to put them on a proper footing.

MR. LLOYD GEORGE said the proper thing was to do as the Germans were doing, and make an intelligent use of the brains of the Jews. He had noticed that half the German Delegates were Jews.

M. CLEMENCEAU said that the Council ought to hear what the Poles had to say about the matter.

MR. HEADLAM-MORLEY said that the Committee had suggested that their report should be communicated officially to the Poles, and that the Committee might then be permitted to receive the Polish Delegation and discuss the matter with them. First, however, they wished to have the report approved in principle.

MR. LLOYD GEORGE urged that the report should be communicated to the Poles in Poland, as the Polish representative in Paris, M. Dmowski, did not represent the democratic opinion in Poland.

PRESIDENT WILSON suggested that the Committee should be authorised to present their report formally to the Polish Delegates in

Paris, and to discuss it with them while the report should also be transmitted to the Polish Government for observations.

MR. HEADLAM-MORLEY raised the question as to the right of appeal by minorities to the League of Nations. They thought that this right was reserved nominally only for the Governments of States. They had, nevertheless, felt that it would not be advisable that the Germans in Poland should only have the right to approach the League of Nations through the German Government.

PRESIDENT WILSON pointed out that one of the Articles of the League of Nations gave the representatives of every State the right to call attention to matters affecting the peace of the world, whether the Government was interested in them or not, and this was not to be regarded as an unfriendly act. By the application of this Article, the Jews of Poland would be able to induce their friends in other countries, such as the United States of America, Great Britain or France, to draw the attention of the League to their position. In any case, however, the League of Nations could not change the minds of the people. Dislike of the Jews in Poland would continue in spite of everything.[10]

MR. HEADLAM-MORLEY asked President Wilson's permission to send him a memorandum on this subject.

PRESIDENT WILSON said he would be glad to receive it.

MR. HEADLAM-MORLEY said he hoped that the economic and financial clauses, which were under consideration by the experts, would be ready very soon. He said that the Committee was about to proceed to its examination of the Preamble to Czecho-Slovakia.

(It was agreed:

1. To approve in principle Report No. 2 of the Committee on New States.

2. That the Committee should communicate the Report officially to the Polish Delegation in Paris, and should confer with them on the subject.

3. That the Secretary-General of the Peace Conference should telegraph the gist of the Report to the Polish Government, and invite its views.)

13. With reference to C.F.14 Minute 4,[11] PRESIDENT WILSON said that M. Vesnitch, when asked for explanation as to the reports of

---

[10] Mantoux, II, 94, attributes the above paragraph to Lloyd George, but the Editors conclude that it was Wilson's. At this point, Lloyd George, *ibid.*, speaks as follows: "We cannot allow propagandist associations and societies from all over the world to flood the League of Nations with their recriminations. The Jews, in particular, are very litigious, and, as we all know too well, unfortunately, the treaty will not make anti-Semitism disappear from Poland overnight. If the Jews of Poland could address the League of Nations directly, there would be perpetual incidents."

[11] See the minutes of the Council of Four printed at May 15, 1919, 11 a.m. (C.F.14).

maltreatment of Montenegrins by the Serbians, replied that King Nicholas was surrounded by bad people. The answer was of course totally irrelevant, since King Nicholas was in France and was not taking any part in the administration of Montenegro. He himself was very anxious to get someone to represent Montenegro at the Peace Conference.[12]

MR. LLOYD GEORGE asked what had occurred in regard to the investigations which President Wilson undertook on January 12th to make.

PRESIDENT WILSON said that the investigation had been undertaken, and that he was expecting the report in the near future.

(It was agreed to adjourn the discussion pending the receipt of the report expected by President Wilson.)

14. With reference to C.F.14 Minute 2,[13] the Council had before them the reply from the Committee composed of Mr. Barnes, Mr. Shotwell, M. Fontaine and M. G. de Grunne[14] to the question referred to them by the Council, namely, as to whether Germany should be admitted to the Labour Organisation before she is admitted to the League of Nations (Appendix III).[15]

MR. LLOYD GEORGE expressed agreement in the report of the Committee.

M. CLEMENCEAU also expressed himself in favour of the proposal that Germany should be admitted immediately after the Washington Conference.

PRESIDENT WILSON agreed, but suggested that it would be preferable to send it to the Washington Conference with a recommendation in its favour.

(It was agreed that the accompanying letter should be remitted to

[12] Mantoux, II, 94-95: "Wilson. One question remaining in suspense is the one of the representation of Montenegro in the negotiations with Austria. Each time I complain to the Serbs about their behavior regarding Montenegro, they reply to me that the King of Montenegro is a scoundrel. If this fact is admitted, it is still true that the Serbs have acted brutally toward Montenegro, arrested some important people, etc., and that adds to our uncertainty about the part that we must take."

[13] See the minutes cited in n. 11 above.

[14] (Victor) Arthur (Léon) Fontaine, Director of Labor in the French Ministry of Labor and Social Security and a technical expert on labor questions in the French delegation, and Count Guillaume de Hemricourt de Grunne, who held the rank of Secretary of Legation in the Belgian foreign service and was a member of the secretariat of the Belgian delegation.

[15] G. N. Barnes et al. to P. E. Dutasta, May 15, 1919, TCL (SDR, RG 256, 180.03401/16, DNA), printed in PPC, V, 684-85. The committee recommended that Germany should enjoy "early participation" in the International Labour Organization, even if she was not allowed initially to join the League of Nations. This was advisable to insure that Germany would be under the same obligations to organized labor as the other advanced industrial countries. The committee suggested that Germany not be admitted to the labor organization in time to attend the initial conference in Washington, since her presence there might create confusion and dissension. However, she should be admitted to membership immediately after the Washington conference and should be entitled to a place on the governing body of the organization.

the Washington Conference with a favourable recommendation from the Council of the principal Allied and Associated Powers. Sir Maurice Hankey was instructed to communicate in this sense with the Secretary-General of the Peace Conference.)

15. At the end of the Meeting a telephone message was received from the Secretariat-General to the effect that Herr Brockdorff-Rantzau was leaving for Spa this evening to confer with his Government and intended to return by Monday evening, May 19th.

16. With reference to C.F.13.A., Minute 8,[16] the following decision was approved as carrying out the intention of the Council and was initialled by M. Clemenceau, President Wilson, Mr. Lloyd George and M. Orlando.

(It was agreed that the Drafting Committee of the Peace Conference shall not accept any decisions of the Council of the Principal Allied and Associated Powers which does not bear the initials of M. Clemenceau, President Wilson, Mr. Lloyd George and M. Orlando. Sir Maurice Hankey was instructed to communicate this decision to the Secretary-General for the information of the Drafting Committee.)

17. At Mr. Lloyd George's request it was agreed to hear the Indian Delegation in the afternoon at 4.30 p.m.

T MS (SDR, RG 256, 180.03401/16, DNA).

[16] See the minutes of the Council of Four printed at May 14, 1919, 4 p.m.

Hankey's Notes of a Meeting of the Council of Four[1]

President Wilson's House,
C.F.17   Paris, May 17, 1919, 4:15 p.m.

1. M. CLEMENCEAU said that he and his colleagues had been considering the action of the Italian Government in landing forces at Scala Nuova and other places on the Coast of Asia Minor, without consulting them. They had prepared a document which was not being reproduced, and which he would hand to M. Orlando. He then made a statement identical with the document. (Appendix 1.)

M. ORLANDO said that on the day when his colleagues had announced to him the decision to disembark forces at Smyrna, Mr. Lloyd George had asked for details of the Italian landings elsewhere, and he had replied he knew very little about them, which was the absolute truth. He had then said he would consult Baron Sonnino. On the same afternoon, he had visited Mr. Lloyd George at his flat, and Baron Sonnino had explained that those landings were carried out for dealing with disorders that had arisen. Nothing more had been said on the matter, which he had presumed to be disposed of. He would receive the communication which his colleagues had to make to him, and would discuss it with Baron Sonnino.

MR. LLOYD GEORGE said that on the previous occasion when this subject had been raised, all that had been heard of was a landing to repair a pier at Scala Nuova, after which, the Italian forces had been re-embarked. This fresh news, however, was of a far more formidable nature, since 500 troops were reported to have been landed, the Italian flag had been hoisted, the Customs House occupied, and some of the troops pushed some distance inland. The occupation of Marmarice had only been reported by the Italian fleet, but these last reports were of definite landings. Moreover, they had occurred at a time when the three principal Powers associated with Italy had expressed themselves rather opposed to Scala Nuova being in the Italian sphere, and in favour of it being in the Greek sphere. It had been a subject of discussion and no final decision had been taken. It was in this state of affairs that the Italian landing had taken place. In such conditions, it was difficult to take a decision in regard to Asia Minor or anywhere else. If such a thing were to happen in any dispute between France and Great Britain, it would create a most difficult situation. What he specially regretted was that this action tended to prejudice a discussion which he had thought was going very well. He and his colleagues had been sincerely anxious to meet the views of Italy as far as they could, and he thought it was a very grave matter that this action should be taken, as it were, to jump the claim, when the matter was under discussion.

M. ORLANDO said he quite understood the feelings of Mr. Lloyd George, and thought, giving the interpretation placed by him on this action by Italy, that he was dissatisfied. He, himself, had not the intention which Mr. Lloyd George had suggested, and he deplored it. He had believed this landing to be merely a repetition of the same sort of thing as had occurred before, namely, a disembarkation to meet some local difficulty. He did not know of any serious landing of any considerable forces. He knew nothing of the landing of troops, the seizure of the Customs House, or the hoisting of the Italian flag, in fact, he had believed this to be a landing without any intention of prejudicing the future disposition of this territory. It was necessary, however, to preserve respect for each other's opinions, and he repeated that he would study the memorandum and take whatever dispositions were necessary.

MR. LLOYD GEORGE said that he would like to add that he and his colleagues had deliberately kept Greek troops away from Scala Nuova, because they thought it would be unfair to Italy for them to land while the question was sub judice.

(At the end of the meeting, the memorandum was communicated to M. Orlando.)

2. PRESIDENT WILSON said he had received a report of a great victory by General Denekin on the Czaritzen front.[2] He claimed to have captured 10,000 prisoners, 128 [120] machine guns, and 28 field guns, which ought to account for a large part of the Bolshevist forces on this front.

MR. LLOYD GEORGE said that coming at the same time as the capture of Samara by Koltchak, this was news of great importance.

SIR MAURICE HANKEY called attention to the expression of opinion by the Foreign Ministers that the Council of the Principal Allied and Associated Powers should consider the question of policy towards Russia.

PRESIDENT WILSON said he had communicated with the United States Ambassador at Tokio, in order to arrange for the despatch of Mr. Morris as promised.

(At this point the Council adjourned to the room upstairs, in order to hear the Indian Delegation, which is dealt with separately in a stenographic report. On the withdrawal of the Indian Delegation there was some conversation in regard to mandates in Asia Minor.)

3. MR. LLOYD GEORGE said that he was much impressed by the accumulating evidence of the unrest that would be caused in the Moslem world by the removal of the Sultan from Constantinople. Neither Great Britain nor France, as great Mohammedan Powers, could afford this unrest, and neither could the United States, if she was about to become a Mohammedan Power. If the Turkish capital were removed to Brussa and the Sultan with the Khalifate was established there, there would always be ferment and intrigue. He, himself, was in favour of keeping the Khalifate at Constantinople. The United States of America, the probable mandatory of Constantinople and the Straits, could be relied on to be absolutely impartial. He felt himself more or less pledged by the declaration he had made on behalf of the Turkish Government. M. Clemenceau had sent him a telegram approving this declaration.

M. CLEMENCEAU said he could not recall it.

MR. LLOYD GEORGE said he would let M. Clemenceau have a copy. The British Empire had nearly a million men fighting the Turks when no-one else had had more than two thousand. He asked his colleagues to consider the desirability of keeping the Khalifate at Constantinople.

APPENDIX TO C.F.17.[3]

The President of the United States and the Prime Ministers of France and Great Britain have been told that Italian troops have occupied Scala Nuova, landing sailors and marines, taking charge of the customs house, and hoisting the Italian colours. They would be very much obliged if the Prime Minister of Italy would inform them as to whether this statement is correct and if so as to the reasons which have influenced him in taking this action without giving his colleagues any previous intimation of the intentions of the Italian Government. They are the more anxious as this landing has been preceded by other landings at Adalia, Marmarice and Budrum about which they have also not been consulted. They would point out that they have never taken any action in Turkey without previous consultation with their Italian colleague. In the case of the recent Greek landing at Smyrna they discussed the proposal with him before orders were given for a single Greek detachment to leave the shores of Greece and Signor Orlando himself agreed to the expedition and to a joint Allied landing to secure the forts. They also feel bound to express their astonishment at the action of the Italian authorities, if it is true, in view of the fact that M. Clemenceau had informed Signor Orlando on Thursday last that, in the opinion of the majority of his colleagues on the Council of Four, Scala Nuova ought not to be included in an Italian sphere of influence in Asia Minor. They would be much obliged if Signor Orlando could give them full information in regard to this matter as they feel it is impossible for the Council of Four to attempt to deal with the problems of the near East if one of its members persistently takes action on its own account without previously consulting the other members.

17 May, 1919.

T MS (SDR, RG 256, 180.03401/17, DNA).
[1] The complete text of these minutes is printed in *PPC*, V, 686-89.
[2] A dispatch from Rear Adm. Mark Lambert Bristol of May 14, 1919, embodied in J. C. Frémont to C. T. Grayson, May 15, 1919, TS MS (WP, DLC). Wilson paraphrases the entire dispatch.
[3] There is a CC MS of this letter, dated May 17, 1919, in WP, DLC.

Two Letters to Herbert Clark Hoover

My dear Hoover: Paris, 17 May, 1919.

Thank you for sending me the copy of the reply of the Bolshevik Government to Dr. Nansen's proposals and also for your promise to let me have a comprehensive memorandum of your own views about the Russian situation.[1]

Cordially and faithfully yours,   Woodrow Wilson

[1] Wilson was replying to HCH to WW, May 16, 1919.

My dear Hoover: Paris, 17 May, 1919.

Thank you for sending me your suggestions with regard to a plan for the financial rehabilitation of Europe.[1] I shall read it with the greatest interest.

Cordially and faithfully yours,   Woodrow Wilson

TLS (Hoover Archives, CSt-H).
    [1] Wilson apparently thought that Hoover had drafted the Enclosure printed with T. W. Lamont to WW, May 15, 1919.

From Bernard Mannes Baruch, with Enclosure

My dear Mr. President: Paris, May 17, 1919.

I enclose herewith copy of the military proposal for the government of the Rhineland provinces during the fifteen years' occupation period. This matter has been under discussion by Messrs. McCormick, Legge, Davis, Robinson, Hoover and myself, and they have asked me to drop you a preliminary note on the subject with the hope that we may have an opportunity of further discussion with you before any action is taken.

Without going into the details of the matter, it amounts to the creation of an effectual military government over practically all aspects of the economic, political and civil life in the Rhine provinces, and is in our belief a proposition for which the United States cannot under any possible circumstances be associated with.

It seems to us fundamental that the normal political and economic life of this territory must proceed as an integral part of Germany and that so far as there is any interference necessary, that interference should be in the hands of a civilian commission, appointed by the four governments concerned; that the military authority should have no relationship whatever to economic or other matters except through such a civilian commission. Of course, if a military situation arose that required military action, and such military action was approved by the four governments, then, no doubt, this civilian commission would have to step into the background; in other words, that the military forces in occupation of the Rhine provinces should have no more relationship to the government of the civilian population in the Rhine provinces than they have to the civilian populations of any other countries.

We cannot emphasize too strongly that we find this proposal, as here outlined, little short of monstrous.

Very sincerely yours,   [B. M. Baruch]

CCL (B. M. Baruch Papers, NjP).

E N C L O S U R E

Supreme War Council,   SECRET.
  Military Representatives.   VERSAILLES, 11th May, 1919.

DRAFT CONVENTION REGARDING THE MILITARY OCCUPATION OF THE TERRITORIES WEST OF THE RHINE.

(NOTE): The use of the terms "Allies" and "Allied" throughout this document must be interpreted to mean "the Allied and/or Associated Powers.")

I. As provided by Section XIV of the present Treaty armed forces of the Allies, will continue in occupation of German territory (as defined by Article 5 of the Armistice of the 11th November, 1918, as extended by Article 7 of the Convention of the 16th of January, 1919)* as a guarantee of the due execution of the provisions of the present Treaty.

No German troops, except prisoners of war in process of repatriation, shall be admitted to the occupied territory even in transit; but after the evacuation by successive stages of such territory police forces of a strength to be determined by the Allied Powers may be admitted for the purpose of maintaining order.

II. *Jurisdiction—*

(a) The existing state of Martial Law with all its consequences shall be maintained in these territories by the Allied military authorities, who shall have the supreme control of the police.

(b) The German courts shall continue to exercise civil and criminal jurisdiction subject to the exceptions contained in paragraphs (c) and (d) below.

(c) The armed forces of the Allies and the persons accompanying them, to whom the General Officers Commanding the armies of occupation shall have issued a pass revocable at their pleasure, and any persons employed by, or in the service of such troops, shall be exclusively subject to the military law and jurisdiction of such forces.

(d) Any foreigner, or any German national, who commits any offence against the armed forces of the Allies, or against any person attached to such forces as defined in the sub-section (c), shall be amenable to the military jurisdiction of the said forces.

III. (a) Any person as defined in Section 2(c) who is accused or guilty of desertion or any offence and who shall pass over from any Allied Army to the German side or who shall take refuge in German territory shall be arrested immediately by German authorities and delivered up to the nearest Commander of Allied Troops.

---

*Proposed by British Military Representative, demurred to by American Military Representative, accepted by French and Italian Military Representatives.

(b) Any person of any nationality accused or guilty of an offence committed in occupied territory who shall take refuge in unoccupied German territory shall be arrested immediately by the German authorities and delivered up to the nearest Commander of Allied troops.

IV. *Administration.*

The civil administration of the provinces ("Provinzen"), Governmental Departments ("Regierungsbezirke"), urban circles ("Stadtkreise"), rural circles ("Landkreise"), and communes ("Gemeinde"), shall remain in the hands of the German authorities under the control of the Allied command. All German administrative authorities shall be obliged to conform to any measures which the General Officers in command of the Allied forces shall consider it necessary to take in the interest of the security, maintenance and distribution of the troops. They shall in particular be entitled to remove any officials whose action may be deemed hostile, and not to accept without enquiry officials coming from the unoccupied or occupied parts of Germany. They shall, moreover, have a vote on all legislation, industrial regulations, awards or agreements, for the purpose of eliminating any such as may be considered dangerous to public order and the security of the armies.

Civil officials shall be attached to the general officers commanding the Allied troops, or appointed to act in conjunction with them whenever the latter may deem it expedient; those civil officials will be placed under the authority of the officers commanding the Allied troops in their respective zones, and will have the direction of such civil matters as may concern the Allied military interests within those zones. The German authorities shall be obliged to conform to any measures which these officials may deem it necessary to take for this purpose.

V. *Requisition.*

The right to requisition, including personnel and material, shall be exercised by the Allied armies of occupation. The charges for the requisition effected in the zone of each Allied army, and the estimate of damages caused by the troops of occupation, shall be determined by local commissions composed both of German civilians appointed by the Allied military authorities on the proposal of the German civil authorities and of Allied military officers, and presided over by an Allied general officer or Field officer.

The German Government shall also continue to be responsible for the maintenance of the troops of occupation upon the same footing as before the coming into force of the present Treaty. In the event of the German Government failing to observe its obligations in either of these respects, the Allied troops shall be entitled to procure what is necessary for their requirements by levying taxes and contributions in the occupied territories.

VI. The Allied troops shall continue undisturbed in the possession of any premises at present occupied by them. They shall have the right to enter without payment on any land or into any building, and to take possession thereof, or to construct any buildings when it shall be necessary for the accommodation of troops or for securing the safety of the same, and do any other act involving the interference with State or private rights of property which may be necessary for these purposes.

VII. (a) The German Government shall undertake, moreover, to place at the disposal of the Allied troops and to maintain in good state of repair, all the military establishments required for the said troops, with the necessary furniture, heating and lighting, in accordance with the regulations concerning those matters in force in the various armies concerned. These shall include accommodation for officers and men, guardrooms, offices, administrative, regimental and staff headquarters, workshops, storerooms, hospitals, laundries, regimental schools, riding schools, stables, training grounds and rifle and artillery ranges, grazing grounds, ground for agricultural training, warehouses for supplies and grounds for military maneuvres, also theatre and cinema premises and reasonable facilities for sport and recreation grounds for the troops.

(b) In the event of the existing military establishments being insufficient or not being considered suitable, the Allied troops may take possession of any other public or private establishment, with its personnel,* suitable for those purposes and billet officers and men, and also their families upon the inhabitants on the basis of the billeting regulations in force in the respective armies. No payment will be made in respect of the matters dealt with in this article.

VIII. Supplies, arms, clothing, equipment and stores of any kind destined for the use of the Allied armies and consigned to the military authorities or to civil authorities attached thereto, or to canteens, officers' messes, individual officers and soldiers, etc., shall be carriage free and subject to no import or excise duty of any description (customs, octroi, etc.).

No German taxes will be payable by Allied armies on their personnel.

IX. The personnel employed on all means of communication, railways, railroads and tramways of all kinds, waterways, including the Rhine, roads and rivers, shall remain under the control of the Commander-in-Chief of the Allied armies.

*Baths, washing places, hotels, etc.

The Commander-in-Chief shall continue to exercise his authority through the intermediary of the Commission for Field Railways and Navigation (Commission de chemin de fer de compagne et de navigation de compagne) which will constitute bodies for supervision and control of the management and operation of communications ensured by the competent German authorities.

The Allied troops shall have the right of requisition in all matters concerning the transport of troops, war material and military supplies, or concerning the postal service and the carriage of staff or material connected with the administrative services. All rolling stock and means of river transport demanded for this purpose by the Allied troops shall be furnished free of charge. Priority shall be given to the demands of the Allied authorities, who may fix the place of entraining and detraining and the routes of the trains. All civil personnel and materials now employed on the maintenance and operation of all the lines of communication shall be maintained in full on those lines in the occupied territories. Officers and soldiers shall be carried free on all occasions on all public tramways.

X. The armies of occupation shall continue to use undisturbed all existing telegraph and telephonic installations, which shall not be allowed to suffer any deterioration. The armies of occupation shall also have the right to continue to instal and use military telegraph and telephone lines, wireless stations and all other similar means of communication which may appear to them expedient; for this purpose they may enter upon and occupy any land, whether public or private. No wireless work shall be carried out within the occupied area without the permission of the general officers commanding the armies of occupation. The personnel of the public telegraph and telephone services shall continue to be under the authority of the commander-in-chief of the Allied armies as regards the execution of their duties, which may be carried out according to the German system, but the Allied military authorities shall have the right to exercise censorship over the telegrams and messages despatched and to supervise the order in which such communications are transmitted. Allied telegrams and messages of an official nature shall be entitled to priority over all other communications and shall be despatched free of charge.

XI. The personnel of the postal service shall continue to be under the authority of the commander-in-chief of the Allied armies as regards the execution of their duties. The public postal service shall continue to be carried out by the German authorities, but this shall not in any way effect [affect] the retention of the military postal services organised by the armies of occupation, who shall have the right to use all existing postal routes for military requirements. The said armies shall have the right to run postal wagons with all necessary personnel on all existing postal routes, and the cost of these services shall be borne by the German Government. The German Government shall transmit free of charge and without examination letters and parcels which may be entrusted to its post offices by or on behalf of the armies of occupation, and shall be responsible for the value of any letters or parcels lost or stolen in the post.

The Allied authorities shall have the right to exercise censorship of letters and full control over the German postal service.

XII. In all matters not covered by the preceding articles the rules and principles laid down in the Hague Regulations of 1907 respecting the laws and customs of war on land shall apply.

GNL. BELIN,[1]
Military
    Representative,
    French Section
Supreme War
    Council.

C. SACKVILLE-WEST,[2]
Major-General,
Military
    Representative,
British Section,
Supreme War Council.

UGO CAVALLERO,
Military
    Representative,
Italian Section,
Supreme War
    Council.

P. D. LOCHRIDGE
Military
    Representative,
American Section,
Supreme War Council.

G. VAN EGROO.[3]
(Belgium)

T MS (WP, DLC).
    [1] Émile Eugène Belin.
    [2] Charles John Sackville-West.
    [3] Capt. Commandant G. van Egroo, member of the Belgian Army General Staff and technical expert on military questions in the Belgian delegation.

From William Christian Bullitt

My dear Mr. President: [Paris] May 17, 1919.

I have submitted today to the Secretary of State my resignation as an Assistant in the Department of State, Attache to the American Commission to Negotiate Peace. I was one of the millions who trusted confidently and implicitly in your leadership and believed that you would take nothing less than "a permanent peace" based upon "unselfish and unbiased justice." But our Government has consented now to deliver the suffering peoples of the world to new oppressions, subjections and dismemberments—a new century of war. And I can convince myself no longer that effective labor for "a new world order" is possible as a servant of this Government.

Russia, "the acid test of good will," for me as for you, has not even been understood. Unjust decisions of the Conference in regard to Shantung, the Tyrol, Thrace, Hungary, East Prussia, Danzig, the Saar Valley; and the abandonment of the principle of the Freedom of the Seas make new international conflicts certain. It is my conviction that the present League of Nations will be powerless to prevent these wars, and that the United States will be involved in them by the obligations undertaken in the Covenant of the League and in the special understanding with France. Therefore, the duty of the Government of the United States to its own people and to mankind is to refuse to sign or ratify this unjust Treaty, to refuse to guarantee its settlements by entering the League of Nations, to refuse to entangle the United States further by the understanding with France.

That you personally opposed most of the unjust settlements, and that you accepted them only under great pressure, is well known. Nevertheless, it is my conviction that if you had made your fight in the open, instead of behind closed doors, you would have carried with you the public opinion of the world, which was yours; you would have been able to resist the pressure and might have established the "new international order based upon broad and universal principles of right and justice" of which you used to speak. I am sorry that you did not fight our fight to the finish and that you had so little faith in the millions of men, like myself, in every nation who had faith in you.   Very sincerely yours,   William C. Bullitt.

TLS (WP, DLC).

From Vance Criswell McCormick, with Enclosure

My dear Mr. President: Paris. May 17, 1919.

I think that the enclosed cablegram is an important one, and needs immediate attention. We have had similar information from a number of different directions, and it looks to me as though it may be possible that the removal of General Graves might relieve the friction which apparently exists and harmonize the situation.

In view of the proposed visit of Morris, I thought that you might want to have him investigate the situation and make you a report.

                Very sincerely yours,   Vance C. McCormick

TLS (WP, DLC).

E N C L O S U R E

Washington. May 9th, 1919.

1920. Highly confidential.

For Secretary of State and McCormick.

Secretary of War has shown me General Graves' telegram No. 281, May 4th,[1] which he transmitted to President with recommendation that forces in Siberia must co-operate with Kolchak or be withdrawn.

I have told the Russian Chargé d'Affaires[2] here that the Omsk military authorities must continue on friendly terms with the American troops and General Graves in Siberia at all costs and that their failure to do so might well lead to a collapse of the railway plan and seriously weaken the prospects of the Omsk Government itself. I put this very emphatically to the Chargé d'Affaires and suggested he might think it advisable to inform the Omsk Government and the Russian representatives at Paris accordingly.

From previous telegrams you have seen the gradual development of what has become a dangerous situation in Eastern Siberia. This has been due primarily to the character of the instructions issued to General Graves which he has interpreted as requiring a rigid and aloof neutrality on his part. The British are concerned by the claim General Graves has announced categorically that so far as his troops are concerned in guarding the railway he is responsible to his Government and to no one else and will not consider orders from the Japanese commander or the railway committee. I understand confidentially the British military authorities in Siberia have told General Graves that in view of their own specific instructions to support the Kolchak Government, they find it difficult to maintain relations with him at all if he considers himself required to keep altogether aloof from Kolchak commander. Secretary of War has been kind enough to show me some of General Graves' written reports to the War Department which to my mind show that he has been, to say the least, tactless in his dealings with the Japanese military commander and, further, that his views of the situation in some instances seem based entirely upon the opinions he has formed as a result of the arbitrary and stupid conduct of General Ivanoff *Rigsbyff* [Rinov] and the bu[c]caneering of the Cossack leaders Kalmikoff and Semenoff. Government officers understand one of the results is that the British regard him as apparently sympathizing with the Bolsheviks rather than with the Omsk authorities.

The American command in Siberia has always required a high degree of tact and large experience in affairs. I cannot help thinking that, in spite of the narrow limitations set by his instructions, General Graves has proved lacking in both these qualifications. I am quite confident that if we decide not to recognize the Omsk Government or determine not to give that government open support, General Graves will be unable to continue to command without open rupture either with the Russians or the Japanese or possibly with both.

I hope you will find it possible to discuss this matter with the President and Mr. Lloyd George and reach some common agreement as to our future course in Siberia. As you know I am in the meanwhile trying to persuade the Japanese to the idea that the railway plan has altogether changed the situation since we sent our combined forces to rescue the Czechs and steady the Russians; that everybody's business now is to restore the railways and emphasize the economic and constructive character of our undertaking and make the military side of it altogether subordinate.

Even if I succeed with the Japanese I still think that first, the matter of coming to a common understanding with the British Government is absolutely necessary, and second, that if we do not somehow relieve the situation in which General Graves finds himself, our policy in Siberia will prove a total failure just at the moment when it seems to promise real success.   Polk,   Acting.

T telegram (WP, DLC).
   [1] See the Enclosure printed with THB to WW, May 9, 1919, Vol. 58.
   [2] That is, Serge Ughet.

From Vance Criswell McCormick, with Enclosure

My dear Mr. President: Paris. May 17, 1919.

I am enclosing a cablegram along the lines of our discussion yesterday, which I thought might interest you.
                Very sincerely yours,   Vance C. McCormick

TLS (WP, DLC).

ENCLOSURE

Washington, May 14, 1919.

1965. Following from Ambassador Morris:

"May 13, 1:00 p.m. Russian Ambassador[1] has informed me that Ivanoff-Rinoff has been recalled by the Kolchak Government, claims being in my opinion a victory for general fusion which might form one of the grounds for recognition of the Omsk Government."

You will recall that Ivanoff-Rinoff was the Russian Commander in

Eastern Siberia who has been responsible for arbitrary and reactionary policies which have been so much complained of by American Representatives and liberal Russians.   Polk,   Acting.

T telegram (WP, DLC).
    [1] That is, Vasilii Nikolaevich Krupenskii.

Vance Criswell McCormick to Frank Lyon Polk

[Paris] 17th May 1919.

2150. Very confidential to Polk from McCormick.

With the concurrence of Secretary Lansing I submitted to the President the telegram given below proposed to be sent to you. The President has replied to me as follows: "I am quite willing that the enclosed should be sent to Polk but beg that you will ask him to consider it in the light of my recent instructions to Morris at Tokio."[1]

The telegram submitted to the President and referred to in his reply above quoted is as follows: "Departments one eight seven seven, May 6, 8 P.M.[2] The President approves of the communication to Koltchak, in such manner as the Department may think best, of a statement substantially as follows: the Government of the United States, animated by a desire to see established in Russia a government responsive to the will of the people which will maintain domestic tranquility and friendly and orderly relations with foreign states, has carefully and sympathetically noted the efforts of the organization headed by Admiral Koltchak to attain this result. The Government of the United States is not disposed to recognize any government in Russia which has assumed and is exercising power without the sanction of the Russian people freely given. The Government of the United States recognizes that conditions in Siberia may now be suitable for an expression of the will of the people and in the event of the securing of an expression of the popular will in favor of a government which satisfies the conditions above referred to, the government of the United States would take under favorable and sympathetic consideration, in the light of the then situation, the question of recognizing such a government as a de facto government of such portions of Russia as might then or thereafter be under its actual control with the consent of the peoples governed."[3]

Ammission

T telegram (WP, DLC).
    [1] That is, WW to FLP, May 14, 1919.
    [2] That is, FLP to the American Commissioners, May 6, 1919, Vol. 58.
    [3] There is a draft, verbatim, of the quoted portion of the final paragraph of this telegram in the V. C. McCormick Papers, CtY.

A Memorandum by Ellis Loring Dresel

MEMORANDUM

URGENT   Paris, May 17, 1919.

Referring to Mr. Dresel's memorandum of May 14th,[1] relative to an interview between himself and M. Dutasta, Mr. Dresel again saw M. Dutasta on May 16th. M. Dutasta stated that he had mentioned the subject of an interview with Count Brockdorff-Rantzau to M. Clemenceau, who had said that his personal opinion was that the Germans were so depressed that any attempt to approach them at the present moment would be useless. However, if the President and the American Commission thought otherwise, no objection of any kind would be interposed. M. Clemenceau expected to see the President at eleven o'clock on Saturday, and any intimation from the latter in favor of the step proposed would meet with his immediate acceptance.

In this connection, attention is drawn to a telephonic communication received by the Commission at 12:30 on Friday from Treves according to which Minister Erzberger had telephoned to Treves that it would be extremely desirable that Mr. Dresel should return at once to Germany. A possible explanation of the message (which is assumed to be genuine) may be found in the theory that Erzberger's relations with Rantzau are very strained, and Erzberger is convinced that the time has come for an entire reconstitution of the Ministry. It is even possible that, being a notorious compromiser and opportunist, he may be planning a union with the Independent Socialists, and an acceptance of the peace terms, and is looking for moral support from the United States in this undertaking.

RECOMMENDATIONS.

It is submitted that an informal interview or interviews with Count Rantzau might be of real value at the present moment. If this view is adopted, M. Clemenceau should be so informed at once.

It is believed that an immediate compliance with Erzberger's request is not advisable, as it might indicate undue anxiety on our part that peace should be signed, and as it might constitute an undesirable interference in a German cabinet quarrel. It is believed that in any event, it would be advisable to approach Rantzau first.

It is recommended that the enclosed telegram to Mr. Dyar,[2] who is in charge of the press work in Berlin and is entirely responsible, be sent (a) if Mr. Dresel's proposed interview with Count Rantzau be disapproved, (b) if after such interview, if approved, it seems unnecessary or undesirable that Mr. Dresel should proceed at once to Germany.

Specific instructions at the earliest possible moment will be greatly appreciated.

Please read this before you meet this morning & let us know. E.M.H.[3]

T MS (WP, DLC).
  [1] It is printed at May 14, 1919.
  [2] Actually, E. L. Dresel to G. H. Harries, May 17, 1919, T MS (WP, DLC). Dresel requested that Harries instruct Charles Bowker Dyar to arrange an interview for himself with Matthias Erzberger "in order to confirm authenticity of request, to ascertain reasons and if possible summary of Erzberger's views on situation." On receipt of Dyar's report, Dresel would consider departure for Berlin if it seemed desirable.
  [3] EMHhw.

From Edwin Samuel Montagu

Very private and confidential.

Dear President Wilson,   Paris. 17th May 1919.

At the last moment as we were going out this afternoon[1] you used the word "mandate" as applied to Turkey. My Mahomedan friends would hate a mandatory because they would be so suspicious that it was disguised annexation. But their attitude of hostility would be largely modified if the mandatory were a country of undoubted integrity and disinterestedness with a length of purse and the capacity to assist the Turk to restart life.

If the mandatory were the Italians, who annexed Tripoli after an unprovoked war and have never succeeded in restoring it to order and who have no money with which to develop Turkey, nothing will convince the Mahomedans that this is not annexation. There would not be a single Turk who would welcome the "friend" appointed to assist her by the League of Nations. The whole mandatory principle throughout the world would be vitiated.

If, however, the mandatory were the Americans, with whom she has never fought, whose history is known in the Philippines, whose disinterestedness is beyond dispute—that would be a different matter altogether.

I was a little inclined to think this afternoon that my friends emphasised too much the Turkishness of Constantinople. As a matter of fact, although the Turks are the largest block of the population, they are not in an absolute majority. But curiously enough the same is true, according to American figures, of the Greeks and Smyrna, and although the Mahomedans will of course resent the loss either of Constantinople or Smyrna, the arguments which give Smyrna to the Greeks make it absolutely imperative for leaving Constantinople to the Turks.

Forgive this note of explanation. We felt that we had taken up too much of your time for me to emphasise these points this afternoon.

Yours sincerely,   Edwin S. Montagu

TLS (WP, DLC).
¹ That is, at the conclusion of the meeting of the Council of Four held at 4:30 p.m. on May 17, 1919, about which see n. 1 to the extract from the Diary of Dr. Grayson printed at this date.

Arthur Hugh Frazier to Edward Mandell House, with Enclosure

My dear Colonel House,   Paris, May 17, 1919.

Professor P. M. Brown has just returned from Budapest where for the past three months he has acted as political observer for the American Peace Delegation. He has furnished me with an interesting oral report of the present situation of Hungary and of the Bela Kun Government. I feel that it might be of importance for the President to hear Professor Brown in this connection, especially in view of the urgency of taking measures to bring about the establishment of a firm and responsible government at Budapest with which the Allies may negotiate peace. Professor Brown, formerly of the American Diplomatic Service, is now Professor of International Law at Princeton University.

Sincerely yours,   Arthur Hugh Frazier.

TLS (WP, DLC).

E N C L O S U R E

A Memorandum by Philip Marshall Brown

THE HUNGARIAN SITUATION

The "Dictatura of the Proletariat" is most unpopular. Even the workingmen are dissatisfied.

The practical application of Socialist theories has resulted in gross abuses, great injustice, some excesses, and general terrorism.

The Red Guard are learning how to convert official perquisitions into pillage. Political suspects are treated as hostages. There have been summary executions of hostages by irresponsible bands of terrorists. The President of the last Hungarian Parliament was recently murdered in a most brutal way.¹

Kun Bela and his Government seem genuinely anxious to avoid excesses and Bolshevist methods, but incapable of controlling the forces they have let loose.

The Government was endeavoring to get rid of the extreme Communists and form a transition Government of Social Democrats. The Rumanian advance made this impossible and stimulated the extremists to fanaticism. The failure of the Rumanians to continue their advance has had the effect of leaving the terrorists a free hand to take vengeance on alleged counter-revolutionists and on "bourgeois" hostages.

A reformation of the Government of Kun Bela now seems quite impossible.

This Government can in no way be said to represent the people of Hungary. It would be cynical to invite that Government to sign the treaty of peace on behalf of Hungary.

The intrigues of the Italians to get a foothold in Budapest and Hungary should be circumvented immediately in order to avoid serious complications.

Recommendations.

1. Military intervention is now the only solution. It would be a simple undertaking as there would be no serious resistance. The great mass of the people, including the majority of the socialists themselves, would welcome intervention.

Kun Bela and his associates constantly are asking that the Entente should let them know clearly what is required. I believe that they would yield to the clear imperative demands of the Entente.

Hungary is drifting into anarchy on account of the failure of the Entente to formulate its policy.

The French at Belgrade are quite ready to occupy Budapest and the rest of the country. They claim to have the troops necessary. I do not think it a formidable undertaking in any way.

2. At the same moment that the French take charge of military occupation, a political mission should be sent in under the head preferably of a man like General Smuts.

This mission should ensure the establishment of a moderate government capable of signing and executing the terms of the proposed treaty. Probably nobody would be better suited than General Smuts for this distasteful task.   Philip M. Brown

T MS (WP, DLC).

[1] Brown was misinformed, at least as to exactly who may have been murdered. The president of the last Hungarian Chamber of Deputies under the old regime, at the time of its dissolution on November 16, 1918, was Károly Szász, who died in 1950.

Two Memoranda by John Charles Frémont for Cary Travers Grayson

Paris 17 May, 1919.

MEMORANDUM for Naval Aid to the President:

In accordance with my telephone conversation with you this morning, I am transmitting herewith a communication from Rear Admiral Andrews, Commander U. S. Naval Forces Eastern Mediterranean, regarding a law passed by the City Council of Fiume, making it treason to do anything to make Fiume Jugo-Slav.[1]

It is requested that, when the President has seen this communication, it be returned to this office in order that the Chief of Naval Operations may see it.   J. C. Frémont   By direction.

[1] P. Andrews to W. S. Benson, May 14, 1919, TLS (WP, DLC). Andrews enclosed A. Bakarcić to [P. Andrews], May 12, 1919, ALS; A. Bakarcić to WW, n.d., T telegram; and an undated clipping from the Fiume *La Bilancia*, all in WP, DLC. Andrews' letter and the two communications from Bakarcić, written on behalf of Croatian residents of Fiume, attacked the so-called "law" of March 27, 1919, the full text of which appeared in the newspaper clipping. The Fiume Municipal Council on October 29, 1918, had transformed itself into an organization called the Italian National Council of Fiume, and it was this latter body which had adopted the "law" of March 27, 1919. As Frémont indicates in the above memorandum, the "law" made it a treasonable act, punishable by several years of imprisonment, to do anything to separate Fiume from Italy.

Paris 17 May, 1919.

MEMORANDUM for the Naval Aid to the President:

In the absence of Admiral Benson I transmit herewith extracts from a letter from Rear Admiral Andrews, Commander U. S. Naval Forces Eastern Mediterranean, dated 14 May, 1919, subject: "General conditions in Adriatic."

FIUME: Since departure of Admiral Andrews from Fiume on 10 May the reports show that city very quiet, situation unchanged.

A report from the Commanding Officer of the U.S.S. MAURY says: "Major Furlong, U.S.A.,—Colonel Watford[1] agrees—that the Italians are markedly more punctilious and careful not to give offense. There have been no further displays of posters or sign painting. General Grazioli has issued a proclamation that anyone displaying an uncensored poster will be subject to the severest penalty."

Referring to the law by the Fiume council, dated March 27, making it treason for Slavs to attempt to advance the Jugo-Slav claim to Fiume, copy of which was forwarded to this office and transmitted for the information of the President, Admiral Andrews says: "Considering the fact that the council of Fiume assumed its functions under the protection of Italian armed force, and the Armistice requirement that Fiume is governed and occupied by *Allied* force, this is a most astounding fact. It is a pity that Allied control of Fiume has not been actual, and not nominal. When I go to Fiume shortly I will take up this matter with the Italian General as to cancelling this law."

POLA: No change at Pola. The deportations from Pola have been reported as far as known. They have been numerous, cruel, unnecessary, and are a grave reflection on Italian character. S.S. GALLICA arrived at Pola on 13 May with 800 Italian troops.

ZARA: Admiral Andrews received a report on 13 May of rioting at Zara on 11 May, in which the Jugo-Slavs were severely beaten up. Many Italian soldiers saw this and did not interfere. This incident has been reported to the President.[2]

Admiral Andrews wrote to Vice Admiral Millo[3] at Sebenico regarding this affair and asked how the perpetrators had been punished. He also informed Admiral Millo that nothing but trivial incidents had as yet occurred in the zone around Spalato, but that reports of such beatings of Jugo-Slavs would inflame the people against the Italians unless they knew that Admiral Millo dealt severely with such conduct.

The President of the local government of Spalato called upon Admiral Andrews to see him about the Zara brutalities, and Admiral Andrews wired to the British Admiral[4] and asked if a British ship could stop at Zara soon for the good effect. The H.M.S. CERES arrived at Zara on the morning of the 15th, in response to this request.

SPALATO: The situation is very favorable at Spalato. Trade has improved very much, being based on the exchange of commodities which Admiral Andrews has established. An officer of the Flagship supervises these exchanges, the larger exchanges being made directly through the Admiral, as neither the Italians nor the Jugo-Slavs trust the integrity of each other. On a recent day 21 large and small steam vessels were at the docks there. Steamers are coming and going all the time, industries are opening up, and there is more work going on.

The incidents of May 8th and May 11th, in which Italian officers were insulted, have been investigated and found to be quite trivial. J. C. Frémont   By direction.

TS MSS (WP, DLC).
    [1] Furlong was Maj. Charles Wellington Furlong. The commanding officer of *U.S.S. Maury* and Col. Watford cannot be identified.
    [2] J. C. Frémont to C. T. Grayson, May 13, 1919, TLS (WP, DLC). The message from Adm. Andrews was as follows: "May eleventh Italian demonstration Zara. Jugo-Slavs beaten up."
    [3] Enrico Millo di Casalgiate, at this time Italian Governor of Dalmatia.
    [4] Probably Adm. Sir Somerset Arthur Gough-Calthorpe.

From Lord Robert Cecil

My dear Mr. President,   Paris. May 17, 1919.

I beg to thank you most cordially for sending me your copy of the proposals of the German Delegates with regard to the League of Nations.[1] I had already given some time to the consideration of them, and the Committee appointed to deal with them met yesterday, the 16th.

A reply has been drafted, and now awaits the final observations of the Committee, after which it will be transmitted, I suppose, to the Supreme Council.   Yours very sincerely,   Robert Cecil

TLS (WP, DLC).
[1] *Vorschläge der Deutschen Regierung für die Errichtung eines Völkerbundes. Proposals of the German Government for the Establishment of a League of Nations*, together with an Appendix, *Entwurf eines Abkommens über internationales Arbeiterrecht. Draft of an International Workers' Charter* [c. May 9, 1919], printed document (WP, DLC). Both the German and English texts of the "proposals" for a league of nations, omitting the draft of a workers' charter, are printed in Miller, *The Drafting of the Covenant*, II, 744-61. The English text only of both items is printed in Miller, *My Diary at the Conference of Paris*, IX, 344-63. The "proposals" were in fact a complete draft of a covenant for a league of nations, and the draft labor charter was similarly comprehensive. The most striking provision of the "proposals" was that all the belligerent nations during the late war were to be admitted to the league at the outset, thus insuring Germany's full participation. In general, the German "proposals" provided for a considerably more complex organizational structure for the league and spelled out in more detail the ways in which the league would operate than did the Covenant adopted by the peace conference.

From Richard Irvine Manning[1]

My dear Mr. President,   London, W.1. May 17th, 1919.

Mrs. Manning[2] & I are sailing for American [America]. I was sorry not to have the privilege of seeing you while in Paris but I understood fully the heavy tasks which required your time & attention. I am taking back to our people the declaration of the tremendous importance & value of the part you have taken in impressing our Allies with the vision of greater justice & security of the rights of the peoples of these countries & in giving them higher ideals. Your firm adherence to such principles & the unfailing courage you have exhibited make us proud of you & makes better Americans of us whom you represent in the best thought & purpose of our people. But for your leadership the League of Nations would not have been adopted & made a part of the Treaty of Peace. Without it our men, who consecrated with their lives the ideals & cause for which we fought, would have given their life-blood in vain. When the Treaty of Peace is signed & men get back to work the just estimate of your achievement will be more fully recognized & the gratitude of the masses, now so strong, will extend & include many who now seem dissatisfied because their vision is obscured. I repeat again that my conviction is strong that our people in American [America] approve and admire your course, & recognize in you the greatest factor in the world for liberty justice & righteousness. With highest esteem I am

Very sincerely   Richd. I. Manning.

Lord Bryce presided last night at a meeting of the League & the speakers called on the Chinese delegates who were present to sign the Treaty—the audience applauded—the sentiment was unmistak[ab]le.

ALS (WP, DLC).
 [1] Recently retired from the governorship of South Carolina.
 [2] Lelia Bernard Meredith Manning.

From the Diary of Colonel House

May 17, 1919.

Orlando and di Cellere were my first visitors. We worked on the Adriatic problem from half past nine o-clock until eleven, but further than "whittling" down the Italian claims, arrived at no definite results. I discussed the subject with the President become [when] they came, but he was inflexible in his determination to yield nothing.

The Italians feel they have have [sic] been mistreated. Self-determination is to be applied, according to them, only when the Italians desire something. When anything is to be given, however, to France, England, Poland or other states, then it is overlooked. They are beginning to be bitter not only against us, but against France and England. I think a great mistake is being made in the way they are treated, for it will surely throw them into the arms of Germany. Their *amour propre* is wounded because they were not asked to join in the Treaty for the protection of France.

From the Peace Conference Diary of George Louis Beer

May 17th, 1919.

Again at 9.30 in Col. House's study with Orlando and de Cellere. Orlando agreed to a marked concession in the Eastern boundary of Istria as laid down in the Treaty of London in the Adelsberg district containing about 60,000 people. House telephoned to Wilson who is evidently not disposed to accept the Italian concessions. He is absolutely doctrinaire on this point. There is some truth in Sonnino's remark that having fornicated with France and England for four months, Wilson is attempting to re-establish his virtue at the expense of Italy.

T MS (G. L. Beer Papers, NNC).

From the Diary of Ray Stannard Baker

Saturday the 17[th May 1919]

After luncheon to-day the President suddenly decided to rearrange the furniture in the gorgeous sitting room of the house.[1] He said the colors of the chairs &c had been bothering him: they did not harmonize. So he & the Admiral went at the purple & green furniture & spent half an hour moving it about to suit the President's taste.

Van Oss[2] the Dutch journalist saw the President, by my appointment, for 20 minutes. Greatly delighted with his talk. Said the President was a man of great dignity: "outward strength, inward gentleness."

J_____ says of the President that he is par excellence the Professor: wants to be surrounded by his inferiors, & expects to instruct.

If a man is explainable he is not great.

The President has remarkable recuperative powers: he will look quite beaten out one day & be as keen & fresh the next as ever.

One reason the President so dislikes publicity while events are in the making is due to a certain artistic repugnance to expose half-done work to the light of day. He wants to present a workmanlike result (in his messages & speech not alone, but in his decisions in conference). He honestly does not believe in old diplomacy, or secret diplomacy, for he is conscious in no way of desiring any dishonest end, or to be working for any selfish interest. He honestly thinks this method of settling the world by secret conferences of 4 men is the best & only way. He does it because it is *his* way of working & he knows no other.

When Hapgood came to me the other day urging that I ask the President to see & confer with a group of liberals I asked him if he had ever heard of Wilson conferring with liberals: that it was too late now to ask Wilson to change his nature or method. He must be accepted as such & such a person, such & such a tool of democracy— the best we've got. We've got to carve our Peace & build our League with him & none other.

My method with the President is to serve him: to give him facts not opinions, honest facts for his swift mind to use—for in serving him I am serving the best instrument America has in these distracted times. I do not see him perfect, he is not a man I love as I love some men, but he is a man I respect & admire enormously. So many men fail with him because they try to use him for advancing their opinions

Hw MS (R. S. Baker Papers, DLC).
¹ Wilson had rearranged the furniture in the parlor also on May 1, 1919. See the extract from the Grayson Diary printed at that date in Vol. 58.
² Salomon Frederik van Oss, editor in chief of the *Haagsche Post (Hague Post)*. His interview with Wilson is printed at June 7, 1919.

From the Diary of Edith Benham

May 17, 1919

Dr. Axson came to luncheon and when he is here we are apt to have something more interesting after. It is a nuisance not to be able to talk freely at the table, but the spies around make it quite impossible. Dr. G. gave the P. quite a lot of despatches, principally Navy. These were confidential and said the Italians were occupying towns in Asia Minor, corroborating reports already received. They have absolutely no right to these places. There are no Italian citizens there and no one knows exactly what they mean by this game. They have occupied the Dodecanese Islands which are inhabited by Greeks and would belong logically to them. The P. says they were among those numerous infamous secret pacts to induce Italy to come into the war. Now, however, Lloyd George and the English (they were promised by England with no show of right) say they don't have to give them to Italy because they promised them if Italy would attack Turkey and she never did, which invalidates the contract. The P. says he has told L.G. and Clemenceau he reserves to himself the right to make these secret pacts public to the world if he feels it is necessary for the world to know why he has done certain things. He says it is particularly irritating the way the Italians are acting as though they saved the war, and he has despatches from Mr. Page begging him to send just a regiment of our men there to steady the line—anything to keep them from breaking any more. At that time they had more than one and one half times (or one half times) men than were necessary to support the line which, you remember, was a short one comparatively. They couldn't trust their own divisions. Some of the worst divisions they brought to France to get them out and the French put them to breaking stones on the road. I forgot to say I asked the P. how they occupied the towns in Asia Minor. He said he supposed with Marines and sailors, but no one can tell, they may have troops for some of their troop ships have sailed.

Someone spoke about the demonstration at the Capitol while the P. was in Rome when the people went there to hear and see him. Baron Sonnino rushed out to the Villa Savoia where we were lunching, represented the demonstration as possibly noisy and unruly, which was not true, it was only enthusiastic. The P. said he would go if only to wave his hand, but not so the wily officials, they said all right, but he was hustled back to the Quirinal by other streets lined with soldiers, and the crowd never saw him. This, however, is just an aside.

Dr. Axson spoke of Belgium and asked if she was not showing more courage in starting up life again and asking less. The P. says quite the contrary, that she is getting more than any of the other countries. When one speaks of Serbia and Poland they say they, the Belgians, haven't suffered in comparison with them. He says they always fall back on L.G. and quote an unfortunate speech of his in which he said her sufferings were so great and the world owed her everything and he is always trying to find other palliatory sentences to relieve himself and when someone reminds him of a sentence in his support he uses his habitual expression, "That's it, that's right!" much lightened in mind.

From the Diary of Dr. Grayson

Sunday, May 18, 1919.

The President arose at nine o'clock, had breakfast, and at 10:15 the President, Mrs. Wilson and I left the house to attend the Scotch Presbyterian Church to hear a sermon by the Reverend Hugh Black.[1] It was an old-fashioned church. You would not realize that you were in a city church, as the edifice reminded you more of a country church. A great many American soldiers were present, and in the same pew with the President, Mrs. Wilson and myself were Lloyd George and his daughter.[2] Clemenceau also had been invited, but he failed to put in an appearance.

The invitation to attend this service was received by the President on Saturday. The President said at the Saturday morning's conference: "I have an invitation to attend the Scotch Presbyterian Church tomorrow, and I move that we have no meeting tomorrow (Sunday) but that we all go to church." The motion not to have a meeting was agreed to. The President said to his colleagues: "When I was President of Princeton University I frequently spent my summers in Scotland bicycling. One Sunday I cycled to church, wearing my bicycle costume. Covered with dust, I entered the church and told the usher that I was an elder in the Presbyterian Church in

America. He looked at me suspiciously, and finally escorted me to a seat in the rear of the church and well to the side, where I worshipped in solitary grandeur."³ Lloyd George seemed to be much amused at this incident. Clemenceau, however, said that he would not have attended services in that costume. Whereupon I said: "Would you have gone in any costume?" Clemenceau answered: "No." Lloyd George then spoke up and said to Clemenceau: "Have you ever been to church in your life?" Clemenceau said: "No, I never have."

The sermon was one of the most impressive to which the President had ever listened. It was a sermon on the Lessons of the War.

We returned to the house at twelve o'clock. Upon our return we found that Colonel House had sent another compromise plan to the President concerning Fiume. The President asked Mr. Miller, who was the bearer of the message, to tell the following story to Colonel House and Orlando—it was a story which the President's father had told him (the President): He (the President's father) was driving along a country road. He came upon a section where a small pig was standing in the middle of the road gazing through a fence at a field of corn. While the President's father watched, the pig moved over to where the fence had been built around the curved trunk of a fallen tree. This tree was hollow but was in the shape of a semi-circle, with both ends pointing out into the road. The pig seemingly believing that he had found a way to the desired food started in at one end of the hollow log and came out a few yards further on in exactly the same roadway from which he had started. The pig gazed back again into the field, and then turned and went back over the original path, coming out the second time exactly where he had started from. This was too much for the pig, who grunted loudly in disapproval and started on the run down the road.

The President made the application to Mr. Miller of the story by saying that every time he was sent a proposal of a compromise in this Italian situation he found that the proposal was very much like the hollow tree in that it seemed to lead in the general direction of the corn-field but after all returned him back to where he started from.

The President, Mrs. Wilson, Dr. Axson, Miss Benham and I had lunch, and after lunch we motored to Barbison, near Fontainebleau. The President got out and walked around the village, visiting the studios of Francis Millet and others. He was not recognized by any one until he passed a bicycle shop in which an American was working. He was without a collar, wearing felt slippers, and his hands were greasy. He walked out of his shop and greeted the President, saying: "If I can be of any assistance to you in showing you around, I shall be glad to do so. I am from New Jersey." He acted as a guide for a few minutes. By this time the native population recognized the

President, and in a short while he was surrounded by a big crowd, which spoiled his fun as a sight-seer. He then entered his motor and proceeded through the beautiful forest to Fontainebleau and the Château there. He got out of his car at the Château, walked through the grounds, visited the carp-pond and other places of interest. We returned to Paris at about seven o'clock.

After dinner the President, Mrs. Wilson and Dr. Axson spent a quiet evening together.

[1] Professor of Practical Theology at Union Theological Seminary in New York.
[2] Megan Lloyd George.
[3] See WW to EAW, July 13, 1908, Vol. 18.

From the Diary of David Hunter Miller

Sunday, May 18th [1919]

I was at the office in the morning after going around to say good-bye to Judge Mack, where I saw Frankfurter. I told Judge Mack that if I heard anything of the decision of the Council of Four I would telegraph him at the Carlton Hotel in London.

At the office I had a message that the President would see Major Johnson and myself at 12:15. I saw Major Johnson a few moments before we went up, and we agreed that the President did not want the details but just the general results. He and I went up together to the President's and saw him for an hour. No one else was there.

The President stood very firmly for the line proposed by Major Johnson and indeed wanted to send word to the Italians that he would not make any concession whatever. I urged him against this showing him that the Italians had conceded a great deal and expressed my belief that they would concede still more. He said that I could talk with them without giving them any ultimatum on the matter and see what progress could be made.

In the afternoon I looked over the Peace Treaty for a while and saw Colonel House a little after five o'clock. I asked him whether he thought we should go on with the Italians and he said, "Yes, in order to keep the negotiations going and in our own hands," and I told him what the President had said. He agreed that it was very unfortunate that the matter had not been settled before, as it could have been.

I then went around to see di Cellere and talked with him until after eight o'clock. I explained to him about the frontier in Istria, which had been most discussed with the President, and he said he would take it up with his people. I told him that Sebenico was not Italian and that the President was opposed to that going to Italy, and that as to Zara, if the President were satisfied that the population wanted it to go to Italy he would consent, although he did not like the idea of an Italian town on the coast. The islands were not much discussed. I suggested that they might be re-examined in detail.

I then went home to a late dinner and to bed.

Miller, *My Diary at the Conference of Paris*, I, 317-18.

From Vittorio Emanuele Orlando

Paris May 18th, 1919.

The landings of Italian Troops in Asia Minor, concerning which the President of the United States and the Premiers of France and Great Britain have asked for information,[1] were determined by imperative reasons of public order and carried out without giving rise to any conflicts such as occurred in [the] case of the Greek landing at Smyrna.

For nearly a month before the Italian occupation, the province of Adalia has been a prey to anarchy. The further occupations are purely military in character, as are the others effected by the Allied Powers in Turkey, and will in no way affect the ultimate decision as to the final disposal of the various territories belonging to the Ottoman Empire.

Furthermore, and although the final settlement of those territories is not now in question, the Italian Prime Minister cannot but draw the attention of the Prime Ministers of France and Great Britain to the provision of article 9 of the Treaty of London of April 26th, 1915, and the rights which, on the basis of this article, were recognized to Italy.

As to the remark that such action was taken without previous consultation with his colleagues, Signor Orlando wishes to point out in his turn that the very cause and the conditions of such landings made any previous consultation impossible. On the other hand it was entirely without Signor Orlando's knowledge that Greece was invited to participate with her troops in the occupation of Smyrna. This action prejudiced "de facto" if not "de jure" the final settlement to be arrived at in the case of this city, concerning which and in accordance with the wishes of the Allied Powers there had been—between the Italian and Greek Governments—conversations which were still pending and showed all the conciliatory spirit by which the Italian Government was animated in the matter.

Likewise no previous notice was given to the Italian Premier of the occupation of Heraclea by French forces.

The Italian Prime Minister wishes to assure the President of the United States and the Premiers of France and Great Britain that he is no less anxious than they are to arrive to a friendly understanding with his colleagues for the final settlement of the Mediterranean problem in a way which, by fulfilling in their letter and their spirit the agreements which determined Italy's entrance into the war, may give Italy, also on this point, the satisfaction the Italian people rightly expect.

T MS (WP, DLC).
    [1] See the Appendix to the minutes of the Council of Four printed at May 17, 1919, 4:15 p.m.

From Robert Lansing, with Enclosure

My dear Mr. President: Paris, May 18, 1919

I am enclosing herewith a copy of a letter in which Messrs. Walsh, Dunn[e] and Ryan present a request that steps be taken with a view to procuring an authorization for certain representatives of Ireland to proceed to Paris, and I shall be glad to receive an indication of your views regarding the reply to be made to these gentlemen in the premises.   Faithfully yours,   Robert Lansing

TLS (WP, DLC).

E N C L O S U R E

Francis Patrick Walsh and Others to Robert Lansing

Sir: Paris Le May 16, 1919.

On behalf of and representing the Irish Race Convention held in Philadelphia on February 22, 1919, we very respectfully request your good offices to procure from the British Government a safe conduct from Dublin to Paris and return for Emon DeValera, Arthur Griffith, and George Noble Count Plunkett, the elected representatives of the People of Ireland so that they may in person present the claims of Ireland for International recognition as a Republic to the Peace Conference. As you know the British Government assented to our going to Ireland. We went there for the purpose of conferring with the representatives of the Irish People, and ascertaining for ourselves at first hand the conditions prevailing in that Country. We have returned therefrom and are now more desirous than ever that the authorized representatives of Ireland shall be given the opportunity to appear and present the case of that Country to the representatives of the assembled Nations.

Awaiting the favor of an early reply we remain,
                          Very truly yours,   Frank P. Walsh
                                              E. F. Dunne
                                              Michael J. Ryan

TCL (WP, DLC).

John Charles Frémont to Cary Travers Grayson

Paris, 18 May 1919.

MEMORANDUM.

For: The Naval Aid to the President.

In the absence of Admiral Benson, I transmit herewith the substance of despatches received today from Rear Admiral Bristol, Commander U. S. Naval Forces, Eastern Mediterranean, in order that the information contained therein may be placed before the President:

"Ser. No. 405. May 15, 9:40 P.M.

Following from Arizona. Smyrna, Turkey quiet. Forts occupied by landing force British, Italian, French, Greek ships. Greek transports with 15,000 troops are expected arrive at 6 G.M.T. Will disembark troops immediately. Landing force Greek naval vessels will land 4 G.M.T. to prepare for disembarking troops. Allied Consulate guards, 20 men each, landed 1 G.M.T. by Allied ships, including Arizona. One Greek destroyer, one Italian destroyer arrived."

"Ser. No. 420.

Following from Arizona. Greek vessels landed landing force 2 GMT and prepared for landing troops. Six Greek transports, one British cruiser, KILKIS, 2 Greek destroyers arrived at 6 GMT. Transports began to disembark troops immediately, no resistance. After the landing, troops began occupation of city. Eight GMT fighting began southeastern part of city noon Wednesday, spread through the city, continued at intervals until 10 GMT. Few scattered shots. Accurate casualties not known, reported 200 Greeks, 100 Turks dead. Impossible to obtain accurate information yet regarding fighting or extent of occupation accomplished. City generally quiet now. Americans have been taken in buildings."

"Ser. No. 429.

Following received from Tchoroum [Tchorlu, or Corlu]. The Turks were anxiously awaiting the results of the execution of the principles of Wilson, while to-day we are told to give up Symrna [Smyrna] to the Greeks. The Turks who have entrusted in the principles of Wilson had also placed their faith in the people of the United States. If Turkey is going to lose Symrna, the Turks are also ready to give up their lives with it. Symrna can be given as a present to a foreign country only after the death of the Turks there. We shall get strength from the spirit of the great president

Washington. Will the Americans accept bloodshed? Sadik on behalf of the inhabitants."

J. C. Frémont
Commander U. S. Navy
By direction.

TS MS (WP, DLC).

From the Diary of Dr. Grayson

Monday, May 19, 1919.

The President arose early, and after breakfast he went for a motor-
ride, returning in time to attend the meeting of the Council of Four,[1]
which took up the question of the disintegration of Turkey as an empire. Many serious questions came up in this connection. The Mohammedans in India have been pointing out to the British representatives that if the Sultan of Turkey is to be entirely deposed and
Turkey dismembered as an Empire, the result may well be a renewal of a Holy War by the Musselmen. The question at issue in
connection with the Turkish problem was, first, whether Turkey
would entirely be eliminated from Europe, and, secondly, whether
the United States would accept a mandatory over what now is Turkey in Europe. The matter was debated at very great length without
a decision being reached, as there were a number of points upon
which the President asked for additional information, both from
Lloyd George and from the latter's Indian representatives.

After the Big Four adjourned the President had as a lunch guest
General John J. Pershing. General Pershing had planned to go to
London to be the guest of the Municipality there on Empire Day,
May 24th, and all arrangements had been made for him to review
there a picked regiment of American soldiers who were to be sent
over from the Army of Occupation to march in review before King
George. General Pershing told the President of his plans, and the latter expressed surprise that the Commander-in-Chief should contemplate being absent from his Army at a time when it was entirely
possible that the German reply to the peace terms would be forthcoming. As a result of the talk between the President and General
Pershing, Pershing canceled the London plan and announced that
he would proceed to Coblenz, there to remain together with General
Hunter Liggett until the question as to whether it would be necessary to renew hostilities against Germany had been disposed of.
There was, however, no business transacted at the luncheon table.
The President told the General a number of good stories. He then
asked: "General, may I inquire to what church you belong?" The

General displayed distinct astonishment and perplexity over the direct question but answered: "Episcopalian." Whereupon Mrs. Wilson applauded with a smile to me. The President then said: "That's too bad; I had hopes that you were a Presbyterian, as I have two Episcopalians here in the presence of Mrs. Wilson and Admiral Grayson, who take sides against me in matters of religion."

The President then referred to the wonderful sermon which we had heard by Dr. Black yesterday, and said to the General: "I wish you could have been present to have heard it. You would have enjoyed it."

After luncheon the President went for a motor ride and returned to the temporary White House to confer with Mr. Bernard M. Baruch and some of the other American economic experts.

After dinner the President, Mrs. Wilson and I spent a quiet evening. The President discussed many things concerning individuals and matters which had to do with the peace negotiations.

Although the President had no personal part in it during the day, the exchange of credentials between the Austrian peace plenipotentiaries and the Allied and Associated representatives took place at St. Germain.

---

[1] The first meeting took place at President Wilson's house at 11 a.m. It was a brief meeting, in which Marshal Foch reported on the forces available for the occupation of Germany. For the full text of these minutes, see *PPC*, V, 702-704.

From the Diary of Edith Benham

May 19, 1919

General Pershing came to luncheon today. He is not a very interesting luncheon guest, for he is heavy and doesn't do his part in a luncheon talk. Conversation turned on Italy and he said he is getting advices from his Intelligence Bureau that the Italians consider the German peace terms too heavy and feel that the French are very heartless in welcoming the Austrians as they have, or not hating them as they want them to. Censoring the German mail in the part we are occupying brings rather strange information, the gist being that the Germans say the terms are hard, but only what they would have made the Allies pay, and more. The P. said it is so hard for the German people to realize now that they must suffer for the sins of their Government. It is always hard, he said, for people to realize that. He went on to speak of the Italians and how they had always had a raw deal in every distribution of territory after a war and in a way they could hardly be blamed for being as tricky as they are. Just before Italy went into war Count Cellere told the P. that his Government had asked both Austria and Germany in 1914 what they intended to do about Serbia, Italy being then of the Triple Alliance, and they said nothing. This was not only once but several times, and then only twenty-four hours before Germany decided to strike did they notify Italy that they intended to go to war. About the Italian Question the P. said he always reminded himself of a story his father told about a little pig he frightened one day driving along the road. The thing saw a tree trunk and decided if he could run into that he could get into the next field and escape, but the trunk was shaped like an elbow so he ran out on the road again. He didn't seem to get any nearer the solution of his difficulty so he repeated the maneuver and arrived on the road again, looking bewildered, and ran down the road as hard as he could.

Hankey's Notes of a Meeting of the Council of Four[1]

President Wilson's House,
C.F.18.B.   Paris, May 19, 1919, 11:30 a.m.

1. MR LLOYD GEORGE read a telegram received from the British General Haking[2] at Spa, communicating a telegram he had received from Berlin. According to this information, some German troops marching past the British Embassy, where the British Military Mission was quartered, had called out "Down with England," but the demonstration had been half-hearted, and the men had been grinning at the time. There had been a protest against the terms of peace, in which 8,000 to 10,000 people had taken part, but they had made no demonstration in passing the Embassy. There was no indication of serious movements of troops westward, and the informant doubted whether the Germans would make any attempt to retake Posen, which would mean starting the war all over again, except in case of great desperation. Great depression was reported in all parts of Berlin.

M. CLEMENCEAU said that his information was of a very similar nature.

2. PRESIDENT WILSON read two telegrams he had received from the American Minister at Warsaw, one containing a message from M. Paderewski. Paraphrases of both these telegrams are reproduced in the appendix.

MR LLOYD GEORGE's comment on this was that it was extremely difficult to establish the facts. General Botha, on review of all the facts in his possession as Head of the Armistice Commission, had

[1] The complete text of these minutes is printed in *PPC*, V, 705-15.
[2] That is, Lt. Gen. Sir Richard Cyril Byrne Haking.

taken the very opposite point of view to that taken in these tele-grams. Clearly, therefore, it would be very dangerous to come to a conclusion without further advice. He considered that General Botha should be asked to summon the Armistice Commission, and to advise the Council of the Principal Allied and Associated Powers on the subject.

PRESIDENT WILSON and M. CLEMENCEAU agreed.

(Later in the Meeting, it was ascertained that General Botha had been called to London, but messages were sent asking him to re-turn at once.)

3. MR LLOYD GEORGE said that the Bolshevist reply to Dr Nansen's letter was another instance of the extraordinary difficulty in eliciting facts. To read this reply gave the impression that the Bolshevists re-fused Dr Nansen's offer because they did not wish to compromise their prospects of military success. All the information he had re-ceived, however, was that the Bolshevists were collapsing in a mili-tary sense.

4. PRESIDENT WILSON read a dispatch from a very experienced United States representative, who had visited Buda-Pest.[3] The gist of this was that Bela Kun's Government wished to avoid bloodshed and murder, but was unable to control its agents, with a result that the "Red Guard" were pillaging, and there was great chaos in the country. The Roumanian advance had increased the disorders, and the failure of the Roumanians to continue their advance had again caused further disorders and attacks on the alleged counter-revolu-tionaries. Some bad instances were given of murders, including that of the President of the late Hungarian Parliament. Attention was also called to Italian intrigues in Hungary. The dispatch concluded by a recommendation that military intervention by the Allied and Associated Powers was essential. It stated that there would be no difficulty in this, because the mass of the people condemned the present Government. Failing intervention, there would be anarchy. The French were at Belgrade, and ready to occupy Buda-Pest, and claimed to have sufficient troops. It was stated that the occupation of Buda-Pest would not be a formidable enterprise. The second rec-ommendation was that simultaneously with the advance, an Allied Mission should be sent under some man like General Smuts.

M. CLEMENCEAU asked if Buda-Pest was occupied, what would happen next?

MR LLOYD GEORGE said the difficulty was to get out after an occu-pation like this.

M. CLEMENCEAU said he would study the possibilities of a French

---

[3] See the Enclosure printed with A. H. Frazier to EMH, May 17, 1919.

advance in concert with the Roumanians. He did not want the French troops carrying out this operation alone.

PRESIDENT WILSON said he would not trust the Roumanians, who had local interests and would excite the hostility of the Hungarian population. He was very doubtful whether an advance was a wise thing to do.

M. CLEMENCEAU said a good deal would depend upon what happened at the expiration of the fortnight given to the Germans, next Thursday. He undertook to have the situation studied from a military point of view, and to report on the following day as to the possibility of occupying Buda-Pest.

5. M. CLEMENCEAU communicated some confidential information he had received as to the probability of the Germans agreeing to sign. This indicated that the Germans would probably ask for a further delay. He believed, however, that Herr Brockdorff-Rantzau knew the Treaty would have to be signed in the end, and would sign it himself if he could not get some-one else to do so. He thought the Germans ought to be given more time if they required it.

PRESIDENT WILSON agreed, and considered that on the whole a demand for delay would be a good sign.

6. MR LLOYD GEORGE reported a visit he had received from M. Orlando on the previous day. One significant point was that M. Orlando had been accompanied by his own chef-de-cabinet[4] and not by Count Aldrovandi, who was Baron Sonnino's chef-de-cabinet. M. Orlando had shown him the proposals he had made to Dr Miller of the American Delegation, and he had shown clearly how much he was affected by the question of Fiume. He had ended by making an appeal for the mandate for the whole of Anatolia. Mr Lloyd George had replied to him that that was quite hopeless. At last M. Orlando had let out that he really did not care a scrap about Asia-Minor if he could get Fiume. Italian public opinion was not really concerned with Asia-Minor, and the Italian Government only wished to have that as compensation if they could not secure Fiume. M. Orlando had admitted that he would rather have Fiume than anything in Asia-Minor. Mr Lloyd George had asked him whether, supposing Italy got Fiume, he would drop Asia-Minor; and he had replied that he would. He had kept reverting all through the interview to the question of Fiume, and had said that Italian public opinion was very much engaged in it. Mr Lloyd George had asked if the Yugo-Slavs could have the use of Fiume while a new port was being constructed at Italian expense.

The more he thought of the problem presented by the presence of

[4] That is, Augusto Battioni.

the Italians in Asia Minor, the more full of mischief the scheme seemed. The Mohammedan deputation, who had given evidence on Saturday, were very alarmed about the whole outlook. They had only been persuaded to come with great difficulty. They had discussed the question until 2 a.m. on Saturday morning and their opinion had been that the whole Mohammedan world would be so upset by what was being done in Turkey that it would be better for them to avoid being mixed up with it. The Turks, while respecting the British, French and Americans, the two former of whom had beaten them, absolutely despised the Italians. To put the Turks under the Italians when they thought themselves better men than the latter, would put the whole Mohammedan world in revolt. At the risk of appearing to vacillate, he would like to reconsider the provisional decision already taken.

PRESIDENT WILSON said he did not in the least mind vacillating, provided the solution reached was the right one.

MR. LLOYD GEORGE said that his present attitude was that it would be best to get the Italians out of Asia Minor altogether. Frankly, he had changed his mind on the question of dividing Anatolia. He thought that it would be a mistake to tear up this purely Turkish province.

PRESIDENT WILSON said that what had impressed him in the evidence of the Mohammedan deputation was what they had said about Turkish sovereignty. He, himself, had forgotten that he had used the word in the 14 points. Those 14 points now constituted a sort of Treaty; in fact in the case of Germany, as Mr. Lloyd George pointed out, they were the basis of the Treaty with Germany. However, it was impossible to work on different sets of principles in the different Treaties of Peace. He was impressed by the fact that the sentiment of the sovereignty of the Sultan was closely connected with the sentiment of Khalifate. He had derived the impression that if the Mohammedan troops, who had fought against the Turks, had thought they were doing more than break the alliance of the Turks with Germany, they would not have fought. They would not have continued fighting to destroy the sovereignty of the Sultan over the Turkish people. Moreover, he and Mr. Lloyd George had said they would not destroy Turkish sovereignty. He had forgotten this until reminded of it on Saturday. (Mr. Lloyd George said he had also forgotten it.) It was true that he had written the 14 points when the situation was altogether different and when there had been a close combination of the four enemy powers, but, nevertheless, this did not affect the essential principles on which they were based. He asked if some way could not be discovered for finding a solution on the following lines? He had not thought it out in detail but this was his idea: Could not the Sultan be left his sovereignty over Anatolia and merely required in certain specific matters to take the advice of, say, the French Government? For example, he might have to take their advice in regard to financial and economic matters and perhaps in regard to international relations. He was not sure that this would not be managed by retaining the Turks in Constantinople, although exercising no sovereignty there. Just as the Pope of Rome lived in Rome without sovereignty and issued his orders to the Roman Catholic Church. Inasmuch as the Mandatory Power at Constantinople would only be responsible for local matters, he saw no reason that there should be any clash.

MR. LLOYD GEORGE said he had been thinking of some similar scheme.

PRESIDENT WILSON said his idea would be to assign some residential district in Constantinople to the Sultan. He would not, of course, be confined there any more than the Pope of Rome was confined to the Vatican for it was of his own volition only that the Pope confined himself. The Sultan would then be separated from his Kingdom merely by a narrow strip of water and territory.

MR. LLOYD GEORGE said that in this case France—and he had no objection to France being entrusted with this—should, in his view, be confined to guiding the Sultan in regard to finance, concessions, and commercial matters. He was opposed to interference with matters of Government as it would only cause great anger in the whole Mohammedan population.

M. CLEMENCEAU said that the terms would have to be drawn very carefully as the Turkish Government was a very bad one.

MR. LLOYD GEORGE said he was reminded that the matter of Gendarmerie would be a difficult one. It had always been found necessary to maintain an International Gendarmerie for the purpose of keeping order. In this case, however, the main Greek and Armenian populations were being withdrawn from Turkish rule and there would only be relatively unimportant minorities under the Turks.

M. CLEMENCEAU suggested that the scheme should be put in writing and examined.

MR. LLOYD GEORGE said he had arranged for a meeting in the afternoon of members of the British Cabinet who were in Paris.

PRESIDENT WILSON said that the Mohammedan deputation who had been received on Saturday had, he had observed, pricked up their ears when something was said about a mandate. It would be difficult for the Turks to distinguish between one sort of mandate and another. What he was suggesting was in effect to give a mandate to France without calling it a mandate. That is to say, France would not be responsible to the League of Nations, she would be in a similar position as an independent friendly country advising the Turkish Government under treaty stipulations. The terms of the Treaty, therefore, would be more limited than the terms of the mandate.

MR. LLOYD GEORGE said that if France took a position of this kind towards the whole of Asia Minor, which would be a very important trust, he would have to ask for a re-examination of the whole question of mandates in the Turkish Empire.

PRESIDENT WILSON pointed out that this solution would leave the Italians out entirely. This brought him back to the question of Fiume. He was inclined to think that this matter had better be left for a few days. He understood that there was a tendency towards changes of opinion in Rome which might take shape in a few days' time. He had heard that the Italians and Jugo-Slav shipping people were getting together on the question of shipping in the Adriatic.

MR. LLOYD GEORGE pointed out that this was at the expense of the British Empire. The Italians were trying to make a negotiation with the Jugo-Slavs to divide the whole of the Austro-Hungarian shipping. It was a most shabby scheme. Great Britain had probably lost hundreds of thousands of tons of shipping in Italy's interest and now Italy was trying to exclude her from any share. Italy would have starved but for the risk that British and French ships had run.

PRESIDENT WILSON said that M. Orlando, in his conversation with Dr. Miller and other American representatives, had, in the end, acceded to the idea of an independent Fiume. If he, himself, were in a position to offer friendly advice to M. Orlando, he would tell him to say to the Italian people that it was not to the interest of Italy to destroy her friendship with the United States. The Americans were willing to take up this position that Italy could have any territory in dispute, the population of which would vote for Italian sovereignty. If Italy declined this offer it would show that she was not sincere in what she had said about the unredeemed Italian peoples.

MR. LLOYD GEORGE said that if the Italians could be got out of Asia Minor altogether it would, in his opinion, be worth giving them something they were specially concerned in, even if it involved the Allies swallowing their words.

PRESIDENT WILSON hoped that Mr. Lloyd George would not press this point of view. He was bound to adhere to his principle that no peoples should be handed over to another rule without their consent.

MR. LLOYD GEORGE said he had assumed that the agreement of the Jugo-Slavs could be obtained. After all, Fiume was a Town with an Italian flavour and an Italian name. Aga Khan had said that no-one who knew Fiume could think of it as anything but an Italian city. It was true that if the suburbs were included there would be a small majority in favour of the Jugo-Slavs. If, however, the Jugo-Slavs were willing to accept another harbour to be constructed by the Italians somewhere else, would it not then be possible to hand Fiume with their consent to the Italians. Surely, this would be worth while if by these means the Italians could be bought off Dalmatia—and in this respect he and M. Clemenceau were in a difficult position owing to the Treaty of London—and if they could also be bought off Asia Minor. This latter was, in his view, most important to the peace of the world.

PRESIDENT WILSON said that this was virtually the proposition that had been put to the Italians by the American group. Their proposal had not been to hand Fiume to the Italians but to have a plebiscite if the Italians had constructed a port at Buccari. This, of course, was subject to the people of Fiume still desiring to become Italian. The difficulty he foresaw was in the Italians being able to finance the construction of a Port.

MR. LLOYD GEORGE pointed out that Italy had an abundance of good engineering labour and he thought they could carry out the scheme.

PRESIDENT WILSON said that in his view the weakest part of the Italian case was their insistence on an Army sustained by compulsory service. In France, conscription, he understood, was both a habit and a preference. This, however, was not Italy's argument. The Italians said they could not get a voluntary Army because they would have to pay so little.

MR. LLOYD GEORGE again insisted on the importance of getting the Italians out of Asia Minor. If this were not done there would always be trouble there as well as in Armenia where America would have the mandate.

MR. LLOYD GEORGE said that the Mohammedan deputation were also very strongly opposed to an Italian mandate in the Caucasus.

(Sir Maurice Hankey was instructed to invite M. Venizelos and Baron Sonnino for a meeting at 4-30 p.m.)

Appendix I to C.F. 18B.
Mr. Gibson, American Minister at Warsaw
to the American Commission to Negotiate Peace.
(Telegram—Paraphrase.)

American Legation,
Warsaw, May 14, 1919.

Mr. Gibson states that the following is a confidential message which Mr. Paderewski sends for President Wilson.
That everything should be done according to the wishes ex-

pressed by you has been my most earnest desire since my arrival here from Paris. In compliance with the request made by you two divisions of the army under General Haller which were on the Volhynian front and marching to assist in defending Lemberg, have been stopped.

Again having convinced myself that the Ukrainians are far removed from being what they have pretended and what the Conference desires to consider them, I must bring this information to your attention and to that of your colleagues. General Oskilko,[5] Commander in Chief of the Second Ukrainian Army, with two of his superior officers, has deserted, and asking protection, has surrendered to the Polish Army. He gives as a reason for this conduct the contamination of the Ukrainian Army by Bolshevism and the necessity of quitting in order that his own life might be saved. General Oskilko is now under the escort of Polish soldiers at Lublin.

Desirous of meeting your wishes, and the wishes of your colleagues, I looked thoroughly into the situation, and I found that the whole of the East Galician country is unanimous in a demand for decisive and energetic action, owing to the numerous crimes which the Ukrainians daily commit in East Galicia, massacres and slaughters which can only be compared to the Turkish crimes in Armenia. Before my arrival, plans had been made and orders had been issued for an offensive without General Haller's co-operation; May 12th was the date set for the beginning of the action. At my insistence, however, action was withheld. On the 11th, General Pavlenko[6] telegraphed a reminder that in Paris the armistice was being concluded, and announced the cessation of all military operations. We credited them with being sincere in their intentions. But they attacked us at two new points on the 12th,—at Vatrzyki they entered our entrenchments, and they bombarded the city of Sanek,[7] hitherto outside of military operations. The Government is now rendered powerless by the excitement throughout the country by the indignation expressed by the most reasonable of the leading people; indeed, it is not possible to ask quiet and patience of a people at the same moment they are being murdered ruthlessly by Ukrainian soldiers who have turned against their own chiefs, by bandits organized in the hope of plunder, with whom Poland is asked to negotiate as with equals. The defence and protection of a population of 1,700,000 is the sacred duty of the military and civilian authorities, is the view held by them, for a portion of this population has practically been exterminated, and any resistance to the just and legiti-

[5] Volodymyr Oskílko (Walery Oskiłtko in Polish).
[6] That is, Mykhailo Omeliánovych-Pavlénko.
[7] That is, Sanok.

mate conclusion reached by those authorities would immediately bring about a revolution covering the whole country. While I am willing to tender at any moment the resignation of my Government, the situation hardly would be improved by this action. Allied military observers to attend the operations would gladly be received by the chief command. Your sure insight, based on your sublime sense of justice, I am confident, will grasp the tragedy of the situation, and your opinion is hopefully and impatiently awaited.

Signed: I. J. Paderewski.

From: Mr. Gibson, American Minister at Warsaw,
To: The American Commission to Negotiate Peace.
(Telegram—Paraphrase)

American Legation,
Warsaw, May 14th, 1919.

Mr. Gibson states that the early attention of the Conference should be given to the situation which has arisen in Poland since the return of Mr. Paderewski from Paris. Mr. Gibson, and the French and British diplomatic representatives[8] have in independent actions pointed out to Mr. Paderewski and to the Foreign Office members the serious attention which the Conference already has given to the Lemburg situation. Upon returning from Paris, and finding that all arrangements for attacks on the Lemberg and Vohynian fronts had been made, Paderewski energetically took the matter up, stating that he had promised upon his honor that no offensive on the Lemberg front should be made with Haller's army, and that he would resign unless the orders were changed. On May 12th the orders were withdrawn, and immediately thereafter Paderewski was attended by a delegation from the Diet and informed that the tales of atrocities committed by the Ukrainians caused the feeling in the country to be so outraged that it was necessary to go ahead with the operations. Paderewski, while striving to maintain views expressed by him, has small hopes of success. He now limits himself to the statement that he will endeavour to obtain the release of the Allies to the promises made by him, but failing in that course and unless the Diet adheres to his viewpoint he would be compelled to resign. On the 15th another conference with the Diet leaders is to be held, and in an effort to bring the situation under control Paderewski will propose the following arrangement:

One. Complete independence of the Lithuanians and White Russians to be formally recognized by the Diet.

Two. The granting of Eastern Galicia to Poland with complete lo-

---

[8] Eugène Léon Pralon and Sir Percy Charles Hugh Wyndham.

cal autonomy to be urged upon the Peace Conference by Paderewski.

Three. For the purpose of maintaining order and obviating additional outrages Paderewski is to ask the Peace Conference that he
and General Pilsudski be permitted discretionary powers in connection with the use of Polish forces. Failure of claims on points mentioned, would place Paderewski government in untenable position,
and his adherents claim that to overthrow him would bring about
immediate revolution and disorder. Mr. Gibson says that his information indicated that even the opponents of Paderewski do not
claim that complete order would be maintained. Mr. Gibson further
says should the government not yield, a general strike of railroad,
post office and telegraph employees would threaten, and that this
movement compared to some forms of political upheaval would in-
voke more danger. Mr. Gibson adds that any of these developments
undoubtedly will find the internal situation ripe, and that it appears
to be plain that unless the dark and more or less hysterical conditions now existing can be taken into consideration at their whole
value, no sound conclusions can be arrived at in regard to Polish
matters. Mr. Gibson further adds that two alternatives may be offered to us, and outlines them as follows:

First. Paderewski's personal responsibility to which he is held on
account of the promise made by him in Paris to be modified, in order
to secure his continuance in office, and assure the continuance of
his wholesome and sincere restraining influence at a time when
there does not seem to be any one of similar characteristics to take
his place.

Second. Paderewski to be held strictly to the fulfillment of the
promise made by him, which would carry with it the possibility of
his enforced retirement, without gaining our point, and with the loss
of the strong personal influence which he has wielded on behalf of
our ideas. This action would permit the government to come into the
control of any of the factions now only too anxious to seize it, on
chauvinistic grounds, which in the present excited state of public
opinion readily appeal to the crowd. Mr. Gibson says that he cannot
think of anyone who might control a majority in the Assembly, and
replace Paderewski with any likelihood of holding it in an orderly
manner.

Public feeling has been aroused by various happenings. The belief is current that in certain Galician villages the entire Polish pop-
ulace has been exterminated by the Ukrainians, and various additional excesses are attributed to them. General Oskilko's surrender
(to which Paderewski referred in his telegram to the President) together with the apparent reasons for same, have been the cause of

further excitement. In addition, there has been the recent surrender to the Poles of several regiments composed of Russian soldiers from the Tula Division, which in April allied themselves with Ukrainian forces in order to support Bolshevism. They say that they want to join Poles so as to down the Ukrainians, who themselves are the advocates of Bolshevism. No matter what the foundation for these stories may be, their effect is definite, giving rise to a situation which we cannot ignore. The opponents of Paderewski in the Diet and elsewhere make use of this situation to influence public opinion in favor of advancing into Galicia in order to protect the lives of over a million Poles, and cause the downfall of Paderewski, who is denounced as submitting to the murder and torture of citizens and soldiers of Poland rather than incur the displeasure of American, British and French statesmen.

Late to-night, accompanied by his British Colleague, Mr. Gibson called on Paderewski and made an appeal that he would endeavour to dominate the situation by a supreme effort, and bring Poland to support and carry out his promises. Mr. Gibson urged the matter on the ground of Polish interests; he stated that if in the face of all obstacles he definitely determines to put an end to offensive operations and carry out the armistice, he will go back to Paris with his prestige greatly augmented; on the other hand, despite the sincerity of his efforts, his position in Paris will be impaired if an advance is made into Galicia. Paderewski admitted to Mr. Gibson the truth of this, and promised to maintain a stiff front and do all he could to fulfil the wishes of the President, but he entertained small hope that a change of heart on the part of the Diet and the people could be forced.

Mr. Gibson adds that he will continue to endeavour to carry out the desires of the Peace Conference according to his understanding of them, and requests that the mission cable him a full expression of its views.

T MS (SDR, RG 256, 180.03401/18½, DNA).

Hankey's Notes of a Meeting of the Council of Four[1]

President Wilson's House,
C.F.19.   Paris, May 19, 1919, 4:00 p.m.

M. Venizelos was introduced.

1. PRESIDENT WILSON drew the attention of M. Sonnino to the memorandum handed to M. Orlando on May 17th (C.F.17. Appen-

---

[1] The complete text of these minutes is printed in PPC, V, 716-31.

dix).[2] He said that what concerned the Council was that the landings seemed to have taken place without any justification.

BARON SONNINO handed round the text of a reply prepared by the Italian Delegation (Appendix I).[3] He doubted if the presence of M. Venizelos would be found helpful. He did not feel justified in assenting to his presence when the communication had been made to M. Orlando, especially in the absence of the latter.

(M. Venizelos then offered to withdraw and left the room.)

PRESIDENT WILSON said he did not quite understand Baron Sonnino's attitude. M. Venizelos was a member of the Peace Conference and equal with all the other members.

BARON SONNINO said he was not speaking in his own name, but for the President of the Council[4] who was ill. He did not feel justified in agreeing to another party who had not been present when the memorandum was handed to M. Orlando taking part in its general discussion. He felt it was not quite fair, either to himself or to the Italian Delegation, more especially as M. Venizelos had a particular interest in all these questions.

PRESIDENT WILSON asked if it was because M. Venizelos was not interested that he should not be present.

MR. LLOYD GEORGE pointed out that because he was an interested party, Baron Sonnino took this view.

BARON SONNINO said he knew very little of the circumstances in which the memorandum had been presented to M. Orlando. He could not understand why it should be discussed in the presence of a fifth party. The Italian Delegation had not been particularly asked to be present to discuss the sending of Greek soldiers to Smyrna.

MR. LLOYD GEORGE said that not a single Greek soldier had left for Smyrna until the Italian Delegation had been consulted.

BARON SONNINO said that M. Venizelos had been invited to send the troops on May 6th.

PRESIDENT WILSON pointed out that the Italian Delegation at that time was not in Paris.

BARON SONNINO said that the Italian Delegation had had a general discussion earlier in the Peace Conference with the Greeks on this subject but it had been suspended pending the discussion of larger questions, including the Adriatic and mandates in Turkey, etc.

MR. LLOYD GEORGE said that the reason for the decision to send Greek troops to Smyrna was that the Greeks were being massacred

[2] That is, the Appendix to the minutes of the Council of Four printed at May 17, 1919, 4:15 p.m.
[3] V. E. Orlando to WW, May 18, 1919.
[4] That is, Orlando.

in that region. He, himself, had received a letter from a British merchant at Smyrna reporting massacres of Greeks. There were two or three hundred thousand Greek inhabitants at Smyrna and it had been necessary to provide some protection. This reason did not apply to the Italian landing at Scala Nuova as there were no Italians there.

M. CLEMENCEAU said that he had had to make an exhaustive enquiry as to why a single Company of French troops had been landed at Heraclea. This landing had not been ordered from Paris and nothing had been known of it there. It had, as a matter of fact, been ordered at the request of the Turks by the Local French Command at Constantinople, the reason being that coal was wanted at Constantinople and, owing to disturbances at Heraclea, it was not arriving. He declared that he was prepared to withdraw this single Company if the Conference demanded that he should.

PRESIDENT WILSON said that the memorandum handed by Baron Sonnino did not explain why 2,000 Italian troops had been landed at Scala Nuova.

BARON SONNINO said that there had been troubles in this district: for example, when the Greeks landed at Smyrna, there had been murders and massacres by the Greeks. In 1917, not only Scala Nuova but even Smyrna had been attributed to Italy. The question was still under discussion when the Greek landing was authorised.

MR. LLOYD GEORGE said that Smyrna was not attributed to Italy by the Treaty of London.

BARON SONNINO pointed out that under Article 9 of the Treaty of London, it was recognised in a general manner that, in the event of the total or partial partition of Turkey in Asia, Italy should obtain an equitable part in the Mediterranean region in the neighbourhood of the province of Adalia.

MR. LLOYD GEORGE said that Italy had shown no anxiety during the war to occupy any part of Turkey, neither Smyrna nor Budrum, nor Scala Nuova. At that time such action on their part would have been very welcome.

M. SONNINO said Italy had offered troops for the Turkish theatre several times.

MR. LLOYD GEORGE said they were only Abyssinian troops, and then only about 1,000, when 200,000 to 300,000 were wanted to fight Turkey.

M. SONNINO said that Italy had her hands full fighting Austria.

PRESIDENT WILSON said he must respectfully remind M. Sonnino that this was not a conversation merely between Allies. The United States had a right to a place there, and further had a right to ask questions, regardless of the Treaty of London. This Treaty did not provide an effective reason why troops should be disembarked on the mainland, or why these places should be occupied.

M. SONNINO said that at Adalia there had been disorders amounting to anarchy.

PRESIDENT WILSON asked if the landings at Scala Nuova, Makri and Budrum had been due to the same cause.

M. SONNINO said there had been disorders at Makri; Marmaris had been occupied because it was necessary to keep ships off the coast of Adalia and Marmaris was the only place at which they could lie in all weather. These landings did not compromise the final territorial decisions.

PRESIDENT WILSON said that although it might not be the Italians' intention to prejudice the decision by this action, in fact it was prejudiced.

M. SONNINO said it was necessary to avoid disorder. At Smyrna, there had been disorder, and he was informed the Greeks had gone to Aidin. That was not in accordance with the recent decision.

M. CLEMENCEAU said they had asked permission to go there, and that was why M. Venizelos was present.

PRESIDENT WILSON said that he and his colleagues had deemed it only courteous to M. Sonnino to invite him to be present when the question was discussed of giving a more extended region of occupation to the Greek troops.

M. SONNINO said that in the present discussion he would have preferred that M. Venizelos should not be present. The Italian Delegation had had discussions with M. Venizelos, and M. Venizelos had published what had occurred in the newspapers. The discussions had then been suspended pending the consideration of larger problems.

MR. LLOYD GEORGE said that M. Venizelos had taken no action without the consent of the Council of Four. If Italy preferred to depend upon her own action she could not expect to take part in the discussions of the Council. As far as he was concerned, unless Italy removed her troops, he would take no further part in the discussion of the Italian claims in Asia Minor. The Italian action was a direct defiance of the Council. It had been done in a way that he did not like to describe. A discussion had actually been in progress with Italy, and the question of Scala Nuova had not been decided. He could not imagine anything more insulting to the Council than this action.

M. SONNINO pointed out that in 1917 Smyrna had been attributed to Italy.

MR. LLOYD GEORGE pointed out that this had been subject to the consent of Russia. Russia, however, had never given her consent, and had gone out of the war. Then the United States of America came in, and the whole situation changed. Mr. Balfour had stated this in writing to the Italian Government.

M. SONNINO said that the French Government had stated that the 1917 agreement held good.

M. CLEMENCEAU said that M. Pichon had never told him so. He had not been consulted.

M. SONNINO said that he recognized that the United States was not bound, but Article 9 of the Treaty of London clearly spoke of the regions round Adalia being attributed to Italy and it was in these regions that the landings had taken place.

PRESIDENT WILSON thought that Italy had taken a very wide interpretation of the phrase. He was sure his British and French colleagues would understand it when he said that the United States did not recognise their right to hand over Turkish populations to Italy. This was a world settlement, and all were partners in it.

MR. LLOYD GEORGE said that the British and French Governments had agreed that the portion of the Turkish Empire for which it had been proposed that they should have mandates should be visited by a Commission. He asked if M. Sonnino was willing that this should apply also to Adalia.

M. SONNINO said that Italy had put no boundary excluding the Commission from Asia Minor.

MR. LLOYD GEORGE said that this was a very important declaration.

PRESIDENT WILSON asked M. Sonnino if it would not be the right thing for Italy to withdraw from Scala Nuova.

M. SONNINO pointed out that there had been massacres at Smyrna, which was not far away.

PRESIDENT WILSON said that M. Sonnino had not even alleged massacres at Scala Nuova, Makri or Budrum.

M. SONNINO said there had been disorders at Makri and very serious disorders at Adalia, amounting to anarchy.

MR. LLOYD GEORGE asked by what right Italy intervened.

M. SONNINO said that the Italians were established at Rhodes.

PRESIDENT WILSON pointed out that Rhodes had not been ceded to Italy.

M. SONNINO said that the Italians had been at Rhodes ever since the war with Turkey. They had been discussing the question of the Dodecanese with the Greeks, but these islands were provisionally occupied. No ill consequences had come from any of those landings, and no person had been hurt. Why, he asked, did the Council want Italy to withdraw their troops. The Italian Government had to consider public opinion in Italy, and there would be very serious agitation if this action was taken. There was no particular object in it. Surely it was not desired to do harm in Italy.

PRESIDENT WILSON said he had only asked for an explanation. He accepted what M. Sonnino had said about disorders at Adalia, but there had not been any serious disorders elsewhere.

M. SONNINO said that in order to retain Adalia, ships were necessary, and this explained the occupation of Marmaris. . . .

PRESIDENT WILSON said that the object of all was to occupy a position of common counsel. To hear that Italy, without a word to anyone, had landed troops in Asia Minor had been very disconcerting.

MR. LLOYD GEORGE said that this was more especially the case as it was obviously done in order to peg out a claim. M. Venizelos had been told that he must not land Greek troops at Scala Nuova, because the question was sub judice. The Italians had done this without saying a word to people who were in the same room with them. He knew what would be said about a man of business who did such a thing. . . .[5]

A few minutes later SIR MAURICE HANKEY read a draft of the dispatch to Admiral Calthorpe, which, after some discussion, was approved in the following form:

"The council of the Principal Allied and Associated Powers has approved that in the event of disorders in the Vilayet of Aidin, anywhere North of Aidin inclusive, Greek troops may be sent to restore order, but only after obtaining the approval of the Senior Naval Officer of the Allied Fleets at Smyrna, who will be the final judge as to whether the circumstances justify the despatch of troops. Greek troops, however, may be sent without special authority to the districts within the Sandjak of Smyrna, but not South of Ayasoluk and within the Kaza of Aivali for the purpose of establishing order and protecting the returning refugees. The Greek military authorities should be given facilities on all railway

[5] At this point Vénisélos returned, and, under questioning from Wilson, revealed that, in addition to the First Greek Division that had been sent to Smyrna, he had now ordered that two more regiments and five hundred gendarmes be sent to assist in maintaining order. He believed that the Greek commander there could now spare some troops to "go up country." He denied that he had ordered any troops sent to Aydin or elsewhere in the interior. The commander on the scene did have authorization to send troops wherever necessary to keep order. However, Vénisélos had instructed the commander not to send troops anywhere if there was any risk of their encountering Italian troops. Wilson asked if Vénisélos did not agree that the Greeks should "await developments" and consult with the Council of Four before "putting in operation any more extended plan for occupation." Vénisélos agreed in principle but suggested that, in order to avoid the lengthy process of securing the approval of the council before Greek soldiers could be sent to any trouble spot, Admiral Calthorpe should have the authority to authorize the sending of troops. The council agreed that either Calthorpe or whoever commanded the Allied fleet at Smyrna should have this authority. Vénisélos also proposed, and the council agreed, that Greek troops should be sent to the Sanjak of Smyrna and the Kaza of Aivali to protect Turkish refugees from those areas who wished to return and recommence farming.

lines radiating from Smyrna for carrying out this movement. M. Venizelos is sending instructions to the Greek authorities to conform to these arrangements."

3. Sir Maurice Hankey was drafting the above dispatch during the following conversation, the notes of which are consequently very brief.

M. SONNINO again reverted to the question of the Italian troops, and asked for the agreement of his colleagues to keep things as they were without withdrawing the Italian troops.

PRESIDENT WILSON said that as far as he was concerned the Italian Government must take the whole responsibility for the retention of these troops.

MR. LLOYD GEORGE said that this was his view.

M. CLEMENCEAU said it was his view also.

MR. LLOYD GEORGE said that the Italian action was most prejudicial to the work of the Conference. M. Orlando, when asked for an explanation, had said he knew nothing about the matter, and it was perfectly clear that he did not. Apparently the Head of the Government had not even been consulted.

M. SONNINO said that of course M. Orlando was kept informed.

(It was at this point that Sir Maurice Hankey read the Draft dispatch quoted above.)

4. The Council had before it Herr Brockdorff-Rantzau's letter on the subject of Reparation (Appendix II), and the draft reply prepared by a Committee under M. Klotz (Appendix III(a)).[6]

(This letter was approved, subject to the following alterations:
In the sixth paragraph, the substitution of the word "claimed" for the word "admitted."
In the seventh paragraph, line 1 to read as follows: "she did not act upon the principle she now contends for either in 1871" etc. * * * instead of "she did not recognise this principle either in 1871" etc.
In the eighth paragraph delete the words "you will not be surprised to learn that" and substitute "in reply we beg to say that").
Sir Maurice Hankey was instructed to see that the necessary alterations were made in the French version and to prepare a copy for M. Clemenceau's signature. (It was further agreed that after

[6] Not printed. At this point, Mantoux, II, 121-22, adds:
"Wilson. Have you formed an opinion of the German note relating to general responsibility for damages? At the time of the Armistice, the Germans acknowledged themselves responsible for damages caused by the aggression of Germany by land, by sea, and in the air. Today they continue to declare that it is not they who caused the war. This attitude is unbelievable.
"Lloyd George. It shows that Germany is still in the hands of her old staff or has not yet got rid of them.
"Wilson. Or at the very least, Germany allows them to speak in her name."

signature Herr Brockdorff-Rantzau's letter, together with the reply, should be published.)

The letter as finally approved is contained in Appx III(b).

5. The Council had before them a letter from Herr BROCKDORFF-RANTZAU, together with a draft reply.

On MONSIEUR CLEMENCEAU's suggestion the subject was adjourned until the draft reply to a second letter from the Germans on the same subject was available.[7]

6. MR. LLOYD GEORGE read the following information he had received in regard to the supply of clothing to German prisoners:

(1) There is no German clothing available of any kind.

(2) All the German prisoners now held by us have underclothing and boots sufficient for them to be sent straight back to Germany.

(3) As regards their civilian clothing, our prisoners of war are wearing prisoners of war coats and trousers. They could be returned to Germany wearing the trousers already supplied, but not the coats.

We have no stocks of civilian clothing available. All available stocks were bought up for the British who have been demobilised and the stocks available for this purpose were insufficient.

Mr. Lloyd George said his attention had been drawn to the suggestion that altered British uniforms might be used. For instance, the military buttons might be cut off and uniforms made for all intents and purposes into civilian suits. He said he was informed that we were actually 200,000 suits short for our own soldiers. Hence he thought that the question should be treated as one in which we were unable to give any help.

PRESIDENT WILSON said that the United States Army had no civilian supplies at all; only military supplies.

M. CLEMENCEAU instructed M. Mantoux to ascertain the state of Prisoners of War in France.

PRESIDENT WILSON suggested that the reply should be that we would supply the prisoners with the best clothing we had, but should explain that we had not enough to give a complete equipment to every prisoner.

SIR MAURICE HANKEY asked whether any repayment was to be exacted for the clothes provided, as contemplated in Herr Brockdorff-Rantzau's letter.

MR. LLOYD GEORGE said that if they were merely to go in the best makeshift that could be arranged, this was unnecessary.

[7] Brockdorff-Rantzau's two letters on the Saar Valley are printed as Appendixes II and III to the minutes of the Council of Four, May 22, 1919, 11:45 a.m., *PPC*, V, 817-22.

(It was agreed that Mr. Lloyd George's draft should be revised in the light of the above discussion.)

7. PRESIDENT WILSON said that he had ordered an enquiry to be sent to Koltchak, direct from the State Department, asking him to specify his programme and policy. He said he had also received information from M. Kerenski.[8] He would not regard this as a good source of information unless it happened to tally with information he had received elsewhere. Kerenski and his friends hoped that there would be no recognition of Koltchak or anyone else as representative of all the Russias and that as a condition of further assistance, certain agreements should be exacted from all the parties opposed to the Bolshevists, by which they would pledge themselves to a certain progressive policy. They should be informed that a departure from this would cause them to lose the support of the Allied and Associated Powers. This seemed to provide the rudiments of a policy.

MR. LLOYD GEORGE agreed that it was important to impose conditions.

PRESIDENT WILSON said that these Russian groups could be broken down at any time by our failure to support them.

MR. LLOYD GEORGE said he was amazed at the amount of material that had been supplied. They had received something like £50,000,000 of armaments and munitions.

8. The following resolution submitted by Sir Maurice Hankey was approved:

> "It is agreed that the Committee which drew up the Articles in regard to Prisoners of War for the Treaty with Germany, should meet again to prepare, for the consideration of the Council of the Principal Allied and Associated Powers, Articles for inclusion in the Treaties with Austria, Hungary, and Bulgaria."

9. PRESIDENT WILSON read a copy of a letter from M. Fromageot, a copy of which had been handed him by Sir Maurice Hankey, who had received it from Mr. Hurst. (Appendix IV.)[9]

(After a short discussion it was agreed that the words "during the period of the belligerency of each as an Allied and Associated Power against Germany" should be reinstated in the French text of Article 232.)

[8] See A. F. Kerenskii *et al.* to WW, May 14, 1919.

[9] H. A. Fromageot to [G. Clemenceau], May 14, 1919, TCL (SDR, RG 256, 180.03401/19, DNA). Fromageot reported that, in the course of the drafting process, the phrase quoted immediately below in the above document, which had been designed to exclude any application of reparation funds to new states such as Poland, had been omitted in the French text while it remained in the English text. He wished to know if the Council of Four desired the clause to remain or to be omitted in both texts.

APPENDIX II TO C.F.19.

Translation.

GERMAN PEACE DELEGATION.

Mr. President,   Versailles, May 13, 1919.

In the draft of a Peace Treaty submitted to the German Delegates, Part VIII, concerning Reparation, begins with Article 231, which reads as follows:

"The Allied and Associated Governments affirm and Germany accepts the responsibility of Germany and her Allies for causing all the loss and damage to which the Allied and Associated Governments and their nationals have been subjected as a consequence of the war imposed upon them by the aggression of Germany and her Allies."

Now the obligation to make reparation has been accepted by Germany by virtue of the note from Secretary of State Lansing of November 5, 1918, independently of the question of responsibility for the war. The German Delegation cannot admit that there could arise, out of a responsibility incurred by the former German Government in regard to the origin of the world war, any right for the Allied and Associated Powers to be indemnified by Germany for losses suffered during the war. The representatives of the Allied and Associated States have moreover declared several times that the German people should not be held responsible for the faults committed by their Government.

The German people did not will the war and would never have undertaken a war of aggression. They have always remained convinced that this war was for them a defensive war.

The German Delegates also do not share the views of the Allied and Associated Governments in regard to the origin of the war. They cannot consider the former German Government as the party which was solely or chiefly to blame for this war. The draft Treaty of Peace transmitted (by you) contains no facts in support of this view; no proof on the subject is furnished therein. The German Delegates therefore beg (you) to be so good as to communicate to them the Report of the Commission set up by the Allied and Associated Governments for the purpose of establishing the responsibility of the authors of the war.

Pray accept, Mr. President, the assurances of my high consideration.   (Signed)   BROCKDORFF-RANTZAU.

APPENDIX III (b) TO C.F. 19.

Translation.

Ministry of Finance,

Minister of Finance to M. Clemenceau.   Paris, 16th May, 1919.

You were so good as to communicate on the 15th May to the Reparations Commission and the Responsibilities Commission a letter from the President of the German Peace Delegation dated May 13th, 1919, relative to the responsibility of the German people in regard to the origin of the war and the obligation to make reparation.

These two Commissions immediately met together at the Ministry of Finance and selected me to preside over their common labour.

After consideration of Count Brockdorff-Rantzau's letter and an exchange of views between the members of the two Commissions these Commissions unanimously approved a draft reply to be submitted to the Council of Four.

I have the honour to transmit to you herewith this draft.

(Signed)   Klotz.

Draft Reply to Principal German Plenipotentiary approved by M. Klotz, Mr. James Brown Scott, Lord Sumner, M. Crespi and M. Sakutaro Tachi, to be submitted to the Council of Four.

"Sir,

In your note of May 3rd [13th] you state that Germany, while 'accepting' in November 1918 'the obligation to make reparation' did not understand such an acceptance to mean that her responsibility was involved either for the war or for the acts of the former German Government.

It is only possible to conceive of such an obligation if its origin and cause is the responsibility of the author of the damage.

You add that the German people would never have undertaken a war of aggression. Yet, in the note from Mr. Secretary of State Lansing of November 5th, 1918, which you approve of and adduce in favour of your contention, it is stated that the obligation to make reparation arises out of 'Germany's aggression by land, sea and air.'

As the German Government did not at the time make any protest against this allegation, it thereby recognised it as well-founded.

Therefore Germany recognised in 1918 implicitly but clearly, both the aggression and her responsibility.

It is too late to seek to deny them today. It would be impossible, you state further, ~~for~~ that the German people should be regarded as the accomplices of the faults committed by the 'former German Government.' However, Germany has never ~~admitted~~ claimed and such a declaration would have been contrary to all principles of international law, that a modification of its political régime or a change in the governing personalities would be sufficient to extinguish an obligation already undertaken by any nation.

She did not act upon the principle she now contends for either in 1871 as regards France, after the proclamation of the Republic, nor in 1917 in regard to Russia after the revolution which abolished the Tsarist régime.

Finally, you ask that the report of the Commission on Responsibility may be communicated to you. In reply we beg to say that the Allied and Associated Powers consider the reports of the Commissions set up by the Peace Conference as documents of an internal character which cannot be transmitted to you."

T MS (SDR, RG 256, 180.03401/19, DNA).

To Richard Irvine Manning

My dear Governor Manning: Paris, 19 May, 1919.

It was a matter of real distress for me that I could not find an interval in my busy days when I could see you and feel the cordial grasp of your hand again, but I am warmly obliged to you for your generous letter which you left behind you and which has just come to my desk.[1] I have had to forego all pleasures and devote myself entirely to the watchful task of trying to get as many things straight as possible in this tremendous settlement.

I am sure you know my warm feeling toward you and how highly and truly I value your generous approval.

With the most cordial good wishes and my sincere respects to Mrs. Manning,   Faithfully yours,   [Woodrow Wilson]

CCL (WP, DLC).
    [1] See R. I. Manning to WW, May 17, 1919.

To Louis Marshall

My dear Mr. Marshall: Paris, 19 May, 1919.

Thank you for your letter of May fifteenth, which I have read with great interest. I think I can assure you that all four of the group with whom I am consulting are equally desirous of seeing genuine guarantees secured for Jewish minorities, and I will take pleasure in laying the points of your letter before them.

                        Sincerely yours,   [Woodrow Wilson]

CCL (WP, DLC).

To Edwin Samuel Montagu

PRIVATE AND CONFIDENTIAL

My dear Mr. Secretary: Paris, 19 May, 1919.

Thank you very much for your confidential note of the seventeenth of May. I was very much impressed and instructed by the interview of Saturday and hope I shall know better how to play my own part in dealing with the critical question of Turkish sovereignty. Your letter gives me the additional guidance I need.

Cordially and sincerely yours,   [Woodrow Wilson]

CCL (WP, DLC).

Two Letters from Tasker Howard Bliss

Dear Mr. President: Paris 19 May, 1919

In my letter of May 9th[1] I reported to you the plan of Marshal Foch for the strength of the Army of Occupation in the Rhenish Provinces after the signature of peace, which was outlined by him at a conference of himself, General Sir Henry Wilson and myself. In that letter I stated that General Pershing's exact knowledge of the situation made his advice necessary in the settlement of this question.

In the conference at Mr. Lloyd George's house, on the afternoon of May 10, you asked me to see General Pershing and obtain his views. In going to General Pershing I had an opportunity of visiting several of the headquarters of his troops in German territory and was able to obtain the opinion of many of his principal officers. Their opinion was in exact accord with that subsequently given to me by General Pershing and I think may be accepted as the general view of the American army in France. This opinion was entirely in favor of continuing the withdrawal of the American army from France on the plan now being executed, and is supported by the following reasons.

1) You will remember that the Marshal's plan calls for four combatant American divisions for the three months following the date of the signature of the Treaty of Peace. This force, organized with all of its auxiliary services, would amount to a total of 162,000 men to be maintained here in France.

2) Under the law providing for our present war-army, the entire drafted force must be mustered out within four months from the date of signature of peace. In order that this may be accomplished, approximately the present rate of movement of American troops home would have to be continued and arrangements made for send-

ing back to France the better part of the above mentioned 162,000 men, to be composed of regular troops.

3) The regular army (which, from statements made by the Chairman of the House Military Committee,[2] is more likely to be reduced than increased), consists of approximately 212,000 men. Leaving out the Coast Artillery and the pre-war garrisons of Hawaii, the Philippines, and Panama, would leave 162,000 men. If the disarmament of Germany should not be completed, to the satisfaction of the French, at the end of three months, they would prolong the occupation for an indefinite period, or until they were satisfied. This would require the entire available regular army of the United States to be kept in the Rhenish Provinces for an indefinite period, leaving not a single man at home for duty on the Mexican border or elsewhere in the interior of our country.

4) The Marshal's plan calls for from one to two American divisions to remain in occupation for from five to fifteen years. This force, together with its auxiliary services, would require a very considerable part of the available combatant troops of the regular army during that period.

The British intend to reduce their force to one battalion (about 1,000 men); I understood you to say that the Americans would not keep more than a nominal force, say, one regiment.

Such a force would not even, in any proper sense of the word, show our flag. It would have to be absorbed in a French organization and subject entirely to French orders. I am informed that the French intend to maintain Senegalese negro troops as a large part of their force of occupation. No one who knows the degraded character of these troops desires to have American troops serve in any way in association with them. This is not on account of color, but because continued occupation by these African troops would be intolerable to any civilized community and will result in incidents for which Americans should not be made to incur even a quasi-responsibility.

5) If the Marshal's plan should be approved by the Supreme Council the transportation of American troops home would have to be stopped in the month of June. Our ocean transports would then have to lie idle or (because of the irresistible demand for their use in commerce) would have to be re-modeled for commercial services. When the transportation of our remaining troops home should then be resumed, we would have to again secure these transports, with the consequent disruption of the peaceful trade in which they would then be engaged, and refit them at great expense as troop transports.

6) The universal desire of the American army in France is to re-

turn home as soon as possible. Officers and men believe that their work here has been accomplished.

7) The American force contemplated by the Marshal for permanent occupation, is of no value from either the moral or the physical point of view. It is so small that it will be absorbed in French organizations and under French control. It will not be strong enough to produce the slightest effect in military operations, should the latter have to be resumed, and could serve only to entangle the United States when it would seem wiser that the latter should have a free hand.

For the above reasons I concur in the views of General Pershing and with what seems to be the universal sentiment of the American army here,—that the withdrawal of the entire American force be continued until completed on the present schedule. If, however, it is absolutely necessary, under any agreement that may have been made, that a nominal American force remain here, it is recommended that the withdrawal of our troops continue on the present schedule until not to exceed one regiment is left in France. I think, however, that even in that case a reservation should be made that will permit the United States to withdraw that regiment whenever in its discretion it thinks such action to be desirable.

As giving General Pershing's views, I quote the following from a memorandum handed to me by him to-day:

"This (referring to the American force requested by Marshal Foch) is relatively so small that the suggestion can not be considered as based upon necessity. Moreover, if, during the occupation, the situation should demand a resort to arms, a small American force of one or two divisions would have to be augmented by new troops from the States.

"As to the retention of a merely nominal force consisting of a regiment or a battalion, that would be for moral effect alone and the desired effect could probably be attained by an understanding or an announcement that the occupying French and British troops would represent all the Allies.

"It should be borne in mind that in such association of troops of different nationalities for any length of time, unless engaged in fighting a common cause demanding full cooperation, there is almost certain to be friction. Any army that we should leave would have to be placed under an Allied command in whose motives we would have little confidence and of whose orders and movements our government could have little or no control.

"The attitude of our Allies toward the German government and the German people is so at variance with our own that an Allied

Commander would be likely to involve us in situations and use our troops under circumstances which we would entirely disapprove.

"The French are planning to use divisions composed half of colored troops and half French, which in itself seems likely to lead to difficulties on account of their race and color. The proposal to use such troops would seem to indicate the small importance they attach to this occupation, as well as a desire to reduce the participation of the French Army to a minimum. The use of such low grade troops by the French would provoke jealousy and adverse criticism by any troops we should leave here who would, of course, be the pick of our Army.

"There are many possible difficulties that might arise that can not be foreseen. Instead, therefore, of having troops here under the very uncertain conditions that exist and take the chance of becoming involved further in European questions, possibly against our will, without an opportunity of prior determination, it seems to me most important that we should decline to leave troops here."

General Pershing tells me that it is very important that he should know as early as possible your decision as to the force, if any, to be retained for purposes of the occupation.

Cordially yours,   Tasker H. Bliss.

[1] THB to WW, May 9, 1919, TLS, enclosing [F. Foch], "Note," [May 9, 1919], T MS, both in WP, DLC. Foch stated that, for the three months following the signature of the peace treaty, thirty army divisions would be needed to insure the disarmament of Germany. This force should include four American divisions. After the disarmament was completed, the occupation force could be reduced to ten divisions, including one or two American divisions.

[2] The new chairman of the House Committee on Military Affairs was Julius Kahn, Republican of California. Kahn, who had just concluded a tour of American military establishments in Europe, had announced in Paris on May 6 that he would introduce bills in Congress to provide for six months of military training for all American boys at eighteen years of age and for an army of 100,000 volunteers. In an interview with Charles Albert Selden of the *New York Times* on May 13, he reiterated his support for universal military training and called for a "regular army" of about 100,000 officers and men to be enrolled on a three-year "volunteer enlistment basis." See *ibid.*, May 7 and 16, 1919.

Dear Mr. President: Paris, 19 May 1919.

Mr. Baruch informs me this morning that on last Saturday he sent to you in writing his objections and those of the American Representatives on the Supreme Economic Council to the provisions of a "DRAFT CONVENTION REGARDING THE MILITARY OCCUPATION OF THE TERRITORIES WEST OF THE RHINE." I understood from him that at the time he sent you a copy of the document itself.

This matter was acted upon during my absence on a visit to General Pershing at Coblenz. En route to Coblenz I stopped at Treves and there had an interview with Mr. Noyes,[1] the American Representative on the Rhineland Commission. I hoped that I would learn from him that his Commission was intended to take control of the civil administration of the Rhenish Provinces during the period of occupation. He informed me, however, that his Commission was intended for the regulation of certain economic questions alone.

An examination of the above-mentioned "DRAFT CONVENTION REGARDING THE MILITARY OCCUPATION OF THE TERRITORIES WEST OF THE RHINE" will show that it carries over into a time of peace the "Laws of Military Occupation" which should apply only in time of war. A *military* government of the Rhenish Provinces should not be permitted in time of war [peace] if American troops are to take any part in this occupation. If there is to be such a military government it is an additional argument for withdrawing every American soldier at the earliest possible moment.

I think that the troops of occupation in the Rhenish Provinces after the signature of peace should be there under the same conditions that a military force exists in any country in time of peace. That is to say, it should be there prepared to quell disorder but to take no part whatever in the civil administration. In my judgment, a strong Inter-Allied civilian Commission should be formed for the purpose of taking over the government of all occupied German territory. This Commission should have sole and absolute control of the civil administration of the country and the military should not be permitted to have any part in it.

I think that the military administration of this territory for from five to fifteen years after the signature of the Treaty of Peace would be an unjustifiable and intolerable burden imposed upon the inhabitants of that territory.   Cordially yours,   Tasker H. Bliss.

TLS (WP, DLC).
¹ Pierrepont Burt Noyes, who had been appointed to the Inter-Allied Rhineland Commission on April 25, 1919. The Council of Five had established the Rhineland Commission on April 14.

To Newton Diehl Baker

Paris [May 19, 1919]

For Secretary of War: "In view of information from many angles about the Siberian situation, I would be obliged if you would get into communication with Polk and ask him to request Morris to form a judgment and confidentially advise us as to whether it would relieve unnecessary friction at Vladivostock if some one else should take the place of General Graves.

You are in touch with Polk and know the difficulties and misunderstandings that are arising there, the most serious of which I learned of in your own message. Morris is going through all the way to Omsk to form an opinion about the situation as a whole."

Woodrow Wilson.

T telegram (J. P. Tumulty Papers, DLC).

From Robert Lansing, with Enclosure

My dear Mr. President: Paris, May 19, 1919.

Will you please advise me what reply you wish to have made to the enclosed telegram from Mr. Polk, with reference to his conversation with Senator Hitchcock?[1]

Faithfully yours,   Robert Lansing

TLS (WP, DLC).
  [1] For Wilson's reply, see WW to RL, May 24, 1919 (first letter of that date).

E N C L O S U R E

Washington. May 17th, 1919.

2014. For the Secretary of State and Colonel House.

Had a long talk with Senator Hitchcock yesterday on the subject of the Covenant of the League of Nations. He reports that from his conversations with Republican Senators he is convinced that the big attack will be made on Clause 10.[1] The two other points that are subject to attack are first the clause in regard to the Monroe Doctrine, which they claim is objectionable. Personally I cannot understand why that is not satisfactory. The criticism it is certain does not go far enough.[2] Seventh paragraph, Article 15, will be also subject of attack and Hitchcock is a little doubtful about that clause himself.[3] I do not know whether any modifications are possible, but my own feeling is that the Covenant would have a better chance of passing if some more or less immaterial modification could be made after the Covenant reaches the Senate. I see many objections to this procedure, but at the same time any change made in the Covenant now will be subject to attack whereas the concessions made as the result of a fight in Senate might have to be accepted by Republicans.

I suggest that some statement should be made in Paris in regard to Article 10 or would it be possible to cable over secret proceedings so I can give them to Hitchcock. Hitchcock is trying to be most helpful.   Polk,   Acting.

T telegram (SDR, RG 256, 185.111/298, DNA).
  [1] He referred to Article X of the Covenant, which is printed at April 28, 1919, Vol. 58.

² This sentence *sic*. It should probably read: "The criticism is certain it does not go far enough."

³ Polk referred to the following paragraph(s) of Article XV, which provided machinery for the settlement of disputes between or among members of the League:

"If the Council fails to reach a report which is unanimously agreed to by the members thereof, other than the representatives of one or more of the parties to the dispute, the Members of the League reserve to themselves the right to take such action as they shall consider necessary for the maintenance of right and justice.

"If the dispute between the parties is claimed by one of them, and is found by the Council, to arise out of a matter which by international law is solely within the domestic jurisdiction of that party, the Council shall so report, and shall make no recommendation as to its settlement."

From the Diary of Vance Criswell McCormick

May 19 (Monday) [1919]

Lunched with Legge,¹ Baruch and Davis. Afterwards discussed financial plans for relief of Europe. Lamont also present. Senator Gerry called to discuss United States politics and at 4.00 o'clock Davis, Baruch, Lamont and I went to discuss with the President the financial plan. President willing to recommend to Treasury and Congress postponing of interest for three years provided Allies agree to a financial plan that is satisfactory.

President in good shape today. Told us of his message to Congress and plans for returning home. Expects to get away about the 1st of June. He will be disappointed, I am afraid. Hopes to be here until Austrian treaty is ready for presentation and expects to carry back with him the signed German treaty.

¹ That is, Alexander Legge.

A Memorandum by Thomas William Lamont

At the President's House,
Paris, May 19, 1919.

Had a talk with the President over the telephone the Saturday previous, about the necessity of explaining to him the memorandum that I had submitted,¹ as per copy attached hereto, upon the financial situation in Europe. He said he would surely send for me on Monday.

The appointment was arranged at 4 o'clock Monday, and there went with me NHD, BHB [BMB] and VMC. I told the President that we had been anxious to talk with him so as to get his word of mouth views on certain points on the whole financial situation. He said that he had read the memorandum with great interest and that it was clear to him we should do something along the lines indicated. We discussed the question of Congressional legislation, and he stated that he could see the necessity for widening the powers of the War Finance Corporation and for securing Congressional action along the line of refunding interest, and possibly securing additional latitude from Congress for direct loans to our Allies. We explained that on this very last point we were not quite as insistent as we had been, except to the necessity for furnishing credit for the stabilization of currencies in the newer countries.

I then asked the President whether he had given consideration to the last paragraph of the memorandum having to do with the question of public opinion in America. He said, "Yes," he had, and noted my suggestion that he should be the one to begin the work of education. He said he had been puzzled to know how this could be undertaken, and wanted to know if I had any idea on this point.

I replied that the way it had lain in my own mind was this: That when the proper time came he could tell the American people in broad, general terms of the situation over here. He should pay a tribute to the American people for the manner in which they had conducted their share in the war, for their magnificent giving, payment of taxes, raising of Liberty loans, readiness to sacrifice everything; but he should point out, in the last analysis America had not really suffered to anything like the degree of her friends over here, that something still remained for us to do, and that was to help them in the present situation as he would have described it. From that go on to say that the help that America could render could be done in this wise: They proved in the last two years that they could save and lend the money to their Government. Let the American people, therefore, continue that habit of saving for another two years, and lend the proceeds to the European nations to set them on their feet.

The President seemed considerably taken with this idea, and we fell into a deep discussion of when such a declaration on his part might best take place. I asked whether it would be best to postpone it until after the Senate had ratified the Treaty, on the theory that perhaps if sprung earlier the Senate would get scared, and perhaps fall down on the Treaty. The President mused on this inquiry for a moment, and then said that on the whole he thought the time to make any such declaration to the American people was at the same time that he asked Congress for what further legislation might be necessary, and that, presumably, would be immediately upon returning home and presenting the Treaty itself. He said that of course he must tell Congress the whole story, and if he told Congress he might just as well take the same opportunity to tell the American people. We all agreed that this was a wise decision.

The President then asked me whether I would have some text

prepared to cover the matter of Congressional and War Finance legislation, which I promised we should do.

The other gentlemen present said comparatively little, as the subject matter was more in my own particular province.   TWL

T MS (T. W. Lamont Papers, MH-BA).
  [1] See the Enclosure printed with T. W. Lamont to WW, May 15, 1919.

From the Diary of Ray Stannard Baker

Monday the 19th [May 1919].

I had quite a talk this morning with Mr. Lansing who is just back from a trip to England where he dined with the King & saw many prominent Englishmen. He looks very fit. He is surprisingly bitter about the treaty & quite frankly told me he thought it almost hopelessly bad. Says, moreover, that most of the Englishmen he saw think so too—regardless of their political convictions: though I suspect that he saw only the tories, and the class there which is opposed to Lloyd-George. Lansing feels strongly that the other American Commissioners have not been properly consulted by the President & are required to bear the odium of a treaty they have had no real part in making. They have not only not been consulted but often they have not been informed as to what was going on. Often times I have known far better the real inside proceedings than any of the Commissioners & have repeatedly told Lansing and White (but only occasionally House, who has been much closer to the President than the others) what was going on in the Council of Four. Certainly I have recently seen more of the President than any of the Commissioners—for even House seems now unable to keep in close contact with him. I don't know how long it will last, for me!

There has also been much jealousy between the "First floor" and the "Third floor"[1]—the Commissioners on the First floor (Lansing and White—I have recently seen little of Bliss) referring ironically to the "Third Floor."[2] This seems small talk—& yet these personal relationships often count largely in affairs.

Secretary Lansing told me he thought there was no hope even in the League of Nations, if it passed the Senate: for it was founded upon an unjust settlement: & the provision requiring unanimous consent in the Council made it an impossible document to change. With section 10, he said, we were called upon to guarantee all the mistakes of the treaty. But then, Mr. Lansing has never really believed in the League! I was also surprised to hear him say—what I truly believe—that he thought the great fault with the Conference from the start was a want of proper publicity: that if the President had from the beginning taken the people of the world into his confidence he might have carried through his program. I was surprised to hear him say this because he is himself one of the most timid & conservative of men regarding publicity.

I had two talks with the President to-day—one over the telephone this morning, in which I urged him to the point of making myself a nuisance, I am afraid, to let us have his message to Congress to put out here & in England. He actually did not want to have any publicity here! Said it concerned only home affairs! I told him that I had cables from London & that half the Paris press had been telephoning me this morning & that if it were not given out here it would be cabled (and garbled!) back from America. He then argued that it was not complete—the paragraph on the prohibition law having been prepared in Washington. It is amazing that he should wish so to try to keep back such a public document. I finally persuaded him to let me have it & get by cable the text of the missing paragraph— and I got it off by courier this evening to London. We will translate it into French & issue it here to-morrow.

This evening, at the usual time, I had quite a talk with him. Sometimes he is very brief & quite impersonal & sometimes, as to-night, he is charmingly discursive & tells with humor the events of the day. We sit facing each other in his study. Admiral Grayson is usually present. He had much to say about the greedy Italians & how they are landing troops in Syria & trying to hold Dalmatia.

"They will never get Fiume," he said, "while I have anything to do with it."

It appears that they wanted to ask Orlando this morning about these military preparations but he did not appear at the Council of Four. Diplomatic sickness? In the afternoon Sonnino came, but was as slippery as an eel or an Italian—and conveyed nothing.

The President seemed much concerned as to whether the Germans would sign. I told him that Brockdorff-Rantzau had come back & he considered it a favorable symptom. He does not like the treaty himself—but hopes fervently that the Germans will sign, & get it over.

When I left he asked me to call a meeting of the Commission at 8 o'clock but I found Lansing & White both out to dinner & could not get them together.

What a man it is! As lonely as God—a slave he is! Rarely anyone in to luncheon or dinner—no social life at all. Yet he is the only great, serious, responsible statesman here: when all is said, a great man: a Titan struggling with forces too great even for him.

We had rumors to-day that certain members of our Commission

were resigning because the treaty does not satisfy them. It is only Bullitt, who wrote what the President characterized as an insulting letter: but Bullitt has spread the news abroad. He does not play the game!

I hear again that both General Smuts & General Botha are bitterly opposed to the treaty.

[1] Of the Hôtel Crillon.
[2] Where House and his entourage had suites, rooms, and offices.

From William Bauchop Wilson and William Cox Redfield

Washington DC [May 19, 1919]

No 131 Secretaries Redfield and Wilson ask me to cable the following letter quote The electric railway problem[1] comma to which your attention has been called on several occasions comma has recently assumed such serious national proportions as to warrant the prompt attention of the federal government period Already fifty or more urban systems comma representing a considerable percentage of the total electric railway mileage of the country comma are in the hands of receivers period The communities affected are among the most important dash New York comma Providence comma Buffalo comma New Orleans comma Denver comma Saint Louis comma Birmingham comma Montgomery comma Pittsburgh comma Des Moines comma Memphis comma Fort Wayne comma Saint Paul comma Spokane comma Chattanooga period paragraph

Other large systems are on the verge of insolvency comma for the industry as a whole is virtually bankrupt period The continued shrinkage in the value of hundreds of millions of electric railway securities held by savings banks comma national banks comma life insurance companies and by the public at large comma threatens to embarrass the nation's financial operations period Furthermore comma the withdrawal of this industry's buying power comma which is said to rank third in magnitude comma involves the unsettlement of collateral industries comma naturally entailing labor dislocation that will affect hundreds of thousands of employees period paragraph

The return to normal conditions is being hampered and the efforts of the government to avert strained conditions in finance comma labor and commerce are being less fruitful of satisfactory results than should be expected comma if some solution of the electric railways' problem were in view period paragraph

What the solution is comma may comma we believe comma be evolved by a thorough investigation of general franchise and operating conditions in their relation to rates comma including service hyphen at hyphen cost hyphen plans comma state and municipal taxation comma local paving requirements comma and internal economies that may be effected period paragraph

We comma therefore comma propose and recommend the appointment by you of a federal board or commission comma whose duty it shall be to study and report upon the entire problem comma in order that the state and municipal authorities and other[s] concerned may have the benefit of full information and of any conclusions or recommendations that may be formulated period Such a study will comma in our opinion comma exert a helpful and constructive force in this critical period of the industry's existence comma and will aid in the readjustment period If you would make such an appointment before June 30th comma your contingency fund could be used to defray the expenses comma which would be about ten thousand dollars period paragraph

The National Association of State Commissioners has already invited federal aid in this matter and the recent Conference of Governors and Mayors[2] adopted a resolution recommending federal consideration of the problem of preventing the financial disaster threatening this country paragraph

We propose that such a commission shall be made up of one representative of each of the following groups colon Treasury Department or War Finance Corporation comma Department of Commerce comma Department of Labor comma National Association of State Commissioners comma American Cities League of Mayors comma Amalgamated Association of Street Railway Employees comma American Electric Railway Association comma Investment Bankers Association of America paragraph

We respectfully urge your authorization for such a commission comma to be followed by your formal proclamation upon the selection of personnel unquote   Tumulty

T telegram (WP, DLC).
    [1] About this problem, see the index references under "transit companies" in Vols. 49 and 51 of this series.
    [2] About which, see the references to "Governors and Mayors, Conference of," in the Index to Vol. 55.

From the Diary of Dr. Grayson

Tuesday, May 20, 1919.

The President after breakfast usually indulges now in a morning walk. I persuaded him to get out in the fresh air more frequently. He generally goes out in the morning and in the afternoon. He has been confining himself too close to the house.

When the President returned from his morning walk he went directly to the conference of the Big Four, which took up the question of the revision of the Treaty of 1839, which defined the boundaries of Belgium and Holland. Belgium is very anxious that this Treaty should be revised so that the Scheldt River should be considered entirely Belgian territory, thus affording Antwerp an open way to the ocean. The representatives of the Dutch government, who were present at the conference, stated that they were willing to make concessions along this line but that they certainly would not consent under any circumstance to any revision of this Treaty that would take away from Holland a single square yard of her territory. The matter was finally referred to the Council of Foreign Ministers, who will endeavor to reconcile the claims of the two nations.

There were no guests for luncheon today, and after luncheon the President worked for a brief period in his study, after which he and I went for a motor ride, which terminated at the Hotel Crillon, where the President held an extended conference lasting for fully two hours with the members of the American Peace Commission.[1]

The President returned to the temporary White House at 7:15 o'clock, when the President and Mrs. Wilson had dinner.

[1] For the subjects of their conference, see H. White to WW, May 22, 1919 (first letter of that date), and EMH to WW, May 22, 1919, and n. 1 thereto.

A Special Message to Congress

[May 20, 1919]

Gentlemen of the Congress: I deeply regret my inability to be present at the opening of the extraordinary session of the Congress. It still seems to be my duty to take part in the counsels of the peace conference and contribute what I can to the solution of the innumerable questions to whose settlement it has had to address itself: for they are questions which affect the peace of the whole world and from them, therefore, the United States cannot stand apart. I deemed it my duty to call the Congress together at this time because it was not wise to postpone longer the provisions which must be made for the support of the government. Many of the appropriations which are absolutely necessary for the maintenance of the government and the fulfillment of its varied obligations for the fiscal year 1919-1920 have not yet been made; the end of the present fiscal year is at hand; and action upon these appropriations can no longer be prudently delayed. It is necessary, therefore, that I should immediately call your attention to this critical need. It is hardly necessary for me to urge that it may receive your prompt attention.

I shall take the liberty of addressing you on my return on the subjects which have most engrossed our attention and the attention of the world during these last anxious months, since the armistice of last November was signed, the international settlements which must form the subject matter of the present treaties of peace and of our national action in the immediate future. It would be premature to discuss them or to express a judgment about them before they are brought to their complete formulation by the agreements which are now being sought at the table of the conference. I shall hope to lay them before you in their many aspects so soon as arrangements have been reached.

I hesitate to venture any opinion or press any recommendation with regard to domestic legislation while absent from the United States and out of daily touch with intimate sources of information and counsel. I am conscious that I need, after so long an absence from Washington, to seek the advice of those who have remained in constant contact with domestic problems and who have known them close at hand from day to day; and I trust that it will very soon be possible for me to do so. But there are several questions pressing for consideration to which I feel that I may, and indeed must, even now direct your attention, if only in general terms. In speaking of them I shall, I dare say, be doing little more than speak your own thoughts. I hope that I shall speak your own judgment also.

The question which stands at the front of all others in every country amidst the present great awakening is the question of labour; and perhaps I can speak of it with as great advantage while engrossed in the consideration of interests which affect all countries alike as I could at home and amidst the interests which naturally most affect my thought, because they are the interests of our own people.

By the question of labour I do not mean the question of efficient industrial production, the question of how labour is to be obtained and made effective in the great process of sustaining populations and winning success amidst commercial and industrial rivalries. I mean that much greater and more vital question, how are the men and women who do the daily labour of the world to obtain progressive improvement in the conditions of their labour, to be made happier, and to be served better by the communities and the industries which their labour sustains and advances? How are they to be given their right advantage as citizens and human beings?

We cannot go any further in our present direction. We have already gone too far. We cannot live our right life as a nation or achieve our proper success as an industrial community if capital and labour are to continue to be antagonistic instead of being partners. If they are to continue to distrust one another and contrive how they can get the better of one another. Or, what perhaps amounts to the same thing, calculate by what form and degree of coercion they can manage to extort on the one hand work enough to make enterprise profitable, on the other justice and fair treatment enough to make life tolerable. That bad road has turned out a blind alley. It is no thoroughfare to real prosperity. We must find another, leading in another direction and to a very different destination. It must lead not merely to accommodation but also to a genuine cooperation and partnership based upon a real community of interest and participation in control.

There is now in fact a real community of interest between capital and labour, but it has never been made evident in action. It can be made operative and manifest only in a new organization of industry. The genius of our businessmen and the sound practical sense of our workers can certainly work such a partnership out when once they realize exactly what it is that they seek and sincerely adopt a common purpose with regard to it.

Labour legislation lies, of course, chiefly with the states; but the new spirit and method of organization which must be effected are not to be brought about by legislation so much as by the common counsel and voluntary cooperation of capitalist, manager, and workman. Legislation can go only a very little way in commanding what shall be done. The organization of industry is a matter of corporate and individual initiative and of practical business arrangement. Those who really desire a new relationship between capital and labour can readily find a way to bring it about; and perhaps Federal legislation can help more than state legislation could.

The object of all reform in this essential matter must be the genuine democratization of industry, based upon a full recognition of the right of those who work, in whatever rank, to participate in some organic way in every decision which directly affects their welfare or the part they are to play in industry. Some positive legislation is practicable. The Congress has already shown the way to one reform which should be worldwide, by establishing the eight hour day as the standard day in every field of labour over which it can exercise control. It has sought to find the way to prevent child labour, and will, I hope and believe, presently find it. It has served the whole country by leading the way in developing the means of preserving and safeguarding life and health in dangerous industries. It can now help in the difficult task of giving a new form and spirit to industrial organization by coordinating the several agencies of conciliation and adjustment which have been brought into existence by the difficulties and mistaken policies of the present management of industry, and by setting up and developing new Federal agencies of advice and information which may serve as a clearing house for the best experiments and the best thought on this great matter, upon which every thinking man must be aware that the future development of society directly depends. Agencies of international counsel and suggestion are presently to be created in connection with the League of Nations in this very field; but it is national action and the enlightened policy of individuals, corporations, and societies within each nation that must bring about the actual reforms. The members of the committees on labour in the two houses will hardly need suggestions from me as to what means they shall seek to make the Federal Government the agent of the whole nation in pointing out and, if need be, guiding the process of reorganization and reform.

I am sure that it is not necessary for me to remind you that there is one immediate and very practical question of labour that we should meet in the most liberal spirit. We must see to it that our returning soldiers are assisted in every practicable way to find the places for which they are fitted in the daily work of the country. This can be done by developing and maintaining upon an adequate scale the admirable organization created by the Department of Labor for placing men seeking work; and it can also be done, in at least one very great field, by creating new opportunities for individual enterprise. The Secretary of the Interior has pointed out the way by which returning soldiers may be helped to find and take up land in the hitherto undeveloped regions of the country which the Federal Government has already prepared or can readily prepare for cultivation and also on many of the cutover or neglected areas which lie within the limits of the older states; and I once more take the liberty of recommending very urgently that his plans shall receive the immediate and substantial support of the Congress.

Peculiar and very stimulating conditions await our commerce and industrial enterprise in the immediate future. Unusual opportunities will presently present themselves to our merchants and producers in foreign markets, and large fields for profitable investment will be opened to our free capital. But it is not only of that that I am thinking; it is not chiefly of that that I am thinking. Many great industries prostrated by the war wait to be rehabilitated, in many parts of the world where what will be lacking is not brains or willing hands or organizing capacity or experienced skill, but machinery and raw materials and capital. I believe that our businessmen, our merchants, our manufacturers, and our captalists, will have the vision to see that prosperity in one part of the world ministers to prosperity everywhere: that there is in a very true sense a solidarity of interest throughout the world of enterprise, and that our dealings with the countries that have need of our products and our money will teach them to deem us more than ever friends whose necessities we seek in the right way to serve.

Our new merchant ships, which have in some quarters been feared as destructive rivals, may prove helpful rivals, rather, and common servants, very much needed and very welcome. Our great shipyards, new and old, will be so opened to the use of the world that they will prove immensely serviceable to every maritime people in restoring, much more rapidly than would otherwise have been possible, the tonnage wantonly destroyed in the war. I have only to suggest that there are many points at which we can facilitate American enterprise in foreign trade by opportune legislation and make it easy for American merchants to go where they will be welcomed as friends rather than as dreaded antagonists. America has a great and honorable service to perform in bringing the commercial and industrial undertakings of the world back to their old scope and swing again, and putting a solid structure of credit under them. All our legislation should be friendly to such plans and purposes.

And credit and enterprise alike will be quickened by timely and helpful legislation with regard to taxation. I hope that the Congress will find it possible to undertake an early reconsideration of Federal taxes, in order to make our system of taxation more simple and easy of administration and the taxes themselves as little burdensome as they can be made and yet suffice to support the Government and meet all its obligations. The figures to which those obligations have arisen are very great indeed, but they are not so great as to make it difficult for the nation to meet them, and meet them, perhaps, in a single generation, by taxes which will neither crush nor discourage. These are not so great as they seem, not so great as the immense sums we have had to borrow, added to the immense sums we have had to raise by taxation, would seem to indicate; for a very large proportion of those sums were raised in order that they might be loaned to the governments with which we were associated in the war, and those loans will, of course, constitute assets, not liabilities, and will not have to be taken care of by our taxpayers.

The main thing we shall have to care for is that our taxation shall rest as lightly as possible on the productive resources of the country, that its rates shall be stable, and that it shall be constant in its revenue yielding power. We have found the main sources from which it must be drawn. I take it for granted that its mainstays will henceforth be the income tax, the excess profits tax, and the estate tax. All these can so be adjusted to yield constant and adequate returns and yet not constitute a too grievous burden on the taxpayer. A revision of the income tax has already been provided for by the act of 1918, but I think you will find that further changes can be made to advantage both in the rates of the tax and the method of its collection. The excess profits tax need not long be maintained at the rates which were necessary while the enormous expenses of the war had to be borne; but it should be made the basis of a permanent system which will reach undue profits without discouraging the enterprise and activity of our businessmen. The tax on inheritances ought, no doubt, to be reconsidered in its relation to the fiscal systems of the several states, but it certainly ought to remain a permanent part of the fiscal system of the Federal government also.

Many of the minor taxes provided for in the revenue legislation of 1917 and 1918, though no doubt made necessary by the pressing necessities of the war time, can hardly find sufficient justification under the easier circumstances of peace, and can now happily be got rid of. Among these, I hope you will agree, are the excises upon various manufacturers and the taxes upon retail sales. They are unequal in the[ir] incidence on different industries and on different individuals. Their collection is difficult and expensive. Those which are levied upon articles sold at retail are largely evaded by the readjustment of retail prices. On the other hand, I should assume that it is expedient to maintain a considerable range of indirect taxes; and the fact that alcoholic liquors will presently no longer afford a source of revenue by taxation makes it the more necessary that the field should be carefully restudied in order that equivalent sources of revenue may be found which it will be legitimate, and not burdensome, to draw upon. But you have at hand in the Treasury Department many experts who can advise you upon the matters much better than I can. I can only suggest the lines of a permanent and workable system, and the placing of the taxes where they will least hamper the life of the people.

There is, fortunately, no occasion for undertaking in the immediate future any general revision of our system of import duties. No serious danger of foreign competition now threatens American industries. Our country has emerged from the war less disturbed and less weakened than any of the European countries which are our competitors in manufacture. Their industrial establishments have been subjected to greater strain than ours, their labour force to a more serious disorganization, and this is clearly not the time to seek an organized advantage. The work of mere reconstruction will, I am afraid, tax the capacity and the resources of their people for years to come. So far from there being any danger or need of accentuated foreign competition, it is likely that the conditions of the next few years will greatly facilitate the marketing of American manufactures abroad. Least of all should we depart from the policy adopted in the Tariff Act of 1913, of permitting the free entry into the United States of the raw materials needed to supplement and enrich our own abundant supplies.

Nevertheless, there are parts of our tariff system which need prompt attention. The experiences of the war have made it plain that in some cases too great reliance on foreign supply is dangerous, and that in determining certain parts of our tariff policy domestic considerations must be borne in mind which are political as well as economic. Among the industries to which special consideration should be given is that of the manufacture of dyestuffs and related chemicals. Our complete dependence upon German supplies before the war made the interruption of trade a cause of exceptional economic disturbance. The close relation between the manufacturer of dyestuffs, on the one hand, and of explosives and poisonous gases, on the other, moreover, has given the industry an exceptional significance and value. Although the United States will gladly and unhesitatingly join in the programme of international disarmament, it will, nevertheless, be a policy of obvious prudence to make certain of the successful maintenance of many strong and well equipped chemical plants. The German chemical industry, with which we will be brought into competition, was and may well be again, a thoroughly knit monopoly capable of exercising a competition of a peculiarly insidious and dangerous kind.

The United States should, moreover, have the means of properly protecting itself whenever our trade is discriminated against by foreign nations, in order that we may be assured of that equality of treatment which we hope to accord and to promote the world over. Our tariff laws as they now stand provide no weapon of retaliation in case other governments should enact legislation unequal in its bearing on our products as compared with the products of other countries. Though we are as far as possible from desiring to enter upon any course of retaliation, we must frankly face the fact that hostile legislation by other nations is not beyond the range of possibility, and that it may have to be met by counter legislation. This subject has, fortunately, been exhaustively investigated by the United States Tariff Commission. A recent report of that Commission[1] has shown very clearly that we lack and that we ought to have the instruments necessary for the assurance of equal and equitable treatment. The attention of the Congress has been called to this matter

[1] United States Tariff Commission, *Reciprocity and Commercial Treaties* (Washington, 1919).

on past occasions, and the past measures which are now recommended by the Tariff Commission are substantially the same that
have been suggested by previous administrations. I recommend
that this phase of the tariff question receive the early attention of the
Congress.

Will you not permit me, turning from these matters, to speak once
more and very earnestly of the proposed amendment to the Constitution which would extend the suffrage to women and which passed
the House of Representatives at the last session of the Congress? It
seems to me that every consideration of justice and of public advantage calls for the immediate adoption of that amendment and its
submission forthwith to the legislatures of the several states.
Throughout all the world this long delayed extension of the suffrage
is looked for; in the United States, longer, I believe, than anywhere
else, the necessity for it, and the immense advantage of it to the national life, has been urged and debated, by women and men who
saw the need for it and urged the policy of it when it required stead-
fast courage to be so much beforehand with the common conviction; and I, for one, covet for our country the distinction of being
among the first to act in a great reform.

The telegraph and telephone lines will of course be returned to
their owners so soon as the retransfer can be effected without administrative confusion, so soon, that is, as the change can be made
with least possible inconvenience to the public and to the owners
themselves. The railroads will be handed over to their owners at the
end of the calendar year; if I were in immediate contact with the administrative questions which must govern the retransfer of the telegraph and telephone lines, I could name the exact date for their return also. Until I am in direct contact with the practical questions
involved I can only suggest that in the case of the telegraphs and
telephones, as in the case of the railways, it is clearly desirable in the
public interest that some legislation should be considered which
may tend to make of these indispensable instrumentalities of our
modern life a uniform and coordinated system which will afford
those who use them as complete and certain means of communication with all parts of the country as has so long been afforded by the
postal system of the Government, and at rates as uniform and intelligible. Expert advice is, of course, available in this very practical
matter, and the public interest is manifest. Neither the telegraph
nor the telephone service of the country can be said to be in any
sense a national system. There are many confusions and inconsistencies of rates. The scientific means by which communication by
such instrumentalities could be rendered more thorough and satisfactory has not been made full use of. An exhaustive study of the

whole question of electrical communication and of the means by which the central authority of the nation can be used to unify and improve it, if undertaken, by the appropriate committees of the Congress, would certainly result, indirectly even if not directly, in a great public benefit.

The demobilization of the military forces of the country has progressed to such a point that it seems to me entirely safe to remove the ban upon the manufacture and sale of wines and beers, but I am advised that without further legislation I have not the legal authority to remove the present restrictions.[2] I therefore recommend that the Act approved November 21, 1918, entitled, "An Act to enable the Secretary of Agriculture to carry out, during the fiscal year ending June 30, 1919, the purposes of the Act entitled 'An Act to provide further for the national security and defense by stimulating agriculture and facilitating the distribution of agricultural products,' and for other purposes," be amended or repealed in so far as it applies to wines and beers.

I sincerely trust that I shall very soon be at my post in Washington again to report upon the matters which made my presence at the peace table apparently imperative, and to put myself at the service of the Congress in every matter of administration or counsel that may seem to demand executive action or advice.

Woodrow Wilson.

Printed in *Message of the President of the United States Communicated to the Two Houses of Congress at the Beginning of the First Session of the Sixty-Sixth Congress* (Washington, 1919).
[2] This paragraph added at Tumulty's suggestion. See JPT to GFC, May 19, 1919, T telegram (WP, DLC).

Hankey's Notes of a Meeting of the Council of Four[1]

President Wilson's House,
C.F.20.   Paris, May 20, 1919, 11:00 a.m.

1. The Council had under consideration the German note on the economic effect of the Treaty of Peace (Appendix 1A), and a draft reply agreed to by American, British, French and Italian representatives. (Appendix 1B.)

MR LLOYD GEORGE considered that, in paragraph 2, a statement should be given as to Great Britain's imports of food and iron ore, in order to show that Germany would only be in the same position as Great Britain had been in for years. In paragraph 5, Mr. Lloyd George suggested that the actual figures of shipping losses should be given, in order to bring home to the German people the reasons

[1] The complete text of these minutes is printed in *PPC*, V, 732-53.

why they would suffer in common with the rest of the world from the shortage of shipping.

PRESIDENT WILSON commented that the last paragraph was somewhat weak. If any part of the German case was true, it was a bad reply to point out that the millions of German citizens who had been engaged in military matters could turn their activities to works of peace.

MR LLOYD GEORGE said that the case of Great Britain was the answer to this part of the German contention.

PRESIDENT WILSON pointed out the omission from sufficient emphasis on the fact that all countries would be embarrassed by lack of raw material owing to the shortage of shipping.

MR LLOYD GEORGE said his general comment on the letter was that this was the most important of the replies to any of the German letters. It was very important to make a thoroughly good case, which should be supported by figures.

PRESIDENT WILSON agreed in this view. It should be pointed out how small the proportion of imports that Germany would lose would be to the total losses due to the war.

M. ORLANDO said that Italy before the war could only import one seventh part of the raw materials she required in Italian bottoms. After the war, she could only import 1 fourteenth in Italian bottoms.

MR LLOYD GEORGE thought that someone with the gift of writing should be asked to re-draft the reply.

(After some discussion, it was agreed that Lord Curzon should be asked to re-draft the reply for the consideration of the Council of the principal Allied and Associated Powers.)

2. M. CLEMENCEAU signed a French translation of the reply to Herr Brockdorff-Rantzau's letter of May 13th on the subject of Reparation and Responsibilities. (The German letter and the reply are contained in Appendix 2A, and Appendix 2B.)[2]

(It was agreed that the two letters should be published as soon as they had been sent.)

3. MR LLOYD GEORGE read extracts from views expressed by Herr Dernburg, German Minister of Finance, on the Peace Terms, to Colonel Thelwall[3] of the British Mission, Berlin.

4. SIR MAURICE HANKEY read a letter from Mr. Headlam Morley urging that the Draft Treaty with Poland attached to Report No. 2 of the Committee on New States[4] should be referred to the Drafting Committee.

---

[2] The text of the German letter is printed as Appendix II, and the reply to it is included in Appendix III to the minutes of the Council of Four printed at May 19, 1919, 4 p.m.
[3] Bernhard Jakob Ludwig Dernburg and Lt. Col. John Walter Francis Thelwall.
[4] For which, see the Enclosure printed with D. H. Miller to WW, May 15, 1919.

(The following resolution was accepted and initialled:

"It is agreed that the Drafting Committee of the Peace Conference should carefully review the draft of a Treaty with Poland attached to Report No. 2 of the Committee on New States. The Drafting Committee should suggest any alterations that may seem to them advisable in order to carry out more effectively the principles and objects with which this Treaty has been drawn up. If there are any material alterations which the Drafting Committee wish to suggest they should confer with the Committee and render a joint report to the Council of the Principal Allied and Associated Powers."

Sir Maurice Hankey was instructed to forward the resolution to the Secretary-General for the Drafting Committee.)

5. MR. LLOYD GEORGE read a telegram from British G.H.Q., Constantinople, dated May 17th, to the effect that the Greeks on landing had been fired on by Turkish gendarmes and that firing had continued all day, the Greeks attacking and killing Turkish soldiers whenever they were seen. It was further alleged in the telegram that the wounded were killed and some of them thrown into the sea and that the Greek Officers had made no attempt to restrain their men.

(Sir Maurice Hankey was instructed to bring this to the attention of M. Venizelos.)

6. The following resolution, carrying out the decision of the previous day, was initialled by M. Clemenceau, President Wilson and Mr. Lloyd George:

"The Council of the Principal Allied and Associated Powers have considered the attached letter from M. Fromageot[5] and have agreed that the following words 'during the period of the belligerency of each as an Allied and Associated Power against Germany,' which had been omitted from the French text but retained in the English text of Article 232 of the Treaty of Peace with Germany, should be re-instated in the French text."

M. ORLANDO, however, pointed out that the question had been examined by an Expert Committee which had voted unanimously an American proposition in favour of the omission of the words quoted and the addition of other words at the end of the article. He asked if this had been in mind when the decision had been taken on the previous day. He suggested that before a final decision was taken, the experts should be seen.

PRESIDENT WILSON said he had some vague recollection of the incident. The proposal had been made by Mr. Dulles, one of the Amer-

5 About which, see n. 9 to the minutes of the Council of Four printed at May 19, 1919, 4 p.m.

ican lawyers, whose thought had been for United States citizens on board the "Lusitania" who, unless some special provision was made, would get no reparation. From a pecuniary, though not from a sentimental, point of view, this was a relatively small matter. Whatever had been the attitude of the experts, however, it was evident that nothing had got into the Treaty.

M. ORLANDO pointed out M. Fromageot's letter explained that the purpose was to exclude the claims by New States.

MR. LLOYD GEORGE said this was not the case. He proposed that the decision of the previous day should be adhered to.

M. ORLANDO reserved his consent, but undertook to consider the matter with experts.

7. The Council had before them a copy of the reply by the Bolshevists to Dr. Nansen's letter,[6] together with a Memorandum agreed to by Mr. Hoover, Lord Robert Cecil, M. Clementel, and Professor Attolico,[7] with a covering letter from Lord Robert Cecil to Sir Maurice Hankey. (Appendix 3.)[8]

[6] It is printed as an Enclosure with HCH to WW, May 16, 1919.

[7] Bernardo Attolico, Director General in the Italian Ministry of Industry, Commerce, and Labor, and a technical expert on economic and financial questions in the Italian delegation.

[8] R. Cecil to M. P. A. Hankey, May 16, 1919, TCL, enclosing a TC of Chicherin's telegram cited in n. 6 above, and a memorandum on the Nansen plan, May 16, 1919, T MS, all in SDR, RG 256, 180.03401/20, DNA. These documents are printed in PPC, V, 743-48. Cecil reported that he, Hoover, and Attolico (Clémentel being unable to attend) had met on May 16 to consider "Lenin's reply," that is, Chicherin's telegram. The three men had agreed on the enclosed memorandum and also that Hoover should send the following telegram to Nansen: "Please inform Nansen that until whole matter has been given further consideration by the Governments here we consider it extremely inadvisable to arrange any meeting with Bolshevik representatives."

The significant portions of the memorandum, which was drafted by Cecil, read as follows:

"Lenin's reply to Nansen really amounts to this:

" 'I shall be very glad to accept supplies but not to cease from fighting, though I would be prepared to enter into negotiations for a general Russian peace.'

"It is now for the Associated Governments to take the next step, and before deciding what that step should be they must make up their minds what is to be their policy in Russia.

"It seems to me they have two courses open to them: They may either decide that so long as the Bolshevik Government is in power there is no hope for Russian peace, and that therefore the first thing to do is to smash the Bolsheviks. If this is to be their line they must strain every nerve to support Koltchak, Denikin, the Letts, the Esthonians, the Poles, and even the Finns in attacking Russia. They must furnish them with supplies and money and instructors, and do everything to make their coming campaign against the Bolsheviks successful. They must also break off all relations direct and indirect with the Bolsheviks, and advise Nansen to say that in view of Lenin's response his scheme for relief is at an end, and that nothing further of that sort can be looked for by the Russian Government. That is one policy. It may be the right one, but it undoubtedly involves much further bloodshed and destruction of material wealth.

"The other policy would be to ask the military authorities to define as nearly as they can what is the position of the various forces fighting in Russia. As soon as the line dividing the combatants has thus been determined, each and all of them should be admonished to retire, say, 10 kilometres on their own side of the line, and to refrain from all future hostilities. They would be told that international commissaries would be sent to the various fronts to see that these directions were obeyed. If, and so far as, they were obeyed, the Associated Powers would do their utmost to supply to the various Governments con-

After a prolonged perusal of this document

M. CLEMENCEAU said he did not see how any change could be made in what the Council had tried to do. There was no doubt that the Bolshevists were now going down hill. Dr. Nansen had suggested a humanitarian course, but Lenin was clearly trying to draw it into a political course.

PRESIDENT WILSON said that Lenin's argument was that the price the Allied and Associated Powers were trying to exact for food was that their enemies should beat the Bolshevists by compelling the latter to stop fighting. What was really intended was to stop aggressive fighting by the Bolshevists, because this was inconsistent with food distribution. They were perfectly correct in claiming that the Allies were supporting Koltchak and Denikin, and not putting pressure on them to stop fighting. Lenin's argument was that for him to stop fighting was to sign his death warrant.

M. CLEMENCEAU pointed out that Lenin was not in the hands of the Allies.

PRESIDENT WILSON replied that if supplies were stopped, Koltchak and Denikin would have to stop fighting too.

M. CLEMENCEAU said it was impossible to stop Lenin fighting, and his word could not be trusted.

PRESIDENT WILSON said he did not feel the same chagrin that he had formerly felt at having no policy in regard to Russia. It had been impossible to have a policy hitherto.

MR. LLOYD GEORGE said there had been very little choice. There had been a lunatic revolution which certain persons, in whom little confidence was felt, were trying to squash. The only reason why the Allies had encouraged them was to prevent Germany from getting supplies. They were, however, now entitled to say, having supported us so far "you cannot leave us in the lurch."

PRESIDENT WILSON said that the Americans had only gone to Siberia to get the Czechs out, and then the Czechs had refused to go.

cerned food and clothing and other necessaries. If some refuse and some accept, those who accept should be supported. Those who refused would be deprived of all assistance. The Governments should further be informed that the Associated Powers or the Council of the League of Nations would immediately take into consideration the whole Russian problem. Their first step would be to call upon all sections of the Russian people, or any part of them who express their adherence to this policy, to elect by free and universal suffrage, under the supervision of the League of Nations, a constituent assembly for the purpose of determining the future constitution of the Russian Government. In the meantime Nansen could be advised to say that so long as the Soviet Government declined to abstain from fighting he was powerless to help them. . . .

"I believe that either of these policies has a fair chance of success, and may be defended by powerful arguments. What is not defensible is a combination of the two: a suggestion that Lenin must cease fighting while we are supplying arms and equipment to Denikin and Koltchak; or, conversely, that Koltchak and Denikin should be encouraged to wage war against Lenin while we are negotiating with the latter to give him economic assistance. Compromise of this kind can only lead to a prolongation of hostilities in Russia, and the spreading in that country of the belief that the Associated Powers cannot be trusted."

MR. LLOYD GEORGE said that his Government's object had been to reconstitute the Eastern front. They had succeeded in doing this, though somewhat East of the line on which they had hoped to establish it. Nevertheless, the reconstitution of the front did prevent the Germans from getting supplies; with which they might have broken the blockade. The feeling in Great Britain was that it was impossible now to leave these people in the lurch.

PRESIDENT WILSON said that at least pledges could be exacted for further support.

M. CLEMENCEAU fully agreed.

MR. LLOYD GEORGE agreed, and said it could be done in either of two ways:

(1) By a formal dispatch;

(2) By summoning the representatives of the various Russian groups now in Paris and putting the conditions to them.

PRESIDENT WILSON preferred the first proposal. The second would be contrary to the idea that had been at the basis of the Prinkipo scheme, namely, that it would not be fair to hear one party without hearing the other. His view was that a formal demand and notice ought to be sent to the various Russian groups. He had himself sent something that was almost equivalent to this,[9] as he felt he was entitled to do.

(After some discussion it was agreed that Mr. Philip Kerr should be asked to prepare a draft for the consideration of the Council.) Mr. Kerr was sent for. While awaiting Mr. Kerr

PRESIDENT WILSON read extracts from a document which had been alluded to at a discussion on the previous day, signed by M. Kerensky and some of his friends, and which contained a number of proposals, including the following:

(i) That the Powers should only help the various Russian groups on certain fundamental conditions for the establishing of Russia on a democratic basis with a constituent assembly, and Governments which declined to agree should not be supported.

(ii) That as a Constituent Assembly could clearly not be called at the present time, Regional Assemblies should be elected on a democratic basis for the re-establishment of Local Government.

(iii) That a representative mission should be sent by the Great Powers to Russia to give assurance of sympathy and assistance.

(iv) That proposals for supplying food were harmful.

[9] See V. C. McCormick to FLP, May 17, 1919.

These proposals in short, PRESIDENT WILSON continued, were that the Powers should obtain an assurance from each group that it would be united with the other groups to form an all Russian Government on a constituent basis, and that in the meanwhile each group should do what it could in its own area.

MR. LLOYD GEORGE was afraid of splitting up Russia.

PRESIDENT WILSON said it was merely proposing to substitute a democratic for an autocratic basis.

(After some further discussion Mr. Kerr entered.)

PRESIDENT WILSON informed Mr. Kerr that the Council desired to make a further effort with Russia along the lines of definite assurance to the several groups as to what they were aiming at. They had been reading a document prepared by certain Russian groups in Paris who, though anti-Bolshevist, were suspicious of reactionary tendencies among the groups fighting the Bolshevists. These suggested that pledges should be demanded from the various groups fighting the Bolshevists to establish a government on a democratic basis. In the meanwhile it was proposed to establish a democratic Government in these Regions by setting up Provincial Central Assemblies. The idea of the Council was to embody these demands in a message to the several Governments, and they hoped Mr. Kerr would prepare a draft for their consideration.

MR. LLOYD GEORGE pointed out that the question of the Baltic Provinces had not been discussed. All the other Russian groups fighting the Boshevists were violently opposed to any recognition of Esthonia and Latvia and the other Baltic provinces. They alleged that to recognise them would be to tear up Russia and to bar access to the sea.

MR. KERR asked what promise was to be given to the various Russian groups to encourage them to give these undertakings.

MR. LLOYD GEORGE said it was not a question of promising more, but of continuing the assistance which was now given.

PRESIDENT WILSON said that the dispatch should intimate that without satisfactory guarantees no further help would be given.

MR. KERR asked if they were to accept the frontiers laid down by the League of Nations.

MR. LLOYD GEORGE said they must.

PRESIDENT WILSON said there was no other solution. He then produced a letter from Mr. Hoover on the subject of the Baltic provinces,[10] where there was an appalling shortage of food. This was due, according to Mr. Hoover, not to lack of financial or shipping facilities, but to the absence of order. He suggested that enough naval

[10] HCH to WW, May 9, 1919, Vol. 58.

force should be given to provide for the protection of relief in the coast towns, and for its distribution along the coast. In this way the established governments should be helped to preserve order. The situation was so appalling from the humanitarian point of view, that he hoped the Council would be willing to hear a deputation composed of the British and United States Naval authorities and himself.

MR. LLOYD GEORGE suggested that in the first instance, Mr. Hoover should discuss the matter with the Admirals.

(This was agreed to.)

(Mr. Kerr withdrew with instructions to draft a letter of [for] consideration.)

8. The Council had before it a draft reply prepared by Mr. Philip Kerr, under instructions from Mr. Lloyd George, to Brockdorff-Rantzau's letter of May 10th[11] on the subject of Prisoners of War. (Appendix 4.)[12]

(The reply was approved.)

(Sir Maurice Hankey was instructed to ask the Secretary-General to translate it into French for M. Clemenceau's signature.)

(It was agreed that Brockdorff-Rantzau's letter, together with the reply, should be published after despatch to the Germans.)

9. The Council had before them a letter from the Serbian Delegation urging that out of the initial one thousand million pounds to be paid by Germany, eighty-million pounds should be specifically assigned to Serbia, together with a Memorandum by the Committee considering the question of Reparation in the Austrian Treaty, to whom it had been referred to May 13th.

(The Memorandum of the Committee was approved, subject to

---

[11] See Appendix III to the minutes of the Council of Four printed at May 12, 1919, 11 a.m.

[12] G. Clemenceau to U. K. C. von Brockdorff-Rantzau, May 20, 1919, TCL (SDR, RG 256, 180.03401/20, DNA), printed in *PPC*, V, 749-50. The letter stated that the Allied and Associated Powers could not agree that prisoners of war and civilian prisoners guilty of crimes during their captivity should be released unconditionally. It declared that all German prisoners had been treated scrupulously according to "the laws of war and the dictates of humanity" and would continue to be so treated until their repatriation. In such matters as the return to prisoners of their personal property, the search for missing persons, and the care of graves, the Allied and Associated Powers were and would continue to do all in their power. However, they could not agree to the German request for full reciprocity in these or any other matters regarding prisoners since there had been "no parallel between the treatment which was accorded to prisoners of war by the German Government on the one side and the Allied and Associated Powers on the other." The Allied powers would do their best to repatriate German prisoners "properly fed and in good condition after the conclusion of peace." However, the needs of "territories recently liberated from the German yoke" would probably make it impossible to honor the German request that prisoners be supplied with full sets of clothing. Finally, the Allied and Associated Powers would be glad to set up commissions to deal with the repatriation of prisoners of war "immediately upon the signature of peace." "They regret, however," the letter concluded, "that they do not see their way to appoint them until they are notified of the intention of the plenipotentiaries of the German Empire to sign peace."

the omission of the first paragraph of Clause 2, and the first four words of the second paragraph.) (Appendix 5.A. and Appendix 5.B.)[13]

APPENDIX I.A. to C.F.20.

SECRET.

TRANSLATION OF FRENCH TRANSLATION OF GERMAN ORIGINAL.

German Peace Delegation,
Versailles.

M. Président, May 13th. 1919.

In conformity with my communication of the 9th instant, I have the honour to present to Your Excellency the Report of the Economic Commission charged with the study of the effect of the conditions of Peace on the situation of the German population.

"In the course of the last two generations, Germany has become transformed from an agricultural State to an industrial State. As long as she was an agricultural State, Germany could feed forty million inhabitants.

In her quality of an industrial State she could ensure the nourishment of a population of sixty seven millions. In 1913, the importation of food stuffs amounted, in round figures, to twelve million tons. Before the war a total of fifteen millions of persons provided for their existence in Germany by foreign trade and by navigation, either in a direct or an indirect manner, by the use of foreign raw material.

According to the Conditions of the Treaty of Peace, Germany will surrender her merchant tonnage and ships in course of construction suitable for overseas trade. German shipbuilding yards will build for five years in the first instance tonnage destined for the Allied and Associated Governments.

Germany will, moreover, renounce her Colonies; all her overseas

[13] Appendix 5A was a "Memorandum on the Request of the Serbian Delegation Enclosed in Sir Maurice Hankey's Letter of May 15, 1919," T MS. Appendix 5B consisted of Secretariat-General of the Peace Conference to the Secretariat-General of the British Delegation, May 11, 1919, TCL, enclosing N. P. Pašić to [G. Clemenceau], May 9, 1919, TCL. All of these documents are in SDR, RG 256, 180.03401/20, DNA, and are printed in *PPC*, V, 751-53. Pašić's letter set forth the arguments in favor of the payment to Yugoslavia of the sum mentioned in the text above. The memorandum suggested that the Serbian claim was exorbitant and, therefore, "inadmissable." On the other hand, Serbia had suffered grievous material and economic damage during the war and deserved prompt assistance. Some aid might come out of "the reparation in specie that can be obtained from Austria, from Hungary, and from Bulgaria." However, the principal suggestion of the memorandum was that the Allies should make "an immediate creation of credit" for Yugoslavia "by an immediate promise of a defined amount from the first sums realised out of the German reparation." It suggested that this promise might consist of "£5,000,000 forthwith or of £1,000,000 every three months for fifteen months."

The paragraph of the memorandum which, as mentioned in the text above, was deleted, read as follows: "There is not in the case of Serbia the special ground, which existed in the case of Belgium, that the damages inflicted on her were caused in a war which was specially a violation of her international status as well as generally aggressive and accompanied by inhuman conduct."

possessions, all her interests and securities in the Allied and Associated countries, and in their Colonies, Dominions and Protectorates, will as an instalment of the payment for part of the reparation, be subject to liquidation, and be exposed to any other economic war measure which the Allied and Associated Powers think fit to maintain or to take during the years of Peace.

By the putting into force of the Territorial Clauses of the Treaty of Peace, Germany would lose to the East the most important regions for the production of corn and potatoes, which would be equivalent to the loss of 21% of the total crop of those articles of food. Moreover, the intensity of our agricultural production would diminish considerably. On the one hand, the importation of certain raw material indispensable for the production of Manure, such as Phosphates, would be hindered, on the other hand, this industry would suffer like all other industries from lack of coal. The Treaty of Peace provides for the loss of almost a third of the production of our coal mines. Apart from this decrease, we are forced for ten years to deliver enormous consignments of coal to various Allied countries.

Moreover, in conformity with the Treaty, Germany will concede to her neighbours nearly three quarters of her mineral production, and more than three fifths of her zinc production.

After this diminution of her products, after the economic depression caused by the loss of her Colonies, of her merchant Fleet, and of her possessions abroad, Germany would not be in a state to import from abroad a sufficient quantity of raw material. An enormous part of German industry would therefore inevitably be condemned to destruction. At the same time, the necessity of importing food stuffs would increase considerably, whilst the possibility of satisfying that demand would diminish in the same proportion.

At the end of a very short time, Germany would, therefore, not be in a position to give bread and work to her numerous millions of inhabitants, who would be reduced to earning their livelihood by navigation and by trade. These persons would have to emigrate, but that is a material impossibility, all the more so because many countries and the most important ones, will oppose any German immigration. Moreover, hundreds of millions [thousands] of Germans expelled from the territories of the Powers now at war with Germany, from the Colonies and territories which Germany must surrender, will return to their native land.

The putting into execution of the conditions of Peace would, therefore, logically bring about the loss of several millions of persons in Germany. This catastrophe would not be long in coming about, seeing that the health of the population has been broken down during the War by the Blockade, and during the Armistice by the aggravation of the Blockade of famine.

No help, however important, or over however long a period it might be distributed, would prevent these deaths "en masse." Peace would impose on Germany numberless human sacrifices that this War of four years and a half did not demand of her, (1,750,000 killed), nearly 1,000,000 dead, victims of the Blockade).

We do not know, and indeed we doubt, whether the Delegates of the Allied and Associated Powers realise the inevitable consequences which will take place if Germany, an industrial State, very thickly populated, closely bound up with the economic system of the world and reduced to the obligation to import enormous quantities of raw material and food stuffs, suddenly finds herself pushed back in the phase of her development which would correspond to her economic condition and the numbers of her population as they were half a century ago.

Those who will sign this Treaty will sign the death sentence of many millions of German men, women, and children."

I thought it my duty, before entering upon a discussion of other details of the Treaty, to bring to the knowledge of the Allied and Associated Delegations this summary exposé of the problem of the German population.

I have at the disposal of Your Excellency statistical proofs of the above statements.

I have the honour &c.

(sgd) BROCKDORFF-RANTZAU.

APPENDIX I. B TO C.F.20.

M.166.

SUGGESTED REPLY TO GERMAN NOTE
ON THE ECONOMIC EFFECT OF THE PEACE TREATY.

(Agreed to by the American, British, French and Italian Representatives.)

1. We have noted the communication of the German Delegation of May 13th with reference to the studies of its Economic Commission as to the Treaty of Peace. Our observations upon the communication are as follows:

2. In general, we would point out that though Germany will lose territories in which grain, iron ore, coal and the like are produced, such commodities are not thereby made unavailable for Germany. The importation of food and materials, which took place on a large scale before the war, may be expected to continue in the future.

3. The German note ignores the great relief to German productive industry which will be afforded by the reduction of armaments, and it takes no account of the diminution of German consumption owing to the transfer of territory with nearly six million inhabitants.

4. The gradual transformation of Germany from an agricultural

State to an industrial State has not affected in the past, nor should its continuance in the future, affect the nourishment of the population; inasmuch as the products of industry are readily exchangeable for the products of agriculture. The severance of agricultural territory which is restored to Poland will not destroy its productivity like the devastation wrought by the German armies in the West. Nothing in the Treaty will prevent the products of these regions from finding a market, as heretofore, in Germany.

5. As to the merchant marine and the Germans employed in that and any coordinate industries, it will be recognized that the destruction of merchant shipping has created throughout the world a shortage, and has added to the sufferings of all those who follow the sea as a means of livelihood. There can be no special consideration evolved for the seamen of Germany at the expense of the seamen of the Allied and Associated Nations, who lost their livelihood, owing to the destruction of a large portion of the world's shipping which German methods of warfare brought about; an amount far in excess of the tonnage which will be transferred under the terms of peace. The transfer of German ships to Allied flags will not prevent Germany from carrying on overseas trade.

6. The statements pertaining to the production of fertilizers are apparently founded on a misconception. Phosphate has always been imported by Germany, and there is no stipulation in the Peace Treaty which prevents such continued importation. As regards Coal, it is to be noted that the transferred territories include important areas of coal consumption as well as of production. Through the destruction of the coal mines of France, the shortage throughout the continent of Europe has been needlessly intensified. The industries of the Allies should not be the first ones to suffer through such wanton destruction.

7. The cession of the Briey Basin containing iron ore deposits is simply a return of those properties to their original owners. All raw materials, such as iron ore, will naturally seek industries to which they are essential. No restrictions are imposed by the Treaty upon Germany's importation of such materials.

8. The world is faced with the necessity of drastic re-adjustments in industry and the means of livelihood; and it is obvious that Germany must, like the other countries, re-adjust itself to changed conditions. When the world's shipping tonnage has again become normal, an adequate supply of raw materials should be available to all countries, including Germany.

9. In the framing of the Treaty of Peace, there has been no intention, on the part of the Allied and Associated Governments, to destroy Germany's economic life. On the contrary, the necessity for a

return to more normal economic conditions has been borne constantly in mind. For example, the Reparations Commission is, in various clauses, charged with specific instructions to this end.

10. The wholesale sacrifice of life and health, and the wanton devastation of territory and the destruction of wealth which have marked this war are bound for many years to impose enormous burdens on the Nations of the world. These burdens are not created or aggravated by the conditions of Peace nor could any conditions be drafted which would remove them. The Treaty certainly does not impose an excessive share of those burdens on Germany. Germany will, moreover, find new resources by reason of the fact that millions of her citizens, who up to now have been employed in military affairs, or in preparation for war, can now turn their whole activities to works of Peace.

T MS (SDR, RG 256, 180.03401/20, DNA).

Mantoux's Notes of a Meeting of the Council of Four

May 20, 1919, 11 a.m.

Examination of the reply to the German note on the economic consequences of the losses of German territories, the cession of the commercial fleet, etc., stipulated in the peace treaty.

Lloyd George. It is necessary to strengthen this document and to redraft it in such a way as to appeal to German public opinion. The German delegation complains that in the future Germany will not possess what is necessary for her economic life. We must show that England and Italy can only live through imports.

Orlando. Of the raw materials necessary to Italy, only one seventh, before the war, was transported by Italian boats. Today that proportion has fallen to one fourteenth.

Lloyd George. It is necessary to ask the facts of the specialists and then to entrust the drafting to someone who is capable of appealing to German opinion.

After an exchange of observations, the drafting of the text is entrusted to Lord Curzon, who will be assisted by Captain Clement Jones.

Lloyd George. I have knowledge of an interview by Herr Dernburg, former German Minister of Colonies. The result seems to be that, for the moment, the Germans are not inclined to sign; Herr Dernburg says they would like to do it, but that they will not be able to do it. Moreover, he complains of imaginary wrongs, for example, the assessment by an Allied commission of the taxes which the Germans will have to pay. There is nothing of the kind in the treaty; it is simply stated that we will have the right to assure ourselves that Germany is assessing her population on a basis at least equal to our own. The Germans also fear that, in a period of twenty or thirty years, the Reparation Commission could impose new obligations upon them which it would be impossible to foresee. Above all, they want to know exactly what they must expect.

Wilson. We have said that the Reparation Commission will make known definitely the sum of our demands in 1921.

Lloyd George. Herr Dernburg says again that Germany cannot accept obligations which she could have barely met when she was still in all her power and in all her prosperity. The present stipulations would turn the Germans into an enslaved people, working for other peoples. In these conditions Germany cannot sign.

There are also some words about the army of occupation, the charge for which is considered too heavy. That question also concerns us, and we are in accord on a reduction of the forces of occupation.

Wilson. I have been told that the French government intends to send some Senegalese to the left bank of the Rhine. Is this true?

Clemenceau. There is exactly one Senegalese battalion there; but I intend to withdraw it and, like you, I think that it would be a grave error to have black troops occupy the left bank of the Rhine.

Orlando. On the subject of the modification of Article 232, which was a question in our last meeting, I do not know if my colleagues are aware that the commission entrusted with studying the same question for Austria-Hungary unanimously voted for a certain American amendment. Did you know about it when you discussed it yesterday? I think that the members of the commission must be questioned about it.

Wilson. I vaguely recall something of this kind. The amendment in question was proposed by Mr. Dulles, who was thinking above all about our losses at the time of the torpedoing of the *Lusitania*. At that time, in fact, we were not belligerents.

Lloyd George. But Mr. Dulles is not a member of the commission?

Wilson. No, but he is one of our legal advisers.

Lloyd George. I do not think that there is anything to change in the decision that we took yesterday.

The decision is affirmed.

Reading of the reply of Lenin to the Nansen proposal for the victualing of Russia: Lenin will not accept the condition of a cease fire. Lord Robert Cecil, after consultation with the Supreme Economic Council, advises the governments to choose between two policies: it is necessary either to crush the Bolsheviks, or to impose upon the different belligerent groups of Russia provisional frontiers and to send them supplies on the condition that a Constituent Assembly will be convened immediately. In all events, one must not try to mix the two systems.

Lloyd George. What do you think of these two documents?

Clemenceau. I do not see how we could modify our current attitude. It is obvious that the strength of the Bolsheviks is on the decline. If the Nansen plan, based exclusively on a humanitarian concern, is rejected by them, there is nothing else to do.

Wilson. Lenin says that we wish to prevent him from defending himself. But all that we asked of him is to cease all offensive action. What he could say is that we are according Kolchak and Denikin material support and that we should enjoin them to stop fighting.

Clemenceau. You can enjoin them as you like—this is not what will stop them. What means of action do we have?

Wilson. We can stop sending them arms.

Clemenceau. If we stop sending arms to Kolchak and Denikin, that will not stop Lenin.

Wilson. Can we not try to sway Lenin morally?

Clemenceau. I have no hope of this kind.

Wilson. I no longer regret as much as I did several months ago not having a policy in Russia; it seems to me impossible to define one in such conditions.

Lloyd George. On the one hand, we have violent revolutionaries without scruples; on the other, people who claim to act in the interest of order, but whose intentions are suspect to us. Nevertheless, we have the duty not to abandon those whom we needed when it was a matter of reconstituting the eastern front in some way, and public opinion would not forgive us for abandoning them when we no longer need them.

Wilson. We should send them a formal summons to pledge themselves to convene the Constituent Assembly. That is what I had intended to do vis-à-vis Kolchak, in order to make very clear the position of the government of the United States. Why should Mr. Balfour not draft a dispatch in this sense in the name of the Allied and Associated Governments?

Lloyd George. I do not know if Mr. Balfour is the ideal drafter for such a dispatch, to which I would like to give a frankly democratic coloring.

Wilson. It is necessary to ask precise questions and to demand precise commitments. We know very well that it is impossible to convene the Constituent Assembly on short notice. But what the document which I mentioned to you yesterday recommends, and which is signed by Kerensky, Avksentev, and some others, is to demand from all the Russian governments the promise of the convocation of the Constituent Assembly, and, meanwhile, the immediate meeting of local assemblies, elected by universal suffrage, which could form among themselves a central delegation to discuss the general interests of Russia.

In sum, it is a question of asking from each one of these groups the assurance that it is ready to unite with the others to reconstitute the Russian Republic. In the meantime, each one of them will guarantee the existence of a local regime based on individual liberty and universal suffrage.

Lloyd George. I have only one objection to make: this system prolongs the division of Russia. Be assured that if Kolchak should arrive in Moscow, the civil war would stop immediately, and the convocation of a National Assembly for all Russia would become possible.

Wilson. Will Denikin rally to it?

Lloyd George. I think so. His chief of staff[1] is a reactionary; but he himself does not appear to have bad intentions. As for Kolchak, he is only a soldier and nothing more.

Wilson. Soldiers most often have very simple ideas about politics.

Lloyd George. Nothing is more true: look at Marshal Foch.

Mr. Philip Kerr is introduced and receives instructions to prepare the draft of the dispatch to be sent to the different governments in Russia.

Lloyd George. We will also have to examine the question of the Baltic countries. The complete independence of these countries would result in cutting Russia off from the sea.

Wilson. I have received a letter from Mr. Hoover about the Baltic provinces. From the economic point of view, he considers that it would be easy to restore the situation if order was assured. He proposes to protect the coast of the Baltic with Allied naval forces and to establish close contact between the mission for economic aid and the naval authorities. The present situation in these countries is terrible.

Lloyd George. But how can we count on these populations? At one time, we sought to distribute arms to them to fight against the Bolsheviks; but we abandoned that because we found too few people whom we could trust.

Hankey. The Serbs have sent a note in which they ask for two billion francs indemnity, under the heading of reparations. The opinion of the experts is against it.

Lloyd George. The note of the experts appears to me rather poorly drafted; it will have to be changed.

Mantoux, II, 125-29.
    [1] That is, Gen. Ivan Pavlovich Romanovskii.

To Tasker Howard Bliss

My dear General Bliss: Paris, 20 May, 1919.

Thank you for your two letters of yesterday about the Rhine Convention and the troops for occupation. General Pershing was at lu[n]ch with me yesterday, and I think I can say that we are all three of one mind with regard to the troops.

I can also say that I entirely agree with you about the Rhine Convention and shall try to obtain a radical modification of it.

Cordially and faithfully yours,   Woodrow Wilson

TLS (T. H. Bliss Papers, DLC).

From Robert Lansing, with Enclosure

My dear Mr. President: Paris, May 20, 1919

I am transmitting to you herewith a copy of an urgent telegram which has been received from Mr. Polk regarding the publication of the text of the Conditions of Peace and I shall be glad to communicate to Mr. Polk your views on this matter.

Faithfully yours,   Robert Lansing.

TLS (SDR, RG 256, 185.182/26, DNA).

E N C L O S U R E

Washington, May 19th, 1919.

2018 VERY URGENT. VERY SECRET. For the Secretary of State, from Polk.

Senator Johnson has announced he will introduce a resolution at once demanding that the text of the Treaty be given out. Despatch from Paris today stated that British and French were prepared to give out statement that the President had vetoed this plan. Despatch also stated that parts of the Treaty were being published in Berlin.

Senator Hitchcock just called up asking what position Democrats should take if such resolution is presented, or what reason they can give as to why text of Treaty is being withheld. Please, if possible, let me have all you can communicate for guidance of Hitchcock. Some answer should be given. Of course it would put Johnson in a hole if Treaty could be published at once, but the reasons for withholding it may of course outweigh.   Polk,   Acting.

T telegram (SDR, RG 256, 185.182/25, DNA).

From Robert Lansing

My dear Mr. President: Paris, 20th May 1919.

I beg to inform you that I have received a copy of the letter addressed to you by Mr. William C. Bullitt[1] in which he states his views in regard to the proposed Treaty of Peace with Germany. I have likewise received a letter from Mr. Bullitt expressing views similar to those stated in his letter to you and tendering his resignation as a Special Assistant in the Department of State, Attached to the Commission. I have, of course, accepted his resignation without making any comment.   Faithfully yours,   Robert Lansing

TLS (WP, DLC).
  [1] W. C. Bullitt to WW, May 17, 1919.

From Felix Frankfurter

My dear Mr. President,   Paris May 20th, 1919.

I wish I could convey to you the feeling of relief and contentment which your letter of generous reassurance,[1] that the Balfour Declaration will eventuate into effective guarantees, has aroused. We are very grateful, indeed.

May I ask you to have word sent me that I may show the letter to all those who are interested—not to be published, of course—and that I may cable its contents to Mr. Justice Brandeis?
                    Faithfully yours,   Felix Frankfurter.

TLS (WP, DLC).
  [1] See WW to F. Frankfurter, May 16, 1919.

A Memorandum by Bernard Mannes Baruch and Others, with Enclosure

[Paris, May 20, 1919]
Memo. for the President.

Loucheur of the French Ministry greatly fears that we are making it impossible for the Germans to sign the Treaty, by reason of the fact that they see no possible hope for their economic life in the clauses as drawn. He believes that the only way in which it is possible to show the Germans that the Treaty can be worked out, without their becoming hopeless slaves, is for a few—a *very* few of our experts (business men) to sit down with similar members of the German Delegation & point out to them *how* their metallurgical & industrial life is *not* to be destroyed. Loucheur fears that unless we give the

Germans some ray of hope that we shall listen to reasonable points that they may raise, they may take a position that will be impossible of solution for both them and us.

We believe there is a very important point in this and we suggest that the Council may see fit to meet it immediately by allowing to become known some statement like the attached. Loucheur thinks that Mr. Clemenceau & Mr. L-George will adopt promptly any suggestion you make on this matter. But Loucheur's name should *not* be brought in.   Respectfully Submitted: B.M.B.
                                                          N.H.D.
                                                          TWL

HwI MS (WP, DLC).

E N C L O S U R E

For the Press

In case the German Delegation, in its communication upon the Treaty which is to be made on Thursday, raises any points which, in the judgment of the Council of Four, justify oral explanations in order to clarify possibly obscure points in the Treaty, the Council will permit its experts to meet members of the German Delegation in person at Versailles, for the purposes indicated.

Hw MS (WP, DLC).

From Sir William Orpen[1]

Dear Mr. President   Paris. 20th May 1919.

I am doing the official picture of the Peace Conference for the British government, and write to know if you would be so good as to share a little of your valuable time to allow me to do a study[.] If you would come here[2] I should only require 2 hours all together at separate times of say ½ or ¾ of an hour each[.] Please forgive me for troubling you, but you understand it would be very much against the picture if all the others are done from life—and yourself from a photograph   Yours obediently   William Orpen

ALS (WP, DLC).
    [1] William Newenham Montague Orpen, British artist and portrait painter. He had most recently served from 1917 to 1919 as an official war artist, with the rank of major in the British Royal Army Service Corps.
    [2] That is, the Hotel Astoria.

From Goldsworthy Lowes Dickinson[1]

Dear Sir,   Cambridge, May 20 [1919]

It is hardly likely that you recollect a visit I paid you years ago, while you were still a professor at Princetown. And certainly I would not advance that as an excuse for addressing you. But I have an object to which I know you will be sympathetic. I am connected with the League of Nations Union in this country, which is the principal, indeed the only organisation of propaganda for the League. It publishes a monthly journal and I recently wrote to Paris to inquire whether any of the American delegation would write us a short article there on the clause in the Covenant which safeguards the Monroe doctrine, and its probable or possible effect upon the working of the League. I received in reply the rather audacious suggestion that I should address myself to you in person. If it were at all possible that you should feel at liberty to send a message to the British public on that or on any other topic connected with the League, I need not point out how much it would help the propaganda of our Union if the message were addressed in the first place to us. But if, as is more than likely, it is out of the question that you should do this yourself, would it be possible for you to authorise the American secretary of the League of Nations Commission in Paris to write us a short article? I do not like to conclude without expressing to you the profound admiration, gratitude and sympathy with which I have greeted every utterance of yours in these last terrible years. It has seemed to me that yours was the only voice among those in authority which spoke the language of sanity, wisdom and hope. And if the treaty drawn up in Paris has filled the friends of civilisation and peace with something like despair, we know at least that whatever be in it that holds out any hope, and in particular, the Covenant of the League, is due in the main to your faithful and untiring efforts.

With the deepest respect, I am
                    Yours very faithfully   G. Lowes Dickinson

TLS (WP, DLC).
   [1] Historian and philosopher, Lecturer in Political Science and Fellow of King's College, Cambridge. He was also a leading publicist for world peace and international organization.

From the Diary of Ray Stannard Baker

                                    Tuesday the 20th [May 1919]

The President came to a meeting of the American Commission at 5:30 & remained until 7. He called me as he was going out & asked me to ride up with him from the Hotel. As we went out the usual crowd around the door—how does the news spread so quickly that the President is inside—cheered loudly and about 20 photographers snapped pictures of us. We rode up in an open car & the President told me of the day's doings. This morning they discussed replies to the Germans' notes. The French love to make the replies as ironically cutting as they best know how, & the President is using his influence to secure modifications. The Reparations note, which we issued to-day, was thus much toned down: and the Economics note, which the Colonel read to me the other day—as the accepted reply— is now being revised by—Lord Curzon: of all men! The President seems a good deal concerned as to whether the Germans will sign— and well he may be. I know he is hearing criticisms of the treaty from all sides. Baruch to-day gave Grayson for delivery to the President a long communication suggesting modifications.[1] Reinsch, in China, has been cabling for information as to what reasons he shall give for the Chinese decision.[2]

I spoke to the President about my Dutchmen:[3] and he said almost shyly: "I fear being misquoted, or interviewed: and if I talk freely, I do not know how to be discrete [discreet]."

I am never quite able to make up my mind whether his unwillingness to meet people—and it is growing upon him—his extreme reticence in talking except in public speeches—or at the other extreme, to his few intimate associates,—is due to a secretiveness of nature, or to a kind of shyness which shrinks from contact with people who are either likely to be hostile or who may crudely misunderstand. He likes to talk to people in the mass—at a distance—but dreads personal contact. He dreads, I think, meeting even the other members of his own peace commission. When I asked him to-day what was done at the Commission meeting, he said that he had "called them into council to discuss some of the problems we are facing." He probably told them what the Council of Four was doing!

[1] BMB to WW, May 17, 1919.
[2] See RL to WW, May 8, 1919 (first letter of that date) and the Enclosure thereto, both in Vol. 58.
[3] Baker here refers to an earlier sentence in the same diary entry where he says: "A group of persistent Dutchmen are bothering the life out of me trying to get to the President."

From the Diary of Colonel House

May 20, 1919.

Just before the President came, Lord Curzon called. He had tried to make an engagement early, but I could not see him. He came to tell me in confidence that the British Government was carrying on negotiations with the Prime Minister of Persia[1] in the settlement of Persian affairs with Great Britain, and he hoped that the President and the American Delegation would not encourage the Persians to get an audience before the Peace Conference. He said the Prime Minister did not wish the Persian Delegates here to know that these negotiations were being carried on, but when they had come to a conclusion, the negotiations would be published and the Delegates brought home. I presented this view to the President and to the other Commissioners. Curzon said that Balfour had sent him to me to convey this information.

I took up with the President the question of the Irish-American Delegation. The President and Lansing were in favor of giving them a brusque refusal to their request, which was that the British Government be asked to give safe conduct to the delegates of the "Irish Republic" so they might come to Paris and be heard by the Peace Conference. I suggested that they be politely told that the British Government had already intimated to us that they would not grant such a request, and largely because the Irish-American delegation had made incendiary speeches in Ireland while they were there.

I had Dr. King[2] today about the Syrian Commission, and I told the President it was something of a scandal that this Commission had not already gone to Syria as promised the Arabs. The honor of Great Britain, France and the United States were at stake, and I hoped he would insist that the Commission leave at once. The President assured me that he had done everything he could in the direction indicated. I then suggested that he set Monday as the time when our Commission would start regardless of the French and English. He adopted the suggestion and said he would tell Clemenceau and Lloyd George tomorrow. There are some letters upon this subject which will be attached to the record.

We discussed the question of the dismemberment of the Turkish Empire and would [what] would become of the component parts. I took occasion to express the hope that the President would not agree to blockade Germany in the event the Germans refused to sign the Treaty. I spoke with considerable feeling and told him that the world, outside of France and perhaps a part of England, would not tolerate such a procedure for the purpose of enforcing a treaty. The President was sympathetic to this view, and I believe will not allow George and Clemenceau to force him into such inhuman warfare.

I handed the President E. W. Scripps'[3] cable from San Diego, Californiam [California] concerning the granting of amnesty to all political prisoners,[4] and I suggested that he let me reply that he would take it under consideration. I urged his favorable action at the proper time, which would seem to me after peace was signed. Scripps' cable and my reply[5] are attached.

The President requested me to see Orlando and get him to sign the agreement relating to the interned German boats, which Lloyd George has already signed.[6] It is the President's purpose to leave Paris after the peace with Germany and Austria is signed, and he has asked me to prepare a memorandum covering the subjects that will be left after these two treaties are out of the way. He desired this memorandum so we might go over it before he left.

[1] Mīrzā Hasan Khān Vosuq od-Dowleh.
[2] That is, Henry Churchill King.
[3] That is, Edward Wyllis Scripps.
[4] See E. W. Scripps to EMH, May 16, 1919.
[5] See EMH to E. W. Scripps, May 20, 1919.
[6] See the three Memoranda of Agreement printed at May 8, 1919, Vol. 58.

From the Diary of Edith Benham

May 20, 1919

Mrs. Wilson told me this morning of an exasperating experience with Baron Sonnino.[1] The "Big Three" had asked Orlando to come and explain why the Italians are doing the different things they are up to in Asia Minor, etc., of which I have written. Orlando sent word that he was ill and the P., who has a genuine liking for him, believes that Sonnino ordered all this without consulting with him and without his knowledge and O. didn't want to say so. The Three didn't want Sonnino so they sent word back as he was ill they would wait. Word came back that Sonnino would come and after some hesitation they decided to let him come. Venizelos had also come to discuss certain subjects and arrived ahead of Sonnino. When S. came in he looked around and said in a tone which the P. described as insufferable that he would only discuss the matter before the three and not before Venizelos, who, of course, is also an Ally. Mrs. W. said she had never seen the P. more annoyed and he said his first impulse was to tell him he could go, but Venizelos, who is a charming person, said he would go out, and went and sat in the little hallway entrance to the P.'s room while they talked. L. George and Clemenceau were furious, and L.G. jumped all over Sonnino for this discourtesy. The P. later, in speaking of the incident, said he had almost lost control of his temper and was on the point of ordering Sonnino out of the house, but fortunately controlled himself.

[1] About this episode, see the minutes of the Council of Four printed at May 19, 1919, 4 p.m.

To Joseph Patrick Tumulty

Paris, 20 May, 1919.

Please say to Secretaries Redfield and Wilson that I am glad to authorize such a commission as they suggest[1] for the investigation of the electric railways problem, and hope that the choice of personnel will be proceeded with at once. In the meantime please say to the Secretary of the Treasury that I authorize the allotment of $10,000 out of the fund for National Security and Defense to the Secretary of Commerce for this purpose and beg that he will immediately place that sum to the Secretary's credit. Written authorization will follow.

Am perfectly willing to lend the Sargent portrait of Roosevelt if I have the authority to do so. Please consult Colonel Ridley.[2]

The following for the Attorney General. I commute the sentence of Wm. J. Kelley to expire at once as suggested in Attorney General's letter of May 12th.

Please tell Goltra[3] that I am quite willing that he should give out his statement in reply to Lewis. I fear however that it will not be possible for me to accept the invitation to Saint Louis and hope he will not make an announcement to that effect.

Woodrow Wilson.

T telegram (WP, DLC).
 [1] See WCR and WBW to WW, May 19, 1919.
 [2] Wilson was replying to JPT to WW, May 19, 1919, T telegram (WP, DLC). Columbia University was holding an exhibition of Theodore Roosevelt memorabilia from May 9 to June 4. Officials of that institution had requested the loan of the White House portrait of Roosevelt by John Singer Sargent to be shown during the remainder of the exhibition. Tumulty commented that he believed that a refusal "would be misinterpreted." About the exhibition, see the *New York Times*, May 10, 1919. Ridley was Clarence S. Ridley, in charge of the maintenance of the White House.
 [3] Wilson was here replying to E. F. Goltra to WW, May 19, 1919, T telegram (WP, DLC). It reads as follows: "Senator [James Hamilton] Lewis back from Tour in the west in Chicago interview yesterday finds western people opposed to League much press comment. I desire to give out interview his [that he is] mistaken[,] that seventy nine out of one hundred and fourteen counties in my state [Missouri] have already endorsed League and pro League sentiment so overwhelming people have invited President make his first address in Missouri which he has accepted."

Edward Mandell House to Edward Wyllis Scripps[1]

[Paris, May 20, 1919]

Please deliver the following message to E. W. Scripps, San Diego, California: "I have presented the matter to the President and have warmly supported your suggestion. He bids me say that he will consider it carefully. I doubt, however, whether he will come to a decision until after peace has been signed. Edward House."

T telegram (E. M. House Papers, CtY).
 [1] Embodied in G. Auchincloss to FLP, May 20, 1919, T telegram (E. M. House Papers, CtY).

From the Diary of Dr. Grayson

Wednesday, May 21, 1919.

The President went for a walk after breakfast, and on his return he held a meeting here of the Big Three at eleven o'clock. Lloyd George and Clemenceau were present, Orlando having gone down to confer with the members of the Italian government over the French boundary in Italy. The question of Asia Minor, which is a very tense one so far as both England and France are concerned, was up for consideration. Before the meeting had much more than started Clemenceau and Lloyd George got into a very serious clash, the question of the secret treaties which had been entered into during the war precipitating it. Clemenceau declared that Lloyd George had made serious misrepresentations, and had in effect charged him with having lied. Finally, Lloyd George declared that he would not allow any such statement to be made and addressing himself directly to Clemenceau he demanded that he apologize and take back his charges. Lloyd George angrily demanded of Clemenceau: "Will you apologize?" In reply Clemenceau said: "That's not my style of doing business." President Wilson finally straightened the pair of them out and managed to get them down to business. Finally, when the meeting came to an end the President jokingly said to them: "You have been two bad boys, and so it would be well for you to shake hands and make up." They stepped towards each other but there was a very apparent evidence on both sides that the bitterness still held, and for a few seconds they confronted each other tense and bitter. At last Lloyd George stuck out his hand and Clemenceau grasped it. They both looked at the President, and seeing him smiling, they laughed heartily and thus wiped out the last trace of any bitterness. The President said to me afterwards: "They remind me of two boys."

The President, Mrs. Wilson and I had lunch, and after lunch the President took an hour's nap, while I gave him some treatment for a headache which had developed as a result of the strain of the morning session.

The Big Three met again in the afternoon and had before them the request from the German delegates for an extension of time in which to consider the treaty terms. The Germans had sent word that they would still have at least six additional notes to communicate to the Allied and Associated governments, and also that they had prepared substitute clauses for various sections of the proposed treaty which they had not yet fully perfected and would require time to do so. The Big Three decided to allow them an additional week in which to consider this matter.[1] The extension of time came very much as a surprise inasmuch as it had been thought that the Germans would be held entirely to the original time limit set. However, the French, running true to form, have now begun to worry and think that the treaty terms have been made so stringent that the Germans would not sign, and they were suggesting certain modifications which could be made to meet the views of the Germans. These modifications as a matter of fact were along the lines for which the President had stood out months ago and were designed to allow economic changes which would make more easy the payment of reparations that have been demanded. The French experts had submitted a report which was before the President and which dealt with these matters. It was considered a coincidence that the majority of the recommendations that the French had arrived at were simply those which the American economic experts had urged from the outset of the deliberations.

After dinner the President went over a number of official papers.

---

[1] For this brief discussion, see the minutes of the Council of Four, May 21, 1919, 4 p.m., printed in *PPC*, V, 772-74

Hankey's and Mantoux's Notes of a Meeting of the Council of Four[1]

President Wilson's House,

C.F.20A.   Paris, May 21, 1919, 11:00 a.m.

1. M. CLEMENCEAU handed round the Attached Note from the German Peace Delegation, asking for an extension of the time limit. (Appendix I.)[2]

(After a short discussion, Colonel Henri[3] was sent for from Versailles, and instructed to ascertain informally from the Germans the extent of the time limit which they desired, in order that M. Clemenceau might have some definite proposition to make to his colleagues.)

---

[1] The complete text of Hankey's minutes is printed in *PPC*, V, 754-71.

[2] U. K. C. von Brockdorff-Rantzau to G. Clemenceau, May 20, 1919, TCL (SDR, RG 256, 180.03401/20½, DNA), printed in *PPC*, V, 767. Brockdorff-Rantzau stated that the German delegation intended to submit to the peace conference during "the next days" communications, or notes, on the following subjects: the "territorial question in the East," Alsace-Lorraine, the occupied territories, the "extent and discharge of the obligation undertaken by Germany in view of reparation," the "further practical treatment of the questions of Labour law," and the "treatment of German private property in enemy countries." In addition, a "syllabus" was being prepared "of the observations which the German Government are called for by the Draft of the Treaty of Peace in its detailed provisions." Since these problems were complicated and required much discussion with experts both in Paris and Berlin, it might not be possible to meet the time limit of fifteen days from May 7 set by the Allies. The German delegation therefore requested that the requisite time be granted for a more detailed exposition.

[3] That is, Lt. Col. Marie Joseph Henry.

GENERAL ALBY[4] was introduced.

2. M. CLEMENCEAU handed a despatch from the French Military Mission at Prague to the Ministry of War, to M. Mantoux, which was translated by him. This despatch stated that General Haller's Polish troops had attacked the Ukrainian troops south of Przemysl and were threatening Borislav. The Polish troops should arrive at Drohorbyez tomorrow. The Galician population were already beginning to retire towards the passes of the Carpathians in order to take refuge in Czecho-Slovakia. The Ukrainian Government had asked for support by the Czech troops in the Borislav district, but this was not likely to be granted. The Czech Government was concerned lest the Bolshevist forces should, owing to the diversion by the Polish attack, overwhelm the Ukrainians. The military command in Czecho-Slovakia under the burden of the demands from the Ukrainian front had no reserves to spare for the Carpathians. Communication from Transylvania to Poland through Czecho-Slovakia was interrupted.

GENERAL ALBY said that this news had been brought to General Pellé[5] by Ukrainian officers. He explained on a map how the Ukrainians, who had been fighting the Bolsheviks for the last two months, were under pressure from Polish, Bolshevik and Roumanian forces.

MR. LLOYD GEORGE said that this was a breach of faith by General Haller, who had absolutely no right to take this action. He said that General Botha had been much impressed with the Ukrainians' case, and had suggested that the Council of Four should see the Ukrainians. The Poles were helping to crush an independent movement against the Bolsheviks.

PRESIDENT WILSON said that Mr. Hoover had suggested that the whole group should be informed that supplies of every kind would stop if fighting did not cease.

MR. LLOYD GEORGE said that Sir Esme Howard, who had always been favourable to the Poles, had sent him memorandum, advising that the Poles ought to be stopped on their present lines.

M. CLEMENCEAU asked if President Wilson's memorandum[6] had been sent to the Poles.

PRESIDENT WILSON reminded him that it had been suspended owing to the receipt of M. Paderewski's telegram.

MR. LLOYD GEORGE urged that the Ukrainian Delegation should be heard. These small nations were going straight to perdition, and

[4] That is, Gen. Henri Marie Camille Edouard Alby, Chief of the French General Staff.
[5] Gen. Maurice César Joseph Pellé, head of the French military mission to Czechoslovakia.
[6] See Appendix I to the minutes of the Council of Four printed at May 21, 1919, 4:15 p.m.

adopting all the worst vices of which the Prussians had been accused.

PRESIDENT WILSON said that the first question seemed to be to define the boundaries. Until that was done, it was difficult for the Council to take up an intelligible position for stopping the fighting between these States.

MR. LLOYD GEORGE advocated the stoppage of food and munitions as a means of bringing the fighting to an end. The Polish Ukrainian Armistice Commission had defined the boundary. General Botha told him that the Polish population in the Lemberg region was only about one-sixth of the total.

PRESIDENT WILSON said that M. Paderewski had told him that Lemberg was Polish.

MR. LLOYD GEORGE said that according to General Botha, Lemberg was a Polish town in the Ukrainian district.

(It was agreed that General Botha and the Members of the Polish-Ukrainian Armistice Commission, as well as the Ukrainian Delegation should be seen on the same afternoon at 4 p.m.)

(General Alby withdrew.)

§ Mantoux's notes:

Clemenceau. We have received a communication from the German delegation in which it requests a delay in the delivery of its observations on the peace treaty, without indicating a time limit.

Wilson (after the reading of the note). That request does not seem unreasonable: it tries only to obtain time to complete the draft in question.

Clemenceau. Yes, but without specifying the time necessary. If we should give our consent under these conditions, that would create an impression which I do not wish.

Lloyd George. Could we not ask the Germans through Colonel Henry when they can be ready? When we have this information, we can fix a time limit for them.

Clemenceau. I can send M. Cambon to them.

Lloyd George. It is better not to do the thing in an official manner, and to try only to know what they desire.

Clemenceau. I am going to summon Colonel Henry.

General Alby is introduced.

Clemenceau. General Alby is going to inform you about the news that he is receiving on the subject of Poland.

Alby. We have received a telegram from Prague indicating that the Poles are advancing into the region of Przemysl and that the Galician populations are fleeing before them into the Carpathians. The Ukrainians have asked the Czechs to assist them against the Polish invasion; but the Czechs have no disposable troops. The situation of the Ukrainians is critical, for they have been fighting against the Bolsheviks for several months and are attacked by the Poles from the rear.

Lloyd George. What the Poles are doing is a flagrant violation of the commitments undertaken; they are only helping the Bolsheviks crush the independence movement of the Ukrainian populations.

Wilson. Mr. Hoover advises us to warn the Poles that if they do not cease their aggression, we will stop the supplies.

Lloyd George. Sir Esme Howard, who is a great friend of Poland, comes to the same conclusion and makes the same recommendation to me.

Clemenceau. Have we not already decided to give a warning to the Poles?

Lloyd George. All these small nations are at this moment heading straight toward their own perdition if they conduct themselves as Poland is doing. It will come to pass that we will judge them as did the Prussians and the Russians: we will conclude that they do not have the right to exist. After having been so oppressed, the Poles think only of oppressing others. Their attitude is the same as that of the Catholic Irish vis-à-vis Ulster.

Wilson. We are forgetting one fact: it is that the frontiers are not yet defined; it is necessary to fix them and then to say that whoever crosses them is against us. As long as that has not been done, the uncertainty in which these populations find themselves is enough to explain the incidents which are taking place.

Lloyd George. We could stop them by refusing them ammunition and supplies.

Wilson. But where would you stop them? That is the point.

Lloyd George. We have already fixed between the Poles and the Ukrainians a boundary which should have marked the separation between their troops during the armistice which we wished to impose upon them. For the moment, it is not possible to determine immediately the ethnographic boundary; but it appears certain that the Poles do not constitute more than one sixth of the population in the contested territories.

Wilson. Is not Lemberg a Polish city?

Lloyd George. Yes, but surrounded by Ukrainian countryside, like Thorn, which is a German city in the middle of Polish territories.

Clemenceau. General Botha and his colleagues on the Commission on Polish Affairs must be seen on this subject. §

3. PRESIDENT WILSON read a draft reply to the German proposals on the subject of the League of Nations. (Appendix II.)[7] This reply

---

[7] "*League of Nations. Draft Reply to the German Proposals*," T MS (SDR, RG 256, 180.03401/20½, DNA), printed in PPC, V, 767-69. The draft stated that the German

had been prepared by the appropriate Committee of the Conference, of which Lord Robert Cecil had acted as Chairman.

(The reply was approved. Sir Maurice Hankey was instructed to inform the Secretary-General, and ask him to prepare a French translation for M. Clemenceau's signature.)

It was at this point that Colonel Henri was seen (see Minute 1).

4. MR. LLOYD GEORGE handed round a scheme in regard to the Italian claims, covering both Fiume and Turkey, which he had prepared for a basis of consideration. (Appendix III.) M. Orlando had been called away to meet his colleagues on the borders of Italy, and had suggested that the opportunity might be taken for a private discussion between the other three members of the Council in regard to Italian claims, and it was for this reason that he had prepared this Scheme.

(There was a short adjournment for reading this proposal.)

MR. LLOYD GEORGE said that perhaps the Council would be glad to hear his reasons. He had discussed the matter for two days with some of his colleagues in the British Cabinet, who had come from London for the purpose. He first referred to the question of Asia Minor. He pointed out that there was undoubtedly a good deal of unrest in the Mohammedan world, in regard to the future of Asia Minor and Turkey generally. Great Britain was, perhaps, the greatest Mohammedan power. There were some 70 millions of Mohammedans in India and several millions in Egypt and the Soudan. There had lately been a good deal of trouble in both these countries. Now Afghanistan was in ferment, and the Amir had declared war. About one and a quarter millions of troops had been raised in India, a large proportion of the fighting men being Mohammedans. These had done the bulk of the fighting against the Turks. It was true there had been some French troops in Gallipoli and a large number of British troops had been used both in Gallipoli and in the subsequent campaigns against the Turks. Nevertheless, in the campaigns subsequent to Gallipoli, the Indian troops had preponderated. The Mohammedan world realised this. Undoubtedly, the partition of Asia

---

proposals had received careful consideration and made the following general comments on them:

"They beg to point out that the proposals of the German Government deal with matters which have been discussed at length by the Commission of the League of Nations. But they consider in general that the proposals of the Covenant are much more practical than those of the German Government, and better calculated to secure the objects of the League.

"They are glad to note that the German Government is in favour of a League for the maintenance of peace which shall be based on, and which shall give effect to, the general principles of democratic government. With that point of view they are in hearty agreement. But they do not consider that all the specific proposals of the German scheme would, in practice, be an advantage for the purpose." The draft then commented specifically on several of the German proposals.

Entering Suresnes Cemetery, May 30, 1919

Speaking at Suresnes Cemetery

A French woman lays flowers
on the graves of American soldiers

Cary Travers Grayson

Ray Stannard Baker at his desk in Paris with Arthur Sweetser

Vance Criswell McCormick

David Hunter Miller

Edith Benham and Charles Seymour

Minor would cause anger in the Mohammedan world. The more he thought the matter over, the less was he, as head of the Power which had done nine-tenths of the fighting against Turkey, willing to agree to the partition of Asia Minor. This was the view of the British Cabinet. Not only would it create permanent trouble in the East, but they had come to the conclusion that it would be unjust. The Allies had no more right to split up Turkey than Germany, in former days, had had to split up Poland. Germany had had exactly the same justification in the case of Poland as there was now in the case of Turkey, namely, that the Government was incompetent. The Allies had a perfect right to say that the Turks should not rule over alien races like the Greeks, Armenians and Arabs, whom they had always misgoverned. But this argument did not apply in these parts of Turkey where the population was overwhelmingly Turk. If Smyrna, and Constantinople and Armenia were ruled out, the population of Anatolia would probably be more than 90% Turk. As an instance of the danger of partition, he mentioned the division of Bengal, which had caused trouble for years. Supposing Anatolia were divided, with the French in the North and the Italians in the South and the Sultan were at Brusa, would it be possible for the French to avoid interference? How could they help it with the Sultan in their sphere?

M. Clemenceau himself had said that this was an impossible situation and had suggested that there should be two Sultans, one in the North and one in the South. But this was unjustifiable to tear the population in half. It would cause constant unrest and trouble throughout the Mohammedan world and the British Delegates could not agree to it. He would like the same power which had the mandate for Constantinople to have the mandate for Anatolia. This was the view of the British Delegation after two days largely devoted to the study of the question. They considered that one power ought to control both, and that power should be the one in Constantinople. In Armenia and Mesopotamia and in Syria where there were non-Turkish races, other powers could govern. But in the case of Anatolia there should be some sort of Government by men of the Turkish race. Some sort of control, however, was desirable. Otherwise there might occur massacres of such Greeks and Armenians and the inhabitants of such other races as remained. The British Delegation would prefer America to exercise this control. The reason for this—and it was necessary to speak very plainly in considering these great problems affecting the future of the world—was that the United States of America would be more acceptable to the Mohammedan world than any other part. One reason was that America was known to have a very great respect for liberty and would consequently be expected to be very fair. Another reason was that America had no past in dealings with Mohammedans. This was not the case either with France or Great Britain. The Mohammedans were honestly afraid lest the Algerian experiment should be tried in Turkey, involving the complete subservience of Mohammedans to Christians. No doubt there would be the same feeling towards Great Britain. A second reason was that if France were given the mandate for Anatolia, Italy would have the right to complain under the Treaty of London. Italy feared lest France should regard herself as the only Mediterranean Power. This was really the basis of the whole of Baron Sonnino's case. Italy must also be ruled out from a mandate for the whole of Anatolia. This was hardly arguable. To give it to France, however, would make the position of Italy impossible. Hence, he could see nothing for it but for the United States of America to accept the mandate.

If, however, the United States could not see its way to accept a mandate, he saw no alternative but to continue the present system with the Turks in entire control. In reality, however, it would not work like the present system. America would have a mandate for Armenia and for Constantinople and it would not be possible for the Turk to remain absolutely free to misrule as he wished. As far as he knew the Turk never had perpetrated any very serious atrocities in Anatolia, even if he had never governed it particularly well. Moreover, the present system included certain restrictions on Turkish administration. There was a debt under an International Board; as France was the largest holder of the debt, the Board had a French President. This would continue. As regards concessions, this was probably a more nominal than real difficulty, since no one, except the United States, had any money. Hence, a scramble for concessions among the European Powers was a scramble for nothing. France had the Cameroons and Togoland to look after, both requiring a good deal of development. Moreover, his proposal gave France a provisional mandate for Syria until the report of the Commission was received. If the report was against France, there might have to be some reconsideration by the Powers in common. It was, however, essential for President Wilson to get home before very long, and the same applied to himself, and some provisional arrangement was necessary. These were his views, which had been prepared in consultation with his colleagues. He did not pretend that he had not vacillated. He had come to the conclusion, however, that any other solution would cause trouble to France and Great Britain, and to the peace of the world. Hence, he could not consent to the partition of Anatolia. Finally, until Russia was settled, he thought it would be necessary for the United States to control the Caucasus also. The British were in control at present, but they could not see their way to remain there.

He wished to point out that these proposals were closely linked up with his proposals in regard to the Adriatic. In the interests of the peace of the world, he thought it would be worth while to press these on the Jugo-Slavs.

PRESIDENT WILSON pointed out certain inconsistencies in Mr. Lloyd George's plan. Very good grounds were found in Asia Minor against handing over the population against its will to a Mandatory. But in the case of Jugo-Slavia the same principle was not applied. The only way to remove that inconsistency was to adopt the principle of the plebiscite which he had advocated. For example, in the case of the Islands, the only way to settle the question of which population predominated was by a plebiscite since the official statistics were disputed both by the Italians and the Jugo-Slavs. Whenever the Jugo-Slavs had been forced to intervene with a plebiscite, the figures had gone against the Italians. Even in regard to Lissa an inhabitant of that Island had told him that the population would not vote for the Italians. He, himself, all along had been willing to say to the Italians you must evacuate the whole territory which will then be put provisionally under the League of Nations, Fiume for the time being becoming a free City giving full access to the district served by the Port.

This access would continue until the construction of a Port of equivalent usefulness at Buccari. Then he would take the vote of the population in regard to Fiume.

In regard to the other territories, the League of Nations would arrange a plebiscite and Italy should be allowed to have any considerable district other than a mere Township that voted for her. This plan would square with the principles proposed by Mr. Lloyd George for Anatolia. His idea was the same as Mr. Lloyd George had suggested in a conversation with him just before the meeting in regard to Silesia, where Mr. Lloyd George had suggested doubts as to whether the population was Polish in sentiment. There might be cases where the preference of the population was stronger than the nationality. For example, there might be people in Silesia, who, though Polish in origin, preferred to remain German. The same principle might apply to the Adriatic. On the coast of Asia Minor on the Aegean littoral there was a considerable Greek population. He was fully in favour of giving the Turks complete access to the sea but he was apprehensive of extending Turkish sovereignty to the coast in the neighbourhood of the Dodecanese. If Turkish sovereignty extended to these shores, the Turks would always remember that the Islands had not long since been taken from them.

To illustrate this, President Wilson brought out an ethnographical map of Turkey pointing out that the population of the coast was very similar to the population of the Island. There was a close similarity between Mr. Lloyd George's plan and his own proposals. He himself, had suggested that the Turks should retain full sovereignty in Anatolia but that the Sultan should be allowed to inhabit a reserved area in Constantinople in the territory of the Mandatory for the Straits. Nevertheless, he would not be hampered in his administration of Anatolia by the Mandatory of the Straits though he might sometimes be guided by the Mandatory's advice. If the United States were the Mandatory of the Straits they would not in the least object if the Sultan were advised in stipulated matters by other Powers on the subject of the government of Anatolia.

MR. LLOYD GEORGE considered that if the United States could not take a Mandatory over Anatolia, it would be better for the Sultan to clear out of Constantinople. The Sultan's Court and guards comprising a very large number of people, would be a great inconvenience to the Mandatory Power.

PRESIDENT WILSON suggested the guards might be limited in number. Since Saturday he had been considering the question very carefully and he doubted the advisability of accepting a Mandate for Anatolia. If the same Power was Mandatory in Constantinople and in Armenia, it would be very difficult for the Sultan to cause much trouble.

He then adverted to the Commission for Syria. The Delegates whom he had nominated were men of such standing that he could not keep them waiting any longer in Paris, consequently he had instructed them to leave for Syria on Monday and to await there their colleagues on the Commission.

MR. LLOYD GEORGE said the same applied to the British Delegates and he thought he would give them the same orders.

M. CLEMENCEAU said in this case he must drop out. He said that the promises made to him had not been kept. General Sir Henry Wilson had apparently not been in a position to discuss with M. Tardieu the question of the sphere of occupation in Syria.

In reply to Mr. Lloyd George, who had asked in what way the promises made to him had not been kept, he said that in the Autumn of 1918, when he saw how the British were acting in Syria, he had come to London and had asked Mr. Lloyd George to say exactly what he wanted. Mr. Lloyd George had said Mosul and Palestine. He had returned to Paris, and in spite of the objections of M. Pichon and the Quai d'Orsay, he had conceded it. Then Mr. Lloyd George had said that France and Great Britain would get along all right. Nevertheless they had not succeeded in getting along all right. Early in the year the proposal had been made for the evacuation of Syria by British troops and the substitution of French troops. Lord Milner had asked him to put this aside for the moment and had undertaken to discuss it with him. He had never done so. Then Lord Milner had promised to help M. Clemenceau with Emir Feisal. He had never carried out his promise. After this, Lord Milner had produced a map by which Syria was divided in order to provide a railway for the British to Mesopotamia. Later, Mr. Lloyd George had suggested that President Wilson should have part of Cilicia. He had even agreed to this. Thus, he had given up Mosul and Cilicia and some more territory for the sake of the British Railway.

MR. LLOYD GEORGE interrupting, asked what M. Clemenceau's grievance was? what constituted a breach of faith?

M. CLEMENCEAU continuing, said that the latest phase had concerned the withdrawal of British troops. It had been agreed to arrange for zones of occupation. It had been agreed that M. Tardieu and General Sir Henry Wilson should study the question. After three days of consultation, General Wilson said that there could be no arrangement unless the limits of Syria were fixed. M. Tardieu had quite properly said that this was not a matter that he could deal with.

France, having given up Mosul and some region required for the Railway and Cilicia, thought she had a right to compensation. He had then suggested that France should have a Mandate over part of Anatolia. Of course he recognised that no promises had been given, but the idea had been proposed in the course of their conversations. He himself, had just listened and had shown no undue hurry about it. Only yesterday it had been suggested that France should have a Mandate for the whole of Anatolia. To-day, however, Mr. Lloyd George came forward with fresh combinations. He knew the cause of this. It was the arrival of Lord Curzon. He had heard all about this from London where Lord Curzon had spoken very freely. Lord Curzon was the fiercest friend France had in England. He regarded it as a good thing to take from France Mosul and part of Syria for a railway and Cilicia, and to do nothing in return. He had another objection. Throughout this Conference his policy had been the closest union between France, Great Britain and the United States of America. He had made great concessions in this respect. Only this morning he had had a meeting of certain representatives from the right of the Chamber and he had reminded them of the great service that Great Britain and the United States had rendered to France, and had insisted that their close cooperation must be continued. Was it a good thing though that France should be excluded from Asia Minor because of the susceptibilities of the Italians? He had public opinion in France to consider. France being the country with the greatest financial interests of any country in the world in Turkey surely ought not to be expelled from Asia Minor on two such grounds as the Mussulman question and the Italian question. He, like his colleagues, had been impressed by the Mohammedan Deputation. He had a genuine respect for the Moslem religion, and the Deputation had made an impression on him. He had thought that something ought to be done for them. He had no proposal to make to-day, but while something might be done for the Turkish people, he was unable to accede to Mr. Lloyd George's proposals. He considered the two hypotheses which he atributed to Lord Curzon dangerous. He considered it dangerous to introduce the United States of America in Asia Minor. To say that the United States were to have a Mandate not only for Constantinople and Armenia, but for the whole country between them would cause a bad ferment and division in the whole of the European world. It would introduce the ideas of men who had not thought of the repercussion of these events in Europe. He did not know what the effect would be in the United States of America, nor could he speak definitely for any country but France, but as regards France, though the feelings in favour of the United States were strong and of long standing, this proposal, if carried out, would not produce a good opinion. He recognised that the United States had done a great deal for France. They had struck the last blow in the war, and France was eternally grateful for it, but if the idea got about that Great Britain had brought the United States in to get France out, public feeling in France would not stand it. He did not say the idea was correct but that it would get about. Rather than sign any such agreement, he would not leave the Conference but it might be necessary for him to leave the Government. He did not say this in order merely to use a threatening argument, but he should not be doing his duty unless he gave this answer. He need hardly say that he was not going to conspire with M. Orlando and M. Sonnino in this matter but it would be impossible to prevent public feeling in France from joining with public feeling in Italy. It should not be forgotten that beyond the military and political decisions to be taken, there were human feelings and hearts to be considered, hence he begged that it would not be decided to keep France out as well as Italy by bringing in the United States of America. He was quite willing to admit, if his colleagues wished him to, that the Government of some other Power might conceivably be better in these regions but it was impossible to ignore Italy and the very bad consequent effect that such exclusion would have in France. When he had begun to speak he had had it in his mind to ask for time to examine the proposition coolly, and to-day he would make no proposal, but after having been led to believe that matters were to be arranged satisfactorily, this proposal had taken him by surprise.

If his colleagues really wished to induce him to believe that Mesopotamia and Palestine should go to Great Britain and Asia Minor to America, he was quite ready to think the matter over. He hoped his colleagues would not think he had forgotten the past. He would never allow any impression to be given outside that he had forgotten what Great Britain and America had done for France. He would do his duty to the Peace of the World, but he hoped before any further discussion, his colleagues would think these matters over.

MR. LLOYD GEORGE said that he must answer one or two of M. Clemenceau's observations. France had no right to complain of the loyalty of Great Britain which had given substantial guarantees for France's security. Great Britain had volunteered to make those guarantees without any pressure being put upon her. She had volunteered to put her whole strength in support of France.

As regards the charge of a break of faith, this was without any foundation. On the occasion of the London visit, Mr. Lloyd George had promised Syria to France provided that he gave up Mosul.

M. CLEMENCEAU said that France had had a definite agreement before as to Syria.

MR. LLOYD GEORGE said that in London it had been agreed that Syria should go to France and Mesopotamia to Great Britain, but that Mosul, which was in the same watershed as Mesopotamia, should form part of that country and go to Great Britain. In his statement M. Clemenceau had entirely ignored the article of his scheme which gave the Mandate for Syria to France. This was clearly stated in the document. Was this a case of bad faith? He recalled the proposal that he had made for a redistribution of the forces in Turkey in order to relieve the British Army which had a very large force there occasioning demobilisation difficulties. He, himself, had gone away to London and for some reason he had never quite understood, the scheme had fallen through. On his return, President Wilson had proposed the Commission to Syria. The United States and Great Britain and Italy had their Delegates all ready. It was France who had never appointed their Delegates.

This was a formal document and had been signed by all of them. M. Clemenceau had not carried out his part of the bargain. He did not say that M. Clemenceau had not kept faith, but he certainly had not carried out the bargain.

As regards General Wilson's conversations with M. Tardieu, his account was that he had gone to M. Tardieu with a map, as it was absolutely essential to delimitate the sphere of occupation. In this map the whole of Syria had been attributed to the occupation of France. M. Tardieu replied he knew about the subject. Surely it was plain common sense to delimitate the spheres of occupation on a map. It was quite unwarrantable to charge him with a breach of

faith because of this incident. As a matter of fact, no counter-proposal had been made by M. Tardieu. As regards the railway to Syria,
this was part of a proposal under which half the oil of Mesopotamia
was to be given to the French. The railway was essential to the
transport of the oil and was in the interests of the French. It had not
been a bargain but was merely a proposal that was under discussion,
and there was no breach of faith here. As regards Asia Minor, he had
never heard of a French claim until the previous day. There had
never been the smallest indication that France wanted a mandate
for Asia Minor. The project had arisen out of a discussion of the Italian claims. M. Clemenceau had himself made the proposal that
France should have a mandate for the northern half of Anatolia.
When the proposal was made, however, it was found that the claim
included priority for concessions. Then President Wilson had
pointed out that under the mandate scheme, priority for concessions
was not permissible. It was not true that France had the greatest
claim in Turkey. Within the last few days he had had the interests
of the various Powers in Turkey examined, with the result that Great
Britain was found to have the largest trade. Germany the second,
France being a bad third. It was true that France had a large claim
in the Baghdad railway, but the Baghdad line would not run mainly
through the part of Anatolia which had been contemplated in the
French mandate. It would run through all the mandated territory,
American, French and British. Hence the basis of this claim was not
in the French zone at all. He did not believe that French public opinion had made any claim for a mandate for Anatolia. He had carefully
studied the French newspapers, and had only found one reference
to it, namely, in the newspaper "Temps," and he believed that to be
Italian propaganda. He did not want to discuss in detail the agreement signed between Lord Grey and M. Cambon, but he meant to
point out that it had always been understood that the two countries
were to do their utmost to attack the Turks. He had tried to carry out
this part of the agreement. He had met M. Ribot and M. Painlevé,
and Marshal Foch at Boulogne, and Marshal Foch had produced a
plan by which the French were to attack from the north and the British from the south. The French Government, however, would not
agree. Afterwards, a document had been prepared by the military
representatives at Versailles. M. Clemenceau, himself, however,
had been against it. Hence, the whole policy was on the understanding of a co-operation in overthrowing the Turks, which had never
been carried out on the French side. All sorts of plans had been discussed. At one time the British would have liked to have landed at
Alexandretta, but could not go there, owing to French susceptibilities. There had been a project for a French landing at Tripoli, but the

French had never gone there. Great Britain was the largest Eastern Power, and now the greatest of all Mohammedan Powers. This was the reason for the objections made to a French mandate over Anatolia. It was not in the least fair to suggest Lord Curzon was anti-French. It was not right to make a just peace in the West and not to make a proper peace in the East. It was solely in the interests of peace in the East that he had been unable to agree to a division of Anatolia. It was for this reason that he had come to the conclusion that the better plan would be for the United States of America to have the mandate. If M. Clemenceau said that this was because Great Britain was jealous of France, he made a suggestion that was not a very worthy one to a Power that had done and guaranteed so much for France.

PRESIDENT WILSON said he hoped, in the first place, the consideration of this question would be postponed for a time, since great issues were involved. He would contemplate with the greatest uneasiness and distress any misunderstanding that might arise in this matter. He must say at once that the United States would find it very difficult to take any part in Asia Minor where they had no material interests. Any part in the sacrifices and burdens of this mandate would be politically disadvantageous to America. Hence, America desired nothing in Asia Minor. What they did desire most of all was first, the accord between the great powers, and second, peace with the world. He hoped, therefore, that the question would be viewed solely from these points of view. Mr. Lloyd George's plan might or might not be the best. But whether they agreed or disagreed in this particular plan, they must find one which would be best for the peace of the world. He had formed no judgement on the scheme for himself, and would think it over. He could only say at this stage, that he feared it was impossible for the United States to take a mandate for Asia Minor. It was difficult for her to take a mandate even for Armenia, where she had permanent interests of long standing, and where a good deal of money had been spent by Americans for the relief of the Armenian people. As regards Constantinople, he thought that even some of the public men who were opposed to him politically would support him in taking a mandate. He did not, however, think that he could persuade them to accept a mandate for Asia Minor. Although he did not exclude the possibility of altering his opinion, his present conviction was, that it would be better not to divide Anatolia, and that the Sultan should be left in Constantinople. If that caused too great complications, he should be removed to Brusa. His present judgement also was that it would be dangerous to bring the Turks to the coast in the neighbourhood of the Dodecanese, supposing that these islands were to go to Greece.

He suggested that instead of a mandate to the United States, something should be laid down to provide for giving advice to the Turks. What had been suggested was that the Sultan should accept advice in regard to certain specific matters, for example, finance, commercial matters and gendarmerie. In discussions with his United States colleagues, he had told them that France was already in the position of advisor as regards the Ottoman debt. He had told his colleagues that he thought the other processes of advice might come from the French Government. He thought that M. Clemenceau had misunderstood his proposal that the United States Delegates on the Syrian Commission should proceed to Syria to await their colleagues. At any rate, they were men of such standing that he could not keep them waiting in Paris. If they did not go to Syria they must go back to the United States.

MR. LLOYD GEORGE said he thought they ought to go to Syria.

M. CLEMENCEAU said that he was ready for the French representatives to go, as soon as the British troops in Syria had been replaced by French. The question had been referred to Sir Henry Wilson and M. Tardieu. He did not think that General Wilson could have reported the result of this interview correctly. General Wilson had said that the limits of Syria must be fixed and M. Tardieu had replied that only the Council of Four could do that.

MR. LLOYD GEORGE said that General Wilson had submitted a document to M. Tardieu. There had been no breach of faith here.

SIR MAURICE HANKEY said possibly the misunderstanding was due to him. The conversation between General Wilson and M. Tardieu had been interrupted in order that certain decisions might be taken, which could only be taken by the Council of Four. On the previous day, just as he was entering the meeting, a large map had been thrust into his hand, containing the proposal for the line of delimitation for Syria, which General Wilson had put forward. At the morning meeting he had had no opportunity to bring this matter forward, and there was no afternoon meeting and the map was still lying in the room.

MR. LLOYD GEORGE insisted that the negotiations in regard to the railway were to the advantage of France. However, he must put a stop to these negotiations until the present misunderstanding was cleared up.

(It was agreed that the Syrian question should be discussed the same evening.)

(The Meeting then ajourned until 4 p.m. the same afternoon.)

§Mantoux's notes:

Lloyd George. I first present the reasons for the proposals relative to Asia Minor the text of which I have just given to you.

The Muslim world is restless; you know our difficulties in Egypt;

Afghanistan is at war with us. During the war, we raised more than a million men in India, almost all Muslims; it is they who bore almost the entire weight of the struggle against Turkey, although supervised by white troops. The Muslim world does not forget that.

The division of the properly Turkish portion of Asia Minor would be unjust and impolitic. After reflection, the British government cannot support it; the cabinet has taken a formal decision on this subject. We must not treat Turkey as Poland was treated a century and a half ago. Will it be said that Turkey does not know how to govern herself? The same could have been said of Poland.

To the extent that the Turks are a domineering people, establishing their government over other races, we have the right to say to them: "It is finished." But if Smyrna and its region, if Armenia, if Constantinople cease to be part of the Turkish Empire, the remainder of Anatolia contains a population of which the Turkish element forms 95 per cent. This purely Turkish part cannot be divided into two without great dangers. I will recall what happened recently in India when Bengal was divided into two administrative zones. It was only a question of a purely internal measure, yet it caused grave difficulties for years, because Bengal would not hear of being divided.

If you divide Turkish Anatolia, what will you do with the different parts? The Italians would establish themselves in the south, the French in the north. But if the Sultan resides in Brusa in the French zone, he will be in the hands of the French, and it will become inevitable that French influence will be felt in the affairs of the northern region. Conflicts between French and Italians would surely ensue.

M. Clemenceau recognizes this; that is the reason why he would prefer to create two distinct states, one of which would have its center at Brusa, the other at Konia. But of the two sovereigns, which would be Caliph? How could we justify that division in the eyes of the inhabitants and of the Muslim world? It is a question there of a homogeneous population, which we could not divide in two without creating constant agitation. The British delegation cannot accept such a system. The mandate over Turkey must be placed in the hands of a single power: such is the conclusion that we have reached.

In Constantinople, in Armenia, in Syria, in Mesopotamia, the European nations must take charge of administration, because these countries, where the Turks are not the majority, have been poorly governed by them. In Anatolia they will govern themselves; it is enough to be at their side, to guide them in the administration of their finances and to insure the protection of the minorities who will remain alongside the Turks.

The solution which seems best to us is to entrust this role to the

United States. Its intervention is the one which the Muslim world will best accept, because of its past as a country of liberty, and also because it has no history as a Muslim power. The Muslims are afraid that the Algerian regime be extended to Turkey; they have suspicions of the same nature with respect to England.

I see another reason against the assignment of this mandate to France. If France is established in that region, Italy would have the right to complain; her impression will be that France is becoming the only great Mediterranean power, and that she herself is almost excluded from the Mediterranean. If Italy receives nothing in Asia Minor, placing France there would put the Italian government in an untenable position. I do not see any solution other than to entrust the task of advising the Turkish government to the United States. If the United States does not think it can accept, I would maintain the regime currently in existence in Anatolia.

Indeed, the presence of the Americans in Constantinople and in Armenia, of the French in Syria, will exercise constant influence and pressure upon the Turkish government and will make it impossible for it to fall back into all the abuses of the past. Moreover, only Turks, or very nearly so, will be governed in Anatolia. Let us not forget that the Turkish regime, such as it is, already tolerates in rather wide measure intervention and advice from foreigners. The Ottoman debt is administered by an international organization under French presidency: that administration must be maintained. An entire system of concessions for public works to foreign enterprises already exists and must continue.

I do not believe, moreover, that we should exaggerate the importance of the interests we might have in these concessions during the period just beginning; for none of us will have capital to invest in these countries for quite a long time, with the exception perhaps of America. France will have nearly the whole of the Cameroons and Togoland to develop her enterprises, and I propose to assign to her immediately a provisional mandate over Syria, until we have received the report of the commission which should serve to guide the final distribution of mandates in western Asia.

I believe that neither we nor France could undertake at the present time the development of a large country like Anatolia; the United States can do it.

Such are the views which I wished to present to you, after consultation with my colleagues. I have presented you with a series of different proposals; I recognize that I vacillated very much. I have reached the conclusion that any solution other than this one will create difficulties for France and the world. We cannot divide Anatolia, and I do not see how, if this country were placed under a

French mandate, we could extricate ourselves vis-à-vis Italy. America is thus the only power to whom we can appeal; as long as Russia is not in a position to shoulder her share of the burden, I consider that the country which will supervise the administration of Anatolia must also administer the Caucasian regions. Furthermore, if Italy is excluded from Asia Minor, I see such an advantage for the peace of the world that that deserves an effort on our part to impose our solution in the Adriatic upon the Yugoslavs.

Wilson. We must not contradict ourselves. You are on solid ground in Asia Minor when you say that you do not have the right to divide a homogeneous population. But how would it be possible to give Italy compensation in the Adriatic against the wish of the peoples involved? The only acceptable procedure appears to me to be the consultation of these peoples by a plebiscite. In this way all the Italian groups, wherever they really exist, will be able to unite with the mother country. But in fact everywhere where a poll has been taken, the result has been unfavorable to Italy. I have a report on Lissa which shows that even that island, which we wished to leave to the Italians, would prefer to be part of the Yugoslav state.

Italy should begin by evacuating all that region and leave it to the disposition of the League of Nations. Fiume, provisionally, would be a free city under the trusteeship of the League of Nations, for a period determined by the time necessary for the creation at Buccari of a Yugoslav port, at the expense of Italy. When that period ended, the population of Fiume would be consulted and would decide itself on the fate of the city. With respect to the remaining contested territories, the plebiscite would determine, commune by commune, what should be Italian and what should remain to the Yugoslavs. This manner of proceeding would be absolutely consistent with our principle.

Similarly, if doubts arose on the subject of the Polish character of certain parts of Upper Silesia, the only way of knowing what the final decision should be is to consult the population. In the end it would not be a question of ascertaining what the race and the language of the population are, but under which regime they prefer to live.

In Asia Minor, it seems to me, as it does to you, impossible to divide the purely Turkish region. I would fear nonetheless extending Turkish domination as far as the coast which faces the islands of the Dodecanese; the Turks have not reconciled themselves to having lost these islands, and we must see to it that future conflicts are avoided.

What was said the other day by the Muslims of India made an impression upon me as upon you, and I believe also that it is necessary to leave to the Turks the government of all of Anatolia. What I myself suggested the day after that meeting was not, moreover, unrelated to what Mr. Lloyd George has just outlined. I proposed to grant Turkish Anatolia its independence by giving the Sultan a residence in Constantinople. That independence of the Turks includes, moreover, the assistance and advice of a western power, with clearly defined functions. I will add that if America had the mandate over Constantinople and another power was the mandatory in Anatolia, I am convinced that there would be no friction to fear.

Lloyd George. There is much to be said in favor of a regime which would leave the Sultan in Constantinople, but are you not afraid to see an independent sovereign, surrounded by his court and guard, in the zone which you would administer?

Wilson. I have doubts about the wisdom of a policy which would place Anatolia under any mandate whatsoever.

Lloyd George. If the Sultan is in Constantinople and you have no power over him, since, from Constantinople, he will be governing that large neighboring region, that will place you in an impossible situation.

Wilson. I believe that he will necessarily be subject to the influence of the power which will administer Armenia, on one side, and the Straits on the other.

The men whom I designated to be part of the commission of inquiry in Syria have been asking to leave for a long time, and I authorized them to go.

Clemenceau. Concerning Syria, if things go against me, I cannot accept. It was said that the zone of occupation in Ottoman Asia would be determined after a conversation between General Sir Henry Wilson and M. Tardieu. They did indeed meet; General Wilson could not reach agreement with M. Tardieu on the occupation of Syria, he told him that he had no instructions. You promised me the settlement of this question. France cannot afford to be treated in this manner.

Lloyd George. What do you mean?

Clemenceau. When I went to London last autumn, I said to you: "Let me know what you want in Asia, in order to eliminate any cause for misunderstanding between us." You said to me: "We want Mosul, which the Sykes-Picot Treaty places in the French zone of influence." I promised you that I would take care of the matter, and I have done it, despite the opposite of the Quai d'Orsay.

You then promised me to evacuate Syria, which was to be occupied by French troops; the boundary of the zones of occupation was to be fixed at Versailles; but Lord Milner brought everything to a halt, and things have remained at an impasse. You also promised me a meeting with Faisal, which never took place.

Then I receive maps from you dividing Syria in a way which we never accepted and which appears unacceptable to us. A little later it is decided that the United States will have a mandate over Armenia and, to give them satisfaction, it is proposed that Cilicia be included in the Armenian mandate instead of being joined to Syria. I accept without difficulty.

I have thus abandoned Mosul and Cilicia; I made the concessions you asked of me without hesitation because you told me that afterward, no difficulty would remain. But I will not accept what you propose today: my government would be overthrown the next day, and even I would vote against it.

Lloyd George. You accuse me of having gone back on my word: I am still waiting to know in what particular I have done so.

Clemenceau. A few days ago, you promised me to study without delay the question of the zones of occupation in Syria; we designated M. Tardieu and General Wilson to settle that question between them. At the end of three days, General Wilson says: "I have no instructions; I must know how the boundaries of Syria are to be fixed."

I believed that in ceding Mosul to you, in accepting that part of Syria be taken in order to let a railroad pass through, and that Cilicia be joined to Armenia, I could have the right to some compensation. It is then that you came up with the idea of the mandate in northern Anatolia entrusted to France. Then all of Anatolia was proposed to us. I am not saying, by the way, that you have taken any commitment toward us. I listened to these proposals. Yesterday, we were discussing a French mandate which extended over all of Anatolia, and today, France is evicted.

I believe that all of that comes from your conversations with Lord Curzon. Lord Curzon is a charming man, and very able, but he is hostile to France. He said everything that I have just heard in London, where someone took note of it before coming to tell it to you here.

You are taking from France Mosul, Cilicia, part of Syria in order to let a railroad pass through, and you exclude her from Anatolia after having almost promised it to her. That seems to me a bit thick.

My constant policy has been to preserve the union of France with Great Britain and with America. In order to do that I have made greater concessions than I first would have thought possible. I am glad to have made them. It is what I was explaining this very morning to a delegation from the Right, which came to present me with certain recriminations. I explained to it that our relations with England and the United States should be determined not only by the immense service that these two countries rendered us during the war, but by the necessary solidarity between them and us after the conclusion of peace.

You say that France must not be in Asia Minor because that would displease Italy: do you not believe there is also public opinion in France? France is, moreover, of all Europe, the country with the greatest economic and financial interests in Turkey—and here she is evicted to please first the Muslims, and then Italy.

I myself was also impressed by what the representatives of Islam said; I make every allowance for their feelings, I respect their religion, I think that we must do something for them. But is it not a fact that the Turks have always proved themselves incapable not only of governing other peoples, but of governing themselves? Both assumptions of Lord Curzon seem to me equally dangerous. I do not see the Turks governing themselves without great disadvantages. As for the idea of introducing America into our disputes, of placing her between the English and French by installing her in all of Asia Minor, I do not believe that that is the way to avoid dangerous frictions. I do not know what the Americans will think of the proposal, but French sentiment would be wounded, in spite of our profound sympathy for America.

The United States did a great deal in this war; she came to help us deal the last blow, the decisive blow, and we are deeply grateful to her. But if our people got the idea that the English placed the Americans in Asia in order to chase out the French, that will create a frame of mind which, for my part, I would dread.

I am the least colonialist of all the French; I cannot be accused of having excessive ambitions in this respect. If this decision was taken, I would not do what our Italian colleagues did, I would not leave the conference, but I would leave the government.

I did not have the least idea of that proposal, so that what I am saying is improvised. My intention is not to plot against you with the Italians; but I would not be able to prevent public sentiment from joining Italian public sentiment and turning against you: that could create great difficulties in the world.

Outside of general political considerations in Syria, there are sentimental considerations. Note that I do not doubt for an instant that American administration in Asia Minor would be an excellent thing; it would perhaps even be better than the administration of that country by any other nation. But you cannot remove in an instant all the results of the past—traditions and interests accumulated over centuries; beware of the reaction that that could produce in the French mind.

If I have not spoken with enough composure, please excuse me. I have no proposal to make. We have agreements concerning Syria; we will hold to them if that is necessary. But what is necessary above all is an arrangement which gives satisfaction to everyone. If Asia escapes us, I will not for that forget the past which binds us, I will continue to do my duty for the peace of the world and vis-à-vis my country. But think about what you wish to impose upon us, and think it over twice.

Lloyd George. I do not think France has the right to complain about the fidelity of Great Britain: she has very recently given proofs of it. If M. Clemenceau has consented to sacrifices on certain claims, it is because England has promised to come to the aid of France if she is attacked.

Clemenceau. Did I not allude to that?

Lloyd George. British opinion willingly offers to place the entire strength of Great Britain at the disposal of France if the latter is in danger. To say that we have not kept our word is without justification, and such a manner of speaking would render all discussion impossible.

In London, Syria having been promised to France and Mesopotamia to Great Britain, I did indeed ask you to have Mosul transferred to the British zone, and you consented to it. I will observe that in the memorandum which I read to you earlier, the first line recalls that Syria will be placed under French mandate.

With a view to making our demobilization possible, I proposed that the occupation of Turkish Asia be divided between us. Upon my return from London, President Wilson proposed to send a commission of inquiry to Syria; he named his experts. I named mine: they remained here because the French government has not appointed its own. I do not say that M. Clemenceau has broken his word to us. It is the French who, for the moment, have not carried out their part of the contract. If there is a breach of promise, it is on the part of the French government, which does not execute a common decision.

General Wilson, you say, stated to M. Tardieu that, in order to establish the zones of occupation, it would be necessary first to know the boundaries. But General Wilson sent you a map which gives the occupation of all of Syria to the French army. Is that a breach of promise? I consider that M. Clemenceau should withdraw what he has said. M. Tardieu can say that he is not in accord with the General; but there is no breach of promise there.

I hear talk of a railroad that must cross Syria; it is a question of transporting petroleum, of which half must go to France. As for Anatolia, I never heard it said, until these last days, that France had territorial claims in that region. To suggest that we did not keep our word in that region is truly intolerable. We held a discussion among ourselves which originated in our desire to settle the Italian question. M. Clemenceau suggested a division of Anatolia; it then appeared to us that that division would lead to serious difficulties.

M. Clemenceau has just said that France holds first place in Asia Minor from an economic point of view. Concerning external commerce, England stands first; before the war, Germany came second and France third, far behind the other two. It is true that there is French money in the railroads of the Levant, including the Baghdad railroad; but the latter crosses territories which will necessarily be placed under different administrations. I do not believe that French opinion demands Anatolia or would be surprised if Anatolia were not placed under the control of France. I have read only one article on the subject, in the newspaper *Le Temps*, and since the conclusion dealt with the concessions to be made to Italy, I concluded from it that that article was only a piece of Italian propaganda.

As for the treaty concerning Syria, its stipulations were contingent, in principle, on common military action. A plan was made by General Foch in 1917. The question was raised upon the assumption of power of M. Clemenceau, who was among those least favorable to this plan. It is England which alone made all the efforts required for the execution of the Sykes-Picot Treaty, even though it had been understood that the action would be made in common.

Clemenceau. Was there ever a written convention relative to our military cooperation?

Lloyd George. No; but we had to refrain from landing at Alexandretta because it was pointed out to us that this port was in the French zone. A plan for a landing at Tripoli was also set aside for the same reason.

Our views on Anatolia are those of a great eastern power which has experience in the Orient. It is that experience which guides Lord Curzon, and not hostile feelings toward France, which you wrongly attribute to him. It is in the common interest that I arrived at the conclusion that an American mandate must be established in Anatolia. M. Clemenceau suggests that that proposal is made only to evict France: I do not understand why he raises a suspicion of this kind against a power which has done so much and which is ready to do so much for France.

Wilson. I believe that our decision must be postponed. Great questions have been raised, and I would view with the greatest apprehension the grave differences that they could create.

I must say without further delay that it will be very difficult for the United States to assume the mission which you propose to it. It has no direct interests in Anatolia; it has not invested capital there. We could only accept the role that you offer us as a burden and against bitter opposition from American opinion. We desire absolutely nothing in Asia Minor. We desire only two things: agreement among the great powers and the peace of the world. We have the duty to find a plan which establishes order in Asia Minor and which helps maintain order in the Mohammedan world.

My opinion is not yet decided. I will study the question; but it appears to me impossible that America will accept this mandate. She will take the Armenian mandate for humanitarian reasons. Americans have already sent missionaries, money, and relief societies to Armenia. American opinion is interested in Armenia. But I do not believe that I could present to Congress plans like the one just outlined. That is enough to rule out America as a possible mandatory in Anatolia.

But we must assist in the solution. I have reached the conviction that it is impossible to divide Anatolia and that the Sultan, if that is possible, should remain in Constantinople. If, however, his presence in Constantinople causes too many complications, it will be necessary that he settle either in Brusa or in Konia. Another point upon which I insist is that the Turks must not be placed too close to the Dodecanese.

The only point upon which there is a divergence of opinion between us is Anatolia. Yesterday, I suggested that Anatolia be not placed under a mandate of the League of Nations, but that we only place alongside the Turkish government a power which will give it advice on matters of finance, on economic matters, and on the organization of the police. France already occupies that position concerning the debt; in my opinion, the same role must be assigned to her in the other areas.

Perhaps we have the impression today of a greater disagreement than that which really exists. I hope that M. Clemenceau will not misunderstand what I said with respect to my representatives on the commission of inquiry on Syria: they have remained here without doing anything for some time; today they must either go to Syria or return to America.

Clemenceau. I am ready to send my representatives to Syria as soon as the relief of the troops of occupation has begun. But I find that it is useless to send a commission to Syria to make an inquiry under the dictatorship of General Allenby. That is why I arranged this meeting between General Wilson and M. Tardieu. General Wilson said that he did not know the frontiers of Syria; M. Tardieu could only reply that that question was in the hands of the heads of government. For the moment, it is only a question of determining the limits of the zones of occupation.

Lloyd George. You received from us a map several days ago. If you do not agree with us on the boundaries indicated on that map, there is nothing to be done, and I warn you that I am going to give instructions that the negotiations regarding the railroad which you mentioned earlier be halted immediately. The French will do what they like. If they consider our attitude to be a breach of promise, we will go our way without worrying further. I have done everything I could to meet the wishes of the French in Syria, and that has only led to an accusation of not having kept our word. I declare that I will make no further effort in that direction. I feel that M. Clemenceau should apologize for having made that accusation against us.

Clemenceau. Do not wait for apologies on my part. But I wish it to be noted that I am ready to discuss the boundaries of the military occupation in Syria this very day. §

T MS (SDR, RG 256, 180.03401/20½, DNA), Mantoux, II, 130-32, 133-43.

To Robert Lansing

My dear Lansing: Paris, 21, May, 1919.

In reply to this letter,[1] I would be obliged if you would give a most emphatic denial that it was my objections which have held up the publication of the text of the Treaty. As a matter of fact, the chief objection has come from the English, and I have concurred because we are, theoretically at any rate, holding the treaty subject to alteration until our discussions with the Germans are finished. That surely is the all-sufficient reason for our not publishing it.

            Cordially and faithfully yours,   Woodrow Wilson[2]

TLS (SDR, RG 256, 185.182/27, DNA).
    [1] RL to WW, May 20, 1919 (first letter of that date), and its Enclosure.
    [2] The gist of this letter was transmitted to Polk in RL to FLP, No. 2194, May 21, 1919, T telegram (SDR, RG 256, 185.182/29, DNA).

To Herbert Clark Hoover

My dear Hoover: Paris, 21 May, 1919.

I read with deep interest and concern your letter of the ninth of May[1] about the situation in the Balkan [Baltic] Provinces, and yesterday had an opportunity to read it to the other members of the

"Council of Four." Mr. Lloyd George suggested that I request you to have a conference with Admiral Hope,[2] or anyone else who represents the British Admiralty here, in order to ascertain whether it was feasible from a naval point of view to carry out the programme you suggest. If the programme were adopted, it would, I suppose, necessarily be the British Navy that executed it, and we would very much appreciate a memorandum from you as to the result of your conference with the British Admiralty.

Cordially and sincerely yours, Woodrow Wilson

TLS (Hoover Archives, CSt-H).
[1] See HCH to WW, May 9, 1919, Vol. 58.
[2] That is, Rear Adm. George Price Webley Hope.

From Herbert Clark Hoover

Dear Mr. President: Paris, 21 May 1919.

Since addressing you on the ninth of May, with respect to the situation in the Baltic States, the matter came up before the Council of Ministers of Foreign Affairs and they appointed a committee comprising representatives of the Army, Navy and food organizations of each of the four governments. This committee has made the enclosed report to the Council of Five.[1] No action has as yet been taken upon it.

With regard to the possible contribution of $12,500,000 from the United States for these purposes, I may say that this entire amount will be covered by our food programme and it will not, therefore, be necessary for the United States Treasury to consider the matter. It is a question of agreeing [to] the policy and of securing that the other Governments do their share in the provision of other materials required in these states.

Faithfully yours, Herbert Hoover

TLS (WP, DLC).
[1] The enclosure is missing. However, it is printed as Appendix C to the minutes of a meeting of the Council of Foreign Ministers, May 23, 1919, 3 p.m., *PPC*, IV, 762-63. For the initial discussion in that body on May 9, 1919, and the establishment of the committee, see *ibid.*, pp. 687-93. For a summary of the committee's report and the action taken upon it by the Council of Foreign Ministers and the Council of Four, see ns. 6 and 7 to the minutes of the latter body printed at May 24, 1919, 4 p.m.

Two Letters from Robert Lansing

My dear Mr. President: Paris, 21 May 1919

I beg to enclose herewith, for your information, copies of several reports prepared by two officers of the Military Intelligence Section of our Army respecting their observations as to the political situation in Germany at the present moment, and reporting the substance of interviews with Mr. Erzberger and Count von Bernstorff.[1] These officers travelled to Berlin at the urgent request of Mr. Erzberger. My colleagues on the Commission and I believe that these reports are extremely valuable as indicating the present sentiment in Germany in regard to the proposed Peace Treaty.

I beg to call your attention particularly to the report by Major Henrotin on the second interview which he had with Mr. Erzberger in which the latter made certain definite suggestions in regard to amending various Articles of the proposed Treaty.

                          Faithfully yours,   Robert Lansing

[1] Two memoranda by A. C. Conger and four memoranda by Maj. Frederick Henrotin, all dated May 20, 1919, and all TC MS (WP, DLC), printed in *PPC*, XII, 124-35. Conger and Henrotin reported on an interview with Matthias Erzberger and Johann Heinrich von Bernstorff on May 18 and on a second interview with Erzberger alone on the following day. In the first interview, Conger had stressed that he and Henrotin spoke only for themselves and took great pains to remove certain German misapprehensions about the attitude of the Americans and the French. Despite rumors to the contrary, Conger said, both Wilson and the American people stood fully behind the terms of the peace treaty. The German government was misinformed in supposing that the French government would compromise on the terms of the treaty. Moreover, the people of both nations would support a renewal of the war should that prove necessary. Bernstorff did most of the talking on the German side and took a belligerent stance. He stated flatly that the German government would not sign the treaty and that the Allies would be invited to enter Germany and take over its government.

In the second interview, Erzberger was more conciliatory. He declared that it was essential for Germany that a peace be signed. He then proposed a series of modifications of the terms of the treaty which would make it possible for Germany to sign it. He warned, however, that he could not sign a treaty which departed too far from the Fourteen Points.

Conger and Henrotin both reported that there was a basic split among the leaders of Germany between those who would sign the treaty with some modifications and those who would not sign it at all. They both believed that the morale of the German civilian population had improved greatly in recent weeks and that the military forces of Germany, both official and informal, were in much better shape, both materially and in esprit, than they had been a few months before.

My dear Mr. President: Paris, May 21, 1919.

The Commission has recently been flooded with declarations from Southern Tyrol protesting against incorporation into Italy.[1] I beg to transmit a number of these protests, as well as certain reports on the question which have been received from Professor Coolidge,[2] our representative in Vienna.

                          Faithfully yours,   Robert Lansing

TLS (WP, DLC).
[1] These documents are missing but see, for example, A MEMORIAL OF GERMAN SOUTH

TYROL TO . . . PRESIDENT WOODROW WILSON, March 24, 1919, printed pamphlet, and "The Memorial of the South Tyroleans to President Woodrow Wilson," March 30, 1919, T MS, both in WP, DLC.
  [2] These reports are also missing but see A. C. Coolidge to the A.C.N.P., April 28 and May 5, 1919, both printed in PPC, XII, 307-309.

From William Linn Westermann and David Magie[1]

Dear Mr. President: [Paris] May 21, 1919.

We would respectfully call your attention to the fact that for eighteen months a group of men has been working in Princeton and in Paris gathering information preparatory to giving technical advice to the American Peace Commissioners upon problems connected with the disposition of the Ottoman Empire.[2]

We know that these problems are now before the Peace Conference. Yet we have no knowledge, except from the daily papers and vague rumor, as to what is being done. The only technical advice which is being heard, so far as we know, is apparently that of British Foreign Office experts and of Mr. Venizelos, all of whom are interested parties. What appears in the daily papers leads us to the conclusion that decisions based upon this advice will result in the looting of the Ottoman Empire in violation of the principles which both you and the American people desire to see enforced.

We feel that our advice and opinions are purely disinterested and that we may be of assistance in bringing about a more equitable solution of some of the problems involved. We respectfully urge that we be granted the opportunity of submitting our opinions to you, personally.   Very sincerely yours,   W. L. Westermann,
                                                    David Magie

TLS (WP, DLC).
  [1] David Magie, Professor of Classics at Princeton University, staff member of the A.C.N.P.
  [2] For the work of The Inquiry's section on "Western Asia," that is, the Middle East, see Lawrence E. Gelfand, *The Inquiry: American Preparations for Peace, 1917-1919* (New Haven, Conn., and London, 1963), pp. 60-63, 103, 145-46, 240-58.

Gilbert Fairchild Close to Felix Frankfurter

My dear Mr. Frankfurter: Paris, 21 May, 1919

The President asks me to say in reply to your note of May 20th that he is entirely willing that you should show his letter to those who are interested and use it in the way that you suggest.
                        Sincerely yours,   [Gilbert F. Close]

CCL (WP, DLC).

Gilbert Fairchild Close to Sir William Orpen

My dear Sir: Paris, 21 May, 1919.

The President asks me to acknowledge receipt of your letter of May 20th and to express his deep regret that his time is so completely taken up with the official work of the Conference that he has been obliged in every case to decline sittings for his portrait. He appreciates very much your desire to make his portrait but unhappily he does not feel that he can find the time necessary for the sittings which you suggest.[1]

                                Sincerely yours,   [Gilbert F. Close]

CCL (WP, DLC).

[1] In fact, Wilson did sit for Orpen on at least four, and perhaps five, separate occasions in June. See the extracts from the Diary of Dr. Grayson printed at June 7, 10, and 13, 1919, and those from the Diary of Colonel House printed at June 10, 11, and 21, 1919.

Hankey's and Mantoux's Notes of a Meeting of the Council of Four[1]

                                    President Wilson's House,
C.F.22.   Paris, May 21, 1919, 4:15 p.m.

PRESIDENT WILSON stated that the reason for the presence of the Ukrainian Delegation was the distressing circumstances existing on the Polish-Ukrainian front and stated that the Council of the Principal Allied and Associated Powers had invited the Delegates to make a statement as to their views on these circumstances. The Council would be glad if the spokesman would set forth these views.

M. SYDERENKO[2] expressed in the name of the Ukrainian Delegation their gratitude to the illustrious representatives of the Great Powers for the interest they were showing in the Ukrainian people. He stated that Ukrainian territory had been devastated, the people had suffered extremely, and that they all deplored the state of war that existed between Poland and Ukrainia. They would like to live with the Poles in peace and harmony, and as brothers. They, however, were not the aggressors, but were only defending the country of their forefathers. They had more than once expressed their willingness to enter into an armistice and repeated that willingness again. They trusted that the Peace Representatives of the Entente would settle this question in accordance with the principles of justice and right as enunciated by President Wilson and as accepted by the Great Powers. Particularly anxious were they that the matter of the Armistice should receive an immediate settlement. The Armi-

[1] The complete text of Hankey's minutes is printed in PPC, V., 775-99.
[2] That is, Gregory Sydorenko.

stice Commission had asked them to express their view and they had accepted the terms of the Armistice proposed by that Commission, but in spite of this they were informed that the Poles had made continuous attacks and had occupied further parts of Ukrainian territory. With regard to this point, Dr. Paneyko[3] the Vice President, would give further information.

MR. LLOYD GEORGE wished to know what the attitude of the Ukrainians was towards the Bolshevists.

M. SYDERENKO, in reply, stated that the Ukrainians were defending their national territory, and that the Bolshevists had invaded and were ravaging their country. They regarded the Bolshevists as their worst enemies, and were doing their best to establish peace and order.

MR. LLOYD GEORGE, to make this point clear, asked whether that statement meant that the Poles were attacking the Ukrainians on the Western side while the Bolshevists were attacking them on the East. The answer was in the affirmative.

DR. PANEYKO stated that the population of Eastern Galicia consisted of about 4,000,000 Ukrainians. These had been given over by the Austrian authorities to Polish domination, and that was the reason why the Ukrainians greeted with joy the collapse of the Austrian Empire and immediately proceeded upon that collapse to establish their own national life and State. This State was founded on the principle of self-determination, as accepted by the Entente, but at the same time guaranteed the rights of minorities. From a social and economic point of view, the State is based upon the principles of democracy, and is introducing moderate reforms, chiefly with reference to the agricultural situation. The estates of the great landowners have not been declared forfeit, but a scheme has been adopted for buying out these land-owners, the object being to obtain a middle class peasantry as the backbone of the State. In spite of the rights of the Poles being guaranteed, the latter, dreaming of the old historical Polish Empire, extending from the Baltic to the Black Sea, proceeded to attack this new State. The Polish population within the borders of the State, chiefly belonged to the bureaucratic and large land-owning classes, but the bulk of the population is Ukrainian.

MR. LLOYD GEORGE asked whether there was any substantial difference between the Polish and Ukrainian languages.

DR. PANEYKO replied that all Slavic languages are closely related, but the Ukrainian language is distinct from that of the Poles. One is not a dialect of the other. The Russian Ukrainians spoke the same language as those in Eastern Galicia. In religion the Galicians are Greek Catholics, owning allegiance to the Church of Rome.

[3] That is, Vasil Paneyko.

Dr. Paneyko, continuing, stated that when the Government, established by the German Military Command in Ukrainia, was overthrown, a movement for liberating the Western Ukraine was commenced by the inhabitants.

MR. LLOYD GEORGE put the question whether, supposing Russian Ukrainia should remain part of Russia, the Western Ukrainians would prefer to remain under Poland or under Russia as an autonomous State.

DR. PANEYKO answered that it was difficult to reply to this question. Their aim and object was complete national independence, and he expressed the opinion that an autonomous State as suggested would not solve the problem, but would only serve to create a situation corresponding to the Balkan States.

M. SYDERENKO pointed out that the Ukrainian people were now all united. At one time they had been divided between Russia and Austria. Now, their common object was national independence. No union with Poland was possible, as the Ukrainians counted a population of some 40,000,000, while the Poles only totalled some 20,000,000. The Russians, on the other hand, had always only used Ukrainia only for their own interests. All the Ukrainian parties from Right to Left were united in the one aim of obtaining complete independence as an indivisible State.

MR. LLOYD GEORGE then asked if it was correct to state that whatever happened to Ukrainia as a whole, the Ukrainians would prefer to throw in their lot therewith. Did they want to be separated from the Eastern Ukrainians? The answer was, No. What they desired was a united independent Ukrainian State.

Mr. Lloyd George farther enquired whether the Ukrainians were prepared to stop fighting if the Poles should do the same, and, if so, would they treat the Polish people fairly and with justice.

DR. PANEYKO stated in reply, that they had been willing to stop and had so stated several times previously. Legislation had also been passed guaranteeing to the Poles minority rights, which legislation had been much appreciated by the latter. To a further query of Mr. Lloyd George, whether, if ordered by the Delegation here in Paris, the Ukrainian troops on the front would obey such order, the reply was, Absolutely, and that the Armies under command of the Ukrainian Government were well-organised and under complete control of the Ukrainian Government.

Mr. Lloyd George enquired whether, if the Ukrainians were relieved on this Polish-Ukrainian front, would these armies be used against the Bolshevists on other fronts.

DR. PANEYKO replied, Certainly. This army was animated with a desire to proceed against the Bolshevists in their country. The Ukrainian Delegation felt that such army would be more successful against the Bolshevists because they understood the population which was at present subject to Bolshevist rule, and would get a sympathetic reception from their co-patriots. The Bolshevists had over-run Ukrainia, because the latter's army had to be withdrawn to defend their homes against the ravaging and pillaging of the Poles. Bolshevism would not find a rich field in Eastern Galicia, as the population there had enjoyed constitutional liberties far more than the Ukrainian population in Russia. The Ukrainians were anxious for the support by the Entente in the way of officers, supplies, munitions of war, etc. and stated that the Poles at the present time, with the assistance of the Allies, were invading Ukrainia and burning and ravaging the country. In the name of humanity, he called upon the Entente to stop the Poles. Every day he received appeals for protection from the Ukrainians.

(The Deputation then withdrew.)

PRESIDENT WILSON requested General Botha to read the report of the Polish-Ukrainian Armistice Commission, (Appendix 4).[4]

The report was then read by Colonel Kisch.

GENERAL BOTHA then pointed out that the Ukrainians had accepted the draft Armistice terms subject to some slight modification, and demonstrated on the map attached to the report,[5] the various lines of demarcation suggested by the Armistice Commission, the Poles and the Ukrainians respectively. The Poles from the beginning had taken up the attitude that it was essential for them, in order to fight Bolshevism, to shorten their line and thus to join hands with Roumania and occupy a line towards the East of the Eastern boundary of Eastern Galicia.

PRESIDENT WILSON wished to have the opinion of General Botha and the Commission as to what effective steps could be taken to make the Poles agree to the draft Convention. As far as he understood the position from the reports that had come in, it appeared that the Poles were continuing their plans of attack regardless of the protests of M. Paderewski, and that Haller's Army was being used on this front.

§Mantoux's notes:

Wilson. The question is to know what the practical means are for bringing the Poles to their senses. Their population is very inflamed.

[4] REPORT (WITH APPENDICES) PRESENTED TO THE SUPREME COUNCIL OF THE PEACE CONFERENCE BY THE INTER-ALLIED COMMISSION FOR THE NEGOTIATION OF AN ARMISTICE BETWEEN POLAND THE UKRAINE, May 15, 1919, printed report (SDR, RG 256, 180.03401/22, DNA), printed in PPC, V, 783-99. The commission reported that it had produced a draft armistice convention between Poland and the Ukraine, as it had been instructed to do, but that conditions demanded by the Polish delegation in Paris raised questions of general policy which were "beyond the competence of the commission." The appendices to the report included the draft armistice convention and the comments of the Polish and Ukrainian delegations in Paris.
[5] It is included in the MS of the minutes.

Paderewski is overwhelmed. General Pilsudski first yielded to our representatives, then annulled the order given. The Diet then urged the new offensive led by General Haller.

Lloyd George. That is what the news provided this morning by General Alby shows.

Kisch. We know furthermore that the Poles have occupied the city of Belsk.[6]

Wilson. The difficulty which faces us is obviously not from the side of the Polish government, which accepts our injunctions, but of the Polish nation, which has truly taken the bit in its teeth. What is General Botha's opinion about the measures to be taken?

Botha. Our commission did not take up the political problem in general terms. We concerned ourselves only with stopping the hostilities and with the terms of the armistice.

Lloyd George. But what is your personal opinion on that question?

Botha. Hostilities must be stopped at any cost. We concluded an armistice with Austria, and, in the Ukraine, Poland is renewing the state of war. The Supreme Council of the Allies must speak to her with force and say to her that our governments will not tolerate the prolongation of this struggle. Whether you should decide today that eastern Galicia should belong to Poland, or, on the contrary, you do not recognize any right for her in that region, everyone must obey you.

In fact, there are in eastern Galicia a million Poles, 700,000 Jews, whom the Poles are claiming, but who are not Polish in any way, and four million Ukrainians: the conclusion is obvious.

President Wilson reads aloud the message prepared to be sent to the Polish government; he adds:

You will notice that it is a question here of a dire warning: we are threatening to starve Poland if she does not obey.

Lloyd George. And also to stop sending her ammunition; I see no other way to force the Poles to listen to us. §

GENERAL LE ROND[7] pointed out that the telegram stating that Haller's Army was being used on the Ukrainian front came from Prague, and without further reliable authority it could hardly be accepted as correct. The same remark applied to the report that the Poles had taken Belsk, well within the Ukrainian lines.

GENERAL BOTHA, in reply to President Wilson stated that, as a Commission, they had not gone into the political question as to what steps should be taken to enforce the Armistice terms. The Commission had impressed upon both parties the urgent necessity for stop-

[6] Now known as Bielsk.
[7] Gen. Henri Louis Édouard Le Rond, Adjutant General to Marshal Foch.

ping bloodshed, had drafted a draft armistice attached to the report, and submitted it to both parties for their acceptance. As Chairman of that Commission, he could only refer to the unanimous conclusion of the Commission, that when the Poles refused to accept the draft armistice their mandate was at an end. He was of opinion that bloodshed should be stopped at once for he feared that if it were allowed to continue peace would never reign in this region. Furthermore, if the Poles would stop this fighting it would give the Supreme Council an opportunity of further considering the question of frontiers and thus enabling a settlement to be obtained.

PRESIDENT WILSON then read a draft telegram which it had been proposed to send to General Pilsudski (Appendix I), before the latest telegrams had arrived from M. Paderewski (Appendix II)[8] and asked whether this telegram met with the approval of General Botha, pointing out that the effect of the telegram might be to create starvation amongst the people and suggesting that the terms of the telegram should be restricted to withholding military supplies.

GENERAL BOTHA suggested omitting all reference to the kind of supplies, thus leaving it open for decision later on, but President Wilson pointed out that such a course would be inadvisable unless the Council had already decided what it would do should the Poles prove obdurate.

GENERAL LE ROND pointed out that the Poles had always maintained that the continuous front from the Black Sea to the Baltic Sea was essential for their safety as against Bolshevism and had alleged that in their present line there was a gap, namely, the Ukrainian front where communications were passing through between Lenin and Bela Khun. If the Poles overthrew Paderewski and no other Government could be established, the only alternatives were either to starve the Poles or force them to become Bolshevists, and he suggested that the telegram should be confined to food supplies. Both sides were filled with ambitious aims but there certainly was some ground for the Polish desire for a continuous front, more especially when the Polish Army seemed to have the better morale.

GENERAL BOTHA pointed out that the Poles stood under the protection of the Supreme Council, and were receiving assistance in the shape of troops, munitions of war and food. The Ukrainians fighting against them had on the other hand not been recognised, were receiving no assistance from the Allies; their country had been devastated by war, and the suffering amongst the population must be great. Yet, both countries were in the same position in this respect,

[8] It is printed as Appendix I to the minutes of the Council of Four, May 19, 1919, 11:30 a.m.

that both owed their present existence to the sacrifices of the Allies. He believed that it would be to the interests of the Poles to listen to the Supreme Council. They had already been told that in the matter of territory they should occupy by force of arms. Such would not be taken into consideration in deciding the ultimate frontiers. He considered the cry of Bolshevism to be a bogey and felt it was impossible for the Supreme Council to allow a small nation to be over-run by its neighbours on the ostensible pretext of a defensive, strategical measure against Bolshevism, which at this point was some hundred miles removed from the present Polish frontier. The Poles owed their very existence to the great sacrifices of the Allies and therefore the Allies had every right to demand that they should be listened to. Furthermore, if the fighting on this front were stopped, it would mean obtaining some sixty thousand men to assist in waging war against the Bolshevists. Looking at the question from the Ukrainian point of view, it must appear to the latter that they are being deceived by the Allies. Military assistance is being sent to the Poles by the Allies in the shape of Haller's Army, and supplies, etc., are being forwarded and being used to over-run a neighbouring State which like Poland owes its existence and continuance to the sacrifices of the Allies. There was plenty of room along the Eastern frontier of Ukrainia for the Poles to fight Bolshevism side by side in agreement with the Ukrainians. He felt that the time had come for the Supreme Council to take active steps. It was impossible after the Ukrainians had expressed their willingness to accept the draft armistice terms to send them home again without a settlement having been reached.

PRESIDENT WILSON sympathised with this argument but expressed the fear that if strong action forced the downfall of the Paderewski Government, Poland would turn Bolshevist, as had happened in other cases. As far as he could judge the present temper of the Diet, Poland would become anarchical if any extreme measure should be adopted.[9]

DR. LORD pointed out that the draft Armistice Terms had as yet not been agreed to by the Supreme Council, but had only been submitted unofficially to the contending parties by the Armistice Commission. He expressed the view that if the Supreme Council should adopt the Armistice with such modifications as they thought fit and

[9] Mantoux, II, 154: "Wilson. My feeling is entirely on your side. The doubt which persists in my mind is this. If Paderewski falls and we cut off food supplies to Poland, will not Poland herself become Bolshevik? Paderewski's government is like a dike against disorder, and perhaps the only one possible. That is the risk that we are running, given the state of mind of the Polish Diet. If I knew what means to use to avoid this risk, I would not hesitate to use it."

formally submit the same to the Poles and Ukrainians, the former would probably accept them.

GENERAL BOTHA feared that delay had been the root of all the trouble, and that every day that passed without a settlement made the problem more difficult.

MR. LLOYD GEORGE agreed that the Supreme Council had hitherto acted rather weakly in this matter. He remarked that it seemed to him that Poles were using Bolshevism as a cloak for their Imperialistic aims. From the experience in Russia he had formed the conclusion that the only way to fight Bolshevism was to use nationals of the country affected. Wherever foreign troops intervened the hands of Bolshevism were strengthened, and therefore to fight Bolshevism in Ukrainia we should rather use Ukrainians than Poles. Ukrainians may naturally say that the Poles in pretending to fight Bolshevism really were pillaging and ravaging their country and the result would be simply to force Bolshevism upon Ukrainia. We are told that the Warsaw mob would overthrow the Paderewski Government if we took strong steps. If that were so it showed pretty conclusively that the Poles were quite unfitted to govern themselves. He hoped that the draft telegram prepared by President Wilson would be sent and suggested that the word "supplies" could be interpreted later. By using the wide term "supplies" some advantage was to be gained and if a decision was necessary the word could be restricted to military supplies. He suggested that a telegram should be sent to General Haller stating that rumours had come to the ears of the Supreme Council that in defiance of their express instructions General Haller had allowed his troops to march against the Galicians.

GENERAL LE ROND suggested that instead of telegraphing to General Haller the telegram should be sent to General Pilsudski of the Polish High Command.

(It was agreed that M. Clemenceau should send a telegram on the above lines to General Pilsudski and at the same time forward through the French Liaison Officer[10] a copy to General Haller for his information. General Le Rond and Colonel Kisch were instructed to submit a draft telegram (See Appendix III).

After further discussion as to the terms of the draft telegram, it was decided that President Wilson should re-draft the same with two additions:

(1) Calling the attention of the Poles to the fact that they owe their legal existence as a State to the Council and

[10] Almost certainly Gen. Paul Prosper Henrys, chief of the French military mission in Poland, 1919-1921.

(2) stating that the draft Armistice Terms had been adopted and confirmed by the Council.

(The meeting then terminated.)

§Mantoux's notes:

Wilson. We could at the same time stop the passage of General Haller's army across Germany.

Le Rond. Instead of sending a telegram directly to General Haller, who only obeys the orders of his government, would it not be better to send this message to Warsaw?

Clemenceau. We must act without delay.

Wilson. Is the army of General Haller not supposed to be part of the French army?

Le Rond. It is now part of the Polish army.

Clemenceau. Its officer corps is French, which we can recall.

Lloyd George. If this message is not sent directly to General Haller, he must in any case be sent a copy.

Wilson. I will modify my telegram by adding that the Polish state can only be fully established with our consent and that the heads of the Allied and Associated governments accept and support the conditions of the armistice proposed by the Commission on Polish Affairs.

Clemenceau. You will speak to them no longer about the blockade?

Wilson. Yes indeed! What I am proposing is only an addition.

Clemenceau. Your text seems to me a bit hard. I understand the Ukrainians, but I would like to hear what M. Paderewski might have to say.

Lloyd George. The Poles are doing everything necessary to revive Bolshevism, just at this time when it is near expiring. We have already heard M. Paderewski; the Ukrainians made their presentation to us for the first time today.

Clemenceau. You have never heard M. Paderewski on the conditions of the armistice. When is he coming to Paris?

Le Rond. He will be here in two days.

Clemenceau. In any case, the message that you have prepared must be sent to M. Pilsudski.

Wilson. And clearly indicate that we, the heads of government, entirely approve of the conditions of the armistice, while reminding them that the existence of Poland and the determination of her frontiers depend upon us.

Lloyd George. We have the right to speak in this manner, at a time when we are going to have to struggle with the Germans in order to impose upon them acceptance of their new frontier on the Polish side.

Wilson. I will revise the draft of the telegram to the Polish government.

Clemenceau. If you wish, I will take care of the telegram to General Pilsudski and to General Haller.

Lloyd George. This latter will have only the object of asking for information about the rumors which come to us on the subject of the Polish offensive.

Wilson. Will you send it to General Haller by General Pilsudski?

Lloyd George. I fear that, in these conditions, it would never arrive.

Clemenceau. I will send it to General Haller through the French liaison officer whom we have placed at his side.§

APPENDIX I TO C.F.22.

TELEGRAM.   Paris, May 19th, 1919.

From: The President of the Peace Conference.

To: General Pilsudski, Head of the Polish State.

The Council of the Principal Allied and Associated Powers feel that it is their duty to call the attention of the Government of Poland to facts which are giving them the greatest concern and which may lead to consequences for Poland which the Council would deeply deplore. The boundary between Poland and the Ukraine is under consideration and it is as yet undetermined, and the Council has more than once informed the Polish Government that they would regard any attempt either by Poland or by the Ukrainian authorities to determine it, or to prejudice its determination, by the use of force, as a violation of the whole spirit and an arbitrary interference with the whole purpose of the present Conference of Peace, to which Poland, at least has consented to leave the decision of questions of this very sort. The Council has, therefore, more than once insisted that there should be an armistice on the Ukrainian front, arranged in Paris and under the advice of Council itself. The Polish military authorities, while acquiescing in principle, have in effect insisted upon such conditions as would amount to a settlement of the very questions in controversy, and have continued to use forces in maintenance of their claims. This has inevitably made the impression on the minds of the members of the Council that the Polish authorities were in effect, if not in purpose, denying and rejecting the authority of the Conference of Peace. The Council feel it their duty, therefore, in the most friendly spirit but with the most solemn earnestness, to say to the Polish authorities that, if they are not willing to accept the guidance and decisions of the Conference of Peace in such matters, the Governments represented in the Council of the Principal Allied and Associated Powers will not be justified in supplying Poland any longer with supplies or assistance of any kind. If it is her deliberate purpose to set at naught the counsel proffered by the Conference, its authority can no longer it is feared be made serviceable to her.

APPENDIX III TO C.F.22.

TELEGRAM.

From: The President of the Peace Conference

To: General Pilsudski, Warsaw.

(Approved by the Council of the Principal Allied and Associated Powers on 21st May, 1919.)

The Council of the Principal Allied and Associated Powers have heard rumours from several sources to the effect that troops of General Haller's Army have recently taken part in operations against the Ukrainian forces in Eastern Galicia, in the region of BELZ or elsewhere.

The Council would be glad to receive early information from the Polish Government with regard to these reports, which the Council is reluctant to believe, since definite engagements were undertaken by General Haller not to take part in the operations against the Ukrainians.

T MS (SDR, RG 256, 180.03401/22, DNA); Mantoux, II, 151-52, 155-56.

Hankey's Notes of a Meeting of the Council of Four[1]

President Wilson's House,

C.F.22A.   Paris, May 21, 1919, 6:15 p.m.

PRESIDENT WILSON read the draft of a reply to the German Note on the Economic Effect of the Treaty of Peace[2] which had been prepared at the request of the Council by Lord Curzon. (Appendix I.)[3]

1. Subject to a few alterations in detail, the Note was approved.

Sir Maurice Hankey was instructed to forward it to the Secretary-General for translation into French for the signature of M. Clemenceau.

It was agreed that the letter should be published after it had been signed and despatched.

2. PRESIDENT WILSON said he would like to intimate to the Germans that the Experts of the Allied and Associated Powers were now ready to discuss with their Experts in regard to Financial and Economic Conditions.

[1] The complete text of these minutes is printed in *PPC*, V, 800-806.
[2] See Appendix I.A. to Hankey's minutes of the Council of Four printed at May 20, 1919, 11 a.m.
[3] There is a TC of this redraft by Lord Curzon in WP, DLC.

M. CLEMENCEAU thought it would weaken the Allied and Associated Powers.

PRESIDENT WILSON said that his object was to demonstrate to Europe that nothing had been left undone which might have induced the Germans to have signed. If they did not sign it would involve sending troops into the heart of Germany and their retention there for a long period. Germany could not pay the costs of this occupation which would pile up the expenses to people who were already protesting against the burden of occupation. People would ask if there was anything reasonable left undone which might have averted this. There would be no loss of dignity by carrying out this plan. The experts of the Allied and Associated Powers would merely explain the meaning of some parts of the Treaty of Peace which, in his view, the Germans had failed to understand. If our Experts could show that no heavier burden has been laid on the German people than justice required, it might make it easier for the German Delegates to explain to their own people.

M. CLEMENCEAU thought that this would serve the objects of the Germans. He agreed that they would probably leave without signing, but when troops began to move, they would sign soon enough. They wanted some excuse with their own people to make them sign.

MR. LLOYD GEORGE thought that sufficient excuse would be given if some concession could be gained. He had nothing particular in mind but there might be some concession which did not matter very much which could be made. The question would not be decided until the German answer to our proposals was available. He had in his mind that they would make proposals perhaps about coal.

M. CLEMENCEAU said we had a very strong answer on this. He had seen some extraordinary effective figures of M. Loucheur's.

MR. LLOYD GEORGE thought they might also make proposals about restoration. He thought before deciding this question, it would be better to await the German reply and to keep an open mind on the subject.

PRESIDENT WILSON said that the letter which had just been considered gave a conclusive reply to the German letter but provided no ray of hope. It merely said that the Treaty was right and nothing more. He had understood that the experts who had discussed with the German Financial Experts at Villette found Herr Melchior a very sensible man. Melchior was now one of the German Delegates, and he was a representative of the kind of people in Germany who wanted to get their industries going again, and he wanted to avoid the chaos and confiscations of property and looting which had occurred elsewhere. These people wanted to get their country started again, and they would listen to what our experts had to say. The

United States Experts had, all along, said that the present scheme of reparation would not yield much. This was Mr. Norman Davis' view, and Mr. Keynes, the British expert, shared it. He himself wanted the Allies to get reparation. He feared they would get very little. If it could be shown to Melchior that the Reparation Commission was allowed to consider the condition of Germany and to adjust the arrangements accordingly from time to time, it might enable him to persuade the German people.

M. CLEMENCEAU said that President Wilson was right, but he did not want to be placed in the position of a man who was begging a favour. He preferred Mr. Lloyd George's idea, of waiting until the German comprehensive reply was received. This would be our "morceau de résistance."

PRESIDENT WILSON said he was afraid ten years hence we should find that nothing had been got out of the Treaty of Peace, and this would cause a reaction in Germany's favour.

3. M. CLEMENCEAU informed his colleagues that he had postponed signing the reply to Brockdorff-Rantzau's letter on the subject of Prisoners of War because he wished to attach to it an admirable report he had received showing the equipment of German Prisoners of War. He hoped to have this on the following day.

4. The attached telegram of General Pilsudski was approved (Appendix II).[4]

(Sir Maurice Hankey was instructed to forward it to the Secretary-General with instructions to translate it into French; to despatch it to General Pilsudski; and to arrange for a copy to be sent to the French Liaison Officer, or any other Officer on the Staff of General Haller, for the information of General Haller.)

APPENDIX I TO C.F.22.A.

Suggested Reply to German Note
on the Economic Effect of the
Peace Treaty.
Redraft by Lord Curzon.

1. The Allied Powers have received and have given careful attention to the report of the Commission appointed by the German Government to examine the economic conditions of the Treaty of Peace.

This Report appears to them to contain a very inadequate presentation of the facts of the case, to be marked in parts by great exaggeration, and to ignore the fundamental considerations arising both out of the incidence and the results of the war, which explain and justify the terms that it is sought to impose.

[4] See Appendix III to the minutes of the Council of Four printed at May 21, 1919, 4:15 p.m.

2. The German Note opens with the statement that the industrial resources of Germany were inadequate before the war for the nourishment of a population of 67 millions, and it argues as though this were the total for which with diminished resources she will still be called upon to provide. This is not the case. The total population of Germany will be reduced by not less than six million persons in the non-German territories which it is proposed to transfer. It is the needs of this smaller aggregate that we are called upon to consider.

3. Complaint is made in the German Note that Germany is required to surrender her merchant tonnage, existing or in course of construction, and that a prior claim is made upon her shipbuilding capacity for a limited term of years. No mention, however, is made of the fact that a considerable portion of the smaller tonnage of Germany is left to her unimpaired; and it seems to have entirely escaped the notice of her spokesmen that the sacrifice of her larger shipping is the inevitable and necessary penalty imposed upon her for the ruthless campaign which, in defiance of all law and precedent, she waged during the last two years of the war upon the mercantile shipping of the world. As a partial offset against the $12\frac{3}{4}$ million tons of shipping sunk, it is proposed to transfer 4 million tons of German shipping. In other words, the shipping which it is proposed to take from Germany constitutes less than one-third of that which was thus wantonly destroyed. The universal shortage of merchant shipping is the result, not of the terms of peace, but of the action of Germany, and no surprise can reasonably be felt if she is called upon to bear her share—and it is a very moderate share—of a loss for which her own criminal deeds have been responsible.

4. Great stress is laid upon the proposal that on the Eastern side Germany shall be deprived of the Regions specially concentrated to the production of wheat and potatoes. This is true. But the Note fails altogether to observe that there is nothing in the Peace Treaty to prevent either the continued production of these commodities in the areas in question, or their importation into Germany. On the contrary the free admission of the products of the Eastern districts is provided for during a period of five years. Moreover, it is fortunate for Germany that these Regions have lost none of their productivity owing to the ravages of war. They have escaped the shocking fate which was dealt out by the German armies to the corresponding territories in Belgium and France on the West, and Poland, Russia, Roumania and Serbia in the East. There appears to be no reason why their produce should not continue to find a market on German soil.

5. Stress is laid upon the proposed restriction in the import of Phosphates. It is, however, forgotten, that Germany has never pro-

duced but has always imported the Phosphates of which she stands in need. Nor is there anything in the terms of peace which will prevent or hinder the importation of phosphates into Germany in the future. Other countries, which do not produce phosphates, are also compelled to import them in common with many other products from the outside; and the only difference in the two situations will arise from the relative degree of wealth or impoverishment in the countries concerned.

6. The German Note makes special complaint of the deprivation of coal, and asserts that nearly one-third of the production of the existing German coal mines will be lost. But it omits to notice that one-fourth of the pre-war consumption of German coal was in the territories which it is now proposed to transfer. Further it fails to take into account the production of Lignite, 80 million tons of which were produced annually in Germany before the war, and none of which is derived from the transferred territories. Neither is any reference made to the fact that the output of coal in the non-transferred districts was rapidly increasing before the war, and that there is no reason to doubt that under proper management there will be a continuing increase in the future.

7. But should not the coal situation be viewed from a different and wider standpoint? It cannot be forgotten that among the most wanton acts of devastation perpetrated by the German armies during the war was the almost complete destruction by her of the coal supplies of Northern France. An entire industry was obliterated with a calculation and a savagery which it will take many years to repair. The result has been a grave and prolonged shortage of coal in Western Europe. There can be no reason in equity why the effect of this shortage should be borne exclusively by the Allied nations who were its victims, or why Germany who deliberately made herself responsible for the deficiency should not to the full limit of her capacity make it good.

8. Stress is also laid upon the hardships alleged to be inflicted upon Germany by the necessity of importing in future iron ores and zinc. It is not understood why Germany should be supposed to suffer from conditions to which other countries contentedly submit. It would appear to be a fundamental fallacy that the political control of a country is essential in order to produce a reasonable share of its products. Such a proposal finds no foundation in economic law or in history.

9. The Allied Powers cannot accept the speculative estimate presented to them in the German Note of the future conditions of German industry as a whole. This estimate appears to them to be characterized and vitiated by palpable exaggerations. No note is taken of

the fact that the economic disaster produced by the war is widespread, and, indeed, universal. Every country is called upon to suffer. There is no reason why Germany, which was responsible for the war, should not suffer also. She must for this reason realise that her economic, in common with her political and military existence, must be conducted henceforward on a reduced and lower plane. The German Note tabulates and aggravates every contemplated deprivation of material, and endeavours to paint a picture of unrelieved gloom. But it fails, as already mentioned, to make any allowance for the fact that the present population of Germany will be diminished by 6,000,000 and that there will consequently be that less number of people to provide for, to feed and to clothe.

10. Similarly, as regards the population of the future, no reliance can be placed on the data which are contained in the German Note. On the one hand, it is sought to prove that emigration from Germany will be necessary, but that few countries will receive the intending emigrants. On the other hand, it is sought to show that there will be a flood of Germans returning their native land to live under the conditions which have already been described as intolerable. It would be unwise to attach too much weight to either speculation.

11. Finally, the German Note rashly asserts that the Peace Conditions will "logically bring about the destruction of several millions of persons in Germany," in addition to those who have perished in the war or who are alleged to have lost their lives in consequence of the blockade. Against the war losses of Germany might very fairly be placed the far greater losses which her initiative and conduct of the war have inflicted upon the Allied countries, and which have left an ineffaceable mark upon the manhood of Europe. On the other hand, the figures and the losses alleged to have been caused by the blockade are purely hypothetical. The German estimate of future losses, which, though it is described as logical, appears to be no less fantastic, could be accepted only if the premises upon which it is presumed to rest are accepted also. But they are entirely fallacious. There is not the slightest reason to believe that a population is destined to be permanently disabled because it will be called upon in future to trade across its frontiers instead of producing what it requires from within. A country can both become and can continue to be a great manufacturing country without producing the raw materials of its main industries. Such is the case, for instance, with Great Britain, which imports at least one-half of her food supplies and the great preponderance of her raw materials from abroad. There is no reason whatever why Germany under the new conditions should not build up for herself a position both of stability and prosperity in the European world. Her territories have suffered less

than those of any other Continental belligerent state during the war. Indeed, so far as pillage or devastation is concerned, they have not suffered at all. Their remaining and untouched resources, supplemented by the volume of import trade, should be adequate for recovery and development on a modest but sufficient scale.

12. The German reply also ignores the immense relief that will be caused to her people in the struggle for recovery by the enforced reduction of her military armaments in future. Hundreds of thousands of her inhabitants, who have hitherto been engaged either in training for armies or in producing instruments of destruction, will henceforward be available for peaceful avocations and for increasing the industrial productiveness of the nation. For no boon should Germany be more grateful.

13. But the first condition of any such recuperation would appear to be that Germany should recognise the facts of the present state of the world, which she has been mainly instrumental in creating, and realise that she cannot escape unscathed. The share which she is being called upon to bear of the enormous calamity that has befallen the world has been apportioned by the victorious Powers, not to her deserts, but solely to her ability to bear it. All the nations of Europe are now bearing burdens and suffering from losses which are almost more than they can carry. These burdens and losses have been forced upon them by the aggression of Germany. It is right that Germany, which was responsible for the origin of these calamities, should make them good to the utmost of her capacity. Her hardships will arise not from the conditions of peace, but from the acts of those who provoked and prolonged the war. Those who were responsible for the war cannot escape its just consequences.
Villa Majestic,
Paris
May 21st, 1919.

T MS (SDR, RG 256, 180.03401/22¼, DNA).

From the Diary of Colonel House

May 21, 1919.

I have had another disagreement [disagreeable] incident over the three Irish-American Delegates. They have published an open letter to the President in which I figure all the way through.[1] They have made many misstatements, but I decided to only deny the essential one. I have given my statement out to the press associations, English, and American, and have notified Lloyd George because it also concerned him. The statements as they will appear in the papers to-morrow will be attached to this record.[2] George express[ed] himself as pleased with what I had done. If I had not come promptly to the rescue, he would have had to make a statement himself.

[1] This letter, F. P. Walsh *et al.* to WW, May 20, 1919, is missing in WP, DLC, but it is printed in *Cong. Record*, 66th Cong., 1st sess., p. 4669, as part of the testimony of Walsh before the Senate Committee on Foreign Relations on August 30, 1919. The significant portion of the letter reads as follows:

"Following the interview courteously accorded by you [Wilson] to the chairman [Walsh] of our delegation on the 17th ultimo, Col. House made the following request of Mr. Lloyd-George:

" 'That safe conduct be given by the Government of Great Britain from Dublin to Paris and return for Eamon de Valera, Arthur Griffith, and George Noble Count Plunkett, the representatives selected by the people of Ireland to present its case to the peace conference.'

"Upon the day following Col. House conveyed the information to us that Mr. Lloyd-George was willing to comply with such request, but desired an interview with the American delegates before doing so, and that it was the desire of Mr. Lloyd-George that arrangements for the meeting with him be made through Mr. Philip Kerr, private secretary to Mr. Lloyd-George.

"After two tentative dates had been set by Mr. Kerr for the meeting with Mr. Lloyd-George, and not yet having met him, we were advised by Col. House to repeat our original request in writing to the honorable Secretary of State, Mr. Robert Lansing, which we did upon the 17th instant.

"At this moment we have been informed by the private secretary of Mr. Secretary Lansing that our request has been referred to you.

"May we not therefore respectfully ask of you that the undersigned, our full delegation, be given an opportunity to present to you in person, in as brief manner as consistent with the importance of the case, suggestions which Messrs. de Valera, Griffith, and Plunkett, the representatives aforesaid, have asked us to convey to you, together with certain facts of grave import now in our possession?

"May we also take the liberty of suggesting, in view of existing conditions in Ireland (which can not and will not be denied), that to foreclose its case by refusing a hearing to its representatives at this time would be disconsonant with the declared purpose for which the war was prosecuted and out of harmony with the common principles of democracy?

"We would gratefully appreciate a response at your convenience."

GFC to F. P. Walsh, May 21, 1919, CCL (WP, DLC), acknowledged the letter of May 20 and stated that, "by the President's direction," Lansing would reply to it.

[2] An extensive summary of the letter of Walsh *et al.* of May 20 appeared in a press report of May 21. This report also summarized House's response as follows:

"Colonel House said tonight that the letter was in error in stating that he had informed the delegation that Mr. Lloyd George was willing to comply with their request for safe conducts for the Irish leaders. The request for safe conducts had been made, he said, but no reply that the request would be complied with. Colonel House said the request was unofficial, except, as the delegates stated, that the President had referred them to him." *New York Times*, May 22, 1919.

From the Diary of Ray Stannard Baker

Paris, May 21, 1919

The President's message which we put out last night is widely published to-day, though not commented upon in the French press.

The Germans asked for more time to present their objections to the treaty & the Council of Four (or three, for Orlando has gone back temporarily to his turbulent Italy) have granted another week. This will mean more delay. In the meantime the Austrian treaty hangs fire. We have been getting up the official summary, but cannot get the treaty!

The Irish-Americans, Walsh, Dunne & Ryan are back here from revolutionary Ireland & like every group of restless agitators came first to our office. They get everybody they come into contact with into hot water. They have written a letter to the Colonel in which they try to involve both him & the President in the squabble. I was busy trying to straighten out the facts this afternoon.

I called on the President as usual this evening. Lloyd George & Clemenceau were just going out. They had the Ukrainians in this afternoon & heard their story: and the President came down stairs correcting a message which is to be sent to the Poles to-morrow.

He told me with a kind of amused satisfaction—he gets very little fun out of his conferences, but he had it to-day—of the discussion this morning of the Syrian question & of a red-hot conflict of view between Lloyd George & Clemenceau. It seems that Lloyd-George calmly proposed to give to Italy (to induce a settlement of the Fiume question) a slice of Syria which Clemenceau had already decided to gobble down. This perfectly frank scramble for territory, which in a moment of anger was fought with all guards down, seemed to amuse the President very much. It has also had the effect of once more reviving the plan for the Syrian Commission (King & Crane). The President told the Four, positively, that *our* commissioners were leaving for Syria on Monday! It has given him his chance. He had no real part in the Turkish settlement, save as America is a pro-spective member of the League of Nations & must guarantee terri-torial integrities. The President had Lord Curzon's redraft of the Economic reply to the Germans. He called it "supercilious." He *hates* to let anything go that is improperly expressed. His literary taste (and true literary taste is only good taste) is one of the elements that delays him. He is ever too much the gentleman for these rough occasions. . . .

Philip Marshall Brown showed me his confidential reports on Hungary & the situation in Central Europe: which I took to the President.[1] He read them carefully, but said: "They are like most of the reports we get: good enough in presenting the facts: but they do not tell us what to do. They all ask us to make more war! He said it sadly.

[1] See, for example, the memorandum by Brown printed as an Enclosure with A. H. Fra-zier to EMH, May 17, 1919.

From the Diary of Edith Benham

May 21, 1919

In speaking of the disposition of Turkey the P. spoke of a delegation of Musselmen he had received in which they pleaded that Turkey be kept as an independent state. He spoke of their dignity and he said that many of their arguments caused him to revise judgments he had already made. In taking leave he said they spoke with "a solemnity of warning" of the consequences which might follow if Constantinople was not allowed to continue the Capitol of the Mohammedan world.

Before going out to dinner last night I stopped in to see the P. and Mrs. W. and say goodnight. As usual they were playing solitaire, and then it was the P. spoke of the Sonnino incident, then laughed at his panacea for rest to his mind and said, "I am afraid you will always think of me as an amiable old gentleman playing solitaire." . . .

We are all interested about the acceptance or rejection by the Germans of the peace terms. Monday, as I wrote you, the P. had Gen. Pershing here to luncheon and discussed with him in another room what was to be done in case of certain eventualities. Before he left the room the Gen. said that he understood that the peace terms gave the military power over the German Courts and Civil Processes, and the P. considered this inadvisable, particularly as it would be the French who would be in command of the joint forces. The P. said he thought that should not be, and the French and other Allies should understand at once this could not be.

After luncheon the P. told us of a very amusing row between Clemenceau and L.G. The question of mandatories for Asia Minor was being discussed, and as Italy had shown such bad faith they didn't want her to have any hand in it. The French want Northern Anatolia, the British Southern, and they want the U.S. to take Armenia. Then there have been various spats because the French felt they were not being treated fairly, then Allenby asked for two French regiments to assist in Syria and they sent them off elsewhere, which made more fusses. Finally the P. got L.G. and Clemenceau to agree to a Commission to go there and for weeks Mr. Charles Crane and another man from Oberlin College[1] have been cooling their heels here waiting for their French and British colleagues to be appointed. Today the P. said he rather precipitated matters quite innocently by asking when the others would be ready, and his two men would go Monday and wait in Syria for their colleagues. L.G. whose cabinet including Lord Curzon had come over here to have an informal sort of meeting with him, said his men would be ready to go Monday and he would direct the Cabinet to appoint them. Clemenceau jumped

around and made an attack on the U. S. and England which he said
wanted to keep France out of Northern Anatolia. While he looked
and talked at the P. the whole thing was directed against L.G. and
he made various accusations of bad faith. Then Mr. L.G. got angry
and unlike Clemenceau, who got cooler as he talked, he got more
and more mad and as the P. says in spats of this kind both bring up
secret agreements which the two countries had made and which
each accused the other of breaking, and of which the P. said he
knew nothing. Disposing of territory not their own to give away was
bad business. Things got very sultry, but the P. said he was able to
pour oil on the waters and Clemenceau when he left held out his
hand. L.G. hesitated, then despite himself, had to laugh and shake.
Sir Maurice Hanky, an ex-marine, whom the P. considers an inval-
uable person, came back for a moment and said he would try to
patch things up, evidently feeling his Chief had made a fool of himself. Sir Maurice the P. says is a fine and honorable gentleman.

¹ That is, Henry Churchill King.

From the Diary of Dr. Grayson

Thursday, May 22, 1919.
The President had an early breakfast and then took a walk, returning in time to sit in with the Council of Four, which took up the
Syrian and the Turkish questions. The Syrian question continued a
source of serious conflict between the French and the British. The
French were very anxious to secure a settlement that would give
them certain paramount rights, and this the British opposed. However, the President refused to take any part in the matter, because of
the fact that it was one which should be settled entirely between the
two parties involved.¹ So far as the Turkish situation is concerned,
the suggestion had been made to the President that the United
States should assume a mandatory over the new Turkish state to be
created out of what has been Turkey in Europe. The President has
been loathe to make a decision on this subject, and the various suggestions relative to the division of Turkey were debated without any
definite action.

The German delegation at Versailles sent a note criticising the
reparations section of the Peace Treaty, and saying that while they
admitted responsibility for all the damage that had accrued to Belgium and northern France as a result of the violation of Belgian neutrality, it was unfair that they should be asked to pay for a lot of damage that had been done by the Allied armies in their advance. The
Council of Four sent a note to Count Brockdorff-Rantzau stating

that they could not furnish repatriated prisoners of war with new civilian suits, underclothing and boots. The Allies have agreed to appoint a Reparation Commission as asked for by the Germans as soon as the Peace Treaty was actually signed.

After the President's conference with the Big Four he told me that it was Foch's ambition to become the Hindenburg or the Ludendorff of the French Army. In this ambition he is backed by Poincaré, and strongly opposed by Clemenceau. Foch seems to have the further ambition of becoming the Military Dictator of the Allies and Associated Powers. General Bliss said that Foch's attitude has changed materially, because he (General Bliss) was present when the Armistice was signed, and Foch was having a "duck fit" for fear that the Allies were making the Armistice terms so strong that the Germans would not agree to sign and stop fighting. The thought of the Germans renewing the war made Foch nervous and tremble with fear at that time. The contrast in his attitude today is most striking. The impression that I gather is that Poincaré is a weak President. His function seems to be practically that of a rubber-stamp. Whatever his clique puts before him, he signs.

The President, Mrs. Wilson and I had lunch, and after lunch we went for a long automobile ride out through the parks adjacent to the city of Paris. Returning to the temporary White House, the President resumed his conference with the Big Four. There was a continuation of a discussion of the questions involved in connection with the Turkish Empire. M. André Tardieu presented the French side of the case but no decision was reached. Tardieu advocated as a solution that Constantinople and the greater portion of Anatolia should remain under the nominal rule of Sultan, but that a commission, to be named by the League of Nations, and preferably composed of Americans, would act as the power behind the throne in directing the affairs of that section of Turkey. Allowing the Sultan to remain in power would be for the purpose of satisfying the Mohammedans in Asia and in India, who are threatening serious trouble to the British Empire.

Lord Reading, the Lord Chief Justice of Great Britain, and the retiring Ambassador to the United States, called today to say good-bye to the President. The Earl was extremely solicitous and told the President that there was something he would like very much to tell him but that he hesitated about doing so. Still, he said, he considered that it was his duty in view of his official status that he should be perfectly frank, and the President told him he hoped that he would be so. The Earl told the President that it was such a rotten and unpatriotic condition in American politics—if not treason—that he believed it was necessary to tell the President all the facts, although he (Lord Reading) was not taking part in American politics. He said that just before he left the United States for England a very prominent Republican United States Senator, one of the party leaders,[2] called upon him and told him that he wanted him to warn Lloyd George that unless he changed his attitude and refused longer to acquiesce in the President's policies and methods in Paris, the Republican party would be compelled much against its will to turn against the British empire and the present British Government and to advocate in the Senate and House of Representatives the recognition of the Irish Republic. It was very plain that this threat had given serious concern to the Earl. The President listened carefully and immediately took steps to get all the facts dealing with the situation. Earl Reading later put all the facts in writing and sent it to the President for his use.

The President spent a quiet evening considering matters that had been sent to him from the United States and retired early.

---

[1] Grayson summarizes Lloyd George's and Clemenceau's continuing wrangling over Syria very well. However, near the end of the discussion, Clemenceau said that he would not push the dispute to the point of endangering the entente between France and Great Britain, nor would he any longer associate himself with the British in the Middle East, "because the harm done to his country was too great."

Coming in at the end of the Clemenceau-Lloyd George exchange, Wilson said that he did not know what part he was to play in this matter, but that he had "never been able to see by what right France and Great Britain gave this country [Syria] away to anyone." For information and advice, Wilson continued, he had to rely upon the King-Crane Commission; and he thought that the question should be adjourned for further consideration.

The minutes of this brief meeting are printed in *PPC*, V, 807-12.

[2] Grayson's account and the one conveyed in FLP to RL, n. d., printed as an Enclosure with RL to WW, May 23, 1919, differ so radically that it is impossible to know who talked to Reading (as Polk's message reveals) on about April 26, 1919. If Grayson's account is accurate, it *might* have been Henry Cabot Lodge. If Polk's account is accurate, he was a leader in the newly organized League for the Preservation of American Independence (about which, see n. 1 to the Enclosure printed with RL to WW, May 23, 1919), most likely Henry Alexander Wise Wood of New York.

A Memorandum by Henry Churchill King

[c. May 22, 1919]

POINTS TO BE TAKEN UP WITH PRESIDENT WILSON.[1]

   I. THE POSITION OF THE COMMISSION:

      1. Is the Commission certainly going? *Yes*[2] If so, how soon should it go?

      2. Are its Official Instructions to be changed?

      3. Would it be well for the Commission to have an American
Yachts.   cruiser at their disposal? That might have the advantage of expediting travel, showing the American flag, and making the whole inquiry a little easier in taking the other members

as guests. Or, would it be better for the American Commission to go by itself?

4. What fund should be set aside for the expenses of the American part of the Commission? What should be the policy as to the salaries of the helpers called in by the Commission?

5. If the Peace Conference dissolves in the meantime, to whom will the Commission report? *To Am. P[lenipotentiaries?]. E[xtraordinary?]. for the Pres.*

6. Who has the responsibility for organizing the whole Commission?

II. THE PRESIDENT'S PERSONAL DESIRES AND PURPOSES AS TO THE COMMISSION:

1. What points in the inquiry does he desire especially to emphasize?

2. Should the Commission go to Syria first?

3. Would the United States be willing to undertake a provisional occupancy of Armenia pending the report of the Commission?

4. Can America be expected to accept a mandate for Armenia or Syria, for example, if that seems best?

III. LIMITATIONS OF TIME AND TERRITORY:

1. Are there definite limitations of time for the Commission? *No.* Is it desired that the Commission should confine itself to a certain time, and do what it can do within that time, or should take such time as seems necessary for intelligent recommendation all around?

2. What is the intended territorial scope of the inquiry?

(1) Do you wish it to include the visiting of all the Areas mentioned in the Official Instructions?[3]

it points
. seem most
l.

(2) Are Adalia and Smyrna and the Peninsula of Arabia to be included?

(3) Should the Commission make any reference to the disposition of Turkey proper, as bearing on the possibility of a single mandatory for Turkey proper and Armenia?

(4) Is it desired that the Commission visit Russian-Armenian and possibly other like regions, as bearing on possible recommendation of a federation of Armenian, Georgian and Kurdish States?

IV EXISTING AGREEMENTS OR UNDERSTANDINGS:

1. How far is the Zionist question closed? *Virtually by Gr. Br. & Pres.*

2. How far is the Mesopotamian question closed? *Virtually*

3. How far is the question of Arabia closed? *No*

4. Is the Commission bound by a pre-Conference or other agreements? If so, what are they? *No*

5. Are there any Conference understandings that close any part of the question; or, is all open? Have mandatories been agreed on? *No*

T MS (WP, DLC).
    ¹ King, Charles R. Crane, and William L. Westermann met with Wilson on the afternoon of May 22. See Harry N. Howard, *The King-Crane Commission: An American Inquiry in the Middle East* (Beirut, 1963), pp. 78-80.
    ² Words in italics are apparently Wilson's replies written by King on a CC MS (H. C. King Papers, OO).
    ³ See Wilson's memorandum, "Future Administration of Certain Portions of the Turkish Empire under the Mandatory System," printed at March 25, 1919, Vol. 56.

From the Peace Conference Diary of William Linn Westermann

INTERVIEW OF MAGIE AND WESTERMANN WITH
PRESIDENT WILSON ON MAY 22, 1919.

The President began by saying that the chief problem was the disposition of Anatolia. He was prepared to propose to the American people that the United States take mandates for Armenia and the State of Constantinople, saying that American sympathy for Armenia pointed to the adoption by Congress of this burden in the case of the former, but that the acceptance of a Constantinopolitan mandate was doubtful. The United States would be the best mandatory for Constantinople because it would be the least likely to foment political intrigue there.

As to Anatolia the Council of Four had had under consideration a plan for the partition of Anatolia between Greece, France, and Italy, giving the Smyrna district to Greece, the northern portion to France and the southern portion to Italy. Mr. Lloyd George, however, had claimed that the promise contained in the Pact of London by which Italy was to receive an "equivalent" to what Great Britain received was invalid, inasmuch as the fulfillment was contingent on Russia's ratification and Russia had never ratified. Westermann interrupted saying that Lloyd George was really speaking of the Saint-Jean de Maurienne Agreement and not of the London Pact, which was signed by Russia. The President was sure that Lloyd George was speaking of the London Agreement.

Last Saturday Mr. Lloyd George introduced some Indian Moslems, who protested against a division of Turkey on the ground that the destruction of the Ottoman Empire and the removal of the Sultan from Constantinople would prove a source of agitation and discontent among all Moslems. These Indians also brought up the

President's declaration of Jan. 8, 1918 (Art. XII of the Fourteen Points) which guaranteed the sovereignty of the Ottoman Empire within the Turkish portion thereof, and cited in addition a speech of Mr. Lloyd George in which the same promise was made. The President then made a proposition to the Four. He said to us that he was not altogether satisfied with it: it was to the effect that the sovereignty of the Ottoman Empire should be maintained in Anatolia, but that France should be given the control of the Finances (through the Public Debt Organization) and of the gendarmery, though not actually to receive a mandate. As a sop to the Moslems the Sultan was to be allowed to remain with his entourage in Constantinople, but without any political power in the state to be formed there, and in a position similar to that occupied by the Pope in Rome. The President said that the great practical disadvantage to this plan was that it made no provision to keep the Italians quiet or satisfy their hopes in Asia Minor; but he stated emphatically that the Italians had no moral claim to any portion of Anatolia.

When asked for his views on the possibility of satisfying the Italians in Transcaucasia, he said that the Italians had already begun to repent of their agreement to send troops there to replace the British forces, and that he was opposed to giving a mandate to Italy over this region. He said that the British asserted that these states must be placed under the same mandate as Armenia. He declared that the Italians might receive something in Africa by which they might be kept quiet, and that both Mr. Lloyd George and M. Clemenceau were ready to give them the British and French territories in Togo Land, but the British and French Foreign Office officials had strongly opposed the suggestion.

He spoke of the landing of Italian troops in Scala N[u]ova and ports between it and Adalia and said that he had tried to force Sign. Sonnino to give the reason for this step, but to every question Sonnino had replied that there had been trouble in Adalia. He said that in connection with Venizelos' request for the landing of Greek forces in Smyrna and below (toward Aidin), Sonnino had suddenly shown great interest and demanded that no Greeks be sent south of a line drawn from Aidin to the coast. In general, he characterized the Italian methods as dirty, condemning also their policy in Dalmatia. In reply to a question whether it might prove a solution if Italy were given special privileges in the matter of obtaining mineral products and raw materials from Anatolia, he said that this would not be possible if Turkey were under a mandate, for the Covenant of the League of Nations provided that there should be no specially favoured nation. If, however, the arrangement described above for France in Anatolia were to be put into effect, such a provision might be made; but he did not believe that the mineral resources of Anatolia were important enough to make such a provision worth while.

Returning to the question of the best mandatory for Turkey, the President said that the United States, if it held mandates over Armenia and Constantinople would be in a strategic position to control that portion of the world, and that, under the Covenant of the League of Nations, it would be the duty of the United States to report to the League any dereliction of duty on the part of the nation in control of Turkey.

When objections were made by us to the retention of the Sultan in Constantinople, the President agreed to the disadvantages which we pointed out and said that the suggestion was made only as an attempt to satisfy the Moslems; and that it had just been brought to his attention in a document written by a Moslem Indian (whose name he had forgotten) and submitted to him by Mr. Crane[1] that the eastern Moslems did not after all set so high a value on keeping the Sultan in his former position. This Moslem also said that the Moslem world was not vitally interested even in maintaining the Caliphate.

Throughout the interview, the President declared himself as strongly opposed to the secret agreements. We think that he will still fight them.

[1] It is missing.

Hankey's Notes of a Meeting of the Council of Four[1]

President Wilson's House,
C.F.23. Paris, May 22, 1919, 11:45 a.m.

1. While the Council was assembling, the Resolution in Appendix I[2] authorizing the Supreme Economic Council to announce that the blockade on Hungary would be suspended as soon as a Government is installed there which gives some assurance of settled conditions, was approved.

SIR MAURICE HANKEY was instructed to forward it to the Secretary General with instructions to arrange for the Supreme Economic Council to take the necessary action.

2. The Council had before them the following documents relating to the Saar Basin:

(1) Letter from Herr Brockdorff-Rantzau to M. Clemenceau dated 13th May (Appendix II).

[1] The complete text of these minutes is printed in *PPC*, V, 813-25.
[2] E. Clémentel to P. E. Dutasta. May 20, 1919, TCL (SDR, RG 256, 180.03401/23, DNA), printed in *PPC*, V, 817.

(2) Letter from Herr Brockdorff-Rantzau to M. Clemenceau dated 16th May (Appendix III).[3]

(3) Draft reply to the letter dated May 13th (Appendix IV).

(4) Draft reply to letter dated May 16th (Appendix V).[4]

MR. LLOYD GEORGE drew attention to the passage in Appendix II, in which the German Delegation take exception to the fact that the restitution of the Saar Valley at the end of fifteen years is made to depend on the ability of the German Government to re-purchase from the French Government, in gold, all the coal mines of the territory and that if this payment is not made, France would acquire the territory permanently even if the population should unanimously vote for Germany. He read the following extract from clause 36 of the Annex to Part III, Section 4 of the Treaty:

"If within the six months following the decision of the experts the price above referred to has not been paid by Germany, the said territory will be finally acquired by France."

This meant that if the Germans could not pay the people of the Saar would remain in servitude. If they could remain independent he would not object to this clause so much, but he felt that at present this was quite wrong.

PRESIDENT WILSON pointed out that the difficulty might be met by providing that if the people of the Saar Valley elected for Germany

[3] U. K. C. von Brockdorff-Rantzau to G. Clemenceau, May 13 and 16, 1919, both TCL (SDR, RG 256, 180.03401/23, DNA), printed in *PPC*, V, 817–22.

In his letter of May 13, Brockdorff-Rantzau suggested that the territorial arrangements of the peace treaty were not compatible with the principles professed by the Allies at the time of the Armistice. While he admitted that the German government saw some justice in the alienation from Germany of territories where the population was largely non-German, such as the province of Schleswig and the predominantly Polish areas of eastern Germany, he stated that his government could not accept such alienation in the wholly German areas on the border of Belgium and, above all, of the Saar Basin. "The German Government," he said, "considers it most of all inadmissible that German territories should, by the Treaty of Peace, be made the subject of bargains between one sovereignty and another, as though they were mere chattels or pawns in a game, in order to ensure the satisfaction of the financial and economic claims of the adversaries of Germany."

He also suggested that the proposed plebiscite for the people of the Saar at the end of fifteen years of occupation was a sham. Even should the population vote to return the Saar to Germany, such a transfer could not take place under the terms of the peace treaty unless Germany could at that time repurchase from France the coal mines of the area with payment in gold, a requirement that it was highly unlikely that Germany would be able to meet, given the reparation provisions of the treaty. "There is in modern history," he asserted, "no example of a civilised Power binding another to subject its own nationals to a foreign domination as the equivalent of a sum of gold."

Germany recognized the justice and necessity of compensation for the coal mines she had destroyed in northern France. However, a far more reasonable and just form of compensation than the permanent alienation of the Saar Basin from Germany would be for Germany to supply coal to France until such time as the damage to the French mines should be repaired, as Germany had undertaken to do. He declared that Germany was prepared immediately to send experts to negotiate the transfer of necessary supplies of coal to France. His letter of May 16 enclosed a plan which outlined the form which these negotiations might take.

[4] Appendixes IV and V are both T MSS (SDR, RG 256, 180.03401/23, DNA), and are printed in *PPC*, V, 823-25.

and the German Government could not pay, they might at least be permitted to remain independent.

M. TARDIEU drew attention to paragraph 6 of Appendix IV from which he read the following extract:

"If, on the one hand, the direct agreement authorised by paragraph 36 came to nothing and if, on the other hand, as you fear, the Commission on Reparations forbade the payment in gold provided for in para. 36, it would then be the duty of the League of Nations to consider the consequences resulting from that refusal both for Germany and for the population of the region under consideration—on condition, of course, that the provisions of para. 37 were carried out."

He then read a text which would meet Mr. Lloyd George's objections.

PRESIDENT WILSON pointed out that the Germans were not so much afraid that they would not have the money, but that the Reparation Commission would not allow them to use it. He understood that the object of this new proposal was to prevent that. No doubt the Germans could borrow the money on the security of the mines if the Reparation Commission allowed them to. President Wilson thought that some special representation should be made to the Reparation Commission on the subject. He then read the following alternative draft handed to him by Dr. Haskins:

"Substitute for the final paragraph of Article 36 on page 38 the following:

The price above referred to shall be paid by Germany within one year after the decision of the experts.

No provision of the present Treaty shall in any way prejudice the right and obligation of Germany to make any payment pursuant to the provisions of this Annex, particularly the provisions of this paragraph and of paragraph 38 thereof. The obligation of Germany to make such payment shall be taken into account by the Reparation Commission and for the purpose of the payment Germany may create a prior charge upon her assets or revenues, upon such detailed terms as agreed to by the Reparation Commission."

MR. LLOYD GEORGE preferred this to the other text.

MR. HEADLAM-MORLEY said he felt that some action of the kind was required, and that if it was not taken there would be a serious situation. The fact of Article 36 quoted above being in the Treaty was producing a bad effect on neutral countries where it was being said "If Germany cannot pay the sovereignty will be transferred to France." He felt that the Allied and Associated Powers ought to get out of this situation and to propose a fresh Article on their own initiative.

PRESIDENT WILSON agreed.

M. CLEMENCEAU said he was of the same opinion.

PRESIDENT WILSON suggested that the words quoted by Mr. Lloyd George should be omitted.

MR. LLOYD GEORGE said that Germany must have some guarantee that this action would not be taken since it constituted something equivalent to servitude for debt.

PRESIDENT WILSON suggested that the best plan would be to leave it to some authority to decide at the end of 15 years, and this authority had best be the League of Nations.

MR. LLOYD GEORGE suggested that the experts should retire and draft a clause to meet the case.

(The Experts withdrew.)

(After an interval the experts returned with a draft clause, which was accepted.)

After a short further discussion the meeting was adjourned in order that the Expert Committee might re-assemble and revise the two draft letters in the light of the discussion.

Note. The various documents referred to, not being available at the time when these Minutes were drafted, they will be contained in the Minutes of the next discussion on the subject.

3. M. CLEMENCEAU reported that he had signed and dispatched the reply approved on the previous day to Herr Brockdorff-Rantzau's letter dealing with the economic effect of the Treaty of Peace.[5]

4. M. CLEMENCEAU reported that he had signed and dispatched a reply to Herr Brockdorff-Rantzau's letter on the subject of prisoners of war.[6]

5. SIR MAURICE HANKEY reported that the Head of the Aerial Section of the British Delegation[7] had strongly urged that wherever the Naval and Military Services were mentioned in the Covenant of the League of Nations, the Air Service should also be mentioned. General Groves[8] had pointed out that elsewhere throughout the Treaty of Peace the Air Service was mentioned whenever the Naval and Military Services were mentioned and he considered that this omission from the Covenant of the League of Nations thereby became conspicuous and might lead to the inference that aerial warfare was excluded.

[5] See Appendix I to the minutes of the Council of Four printed at May 21, 1919, 6:15 p.m.

[6] See n. 12 to Hankey's minutes of the Council of Four printed at May 20, 1919, 11 a.m.

[7] Maj. Gen. Sir Frederick Hugh Sykes, Chief of Staff for Aviation.

[8] Brig. Gen. Percy Robert Clifford Groves, Assistant Chief of the Aviation Section of the British delegation.

MR. LLOYD GEORGE pointed out that the change could not be made without summoning a Plenary Meeting of the Allied and Associated Powers represented at the Peace Conference.

PRESIDENT WILSON pointed out that Aerial warfare in its belligerent forms was included either in the Naval or in Military warfare and he did not think that any misunderstanding could arise from this omission. He thought it was unnecessary to introduce the change which, as Mr. Lloyd George had pointed out, could only be effected by a Plenary Conference.

SIR MAURICE HANKEY pointed out that the British Air Service was entirely separate from the Naval and Military Services and he was under the impression that the same was true in Germany. He also understood that the French were contemplating a separation of their Air Service from the Naval and Military Services.

(It was agreed that the alteration in the Covenant of the League of Nations should not be made.)

6. The Council had under consideration the following clause, submitted by the Committee on New States for insertion in the Treaty with Austria, together with corresponding clauses for insertions in the Treaties with Hungary and with Bulgaria:

"The Kingdom of the Serbs, Croats and Slovenes accepts and agrees to embody in a Treaty with the Principal Allied and Associated Powers such provisions as may be deemed necessary by the said Powers to protect the interests of inhabitants of Serbia, who differ from the majority of the population in race, language, or religion. The Kingdom of the Serbs, Croats and Slovenes further accepts and agrees to embody in a Treaty with the said Powers such provision as they may deem necessary to protect freedom of transit and equitable treatment of the commerce of other nations."

(The above clause was approved and initialled by the Four Heads of Government.)

(Sir Maurice Hankey was instructed to forward it to the Secretary General for communication to the Drafting Committee together with an intimation that the initials to the clause for the Austrian Treaty would cover the clauses for Treaties with Hungary and Bulgaria.)

T MS (SDR, RG 256, 180.03401/23, DNA).

Mantoux's Notes of a Meeting of the Council of Four

May 22, 1919, noon.

Lloyd George. Here is the question which we wish to resubmit for study by the experts. The German delegates say that, according to the present wording of the treaty, the territory of the Saar would remain with France, even if the population, by plebiscite, pronounced itself in favor of Germany, in case the latter could not pay back in gold, in six months, the value of the mines. Thus, for an economic reason, this population would be in a position of veritable political servitude. We recognize that the German objection is admissible.

Wilson. At the time of the plebiscite, the population will have to choose among three solutions: annexation to France, return to Germany, or continuation of the regime provided for by the treaty. Could we not amend the clause in question by saying that, if the population votes for return to Germany and Germany is incapable of paying, the regime provided by the treaty would be prolonged during the time necessary to assure payment?

Tardieu. We have prepared a reply to Count Brockdorff-Rantzau, indicating that in case this difficulty should arise, the question would be brought before the League of Nations. It is our American colleagues who proposed an amendment of three lines to this effect, and we have no objection to it.

Wilson. What the Germans fear is not that they will not have the means to pay, but that they will not be able to apply them to that particular object, and they fear the opposition of the Reparation Commission. The necessary amendment must have the effect of preventing that opposition. It will always be easy to borrow money on the security of the mines themselves, and we could address a special recommendation to that effect to the Reparation Commission.

Lloyd George. Our reply must clearly show that the sovereignty established over this territory and the right of the people to self-determination do not depend, either one of them, on a payment made or not.

Clemenceau. The new text proposed satisfies you.

Lloyd George. It is certainly much better than the former one.

Headlam-Morley. We will remove the sentence which says that, if Germany does not pay in the desired time, sovereignty will pass to France. Even if this eventuality cannot take place, the single fact of envisaging it would produce a deplorable effect in Germany.

Wilson. The only question which remains is to know if a certain pressure should not be maintained in order to oblige the Germans to carry out their obligations.

Lloyd George. In any case, the present wording cannot stand.

Wilson. It is better to change the wording of the entire paragraph.

Lloyd George. Certainly, we must require guarantees; but imprisonment for debt is not one which we can exact.

Clemenceau. I think absolutely as you do: we cannot make the liberty of a people security for a debt.

Tardieu. Could we not confine ourselves to saying that the territory will not become German as long as the debt has not been paid?

Lloyd George. It is better that the article alludes exclusively to the ownership of the mines.

Clemenceau. I am of that opinion.

Tardieu. We could draw up an amendment indicating that, within one year after the plebiscite, the Reparation Commission will settle the question of payment, if need be, by the liquidation of the mines.

Lloyd George. Thus the last line would disappear?

Tardieu. Yes.

Lloyd George. It is important to inform the Germans of this amendment.

Wilson. This is an excellent solution. We would have to modify not only the article, but the letter in answer to the German note.

Lloyd George. It must be clearly stated that it was never our intention to exchange people for gold.

Tardieu. We will take up the wording of Paragraphs 1 and 6 again and make the change indicated.

Lloyd George. We must be able to make the best of the concession we are making to the Germans; that could have an effect on German opinion. They are told that our stipulations concerning the Saar only disguise an annexation; we must seize this opportunity to affirm the contrary. Men who, like Bernstein,[1] are advising the Germans to sign the treaty, will take note of our rectification.

Clemenceau. There is another letter in reply to the second German note.

Wilson. It must be reread in the light of the modifications made in the first letter and modified as a consequence.

Mantoux, II, 165-67.
[1] Eduard Bernstein, leader of the German Social Democratic party.

Tasker Howard Bliss to Bernard Mannes Baruch

My dear Mr. Baruch: Paris 22 May, 1919

Yesterday morning the question of the "Draft Convention relating to the Administration of the Rhenish Provinces after signature of Peace" came before the Military Representatives at Versailles. It had already been before them (during my absence from Paris) on reference from the Supreme War Council and they had submitted to the latter their memorandum on the subject, approving the original document before the Supreme War Council.

It seems, however, that there were various modifications that the British and French desired to introduce into the document (in the way of making it more stringent) and for that reason the Military Representatives took it up again at Versailles yesterday morning. The day before, I had asked the President what attitude I should take. He told me to say that the United States government dissented from the draft convention as proposed (I suppose for the reasons which you gave him in your letter of last Saturday and which I gave him in a letter on Monday). In my letter to the President I suggested (and I think you did also) that instead of the military administration of the occupied territory, there be provided a strong Inter-Allied *Civil* Commission which would be superior as a governing body to the military. I understand that some such idea is the one which the President will propose to the Supreme War Council. What his success will be, I do not know.

I made a statement to my colleagues at Versailles to the above effect and told them that I could take no part in any discussion on the subject of the proposed military administration until the Supreme War Council should refer back to us the original document which is now pending before it.

Last night I received a note from the President in which he says "I can also say that I entirely agree with you about the Rhine Convention and shall try to obtain a radical modification of it." As a matter of fact, it is not a modification that is desired but rather a complete substitution of civil control for military control.

I think this is a matter of very great importance and that you ought to take every opportunity, in view of your personal relations with the President, to impress upon him the necessity for this civil control and not some mere modification of the proposed military control.

Cordially yours,   Tasker H. Bliss

TLS (B. M. Baruch Papers, NjP).

From the Diary of Vance Criswell McCormick

May 22 (Thursday) [1919]

Lunched with Hoover and Davis in Hoover's room. Hoover very much exercised because he had had a talk with General Smuts of British delegation who said he would not sign the Peace Treaty as his conscience would not permit him to do so and reported that Barnes,[1] another British delegate, would not sign and that there is a revolution on, and among our delegates also, and that he had talked with House, Lansing and Bliss and that they did not approve of the Treaty and were considering not signing. I suggested the latter was incredible as all the above discussed the Treaty with the President and approved it before it was submitted to all the Allies at the Quai d'Orsay and voted for it in the Plenary session and I thought this was a pretty late date to criticize and balk. Hoover had nothing to say, except he said everyone was displeased and the Treaty was unworkable and would never be signed and he thought Lloyd George would attempt to take the world leadership away from President Wilson and come out in about a week and denounce the Treaty and stand for a new deal. I told Hoover I did not think he had the courage to do this and besides he was largely responsible for the clauses most criticized. It is amusing to hear criticism from Davis, Keynes and others who, when they have been talking to the Big Four, agree with everything they say and make no strong protest. I told them the time to fight is before they are committed.

At 4.00 o'clock went to the President's house to discuss Austrian Reparation clauses. The Big Four did not agree with us about relieving new countries from reparations for ceded territories and I guess they are right; otherwise treaty clauses accepted.

The Big Four were all present and seemed still to be working harmoniously. I thought Lloyd George looked old and tired. The old "tiger" as spry as could be and as usual wore gray gloves which he does at all the meetings.

I had a chance to say a word to the President about my conversation with Hoover. He said he had heard about some of the British delegates not signing but did not take much stock in the report about the American delegates. He said they certainly would have told him as, in fact, he showed them all the clauses and they said they approved. He asked me to talk to Mr. Lansing and sound out the situation.

[1] That is, George Nicoll Barnes.

From Thomas William Lamont

Dear Mr. President   [Paris] May 22-19

The attached letter[1] is of importance, in view of the meeting which we have been summoned to attend at your house at 4 p.m. today.

Sincerely yours   T W Lamont

ALS (WP, DLC).
[1] T. W. Lamont to WW, May 22, 1919, TLS (WP, DLC). Lamont also questioned the wisdom of imposing reparation liability upon the successor states of the Austro-Hungarian Empire. He stated that the American financial experts had estimated that Czechoslovakia, Yugoslavia, Rumania, and Poland would, under the proposed reparation clauses, have a per capita liability which, in proportion to per capita wealth, would be in excess of the per capita liability for the war debts of France and Great Britain. Moreover, the new states had no established financial organizations and international connections to deal

with such debts. Lamont warned that some of these states might refuse to sign the Austrian peace treaty unless the Council of Four reconsidered its decisions on this subject. "I venture to suggest," he concluded, "that the Supreme Council may wish to consider whether it is wise to insist upon the principle that reparation liability attaches to Allied States acquiring enemy territory. The immediate political difficulties will be serious. If they are overcome, there is the further political danger of creating that community of interest with Germany which would tend to result from making these lesser Allied States practically co-debtors with Germany. On the other hand, the practical advantage to the other Allied States seems very problematic, as it is hardly to be expected that these lesser States can for many years make any external payments above the amounts necessary to insure imports necessary to maintain their economic life. Indeed, the rehabilitation of the economic life of these countries, which depends largely on credit facilities, would be jeopardized were these States subjected to a liability, even contingent, for a substantial external payment by way of reparation. I have gone over this matter carefully with Messrs. Baruch, Davis and McCormick. We are all in accord with its importance, and join in recommending that you consider asking the Supreme Council to modify its decision . . . so that Allied States acquiring portions of enemy territory be relieved from reparation liability."

Hankey's Notes of a Meeting of the Council of Four[1]

President Wilson's House,
Paris, May 22, 1919, 4 p.m.

C.F.24.

1. During the assembly of the meeting on the Reparation Clauses for the Treaty with Austria, the Council examined the re-drafts of the letters prepared by the Committee in reply to the letters from the German Delegation on the subject of the Saar Valley, dated May 13th and May 16th.

After a short discussion the letters attached in the Appendix[2] were approved, a few small modifications being introduced.

Sir Maurice Hankey was instructed to communicate these letters to the Secretary-General of the Peace Conference for the following action:

1.   For preparation of a fair copy for signature by the President of the Conference and despatch.
2.   For communication to the Drafting Committee, in order that the necessary alteration might be made in the Treaty of Peace.
3.   For publication after despatch.[3]

T MS (SDR, RG 256, 180.03401/24, DNA).

[1] The complete text of these minutes is printed in PPC, V, 826-29.

[2] "Draft of Proposed Answer to Letter of Count Brockdorff-Rantzau of May 13th, 1919" and "Draft Answer to the Letter of Count Brockdorff-Rantzau, dated 17th [16th] May, 1919," T MSS (SDR, RG 256, 180.03401/24, DNA), printed in PPC, V, 827-29.

[3] These were not the final drafts. The final reply to both letters is printed as an Appendix to the minutes of the Council of Four printed at May 24, 1919, 11 a.m.

Hankey's Notes of a Meeting of the Council of Four[1]

President Wilson's House,
C.F.24/1.   Paris, May 22, 1919, 4:15 p.m.

1. The Council had before them the draft of Reparation clauses for inclusion in the Treaty of Peace with Austria (Appendix).[2]

2. PRESIDENT WILSON called attention to the proposal, in the draft Reparation clauses for insertion into the Treaty with Austria, that the new states arising out of the former Austro-Hungarian Empire should bear a share in the Reparation debt. He considered that this would place an overwhelming burden on these States. He said that he was advised that if those countries took over the pre-war debt attaching to their territory and a Reparation liability also this would constitute a "per capita liability exceeding that of France and Great Britain.["]

MR. LLOYD GEORGE said he could not accept such an estimate and pointed out that the amount of the Reparation liability affecting those countries had not been fixed: this was left to the proposed Reparation Commission.

PRESIDENT WILSON said he was assuming that it was intended that these States should pay their share of the Reparation liability in full. This, in his opinion, would be an unduly heavy burden, and he was informed that, if it were imposed, some of these States would refuse to sign the Treaty. He pointed out that there was a danger that these States, being placed in a position of co-debtors with Germany, might turn in that direction for their economic development. He added that it was not so much the amount of the liability but the principle of its imposition that would have so damaging an effect on the immediate credit of those countries.

MR. LAMONT said that no doubt the proposal that these States should pay was just in principle: but the demands of the Reparation Commission seemed scarcely consonant with the aims of the Committee which had been set up with a view to assisting these States to establish their credit. Further he doubted whether they would be able to pay any sum of importance.

MR. LLOYD GEORGE pointed out that the greater number of the nationals of these States had fought against the Allies right up to the end of the war; they would never have achieved their freedom but for the war. If they had remained neutral the war might have been shortened by two years. Why should they get their freedom without paying for it? It would surely be unjust that they should do so, when in Great Britain there would be a "per capita" liability of £800 per

[1] The complete text of these minutes is printed in PPC, V, 830-58.
[2] Printed in PPC, V, 836-57.

house as a result of the war. Those states ought to bear the same burden as those who helped them to get their freedom. The Allies had advanced large sums to Serbia; was it intended that the Jugo-Slav State should bear none of this? He pointed out that some of these countries, e.g. Bohemia and Transylvania, had very large resources.

PRESIDENT WILSON pointed out that under the Financial Clauses of the Treaty these States are intended to share in the debts of the former Austro-Hungarian Empire, both the debts incurred during the war and previous to it. He agreed that Mr. Lloyd George was quite right in principle but he did not see how these countries could take a part in the credit system of Europe if they were pressed too hard and especially if they were not to know the extent of their indebtedness for two years.

M. ORLANDO said that it seemed to be suggested that the decision of the Council of Four that the former Austro-Hungarian Empire should be responsible for its indebtedness should now be reversed. He pointed out that Italy was undertaking the liability for her annexed territories. Mr. Lloyd George had referred to the shipping of Trieste as enemy shipping; but it could scarcely be properly so described if these new States were to get off their liability. Very possibly they could not pay much but the establishment of the principle was important. He could not go to his country and say that four-fifths of the Austro-Hungarian Empire was getting off its liabilities.

PRESIDENT WILSON said that it was not suggested that those States should pay nothing. But he thought they ought to know at once what they have to pay.

M. KLOTZ said that in the proposed Reparation Clauses there were special advantageous provisions for these States, e.g. they are not required to issue bonds of guarantee: they are to pay nothing for two years: their liability having been fixed in 1921 may not subsequently be increased—i.e. there is no joint liability: they are allowed to use any payments they may be entitled to from enemy States as a set-off against their indebtedness.

MR. LLOYD GEORGE agreed with President Wilson that it was not desirable that these States should have an indefinite liability hanging over them for so long. He thought the amount could be fixed in a shorter time than two years: six months should be enough. The problem was not a gigantic one as in the case of Germany. He thought further that the Austrian debt to the Allies should be provided for before her own internal debts. He doubted whether it was a good thing to have the same Reparation Commission to deal with Austria and Germany. He thought this might involve delay.

3. PRESIDENT WILSON said that he understood that this question

had been thoroughly discussed before settlement. He thought that the main directing Commission should be the same in both cases though they would, of course, have experts to assist them on special places and questions.

MR. LLOYD GEORGE said that the decision to have the same Commission in both cases had been taken in view of the interval of two years adopted in each case for the fixation of liability: but the adoption of a time limit of six months in the case of Austria would involve the appointment of a separate Commission. Further, it would not be necessary to work on quite such rigid principles in the case of Austria.

MR. LAMONT pointed out that if there were two Commissions and they were empowered to deal in the bonds to be issued they might compete against each other.

M. ORLANDO thought that a number of Sub-Committees etc. would be necessary but thought that there should be one Supreme Commission.

M. KLOTZ thought it would be difficult for the same Commission to deal with both debts in view of the shorter interval now proposed for the fixation of the Austrian debt. He suggested that the Main Commission might constitute a special section to deal with Austria.

PRESIDENT WILSON said there now seemed general agreement in principle and suggested that the present Commission on Reparation should settle the point.

4. M. CRESPI called attention to the last paragraph of Article II of the proposed Reparation Clauses and the note attached thereto, as follows:

"Damage done to persons or the property of persons who, at the moment when the damage took place, did not belong to the population of a State which, at the period in question, was recognised by the majority at least of the principal Allied and Associated Powers is not included herein."

NOTE:

"In the Conditions of Peace transmitted to Germany, the English text limits the right of the Allied and Associated Powers to the recovery of damage suffered 'during the period of the belligerency of each as an Allied and Associated Power against Germany.' There is no corresponding phrase in the French text. The phraseology of the English text appears to have been introduced by the Drafting Committee of the Peace Conference as the result of a communication to the effect that the Supreme Council had decided not to accord the right of recovery for damage suffered by new States which, at the times the damage was suffered, had not yet been recognised. The English text adopted does not appear to be entirely in accordance with the decision of the Supreme Council, since its effect, among other things, is to prevent recovery for damage suffered from acts of aggression leading up to a declaration of war against Germany, and to prevent recovery for damage suffered by Allied and Associated States during the period when they were at war with Austria-Hungary but not yet with Germany. Accordingly, the Commission charged with the preparation for submission to the Supreme Council of Reparation Clauses for the Treaty of Peace with Austria has in the above text eliminated the words 'during the period of the belligerency of each as an Allied and Associated Power' and has substituted the above sentence, which it is believed will more accurately express what is understood to be the intention of the Supreme Council."

He pointed out that some States though not actually at war with Germany had suffered damage at German hands: similarly with Austria. He thought that in such cases a claim for damage should be established.

M. ORLANDO pointed out that the question was the same for Austria and Germany: there must be a uniform text.

MR. LLOYD GEORGE said that the text suggested in the Reparation Clauses would exclude Poland. He pointed out that this text would enable Italy to claim against Germany in respect of a period during which she was not at war with Germany. He thought such a claim could not be substantiated.

M. ORLANDO said that Reparation was based on the principle of solidarity. As regards the Adriatic Italy accepted the view that this principle prevented any special claims. He thought it would be very difficult to distinguish damage caused by Austrian from that caused by German agency.

M. CRESPI said that German aeroplanes had bombarded his factory before the declaration of war by Italy against Germany, and there was no doubt that German U Boats had sunk Italian ships before this date. On the principle of solidarity Germany should be regarded as responsible for all damage.

MR. LLOYD GEORGE said that Italy, no doubt for very good reasons, did not for a considerable period, declare war on Germany, though urged to do so by the Allies. This was a considerable hindrance to the Allies in the effective application of the blockade. He further pointed out that U Boats sunk neutral as well as Allied shipping. He did not think that claims by Italy for damage against Germany before she declared war on Germany could be justified.

On the proposal of M. KLOTZ it was agreed that the words "during the period of the belligerency of each as an Allied and Associated Power against Austria" should be inserted in Article II and the last paragraph omitted. It was further agreed that the same form which had been omitted from the French text but retained in the English text of Article 232 of the Treaty with Germany should be inserted in the French text.

Consequent on this discussion M. ORLANDO initialled the Resolution given in the Appendix hereto which had already been initialled by his three colleagues, and Sir Maurice Hankey was instructed to forward it to the Secretary-General for the information of the Drafting Committee.

5. M. KLOTZ then called attention to Annex III of the proposed Reparation Clauses for Austria, dealing with merchant shipping. He pointed out that as Austria becomes a land-locked country it was proposed that she should surrender her entire merchant fleet. He called attention to the Italian objection to this proposal and to the recommendation made by the French and American representatives on the Reparation Commission that an arrangement should be made to leave a larger percentage of shipping in the Adriatic than would normally be the case under the pool.

M. ORLANDO expressed the thanks of Italy for the French and American proposals. He said, however, that he failed to see why the Adriatic should be worse off as regards shipping than Germany who is to be left with a proportion of her smaller tonnage and fishing vessels. He pointed out that the smaller craft and coasting vessels were an important part of the economic life of the coastal population and he thought it unjust and dangerous to take them away from their owners. It was true that Austria was to have no ports but the sea and the sea-faring population remain. The tonnage in question—some 60,000 tons—was a relatively small matter.

MR. LLOYD GEORGE said he thought there would be no difficulty over the fishing vessels. But shipping was an especial concern of Great Britain owing to her very heavy lossess—nearly 8 million tons. The Greeks had also been very heavy losers and moreover had lost precisely the kind of ship which it was proposed should be given to Italy and the Jugo-Slavs. He reminded the Council that Great Britain had lost her ships in carrying for Italy and France etc. British tonnage had been placed at the disposal of the whole world and none of it used for private enterprise. The recent withdrawals for various reasons by various countries, e.g. the United States of America, Brazil and Portugal, of shipping from the pool was making a very bad impression in Great Britain. The country was very short of shipping, and probably, taking all things into account, it was the most important British industry. He asked the council not to force a concession on Great Britain at that meeting. He suggested there should be a conference between the parties interested, including Greece, with representatives of the British Board of Trade who would not be found indisposed to make concessions.

It was agreed that the text of the Annex should stand and that a special arrangement for the Adriatic should be considered by representatives of France, Italy, Greece and Great Britain.

LORD SUMNER said that he had been approached by representatives of Jugo-Slavia who wished to secure a share for Jugo-Slavia of the libraries and learned materials of all kinds now in Vienna. He did not think that this matter fell within Reparation but he had drawn up the following clause providing, not for the division of this material, but securing that Austria should maintain it in good condition, allow reasonable access to it, etc.

"With regard to all objects of an artistic, archaeological, scientific or historic character, forming part of collections, which formerly belonged to the Government or to the Crown of the Austro-Hungarian Empire and are not otherwise provided for in this present Treaty, Austria undertakes:

(a) to negotiate, when required, with the States concerned, for an amicable arrangement, whereby any portion thereof or any objects belonging thereto, which ought to form part of the intellectual patrimony of the ceded districts, may be repatriated to their districts of origin on terms of reciprocity, and

(b) for twenty years, unless such an arrangement is sooner arrived at, not to alienate or disperse any of the said collections, or to dispose of any of the above objects, but at all times to ensure their safety and good condition and to make them available at all reasonable times to students, who are nationals of any of the Allied and Associated Powers."

This clause was adopted.

On the suggestion of Mr. Lloyd George the drafting of Reparation Clauses for Bulgaria was referred to the Reparation Commission.

PRESIDENT WILSON said that, having regard to the fact that the rights of small States deserve special consideration, he thought that the representatives of the States previously forming part of the Austro-Hungarian Empire should have an opportunity of giving their views before the text of these Clauses of the Treaty with Austria was definitely adopted.

This was agreed.

This meeting terminated at 6:45 p.m.

T MS (SDR, RG 256, 180.03401/24½, DNA).

Hankey's Notes of a Meeting of the Council of Four[1]

President Wilson's House,
C.F.25.   Paris, May 22, 1919, 6:15 p.m.

1. PRESIDENT WILSON read the despatch attached in the Appendix,[2] which was a revision of the earlier draft prepared as a result of the meeting on the previous day.[3] The revised despatch was agreed to.

PRESIDENT WILSON raised the question of whether it should be sent to Poland or handed to M. Paderewski on his arrival in Paris.

As there was some doubt as to the date on which M. Paderewski was due to arrive, the question was adjourned till the following day.

APPENDIX TO C.F.25.

TELEGRAM   Paris, May, [blank] 1919
From: The President of the Peace Conference.
To: General Pilsudski, Head of the Polish State, Warsaw.

The Council of the Principal Allied and Associated Powers feel that it is their duty to call the attention of the Government of Poland to facts which are giving them the greatest concern and which may lead to consequences for Poland which the Council would deeply deplore. The boundary between Poland and the Ukraine is under consideration and is as yet undetermined, and the Council has more than once informed the Polish Government that they would regard any attempt either by Poland or by the Ukrainian authorities to determine it, or to prejudice its determination, by the use of force, as a violation of the whole spirit and an arbitrary interference with the whole purpose of the present Conference of Peace, to which Poland, at least, has consented to leave the decision of questions of this very sort. The Council has, therefore, more than once insisted that there should be an armistice on the Ukrainian front, arranged in Paris and under the advice of the Council itself. Full conferences in that matter have been held between a carefully selected Inter-Allied commission and representatives of Poland and the Ukraine, and terms of armistice drawn up which have been formally approved by the Council of the Principal Allied and Associated Powers. The representatives of the Ukraine have accepted those terms, but the Polish military authorities, while acquiescing in principle, have in effect insisted upon such conditions as would amount to a settlement of the very question in controversy, and have continued to use force to maintain their claims. This has inevitably made the impression on the minds of the members of the Council that the Polish authorities were in effect, if not in purpose, denying and rejecting the authority of the Conference of Peace. The Council feel it their duty, therefore, in the most friendly spirit but with the most solemn earnestness, to say to the Polish authorities that, if they are not willing to accept the guidance and decisions of the Conference of Peace in such matters, the Governments represented in the Council of the Principal Allied and Associated Governments will not be justified in furnishing Poland any longer with supplies or assistance. If it is her deliberate purpose to set at naught the counsel proffered by the Conference, its authority can no longer, it is feared, be made serviceable to her. The Council will, of course, insist upon an absolute cessation of hostilities on the part of the Ukrainian military forces.

T MS (SDR, RG 256, 180.03401/25, DNA).
    [1] The complete text of these minutes is printed in *PPC*, V, 859-60.
    [2] There is a MS of this document, typed by Close, in WP, DLC.
    [3] See Appendix I to the minutes of the Council of Four printed at May 21, 1919, 4:15 p.m.

Two Letters from Robert Lansing

My dear Mr. President: Paris, May 22nd, 1919.
    I am sending you herewith a copy of a letter which I have just received from Frank P. Walsh, Chairman of the American Commission for Irish Independence, in which he quotes a letter addressed to M. Clemenceau by Eamon de Valera, Arthur Griffith and Count George Noble Plunkett.[1]

                    Faithfully yours,   Robert Lansing.

    [1] F. P. Walsh to RL, May 22, 1919, TCL (WP, DLC). As Lansing indicates, this letter embodied one from De Valera, Griffith, and Plunkett to Clemenceau, datelined Dublin, May 17, 1919. They warned Clemenceau and the peace conference that the people of Ireland would not be bound by any treaty or agreement made by the British government claiming to act on behalf of Ireland. They reiterated that they were the duly appointed delegates authorized to speak and act on behalf of the Irish government before the peace conference.
    The identical message was also embodied in F. P. Walsh to WW, May 22, 1919, TLS (WP, DLC).

My dear Mr. President: Paris, May 22nd, 1919.
    I am transmitting to you herewith a letter which, subject to your approval, I propose to send to Mr. Frank P. Walsh in reply to the communication which he and Messrs. Dunne and Ryan addressed to me regarding safe conduct for the so-called Representatives of the People of Ireland to proceed to Paris.[1]
    In view of the involved state of this case and the tactics which

these gentlemen are employing, I thought it best to deal with their request from a purely technical standpoint.

Faithfully yours,   Robert Lansing.

TLS (WP, DLC).
    [1] See the Enclosure printed with RL to WW, May 18, 1919.

To Robert Lansing, with Enclosure

My dear Lansing: Paris, 22 May, 1919.

Pardon me for not having sent you the enclosed letter before.[1]

And may I remind you of the general outline of what we agreed upon as what we would say? In substance it was as follows:

That although it had not been possible to extend official assistance to these gentlemen, every effort had been made to bring them into friendly communication with the British representatives here and through these friendly offices Mr. Lloyd George had consented to see them. But that the utterances which they had made while in Ireland[2] had been of such a character as to give the deepest offense to those with whom they were seeking to deal and had rendered it impossible for us to serve them any further. In brief, the statement (which you can easily elaborate, with House's assistance) ought to show that the whole failure of their errand lies at their door and not at ours.

Cordially and faithfully yours,   [Woodrow Wilson]

I think on the whole it would be better to send the answer which is here suggested than the rather formal one which you sent me.   W.W.[3]

CCL (WP, DLC).
    [1] That is, the letter cited in n. 1 to the previous document.
    [2] See D. Lloyd George to EMH, May 9, 1919, printed as an Enclosure with EMH to WW, May 9, 1919, Vol. 58.
    [3] For the letter which Lansing sent, see the Enclosure printed with RL to WW, May 26, 1919 (first letter of that date).

E N C L O S U R E

Robert Lansing to Francis Patrick Walsh

Sir: Paris, May 22nd, 1919.

I have received the letter which you and Messrs Dunne and Ryan addressed to me on May 16th, regarding the issuing of safe-con-

ducts by the British Government to enable certain persons to proceed from Ireland to France and return and desire to explain to you
that inasmuch as it appears that the persons in question are British
subjects and as I believe that regular channels exist for the filing of
applications by subjects of Great Britain for permits to travel from
the different portions of the British Empire, the American authorities are not in a position to approach the British authorities officially
in connection with this matter.

    I am, Sir

Your obedient servant,

T MS (WP, DLC).

From Edward Mandell House

Dear Governor: Paris, 22 May 1919.

    I enclose herewith the memorandum you asked each of us for at
the last meeting you had with the Commissioners.[1]

Affectionately yours,   E. M. House

TLS (WP, DLC).
  [1] EMH, "MEMORANDUM FOR THE PRESIDENT: Questions Remaining to be Settled After
German and Austrian Peace Treaties are Disposed of," [c. May 22, 1919], TS MS (WP,
DLC). This sixteen-page memorandum set forth the "questions" under six headings: territorial matters; naval matters; commissions, etc., to be appointed under the peace treaty
with Germany; a miscellaneous category including prewar debts, enemy property, and
contracts; treaties with new states and states acquiring new territories; and shipping
matters.

From Henry White

My dear Mr. President: Paris 22 May 1919

    I have been thinking a good deal of what you said to us on Tuesday
in respect to possible arrangements for the government of Turkey
which were passing through your mind, and I cannot but feel that
there are very serious objections to the Sultan's continuing to reside
in Constantinople as head of the Mohammedan religion and also as
ruler of Anatolia or other part of Turkey. These objections would, I
think, be still greater if a number of foreign advisers in connection
with his temporal power were to be established in that city, while the
latter, with the Dardanelles district, was being governed by a mandatary of the League of Nations.

    I very much question whether Congress, which apparently is not
strongly in favor of our accepting any mandates, could be persuaded, in view of the general feeling in the United States against

the Turkish Government, to consent to our becoming the mandatary for Constantinople, were the Sultan to remain there as the Pope does in Rome or under any circumstances whatever.

In view of the capacity for intrigue, based upon centuries of training therein, which exists in Constantinople, I cannot imagine that any mandatary could escape constant opposition in the prosecution of his work from intriguers connected with the Sultan's surroundings, with one or more of the foreign advisers aforesaid, or with the officials of the old régime. These intrigues would not improbably be more or less connected with the Ottoman Public Debt Organization, which has exercised for many years past a very powerful underhand influence upon the government of Turkey and of Constantinople in particular.

Since I ventured on Tuesday to suggest some doubt as to how much confidence should be placed in the opinions of the representatives of India who spoke before the Council of Four on Monday, I have been informed that the Maharajah of Bikanir, who appeared as a representative of Indian Mohammedanism, is not a member of that religion. After expressing himself so strongly before you, as I understand he did, as to the harm which would be done to the Sultan's prestige by the removal of his residence from Constantinople to another part of Turkey and by his being deprived of all temporal power, Bikanir was asked how he came to make a statement in the matter, not being a Mohammedan. He replied that, as a representative of India at the Conference, it was his duty to do so, otherwise great indignation would have been caused among the Mohammedans by his not having spoken in their behalf, and the more so as he is of another religion. Furthermore, Lord Curzon, who has a thorough knowledge of all matters connected with India, of which he has been Governor General, and Balfour, are of the opinion that the Sultan's religious prestige would not be damaged by either of the causes aforesaid, but that he could perfectly well be transferred to the city of Broussa without loss of his prestige as chief of Islam. I understand, also, that one of the causes, if not the chief cause, of Lord Curzon's brief visit to Paris was to impress this view upon the Prime Minister—a view which is in opposition to that of Mr. Montagu, the present Secretary of State for India.

The foregoing information was imparted to me in confidence by Eyre Crowe, the Permanent Under-Secretary of the British Foreign Office, who says that his Office and the military authorities connected with India are of the same opinion as Curzon and Balfour. I rather suspected, when you mentioned the statement of the Indian Representatives, that they had been brought before the Council of Four by some individual or government interested in impressing certain views upon the Council; and it turns out that they appeared at the instance of Montagu, who has not had much personal experience of India.

In view of these circumstances, I am of the opinion that the American mandatary, if there be any such, would have but little chance of success if the Sultan were to remain in Constantinople, and still less so, if advisers of several nationalities were also settled there, who would almost certainly—one or more of them, in any case—be intriguing for their respective countries in opposition to the wishes or decisions of the mandatary. Mr. Lansing, General Bliss and Colonel House authorized me to say that they concur fully in the views which I have expressed in this letter.

Yours very sincerely,   Henry White

TLS (WP, DLC).

From Henry White, with Enclosure

My dear Mr. President: Paris 22 May 1919

I send you herewith the copy of a letter which I have received this morning from our old friend, Lord Bryce, as I think it may be of interest to you.

I propose writing to him at once that I consider the demonstration which he suggests in the House of Lords in favor of the League, would be in the highest degree inexpedient. My feeling is that it would materially enhance the idea which appears to be now prevalent in certain circles in the U. S. that the provisions of the League are chiefly in the interests of the British Empire and for the protection of its boundaries.

On the other hand, it seems to me that there is a good deal to be said for his suggestion of impartial commissions to examine the questions at issue relative to the Balkans, during the summer, with a view to a re-assembling of the Conference in the autumn, to receive and act upon the reports of these commissions.

Should this plan turn out feasible and meet with your approval, it might perhaps be well to suggest that the Conference re-assemble in London, rather than here, for reasons which you will not fail to understand.

Yours very sincerely,   Henry White

TLS (WP, DLC).

ENCLOSURE

James Viscount Bryce to Henry White

My dear White: London, S.W. 19 May 1919

You are doubtless better informed than I am here as to what is passing in the U. S. A. but from what reaches me, the League of Nations is not yet "out of the wood," so far as the Senate is concerned, whether from conviction or from political party motives, there seems to be still so much disposition to oppose left in that Body that nothing less than a clear and strong manifestation of popular feeling will suffice to push it through. It has occurred to some of us that a demonstration in favor of it in the House of Lords might possibly be of some use. If so, we would make it about the time when the matter is nearly ready to come before the Senate. With a view to that, I should be grateful to you if you could let me know when the President is likely to return to America. I presume he will not do so until Peace has been signed with Germany. But will he do so forthwith thereafter? Or will he wait till the minor questions, such as the Balkans, and Baltic States, and the Turkish Empire, have been dealt with? It has seemed to me that in view of the many difficult questions of boundaries, the best course would be to create small impartial commissions to examine these questions of frontiers in debate between Greeks, Slavs, Bulgarians, etc. and such as questions of nationality as is involved in Italy's claim to annex some 200,000 German-speaking Tyrolese and let the Conference meet later in the year to receive the reports of these commissions before settling the delimitations. As I think I have already written to you, to hand over Tyrolese of German race to Italy, and the Bulgarians of Macedonia to the Greeks or Serbs will be to sow the seeds of future war.

We were very glad to have news of you from Owen Wister,[1] who lunched with us on Friday, and was in very good form. He is uneasy about the effect in America of the still open sore of Ireland.

I hope you have good news of your daughter and her children.[2]

Ever yours,   Bryce

P.S. You may like to know that many of us here doubt the prudence of imposing such harsh terms on Germany. We suppose it was difficult to resist the exigence of France. But we fear that their very harshness may not only prevent the recovery of as large an indemnity from Germany as both France and we desire, but may also produce a spirit in Germany of a general resentment and bitterness which will be, when Germany begins to recover her strength, a standing menace to France, obliging her, and ourselves also, to maintain a permanently large force. This the English masses are most unwilling to do. When they come into power, will they do it? Neither a man nor a nation always gets most by demanding most. Here if we ask less, we should probably get more. However, we in England are "keeping silent, even from good words," lest by saying all we think we should make the position worse.

I am glad to hear it has been decided to turn the Turks altogether out of Armenia, it now only remains to hope that the U. S. will accept a mandate for that country.

TCL (WP, DLC).

¹ That is, the American novelist, short story writer, and biographer.
² Muriel White, Countess Seherr-Thoss, wife of Hermann Roger Hans Christow, Count Seherr-Thoss. Their children were Hans Christoph, Margaret, and Hermann Seherr-Thoss.

From Robert Lansing, with Enclosures

My dear Mr. President: Paris May 22, 1919

I enclose to you a copy of a letter and memorandum from Lord Bryce, of which I spoke to you the other day.

Faithfully yours, Robert Lansing

TLS (WP, DLC).

E N C L O S U R E I

James Viscount Bryce to Robert Lansing

You are of course at liberty to show this to the President of [or] any of your Colleagues.

My Dear Mr. Lansing: [London] May 15th, 1919.

I greatly regret not to have had the opportunity of a longer talk with you, but as I know how busy you are, I have put on paper a brief abstract of what I would have said to you on some matters not yet settled by the Conference. The U. S. Delegation has, as we all feel, been absolutely disinterested and impartial, desiring, as the President has repeatedly and forcibly stated, only the application of the principles of Nationality and Self Determination. As I know that you all desire that everywhere there should be that contentment with their rulers which is the necessary basis of peace, I am sure you will wish that the working of the League of Nations should have a fair chance of success by starting from that basis. Having travelled in the countries to which the enclosed Memorandum relates, I have grave fears lest this basis should not be laid if the demands of some of the Powers represented at the Conference to appropriate territories which do not rightfully belong to them, should be granted. It may, in some cases, need firmness to resist those demands, but I venture to suggest that a convenient and eminently fair way to meeting the difficulties may be found by appointing small impartial Commissions to investigate the facts on the spot and report to the Conference at its later sittings.

If, as seems probable, it will be impossible for the Conference to despatch all the many questions it has to solve before the President leaves for the U. S., there would be ample time for these commissions to present their reports after his return.

Many of us here feel especially anxious regarding the Bulgarian population in Macedonia. If they are put under Greece or Serbia, there is sure to be future trouble. A plaintive appeal has reached me from the Bulgarian Minister at the Hague,[1] whom I know, and who did his best to keep Bulgaria on the side of the Allies. He has given me a memorandum of facts which I could transmit to you if your Delegation has not already received a copy of it.

Believe me,   Very sincerely yours,   James Bryce.

[1] Pantcho Hadji-Mischef. He had served briefly as the last Bulgarian Minister to Great Britain just before Bulgaria entered the war.

E N C L O S U R E   I I

A Memorandum by James Viscount Bryce

Confidential.

Memorandum on questions before the Conference.

I. *Bulgarian population in Macedonia and S.E. Thrace.*

It will be a serious menace to future peace if this population is delivered over to the tender mercies either of Greece or of Serbia. The latter wishes to have a large part of Macedonia between the river Vardar and the Lake of Ochride which is Bulgarian by speech, by race and by national sentiment. It ought to be added to Bulgaria, but if this cannot be done, it ought to be constituted into a separate autonomous area. Similarly, S.E. Thrace, including Adrianople and Dedeagatch, is far more Bulgarian than Greek, and the inhabitants will be restless and angry under Greek rule. Under such conditions there will not be peace.

II. *Tyrol.*

The Italian Government seeks to annex, alleging strategic arguments, a large region of Central Tyrol, including Meran, Botzen and Brixen, which speaks German and is Germanic by race. The Tyrolese are a brave, simple, honest people, whose only fault was that they have been ruled by the Hapsburgs. They fought bravely against Napoleon when he handed them over to Bavaria. To give them to Italy would be bitterly resented by them, and altogether inconsistent with the principle of Nationality.

III. *Hungary and Transylvania.*

Part of S.E. Hungary, and a half at least of Transylvania, is inhabited by a population mainly of Rumanian stock, and may properly be given to Rumania. But she claims also a large region up to the Thein river, and including N. Transylvania, which is chiefly and in parts, entirely of Magyar race. The Rumanian army has already occupied these districts and is reported to be treating the Magyar inhabitants with great harshness. The just course would seem to be to appoint an impartial commission to proceed to the country and draw the frontier after a careful enquiry in accordance with the principles of Nationality and Self-determination.

IV. *Armenia.*

As it is understood that all Turkish rule in Armenia is to cease, I need only say that her friends in this country would regret to see any part of Armenia or Cilicia delivered by way of Mandate either to France or to Italy. Neither Power could be trusted to administer the Country with a sole view to the welfare of the inhabitants, as America would do. There would be financial exploitation and wide R. Catholic religious orders would make trouble with the ancient National churches. The Christians, though reduced by recent massacres, now equal or outnumber the Turkish Moslems, because that population also has been immensely reduced by the War.

T MSS (WP, DLC).

From John Joseph Pershing

Personal.

Dear Mr. President: Paris, May 22, 1919.

I have just received a message from the Commanding General of the Army of Occupation[1] to the following effect:

"This morning, General Mangin,[2] Commanding General of the French Army at Mayence [Mainz], sent a Colonel of his Staff[3] to General Liggett's headquarters at Coblentz to inquire what our attitude would be toward a political revolution on the west bank of the Rhine for the establishment of an Independent Rhineland Republic, free from Germany.[4] He inquired what the American attitude would be toward such new Republic. The Staff Officer stated that they had fifty deputies ready to send into the American sector to assist in starting the revolution. The meaning of the word deputies in this connection is not clearly understood, but it was made clear that they were to be French."[5]

General Liggett very properly declined to consider the proposition, and his action has been approved by me. I have given him instructions not to permit the entry of political agitators into our sector, no matter by whose order they might claim to be operating.

Faithfully yours,   John J. Pershing.

TLS (WP, DLC).
[1] That is, Lt. Gen. Hunter Liggett, since May 2, 1919, commander of the United States Third Army, the American army of occupation.
[2] Gen. Charles Marie Emmanuel Mangin, commander of the French Tenth Army, with headquarters at Mainz.
[3] Col. Joseph Cyrille Magdalaine Denvignes, deputy delegate on the inter-Allied commission in Rhenish Hesse.
[4] A Rhineland separatist movement, looking toward either an autonomous Rhineland province within Germany or an entirely independent Rhineland Republic, had begun as early as October 1918. It acquired some momentum in early 1919 with the increasing disorders in Germany and fears that the Berlin government might be seized by German followers of the Bolsheviks. Even Konrad Adenauer, then Mayor of Cologne, toyed with the idea of an autonomous or independent Rhineland, although he soon abandoned the project.
The principal, self-appointed, leader of the separatist movement was Dr. Hans Adam Dorten, a former public prosecutor of Düsseldorf, who had served in the war as a captain of antiaircraft batteries on the Verdun front. Although Dorten was active in all of the Allied zones of occupation, he concentrated his efforts in the French zone and made a special effort to cultivate the support of General Mangin and of General Augustin Grégoire Arthur Gérard, commander of the French Eighth Army, with headquarters at Landau. Dorten correctly surmised that the French military leaders would be most receptive to a Rhineland separatist movement. It is an open question how much the French government knew about the movement, but it is clear that Generals Mangin and Gérard kept Marshal Foch well informed as to its progress.
Dorten first met with Mangin in early April 1919 and, with the General's support, the scheme developed rapidly. Dorten and the other leading conspirators drew up a plan for a Rhenish state which was to be largely, but not quite totally, independent of Germany and would comprise at least Rhenish Prussia, Rhenish Hesse, the Bavarian Palatinate, Nassau, and perhaps the Saarland. They proposed to proclaim their new state on May 24 in Coblenz, which was to be its capital. They believed that placing the capital in the American occupation zone would conceal the French influence. General Mangin met with Dorten and the other leaders in Mainz on May 17, approved their plans with some changes, and agreed to get into contact with General Liggett, whose acquiescence in the scheme was obviously crucial to its success. Mangin approved a final version of the plan on May 21 and sent Denvignes to see Liggett on May 22.
Meanwhile, a totally separate group of conspirators, abetted by General Gérard, had put up posters on May 20 throughout the Palatinate calling upon its inhabitants to form a republic. This effort brought no response and was a total fiasco.
The dénouement of the Dorten-Mangin affair will appear in later documents in this and the following volume. For a detailed discussion of the Rhenish separatist movement, see Jere Clemens King, *Foch versus Clemenceau: France and German Dismemberment, 1918-1919* (Cambridge, Mass., 1960), pp. 28-43, 73-106, and Keith L. Nelson, *Victors Divided: America and the Allies in Germany, 1918-1923* (Berkeley and Los Angeles, Calif., and London, 1975), pp. 110-12, 305-307.
[5] These "deputies" were to be German, not French. This error was the result of a misunderstanding during the telephone conversation in which the message quoted in the above document was transmitted from Coblenz to Paris. See Nelson, *op.cit*, p. 306, n.64, and the Enclosure printed with G. Clemenceau to WW, June 1, 1919. The original transcription of the telephone message is printed in United States. Department of the Army, *The United States Army in the World War* (17 vols., Washington, 1948), X, 1129.

From Sherman Miles[1]

Memorandum for the President: Paris, 22 May 1919.

From: Colonel Sherman Miles, General Staff.

SUBJECT: CARINTHIA

1. By the verbal direction of Colonel House, I submit the following memorandum for your information:

2. Last January Major Lawrence Martin,[2] Professor Kerner,[3] Lieutenant Leroy King[4] and I conducted an investigation in Carinthia to determine the political will of the people in the southeastern corner of that province. This small district is claimed by both Yugo-Slavia and Austria. We had an unique opportunity to apply the principle of self-determination practically, in the field. For ten days we covered the district, visiting towns and hamlets unexpectedly and talking to people of all classes. We had with us one representative of each of the two sides, and were ourselves able to question the people both in the German and Slovene languages.

3. We found that the majority of the people in the disputed district, though Slovene by blood, called themselves "Wendish" and desired to remain under Austrian rule. This desire of the people is largely the result of the geographic and economic unity of the province. The attached map[5] shows that the basin of the Drau is entirely surrounded by high mountains, which are particularly precipitous on the southern border. The entire economic life of the province centers around this basin, and the people in the disputed area south of the Drau and the Wörther See are economically dependent on the markets of Villach, Klagenfurt and Völkermarkt to the north.

4. The Yugo-Slav authorities tried to convince us that the people were influenced by Austrian terrorism. We carefully investigated this, and found it to be utterly unfounded.

5. Just before our investigation, the Yugo Slav forces had been driven out of the western part of the disputed area. We investigated this, and were convinced, as soldiers, that the few score ill-armed and irregular Austrian troops could not have accomplished the result, and that the district was freed of Yugo Slav control largely by the action of the inhabitants themselves. During the past month I am informed that the same thing has happened in the eastern part of the disputed area, and that now the entire province is in the hands of the Carinthian (Austrian) authorities—a result largely attributable to the will of the people themselves.

6. Of the four Americans who made the investigation in January, three were absolutely convinced that self-determination, economics and geography all demanded that southeastern Carinthia should remain politically with the rest of the province, that is to say with Aus-

tria. The fourth member of the investigation, Professor Kerner, considered that the province should be divided by the River Drau between Austrian [Austria] and Yugo-Slavia. I am informed by Professor Seymour that the American, British and Italian experts who studied Carinthia all arrived at the same conclusion independently—that Carinthia was a political entity which should not be divided. This conclusion was reached before our investigation in January, though we knew nothing of it. It was further strengthened by our reports and by those of Professor A. C. Coolidge.[6] It was adopted by the Territorial Commission.[7] It was also adopted unanimously by the Council of Five,[8] and later by the Council of Ten.[9] Only within the last ten days has it been upset, under Yugo-Slav pressure, by the idea of making a political concession in favor of the Slovenes.

7. I understand that the present intention is to permit the people of the disputed area to express their will by a plebiscite five years hence. I believe that this should be done. But the question now is, under which Government (Yugo-Slav or Austrian) should the disputed area rest during the next five years? The proposed compromise is to give to the Yugo-Slavs, for the next five years, that part of the province south of the Wörther See and the Drau (red line on the map). This is more than any unbiased investigation or expert has ever recommended, and would mean that the people in the district handed over to the Yugo-Slavs would be cut off from their natural markets for the next five years. I understand that this proposition now has the support of the British, French and (conditionally) Italian experts, and also Professor Johnson (American), but solely on the ground of political expediency, as a compromise to the Slovenes.

8. I submit that in this case we know, by American investigation in the field, on which side the principle of self-determination lies. We also know that in this case self-determination co-incides with the natural forces of geography and economics. To draw an artificial line through this province, disregarding the present will of the people, economics and geography, and to force these people to live for five years under these artificial conditions appears to be a complete surrender of principle. I realize that under either government the people will be subjected to propaganda in preparation for the plebiscite. But our investigation convinces me that severe political measures, such as deportations and economic privileges or deprivations, are more to be feared from the Yugo-Slav authorities than from the Austrians. I also realize that the element of political expediency has now entered into the question, and that the Yugo-Slavs are making a strong plea to the effect that something must be given the Slovenes on their northern border to compensate for their losses to Italy in the west. Nevertheless, the principles in the case of Carinthia are

clear, and have been recognized by independent investigations of the British, Italians and ourselves, and have been adopted unanimously by the Council of Five and the Council of Ten. I therefore submit that it would be the greatest misfortune to compromise to political expediency on an issue the principles of which have been so clearly established.

Sherman Miles

TS MS (WP, DLC).
  [1] A member of the Coolidge mission in Vienna. He had recently conducted a number of investigations in several of the contested areas of the former Hapsburg Empire.
  [2] Associate Professor of Physiography and Geography at the University of Wisconsin and a junior geologist of the United States Geological Survey; at this time, on military duty at the general headquarters of the A.E.F. and assigned to the A.C.N.P.
  [3] Robert Joseph Kerner, Associate Professor of European History at the University of Missouri and a member of The Inquiry specializing in eastern Europe; he had been with the Coolidge mission in Vienna until early March.
  [4] In civilian life, a lawyer of New York and Newport, Rhode Island.
  [5] Not reproduced.
  [6] For these reports, see *PPC*, XII, 498-523.
  [7] That is, the Commission on Rumanian and Yugoslav Affairs, which had been appointed on February 1 and February 18, 1919. For the reports of this commission, see the minutes of the Council of Foreign Ministers, May 9, 1919, 3 p.m., printed in *PPC*, IV, 680-81, and Annexure A to the minutes of the Council of Foreign Ministers, May 10, 1919, 4 p.m., printed in *ibid.*, pp. 701-703.
  [8] See the minutes of the Council of Foreign Ministers, May 10, 1919, 4 p.m., printed in *ibid.*, pp. 696-703.
  [9] See the minutes of the Council of Ten printed at May 12, 1919, 4 p.m.

Clive Day and Charles Seymour to the American Commissioners

[Paris] May 22, 1919.

From: Dr. Day and Dr. Seymour
To: The Commissioners
Subject: Change in the frontier recommended between Jugo-Slavia and German Austria.

1. As a result of a hearing of Jugo-Slav representatives before the Jugo-Slav Territorial Commission held on May 20th the British, French and Italian representatives approved a new frontier proposed by the Jugo-Slavs in the Klagenfurt basin. The American delegation, because of a disagreement between themselves and Dr. Johnson, reserved their opinion.

2. The undersigned herewith present their arguments for maintaining the first decision of the Territorial Commission, which has been approved by the Council of Foreign Ministers and the Chiefs of the Five Governments.

The frontier first recommended (the Karawanken Mountains) was unanimously agreed upon by all the American experts and independently recommended by the Coolidge mission in Austria after an investigation on the spot. It was agreed to by representatives of all the powers on the Territorial Commission.

This frontier, because of the character of the mountains, forms a natural barrier; it has long been an administrative boundary between provinces of Austria.

The frontier suggested by the Jugo-Slavs would cut across the Klagenfurt basin, which all the delegates agreed was an economic unit which could not be divided without serious detriment to the interests of the population on both sides of the line.

The German-speaking population in the basin is in an enormous majority (170,000 German-speaking; 70,000 Slovene-speaking). According to the reports of Colonel Miles, representing the Coolidge mission, the greater part of the Slovene-speaking population is opposed to incorporation within Jugo-Slavia.

Since the drafting of the Commission's report no new fact has been brought to its attention. The desire of the French and British delegates to change the report is the result of Jugo-Slav insistence.

For these reasons the undersigned recommend the maintenance of the original report as approved by the Council of Ten, unless for political reasons of a general nature it seems advisable to satisfy Jugo-Slav demands in this region.

Clive Day
Charles Seymour
United States Delegates
on Jugo-Slav Commission.

TS MS (WP, DLC).

Douglas Wilson Johnson to the American Commissioners

[Paris, c. May 22, 1919]

MEMORANDUM

From: Douglas Johnson
To: The Commissioners
Subject: American attitude re disposition of Klagenfurt Basin

The French, British, and Italian delegations (the latter with an important reservation) are in agreement that the Klagenfurt Basin should be assigned to Jugo-Slavia.

The American delegation is divided in its opinion. Mr. Seymour and Mr. Johnson were charged with the study of this problem and with presenting the American view before the Roumanian Commission.[1] Mr. Seymour is of the opinion that the basin should be assigned to Austria, whereas Mr. Johnson agrees with the French, British, and Italian opinion that the basin should go to Jugo-Slavia. In view of this difference of opinion it seemed best for both of us to take the position, in the Roumanian Commission, that the solution of the problem involved political considerations beyond our competence; and for each to present to the American Commissioners to negotiate peace the grounds for his opinion. The present memorandum outlines the views of Mr. Johnson.

When the Klagenfurt problem first came before the Roumanian Commission, I (as well as Mr. Seymour) favored attributing the region to Austria, as did also the British and Italian delegations. The French alone favored attribution to Jugo-Slavia, in the form in which the problem then presented itself. My own reasons for a change of view are as follows:

1. *The ethnographic argument.* The Klagenfurt geographic basin contains within its natural limits approximately 170,000 Germans and 70,000 Jugo-Slavs. It appears, further, that a considerable although unknown number of the Jugo-Slavs are Germanophile. Under these conditions it was reasonable to believe that a plebiscite would result in favor of Austria. Nevertheless, when the frontier was fixed on the crest of the Karawanken mountains, opportunity was afforded for a consultation or plebiscite in the basin, in view of the doubt entertained by some members of the Commission as to whether a majority of the population would really prefer Austrian rule.

The geographic unity of the basis was impaired when the Council of Ten accepted the Italian proposition to reduce the area of the plebiscite in such manner as to leave the Villach-St. Veit railway outside the voting district. The effect of this was to reduce by nearly 100,000 the number of Germans voting, and to render less certain a vote in favor of Austria. The Jugo-Slav delegation next submitted a proposition for a frontier, geographically not seriously inferior to that accepted by the Council of Ten for the northern limit of the plebiscite area, and which by excluding large German populations changed the Jugo-Slav minority to a Jugo-Slav majority of more than 2 to 1 (Jugo-Slavs 56,600; Germans 24,600). It is my opinion (after studying carefully the reports of Colonel Miles as to the existence of Germanophile sentiments along the Jugo-Slav population) that there is not sufficient evidence before us to warrant the assurance that this Jugo-Slav majority would prefer Austrian rule. Since the doubt exists, it should be resolved in favor of the Jugo-Slavs rather than in favor of the Austrians.

2. *The geographic argument.* There can be no doubt that the best natural frontier between Austria and Jugo-Slavia would lie along the

crest of the Karawanken mountains; and that it is unfortunate to divide the natural unit, geographic and economic, which the Klagenfurt basin constitutes. On the other hand, the proposed frontier separating the Jugo-Slav part of the basin from the German part, follows easily recognizable geographic lines,—lake, rivers, and watersheds; and it corresponds very closely with the linguistic boundary. Under the circumstances it seems to me wise to sacrifice geographic and economic considerations to a solution which possesses marked ethnographic, strategic, and political advantages. This would be particularly true if the attribution of the area to Jugo-Slavia were accompanied by a provision that after a period of years the population should have a right to protest in case it found by experience that the arrangement was economically unsatisfactory.

3. *The strategic argument.* The present proportion of Germans in the Klagenfurt basin is the result of a very marked Germanization of the area, which formed part of the definite German policy of expansion toward the Adriatic. If the line of the Karawanken mountains is accepted as the boundary between Austria and Jugo-Slavia, the process of Germanization will continue south of the Drave,[2] the compact Jugo-Slav population of that area will be eliminated, and the advancing German wave will top the last important barrier separating it from the southern sea. In my opinion it is in the interest of world peace to check this German advance where it now stands, rather than deliberately to aid its extension to the summit of the last serious obstacle to its progress.

4. *The political argument.* The Slovene population suffers from the fact that it is being encroached upon by Italy on the west, Austria and Hungary on the north. It has seemed necessary to assign to Italy a very large number (225,000) of Slovenes in order to assure her a frontier geographically and economically possible (the line referred to in the President's published memorandum).[3] Such a sacrifice by a small people might be almost insupportable if accompanied by further sacrifices to Austria and Hungary. The sacrifice to Hungary has been reduced by the unanimous consent of the Roumanian Commission to restore to Jugo-Slavia a part of the Prekmurje.[4] The Jugo-Slav delegation asserts its willingness to accept the sacrifice to Italy if it can also be saved from sacrifice to its old oppressors, the Austrians. Under these circumstances it seems to me advisable to resolve the doubtful point of the Klagenfurt basin in favor of the Slovenes, who must under the best obtainable conditions suffer more severe losses than any other element of the Jugo-Slav peoples.

T MS (WP, DLC).
  [1] That is, the Commission on Rumanian and Yugoslav Affairs.
  [2] That is, the Drau, or Drave, River.

3 Printed at April 14, 1919, Vol. 57.
4 A region in northeastern Slovenia, also known as Prekomurje or Prekumurje, which, at this time, was part of Vas County, Hungary.

Gordon Auchincloss to Gilbert Fairchild Close, with Enclosure

Dear Mr. Close: Paris 22 May 1919.
    Enclosed please find a telegram which came through this morning for the President.
                    Faithfully yours,   Gordon Auchincloss

TLS (WP, DLC).

E N C L O S U R E

Washington. May 21 [1919]

86. For Auchincloss only from Polk.
    Secret. Please deliver the following message confidentially to the President from the Secretary of War.
    "I have received your message[1] and conferred with Polk about the Siberian situation. He has cabled Morris in the sense you suggest. I feel from all the information we have that General Graves is carefully and intelligently carrying out orders under trying circumstances, and that the efforts made to involve him in hostile operations against some part of the Russian population are insidious and baffling. He seems to have displayed firmness and good judgment. Polk feels that he is careful and firm but that he has been too rigid in following instructions and that he has made unnecessary issues which could have been avoided by the exercise of tact. This seems to me difficult to judge at this (distance?) and I am particularly conscious of the stringent instructions I gave him[2] as the reasons for his unbending attitude. We both feel that Morris' views will be valuable. The despatches made it clear that there is a wide difference of policy among the nations represented in Siberia. Polk and I both feel that Graves' removal at this time would create the impression that the United States Government was dissatisfied with his conduct and would be used to show our approval of other policies with which we are not in sympathy. If it is deemed wise to direct some form of government cooperation with the Omsk government his stiffness with which seems most criticised[3] whether with or without recognition of [either with or without recognition, your][4] views could be in-

stantly conveyed to General Graves and of course would be immediately complied with by him. Up to the present time he has no orders (except?) to guard the railroad and preserve local order without taking sides as between the various Cossack groups, local self-governments and claimants to general jurisdiction throughout the country. Such clashes as have occurred between him and others have for the most part been caused by violence toward local populations."

Polk   Acting.

T telegram (WP, DLC).
  [1] See WW to NDB, May 19, 1919.
  [2] See RL to FLP, April 1, 1919, Vol. 56.
  [3] *Sic* also in the CC of this telegram in the N. D. Baker Papers, DLC.
  [4] Correction here from *ibid.*

From Roland Sletor Morris

My dear Mr. President: Tokyo, May 22nd, 1919.

I am taking advantage of Dr. Teusler's[1] trip to Washington to send you this personal word of deep and lasting gratitude for the opportunities you have given me during the past two years. May I also thank you for your telegram from Paris approving in such generous terms my part in the Siberian Railway negotiations.[2] I cannot without seeming to exaggerate express to you how much I value any word of commendation from you. My thoughts have been so constantly with you during the trying days you have spent in Paris. I can appreciate in some small measure the difficulties you have met and I am so happy in the victory you have achieved for a more liberal and I hope a lasting peace.

I cannot resist telling you what splendid work Dr. Teusler has done in Siberia. His energy, his enthusiasm and his judgment have enabled him to solve all sorts of perplexing problems and have made our Red Cross efforts the most effective help which we have been able to offer Russia during the past year. I hope you may find time to hear some of his personal experiences. They will add color to the dull reports of conditions in Siberia which you are obliged to read.

Mrs. Morris,[3] joins me in kindest regards to Mrs. Wilson.
Faithfully and Sincerely yours,   Roland S. Morris

TLS (WP, DLC).
  [1] That is, Rudolf Bolling Teusler, M.D.
  [2] See WW to R. S. Morris, April 16, 1919, Vol. 57.
  [3] Augusta Shippen West Morris.

Felix Frankfurter to Gilbert Fairchild Close, with Enclosure

My dear Mr. Close: Paris, May 22nd 1919.

I wonder if this is not a letter that the President would like to read. It comes to me from one of the most dependable observers I know. The writer has a disciplined mind. He is not too fastidious in his demands on life—neither one of the proletariat nor a "parlour socialist." That he should write as he does is profoundly significant.

Cordially yours,   Felix Frankfurter

TLS (WP, DLC).

ENCLOSURE

An Unknown Person to Felix Frankfurter

Warsaw, May 12th, 1919.

I don't know what you people are doing in Paris, but I know what you ought to be doing. There are more than a million Jews in the New Poland being starved, and persecuted to death. There are more than six hundred thousand in Eastern Galicia, now partly battle ground between the Poles and Ukrainians, partly what is almost as bad, Ukrainian territory subject to all kinds of lawlessness. These six hundred thousand are slowly also rotting to death. I have reported on this matter very fully to Mr. Lewis Strauss.

In Poland the situation is indescribable. Ask Strauss to show you what Dr. Bogen[1] has written. Unfortunately Bogen has not perhaps the gift to make you see and hear and smell the horrors of what he saw during his recent trip. Here in Warsaw there is filth and rags and disease and starvation. Twenty-five percent of all the Jewish children that go to school are always sick, because of the under nourishment and lack of proper care.

Only twenty-five percent of all the Jewish children go to school anyway. Of those that don't go to school, probably fifty percent are under normal. The filth and poverty are indescribable. Further out in the country, the Jews not only starve, but they also have to suffer directly from the terrific persecution with which the new Republic tries to solve the race question. Talaat and Enver and Djemal[2] have nothing on the Poles. Nor had the Germans. A thousand Jews were murdered in Vilna when the Poles took it. In Lida the death roll was in proportion and so all through the country that the Poles are taking back from the Bolsheviks. They are treating the Lithuanians as badly. In short, when it comes time for self-determination, there ain't going to be no Lithuanians or Jews or nothing but a few Poles.

I am not talking from what Bogen saw only, but from what all the Yiddish papers print from eye-witnesses. In the small villages in the North east, the people have absolutely nothing to eat. The bread sold at so many marks a pound in Vilna consists of straw, dung, and dirt. Like Nebuchednezzar the poor Jews in the little villages, who are not allowed to go out of the villages bounds to get food, have gotten down to eating grass, and, what is worse, poison ivy soup. This sounds funny, unless it has happened to you, when it is damn serious.

The whole race is being rooted out, and what will be left, will be so inferior physically, that it will not be good for anything substantial for the next fifty years. Already all the teachers in the schools, and all the doctors, and all the doctors tell you that the Jewish children are much weaker and more sickly than gentiles, and that the general standard of Jewish health is lower, much lower than that of the general population.

Allow me to impress upon you, that if something is not done of a radical nature to relieve the situation, there will be no Jews left to go to Palestine. At any rate the flower of the race will have been destroyed.

Three things must be done, and with all possible speed.

1. The Polish Government must be bullied and brow-beaten into quitting its Policy of extermination and persecution. This cannot be accomplished by Polish promises. American Jews must be allowed to go over the whole country and see that the Jews do not suffer; especially along the battle front. The Polish Army must agree to their being attached to the Polish military forces. If this does not happen, not another grain of American Food or stiver of American money should go to Poland, which should be let stew in its own juice.

2. The Peace Conference must give effective minority rights g[u]arantees. Proportional representation. Some category of local tribunal on which Jews shall sit and to which Jews may appeal in case of persecution. Protection of Jewish merchant class against boycott and governmental discrimination. In all the Slav countries, Russia excepted, the Jews now suffer because the Government in various ways makes business impossible for them. Result, all the Jews tend to become proletariatized. And lastly, a section of the League of Nations which shall have the duty to hear minority grievances and enforce its decisions against tyrannous majorities.

3. Organization of tremendous relief and constructive enterprises to save the remnant of the Jewish Population. One such enterprise

and the most fruitful, I believe, would be transfer of large numbers of Jews, all of whom want to emigrate, to parts of the world, nearer Palestine, perhaps, say in the depopulated parts of Asia Minor, where they will at least be out of reach of Slav race hatred. Palestine can't take them now, either in the quantities or qualities in which they wish to come. A half way station ought to be found for them, an expense, even the classic thirty-three thousand dollars a family which it cost the Baron de Hirsch Fund[3] to get a family to Argentina, would be warranted. Every young man, and many of the older, that I meet, wants to go right away to Palestine. All, practically without exception wish to emigrate.

I tell you quite plainly that Zionism will have to show the Jews of the world that it has saved the Jews in the Diaspora and made their life possible, as well as that it has gotten us back Palestine. A terrible storm is brewing in the press against the day when the full truth about the fate of our Jews in Middle Europe gets to be known. Since I have been in Middle Europe I quite understand the lure of Bolshevism. You will soon have all decent men, Bolsheviks, and in jail.

T MS (WP, DLC).
   [1] Boris David Bogen, Russian-born naturalized American citizen, at this time an agent of the American Jewish Joint Distribution Committee in Poland. For a later discussion of what he had seen and written about in Poland, see his autobiography, *Born a Jew* (New York, 1930), pp. 124-201.
   [2] That is, Talat Paşa, Enver Paşa, and Cemal Paşa, about whom see n. 1 to F. Frankfurter to WW, May 8, 1919, Vol. 58.
   [3] Founded by Baron Maurice de Hirsch (1831-1896), a wealthy, German-born financier of Paris, who, in 1891, established the Baron de Hirsch Fund to assist Jewish immigrants to the United States and the Jewish Colonization Association to promote and assist the emigration of Jews from Europe and Asia for settlement in agricultural colonies in both North America and South America. It appears that the author of the above letter has confused these two philanthropic organizations.

Jan Christiaan Smuts to David Lloyd George

The Prime Minister.   [Paris] 22nd May, 1919.

I append a list of the most important provisions of the Peace Treaty which in my opinion call for amendment.

   1. *The Occupation Clauses*: (paras. 428-432).

The most dangerous provision of the whole Treaty is *the occupation of the left bank of the Rhine* for 15 years—and even thereafter,—at the option of the Allies, or in case the Germans have not (as they will not) have fulfilled all the terms of the Treaty. In the first place the size of the French army is not fixed, and it would be possible for France for the next 15 years to put most of her military expenditure on to German shoulders by keeping the bulk of her troops in the occupied area. In the second place the military régime to be followed is not fixed, and a system of martial law may and probably will be adopted which will be most irksome and irritating to the population and hampering to industry. The least that should be done if the Occupation Clauses are to remain is that the French army of occupation should be limited to reasonable numbers, that provision should be made that the civil population and administration should not in any way be under military law, order or regulation, and that the German Government should remain in undisturbed civil administration of the occupied area. Both this area and the Saar basin should remain in the German Customs system.

Military occupation and martial law for such a long period will, however, be so productive of friction and mischief, and involve such risks to Peace, that I would very strongly urge that the occupation be dropped in favour of the proposed Treaty of Guarantee. France should not have the double insurance of both the occupation and the guarantee. The Allies will have military, naval, and air Commissions going over Germany with full powers for an indefinite time. The League of Nations also has powers of investigation. The Reparation Clauses will effectively prevent military manufacture for 30 years. All fortifications are to be razed and no troops may be assembled within 50 km. east of the Rhine (paras. 42-3). In view of all this, and also of the proposed Guarantee, the Occupation provisions should be deleted.

2. *The Saar Basin.*

With the Occupation Clauses are associated the special provisions for the administration of the Saar Basin for 15 years. The German character of the great bulk of the population is beyond question, and there is no necessity to hold a referendum at the end of fifteen years. I consider the special administration a clumsy device and really uncalled for so long as France has full powers in respect of the coal mines. But if the special administration is to be established, it should automatically cease after fifteen years as soon as Germany can repurchase the coal mines. (I understand that the drastic penalty Clause in case the mines are not paid for in gold in six months after the valuation will be dropped.)

3. *The Reparation Clauses.*

I am advised that while a very large amount of reparation could be obtained from Germany in the long run, the actual scheme adopted in our Reparation Clauses is unworkable, and must kill the goose which is to lay the golden eggs. We could not get anything like one milliard sterling out of Germany within the first two years. Apart from ships, foreign securities and certain raw material, we could get nothing but worthless paper. So far from getting anything more out of Germany the first couple of years, the real practical problem is to find credit for Germany wherewith she could purchase food and the necessary raw materials to re-start her industrial life. There is actually sitting a Commission,[1] whose object it is to find out how to finance Germany and other European countries in the immediate future.

Besides the impossibility of paying this milliard in two years, I am also advised that the scheme of the five milliard bonds is unworkable and should be scrapped.

I think we should be prepared to listen to what the Germans have to say in criticism of our scheme of Reparation, and to modify it with a view to making it practicable and not crippling German industry irreparably in the next few years. Our policy should rather be to begin nursing German industry and finance in order to obtain heavy contributions from them when they have become productive.

In particular I think the coal demands we are making on Germany are too heavy, and must seriously cripple her industry. Three separate commissions have taken coal from Germany: one confiscated the Saar Basin, another cut off the Silesian coal fields, and the third laid heavy contributions on the Westphalian fields in favour of France, Belgium and Italy. The combined result of all this is a burden which it will probably be too heavy for German industry to bear. All this requires reconsideration, and would probably have received it but for the hurry in which the Treaty was finally put together from the various Commission Reports.

While sticking generally to our scheme of Reparation, I would eliminate the above objectionable or unworkable features, and in particular I would scrap the schedules dealing with the future delivery of coal and coal products, and the future construction of ships. I would give the Reparation Commission full power to settle not only the amount but also the form in which the payments are to be made (in money or kind). I would certainly take away the power from the French and Belgian manufacturers to rove about German factories in order to despoil them of machinery which they may allege to be necessary for their works (para. 4 of the Fourth Annex to Reparation Clauses). This industrial looting would be most mischievous, and could not in peace time be justified as a reprisal for crimes committed in war time. The proper reprisal is to make the Germans pay.

4. *Germany's Eastern Frontier.*

I am convinced that in the undue enlargement of Poland we are not only reversing the verdict of history, but committing a cardinal error in policy which history will yet avenge. The new Poland will include millions of Germans (and Russians) and territories which have a German (or Russian) population, or which have for very long

[1] He presumably referred to the Supreme Economic Council and, perhaps more especially, to its Financial Section.

periods been part of Germany (or Russia). It is reasonably certain that both Germany and Russia will again be great Powers, and that, sandwiched between them the new Poland could only be a success with their goodwill. How, under these circumstances, can we expect Poland to be other than a failure, even if she had that ruling and administrative capacity which history has proved she has not? Even now while the Conference is sitting, the Poles are defying the Great Powers. What is going to happen in future with the Great Powers divided and at loggerheads? I think we are building a house of sand. And in view of these and many other considerations, I would revise the boundaries of Poland as provisionally settled in the Treaty, leave Upper Silesia and all real German territory to Germany, contract the boundaries of the Free City of Danzig, and instead of placing her under the suzerainty of Poland as we propose doing, leave her under the suzerainty of Germany with an administration under the League of Nations. I think the two cardinal errors in policy of this Treaty are the long occupation of the Rhine, and the enlargement of Poland beyond anything which we had contemplated during the war. Those two errors are full of menace for the future peace of Europe, and I urge that every means be taken to remove them before it is too late. It is not yet too late. There is no doubt that the German Delegates are going to make a stiff fight, perhaps a condition for signature of the Treaty, that the settlement of their Eastern frontiers in Silesia, East and West Prussia should be revised. I would advise that we consider the case to be put forward by them most carefully on its merits.

5. *The Punishment Clauses.*

While I am all in favour of the policy laid down in the Punishment Clauses, I feel that for the German Government to agree to them as they stand must be almost, if not quite, impossible. An indefinite obligation to surrender *any* person whom *any* Ally might name, and actually to have to supply the evidence for his conviction, is more than any Government with a sense of honour and regard for its people could sign. The demand should be limited to a definite, reasonably short list of war criminals, whose position or whose crimes were really outstanding. And when the German press for such an amendment I hope we shall meet them fairly.

The above are the most important alterations which I would suggest to the Peace Treaty. There are, however, a number of other more or less important provisions to which I wish to draw attention.

6. *The Military and Air Clauses.*

I think we are doing wrong in trying to bind down Germany to a maximum army of 100,000 men. For a population so large, and in such a state of internal ferment, and with frontiers and neighbours such as Germany has, I think such a force totally inadequate for necessary police and defence purposes. It took us more than 100,000 men to maintain order in Ireland during the latter part of the war, and Germany's case is much more serious. We should be prepared to listen to the case which the German delegates may make on this matter.

I think it is also quite wrong to deprive her completely of tanks and military aircraft. These things have become part of the equipment of a properly organised army, and we should be prepared to leave her the necessary quota of tanks and aircraft for her small army. A similar argument applies to the airships and seaplanes necessary for her reduced Navy.

There is a provision that all aerodromes within 150 km. of the eastern, western and southern boundaries of Germany should be demolished. This is far too drastic, and indeed unnecessary, if not impracticable. The Treaty bristles with similar pinpricks which embody merely the whims of minor officials, and should not remain in the Treaty in its final form.

7. *International Rivers and Railways.*

While the internationalisation of the rivers and railways of Germany which provide outlets for the new States is perfectly sound in principle, the administration laid down for these rivers and railways is entirely indefensible. These rivers are to be administered by Boards which contain a small minority of German representatives, and this even in the case of rivers which are exclusively German. English, Italian, French, Scandinavian and Belgian representatives form a great majority in these Boards. It is as if the Thames Conservancy consisted almost entirely of representatives of foreign Governments! Principles are laid down for the fixing of rates over German railways which are almost unintelligible, and, so far as I understand them, unworkable. Generally most of the provisions in respect of German rivers and railways are hopelessly one-sided, and seem intended merely to bring the whole principle of internationalisation into disrepute. They require drastic revision. I would suggest that the principle laid down in the case of the Kiel Canal be generally followed. That is to say, the administration of these international rivers and railways in German territory should be German, but a right given to an aggrieved party to appeal to the League of Nations, who shall have power to appoint an administering Commission in a proper case.

8. *Pin-pricks.*

As I have said, the Treaty is full of small, comparatively unimportant provisions which serve no useful purpose, but must be unnecessarily galling and wounding to the feelings of a defeated enemy.

While making the Treaty as hard and stiff as Germany deserves after the manner of her warfare, we should be careful to eliminate from it all trace of petty spite and ill-feeling, which cannot serve so great a cause as ours, nor promote the interests of future goodwill and peace. I am for drastic revision of all such pin-pricks; they relate largely to the treatment of German nationals and German property and rights. But they are found in almost every chapter of the Treaty.

Procedure for Alterations.

I have set out what I think should be done with this Treaty. I add a few words as to the method which I think should be followed in the necessary revision.

I am very anxious, not only that the Germans should sign a fair and good Peace Treaty, but also that, for the sake of the future, they should not merely be made to sign at the point of the bayonet, so to speak. The Treaty should not be capable of moral repudiation by the German people hereafter. And for this purpose I consider it important that we should as far as possible carry the German Delegates with us, that we should listen to what they have to say, that we should give all necessary explanations to them, and that where our Clauses appear really untenable, we should be prepared to accept alterations or compromises. In order to do this, it will be necessary to meet them in oral discussion. And the suggestion I would make for this purpose is that a small Committee of minor delegates be appointed to meet the Germans after they have handed in their final note on the 29th May, and confer with them in regard to the Treaty as a whole. This Committee to make a report to the Supreme Council of the alterations they recommend after hearing the German side. In this way the Supreme Council will avoid direct negotiations with the German Delegates, but will have before them recommendations arrived at after full cognisance has been taken of the German case. Necessarily much will depend on the personnel of this Committee. I would suggest that it consist of three delegates, one nominated by the United States, the British Empire and France respectively. It is essential for rapid work that the Committee be as small as possible, and Italy and Japan are not sufficiently interested in the German Treaty to make it worth while overloading the Committee with two additional representatives. If the three Delegates are carefully selected, their work may be of first-class importance, not only in securing the necessary modifications in the Treaty, but in listening to and considering the German case, and thereby removing from the making of the peace all appearance of one-sidedness and unnecessary dictation. The moral authority of the Treaty will be all the greater and more binding on that account. And not only the enemy, but the public opinion of the world will accept it more readily as an honourable ending of the most awful and most tragic dispute in history. The final sanction of this great instrument must be the approval of mankind.

(Sd)   J. C. Smuts

CCL (WP, DLC).

From Joseph Patrick Tumulty

[The White House, 22 May, 1919.]

No. 138 Great demonstration New York City last night, addressed by Hughes, to protest against killings in Poland, Galicia, Roumania and elsewhere.[1] Feeling in this matter growing more intense throughout country. Cannot something be done?

It is evident that Germany is doing everything to separate the Allies. A great many newspapers in this country are worried lest you be carried away by the pleadings of Germany for a "softer peace." I know you will not be led astray.

There is an intense feeling in the Senate in favor of the publication of terms of the treaty. Can anything be done to straighten this out?   Tumulty.

T telegram (WP, DLC).
[1] A day of parades and demonstrations in New York to protest against the killing of Jews in Poland, Galicia, and Rumania culminated in a mass meeting in Madison Square Garden in the evening of May 21. Abram Isaac Elkus served as chairman of the meeting, and the speakers included Nathan Straus, Charles Evans Hughes, Jacob Henry Schiff, and Mayor John Francis Hylan. The audience included many Jewish veterans of the World War. For a description of the day's events and extracts from some of the speeches at the evening meeting, see the *New York Times*, May 22, 1919. See also L. Marshall to WW, May 26, 1919, n. 3.

From the Diary of Dr. Grayson

Friday, May 23, 1919.

The President arose early and after breakfast went for a short automobile ride before the meeting of the Big Four. Today's session was devoted to a discussion of the military conditions that are to be made a part of the Austrian peace terms. The question of the size of the Austrian Army that would be permitted under the Treaty was a knotty one inasmuch as it involved the question as to whether Austria should not be allowed a sufficient force to withstand any effort on the part of the Hungarian Bolshevists to invade the former Hapsburg Monarchy.

A map is in the President's room which is so large that they cannot hang it on the wall. So whenever it is necessary to consult the map they lay it down on the floor. The President wanted me yesterday morning, and when I entered the room I found the Big Four down on all fours studying this map. They were unable to stand up and examine it. It had every appearance of four boys playing some kind of a game.

The President, Mrs. Wilson, Miss Benham and I had lunch as usual. After luncheon the President held a conference with Charles R. Crane and Dr. King of Oberlin University, whom he had selected as the American members of the Inter-Allied Commission which is to be sent to Syria the first of next week to examine local conditions there on behalf of the Conference.

After the conference the President attended the meeting of the Big Four, when the Inter-Allied military chiefs, including General Bliss, the American representative, presented their views of the Austrian military situation.

At the conclusion of the Big Four meeting the President went for a brief automobile ride, returning in time for dinner, at which there were no guests. In the evening he played Canfield and retired early.

From the Diary of Edith Benham

May 23, 1919

I think I rather wrote myself out yesterday or the day before, for nothing much went on yesterday. The P. was quite amusing about the Big Four and the way they would look if photographed. They have had to use a huge map and there is no table large enough in the room to hold it when spread out, so it has to go on the floor and he says most of them spend their time on all fours poring over it. Yesterday he sat on a chair while L.G. and Clemenceau renewed again, but more amicably, their fight of the day before. He was a sort of umpire and he said it was fun to watch the two pointing out places on the map and one saying to the other, "You promised us this or that in Asia Minor for this thing or the other," and "I sat there quite out of sympathy or understanding, as I told them, of the bargaining away of peoples."

Hankey's Notes of a Meeting of the Council of Four[1]

President Wilson's House,
Paris, May 23, 1919, 11 a.m.

C.F.26.

1. M. CLEMENCEAU reported that he had received from Herr Brockdorff-Rantzau a letter on the subject of private property, dated May 22nd, 1919. (Appendix 1.)[2]

(It was agreed:

That this letter should be referred in the first instance to the Committee which has been advising the Council of the Principal Allied and Associated Powers on the subject of Reparation in connection with the Treaties of Peace with Austria and Hungary, who should be asked to draft a reply for consideration. See below, Minute 6, regarding the composition of this Committee.)

2. M. CLEMENCEAU said he had received a further note from Herr Brockdorff-Rantzau, dated May 22nd, 1919, on the subject of International Labour.[3] (Appendix II.)

(It was agreed:

That this letter should be referred in the first instance to the Committee which had dealt with the previous letter from the German Delegation on this subject, and which should be asked to draft a reply for the consideration of the Council of the Principal Allied and Associated Powers.)

3. M. CLEMENCEAU said he had reason to believe that the Japanese Government were about to propose to the Allied and Associated Governments the recognition of the Omsk Government. He thought that these Governments ought to anticipate them. He did not like to leave it to Japan to take the initiative.

PRESIDENT WILSON asked whether it was proposed to recognise this Government as representing all Russia, or merely as a local Government.

M. CLEMENCEAU replied as representing all Russia.

PRESIDENT WILSON said he could not do that.

MR. LLOYD GEORGE said he also was opposed to that. Mr. Kerr's draft despatch to the Russian *de facto* Government was ready, and he thought that it ought at once to be considered.

(It was agreed:

To discuss Mr. Kerr's draft letter in the afternoon.) . . .[4]

5. There was a short discussion on the subject of the military forces of Austria.

M. CLEMENCEAU said he thought the question was a very delicate one. He, himself, was prepared to come rather nearer than he had been to the views of President Wilson. In regard to the small States, there were two aspects, one financial and one political, apart from the military. The financial had been discussed yesterday. He was glad, however, that the report of the Reparation Committee had not been finally approved, and that it had been referred back for further drafting. He thought that the financial authorities had viewed it too much from a purely financial point of view and had not sufficiently taken political considerations into account. The question was really not disconnected from the question of the number of troops that small countries like Poland and Czecho-Slovakia should have. He agreed to a limitation of their armaments, but thought that they should not be reduced at once and too hastily.

PRESIDENT WILSON suggested the possibility that some gradual system of reduction might be introduced pending the solution of the Russian question, and that the reduction to the final figures might depend on the settlement of that question.[5]

(It was agreed:

To adjourn upstairs and discuss this question in the first instance with experts.)

6. Arising out of the previous discussion, M. CLEMENCEAU said he wished to add a further political element to the Reparation Committee.

MR. LLOYD GEORGE and PRESIDENT WILSON said they had no objection.

M. CLEMENCEAU proposed to add M. Loucheur and M. Tardieu.

MR. LLOYD GEORGE said that, in that case, he would add General Smuts and Mr. Keynes.

(It was agreed:

That the Committee appointed to advise the Council of the Principal Allied and Associated Powers on the question of Reparation with Austria, Hungary and Bulgaria should be composed as follows:

United States of America.	Mr. Norman H. Davis.
	Mr. B. M. Baruch.
	Mr. T. W. Lamont.
	Mr. J. F. Dulles.
	Mr. V. McCormick.
British Empire.	Lord Cunliffe.
	Lord Sumner.
	General Smuts.
	Mr. J. Keynes.
France.	M. Klotz.
	M. Loucheur.
	M. Tardieu.
	M. Jouasset.[6]
Italy.	M. Crespi.
	M. D'Amelio.)[7]

T MS (SDR, RG 256, 180.03401/26, DNA).

[1] The complete text of these minutes is printed in *PPC*, V, 861-72.

[2] U. K. C. von Brockdorff-Rantzau to G. Clemenceau, May 22, 1919, TCL (SDR, RG 256, 180.03401/26, DNA), printed in *ibid.*, pp. 865-69. The German delegation stated that it could not accept in principle the provisions in the preliminary peace treaty which dealt with German private property within the reach of the Allied and Associated governments, since they violated "the most elementary conceptions of a peace of Right." The

German delegation claimed that the entire matter involved questions of private law which ought to be excluded from considerations motivated by political power. In particular, the German delegation objected to the provisions of Articles 297 and 298 which stipulated that, whereas all Allied nationals would be entitled to full compensation from Germany for damages caused to them during the war by Germany's enemy alien laws, all measures taken against German private property in enemy countries during the war were to remain legally binding even after the signing of the treaty, and German nationals in enemy countries were denied any claim to compensation.

The articles further provided that, since the measures taken by the Allied and Associated powers during the war would not suffice to appropriate all available German property for the purpose of compensation, German property in the Allied and Associated countries could still be liquidated after the conclusion of peace and that "new war measures" could even be enacted to that effect. In addition, Articles 53, 121, and 260 stated that all German private property in territories to be ceded by Germany and in the former German colonies, as well as in Russia, China, Austria, Bulgaria, and Turkey, would be subject to confiscation.

In its criticism of these provisions, the German delegation argued that, if the proposed actions taken against private property were to be undertaken, the principles of public law underlying them should apply to both parties. Moreover, such actions should involve only those measures actually adopted during the war. All measures of this kind taken after the Armistice were clearly illegal, and to continue them after the conclusion of peace would, in fact, mean a perpetuation of economic warfare.

Brockdorff-Rantzau's letter then claimed that the proposed expropriation of German property abroad would amount to such an extensive confiscation that it would undermine the fundamental principles of international law which guaranteed the inviolability of private property whose legitimacy had been expressly acknowledged by both the highest British and German courts during the war.

However, the German note continued, Germany recognized that, due to the burden on its future economic life resulting from the peace treaty, German property abroad could not be "maintained in its former extent." Thus, in order to discharge her financial obligations, Germany was prepared to sacrifice this property in a large measure but had to insist that its disposal be regulated according to international legal principles. The German delegation was confident that a compromise could be found if the Allies would acknowledge the principle of reciprocity and were willing to have the other issues discussed directly between the experts of both sides.

³ U. K. C. von Brockdorff-Rantzau to G. Clemenceau, May 22, 1919, TCL (SDR, RG 256, 180.03401/26, DNA), printed in *ibid.*, pp. 869-72. In this comment on the reply of the Allied and Associated governments of May 14, 1919 (see n. 5 to the minutes of the Council of Four printed at May 14, 1919, 12:15 p.m.) to the German note on international labor legislation of May 10, 1919 (see n. 2 to the minutes of the Council of Four printed at May 12, 1919, 11 a.m.), the German delegation affirmed its opposition to the proposed treaty's provisions for an international labor organization. It repeated its previous demand for the convocation of an international labor conference at Versailles as part of the peace negotiations in order to enable the representatives of the workers of all countries to vote on the issues concerning them and to reconcile the labor provisions of the peace treaty with the proposals of the German government and the resolutions adopted by the International Trade Unions Conference in Bern in February 1919. The labor conference planned by the Allies to be held in Washington in October 1919, the German note continued, could be no substitute for an immediate discussion, since any future conference would be based entirely on the terms embodied in the peace treaty, which differed from the demands of the Bern Conference in two essential aspects: the proposed treaty's terms gave at most only one fourth, instead of one half, of the total votes to the representatives of the workers; and they failed to make resolutions adopted by the international labor conference legally binding on all member states. Should the Allied and Associated governments again reject the request for an immediate conference, Brockdorff-Rantzau's letter concluded, it was necessary at least to seek the opinions of the labor unions of all countries and to assure that they approved the labor provisions of the treaty.

⁴ Here follows a discussion of the future of the Grand Duchy of Luxembourg. It was agreed that the Council of Four should enter into direct negotiations with the government of Luxembourg.

⁵ Mantoux, II, 181: "There is in that part of the world an unknown factor: it is Russia. Can we not say that, wherever this factor can make itself felt, military forces could be maintained sufficient to guard against any eventuality?"

⁶ Georges Jouasset, Inspector of Finance and financial expert in the French delegation.

⁷ Mariano d'Amelio, Counselor to the Court of Cassation and adviser on legal questions in the Italian delegation.

Hankey's Notes of a Meeting of the Council of Four[1]

President Wilson's House,
Paris, May 23, 1919, 11:30 a.m.

C.F.27.

1. PRESIDENT WILSON pointed out that the draft clauses of the Treaty of Peace with Austria, referring to Prisoners of War (Annex A)[2] had been drawn up on the same lines as the corresponding clauses of the Treaty of Peace with Germany.

The clauses in question referred only to the release of prisoners belonging to Austria proper. For good and sufficient reasons, no reference had been made to those prisoners who were nationals of territories which had belonged to the former Austro-Hungarian Monarchy, such as Czecho-Slovakia, Jugo-Slavia, and Austrian Poland. The Prisoners of War Commission had, however, in their report to the Supreme Council embodied a definite proposal, which read as follows:

"Austro-Hungarian prisoners of war, and interned civilians who were nationals of territories which belonged to the former Austro-Hungarian Monarchy, and which are to be allotted to Allied and Associated States shall be set at liberty forthwith. All necessary facilities shall be given by the Allied and Associated States to delegates of the Legations and Consulates of new States, in order that they may enter into direct communication with their nationals who are prisoners of war or interned civilians and may facilitate and accelerate their repatriation."

M. CAHEN[3] said he would read the following statement, which expressed the views of the Prisoners of War Commission on this point:

"The Commission thought that the question thus raised was of the greatest interest, and discussed it at length. The question is indeed nothing less than that of deciding the fate of prisoners and interned civilians who were nationals of the former Austro-Hungarian Empire; should this question form the subject of a special stipulation in the Treaty of Peace concluded with the new Austrian State, or on the other hand, since it is a question of interallied interests, should any general decision be deferred and the Allied and Associated Governments be left to deal with the question in due season and to settle it by special agreements?

In view of the fact that, according to instructions received by the Italian Delegation, the Commission was only appointed to

---

[1] The full text of Hankey's minutes, including all appendices and annexes (which are not reproduced here), is printed in PPC, V, 873-98.
[2] Printed in ibid., pp. 882-85.
[3] That is, Georges Joseph Ernest Cahen-Salvador, director of the General Service of Prisoners of War in the French Ministry of War and president of the Commission on Prisoners of War.

study conditions to be inserted in the Treaty of Peace with the new Austrian State, concerning the repatriation of prisoners of war who were subjects of that State, the Italian Delegation was of opinion that the Commission was not competent to accept the amendment proposed by the Serbian Delegation. That amendment dealt with a question which was not of direct interest to the new Austria and which must be decided by direct arrangement between the Governments concerned.

It therefore thought that the Commission could express no opinion on the said amendment and must confine itself to transmitting it direct to the Governments of the principal Allied and Associated Powers through their delegates on the Commission.

The Italian Delegation, for its part, was willing to transmit the amendment to the Italian Government.

The majority of the Commission considered, on the contrary that as it was instructed to determine the date and method of repatriation of enemy prisoners of war, it was not justified in indifference to the fate of nationals of Allied and Associated countries retained in captivity.

While doubtless holding that the Treaty of Peace regulating relations with the new Austrian State should not include special stipulations with regard to the liberation of Czecho-Slovaks, Jugo-Slavs, Poles and Transylvanians, the Commission considered it inadmissible that Austrian prisoners should be repatriated unless Czecho-Slovaks, Jugo-Slavs, Poles and Transylvanians were certain of benefiting in the same way.

It therefore deemed it essential to call the attention of the Supreme Council to the necessity and urgency of a general decision, common to all the Allied and Associated Powers, in favour of all prisoners captured in the ranks of the Austro-Hungarian armies, and who no longer belong to the Austrian State. The insertion of such a clause in the text would moreover have caused the postponement of its application until the Treaty came into force. While recommending it to the favourable consideration of the Supreme Council, the majority of the Commission thought that the decision was not inseparable from the Treaty of Peace and might even precede it.

This decision, which is claimed as an act of justice and impatiently awaited, will when backed by the authority enjoyed by the resolutions of the Supreme Council, ensure the immediate release of prisoners who were nationals of the former Austro-Hungarian Monarchy and have become nationals of new Allied and Associated States."

M. ORLANDO said that the members of the Prisoners of War Com-

mission were unanimously agreed that the question under reference did not directly concern the Treaty of Peace with Austria. In his
opinion, the question would have to be considered from two points
of view, namely, from the point of view of fact and from the point of
view of right.

In regard to the question of fact, Italy had not been in any way be-
hindhand in according special treatment to the prisoners of war and
interned civilians in question. Nearly the whole of the Czechs, some
40,000, had already been liberated. Similarly, Poles, Roumanians of
Transylvania, and even Jugo-Slavs, had also been liberated. The
prisoners of war who were nationals of territories which had belonged to the late Austro-Hungarian Monarchy, still remaining in Italy, had been concentrated in special camps, where they enjoyed
special treatment. A very much larger number would already have
been liberated; but at the present moment very great difficulties existed in regard to transportation. The policy of the Italian Government was to send home as many of these people as possible. From
the point of view of fact, therefore, the Italian Government had already taken steps to give effect to the recommendations of the Commission. Moreover, it would continue the repatriation of these prisoners as quickly as the existing transportation conditions permitted.

In the second place, in regard to the question of right, a difficulty
at once arose since the repatriation of prisoners of war was dependent upon the conclusion of peace. Naturally, as soon as Peace was
concluded all prisoners of war would be set free. Consequently, the
problem resolved itself into one of deciding at what particular moment peace could be considered to have been concluded with the
new States of Jugo-Slavia, Czecho-Slovakia, Poland, etc. In regard
to the territories included in Austria proper, and in Hungary, a separate Peace would be signed, and from that moment the prisoners of
war belonging to these territories would be repatriated. But in regard to the new States which previously had formed part of the Austro-Hungarian Monarchy, peace would in his opinion exist only
when these territories had been finally delimited, and at that moment the prisoners would by right be released. That being the case,
he could not accept the resolution of the Commission, wherein it
was laid down that all Austro-Hungarian Prisoners of War and interned civilians who were nationals of territories which belonged to
the former Austro-Hungarian monarchy should be set at liberty
forthwith. In the first place he could not accept such a legal international obligation, before Peace had been declared. Furthermore,
it would as a matter of fact be impossible for him to comply with
such a resolution because until the frontiers were determined it
would be impossible to know to what particular country a prisoner

of war in reality belonged, that is, it would be impossible to say whether he was a friend or a foe. For instance, in the case of an inhabitant of the Banat, or of Galicia, it would be impossible to say whether he was to be considered a Roumanian or a Hungarian, or something else.

To sum up, in regard to the question of fact, Italy had already set free a large number of the Austro-Hungarian Prisoners of war and interned civilians, who were nationals of territories which belonged to the former Austro-Hungarian Monarchy, within the limits possible under existing transportation facilities. And, in regard to the question of right, he felt unable to accept any formal obligation, as no nation could be compelled to free all prisoners until peace was signed.

Under those circumstances, he thought that no formal decision should be taken on this question. Should his colleagues, however, favour the acceptance of the draft clauses proposed by the Commission, the matter should be discussed solely from a political point of view.

PRESIDENT WILSON expressed the view that the prisoners of war in question should be liberated as soon as possible, whether they were by right entitled to repatriation or not.

M. ORLANDO replied that that was exactly what Italy had been doing. In other words, he was prepared to accept the principle involved in the recommendation made by the Commission; but he could not accept a formal obligation.

PRESIDENT WILSON thought that if after liberating the prisoners that belonged to Austria proper, any of the Allied powers should continue to detain prisoners which belonged to other parts of the former Austro-Hungarian Monarchy, the impression would be created that States which were friendly were being treated more harshly than enemy States, and the situation in Southern Europe would thereby be still further complicated.

M. ORLANDO thought that the hypothesis put forward by President Wilson was an impossible one. He assured the Council that as far as Italy was concerned, the moment the nationals of Austria proper were liberated, the nationals of all those other territories which had belonged to the former Austro-Hungarian Monarchy would obviously also be set free. On the other hand, he could not possibly take a formal obligation to release *forthwith* all prisoners of war at present interned in Italy. That was the only engagement which he could not accept.

PRESIDENT WILSON thought that the Allied and Associated Governments need only be required at the present moment to accept the policy without taking any definite formal obligation.

M. ORLANDO said that under these circumstances he accepted the proposal. He would do his best to liberate as many of the prisoners of war as possible. The present difficulty lay wholly in want of transport.

(The Supreme Council approved the articles relating to prisoners of war to be inserted in the conditions of Peace with Austria. (Appendix A.) The Heads of the Governments further agreed that all prisoners of war who were formerly nationals of the Austro-Hungarian monarchy and have now become nationals of an allied or associated country must be liberated immediately, subject to the possibilities of transportation and the final settlement of the frontiers of the new states. In any case they should not be liberated later than the prisoners of war who are nationals of the new Austrian state.)

2. PRESIDENT WILSON said that the Military representatives of the Supreme War Council at Versailles had submitted, in accordance with the resolution taken by the Supreme Council of the Allied and Associated Powers on the 15th May, 1919, a report on the strength of the Armies to be allowed for Austria, Hungary, Bulgaria, Czecho-Slovakia, Jugo-Slavia, Roumania, Poland, and Greece. (Appendix B.)[4]

M. ORLANDO suggested that the Military representatives present should be asked to make a reasoned statement, showing the grounds for their recommendations.

MR. LLOYD GEORGE expressed the view that the reasons for the recommendations made by the military representatives were set forth very clearly in the Report, which had been circulated. He thought the report in question gave a very good summary of the arguments relating to difficulties of the question.

PRESIDENT WILSON called on General Bliss to make a statement.

GENERAL BLISS stated that the original draft of the Military Clauses for insertion in the Conditions of Peace with Austria had been prepared by the Military Representatives, Versailles, during his unavoidable absence. On his return to Versailles, he had found that the draft submitted by the Military Representatives had already received consideration by the Supreme Council, which had decided to return the same to the Military Representatives for modification along certain fixed lines. As a result of a careful study of the labours of his colleagues, he wished to state that he accepted without qualification their conclusions. The figures originally arrived at by the Military Representatives were necessarily based almost entirely on

---

[4] Printed in *PPC*, V, 885-91.

military considerations. He fully realised, however, that in the end
the question must be, and would be, settled chiefly on political
grounds. In studying the question, the Military Representatives had
given full value to all connected questions such as the population of
the territories; the character of the territory; the frontiers and the relation between land and maritime frontiers; the character of the local industries (e.g. whether chiefly agricultural or industrial); the
general character of the population; the existence of large cities and
so forth. Each of the Military Representatives working independently had formed his own estimates. These had naturally differed to
a certain extent in details; but the results reached had been practically the same.

He fully realised that the Supreme Council was bound by its decision in regard to the strength of the military forces to be allowed to
Germany; and on that account the Military Representatives had received definite instructions to take the German figures as a proportional standard in fixing the forces to be allowed to Austria-Hungary, Czecho-Slovakia, Yugo-Slavia, Roumania, Poland, Bulgaria
and Greece. He felt that it might be somewhat hackneyed to re-state
the fact that the figures accepted for Germany had not been based
on military advice. The Military Committee, presided over by Marshal Foch, had originally been unanimous in recommending to the
Supreme Council that a total force of 200,000 men should be allowed to Germany: the whole force to be raised by conscription. The
recommendation of the Military Committee had been referred back
by the Supreme Council, with instructions that a system of voluntary enlistment should be substituted for the compulsory system
proposed. In consequence, the Committee had recommended that
the total number of effectives and reservists in the army, to be organised on a basis of a long term compulsory service, should not exceed 140,000. The French Representatives, whilst accepting this
figure, expressed a strong recommendation that it should be reduced from 140,000 to 100,000 effectives. When the question again
came under the consideration of the Supreme Council, the British
Prime Minister had made some very carefully considered remarks
which indicated a reluctant dissent from the views of his military advisers. He laid great stress on the apprehension of a renewed attack
by Germany which existed in France; he believed that this apprehension was a factor that must be taken into account, and in consequence he proposed that the Council should accept the figure recommended by the French representatives, and that the force should
be brought down to 100,000 effectives. He (General Bliss) had never
heard an argument which convinced him that the figure 100,000

was correct from a military point of view, and he personally could not bring himself to relinquish his military judgment except as the result of convincing argument.

Finally, when the whole question was referred back to the Military Representatives on the 15th May last with a mandate that the force for Austria should not exceed 15,000 men, the case appealed to him in the following way. An intelligent survey of the situation in Central and Southern Europe would inevitably justify the anticipation that considerable trouble must in the near future arise in those regions, especially as a result of the application of the Peace Conditions. Now, should the Allied and Associated Governments prevent those States from maintaining a sufficient force for the maintenance of order, who would be responsible for doing the work? The total strength of the forces to be maintained by Austria as originally recommended by the Military Representatives for military reasons was much less than the force which even the weakest of the Entente Powers proposed to maintain. In his opinion, the strength of the forces recommended by the Military Representatives was exceedingly small for the purpose of maintaining order in those turbulent regions. He fully acknowledged that eventually the question would have to be settled chiefly from political considerations, but he felt very strongly that by radically reducing the forces of Austria-Hungary, Czecho-Slovakia, Jugo-Slavia, Roumania, Bulgaria and Greece, as proposed, those States would be converted into mere vassals of the two Continental Powers of the Entente. Should disorders then occur, and the States be unable to cope with the same through want of forces, the inevitable result would be that stronger armies would have to be maintained by France and Italy, following in the occupation from time to time of the territories in question for the purpose of quelling disorders. He did not think that such a situation pointed to the maintenance of the Peace of Europe in the future. The Council no doubt realised the danger of future combinations between Germanic, Slavonic and Asiatic races, which might eventually sweep the civilization of Western Europe out of the way. He personally had never believed in the possibility of the extinction of all traces of Anglo-Latin civilization from Western Europe, but he thought that by eliminating the possibility of the maintenance of order in Central and Southern Europe, the Council were formulating a possible scheme to bring this about. The brilliancy of the military glory which now lightened up certain of these Western nations of Europe might in reality not be an evidence of health but only the hectic flush of disease which would eventually result in the downfall of our strip of Latin and Anglo-Saxon civilization along the Western coast of Europe.

In conclusion, he wished to lay stress on the fact that the acceptance of the figures based on the instructions issued by the Supreme Council would inevitably reduce these States to a condition of vassalage to the Western Powers of the Entente.

MR. LLOYD GEORGE asked General Bliss to state his proposal.

GENERAL BLISS replied that his suggestion was that the Council should accept the figures recommended by the Military Representatives.

PRESIDENT WILSON said that it had been assumed that the Supreme Council had instructed the Military Representatives to act on the basis of 15,000 effectives for Austria. He himself had never agreed to that figure and, in fact, he had suggested 20,000. The considerations which General Bliss had urged were, he thought, very serious and large, and required to be very carefully considered. In his opinion, the Supreme Council could not proceed to accept or alter the figure off-hand. He proposed, therefore, that this question should be reserved for discussion from a political point of view.

M. CLEMENCEAU associated himself with what President Wilson had said. He would ask, however, that a copy of General Bliss' speech be circulated so that each of the members of the Supreme Council might have his remarks before them.[5]

M. ORLANDO agreed. He added that General Bliss' speech had made a considerable impression on him.

MR. LLOYD GEORGE thought that without doubt the Supreme Council would very shortly receive from Germany some protest in regard to the strength of the authorised forces, which had been fixed at 100,000 men. In his opinion, the Germans would never accept that figure. At the present moment, he personally was disposed to agree with General Bliss' statement that 100,000 men would be an inadequate force for Germany. He had originally accepted that figure as a compromise in view of the fact that Marshal Foch had pressed the matter. The French were the nearest neighbours to Germany, and he thought that their wishes should as far as possible be conceded. He felt certain, however, that the Supreme Council would receive within the next two or three days the German view of the matter. He thought, therefore, that it would be best to consider the problem from the point of view of Germany, Austria, Hungary, and the other States as a whole. He did not think it possible to take Austria and Hungary separately.

PRESIDENT WILSON invited attention to the following statement which occurred in the Report of the Military Representatives, namely:

[5] A separate T MS of Bliss' remarks is in WP, DLC.

"On their Eastern frontier these two nations, Poland and Roumania, are in contact with Bolshevist Russia. Not only are they themselves directly menaced by this, but they in fact constitute a barrier which defends Europe against Bolshevism. They must therefore be left in a condition to continue war against the Russian Maximalists with all possible means at their disposal. It is indispensable that Poland and Roumania should be authorised to keep all their forces mobilised under the control of the League of Nations until the Russian question is definitely settled."

MR. LLOYD GEORGE adhered to his statement that the question of the strength of the armies to be allowed for Austria, Hungary, Bulgaria, Czecho-Slovakia, Yugo-Slavia, Roumania, Poland and Greece, must be considered as a whole. Should Czecho-Slovakia be allowed to raise a conscript army without limitations, she would have an army of 1¼ millions as compared to the army of 100,000 allowed to Germany. In his opinion, it was quite impossible to restrict Germany without at the same time restricting the other countries; otherwise Germany would be forced into an offensive alliance with the Balkan States aimed at the Western Powers. In this connection, he had been greatly impressed by the remark made by General Bliss in the course of his statement, in regard to the possible formation of a Germano-Slav alliance.

(It was agreed to adjourn the further consideration of the Military Clauses of the Conditions of Peace with Austria.)

MR. LLOYD GEORGE said that the only question in regard to the Naval Clauses, which called for a decision, related to the following reservation made by Admiral Benson, the American Representative:

"That the Naval Terms should contain no prohibition against the manufacture within the limits of States formerly a part of the Austro-Hungarian Empire of naval war material on foreign order."

In his opinion, the matter was a very small one, and he personally was quite indifferent as to the inclusion or exclusion of the condition in question.

PRESIDENT WILSON said that at the last Meeting he had been under the impression that the point raised was a very serious one. Since then he had consulted his experts, and he agreed that the question was one of only slight importance. On the other hand, he doubted whether it was worth while to include in the Conditions of Peace, clauses which were of no real importance. On this account he proposed that the condition in question should be omitted.

(It was agreed that the Naval Terms should contain no prohibition against the manufacture within the limits of States formerly a part of the Austro-Hungarian Empire of naval war material on foreign order

Note:

This entails the deletion of paragraph 2 of Article 25.

The Naval Clauses, as amended, were adopted. For text see Appendix C.)[6]

(The Air Clauses were adopted without amendment. For text see Appendix D.)[7]

(The Clauses dealing with Inter-allied Commission of Control, and the general clauses were adopted without amendment. See Appendix E and F.)[8]

(The Meeting then adjourned.)

T MS (SDR, RG 256, 180.03401/27, DNA).

[6] Printed in *PPC*, V, 891-92.
[7] *Ibid.*, pp. 892-95.
[8] *Ibid.*, pp. 895-98.

Hankey's Notes of a Meeting of the Council of Four[1]

President Wilson's House,

C.F.28.   Paris, May 23, 1919, 4:00 p.m.

1. MR. LLOYD GEORGE read a communication which had been circulated by the Secretary-General from Marshal Foch, the gist of which was that the Germans would not sign a peace of violence, and were preparing a new war, especially against the Poles; that negotiations had been carried on with the Soviet with satisfactory results; and that German non-commissioned officers, who had volunteered to help the Bolshevists, would be collected at Königsberg. (W.C.P. 838.)

He also read a telegram he had just received from Cologne, where the British representative had had an interview with the Burgomaster[2] just returned from Berlin. The trend of this information was that the German Government would refuse to sign the terms, but that after the advance, the hopelessness of the situation would be realised, and peace would be signed under protest.

2. M. CLEMENCEAU handed to M. Mantoux, who read it, an interview between the French General Desticker[3] and Dr. Heim,[4] the Ba-

[1] The complete text of these minutes is printed in *PPC*, V, 899-911.
[2] Konrad Adenauer, Lord Mayor of Cologne.
[3] Col. Pierre Henri Desticker, assistant chief of staff to Marshal Foch and one of Foch's closest advisers.
[4] That is, Dr. Georg Heim, about whom see n. 2 to the minutes of the Council of Four printed at April 12, 1919, 11 a.m., Vol. 57. For a discussion of the efforts by Heim and his Bavarian People's party to establish a postwar Bavaria free from Prussian dominance by pursuing a federalist, particularist, and, on occasion, openly separatist policy, see Allan Mitchell, *Revolution in Bavaria, 1918-1919: The Eisner Regime and the Soviet Republic* (Princeton, N. J., 1965), pp. 190-92, and Karl Schwend, *Bayern zwischen Monarchie und Diktatur* (Munich, 1954), pp. 58-68.

varian Deputy, which took place at Luxemberg on 19th May, 1919, in the course of which, Dr. Heim urged that the tendency of the Treaty of Peace was to assist the domination of North Germany, which was Protestant and Socialistic, and dangerous, instead of promoting what he urged would be a better policy, namely, the formation of a separate Catholic, and consequently Anti-Bolshevik Confederacy in South Germany.[5] (Appendix 1.)[6]

3. (The Naval Clauses for inclusion in the Treaty of Peace were initialled.

Sir Maurice Hankey was instructed to forward them to the Secretary-General, for the information of the Drafting Committee of the Peace Conference.)

4. M. CLEMENCEAU said that he had information that Italian public opinion was very bitter against France. It was a fact, the reasons of which he did not wish to discuss. M. Barrère, the French Ambassador at Rome, who was notoriously a firm friend of Italy, had sent him very unpleasant despatches within the last few days. The Marseillaise had been whistled down in Turin, and officers insulted in other places. M. Barrère had made representations to the Italian Government, and suggested that they ought to interfere, in order to stop the storm of abuse in the Press. Today, M. Barrère reported that French officers had been so seriously insulted at Milan that they ought no longer to be left there. There were altogether 1,200 French soldiers at Milan. M. Clemenceau had asked the French War Office if they could not be withdrawn, and had received the reply that Milan was the base of the French troops in Italy, and if the base was withdrawn, the whole of the troops must be withdrawn also. He did not like to do this without consulting M. Orlando. He felt it was dan-

[5] Mantoux, II, 187-88: "Clemenceau. . . . I also have a communication to impart to you. General Desticker saw Dr. Heim at Spa, that Bavarian deputy of whom we have already spoken. The General gives me an account of their conversation.

"M. Clemenceau reads the report aloud: Dr. Heim advocates the division of Germany into two states. Southwestern Germany, which would include Austria, with a Catholic majority, is the only force which can resist anarchical tendencies.

"Concerning reparations, Dr. Heim thinks that the Allies are harboring illusions about what they will be able to obtain from Germany, because the conditions imposed upon that country will halt its productive power.

"Wilson. It is a remarkable document. Like Count Brockdorff, Dr. Heim claims that, if Germany does not keep everything currently produces on her own soil, all her industries will shut down. It is a difficult argument to sustain.

"Lloyd George. I received a telegram relating a conversation with the Mayor of Cologne. Scheidemann, whom he saw recently, has decided to let the Allies renew the offensive and then to sign, after a protest.

"One would say that Germany is going to fall to pieces. That would mean that our conditions will not be executed; on the other hand, Germany would be significantly weakened. We have to choose between these two alternatives.

"Clemenceau. If Germany dissolves, I will do nothing to prevent it.

"Lloyd George. I think that, under these conditions, Bavaria will not remain with Germany. It is possible that we may have a decision to take on this subject."

[6] A translation from the French is printed in PPC, V, 906-909.

gerous to withdraw, because it would indicate a separation between France and Italy. On the other hand, if he did not withdraw, there was the risk of a very serious incident. He could not take the responsibility of risking such trouble. Today, there was to be a solemn demonstration in the French Chamber and Senate to celebrate the fourth anniversary of Italy's entry into the war. This had the full approval and support of the French Government. It was at this very moment that these insults to French officers were taking place. He did not accuse the Italian Government, as he knew that M. Orlando had no part in the matter.

M. ORLANDO said he greatly regretted that he could not deny that the state of feeling in Italy was one that gave cause for anxiety. There were signs of exasperation, partly due to war weariness, and partly to anxiety created by the fact that the questions most interesting to Italy had not yet been settled, and the people could see no way out. Hence, there was a certain mania that Italy was being persecuted. The Government, of course, had nothing to do with these movements, which had latterly been turned against the Italian Government itself. This was the reason of his recent journey to meet his colleagues. On this occasion, he had been told that the situation within the last few days was somewhat better, and that there was a certain calm. He had, at M. Clemenceau's request, made enquiries about the alleged incident at Genoa, and had been told by the Prefect that there was nothing in the allegation. This was the first he had heard of these latter incidents, and he had not heard of M. Barrère's representations to the Italian Government. He was informed by Count Aldrovandi that no despatch on the subject had come from the Italian Foreign Office.

M. CLEMENCEAU said that M. Barrère had mentioned the probability that this information might have been kept at Rome, and had asked M. Clemenceau to speak to M. Orlando about it.

M. ORLANDO said he would make enquiry, and give a reply at once. He learned of these incidents with the greatest sorrow and regret.

M. CLEMENCEAU asked that no time might be lost, as he ought to take away the troops at once, if there was not to be a serious incident. In reply to Mr. Lloyd George, he said that he saw no particular object in leaving the French troops in Italy, except that the moment was inopportune to take them away. It would also involve the withdrawal of the two Italian divisions from France.

M. ORLANDO said that he believed there was only one brigade of French troops and one brigade of British troops now in Italy.

5. (Mr. Philip Kerr entered.)

PRESIDENT WILSON, at the request of his colleagues, read the attached draft despatch to Admiral Koltchak, prepared by Mr. Kerr, at the request of the Council. (Appendix II.) President Wilson expressed doubts as to whether the memorandum would be acceptable to General Denikin and M. Tchaikowsky.

MR. KERR said that both these de facto Governments had recognised Admiral Koltchak as the central Government of Russia.

MR. LLOYD GEORGE suggested that a copy of the despatch might be sent to General Denikin and to the Archangel Government.

M. CLEMENCEAU objected to the proposed abolition of conscription as one of the conditions.

M. ORLANDO agreed.

PRESIDENT WILSON said that although he had been in favour of it, he regretted that the Covenant of the League of Nations had not abolished conscription.

MR. LLOYD GEORGE said that he did not wish to press the use of these particular words in this document, but he was convinced that somehow or other, conscription must be got rid of in Russia. Otherwise, he was apprehensive lest Russia might raise six millions of soldiers and, sooner or later, Russia might come into the German orbit.

PRESIDENT WILSON asked if Mr. Kerr was sure about the alleged declaration by Admiral Koltchak, recognising Russia's debt as an obligation.

MR. KERR then read the following telegram from Mr. Kliotchnikoff[7] to the Ambassador in Paris:[8]

November 27th, 1918.

Please communicate the following to the Government to which you are accredited:

"The Russian Government at the head of which stands Admiral Koltchak remembering that Russia always kept all her obligations towards her own people as well as other nations to which it was bound by conventions, presumes it necessary to announce in a special declaration that it accepts all obligations incumbing to the Treasury and will fulfill them in due time when Russia's unity will be again achieved. These obligations are the following: Payments of interests, redemption of inner State debts, payments for contracts, wages, pensions and other payments due by law, and other conventions. The Government declares at the same time all financial acts promoted by the Soviet Powers as null and void, being acts edicted by mutineers."

PRESIDENT WILSON observed that Lenin's suggestion, that the Russian debt was our principal pre-occupation, had been resented.[9]

---

[7] Iurii Veniaminovich Kliuchnikov, Acting Foreign Minister of the Kolchak government.

[8] That is, Vasilii Alekseevich Maklakov.

[9] Mantoux, II, 190-91: "Wilson. Recognition of the Russian debt is mentioned in this

MR. LLOYD GEORGE pointed out that in this draft, it was only mentioned that Koltchak had made this statement, but it was not made a condition.

M. CLEMENCEAU again earnestly asked that the reference to the abolition of conscription might be removed.

PRESIDENT WILSON asked if recognition of Admiral Koltchak depended on the conditions laid down in the despatch.

MR. KERR replied that it did not. Acceptance of these proposals was a condition of the continuation of assistance and no mention was made of recognition.

PRESIDENT WILSON pointed out that the versions which had previously been suggested, insisted not only on the free election of the Central Legislature, but also of regional bodies, for example, in the territory administered by Koltchak, Denikin and the Archangel Government.

MR. LLOYD GEORGE said that para. 2 went as far in this direction as was now possible. To ask the Russian groups to hold elections in the middle of a war, when great confusion must prevail, would be to ask too much.

PRESIDENT WILSON suggested the substitution of the words "to promote elections" instead of "to permit elections."

MR. LLOYD GEORGE asked whether this was fair. Koltchak had latterly made a very big advance and there must be considerable confusion in his rear. In these circumstances, he could not fairly be asked to promote an election. It had not been found possible to hold an election even in the United Kingdom during the war. Much less was it possible in France or in Italy. In Russia a Constituent Assembly had been elected within the last two years or so by universal suffrage, and had only been got rid of by the Bolshevists, because it was not sufficiently extreme. Nevertheless, it had been a thoroughly democratic body.

M. CLEMENCEAU said Russia should be allowed to choose.

MR. LLOYD GEORGE pointed out that the memorandum permitted this. It provided that if an election could not be held, the Constituent Assembly should be summoned when Koltchak reached Moscow.

PRESIDENT WILSON pointed out that the memorandum could only with complete truth be applied to the British Government, which, he believed, alone had supplied Russia with munitions etc. The United States had only supplied the Czechs, but this supply had stopped. They had not furnished supplies to Koltchak.

M. CLEMENCEAU thought that France had sent very little, mainly

message. When Lenin made us an offer of this kind, we reproached him for it as a maneuver whose purpose was to show that the bourgeois governments were ready to recognize any regime, provided that it guaranteed the payment of coupons."

because Great Britain had to supply the shipping. He would like to make enquiries on this.

PRESIDENT WILSON suggested that the declaration might be made by the British Government only, since they alone were literally in a position to make this declaration, but it should be made with the avowed approval of the Associated Powers.

MR. LLOYD GEORGE suggested that the difficulty might be surmounted by stating in the text that it was the British Government that had supplied more than £50,000,000 worth of munitions.[10]

PRESIDENT WILSON explained that he was in an awkward situation. The British and French Governments had both dealt with Koltchak as a de facto, though not as a de jure Government. Meanwhile, the United States had looked on, and had only helped to guard the railway which was under an International Commission, of which an American engineer was President.[11] His position, therefore, was very anomalous. He would like to consult Mr. Lansing on the subject of how the United States could associate themselves in this declaration without getting into a still more anomalous position.

M. CLEMENCEAU said he would like time to consult M. Pichon. He again raised the question of the inclusion of the abolition of conscription among the conditions which he asked should be removed.

PRESIDENT WILSON suggested the phrase "limitation of armaments and of military organization."

M. CLEMENCEAU said he would accept that.

M. ORLANDO also accepted.

MR. LLOYD GEORGE agreed to make this alteration in Mr. Kerr's draft.

(The subject was adjourned for further consideration.)

6. (It was agreed that the Commission on the International Regime of Ports, Waterways, and Railways should be asked to prepare for consideration, clauses for insertion in the Treaty with Bulgaria.) Sir Maurice Hankey was instructed to notify the Secretary-General of this decision.

PRESIDENT WILSON said that he had instructed the representatives of the United States of America on the various Commissions, that as the United States of America was not technically at war with Bulgaria, strictly speaking, the American representatives ought not to sign the Treaty of Peace with that country. Since, however,

---

[10] Mantoux, II, 192: "Lloyd George. The text says that Great Britain has furnished fifty million pounds sterling in arms, war matériel, and provisions to the anti-Bolshevik governments. There are people at home who will not like this sentence; but it states the facts."

[11] That is, John Frank Stevens, president of the Inter-Allied Technical Board supervising the Trans-Siberian Railway.

through the operation of the League of Nations Covenant, which he presumed would be included in this Treaty, the United States became in some degree a guarantor of the results of the Treaty, the American plenipotentiaries would be entitled to sign, and on this understanding the experts had been authorised to take part in the various enquiries.

7. PRESIDENT WILSON drew attention to the statement made by General Bliss at the morning meeting, which seemed to him to carry considerable weight.

M. CLEMENCEAU agreed, but pointed out that it only affected one side of the question.

MR. LLOYD GEORGE urged that the Great Powers should not allow the small States to use them as catspaws for their miserable ambitions. Prussia had begun just as these States were beginning, and at that time, had not a population as large as Jugo-Slavia. Peace had to be made with Austria. Were we to say that Austria was only to have a few thousand men and that Germany was only to have 100,000 men, and yet Czecho-Slovakia was to be allowed 1½ million troops, and Poland, who was insisting at this very moment against the decision of the Great Powers on embarking on imperialistic enterprises, an army of two millions? This was an outrage on decency, fair-play and justice. We ought to be fair even to the German people.

PRESIDENT WILSON agreed that the whole armaments question ought to be settled as a whole.

M. ORLANDO said he had been thinking the matter over. The consequences of the decisions taken now would be various and of very great importance. The reduction proposed by the military representatives at Versailles would bring the effectives of these States down to the same standard of military strength as Italy had had before the war. Czecho-Slovakia was to have 50,000 men; Italy's peace effectives had been 180,000 men, although the Italian population was three times the size of that of Czecho-Slovakia. The numbers proposed by the military representatives at Versailles did not amount to disarmament. If compared with the numbers to be allotted to Germany, the Czecho-Slovak army would be immensely larger in proportion, half, indeed, as large as the German army, although Germany was many times larger than Czecho-Slovakia. All the world must reduce their armaments.

M. CLEMENCEAU said his view was that this was the most difficult question of all that had to be decided. He saw the point of what Mr. Lloyd George said, but he also saw the other side of the question. He thought they ought to hear what these small nations themselves had to say. At the very moment when they were being charged with part of the debt of Austria-Hungary, they would not be very well disposed towards the Great Powers if they were asked to reduce their armaments.

One of the strongest guarantees against German aggression was that behind Germany, in an excellent strategic position, lay these independent States—the Poles and the Czecho-Slovaks. This fact would make it much harder for Germany to renew the policy of 1914. His Military Advisers were opposed to reducing the Polish army owing to the danger to Poland from Russia. The same applied to Roumania. After all that she had suffered would Serbia be content to be reduced to 20,000. The same applied to the Czecho-Slovaks and the Jugo-Slavs. While he fully recognised the force of Mr. Lloyd George's remarks he did not quite see how this policy could be carried out.

PRESIDENT WILSON said he had added up the total figures proposed by the Military Representatives and they would only amount to 350,000 men for the whole of Eastern Europe.

MR. LLOYD GEORGE said that the figures given by the Military Representatives were not really an indication of the strength of the armies proposed. Except in the case of Germany, Austria and Hungary, where only volunteer armies would be allowed, the figures would be practically annual figures. For example, if Czecho-Slovakia had an army of 50,000 men and this number was trained for a year, in 12 years she would have an army of half a million.

PRESIDENT WILSON said that he understood from his Military advisers that part of the plan was to limit military equipment.

MR. LLOYD GEORGE pointed to the experience of Great Britain which had had very little military equipment at the beginning of the war, and said that it was very difficult to guarantee that these nations would not manage to provide themselves somehow with equipment.

(The question was adjourned.)

APPENDIX II

DRAFT DESPATCH TO ADMIRAL KOLTCHAK.

(*Prepared by Mr. Philip Kerr for consideration at the request of the Principal Allied and Associated Powers, 23rd May, 1919.*)

The Allied and Associated Powers feel that the time has come when it is necessary for them once more to make clear the policy they propose to pursue in regard to Russian affairs.

It has always been a cardinal axiom of the Allied and Associated Powers to avoid interference in the internal affairs of Russia. Their original intervention was made for the sole purpose of assisting those elements in Russia which wanted to continue the struggle against German autocracy and to free their country from German rule, and in order to rescue the Czecho-Slovaks from the danger of annihilation at the hands of the Bolshevik forces. Since the signature of the Armistice on November 11th 1918 they have kept forces in various parts of Russia and the British Government have sent munitions and supplies to assist those associated with them to maintain their position to a total value of more than £50,000,000 (?). No sooner, however, did the Peace Conference assemble than they endeavoured to bring peace and order to Russia by inviting representatives of all the warring Governments within Russia to meet them in the hope that they might be able to arrange a permanent settlement of Russian problems. This proposal and a later offer to relieve the distress among the suffering millions of Russia broke down through the refusal of the Soviet Government to accept the fundamental condition of suspending hostilities while negotiations or the work of relief was proceeding. They are now being pressed to withdraw their troops and to incur no further expense in Russia on the ground that continued intervention shows no prospect of producing an early settlement of the Russian problem. They are prepared, however, to continue their assistance on the lines laid down below, provided they are satisfied that it will help the Russian people to recover control of their own affairs and to enter into peaceful relations with the rest of the world.

The Allied and Associated Governments now wish to declare formally that the object of their policy is to restore peace within Russia by enabling the Russian people to resume control of their own affairs through the instrumentality of a freely elected Constituent Assembly and to restore peace along its frontiers by arranging for the settlement of disputes in regard to the boundaries of the Russian state and its relations with its neighbours through the peaceful arbitration of the League of Nations.

They are convinced by their experiences of the last year that it is not possible to secure self-government or peace for Russia by dealings with the Soviet Government of Moscow. They are therefore disposed to assist the Government of Admiral Koltchak and his Associates with munitions, supplies, food and the help of such as may volunteer for their service, to establish themselves as the government of all Russia, provided they receive from them definite guarantees that their policy has the same end in view as that of the Allied and Associated Powers. With this object they would ask Admiral Koltchak and his Associates whether they will agree to the following as the conditions upon which they accept the continued assistance from the Allied and Associated Powers.

In the first place, that, as soon as they reach Moscow they will summon a Constituent Assembly elected by a free, secret and democratic franchise as the Supreme Legislature for Russia to which the Government of Russia must be responsible, or if at that time order is not sufficiently restored they will summon the Constituent Assembly elected in 1917 to sit until such time as new elections are possible.

Secondly, that throughout the areas which they at present control they will permit free elections in the normal course for all local and legally constituted assemblies such as municipalities, Zemtsvos, etc.

Thirdly, they will countenance no attempt to revive the special privileges of any class or order in Russia. The Allied and Associated Powers have noted with satisfaction the solemn declarations made by Admiral Koltchak and his associates that they have no intention of restoring the former land system. They feel that the principles to be followed in the solution of this and other internal questions must be left to the free decision of the Russian Constituent Assembly; but they wish to be assured that those whom they are prepared to assist stand for the civil and religious liberty of all Russian citizens and will make no attempt to reintroduce the regime which the revolution has destroyed.

Fourthly, that the independence of Finland and Poland be recognised, and that in the event of the frontiers and other relations between Russia and these countries not being settled by agreement, they will be referred to the arbitration of the League of Nations.

Fifthly, that if a solution of the relations between Esthonia, Latvia, Lithuania and the Caucasian and Transcaspian territories and Russia is not speedily reached by agreement the settlement will be made in consultation and co-operation with the League of Nations.

Sixthly, that as soon as a government for Russia has been constituted on a democratic basis, Russia should join the League of Nations and co-operate with the other members in the limitation of armaments and of military organisation throughout the world.

Finally, that they abide by the declaration made by Admiral Koltchak on November 27th 1918 in regard to Russia's national debts.

The Allied and Associated Powers will be glad to learn as soon as possible whether the Government of Admiral Koltchak and his associates are prepared to accept these conditions, and also whether in the event of acceptance they will undertake to form a single government and army command as soon as the military situation makes it possible.

T MS (SDR, RG 256, 180.03401/28, DNA).

To John Joseph Pershing

My dear General Pershing: Paris, 23 May, 1919.

I am very much disturbed by what you tell me about the message from General Mangin to General Leggett,[1] and I am going to take the matter up at once with the French Prime Minister.

I note what you say about Marshal Foch being entirely satisfied with the retention of the Fourth and Fifth Divisions, leaving the Sixth free to continue its movement, and approve of your decision in that matter.[2]

Cordially and faithfully yours,   Woodrow Wilson

TLS (J. J. Pershing Papers, DLC).
  [1] See J. J. Pershing to WW, May 22, 1919.
  [2] Wilson was here replying to J. J. Pershing to WW, also May 22, 1919, TLS (WP, DLC).

To Georges Clemenceau

My dear Mr. President of the Council: [Paris] 23 May, 1919.

I have just received a message from the Commanding General of our Army of Occupation which gives me very serious concern. It is to the following effect:

"This morning General Mangin, Commanding General of the French Army at Mayence, sent a Colonel of his Staff to General Liggett's headquarters at Coblentz to inquire what our attitude would be toward a political revolution on the west bank of the Rhine for the establishment of an Independent Rhineland Republic, free from Germany. He inquired what the American attitude would be toward such new Republic. The Staff Officer stated that they had fifty deputies ready to send into the American sector to assist in starting the revolution. The meaning of the word deputies in this connection is not clearly understood, but it was made clear that they were to be French."

General Liggett very properly declined to consider the proposition, and his action has my entire approval. He has been given instructions not to permit the entry of political agitators into our sector no matter by whose order they may claim to be operating, and I feel confident that these orders meet with your own approval.

Cordially and faithfully yours,   [Woodrow Wilson]

CCL (WP, DLC).

To John Joseph Pershing

Dear General Pershing,   [Paris, c. May 23, 1919]

M. Jeanneney,[1] Under Sec'y of War, is leaving Paris to-night to go to Gen'l Liggett's headquarters to make inquiries about the matter (revolution in the Rhine provinces) we spoke of this afternoon.[2] Will you not be kind enough to request General Liggett to answer fully any questions M. Jeanneney may ask and oblige

Your friend   Woodrow Wilson

Excuse pencil

ALS (J. J. Pershing Papers, DLC).
[1] Jules Émile Jeanneney. Actually, he was Undersecretary of State in the Presidency of the Council (not Undersecretary of War).
[2] For Jeanneney's report, see the Enclosure printed with G. Clemenceau to WW, June 1, 1919.

To Henry White

My dear Mr. White: Paris, 23 May, 1919.

Thank you sincerely for the letter and memorandum from Lord Bryce,[1] and also for letting me see a copy of the letter from Lord Bryce under date of May 19th with regard to a possible demonstration in the House of Lords in favor of the League of Nations.[2] You were absolutely right in the reply you made to him.

I realize the force of the objections that you urge to allowing the Sultan to remain in Constantinople,[3] and just such arguments are beginning to prevail in my mind, after further consideration of the matter.

I am going to try to see the Minister of Colombia, and thank you for the suggestion.[4]

In haste,

Cordially and sincerely yours,   [Woodrow Wilson]

CCL (WP, DLC).
[1] Actually, the Enclosures printed with RL to WW, May 22, 1919 (third letter of that date).
[2] That is, the Enclosure printed with H. White to WW, May 22, 1919 (second letter of that date).
[3] H. White to WW, May 22, 1919 (first letter of that date).
[4] H. White to WW, May 22, 1919, TLS (WP, DLC). White repeated an earlier request that Wilson receive briefly the Colombian Minister to Great Britain, Dr. Ignacio Gutiérrez Ponce. See H. White to RL, May 8, 1919, TC MS (WP, DLC). The Minister intended to present a letter to Wilson which stated that the Colombian government was ready to join the League of Nations and would ask the National Congress to approve and ratify an act to that effect. Although Wilson had previously agreed to see Gutiérrez Ponce, several appointments had apparently fallen through. However, Close subsequently scheduled a new meeting for May 28. GFC to I. Gutiérrez Ponce, May 16 and 27, 1919, both CCL (WP, DLC).

From Louis Marshall

Dear Mr. President: Paris, May 23, 1919.

Your very kind letter of the 19th inst., just received, is most encouraging. The hopes of all minority groups of Eastern Europe rest upon that whole-hearted sympathy that you have unfailingly evinced for the oppressed. It is, therefore, that I venture to call your attention to the atrocities to which the Jews of Poland and Galicia have recently been subjected—even at the very moment whilst the Peace Conference is engaged in bestowing sovereign powers and extensive territories upon Poland.

Last November the Poles attacked, murdered and plundered the Jews of Lemberg. Mr. Paderewski and Mr. Dmowski were then in New York, representing the National Polish Committee. They were requested by Judge Mack and myself and others to issue a declaration expressive of their abhorrence of the brutalities that had been committed and admonishing the Poles to refrain from such outrages. Although they conceded that a boycott had for six years been maintained by the Poles against the Jews, admittedly initiated by Mr. Dmowski, they refused to make any public statement, dismissing the request with the remark, contrary to the historic facts, that pogroms had never taken place in Poland. Since then a series of massacres and crimes of violence have been launched against the Jews in ever increasing volume and virulence. They have been either perpetrated, sanctioned, or suffered by the military authorities. A few recent instances will suffice:

In April last, while a committee of Jews was peaceably engaged, at Pinsk, in arranging for the distribution of food among the starving poor of the city, under the auspices of the American Jewish Relief Committees, a squad of soldiers under the command of a Major of the Polish Army, an avowed anti-semite, on the pretext that the men and women present, all of whom were unarmed, were Bolsheviks, arrested them, led them to the market place, selected from their number 37 young men of unblemished reputation, and without trial or hearing summarily executed them. The survivors, after being compelled to witness this horror, were imprisoned over night and severely beaten and were discharged on the following day on the assurance of the Rabbi that they were of good character. Not content with this outrage the military authorities arbitrarily imposed a fine of 100,000 marks upon the Jewish Community, and, I am informed, subsequently seized a like sum sent by our American Relief Committees for the succor of the unfortunates who were struggling against famine and disease.

Shortly after this occurrence pogroms accompanied by serious loss of life occurred in Lida, and other Polish towns.

Now comes an account from reliable sources that at Wilna more than two hundred Jews, principally women, old men, and young children have been done to death by a mob armed by the Polish legionaires; that every Jewish house in Wilna has been pillaged; that an entire congregation was murdered while engaged in religious services in a synagogue; that 5,000 Jews have been deported, one knows not whither; that the sale of food to the Jews is refused, and that they are even prohibited from leaving the city to secure sustenance. The Chief Rabbi and other prominent men were cruelly castigated and a prominent writer murdered by the wayside.

In Galicia similar pogroms have been conducted on a large scale as the result of careful preparation. The peasants came to the towns where the Jews reside with carts to bear away their booty. Persecution is widespread, and yet the Polish Government has consistently ignored these monumental crimes.

My object in directing your attention to these facts, in part evidenced by accompanying copies of communications received here,[1] is two-fold:

1. To urge our Government, either alone or in conjunction with the other Great Powers now represented at the Peace Conference, to notify the Polish Government that such atrocities must cease; that the perpetrators be punished and that the necessary steps be forthwith taken to prevent the repetition of these crimes against humanity;

2. To make provision in the several treaties about to be entered into with Poland and other East European lands whereby the inhabitants may be adequately safe-guarded against pogroms. That can best be accomplished by applying the principle recognized in various jurisdictions whereby responsibility for the consequences of the acts of a mob is made to rest upon the communities wherein their outbreaks occur, and by compelling them fully to indemnify the sufferers for the loss and damage sustained.

It would afford me great satisfaction were the opportunity afforded me to confer with you briefly on this grave subject and incidentally with respect to a few other points essential to the protection of racial and linguistic and religious minorities.

Gratefully yours,   Louis Marshall

TLS (WP, DLC).
[1] "Communication from Mr. Rosenbaum, Under Secretary of State of Lithuania," n.d., TC MS (WP, DLC); Polish Jewish Information Office to Lucien Wolf, [May 9, 1919?], TC telegram (WP, DLC); and Jewish Polish Information Office to Lucien Wolf, May 16, 1919, CC telegram (WP, DLC).

From the Diary of Ray Stannard Baker

Friday May 23rd [1919].

Much restlessness in our Commission over terms in the treaty. Reports have gone out that there have been 9 resignations: but actually only one man—Bullitt—has resigned & he on the Russian issue. A group of younger men have sent a letter expressing their disapproval of the treaty & asking to be relieved if the Commission thinks it necessary[1]—which is a very different thing from resigning. No one that I know approves the treaty—not even the President. Secretary Lansing thinks it bad & a League of Nations founded upon it impossible. At a dinner I attended this evening I talked with Hoover: & he says that the treaty is wholly unworkable & that if the economic terms are enforced it will mean ruin in Germany & probably Bolshevism, to say nothing of the impossibility of getting Reparations out of the Germans. He doesn't believe that this government will sign the treaty unless there are material changes.

Hapgood, Morgenthau, Frankfurter, Steffins,[2] & other liberals were in my office to-day arguing that changes were necessary in the treaty & that the President could still get the liberals of the world behind him in such a program if he wanted them. They suggested that I bring the matter to the President's attention, which I did this evening. I assumed quite frankly that the President would like the treaty somewhat modified (which he does not deny) and asked in what way the liberal groups could help him:

"Baker," he said, "it is like this. We cannot know what our problem is until the Germans present their counter proposals."

I spoke of the criticism among liberals in Europe who had all along been his sincere supporters.

"There does not seem to be much criticism in America."

"No," I replied, "the treaty there has so far had a good press, but I wonder if they know what is really in the treaty." I also suggested that we were not so specifically interested in America as in Europe & that the defects of the treaty would be slower in reaching our intelligent opinion.

"Tumulty cables that opinion will not support any material relaxation of the terms."

Well, I could not pursue the argument further. The President is evidently now keenly aware of his problem in getting the treaty—with the League—adopted by the American Congress. He has had to accept a treaty that was a terrible compromise—& now hopes to get it by, not because it is just, but because the American people don't know, don't care, and are still dominated by the desire to "punish the Hun."

I made an opportunity, also, in my talk with him, to suggest again that the treaty be released in America, so that our people could be really informed. This he objected to, saying that it would hamper them (the Council of Four) in making changes. I do not quite see how. Hoover told me to-night that he bought at Rotterdam for 2 francs fifty each a half dozen copies of the treaty printed in English, French & German. How absurd it is, under such circumstances to make a mystery of the business. It is all coming out through German sources & any day may be published in full by some enterprising New York paper! I cannot understand the position of the Big Four!

When I reported what the President had said about help from the Liberals, one of them said:

"Apparently he wants no help—"

"He never does," said another.

---

¹ They were John Storck, secretary and confidential clerk to Isaiah Bowman; Lt. George Bernard Noble, assistant in the Division of Current Intelligence Summaries; and Lt. Adolf Augustus Berle, Jr., Joseph Vincent Fuller, and Samuel Eliot Morison, assistants to Robert H. Lord in the territorial group on Russia and Poland. They had, in fact, sent individual letters to J. C. Grew on May 14 and 15, respectively. See *PPC*, XI, 569-72. In their meeting on May 19, 1919, the commissioners had instructed Grew to reply that they needed further time to consider what course should be pursued in the circumstances. *Ibid.*, pp. 179, 575. Four weeks later, Berle and Morison, citing their opposition to the policy of the United States toward Russia, renewed their requests, and the commissioners decided to relieve them of their duties. *Ibid.*, pp. 235-36, 244, 591; Beatrice Bishop Berle and Travis Beal Jacobs, eds., *Navigating the Rapids, 1918-1971: From the Papers of Adolf A. Berle* (New York, 1973), pp. 13-14.
² That is, Lincoln Steffens.

From the Diary of Vance Criswell McCormick

May 23 (Friday) [1919]

Called on Lansing about General Graves' withdrawal from Russia and took occasion to question him about Hoover's statement that he and other American delegates were going to refuse to sign and as I had supposed Hoover let his imagination run wild which I find is frequently the case. Lansing said he told Hoover he did not approve of all the Treaty but he had no thought of raising any objection to signing; in fact, he said they were appointed by the President and as Plenary Commissioners would, therefore, have to sign unless they resign. I could see Lansing was a bit sore at not being consulted more. He also told me that Lloyd George was largely responsible for the giving up of [on] the Council of Ten and substituting the Big Four because he, Lansing, argued to a finish too many of the questions in dispute and thereby blocked Lloyd George's game. He said this information came from an English source. As a matter of fact, my own guess is that Colonel House was largely instrumental in breaking up the Council of Ten because it left him out and the Colonel could not bear it as he and Gordon have certainly been obsessed to be the whole show.

From the Diary of Colonel House

May 23, 1919.

This morning rumor was rife that the Irish Delegates intended putting out a "blast" against me. Several of my friends among the newspaper people and others went to them and told them, as far as they could find out, I had been the only friend they had had in Paris, and they were now trying to alienate me. They also said it was a well known fact that I was more of a friend of the small nations than any Delegate connected with the Great Powers.

The Irish Delegates came at five and after some conversation they decided to drop the controversy. Before they told me this conclusion, I remarked that there was nothing the British would like better than to have them fall out with me. This phase of the situation evidently had never occurred to them. We parted friends. I am wondering how long this will last, for they still have another two weeks in Paris.

Dr. King, one of our Commissioners to Syria, was a caller. He came for advice as to many matters connected with his duties. Every day someone like King comes, stating that they do not wish to disturb the President and that it will answer every purpose if they get instructions from me. Just why I do not get into serious trouble I do not know. Someday I suppose I will, for the President is intolerant of anyone excepting myself acting for him. He wishes to do everything himself.

To Joseph Patrick Tumulty

Paris, 23 May, 1919.

I approve of the Attorney General's suggestions as to the appointment of Samuel J. Graham[1] as judge of the Court of Claims and Francis P. Garvan[2] to take his place in the Department of Justice.

Please say to Polk and Baker that I entirely concur in the conclusions of their message about General Graves and feel we must all wait for a judgment until we hear Morris's impressions in full.

Woodrow Wilson.

T telegram (WP, DLC).

[1] Samuel Jordan Graham, Assistant Attorney General since 1913.

[2] Francis Patrick Garvan, former Director of the Bureau of Investigation of the Office of the Alien Property Custodian, who had been appointed Alien Property Custodian on March 4, 1919.

From Joseph Patrick Tumulty

[The White House, May 23, 1919]

No. 139 Mr. Taft in signed article this morning says, "Find it hard to believe President sent sympathetic note to women who played [pleaded][1] for Huns."[2] I think this matter of sufficient importance to be cleared up from this side. There is great deal of unrest here owing to talk in newspapers of return to Great Britain of German ships found in our harbors at beginning of the war.

Tumulty.

T telegram (WP, DLC).
[1] Correction from the "original" copy in the J. P. Tumulty Papers, DLC.
[2] Taft's sharp criticism of Wilson's reply to the message from the Women's International Conference for Permanent Peace (see Jane Addams to WW, May 13, 1919, and WW to Jane Addams, May 16, 1919), which was published on the front page of the *Washington Post* on May 23, 1919, had been the result of his confusion about what kind of appeal Wilson had answered. On May 20, 1919, the *New York Times* had reported that Jane Addams had read to the women's conference "President Wilson's reply to an address sent him at Paris relative to modification of the terms of peace." Several days earlier, the conference had indeed adopted a resolution which had vehemently denounced the peace terms as contrary to the principles of a just and lasting peace and a gross violation of the Fourteen Points and had called for their radical revision. See the *New York Times*, May 15 and 16, 1919. If a copy of this resolution was ever sent to Wilson, it is missing in WP, DLC. However, Taft had assumed that it was this resolution which Wilson had endorsed in his telegram to Jane Addams of May 16. His article strongly defended the peace terms, argued that the few deviations from the principles of the Fourteen Points had been absolutely necessary, attacked the women assembled in Zurich as "these Alices in Wonderland" who had no regard for facts or for logic, and wondered how Wilson could possibly "sympathize with such blindness." For Wilson's response, see WW to JPT, May 25, 1919.

From Robert Lansing, with Enclosure

My dear Mr. President: Paris May 23rd, 1919

I did not fail to communicate to Mr. Polk the substance of your letter dated May 21st, 1919, regarding the publication of the text of the Conditions of Peace, and I am transmitting to you herewith copy of a message which I have received from Mr. Polk on this matter.

Faithfully yours,   Robert Lansing.

TLS (SDR, RG 256, 185.182/29, DNA).

ENCLOSURE

Washington. May 22nd, 1919.

2057. For the Secretary of State from Polk.

SECRET. Your 2194, May 21st.[1] Many thanks for information. Senator Pomerene called this morning and asked me to have his views on the subject of publication of the treaty laid before the President. He feels Democrats have no adequate answer to the Republican at-

tack and urges (most?) if not all of the treaty be given out provided
of course there is no compelling reason for withholding the publication of the treaty. He and Hitchcock both urge that they (should?)
have as much light on the subject as possible. I explained to Pomerene that I assumed that the British and French were unwilling to
have the terms known for reasons of domestic politics.

Polk, Acting.

T telegram (SDR, RG 256, 185.182/28, DNA).
  ¹ See WW to RL, May 21, 1919, n. 2.

From Robert Lansing, with Enclosure

My dear Mr. President: Paris May 23, 1919

  I enclose to you a copy of a memorandum sent me by Mr. Polk. It
shows how far the bitterness of opposition is being carried by our political opponents in America.

Faithfully yours,   Robert Lansing

TLS (WP, DLC).

E N C L O S U R E

Department of State
OFFICE OF THE COUNSELOR.

  The BRITISH AMBASSADOR called on me on the twenty-sixth and
twenty-ninth of April. After some hesitation, he said he had something on his mind which he felt he should discuss very frankly with
me, and that was the attitude of the Republicans in the United
States toward the British. He assured me he was bringing the subject up not because he believed the matter would seriously embarrass his Government, but he felt it was his duty to inform me so the
President and the Secretary of State would have such information as
he possessed on the subject.

  He told me that a well known Republican and an officer of the
organization¹ recently formed by Henry Watterson and George
Wharton Pepper, and others, had called on him, after being properly
introduced, and frankly said that he (the speaker) was disturbed
over the attitude the Republicans would have to take in view of what
was going on in Paris. Apparently, Mr. Lloyd George and the other
representatives of the British Government were very close to the
President and were following his lead. For that reason, it would be
necessary for the Republicans for their own protection to attack the
British Government; that they did not wish to indulge in tail-twist-

ing, nor were they unfriendly at the bottom to the British people, but in their fight against the President it would be necessary to attack all who stood with him, and if the British Government stood with him, they would be attacked. He even went so far as to intimate that it might be necessary for the Republicans to take sides with the Irish, and with anyone else that was opposed to the present British Government.

Reading said he declined to be drawn into any discussion with the man, but in order to make it perfectly clear, he asked him on two occasions a direct question as to whether he (the speaker) meant to tell him (the British Ambassador) that the opponents of the President would find it necessary to fight the British Government if it continued to work in harmony with the official head of the United States. The speaker in both instances replied that was what he intended to say. Reading refused to discuss the matter with him in any way, and refused to see him again, although the man sought another interview.

Reading showed me in confidence a memorandum prepared by the man of their conversation, and it confirmed all Reading told me.

Reading said this was the only case where anyone had been quite so frank, but he gathered from the tone of some of the Republican papers and from conversations with certain Republicans in Washington, that there was real feeling on the part of the Republicans because of the harmony which existed between the President and the British representatives.

Lord Reading thought it a most astonishing state of affairs and one which he felt he should in confidence draw to the attention of the American officials.

I have reason to believe the man who saw Lord Reading was Henry A. Wise Wood, who has been a windy critic of the President's for some time.   F.L.P.

T MS (WP, DLC).
  [1] The League for the Preservation of American Independence, founded on March 7, 1919, by Henry Alexander Wise Wood of New York as a propaganda organization to oppose America's entry into the League of Nations. George Wharton Pepper, a distinguished Philadelphia lawyer and legal scholar, was the league's director; Henry Watterson, former editor of the Louisville *Courier-Journal*, was its president. Its advisory council included five Republican senators: Miles Poindexter of Washington, George Higgins Moses of New Hampshire, Joseph Irwin France of Maryland, Harry Stewart New of Indiana, and Howard Sutherland of West Virginia. William Edgar Borah of Idaho and James Alexander Reed of Missouri agreed to cooperate with the organization, and Philander Chase Knox of Pennsylvania and Henry Cabot Lodge of Massachusetts expressed approval of its purposes. For a detailed discussion, see Ralph Stone, *The Irreconcilables: The Fight against the League of Nations* (Lexington, Ky., 1970), pp. 78-82.

From the Diary of Dr. Grayson

Saturday, May 24, 1919.

The President arose early, and after his usual morning walk, which I have persuaded him to take whenever the weather is favorable in order that he may keep in excellent physical condition, went into session with the Council of Four. The Russian question was under consideration.[1] The British and French have been urging the President to recognize the government of Admiral Koltchak, which is driving the Bolshevists out of control in Russia. The President has refused to accept the government as a "pig in a poke," but declares that there must be assurances which will show that not only will Koltchak agree to the calling of a constitutional assembly to decide what form of government shall be created in Russia, and who shall direct that government, but that he (Koltchak) shall give such assurances as will prevent him from establishing a military dictatorship in Russia. The matter was discussed in all of its aspects without a final decision being reached.

The President had no luncheon guests and was able to take a brief motor ride before resuming the sessions of the Big Four. The afternoon session of the Big Four was very brief, it being devoted simply to an approval of the reply of the Allies to the German demands for concessions in connection with the Saar Valley. The Germans were told that they had been assessed the mineral wealth of the Saar Valley for a period of fifteen years as a matter of retribution, and that they would not be allowed to send coal from the Valley and from other sections retaining their control. One concession, and a very great one, that was made, however, was that at the end of fifteen years the Allied Economic Commission and the League of Nations should decide in what form Germany should buy back her Saar Valley holdings. The original clause had compelled payment in gold and Germany in her protest had pointed out that this would be impossible if the other terms of the economic demands were to be met.

At five o'clock the President and I left the house for a walk on the Avenue du Bois de Boulogne. We sat down on the chairs and watched the pedestrians, equestrians and motor-cars pass by. The President loves to watch a crowd, especially if he is unrecognized and the crowd treats him as one of their number. He loves to elbow with his fellowman, so to speak. He has the most observing eye. He can see more things than any man I know. If there is any freak costume of any kind, it catches his eye, notwithstanding the fact that his vision is not good, especially in one eye. He repeatedly pointed out various individuals, making comment regarding their appearance. For instance, pointing to a passer-by, he said: "That fellow passing there I think is an American actor." I said: "Why do you say that?" He replied: "Look how he walks; look at his clothes, his self-satisfied stride and carriage and manner; they are all peculiar to one who is accustomed to the stage." "The cut of his clothes," the President said, "gives me the suggestion that he is on the stage." I agreed fully with the President; I should not have made this observation without the President's suggestion. The extreme costumes worn by women could not, in the President's opinion, last long because they were not attractive and showed a tendency to immodesty. It was an enjoyable and restful half-hour for the President. Little children accompanied by their nurses were objects of the President's attention. They were attired in all colors, which interested the President very much. The arrangement of houses that were being built with gardens in the rear was commented upon by the President. He thought it was an attractive and sensible arrangement, because it gave privacy to the occupants of the houses; it gave them a chance to sit in the gardens and not be observed by the public. This is just the reverse of what we have in our cities in America.

In discussing individuals connected with the American Peace Commission, the President said: "I have given representation to Wall Street which may be misunderstood at home, especially by Democrats and Progressives. I chose, purposely, for instance, Tom Lamont, of Morgan & Company, because I wanted him to see at first hand exactly the plans and purposes and manner of the administration's way of doing business. I wanted him to be a partner of reform for the country. If Wall Street continues to try to run the finances and economic conditions of the country a revolution is inevitable. And I do not want to see a revolution. Therefore, I hope that they will grasp the situation and become a partner in this reform plan of government. It gives them a good opportunity to see the workings of the government at first hand, and then if they refuse to become partners for the good of all the people, they know what to expect."

After dinner the President spent a very quiet evening.

¹ Grayson was confused here. As the reader will see from the minutes printed below, Grayson's account transposes the meetings of the Council of Four of 11 a.m. and of 4 p.m. In addition to these two meetings, the Council of Four met at 11:15 a.m. to discuss a draft of the economic clauses to be included in the treaties of peace with Austria and Hungary. The minutes of this meeting, which we do not reproduce, are printed in PPC, VI, 1-14.

To Sidney Edward Mezes

My dear Doctor Mezes: Paris, 24 May, 1919.

Thank you for calling my attention to the difference between the draft and the treaty in the matter of Dantzig.[1] I will take the matter up very promptly.

Cordially and sincerely yours,   Woodrow Wilson

TLS (E. M. House Papers, CtY).
    [1] It is printed in the following document.

Hankey's Notes of a Meeting of the Council of Four[1]

President Wilson's House,

C.F.29.   Paris, May 24, 1919, 11:00 a.m.

N.B. The following business was transacted during the assembly of the larger meeting for discussion of the Economic Clauses in the Treaty of Peace with Austria.

1. (M. Tardieu and Mr. Headlam-Morley were introduced.)

MR. HEADLAM MORLEY reported that, after further consideration, the Committee had come to the conclusion that the two replies to Herr Brockdorff-Rantzau's letters of May 13th and May 16th, approved by the Council on May 22nd, (C.F.24)[2] and which had been prepared somewhat hastily, were susceptible of improvement in drafting. They had therefore ventured to incorporate the two replies in a single draft, which he now submitted. He and M. Tardieu were in complete agreement and Dr. Mezes had approved it in place of Dr. Haskins, who was away.

(The revised reply (Appendix) was approved, and Sir Maurice Hankey was instructed to forward it to the Secretary-General, as superseding the reply forwarded on May 22nd, and for the following action:

(1) To prepare a reply in French for M. Clemenceau's signature and for despatch.

(2) To communicate to the Drafting Committee in order that the necessary alteration may be made in the Treaty of Peace with Germany.

(3) For publication as soon as signed and despatched.

(M. Tardieu and Mr. Headlam-Morley withdrew.)

2. The Articles regarding the return of Prisoners of War, approved

    [1] The complete text of these minutes is printed in PPC, V, 912-17.
    [2] See the minutes of the Council of Four printed at May 22, 1919, 4 p.m. For Brockdorff-Rantzau's letters, see n. 3 to the minutes of the Council of Four printed at May 22, 1919, 11:45 a.m.

on the previous day for inclusion in the Treaty of Peace with Austria (C.F.27)[3] were initialled by the four Heads of Governments.

(Sir Maurice Hankey was instructed to forward them through the Secretary-General to the Drafting Committee.)

3. The Air Clauses approved on the previous day (C.F.27)[4] for inclusion in the Treaty of Peace with Austria, were initialled by the four Heads of Governments.

(Sir Maurice Hankey was instructed to forward them to the Drafting Committee through the Secretary-General.)

4. PRESIDENT WILSON asked that the clauses in regard to Inter-Allied Commissions of Control, recorded as approved on the previous day (C.F.27),[5] might not be submitted for initials. He wished to reserve them for the present, as he was inclined to think that United States officers ought not to take part.

5. After M. CLEMENCEAU, PRESIDENT WILSON and MR. LLOYD GEORGE had initialled the General Clauses, namely, Articles 47 to 50 of the Military, Naval and Air Terms with Austria,[6]

M. ORLANDO withheld his initials, on the ground that the Armistice of 3rd November, 1918, which had been drawn up hastily, had been found to omit certain of the islands included in the Treaty of London, and he wished to have the Clauses re-examined by his military advisers.

(NOTE: This Meeting was continued after the conclusion of the discussion of the Economic Clauses with the Economic Experts.)

6. PRESIDENT WILSON read the following memorandum which he had received from Dr. Mezes, pointing out alterations made by the Drafting Committee in Articles 102 and 104 of the Treaty of Peace with Germany:

"The Articles as drafted and as they appear in the Treaty are given below in parallel columns, the divergencies of importance being underscored:

DRAFT.	TREATY.
Article 2.	*Article 102.*
The Five Allied and Associated Great Powers underbreak to establish the town of Danzig together with the rest of the territory described in Article I as a free city.	The City of Danzig, together with the rest of the territory described in Article 100 is established as a free city and placed under the protection of the League of Nations.

---

[3] See the minutes of the Council of Four printed at May 23, 1919, 11:30 a.m. The articles mentioned are printed in *PPC*, V, 882-85.

[4] They are printed in *ibid.*, pp. 892-95.

[5] They are printed in *ibid.*, pp. 895-97.

[6] They are printed in *ibid.*, pp. 897-98.

Article 4.

The Five Allied and Associated Great Powers undertake to negotiate a Treaty between the Polish Government and the Free City of Danzig, <u>which shall come into force at the same time as the establishment of said free city</u>.

Article 104.

A Convention, the terms of which shall be fixed by the principal Allied and Associated Powers shall be concluded between the Polish Government and the free city of Danzig.

The effect of the changes is to bring Danzig into existence as a free city as soon as the Treaty is signed. According to the draft, Danzig comes into existence as a free city only after its representatives and representatives of the Five Principal Powers have worked out its constitution, and further have negotiated a satisfactory Treaty between it and Poland. It may well be more difficult for the Five Great Powers to provide Danzig with a constitution drafted with the general interest in view, and also difficult, maybe impossible, to negotiate a satisfactory Treaty between Danzig and Poland if the former is set up as an autonomous and going concern immediately upon the signing of the Treaty and without further need of assistance on the part of those Powers.

If these points are well taken, it is important that the articles of the Treaty above set forth, should be modified so that they may accord with the draft."

M. CLEMENCEAU, after consulting the French text, said that it was obviously a translation from the incorrect English text.

MR. LLOYD GEORGE thought it possible that the Germans would make a strong resistance to the whole of the Clauses of the Treaty of Peace dealing with Poland. This would give an opportunity to the Allied and Associated Powers to make a correction.

(It was agreed that the Drafting Committee should be instructed to revise the articles in the final erratum or in the final Treaty of Peace handed to the Germans.)

(Sir Maurice Hankey was instructed to prepare an instruction to the Drafting Committee for the initials of the four Heads of Governments in the afternoon.)

7. PRESIDENT WILSON said that he had sent a copy of Mr. Philip Kerr's draft despatch to Mr. Lansing, who had replied[7] that he considered the statement right, and that the United States were justified in joining in it. Mr. Lansing would have preferred to withhold the despatch until a reply had been received from Mr. Morris, who

---

[7] If Lansing made his response in a letter, it is missing. There is, however, an undated T MS of the draft of Kerr's despatch to Kolchak, with both WW and RL Hw emendations, in WP, DLC.

had been sent to Omsk. He himself, however, did not agree in this. He agreed, however, to the following addition to the paragraph numbered "fifthly," at the top of page 5, which Mr. Lansing had proposed:

"and that until such settlement is made, the Government of Russia agrees to recognise those territories as autonomous, and to confirm the relations which may exist between the Allied and Associated Governments and the de facto Governments of those territories."

(This was accepted.)

(It was agreed to discuss the question in the afternoon.)

8. PRESIDENT WILSON read a despatch from the American Diplomatic Representatives in Warsaw,[8] showing M. Paderewski still to be strongly favourable to the views of the Allied and Associated Powers, ending with a message that he had strongly defended President Wilson's views.

MR. LLOYD GEORGE read telegrams showing that General Haller's Army was now being moved from the Ukraine to the Polish front, and that the Ukrainians had sent envoys to negotiate peace with the Polish Government.

APPENDIX TO C.F.29.

REVISED REPLY TO LETTERS FROM HERR BROCKDORFF-RANTZAU
of 13th and 16th May, 1919.

Sir,

I beg to acknowledge receipt of your letter of May 13th, 1919, and also of your further letter of May 16th; as these two communications concern the same subject, it will be convenient that I should answer them in one letter.

With regard to the more general observations contained in your first letter, I must emphatically deny on behalf of the Allied and Associated Governments the suggestion contained in it that "German territories are by the Treaty of Peace made the subject of bargains between one sovereignty and another as though they were mere chattels or pawns in a game." In fact the wishes of the population of

---

[8] H. S. Gibson to A.C.N.P., No. 60, May 19, 1919, T telegram (SDR, RG 256, 186.3111/87, DNA):
"CONFIDENTIAL.
"Paderewski told me this afternoon he was most hopeful Diet would pass motion declaring free determination for Eastern Galicia. He is working for a resolution from the Diet stating in so many words that he is empowered to settle eastern frontiers and especially Galician question in accordance with principles of President Wilson. In conclusion he said: 'Please send a message to the President for me to say that I have been the consistent champion of his ideas in this situation and that I shall have to defend them with all my heart and soul.' "

all the territories in question will be consulted and the procedure followed in such consultation has been carefully settled with special regard to local conditions.

In the territories ceded to Belgium, full liberty is ensured for the popular opinion to express itself within a period of six months. The only exception that has been made applies to that part of the territory of Prussian Moresnet lying west of the road from Liège to Aix-la-Chapelle, the population of which numbers less than 500 inhabitants, and in which the woods are transferred to Belgium as part reparation for the destruction of forests by Germany on Belgian territory.

As to Slesvig, I am to explain that this question was taken up by the Peace Conference on the request of the Danish Government and the population of Slesvig.

As regards the inhabitants of the Saar Basin, the "domination" which is termed "odious" in your letter is the administration of the League of Nations. The scheme contained in Section IV has been drawn up with the greatest care so that, while it provides compensation for the destruction of the coal mines in the North of France, it also secures the rights and welfare of the population. They are assured of the maintenance of all their present liberties and in addition there are guaranteed to them in financial and social matters a number of special advantages; moreover, definite provision is made, after a period of 15 years, for a plebiscite which will enable this population, which is of so complex a character, to determine the final form of government of the territory in which it lives, in full freedom and not necessarily to the advantage either of France or of Germany.

As a larger part of your two communications are devoted to observations on the scheme concerning the Saar Basin, I must explain that the Allied and Associated Governments have chosen this particular form of reparation because it was felt that the destruction of the mines in the North of France was an act of such a nature that a definite and exemplary retribution should be exacted; this object would not be attained by the mere supply of a specified or unspecified amount of coal. This scheme therefore in its general provisions must be maintained, and to this the Allied and Associated Powers are not prepared to agree to any alternative.

For this reason the suggestion you make in your first letter for some other means of making good the deficiency of coal—a suggestion which is developed with more precision in the annex to your second letter—cannot be accepted. In particular, I would point out that no arrangement of the kind put forward could give to France the security and certainty which she would receive from the full exploitation and free ownership of the mines of the Saar.

Similarly, the proposed handing over of shares in German coal mines situated in German territory and subject to German exploitation would be of doubtful value to French holders, and would create a confusion of French and German interests which, under present circumstances, could not be contemplated. The complete and immediate transfer to France of mines adjacent to the French frontier constitutes a more prompt, secure and businesslike method of compensation for the destruction of the French coal-mines; at the same time, by securing that the value of the mines should be credited to the reparation account due from Germany, it makes full use of them as a means of payment on the general account of reparation.

In some points your letter of the 13th seems to have been written under a misapprehension as to the meaning and purport of certain articles in the scheme. There is not, as you suggest, in the Treaty any confusion between trade contracts to be established for delivery of coal from the Ruhr districts (see Annex 5 of Part VIII) and the cession of the Saar mines; the two questions are essentially distinct.

The interpretation which you in your letter place upon Clause 36 of the Annex assumes that the effect of this clause will be to bring about a result which emphatically is not one which the Allied and Associated Governments ever contemplated. In order to remove any possibility of misunderstanding, and in order to avoid the difficulties which you apprehend as to Germany's ability to effect the payment in gold contemplated in this clause, the Allied and Associated Governments have decided that some alteration is desirable; they propose, therefore, to substitute for the last paragraph of the said clause the following:

"The obligation of Germany to make such payment shall be taken into account by the Reparation Commission, and for the purpose of this payment, Germany may create a prior charge upon her assets or revenues upon such detailed terms as shall be agreed to by the Reparation Commission.

If, nevertheless, Germany, after a period of one year from the date on which the payment becomes due, shall not have effected the said payment, the Reparation Commission shall do so in accordance with such instructions as may be given by the League of Nations, and if necessary, by liquidating that portion of the mines which is in question."

May 24th, 1919.

T MS (SDR, RG 256, 180.03401/29, DNA).

Hankey's Notes of a Meeting of the Council of Four[1]

President Wilson's House,
C.F.31.   Paris, May 24, 1919, 4:00 p.m.

1. The Council had under consideration a draft despatch for Admiral Koltchak prepared by Mr Philip Kerr at the request of the Principal Allied and Associated Powers. (Appendix I.)

PRESIDENT WILSON explained to Viscount Chinda that he and his colleagues had felt some misgivings lest Admiral Koltchak might be under reactionary influences which might result in a reversal of the popular revolution in Russia. They also feared a Military Dictatorship based on reactionary principles, which would not be popular in Russia and might lead to further bloodshed and revolution. This despatch had been prepared for consideration in order to lay down the conditions of support for Admiral Koltchak and the groups working with him at Archangel and in South Russia. Should Admiral Koltchak accept the conditions, he would continue to receive the countenance and support of the Principal Allied and Associated Powers, otherwise he would not. The substance of the document was contained in the six conditions laid down in the last half.

VISCOUNT CHINDA said that he had only received the document a short time before leaving the Embassy, and consequently had not been able to study it in detail. Unfortunately, Baron Makino was on a visit to the devastated regions, and would not be back until the following day. He would be very much obliged if he could be allowed time to discuss the despatch with his colleagues before giving a final reply. Nevertheless, speaking personally, he felt that in all probability his Government would be prepared to associate themselves in this despatch. His reason for this belief was a despatch which had recently been addressed by his Government to the Japanese Ambassadors in Washington, London, Paris and Rome, which he proceeded to read not as a proposal, but only as a matter of information. The gist of this dispatch was somewhat as follows: More than six months have elapsed since the provisional Government under Admiral Koltchak was organised at Omsk to restore order in Siberia. It has so far accomplished its extremely difficult task with admirable tact and determination. Its position had lately been strengthened by its recognition by other anti-Bolshevist groups in Russia as the central organisation in Russia. Having regard to the general desire to see the restoration of an orderly and efficient Government in Russia, and believing that official recognition will materially conduce to this end, the Japanese Government feels that the time has come for a provisional recognition to be accorded, on condition of a promise by

[1] The complete text of these minutes is printed in PPC, VI, 15-24.

the Omsk Government to safeguard the legitimate interests of the Allied and Associated Powers, and that it will assume responsibility for the debts and financial obligations of the former Russian Government.

The message concluded with an instruction to bring this declaration to the notice of the Governments to which the Ambassadors were respectively accredited, and to suggest to them that the question might conveniently be discussed among their delegates at Paris. On concluding the reading of this despatch VISCOUNT CHINDA remarked that the policy in the draft despatch which had been handed to him seemed to be a preliminary step towards the policy proposed by the Japanese Government. This was the reason for his confidence that the Japanese Government would accept it. Nevertheless, he would like to discuss the matter with his colleagues.

One point of detail in the dispatch to which he wished to draw attention was the following statement:

"Finally, that they abide by the declaration made by Admiral Koltchak on November 27th, 1918, in regard to Russia's national debts."

He asked what the declaration was to which this referred.

MR LLOYD GEORGE, who had sent for the document containing the declaration, read the following:

"Telegram from M. Klioutchnikoff to the Ambassador in Paris:

November 27th, 1918.

Please communicate the following to the Government to which you are accredited:

"The Russian Government at the head of which stands Admiral Koltchak remembering that Russia always kept all her obligations towards her own people as well as other nations to which it was bound by conventions, presumes it necessary to announce in a special declaration that it accepts all obligations incumbing to the Treasury and will fulfil them in due time when Russia's unity will be again achieved. These obligations are the following: Payments of interests, redemption of inner State debts, payments for contracts, wages, pensions and other payments due by law, and other conventions. The Government declares at the same time all financial acts promoted by the Soviet Powers as null and void, being acts edicted by mutineers."

(Sir Maurice Hankey undertook to send a copy to Viscount Chinda.)

VISCOUNT CHINDA supposed that the responsibility for sending supplies to Russia would be divided between the various Governments according to their respective capacity.

MR LLOYD GEORGE said that up to now Great Britain had supplied the great bulk of the war material. He would be very glad to adopt Viscount Chinda's proposal, as then the United States of America would have to supply the greater part.

VISCOUNT CHINDA said he had only mentioned it because of the limited resources of Japan for such supplies.

PRESIDENT WILSON said that this was a matter for Congress. He hoped, however, he might induce Congress to take a share when the whole matter was explained to them.[2]

MR LLOYD GEORGE said that substantially the conditions in this dispatch had been read to the British Trades Unionists, who had been satisfied on the whole.

VISCOUNT CHINDA then drew attention to the following message in the despatch:

"They are therefore disposed to assist the Government of Admiral Koltchak and his Associates with munitions, supplies, food, and the help of such as may volunteer for their service, to establish themselves as the Government of All Russia," etc.

He thought that Japan, having a standing army, might find it difficult strictly to conform to the letter of this proposal.

PRESIDENT WILSON said he did not understand this phrase to mean Government help. It had not been in contemplation to send formed troops. His interpretation of the words was that it meant such individuals as might volunteer.

MR LLOYD GEORGE said the phrase had been inserted to meet the case of Great Britain. There was a very strong feeling against sending forces to Russia, and it was necessary to give guarantees to the soldiers that they would not be sent. Nevertheless, a good many men in the British Army had volunteered to go to Russia to take part in the operations; indeed, sufficient numbers had volunteered to supply the Archangel force. That was the reason for this provision.

VISCOUNT CHINDA said it would be very difficult for the Japanese Government to undertake their help in that sense. There were technical difficulties in the way of employing Japanese forces as volunteers. They could only send regular troops.

PRESIDENT WILSON said Mr Lloyd George's interpretation showed that he had not read it aright. He understood it had been agreed that the Allied and Associated forces should be withdrawn from Archangel.

MR LLOYD GEORGE said that the difficulty in withdrawing the men who had volunteered from England was that they were mostly men

---

[2] Mantoux, II, 202: "Wilson. It is not I who needs to be persuaded but the Congress of the United States, which until now has shown itself hostile to the idea of any intervention in Russia. I believe that that attitude could change if Admiral Kolchak replies satisfactorily to the questions which we are going to ask him."

in technical services, such as artillery and aircraft, who could not well be spared. If they were withdrawn, it would place both the Archangel forces and Denikin in great difficulties.

VISCOUNT CHINDA said that the Japanese forces in Siberia were regulars, and they could not be converted into volunteers.

PRESIDENT WILSON said that the answer was that the United States and Japanese troops who were in the rearward services were not affected. This phrase only concerned the troops taking part in regular operations. The United States and Japanese forces were on the lines of communications. He suggested that the difficulty should be met by the substitution of some such words as the following:

"Such other help as may prove feasible."

MR LLOYD GEORGE said that he thought the phrase had better be left out rather than amended.[3]

(It was agreed that the words: "And the help of such as may volunteer for their service," should be omitted.)

M. CLEMENCEAU said that he learnt that the Japanese had furnished a considerable amount of munitions to Admiral Koltchak, but he could not specify the exact amount.

MR LLOYD GEORGE said that on the whole he thought it would be better to omit the following words from the second paragraph of the letter:

"The total cost of which exceeds £100,000,000." (It was agreed to omit the above words, and to substitute the following:

"at a very considerable cost.")

Conclusion:

(It was agreed that the draft despatch should be provisionally approved, subject to the above corrections, but that no action should be taken until it had received the formal approval of the Japanese Delegation.

Viscount Chinda undertook to notify Sir Maurice Hankey if the despatch was approved, and Sir Maurice Hankey was instructed in that event to submit a copy for signature by the representatives of the Five Powers, after which it would be dispatched in their name to Admiral Koltchak by M. Clemenceau.)

2. (Colonel Kisch was introduced.)

---

[3] Mantoux, II, 202: "Wilson. Our reply to the question put by Viscount Chinda is thus: it is not a question of sending regular forces to Russia. I add that this decision does not affect the troops who are guarding the railroad in Siberia. But in order to help Admiral Kolchak on his march to the West, we will only furnish him with material means, leaving to individuals the right to enlist voluntarily in the Russian armies.

"Lloyd George. It is perhaps better not even to mention these volunteers in our despatch, since their action does not depend on the governments.

"Wilson. That is better indeed."

COLONEL KISCH gave a description with a map of the military situation in Siberia. He explained that Admiral Koltchak's main operations were on his northern wing with the immediate object of effecting a junction at Kotlas with the forces based on Archangel. His subsequent objective would be Viatka. The Bolshevists had been forced back in this district, and, in order to meet the menace, had withdrawn 20,000 men from opposite the forces at Archangel. With those reinforcements they would be able to oppose Koltchak's 36,000 men on his northern wing with about double strength, though the morale of the Bolshevist troops, who had been severely handled, was low. The Bolshevists had countered this attack by Admiral Koltchak by a counter-attack against his southern wing, where they had made a total advance in the region of Samara, which had been threatened by Koltchak, of some 60 miles. Denikin was creating a diversion to check this counter-attack by an advance towards Tzaritzin, and Admiral Koltchak was putting in his last reserves to check this Bolshevist advance, and meanwhile was pressing on in the north. On the west the Esthonians had made a considerable advance, and, if aided by a rising in Petrograd, might even hope to capture that city. The inhabitants in the districts recently over-run by Admiral Koltchak had received him favourably. In the northern part of Russia there was close affinity between the population west of the Urals and the Siberian population, but before long Koltchak, if he continued his successes, would be entering the really Bolshevist regions of Russia.

(Colonel Kisch then withdrew.)

3. MR LLOYD GEORGE said that if a satisfactory answer was received from Koltchak, the following decisions would have to be taken:

(1) Whether the Allied and Associated Powers should confine themselves to rendering him assistance.
(2) Whether they should recognise the Omsk Government as the Government for the area occupied by Koltchak's troops.
(3) Whether the Omsk Government should be recognised as representing the whole of Russia.

PRESIDENT WILSON said that he hoped, before Koltchak's reply was received, to have Mr Morris's report.

MR LLOYD GEORGE suggested that someone ought to be sent to see Denikin.

4. SIR MAURICE HANKEY said he had received a letter from M. Berthelot, stating that the Committee on New States would be glad if a Japanese representative could be added. This would be more especially important when commercial matters were under consideration.

VISCOUNT CHINDA said he would be glad to arrange for a Japanese representative.

(It was agreed that a Japanese representative should be added to the Committee.)

5. PRESIDENT WILSON read a letter addressed to Sir Maurice Hankey by Sir Esme Howard[4] on behalf of the Commission on Baltic Affairs. (Appendix II.)[5]

(It was agreed that the Commission on Baltic Affairs should be authorised to examine the future relations of all the Baltic States to Russia, and to submit recommendations thereon.)

6. SIR MAURICE HANKEY drew attention to the following reference from the Council of Foreign Ministers at their Meeting on the 23rd May, 1919 (I.C.190, Minute 4):[6]

---

[4] Esme William Howard, who had been British Ambassador to Sweden until the peace conference convened, was an adviser on political and diplomatic questions in the British delegation. He had also been British civil commissioner on the Inter-Allied Special Commission to Poland in February and March 1919.

[5] E. W. Howard to M. P. A. Hankey, May 24, 1919, TCL (SDR, RG 256, 180.03401/31, DNA); printed in PPC, VI 23-24. Howard stated that the Commission on Baltic Affairs, which had been established on April 28, 1919, had begun its examination of the Baltic question but had concluded that its mandate was somewhat vague and that more precise instructions were required before it could make any definite recommendations on questions which, to some extent, involved the study of a part of the Russian problem. The commission asked to be authorized, therefore, to examine in particular the future relations of the Baltic states to Russia. This question, the commission believed, was all the more urgent, since the Allied and Associated governments were currently considering a *de facto* recognition of the Kolchak government. Howard concluded: "But if this government is to be recognised some security should first be obtained from Koltchak, as a condition of recognition, for the future of the Baltic provinces to which the Allied Governments have given assurances that their status will be determined as far as possible in accordance with the wishes of the population. Unless this is done at once it may be difficult to ensure that Koltchak, after victory over the Bolsheviks, would allow us to make good the assurances given by us to the Baltic States."

[6] Printed in PPC, IV, 752-57, 762-63. The council discussed a report by a committee of American, British, French, and Italian economic, military, and naval representatives, appointed on May 9, 1919, to examine "the best means of establishing and maintaining order in the Baltic Provinces and of revictualling the population." The committee believed that the maintenance of order was a necessary condition for the distribution of food in the Baltic countries; that the presence of the German army in Lithuania and Latvia was an intolerable situation that should be terminated as soon as possible; and that, since the dispatch of Allied troops to the Baltic countries was out of the question, the only alternative was the organization of local troops, supplemented by volunteers from the outside. The committee then made the following recommendations: (1) all German troops should be required to withdraw from Latvia and Lithuania as soon as local forces could be organized to replace them; (2) a military mission, under British command, should be established in Libau or Reval to advise the governments of Estonia, Latvia, and Lithuania on the organization, equipment, and training of the local forces and on the best means of defending themselves against German and Bolshevik aggression; (3) all volunteers should be recruited in the Scandinavian countries; (4) a credit of ten million pounds sterling should be placed at the disposal of the Baltic states to be used as decided upon by the military and political missions; (5) food, equipment, clothing, arms, munitions, etc. should be provided by the Allied and Associated powers and should be paid for by the credit mentioned in the previous article; and (6) the political and economic missions should inquire as to what collateral guarantees could be obtained from the Baltic countries to cover the above-mentioned credit.

In presenting the recommendations of the committee, Hoover quoted a telegram which he had received from Major Ferry K. Heath, the chief of the food commission of the American Relief Administration in Finland, to the effect that White Russian and Es-

"The Articles 1-3, 5-6, of the Committee's Report were accepted. Paragraph 4 and the question formulated by Mr Balfour regarding the advance on Petrograd, together with the 7th Article proposed by Mr Lansing, were referred to the Council of Heads of Governments.

Mr Lansing made a reservation to the effect that Article 7 as proposed by him would fulfil all the necessary purposes and render Mr Balfour's suggestion unnecessary."

(After the procès-verbal and the various documents referred to in the above conclusion had been consulted, it was agreed to adjourn the subject for discussion with the Foreign Ministers.)[7]

7. (The following resolution, submitted by Sir Maurice Hankey, was accepted:

It was agreed:

1. That the Economic Commission shall be asked immediately to prepare, for consideration by the Council of the Principal Allied and Associated Powers, Articles for insertion in the Treaty with Bulgaria.

2. That the Financial Commission shall be asked immediately to prepare, for consideration by the Council of the Principal Allied and Associated Powers, Articles for insertion in the Treaty with Bulgaria.

---

tonian troops had completely routed the Bolshevik forces on the Narva front and were facing the opportunity of a rapid advance toward Petrograd. A decision would have to be made by the Omsk government whether to encourage this advance, and Heath asked for definite assurances that the Allied governments would provide food for the anti-Bolshevik troops and the population of Petrograd in the event that the city should be occupied.

After a lengthy discussion, the Foreign Ministers adopted the committee's recommendations, with the exception of the fourth point, which was referred to the Council of Four. In addition, Lansing wanted to include a seventh article recommending that "the Director General of Relief should continue to extend *ravitaillement* in all nonBolshevik areas of the Baltic region without respect to political control." He stated that he preferred not to refer the question of the advance on Petrograd to the Council of Four until he had seen a "definite formula." He argued that the article suggested by himself would make a decision on this question unnecessary, and he objected to a resolution introduced by Balfour, which asked the Council of Four to determine which directions should be given to the Russo-Estonian forces and whether a communication on this subject should be sent to Admiral Kolchak.

[7] At this point, Mantoux, II, 203, adds: "Hankey. Mr. Hoover proposes to advance ten million pounds to the Baltic states, which would be furnished by all the Allied and Associated powers.

"Lloyd George. Why do that? We are sending arms, ammunition, and provisions directly to them.

"Wilson. Mr. Hoover proposes also that we should take charge of provisioning the Baltic countries invaded by the Bolsheviks, without considering their present political status.

"Lloyd George. Concerning the ten million pounds, I will observe that we are giving money neither to Admiral Kolchak nor to General Denikin. Admiral Kolchak is at this time seeking a loan in London, and Lord Revelstoke has undertaken to float it. When consulted on the matter, we did nothing other than state that the British government would raise no objection.

"Hankey. Mr. Balfour and M. Pichon also had reservations about the ten million pounds."

Lord Revelstoke was John Baring, 2d Baron Revelstoke, a partner in Baring Brothers and Co., Ltd., London merchant bankers.

2 [3]. That the Reparation Commission shall be asked immediately to prepare, for consideration by the Council of the Principal Allied and Associated Powers, Articles for insertion in the Treaty with Bulgaria.

4. That the Military Representatives of the Supreme War Council at Versailles, with whom shall be associated Naval and Aerial Representatives of the Principal Allied and Associated Powers, shall be asked to prepare, for the consideration of the Council of the Principal Allied and Associated Powers, Military, Naval and Air Clauses for insertion in the Treaty with Bulgaria.)

(Sir Maurice Hankey was instructed to communicate these decisions to the Secretary-General for the necessary action.)

8. M. CLEMENCEAU reported that M. Venizelos had applied to be heard on the subject of the frontiers of the territory to be allotted to Greece.

9. With reference to C.F.29,[8] Minute 6, the instructions to the Drafting Committee in regard to the alterations in Articles 102 and 104 of the Treaty of Peace with Germany were initialled by the four Heads of Governments.

(Sir Maurice Hankey was instructed to forward the initialled copy to the Drafting Committee.)

APPENDIX I

DRAFT DESPATCH TO ADMIRAL KOLTCHAK.

*(Prepared by Mr Philip Kerr for consideration
at the request of the Principal Allied and
Associated Powers, 23rd May, 1919.)*

The Allied and Associated Powers feel that the time has come when it is necessary for them once more to make clear the policy they propose to pursue in regard to Russia.

It has always been a cardinal axiom of the Allied and Associated Powers to avoid interference in the internal affairs of Russia. Their original intervention was made for the sole purpose of assisting those elements in Russia which wanted to continue the struggle against German autocracy and to free their country from German rule, and in order to rescue the Czecho-Slovaks from the danger of annihilation at the hands of the Bolshevik forces. Since the signature of the Armistice on November 11th 1918 they have kept forces in various parts of Russia. Munitions and supplies have been sent to assist those associated with them, the total cost of which exceeds £100,000,000. No sooner, however, did the Peace Conference assemble than they endeavoured to bring peace and order to Russia by

---

[8] That is, the minutes of the Council of Four printed at May 24, 1919, 11 a.m.

inviting representatives of all the warring Governments within Russia to meet them in the hope that they might be able to arrange a permanent solution of Russian problems. This proposal and a later offer to relieve the distress among the suffering millions of Russia broke down through the refusal of the Soviet Government to accept the fundamental condition of suspending hostilities while negotiations or the work of relief was proceeding. They are now being pressed to withdraw their troops and to incur no further expense in Russia on the ground that continued intervention shows no prospect of producing an early settlement. They are prepared, however, to continue their assistance on the lines laid down below, provided they are satisfied that it will really help the Russian people to liberty, self-government, and peace.

The Allied and Associated Governments now wish to declare formally that the object of their policy is to restore peace within Russia by enabling the Russian people to resume control of their own affairs through the instrumentality of a freely elected Constituent Assembly and to restore peace along its frontiers by arranging for the settlement of disputes in regard to the boundaries of the Russian state and its relations with its neighbours through the peaceful arbitration of the League of Nations.

They are convinced by their experiences of the last year that it is not possible to attain these ends by dealings with the Soviet Government of Moscow. They are therefore disposed to assist the Government of Admiral Koltchak and his Associates with munitions, supplies, food, and the help of such as may volunteer for their service, to establish themselves as the government of All Russia, provided they receive from them definite guarantees that their policy has the same object in view as that of the Allied and Associated Powers. With this object they would ask Admiral Koltchak and his Associates whether they will agree to the following as the conditions upon which they accept continued assistance from the Allied and Associated Powers.

In the first place, that, as soon as they reach Moscow they will summon a Constituent Assembly elected by a free, secret and democratic franchise as the Supreme Legislature for Russia to which the Government of Russia must be responsible, or if at that time order is not sufficiently restored they will summon the Constituent Assembly elected in 1917 to sit until such time as new elections are possible.

Secondly, that throughout the areas which they at present control they will permit free elections in the normal course for all local and legally constituted assemblies such as municipalities, Zemtsvos, etc.

Thirdly, they will countenance no attempt to revive the special privileges of any class or order in Russia. The Allied and Associated Powers have noted with satisfaction the solemn declarations made by Admiral Koltchak and his associates that they have no intention of restoring the former land system. They feel that the principles to be followed in the solution of this and other internal questions must be left to the free decision of the Russian Constituent Assembly; but they wish to be assured that those whom they are prepared to assist stand for the civil and religious liberty of all Russian citizens and will make no attempt to reintroduce the regime which the revolution has destroyed.

Fourthly, that the independence of Finland and Poland be recognised, and that in the event of the frontiers and other relations between Russia and these countries not being settled by agreement, they will be referred to the arbitration of the League of Nations.

Fifthly, that if a solution of the relations between Esthonia, Latvia, Lithuania and the Caucasian and Transcaspian territories and Russia is not speedily reached by agreement the settlement will be made in consultation and co-operation with the League of Nations, and that until such settlement is made the Government of Russia agrees to recognise these territories as autonomous and to confirm the relations which may exist between these *de facto* Governments and the Allied and Associated Governments.

Sixthly, that as soon as a government for Russia has been constituted on a democratic basis, Russia should join the League of Nations and co-operate with the other members in the limitation of armaments and of military organisation throughout the world.

Finally, that they abide by the declaration made by Admiral Koltchak on November 27th, 1918, in regard to Russia's national debts.

The Allied and Associated Powers will be glad to learn as soon as possible whether the Government of Admiral Koltchak and his associates are prepared to accept these conditions, and also whether in the event of acceptance they will undertake to form a single government and army command as soon as the military situation makes it possible.

T MS (SDR, RG 256, 180.03401/31, DNA).

Two Letters to Robert Lansing

My dear Lansing: Paris, 24 May, 1919.

The attacks here referred to[1] are all parts of the general plan to make as much mischief as possible, and I think the only way to handle them is to make a direct frontal attack in reply. Article X of the Covenant is the king pin of the whole structure. It is, as you know, the guarantee of political independence and territorial integrity. Without it, the Covenant would mean nothing. If the Senate will not accept that, it will have to reject the whole treaty.

It is manifestly too late now to effect changes in the Covenant, and I hope that Polk will urge Hitchcock and all our friends to take a most militant and agressive course, such as I mean to take the minute I get back.

Cordially and faithfully yours, Woodrow Wilson[2]

TLS (SDR, RG 256, 185.111/307, DNA).
[1] See FLP to RL and EMH, No. 2014, May 17, 1919, printed as an Enclosure with RL to WW, May 19, 1919.
[2] The gist of Wilson's letter was repeated to Polk in RL to FLP, No. 2276, May 26, 1919, T telegram (SDR, RG 256, 185.111/307, DNA).

My dear Lansing: Paris, 24 May, 1919.

I think that our friends in the Senate ought to be furnished very frankly with the following reason which seems to me quite convincing:[1] namely, that if our discussion of the treaty with the Germans is to be more than a sham and a form, it is necessary to consider at least some of the details of the treaty as subject to reconsideration, and that therefore it would be a tactical blunder to publish the details as first drafted, notwithstanding the fact that there is no likelihood that they will be departed from in any substantial way.

The last reason that Polk mentions is also undoubtedly present in the minds of our colleagues. There are reasons of domestic politics which make them unwilling to publish just now.

Cordially and faithfully yours, Woodrow Wilson[2]

TLS (SDR, RG 256, 185.182/31, DNA).
[1] Wilson was replying to RL to WW, May 23, 1919 (first letter of that date) and its Enclosure.
[2] The gist of Wilson's letter was repeated to Polk in RL to FLP, No. 2289, May 27, 1919, T telegram (SDR, RG 256, 185.182/32-A, DNA). Wilson sent an almost verbatim copy of the first paragraph of this letter to Tumulty in WW to JPT, May 24, 1919, T telegram (WP, DLC).

To Louis Marshall

My dear Mr. Marshall: Paris, 24 May, 1919.

I fully appreciate the gravity of the situation in Poland and elsewhere to which you call my attention in your letter of the 23rd, and beg to assure you that the Council is exercising every sort of influence it can exercise to remedy these distressing conditions.

Sincerely yours, [Woodrow Wilson]

CCL (WP, DLC).

From Henry White

Dear Mr. President: Paris 24 May 1919

I enclose herewith the copy of a letter which I have received from the Danish Minister and which speaks for itself.[1] I ought to add that the Minister called upon me a few days ago to say that the Danes are in an uncomfortable position with respect to the extension made by the Council of Four of the zone in which the Danish Government asked that a plebiscite be taken. He says that the Danes have no desire that a large German population be imposed upon them and that a plebiscite held in the third and added zone may result in favor of its union with Denmark, but if so, it will only be with a view to escaping the heavy taxation which will fall upon all parts of Germany as a result of the Peace Terms.[2]

On the other hand, the Danish Government feels that it would be very awkward, in the event of such a decision being arrived at, as the result of a plebiscite, to decline to accept it. Consequently they would greatly prefer that a plebiscite be not insisted upon in that zone.

I hope it may be possible for you to grant the Danish Minister's request to see you, as his Government has been extremely moderate in its demand and, like most of his countrymen of good family, he is a courteous, sensible gentlemen, who will not, I am sure, take very much of your time.

It occurs to me that perhaps advantage might be taken of the Danish Government's views in this matter to make a "concession" to Germany when we answer the objections that her Delegation may make, on or before the 29th instant, to the provisions of the Treaty. The opportunity of giving satisfaction to two countries antagonistic to each other might be worth considering!

In the event of your being able to see the Danish Minister, perhaps Mr. Close will kindly let him know when he may present himself at your house, unless you prefer that I should do so.

Yours very sincerely,   Henry White

TLS (WP, DLC).
[1] Herman Anker Bernhoft, Danish Minister to France, to H. White, May 22, 1919, TCL (WP, DLC). Bernhoft had asked White to arrange an interview with Wilson for him in order to discuss the problem described by White in the balance of this letter.
[2] About this matter, see the minutes of the Council of Four, April 15, 1919, 4 p.m., Vol. 57, and Miller, *My Diary at the Conference of Paris*, X 211-28.

From William Shepherd Benson

My dear Mr. President,   Paris, 24 May 1919.

I have the honor to quote below a despatch received for you from Rear Admiral Bristol, Senior U.S. Naval Officer Present at Constantinople:

"Following received for President:

'Mr. President. The occupation Smyrna by Greecian troops has cruelly affected the Ottoman nation and has plunged it to the depths of despair. According to the principles which you solemnly proclaimed in your different messages, the parts of which regarding Turkey were clearly defined, the Ottoman people were convinced that its future destinies were assured by the application of these principles. The recent decision, however, of the allied powers regarding the Smyrna provinces, of which 83 per cent of the population is essentially Turkish, proves that the aspirations and desires, of which the Turkish territories were always the object, are on the point of being put into execution under forms of mandates conceded to the different powers without taking into consideration the right of existence of the Ottoman nation. Such decisions create dangerous rivalries, and they will drive the Ottoman nation to exasperation, causing grave complication which it is Europe's interest to avoid in the near East. In exposing to you the consideration which precedes the League of National Ottoman Unity, I consider it my duty to add that the allied powers in ceding Smyrna to the Greeks, the only important outlet other than Eastern Mediterranean Sea, causes the economic ruin of several thousand Turks and creates in Asia Minor a new Macedonia. Furthermore in thus granting full liberty to Greek Imperialism, the hatred of the race will be received [revived] and security and order can not be guaranteed. Signed Ahmed Riza, Senator President of the National Unity League.' "

Very sincerely yours,   W S Benson

TLS (WP, DLC).

From Kim Kyu-sik[1]

Mr. President,   Paris May 24th, 1919.

The Delegation of the Provisional Government of the Republic of Korea, which is headed by J. Kiusic S. Kimm, has the honour to address Your Excellency in asking you to use your good influence in bringing before the attention of the Peace Conference the following note from Syngman Rhee,[2] President of the Cabinet of the Provisional Government of the Republic of Korea:

"I am authorised by the Provisional Government of the Republic of Korea to lay before your honourable body the following communication:

" 'The Provisional Government of the Republic of Korea requests the Peace Conference to recognize the newly formed Republic of Korea and its Provisional Government as the legitimate body representing the entire people of Korea.

" 'This Provisional Government is established as the result of their present independence movement against the rule of Japan. With the Declaration of Independence on the 1st of March, 1919,[3] and the heroically patient resistance against the Japanese military oppression by the entire population, as events have proved, the will of the Korean people has been clearly manifested that they are determined to be free from the Japanese rule at all cost and that their own affairs within and without the Korean soil shall be determined by the people of Korea.

" 'It is the unanimous and passionate desire of the Korean people to have a free and absolutely Independent Republican Government of their own choice, as it is their belief that without such a government they cannot develope themselves as a free and responsible people among the civilised nations of the world.

" 'This Provisional Government is the only Government which represents the will of the Korean people. From the date of Declaration of Independence any international agreement, engagement or contract which may be entered into by any other authority than that of this new Provisional Government, will not be recognized by the Korean people.

" 'The Korean people have solemnly sworn to resist all existing authorities in Korea other than those of their own Provisional Government. If the Korean people are compelled to submit to the existing Japanese rule by brutal force, they declare—believing in the principle of self-determination—that such process is illegal, immoral and invalid.

" 'It is however a regrettable fact that our Independence movement is being ruthlessly suppressed by the Japanese authorities who are resorting to such brutal, cruel and barbarous treatment on the defenceless people—including women and children—for the sole purpose of imposing her will upon them.

" 'The Provisional Government has sent to Paris a delegation, headed by J. Kiusic S. Kimm, as the direct and duly accredited representatives of the entire Korean people for the presentation of the case of Korea before the Peace Conference.'   "It is the sincere wish of my Provisional Government that Your Excellency will exert your good offices so that the Peace Conference may accord Mr. Kimm the privilege of an audience and recognize our just claim to be free from the illegal foreign domination."

We have the honour to be, Mr. President,

Yours very respectfully,   FOR THE KOREAN DELEGATION.

J. Kiusic S. Kimm.

TLS (WP, DLC).

[1] Also known by his western name, John Kiusic Soho Kimm. He was the Minister of Foreign Affairs in the Korean Provisional Government, which had been proclaimed by exiled nationalist leaders in Shanghai on April 13, 1919. At this time, Kim, who had been educated in the United States and was a graduate of Roanoke College, was in Paris as the representative of the Provisional Government to promote the cause of Korean independence.

[2] Educated at the George Washington University, Harvard, and Princeton (Ph.D. 1910) and a former student of Wilson's, Syngman Rhee (Yi Sŭng-man) was one of the most prominent Korean nationalist leaders. He had been elected President of the Korean Provisional Government on April 10, 1919. Living in exile in Hawaii since 1913, Rhee, officially a subject of Japan, had been unable to go to Paris due to the refusal of the Japanese authorities to issue a passport for him and the State Department's unwillingness to intercede on his behalf. Throughout the 1920s and 1930s, Rhee continued his efforts for Korean independence, and he was elected the first President of the Republic of Korea in 1948.

[3] About the movement for Korean independence and the events connected with the declaration of independence, see FLP to the American Commissioners, March 22, 1919, n. 2, Vol. 56.

Lord Robert Cecil to Edward Mandell House

Dear Colonel House,   Paris. 24th May, 1919.

In accordance with the President's suggestion,[1] I enclose for his consideration drafts of model uniform clauses for the three types of mandate.[2] In the "Class C" draft, Samoa and New Zealand are specifically mentioned, but the same terms will apply to the cases of the other German possessions which are to be administered as "integral parts" of the territory of the Mandatory Power. This draft has, I understand, been agreed to by the Dominion Prime Ministers, and I have therefore not attempted to redraft it.

With regard to the other drafts, the details of their provisions are, in part, the result of prolonged consideration by various sections of our Delegation, *but all the drafts as a whole must be regarded merely as my personal suggestion as to what the Mandate Conventions ought to be.*

I will not trouble you with a reasoned explanation of the objects of the several clauses, but I shall of course be delighted to discuss them at any time. I am sure I need not remind you how important I believe it to be that we should insert, if necessary against opposition, such terms as will give the League real opportunities of securing that the mandates shall not be looked upon as a disguise for annexation.   Yours very sincerely,   Robert Cecil.

P.S. With regard to Class A—the Turkish mandates—it is impossible to say how far the form herewith enclosed will be suitable in each case till it is known what precisely is intended. For instance, the Mandate for Palestine may require very special provisions since the native government of that country must provide for some kind of cultural or other autonomy for both Arabs and Jews. Similarly it is uncertain what, if any, native government Constantinople is to have and whether it is to be treated by itself or as part of the remaining Turkish dominion. The racial position in Armenia will also cause great difficulties.

TCL (WP, DLC).
  [1] WW to EMH, May 19, 1919, TLS (E. M. House Papers, CtY).
  [2] T MS (WP, DLC). Cecil's "proposed model clauses" for mandates over the former Turkish territories in the Middle East ("Class A"), the former German colonies in Central Africa ("Class B"), and Samoa ("Class C") spelled out in detail the rights and responsibilities of the mandatory powers and the native populations and elaborated upon the administrative arrangements pertaining to each class of mandates.

From the Diary of Colonel House

May 24, 1919.

Lansing sent up a letter he proposed sending the Irish Delegation. He had laready [already] written one and had sent it to the President for his approval. The President thought it too formal and requested that he frame another and consult with me. There was little or nothing left of the Lansing effort when I had revamped it.[1] If he had sent it as prepared it would have opened up an endless controversy. I tried to eliminate in the one I substituted every possible point of controversy.

  [1] The revised version is printed as an Enclosure with RL to WW, May 26, 1919 (first letter of that date). We have not found Lansing's original draft.

To Joseph Patrick Tumulty

Paris, 24 May, 1919.

Please ask Michael Francis Doyle,[1] Philadelphia, to assure the representatives of the shipyard workers who had a demonstration in Philadelphia the other day that they can certainly count upon my continued interest in the industry which we have so greatly stimulated and thank them very warmly for their message to me.[2]

Woodrow Wilson.

T telegram (WP, DLC).
  [1] Lawyer of Philadelphia, long involved with civic and social problems and active in

Democratic party politics; at this time, among other things, counsel for the employees in the Delaware River shipyards.

² Wilson was replying to Edward Kenan and M. F. Doyle to WW, received May 20, 1919, T telegram (WP, DLC). The telegram informed Wilson that 78,000 shipyard workers in Philadelphia had held a "monster parade and demonstration" under the auspices of the Delaware River Shipbuilding Council in favor of the building of a "great American merchant marine" in order to keep the shipyards busy. The workers congratulated Wilson on his "splendid achievements" and urged him to continue his interest on their behalf.

From the Diary of Dr. Grayson

Sunday, May 25, 1919.

The President was feeling the strain of the hard week through which he had gone, and last night I asked him to forego his usual Sunday at church and to rest as long as possible. The result was that he remained in his room until nearly eleven o'clock, and came out very much refreshed.

Mrs. Wilson, as a result of trimming a bunion, developed a severe infection (blood poison) in her right foot. It was necessary for me, under a local anesthetic, to make a free incision in order to evacuate the pus and provide for thorough drainage. The President showed that he was extremely uneasy and disturbed over her condition. No one could have been more sympathetic, tender and attentive.

After lunch the President, Mrs. Wilson, Dr. Axson and I motored to Fontainebleau. We went all through the Forest of Fontainebleau. It was a most pleasant ride. On our return Mrs. Wilson was helped from the car into her bed. The President spent the evening in her bed-room, going over a number of official matters that required his attention.

I attended a dinner at the Ritz Hotel given by Mr. Coromilas,¹ the Minister from Greece. There were about thirty guests—more men than women. I had a seat next to Hon. Arthur James Balfour. He discussed the President at great length during the dinner. He told me that he thought the President was not only the most scholarly and polished speaker that he had ever listened to but that he was the most profound and logical debater he had ever heard. Mr. Balfour said: "According to my way of thinking, he is the greatest statesman of any time. I can never tire seeing too much of him. It is always an intellectual treat to be with him. Can't you persuade him to go to Scotland for at least a week's recreation; play golf, relax, and enjoy a vacation thoroughly free from officialdom? I would love to have him as my guest, and I would count it as the greatest treat of my life. I feel sure that you as a physician would find that such a vacation would prove to be an excellent tonic for him. Do see if you can't arrange this."

Mr. Balfour and I talked about the President's aptitude in framing stories and anecdotes to meet situations as they arose. I then told him the "pig" story.[2] Mr. Balfour said that he was afraid Orlando did not appreciate such an appropriate story, first, because he missed the humor of it, and, second, he missed the wonder [wider?] application, which he would pretend not to see in the circumstances.

[1] Lambros A. Coromilas (or Koromilas), former Greek Minister to the United States (1907-1910) and Foreign Minister (1912-1913); at this time, Greek Minister in Rome and a technical adviser in the Greek delegation at the peace conference. He was married to Anna Ewing Cockrell, daughter of the late Senator Francis Marion Cockrell, Democrat of Missouri.
[2] See the extract from the Diary of Dr. Grayson printed at May 18, 1919.

From the Diary of Colonel House

May 25, 1919.

Tardieu was my most interesting caller. He came from Clemenceau to tell me that Orlando had just been to the War Office to notify him that the Italians intended at tomorrow's meeting to demand from the French and British the Treaty of London. Tardieu was in a great state of mind and wished me to communicate at once with the President, which I did over the private telephone. I had just left the President at the "Paris White House" but at that time neither of us knew of this latest *denouement* in the Adriatic situation.

The President was disturbed but not "panicy." He thought a way out would be found. In my conversation with the President at his house, I told him that I considered it essential to keep my hand upon the organization of the League of Nations for if that was a failure he would be condemned for paying such a price for it. If, on the contrary, the League was a success, then it would be considered that no price was too high. He agreed to this and told me to use my own pleasure as to when I should go,[1] but he wanted to think about it and talk with me further before I actually came to a decision.

[1] To London.

To Joseph Patrick Tumulty

[Paris, May 25, 1919]

Please give following message to Glass: "You may take it for granted that I will sign the Urgent Deficiency Bill and go forward with the plans you mention in your cable."[1]

For yourself: No one need have any concern about the return of the German ships in our possession. Full understanding has been reached about them. As for Mr. Taft's criticism, I am quite willing to be responsible for any sympathetic reply I make to appeals on behalf of starving women and children.[2]   Woodrow Wilson

T telegram (WP, DLC).
    [1] Wilson was replying to FLP to Ammission, No. 2079, May 24, 1919, T telegram (WP, DLC), transmitting a message from Glass to Wilson to the effect that Congress had passed the urgent deficiency bill. The bill had appropriated more than $40,000,000 to the Bureau of War Risk Insurance, to be used, for the most part, for family allowances. Glass had taken the liberty of assuming Wilson's approval of the bill, and he had begun to release checks for family allotments and allowances. He now asked Wilson to confirm that he would, indeed, sign the bill once it reached him.
    [2] See JPT to WW, May 23, 1919.

From the Diary of Dr. Grayson

Monday, May 26, 1919.

The President had an early breakfast and immediately went to his study. He remained there for a short time and then went for a motor ride, returning for the meeting of the Big Four, at which the question of the Dalmatian Coast and Fiume was again taken up. This meeting developed a very sharp controversy between the President and Premier Orlando of Italy. Orlando had announced that while he was willing to make Fiume a free city, he was not willing to concede anything else in that connection, and declared that unless his view was accepted he would insist that the Treaty of London should be followed out to the very letter. The President in an impassioned speech characterized the Treaty of London as an "infamous bargain," and served frank notice on his conferees that under no circumstance would the United States be a party to fixing the boundaries of the Jugo-Slav Republic under the limitations laid down by the disputed pact. The President's attitude was extremely firm and Clemenceau expressed grave concern, telling Orlando that he believed it would be absolutely necessary that something should be done by Italy to meet the President's views. Clemenceau warned Orlando that disregard to America under such conditions would certainly prove disastrous later on. Lloyd George sympathizes with the Italian viewpoint, however, and the conference adjourned without a definite agreement being reached.

The President had luncheon with Mrs. Wilson in her room, and after lunch the President and I went for a motor ride. The afternoon session of the Big Four was again devoted to the discussion of whether the Koltchak regime in Russia should be recognized.

The President was the chief speaker at a dinner which was given at the Hotel Meurice by the representative of the South American states at the Peace Conference in honor of Senor Epitacio Pessoa, the President-elect of Brazil, and the chief Brazlian delegate at the Peace Conference. The President's address was freely commented upon as being a very wonderful one.

From the Diary of Ray Stannard Baker

Monday the 26th [May 1919]

A feeling of great irritation & impatience is in the air. No one is satisfied with the treaty. Norman Hapgood was in to-day writing a letter to the President on the Russian situation which I took up to-night.

The Italian situation is very acute again. The Italians announce that they will stand on the London treaty. The President told Orlando to-day (he explained to me afterwards) that the London treaty was of a past era, & that he could not countenance it in any way, that no one had the right to pass to Italy by treaty or otherwise lands in Dalmatia without respect to the wishes of the people who inhabited those lands. . . .

From what he said to me tonight the President evidently believes that the treaty is in the main based securely upon the 14 points—his interpretation of them.

From Robert Lansing and Others

Dear Mr. President: Paris 26 May 1919

We have just been confidentially informed by Colonel House that the Italians propose demanding, in the Council of Four this morning, the fulfillment of the Treaty of London in its entirety.

In view of the fact that when we discussed with you a fortnight ago, or thereabouts,[1] the possibility of such a demand, and of the further fact that you seemed inclined at that time to inform the British and French Prime Ministers that the American Delegation would withdraw from the Conference rather than assent to the recognition of the Treaty of London, we venture to express the hope that you will not take any final step in the matter without a further conference with us.

We feel that circumstances, which we shall be glad to explain to you in conversation, have occurred during the last few weeks which would not justify our breaking up the Conference now on account

of the Adriatic situation, and that we should not have the support of
our own people in doing so.

Yours very sincerely,   Robert Lansing.

Henry White

Tasker H. Bliss

TLS (WP, DLC).
¹ On May 12, 1919. See the extract from the Diary of Colonel House printed at that
date.

Hankey's Notes of a Meeting of the Council of Four[1]

President Wilson's House,
C.F.32.   Paris, May 26, 1919, 11:00 a.m.

... 3. With reference to C.F.31, Minute 1,[2] SIR MAURICE HANKEY
stated that the Japanese Delegation had agreed to the draft despatch
to Admiral Koltchak (Appendix III),[3] subject to two very small
amendments, namely, in paragraph 2 instead of the words "they are
now being pressed to withdraw etc.," was substituted the following:
"some of the Allied and Associated Governments are now being
pressed to withdraw etc.," and paragraph 4 instead of the words "the
last year" was substituted "the last 12 months."

(These alterations were approved and the letter was signed by the
Four Heads of States. The letter was then taken by Mr. Philip Kerr
to the Japanese Embassy, where it was signed by the Marquis
Saionji. Sir Maurice Hankey was instructed to communicate the
letter to the Secretary-General with instructions to dispatch it, in
the name of the Conference to Admiral Koltchak.

NOTE. The Marquis Saionji, when appending his signature, particularly asked that the letter should not be published until
a reply was received. Sir Maurice Hankey made a communication in this sense to the Secretary-General.)

4. The general clauses, namely, Articles 47 to 50 of the military,
naval and air clauses for inclusion in the Austrian Treaty, which had
previously been initialled by the other three Heads of Governments,
were initialled by M. Orlando, who withdrew his previous objections.

(Sir Maurice Hankey was instructed to forward them to the Secretary-General, for the information of the Drafting Committee.)

¹ The complete text of these minutes is printed in *PPC*, VI, 25-42.
² That is, the minutes of the Council of Four printed at May 24, 1919, 4 p.m.
³ Printed in *PPC*, VI, 34-36. Except for the two changes adopted in the meeting of the Council of Four on May 24, 1919, 4 p.m., this draft was identical to the one printed as Appendix I to
that meeting.

5. The letter from the Austrian Delegation at St. Germain contained in Appendix IV[4] was read.

MR. LLOYD GEORGE said he thought a different procedure ought to be adopted with Austria from that adopted with Germany. The two cases were not really comparable. The Austro-Hungarian Empire had broken up, one half was friendly, and the other half, consisting of Austria and Hungary, he believed at any rate was not unfriendly. They were not in the same category as Prussia. Consequently, would it not be worth while, he asked, to give a different reply to what had been given to Germany? In his view, the question of compensation and the question of the military terms could not be ready for sometime, perhaps 9 or 10 days. But a good many parts of the Treaty were ready, for example, the boundaries with Austria and with Hungary.

PRESIDENT WILSON said that the southern boundary of Austria was not yet ready.

MR. LLOYD GEORGE said it could be settled in a very short time. Ports, Waterways and Railways were ready, as were the Economic Clauses. He suggested that these should be handed to the Austrians, but that the question of reparation and the military clauses should be reserved and that the experts of the Allied and Associated Powers should be asked to meet the Austrian experts in regard to these. He did not mean that the Council of Four itself should meet the Austrians, but that our experts should meet their experts in regard to compensation and the military terms, which they should discuss with them on general lines.

M. CLEMENCEAU said that the experts would require very precise instructions.

PRESIDENT WILSON said that we know exactly what the experts thought on the subject. He then read a weekly list of outstanding subjects which had been prepared by Sir Maurice Hankey. He noted Sir Maurice Hankey's statement that no communication had

[4] Karl Renner to G. Clemenceau, May 24, 1919, TCL (SDR, RG 256, 180.03401/32, DNA); an English translation of the French text is printed in *PPC*, VI, 37-38. In this letter, Renner complained that the delegation of the German Austrian Republic, which had been invited to the peace conference on May 2 and had arrived in St. Germain-en-Laye on May 14, had so far received no word about the opening of the negotiations. The long delay in the conclusion of the peace, Renner stated, had given rise to a general uneasiness among the people of German Austria. The uncertainty about the country's future was provoking all kinds of rumors and fears, was threatening peace and order in the large industrial centers and in the contested areas of the former empire, and was creating a situation which might lead to an "irritation of the masses" and the fermentation of "unhealthy ideas." In addition, Renner continued, the expenses entailed by the long stay abroad of the large number of officials of the German Austrian delegation were out of proportion to the country's more than precarious economic condition. Thus, Renner appealed to Clemenceau to open the negotiations with German Austria as soon as possible and not to adjourn before a decision about the fate and the future of his country had been reached.

been made to the Drafting Committee about the boundaries between Italy and Austria.

MR. LLOYD GEORGE suggested that these should be settled today.

PRESIDENT WILSON said that, according to his recollection, there had been a general understanding that Austria should be treated somewhat differently from Germany. Consequently, he agreed with Mr. Lloyd George's proposal to get the experts together.

M. ORLANDO asked if it would not be possible to have these questions roughly settled. He thought the outstanding questions could be arranged in 2 or 3 days, and then the negotiations could start. The difference of treatment to the Austrian Delegation would not be well understood in Italy, where Austria had always been regarded as the principal enemy. The Austro-Hungarian Empire had dissolved and the different States forming out of it were regarded with mixed feelings by Italy, some friendly and some otherwise. Austria, however, was regarded as the principal enemy. To adopt a different procedure would create a very painful impression in Italy. It would be felt there that the Italian contest with Austria was not taken very seriously. He agreed that a very rapid decision was necessary, but he did not see why one or two questions should not be left in suspense while proposals as to the remainder of the Peace Treaty were handed to the Austrians. To adopt a totally different procedure would create a very bad impression in Italy without any useful result. If in 3 or 4 days, a sufficient portion of the Treaty could be assembled and handed to the Austrians, so as not to give an impression of a piecemeal presentation, he would not object.

MR. LLOYD GEORGE said that Italy must really understand the fact that the peace of Austria was entirely different from that of Germany. Supposing Bavaria and Saxony had broken off from Prussia before the war came to an end and had perhaps even fought against Prussia, it would have been impossible for the Allies to take the line they had. For one thing, there would have been no representatives of the German Empire to meet. Consequently, a different line must be pursued and he could not see why Italy should not agree to a different procedure. He doubted if either the question of the military terms or the compensation could be settled in 3 or 4 days. If so, the settlement would be a bad one.

M. CLEMENCEAU said that he was ready to make every effort to meet M. Orlando, because he had learned from experience that, when the Allies were not in agreement with Italy, the immediate result was anti-French and sometimes even pro-German demonstrations in Italy that were extraordinarily disagreeable. He wanted, above all things, to avoid any differences with Italy. When, however,

M. Orlando suggested that it had been agreed to adopt the same procedure for Austria as that for Germany, this was not the fact. M. Orlando had not been present when the decision had been taken, for
reasons over which his colleagues had no control. It was in his absence that the new procedure had been agreed on. All he sought was
a reasonable agreement in a reasonable way. The Austrian Peace
was very different from, and, in many respects, much harder to arrive at, than the German, for the reason that the country had fallen
to pieces, raising all sorts of questions of boundaries and there were
conflicts arising on the Polish front and elsewhere in the late Austro-
Hungarian Empire. In Istria, he learned that trenches and barbed
wire were being put up by both sides. President Wilson had come to
Europe with a programme of peace for all men. His ideal was a very
high one, but it involved great difficulties, owing to these century
old hatreds between some races. We had in Central Europe to give
each what was his due not only between them, but even between
ourselves. For example, to take the question of disarmaments. M.
Orlando had been good enough to visit him on the previous day to
discuss the question of Dalmatia; but the Yugo-Slavs would not
agree to disarm themselves while Italy adopted her present attitude.
He, himself, was not in a position to oppose Italy in this matter, because France had put her signature to the Treaty of 1915, but it was
not a question that could be decided in two or three days. Referring
again to M. Orlando's visit, he said the principal subject for discussion had been the anti-French manifestations in Italy. M. Orlando
said that there was an improvement, but since then he had received
two despatches from M. Barrère, which indicated the situation to be
worse. There was a pronounced pro-German propaganda in Italy,
where enormous sums were being expended by Germany. All this
ought to be stopped and there was only one way to stop it. It was necessary to have the courage to tackle and solve the most difficult
questions as soon as possible. It was not at all easy to do so and could
only be done if M. Orlando would take the standpoint that he must
preserve the Entente with his Allies. He recalled that, in the previous weeks, he had a serious disagreement with Mr. Lloyd George
on the question of Syria when both had spoken very frankly. Nevertheless, both had concluded by saying that they would not allow
their differences to upset the Entente.[5] The same was not said in
certain quarters in Italy. Hence, he maintained that these questions
could not be settled in three days. Consequently, it was impossible
to meet the Austrians with a complete Treaty as had been done in
the case of the Germans. If M. Orlando would agree, he thought a

[5] See the extract from Grayson Diary printed at May 22, 1919, n.1.

start might be made by getting discussions between the experts, which would gain time. It was very hard to settle all these extraordinarily difficult questions rapidly. President Wilson adhered to his principles as applicable to the Austrian Treaty. France and Great Britain admitted the principles, but also did not deny that they were bound by their signature of the Treaty of 1915. If M. Orlando wanted a settlement, he must discuss it with the supreme desire to maintain the Entente and meanwhile a plan must be found to keep the Austrian Delegation quiet. We should tell them that the Treaty was not ready, but that it would be useful to have certain discussions with their experts. He did not want to embarrass M. Orlando in Italy and if this would be the result, he would withdraw every word he had said, but he was very anxious that the Austrian Delegates should not return to Vienna.

M. ORLANDO thanked M. Clemenceau most sincerely for what he had said, which was absolutely frank and clear. He did not wish to refer in detail to the troubles in Italy. The impressions he had received from Italy differed from M. Barrère's reports, which, according to his own account, were exaggerated. Nevertheless, he did not deny that the situation in Italy was extraordinarily grave. It could be excused and justified if it was recalled how Mr. Lloyd George before his visit to London had informed his colleagues that if he had to return to England without being able to show a considerable step towards peace, the position would be very serious. It was exactly the same now in regard to Italy. The trouble there arose from uncertainty. Once the Italian claims were settled, it would be found that Italy was as sincerely loyal to the cause of the Entente as before. He was absolutely sure that the present disquieting phenomena in Italy were due to anxiety and uncertainty. Like M. Clemenceau, he, himself, had decided to remain always with the Entente and to run all the personal risks involved. He felt he could not be accused of adopting too uncompromising a spirit. He had always made every effort to reach an agreement, including the recent conversations with Colonel House and Mr. Miller, where he had discussed proposals involving very grievous renunciations by Italy.[6] He thanked M. Clemenceau for his courageous words in favour of tackling the main problems, difficult and complex as they were. But, having regard to the excitement of public opinion, he asked why this should be still further excited by questions of procedure. In the present exciting state of affairs and in view of the exasperation in Italy, if questions of procedure were added, an irritation would be caused which would

[6] See the extracts from the Diary of Colonel House printed at May 13, 16, and 17, 1919, and those from the Diary of D. H. Miller printed at May 12, 13, and 14, 1919.

produce an effect contrary to what was desired. This was his only reason for anxiety.

PRESIDENT WILSON asked whether M. Orlando in his remarks had not really suggested the way out. He had suggested to say to the Austrians that by Wednesday or Thursday all matters would be laid before them which could be settled directly, but that some questions that could not be settled directly would be reserved.

M. ORLANDO said that President Wilson had correctly interpreted his views and he would accept his suggestions.

MR. LLOYD GEORGE said it only remained to divide the Treaty of Peace into two categories.

PRESIDENT WILSON said he had assumed that the only reserved question would be the military terms and reparation.

SIR MAURICE HANKEY said that Mr. Headlam Morley had come to him that morning and had told him that the Economic Clauses were based on the assumption that Austria was to be a continuation of the old Austro-Hungarian Empire, but that the Financial Clauses were drawn on the assumption that Austria was a new state. He had urged that the whole Treaty of Peace wanted examination from this point of view.

MR. LLOYD GEORGE questioned whether Mr. Headlam Morley's description of the Economic Clauses was correct.

(It was agreed:

That the Treaty of Peace should be handed to the Austrians in the course of the present week, but that the military terms and reparation clauses should be reserved for discussion with Austrian experts. Sir Maurice Hankey was instructed to draft a reply to the Austrian Delegation to give effect to this decision.)

6. PRESIDENT WILSON drew attention to a copy of a letter he had received, which had been addressed by the Secretary-General to Mr Barnes in regard to the participation of Germany in the new Organisation contemplated for Labour. From this letter he read the following extract:

"Consequently, I would be grateful to you for informing the Washington Conference that Germany will be admitted after the closing of the Conference, and under conditions expressed in the letter of May 15th of the Labour Commission."

This letter, President Wilson pointed out, did not carry out the decision of the Council, which had merely consisted in a recommendation to the Labour Conference at Washington that Germany should be admitted, but had left the final decision to the Conference.

(Sir Maurice Hankey was instructed to call the attention of the Secretary-General to this error.)

7. A letter was read from Marshal Foch somewhat in the following sense:

At the Meeting of the 19th inst. the Council communicated to the Marshal a decision that after May 27th the Army under his command should be ready to advance, in the event of the German reply calling for immediate action. He was instructed to make his dispositions so that the advance might be in the best possible conditions. This implied the following:

(i) Administrative measures to ensure that the effectives were completed, by bringing back personnel on leave.

(ii) Tactical movements; that is to say, concentration of all the necessary forces.

(iii) Not to keep the troops waiting too long in expectation of movements; that is to say, it was desirable to take the last measures as late as possible, and not more than three days before they should be executed.

He recalled that he had been instructed to delay until May 30 the final measures so far as the French Army was concerned. Tactical measures, however, must begin on May 27th, hence it was necessary that he should receive orders before 4 p.m. today, so that he could either give a counter order or confirm his previous orders. Consequently, he asked to have May 30th confirmed as the date on which he was to resume his march, or otherwise.

PRESIDENT WILSON suggested the reply should be that three days' notice would be given to Marshal Foch as soon as the Council knew if action was necessary.

MR LLOYD GEORGE and M. CLEMENCEAU agreed.

(M. Clemenceau undertook to instruct Marshal Foch accordingly.)

8. M. CLEMENCEAU said he had received a letter from Dr. Beneš, who wanted to be heard on the Military and Financial questions.

(It was agreed that Dr Beneš should be heard, and Sir Maurice Hankey was instructed to draft a reply.)

9. M. CLEMENCEAU handed Sir Maurice Hankey a Note prepared for the Council of the Principal Allied and Associated Powers by the Council of Foreign Ministers, dealing with Boundaries in the Banat.

(Sir Maurice Hankey was instructed to translate and circulate the Note.)

10. M. CLEMENCEAU handed Sir Maurice Hankey a letter received from the Marquis Saionji, asking that in ordinary circumstances Japan might be represented on the Council of the Principal Allied and Associated Powers.

(Sir Maurice Hankey was instructed to draft a polite reply to the effect that Japan would be invited whenever questions particularly affecting her were under consideration.)

11. M. CLEMENCEAU read a Note from the Secretary-General, suggesting that the letter forwarded by the German Delegation of May 17th concerning the provisions contained in Article 438 of the Conditions of Peace (Religious Missions)[7] should be referred to the Committee appointed to deal with political questions outside Europe, composed of Messrs. Beer (America), Macleay (British Empire),[8] de Peretti (France),[9] della Torretta (Italy),[10] Chinda (Japan).

(This proposal was approved, and Sir Maurice Hankey was instructed to notify the Secretary-General accordingly.)

12. A letter from the German Delegation, dated May 24th, on the subject of responsibility for the consequences of the war and reparation, was read. (Appendix V.)

(It was agreed that the letter should be sent to the Commission dealing with Reparations in the Austrian Treaty, which should be asked to advise the Council of the Principal Allied and Associated Powers as to the nature of the reply to be sent.)

APPENDIX V TO C.F.32.
RESPONSIBILITIES.
TRANSLATION OF NOTE FROM HERR BROCKDORFF-RANTZAU.

GERMAN PEACE DELEGATION,
VERSAILLES.

Sir,   May 24th, 1919.

The contents of your Excellency's note of 20th inst., concerning the question of Germany's responsibility for the consequences of the war,[11] have shown the German Peace Delegation that the Allied and Associated Governments have completely misunderstood the sense in which the German Government and the German nation tacitly gave their assent to the note of Secretary of State Lansing of November 5th 1918. In order to clear up this misunderstanding the German Delegation find themselves compelled to remind the Allied and Associated Governments of the events which preceded that note.

The President of the United States of America had several times solemnly declared that the world-war should be terminated not by a

[7] It is printed in PPC, VI, 779-780.

[8] That is, James William Ronald Macleay, a technical expert on political and diplomatic questions relating to the Far East in the British delegation.

[9] Count Emmanuel de Peretti de la Rocca, chief of the African section in the French Foreign Ministry and an adviser on political and diplomatic questions in the French delegation.

[10] Pietro Paolo Tomasi, Marchese della Torretta, former Chargé d'Affaires in Russia; at this time, an adviser on political and diplomatic questions in the Italian delegation.

[11] It is included in Appendix III (b) to the minutes of the Council of Four printed at May 19, 1919, 4 p.m.

Peace of Might, but by a Peace of Right, and that America had entered the war solely for this Peace of Right. For this war-aim the formula was established:

"No annexations, no contributions, no punitive damages"! On the
other hand, however, the President demanded the unconditional
restitution of the violated Right. The positive side of this demand
found expression in the fourteen points which were laid down by
President Wilson in his message of January 8th 1918. This message
contains two principal claims against the German nation: firstly, the
surrender of important parts of German territory in the West and in
the East on the basis of national self-determination; secondly, the
promise to restore the occupied territories of Belgium and the North
of France. Both demands could be acceded to by German Government and the German Nation, as the principle of self-determination
was concordant with the new democratic constitution of Germany,
and as the territories to be restored had by Germany's aggression,
undergone the terrors of war through an act contrary to the Law of
Nations, namely by the violation of Belgium's neutrality.

The right of self-determination of the Polish nation had, as a matter of fact, already been acknowledged by the former German Government, just the same as the wrong done to Belgium.

When, therefore, in the note the Entente transmitted by Secretary of State Lansing on November 5th 1918 to the German Government, a more detailed interpretation was given of what was meant
by restoration of the occupied territories, it appeared from the German point of view to be a matter of course that the duty to make
compensation, established in this interpretation, could not relate to
territories other than those the devastation of which had to be admitted as contrary to Right, and the restoration of which had been
proclaimed as a war-aim by the leading enemy statesmen. Thus
President Wilson, in his message of January 8th 1918, expressly
termed the reparation of the wrong done to Belgium as the healing
act without which the whole structure and validity of international
law would be for ever impaired. In a like manner the English Prime
Minister, Mr. Lloyd George, in his speech held in the House of Commons on October 22nd 1917 proclaimed:

"The first requirement always put forward by the British Government and their Allies has been the complete restoration, political,
territorial and economic, of the independence of Belgium and such
reparation as can be obtained for the devastation of its towns and
provinces. This is no demand for war indemnity, such as that imposed on France by Germany in 1871. It is not an attempt to shift
the cost of warlike operations from one belligerent to another."

What is here said of Belgium, Germany had to acknowledge also with regard to the North of France, as the German armies had only reached the French territories by the violation of Belgium's neutrality.

It was for this aggression that the German Government admitted Germany to be responsible: it did not admit Germany's alleged responsibility for the origin of the war or for the merely incidental fact that the formal declaration of war had emanated from Germany. The importance of State Secretary Lansing's note for Germany lay rather in the fact of the duty to make reparation not being limited to the restoration of material value, but being extended to every kind of damage suffered by the civilian population in the occupied territory, in person or in property, during the continuance of warfare, be it by land, by sea or from the air.

The German nation was certainly conscious of the one-sidedness in their being charged with the restoration of Belgium and Northern France, but being denied compensation for the territories in the East of Germany which had been invaded and devastated by the forces of Russian Tsarism, acting on a long premeditated plan. They have, however, acknowledged that the Russian aggression must, according to the formal provisions of the Law of Nations, be placed in a different category from the invasion of Belgium, and have therefore desisted from demanding compensation on their part.

If the Allied and Associated Governments should now maintain the view that compensation is due for every act contrary to the Law of Nations which has been committed during the war, the German Delegation does not dispute the correctness in principle of this standpoint; they beg, however, to point out that in such case, Germany also has a considerable damage-account to set up and that the duty to compensate incumbent on her adversaries—particularly in respect of the German civilian population, which has suffered immeasurable injury from starvation owing to the Blockade, a measure opposed to the Law of Nations—is not limited to the time when actual warfare was still being carried on from both sides, but has special effect in regard to the time when a one-sided war was being waged by the Allied and Associated Powers against a Germany which had voluntarily laid down arms. This view of the Allied and Associated Governments, at any rate, departs from the agreement which Germany had entered into before the Armistice was concluded. It raises an endless series of controversial questions on the horizon of the Peace negotiations and can only be brought to a practical solution through a system of impartial international arbitration, an arbitration as provided for in Article 13, part [para.?] 2, of the Draft of the Conditions of Peace.[12] This clause prescribes:

"Disputes as to the interpretation of a treaty, as to any question of international law, as to the existence of any fact which if established would constitute a breach of any international obligation, or as to the extent and nature of the reparation to be made for any such breach, are declared to be among those which are generally suitable for submission to arbitration."

Your Excellency has further pointed out in your note of the 20th instant that according to the principle of international law no nation could, through an alteration of its political form of government or through a change in the persons of its leaders, cancel an obligation once incurred by its government. The German Peace Delegation is far from contesting the correctness of this principle; they also do not protest against the execution of the agreement introduced by the former government in their proposal of October 5th 1918, but they do take objection to the punishment, provided for by the Draft of the Peace Treaty, for the alleged offences of the former political and military leaders of Germany. The President of the United States of America on December 4th 1917 declared that the war should not end in vindictive action of any kind, that no nation of people should be robbed or punished because the irresponsible rulers of the country had themselves done deep and abominable wrong. The German Delegation does not plead these or other promises to evade any obligation incumbent on Germany by the Law of Nations, but they feel entitled to call them to memory if the German nation is to be held responsible for the origin of the war and made liable for its damage.

Whilst the public negotiations immediately preceding the conclusion of the Armistice were still going on, the German nation was promised that Germany's lot would be fundamentally altered if it were severed from the fate of its rulers. The German Delegation would not like to take your Excellency's words to mean that the promise made by the Allied and Associated Governments at that time was merely a ruse of war employed to paralyse the resistence of the German nation, and that this promise is now to be withdrawn.

Your Excellency has finally contended that the Allied and Associated Governments had the right to accord to Germany the same treatment as had been adopted by her in the Peace Treaties of Frankfort and Brest Litowsk. The German Delegation for the present refrains from examining in what respects these two Acts of Peace differ from the present Peace Draft, for it is now too late for

[12] The Covenant of the League of Nations, Art. 13, Par. 2, printed at April 28, 1919, Vol. 58.

the Allied and Associated Governments to found a claim of right on these precedents. The moment for so doing has come when they had before them the alternative of accepting or rejecting the fourteen points of the President of the United States of America as a basis of Peace. In these fourteen points the reparation of the wrong done in 1870/1871 was expressly demanded and the Peace of Brest Litowsk was spoken of as a deterrent example. The Allied and Associated Governments at that time declined to take a peace of violence of the past as a model.

The German nation never having assumed the responsibility for the origin of the war, has a right to demand that it be informed by its opponents for what reasons and on what evidence these conditions of Peace are based on Germany being to blame for all damages and all sufferings of this war. It cannot therefore consent to be put off with the remark that the data on the question of responsibility collected by the Allied and Associated Governments through a special Commission are documents concerning those Governments alone. This, a question of life or death for the German nation, must be discussed in all publicity; methods of secret diplomacy are here out of place. The German Government reserve to themselves the liberty of reverting to the subject.

Accept, Sir, the assurance of my high esteem.

(Signed)   Brockdorff-Rantzau.

T MS (SDR, RG 256, 180.03401/32, DNA).

Mantoux's Notes of a Conversation among Wilson, Clemenceau, and Lloyd George

May 26, 1919, 3:30 p.m.

Lloyd George. M. Orlando did not take the opportunity which was offered to him this morning. I will make him speak.

Clemenceau. M. Tardieu has seen M. Crespi: the latter mentioned the desiderata of Italy touching the Tarvis Pass and Albania. If the Italian argument was accepted on these two points, that would help in the solution. As for M. Orlando, he no longer knows where he is. If this course is opened to him, I believe that one can make him move.

Lloyd George. The difficulty is that, when an agreement is reached with M. Orlando, he returns to see Baron Sonnino, and it becomes apparent that nothing has been done. Baron Sonnino has ideas of expansion in Asia.

Clemenceau. On this point, I will tell you that I have been notified that the Italians have seized two more points in Asia Minor. If things go on in this way, I do not see how far it will take us. I will tell M. Orlando today: "You must speak; we have the right to ask you to make known in writing what you want."

I told him in our conversation yesterday: "You failed to inform your Chamber of Deputies that, in the Treaty of London, Fiume was promised by the Italian government to the Croatians, and because we did not wish to embarrass you, the British Prime Minister and I have not been able to explain that to our own parliaments."

M. Orlando must speak now and give us his proposals in writing. We ourselves will reply in writing.

Lloyd George. Shall we raise the question of Asia Minor at the same time?

Clemenceau. That would seem to me more difficult. The public does not understand anything about it, and I must tell you that the Greek landing was rather poorly done. There were difficulties, people were killed. I fear that the Greeks are behaving a little like the Poles.

Lloyd George. M. Vénisélos holds his Greeks in hand better than M. Paderewski his Poles. But I fear that the Greek army is worse than the Italian army, and there are also discussions which I do not like among our representatives in Constantinople. We must beware of all that.

Wilson. It is better to separate the question of Asia Minor from the question of the Adriatic. For the peace of the world, I believe that Italy must remain outside Asia Minor.

Clemenceau. We will repeat that there can be no question of the Treaty of London if Italy insists upon Fiume. The Italians must be obliged to speak: the public knows nothing.

Lloyd George. Perhaps things would go better if the public knew even less about it.

Clemenceau. The French public does not know the facts. The demonstration which has just taken place in both Chambers[1]—and which, in my opinion, is useful—rests upon a complete misunderstanding.

Lloyd George. In fact, I believe that here, as at home, one thinks rather little about Italy.

Clemenceau. The only way out is to ask the question clearly, and I have told M. Orlando to consider the consequences if Italy should break with the United States.

Wilson. What I fear is that publicity might make a retreat more difficult for the Italian statesmen, because people who are at once weak and obstinate believe that it is impossible to draw back once it is known what position they have taken.

Lloyd George. I am completely reassured regarding the repercussion on British opinion.

Clemenceau. I said to M. Orlando: "You have bought our newspapers." He disputed the fact. I replied to him: "Do you want proof?" My opinion is that all this must be brought into full light.

Lloyd George. Concerning the treaty with Austria, I suggest communicating to the Austrian delegation the parts of the treaty which will be ready next Wednesday. We cannot prolong indefinitely the present state of affairs. The British government is divided between Paris and London, and one or another of our ministers is obliged to make the trip each week.

Clemenceau. If Italy claims Dalmatia, we will see what we have to do.

Wilson. The Italians must realize, furthermore, that they cannot have what they want without the consent of the United States. If their only preoccupation is to save their pride, they are throwing themselves into an impasse.

I adhere to the principle that one cannot dispose of peoples without their consent: it is necessary for the Italian government to begin by admitting this as we do. I will say to M. Orlando: "Can you ask the United States, as a member of the League of Nations, its guarantee of a frontier, the layout of which it would disapprove?"

It is absurd to insist upon the execution of the Treaty of London, when Russia, which signed it, is no longer in the ranks of the Allies and when, among the powers which will make peace tomorrow is the United States, which did not sign the Treaty of London—while the enemy against which this treaty was directed, Austria-Hungary, has disappeared!

Lloyd George. In spite of that, we are bound by our signature. The Italians have taken their part of the reciprocal commitment: they have lost 500,000 men.

Clemenceau. Are you sure of this? M. Pašić told me the other day on this subject, while stroking his long beard, "It is in retreats that most men are always lost."

Wilson. Did not Italy declare war on Germany a year after the time she had agreed to break with all your enemies?

Clemenceau. Should I ask M. Orlando this question?

Wilson. Yes, but it is better not to ask for anything in writing, for the reason which I have just mentioned.

Clemenceau. Not yet.

[1] "FRENCH TRIBUTE TO ITALY . . . Paris, May 23. On the occasion of the anniversary of the entrance of Italy into the war, the French Chamber of Deputies and Senate today adopted unanimously a resolution asserting the continued fraternity of the two nations, and declaring they

would remain united in a just and durable peace. The Government associated itself with the resolution." *New York Times*, May 24, 1919.

Hankey's Notes of a Meeting of the Council of Four[1]

President Wilson's House,
Paris, May 26, 1919, 4:00 p.m.

C.F.33.

M. LAMONT, M. TARDIEU and M. CRESPI attended to present the attached note from the Reparation Commission (Appendix).

MR. LLOYD GEORGE asked that his decision on the first point might be reserved, as he had received a letter from General Smuts, and wished to discuss the whole question with him, before giving a reply.

In regard to the second point it was agreed:

That the Commission was empowered to discuss the remarks made by the Delegation of the Powers having special interests, and eventually to present before the Supreme Council new proposals both as regards the Reparation Clauses and the Financial Clauses, and particularly as regards the recommendation of the participation of small Nations in the burden of reparation.

MR. LLOYD GEORGE expressed the hope that the question should be rediscussed with an open mind, as though no decision had already been taken. He expressed his intention of instructing the British representatives in this sense.

At this point the members of the Committee on New States were introduced. The proceedings of this part of the Meeting are recorded as a separate Meeting.

APPENDIX TO C.F.33.

26th May 1919.

The Commission, sitting this morning, has heard the Delegations of the Powers having special interests.

After the departure of these Delegates, the Commission, as a result of an exchange of views between Messrs. LAMONT, Lord SUMNER, M.M. LOUCHEUR & TARDIEU, think it necessary to ask the Supreme Council:

1°—Whether General SMUTS and Mr. KEYNES, who have not attended this morning's meeting, have been officially appointed by Mr. LLOYD GEORGE, in the same way as M.M. LOUCHEUR & TARDIEU have been appointed by M. CLEMENCEAU, and Messrs. LAMONT, BARUCH & DAVIS by President Wilson.

2°—Whether the Commission is empowered to discuss the remarks made by the Delegation of the Powers having special interests, and eventually, to present before the Supreme Council new proposals both as regards the Reparation Clauses and the financial Clauses, and particularly as regards the reconsideration of the participation of small Nations in the burden of Reparations.

T MS (SDR, RG 256, 180.03401/33, DNA).
  [1] The complete text of these minutes is printed in *PPC*, VI, 43-44.

Hankey's and Mantoux's Notes of a Meeting of the Council of Four[1]

President Wilson's House,
C.F.34.   Paris, May 26, 1919, 4:15 p.m.

1. The Council had before them the draft articles prepared by the Committee on New States for inclusion in the Treaties with Austria and with Hungary. (Appendix I.)

It was pointed out that the clauses were the same as those already approved for Poland, except that the special clauses relating to the Jews were not included. These were believed to be unnecessary in the case of Austria, where the situation was different in that respect to the situation in Poland.

PRESIDENT WILSON raised the question whether it would not be better to include these clauses, even if unnecessary, in the Treaty with Austria to avoid giving offence to Poland, but did not press the point.

MR. HEADLAM-MORLEY asked whether Austria was regarded as a New State or as an old State, the inheritor of the Austro-Hungarian Empire. Some parts of the Treaty appeared to have been drafted on the former hypothesis, some on the latter. It was dangerous to treat Austria as possessing the rights formerly belonging to the Austro-Hungarian Empire. He produced a Memorandum and some draft articles which he had prepared on the subject.

MR. LLOYD GEORGE thought that there was a good deal in this idea, and proposed that the point should be examined by the Drafting Committee.

M. ORLANDO said that the question would require careful consideration and that at first sight he was not favourably impressed by the suggestion. He thought it was creating a new precedent.

M. CLEMENCEAU entirely supported M. Orlando.

PRESIDENT WILSON thought that M. Orlando had not entirely realised the difficulty. The Austro-Hungarian Empire was in an entirely special position.

  [1] The complete text of Hankey's minutes is printed in *PPC*, VI, 45-59.

(It was decided to refer this point to the Drafting Committee who should be authorised either to deal with the matter themselves or to take such advice as might seem to them requisite.)

(The draft clauses relating to minorities were approved.) . . .

§ Mantoux's notes:

The members of the commission charged with studying the problem of reparations in view of the treaty with Austria are introduced. After an exchange of views, it is agreed that the commission should take up the entire question again, without taking any earlier decisions into account.

The members of the commission on national and religious minorities are introduced.

Wilson. For the guarantees to the minorities, shall we write the same stipulations into the Austrian treaty which we wish to impose on the Poles, Czechs, etc.?

Headlam-Morley. It would seem very difficult not to impose on the Austrians and the Hungarians the same conditions as on friendly states, although the problem of minorities does not arise in either Austria or Hungary, within the boundaries that these two countries will have, as it arises in certain others.

Wilson. Mr. Miller explained to me that the conditions relative to the Jews have not been inserted into the Austrian treaty, because the question arises in a totally different way than in Poland.

Headlam-Morley. Everyone tells me that the situation of the Jews in Poland is quite peculiar to that country.

Wilson. The experts appear to agree on all points; but what we wish to avoid is the impression that we are imposing on friendly states conditions which we have omitted in a treaty with enemies. Will the Poles be able to complain if certain clauses relative to the Jews do not appear in the Austrian treaty?

Headlam-Morley. I do not think so.

Berthelot. There will nevertheless be a question of national minorities in Austria, for about 500,000 Czechs will remain in the interior of that country. As to the Jews, the question arises in a completely different manner than in Poland, where they constitute 14 per cent of the population.

Wilson. What I mean is this: even if the clauses concerning the Jews are not necessary in the treaty with Austria, is it not politically desirable to insert them in the treaty anyway, to avoid a complaint on the part of the Poles?

Headlam-Morley. I have another question to submit to you. In our work, we have treated Austria as a new state. It is necessary that the question be put; for, in the entire treaty, except in the financial clauses, the Austrian Republic has been considered heir to the former Austrian Empire. If Austria is a new state, she cannot cede territory to the Yugoslavs, the Czechs, or the Poles.

The former Austria has disappeared from the face of the earth: the present Austrian state must not be asked to renounce, for example, the Treaty of Algeciras,[2] because that state did not participate in it any more than did the Czech or the Polish states.

Wilson. What you indicate is true from a historical point of view. But from the juridical point of view, has not the present Austria succeeded the former Austria?

Headlam-Morley. German Austria never had supremacy over the Kingdom of Bohemia.

Lloyd George. All the constituent parts of Austria-Hungary will sign the treaty one after the other.

Headlam-Morley. The present Austria is only a part of the former empire; she is not the former empire diminished.

Wilson. In this case, why are we treating her as an enemy state?

Headlam-Morley. In fact, she is in that situation. But I insist upon my point of view, because it is important not to let Austria speak in the name of the Germans of Bohemia. She must be told clearly: "You are a new state, and you have no right over your neighboring states."

Wilson. In that case, Austria would not have to cede any territories.

Headlam-Morley. No; she would only have to renounce her union with other nationalities, whose frontiers we would indicate.

Miller. It seems to me that Austria and Hungary are enemy states, not only in fact, but juridically: a state of war exists between us and these states. Like Mr. Headlam-Morley, I think that there exists no successor to Austria-Hungary; the right of Austria to speak for the Germans of Bohemia is inadmissible. The Germans of Bohemia are a minority in another state.

Headlam-Morley. In asking Austria to renounce her rights over this or that territory, you implicitly recognize those very rights.

Lloyd George. I recognize that there is much to be said in favor of this argument, which deserves to be studied closely. What would satisfy Mr. Headlam-Morley would be a preamble recalling that the Austro-Hungarian Monarchy has ceased to exist by the will of the populations, that the different parts of the Austro-Hungarian Empire are becoming states or are joining pre-existing states, Austria being nothing other than one among them. It is a question which must be referred to the experts.

Orlando. The problem is important and deserves to be studied

[2] The so-called Act of Algeciras, the result of the Conference of Algeciras held by the major European powers from January 16 to April 7, 1906. It had settled the first Moroccan crisis and recognized the dominant position of France in Morocco.

closely. I will simply observe that, if we adopt the views of Mr. Head-lam-Morley, we shall depart from what we have done heretofore: the credentials have already been exchanged without this point of view having been taken into account.

As for the disappearance of the former state of Austria, it is a debatable fact. We were then in the presence of two states, the Austrian state and the Hungarian state, with distinct sovereignties, two parliaments making their laws separately. Does the fact that many territories cease to be part of Austria result in the disappearance of the Austrian state? That is very debatable.

In law, changes in quantity do not change the quality of the object. Germany, deprived of Silesia, of Alsace-Lorraine, of the Saar, of Schleswig, remains Germany. Is not Austria simply a diminished state?

We have a precedent, that of Turkey. When European Turkey was reduced to a bit of Thrace, it was a radical amputation; it was never said, however, that Turkey had disappeared. Since 1878, when Serbia became independent, and Bulgaria received her autonomy, Turkey has been cut up bit by bit: the Ottoman state has nevertheless survived.

My conclusion is that that question is so serious that it would be dangerous to formulate a conclusion without a very thorough study.

Clemenceau. I completely support what M. Orlando has just said.

Wilson. The difference between the cases which have just been cited and that of Austria is greater than M. Orlando appears to believe. Turkey constitutes a single state; the same thing was true of Germany, despite the federal character of her government. But Austria was one of two states, bound to each other by a personal union and by the compromise of 1867, which regulated their relations and instituted, for questions of common interest, a sort of federal government, the Austro-Hungarian Delegations.

This dual monarchy dissolved itself. Take Bosnia-Herzegovina: I cannot remember if she was assigned to Austria or to both states at once.

Headlam-Morley. It was a country of the empire, which belonged jointly to Austria and to Hungary.

Wilson. This complicates the situation even more; for here is a territory which neither of the two states could alone cede to a foreign state. Such a complicated situation is very different from that of Turkey or of Germany.

Lloyd George. M. Orlando has said that in law, quantity cannot affect quality; but there is a point where quantity subsumes quality. If you take Alsace-Lorraine and a part of Silesia away from Germany, Germany subsists. But Czechoslovakia is going to be a country of thirteen million inhabitants, and Austria will only have eight millions. Galicia was also a part of Austria. When one takes away from a state three quarters of its territory, can one say that that state subsists? If Germany lost Bavaria, Saxony, Württemberg, Hannover, and the Rhenish provinces, would she still be Germany?

There is much to be said for Mr. Headlam-Morley's argument: Austria does not even retain—like the Greek Empire when it possessed only Constantinople—the prestige of a center recognized as the national center par excellence.

Clemenceau. How should the question be presented to the experts?

Orlando. Can we not present it to those who are studying the problem of national minorities? It is not necessary to involve ourselves in a purely academic question.

Clemenceau. I will ask that they examine it at the same time when they discuss the name that the Austrian state should take. I would not accept the appellation of German Austria.

Wilson. We could say: "New Austrian State."

Lloyd George. If the Drafting Committee is too busy to settle that question, we will ask it to appoint jurists who can deal with it.

The experts withdraw.

Wilson. I have received a letter from the Luxembourg government, announcing to me that it is ready to send a delegation to us and asking at what date it could be received.[3]

Lloyd George. When will the treaty with Austria be ready?

Hankey. Not before Saturday, taking into account the time necessary for printing and corrections.

Wilson. Do you want to summon the Luxemburgers for Wednesday evening?

Lloyd George. It is agreed.[4]

Clemenceau. Must not the Belgians be present?

Lloyd George. I believe that they must be invited.

Hankey. So I am to ask the Secretariat to inform the Austrian delegates about the date when the treaty can be communicated to them—toward the end of this week. At the same time, one could invite the Austrian delegation to designate experts who would be consulted on the question of reparations and on the military clauses.

Wilson. The reason why we are negotiating these two questions apart from the rest must be indicated. That reason is the division of Austria-Hungary into several states and the necessity of taking into account the respective rights and interests of these states.

[3] E. Reuter to WW, May 26, 1919, T telegram (WP, DLC).
[4] Wilson conveyed this invitation to the delegation from Luxembourg in WW to E. Reuter, May 26, 1919, T telegram (WP, DLC).

Orlando. Why ask the Austrian delegation to name its experts immediately? We can wait a bit. The important thing is to make clear the distinction which justifies the separate treatment of these two questions.

Wilson. It is easy to show that it is the consequence of the division of the Austro-Hungarian Empire and of the relations which must be anticipated among the different states of Central Europe.

President Wilson reads from a memorandum on Carinthia.[5]

Wilson. You remember that we gathered at the Quai d'Orsay with the Ministers of Foreign Affairs in order to study that question.[6] On the triangle of Tarvis, we adopted the recommendations of the Ministers of Foreign Affairs. Since then, the question of the plebiscite in Klagenfurt has arisen. The insistence of the Yugoslavs has modified the opinion of our experts: they now suggest to cut this district into two parts, the south being given to the Yugoslavs without plebiscite.

On the region of Klagenfurt, I have an interesting report supplied by four Americans who visited this area.[7] The feeling of the population, they say, is Austrian. Carinthia, whatever the origin of its populations, forms a geographic and economic entity. If we place under the government of the Yugoslavs the area to the south of the Drava, with a plebiscite at the end of five years, they fear pressure and frauds which could falsify the popular vote.

Lloyd George. That means that the triangle should go to Austria?

Orlando. I know that today there was supposed to be a meeting of the experts to deliberate on the substance of this question: should not this so interesting document be communicated to them?

Clemenceau. We have a document to the contrary, furnished by M. Pašić.

Orlando. The most urgent thing is to stop the fighting which goes on at this moment between the Yugoslav and German populations in that region; it is necessary, as at Lemberg, to seek to impose an armistice. Should we not, as with the Poles and the Ukrainians, give a warning to the two parties face to face?

Wilson. The American experts had recommended what we had approved together at the Quai d'Orsay; but their opinion was changed.

Lloyd George. I propose to put over until tomorrow the study of this question.

Orlando. But what will you do to stop the hostilities? That is an urgent necessity.

Wilson. Make a proposal.

[5] C. Day and C. Seymour to the American Commissioners, May 22, 1919.
[6] See the minutes of the Council of Ten printed at May 12, 1919, 4 p.m.
[7] S. Miles to WW, May 22, 1919.

Orlando. I will seek a formula with a view to a proposal for an armistice.

Wilson. My opinion is that one can only stop the hostilities in Carinthia by fixing the frontiers.

Clemenceau. Can we not send a dispatch to Agram and another to Vienna?

Orlando. The Austrian delegation raises the question insistently; a reply must be given.

Clemenceau. The Austrians are indeed making this request; they even insist on having interviews with us. The Secretariat replied by asking them to send a written note.

Orlando. It is not a question of study but of immediate action.

Wilson. We can address ourselves to the Austrian and Yugoslav delegations in Paris, demanding that they cease hostilities.

Lloyd George. They will both ask: "Where will you stop us?" It is always the question of the frontier which is asked.

Wilson. They must be told: "Stop your fighting at once."

Orlando. That's right. For us, it is a matter of conscience not to allow this situation to be prolonged.

Clemenceau. I am willing to try.

Lloyd George. Can we not form a very small commission, as we have already done in a similar case, to settle the question of the frontier quickly?

Orlando. The simplest thing is to hasten the work of the commission which has studied that question in detail.

Wilson. I believe that it should be asked to name a limited subcommission, which will reach conclusions more quickly.

Lloyd George. And to summon the Austrians and the Yugoslavs.

Orlando. Once the frontier has been fixed, the fighting will obviously cease.

Wilson. The simplest thing is for us to take the matter in hand, to fix the frontier, and then invite them both to withdraw into their respective territories.

Clemenceau. We could hold another meeting with the Ministers of Foreign Affairs on this subject.

Wilson. That's fine, tomorrow for example. §

7. M. CLEMENCEAU said he wished to make a last appeal to his Italian colleague. The situation had fortunately not as yet reached the worst point of gravity. Nevertheless, it was necessary to present the terms to the Austrians very shortly, and consequently it was impossible to leave them much longer at St. Germain without a conversation. Yesterday he had seen M. Orlando, and had explained to him the gravity of the present situation for France as well as for Italy. M. Orlando, with his usual open-mindedness, had said that some pro-

posal must be made. First, however, some definite conversations must take place. He did not want to anticipate M. Orlando's proposals, but he hoped that some proposal would be made to get out of the difficulty. It would be an immeasurable relief, even if an unsatisfactory solution could be reached, and this relief would extend not only to Governments, but to people. If M. Orlando was not prepared to propose anything today, he hoped he would do so as early as possible.

M. ORLANDO said that, as he had remarked this morning, it would be a veritable liberation to get a solution, and he was fully in accord with M. Clemenceau on this, and he thanked him for raising the question. M. Clemenceau had stated his own sentiments perfectly. M. Clemenceau asked what was the decision of Italy? When this question had been discussed here between April 15th and April 20th, a marked difference had been shown between the maximum[8] demands of Italy and the common views of all the Allied and Associated Powers. On April 20th he himself had said that, given the situation in which Italy had to renounce everything outside the Treaty of London, he would insist on adherence to the Treaty of London with all that it involved.[9] He recognised, however, that this would divide him and his Allies from President Wilson, for the Allies stated that they would adhere to the Treaty although they were not perhaps in accord with it. But President Wilson said that he was not in accord with it and not bound by it. Thus, a difference would be created between the United States on the one hand, and France and Great Britain on the other, and this was very undesirable. From the Italian point of view, what he desired was some transaction which would involve an agreement, but, failing that, he must claim the Treaty, however undesirable. He would seek every way of conciliation. For example, there had been the proposals of Mr Lloyd George between April 20th and 23rd.[10] Later, there had been the discussions between Col. House and Mr Miller and himself.[11] He desired ardently to get out of the difficulty with the agreement of everyone. But, if not, he must demand the Treaty of London.

PRESIDENT WILSON said that he feared they were somewhat in danger of getting into a *cul de sac*. He wanted very earnestly to point out to his Italian colleague the situation as it presented itself to him as a whole. We could not move in two opposite directions at once, and yet the Italians appeared to be trying to do so. The Treaty of Lon-

[8] "minimum" in Mantoux, II, 221.
[9] See the minutes of the Council of Four printed at April 20, 1919, 10 a.m., Vol. 57.
[10] See, for example, the minutes of the Council of Four printed at April 22, 1919, 4 p.m., *ibid.*
[11] Again, see the extracts from the Diary of Colonel House printed at May 13, 16, and 17, 1919, and those from the Diary of D. H. Miller printed at May 12, 13, and 14, 1919.

don was made in circumstances which had now altogether altered. He was not referring now to the fact of the dissolution of the Austro-Hungarian Empire, but to the partnership of the world in the development of peace, and the attention which had been directed by plain work-a-day people to this partnership as a basis of peace. When the Treaty of London had been entered into, there had only been a partnership between a few Great Powers—Russia, France, Great Britain, with Belgium and Serbia, against Germany, Austria and Turkey. As Belgian and Serbian soil had been violated, the only voluntary partners were France, Great Britain and Russia. He understood that these Powers had wished to induce Italy to become a partner, and for this reason had entered into the Treaty of London. At that time the world had not perceived that the war was a matter of common concern. He knew this because his own people had gone through this phase. He himself, probably before most of his people, saw the effect that the war was going to have on the future destinies and political development of the world. Slowly, at first very slowly, the world had seen that something was being done which cut at the roots of individual liberty and action. When that was realised, there was a common impulse to unite against the Central Empires. Thus, there came into the war many peoples whose interest was absolutely separate from any territorial question that was European in character. They came in for motives that had no connection with territory or any advantage. They sought only the emancipation of the world from an intolerable threat. Then there came new ideas, and the people of the world began to perceive that they had a common purpose. They realised that it was not only Belgium and Serbia, but all the small States that were threatened. Next there was a realisation of the rights of minorities and small groups of all kinds. The light broadened out into a perception of the final settlement that was at hand. It was about this time that he himself had made his address to Congress on the results of the war. His own address had taken place, he thought, three days after Mr Lloyd George's address to the House of Parliament.[12] The only difference between the two addresses was that he summed up his in 14 points. Both his speech and that of the Prime Minister of Great Britain contained the same line of thought and ideas. They stated in their speeches what was coming into the consciousness of the world. When the Armistice was reached, his own statements had been accepted as the basis not only of the Armistice, but also of the peace. These ideas had by this time taken possession of all the world, and even the Orient was beginning to share them. Then came the League of Nations as a prac-

[12] About Lloyd George's speech of January 5, 1918, see British embassy to WW, Jan. 5, 1918, n. 2, Vol. 45. Wilson's Fourteen Points address is printed at January 8, 1918, *ibid.*

tical thing,—up to then, it had been regarded as of academic interest,—and the nations of the world desired to achieve peace on that
basis; hence, when the Peace Conference began, the whole platform of the Peace had been laid down. This platform had no relation
to the ideas which belonged to the old order in European politics,
namely, that the stronger Powers could dispose of the weaker. Great
Britain and France had no right because they were strong to hand
over peoples who were weak. The new conception did not admit of
this. If these principles were insisted on, they would violate the new
principles. There would then be a reaction among the small nations
that would go to the very heart of the Peace of the world: for all those
small nations, when they saw other nations handed over, would say,
"Our turn will come next." One of the reasons for which the United
States people had gone to war was that they were told that the old-
fashioned methods were dead. Hence, if Italy insisted on the Treaty
of London, she would strike at the roots of the new system and undermine the new order. The United States would be asked under the
Covenant of the League of Nations to guarantee the boundaries of
Italy, and they could not do so if this Treaty were insisted on. There
was one question which would not be susceptible of solution. If Italy
insisted on the Treaty of London, as M. Clemenceau had pointed
out, we could not ask Yugo-Slavia to reduce her army below the
point necessary to maintain her safety against Italy. Yugo-Slavia
would never do it. It would be impossible to use force against her—
against the very power whose violation had caused the outbreak of
the present war. This process could not be repeated to accomplish
the ends the Italians had in view. If he was to be the spokesman and
the spiritual representative of his people, he could not consent to
any people being handed over without their consent. But he could
consent to any people being handed over who stated that they
wished to be. He was willing that Italy should have any part on the
eastward slope of the Istrian Peninsula whose population would vote
to be attached to Italy. Only he could not assent to any population
being attached that did not so vote. He wanted to point out to M. Orlando that Great Britain and France could not hand over any part of
Yugo-Slavia to Italy, and that it could not be a legal transaction, except in accordance with the general peace; that is to say, only in the
event of all parties being in agreement. It was constantly urged in
the Italian Press and by Italian spokesmen that they did not want to
abandon the Italians on the other side of the Adriatic. Was it not possible to obtain all she desired by means of a plebiscite? There would
be no risk to Italy to leave the operation of a plebiscite to be carried
out under the League of Nations. Italy herself would be a member
of the League of Nations, and there would be no possibility of her

being treated unfairly. If Italy did not take advantage of this, she would be establishing her enemies on her eastern borders. Thus there would be a beginning again of the evils that had arisen in the Balkans. Beyond the boundaries of Italy would be the Yugo-Slavs with their eyes turned toward the population which had been placed under Italy by the powerful Western nations. It was impossible for Italy to adopt both methods. Either she must abandon the new methods altogether, or else she must wholly abandon the old methods and enter into the new world with the new methods under conditions more hopeful for peace than had ever before prevailed.

M. ORLANDO said he had no difficulty in recognising that President Wilson's speech was perfectly logical, provided that his hypotheses were correct. What he disputed, however, was the correctness of those hypotheses. He could not admit that the Treaty of London was a violation of the principles of justice and right. The Treaty of London had merely anticipated the boundaries which would have to be drawn. All through the present Conference terrible problems had presented themselves, involving ethnical, geographical, strategical and other considerations, and in every case great difficulties had had to be surmounted in order to reach a solution. The Treaty of London had merely anticipated these difficulties. The Treaty of London was indeed a compromise transaction. It was a compromise because of the renunciation by Italy of Fiume and half of Dalmatia, including the Italian towns of Spalato and Trau. It was a compromise because of the admixture of races. Hence, he could not admit the premise of President Wilson that the Treaty of London was, without discussion, a violation of right and justice. Whether it was good or bad, it was a compromise. Experience showed that for Italy it was a bad compromise, because Italy did not get satisfaction on Fiume. He deeply regretted this, but accepted it in a spirit of compromise. However, if the Treaty was not acceptable another solution must be sought.[13] He much regretted that he could not possibly accept a plebiscite. His first reason for rejecting it was that it would prolong the present state of anxiety in Italy. His second objection was the complexity of the problems. He could not deny, for example, that on the eastern slope of the Istrian Alps, the majority of the inhabitants were Slavs. Consequently, a plebiscite would not give the right result to Italy. But in this case he had to seek a different principle from the ethnographical principle, namely, that the line of the Alps was the defence of his country. His third reason—and he did

[13] Mantoux, II, 224-25: "I know the absolute opposition of President Wilson to the Treaty of London. It is an agonizing fact that this compromise, whatever its intrinsic value, should not have the approval of a power which has served the entire world and Italy herself so well, that it be rejected by a man whom I respect, and so I say: it is necessary to look for something else."

not wish to make comparisons detrimental to other peoples—was that there was a different state of culture in Jugo-Slavia from Italy, because there was a different state of civilisation. It was quite true that Italian military authorities had, in many places, got on perfectly well with the inhabitants. But, nevertheless, in these conditions he could not count with any confidence on the sincerity of the plebiscite. These were the three reasons why he could not accept the proposal for a plebiscite. He was ready to try and find a solution, but he could not see one at present. His conclusion unfortunately, therefore, was that an *impasse* had been reached. In these circumstances, what course was open to him? He had only his Treaty to make an appeal to. He was not a Shylock, demanding his pound of flesh from the Jugo-Slavs. Great Britain and France had given their adhesion to this arrangement. He could not say he was satisfied with the Treaty and he regretted profoundly the difficulty it had created with the United States. But as no other way could be found out, he was bound to adhere to this attitude.

PRESIDENT WILSON said that he did not characterise the Treaty in the manner M. Orlando had suggested, but only as inconsistent with the new order of settlements, namely, that the ethnical principle should be adopted except where other paramount considerations, such as the existence of the Alps, were introduced. If there was no doubt the principle of self-determination should be followed. He reminded M. Orlando that, in the case of the Polish corridor, where very strong strategical considerations had applied, this territory had not been assigned to Poland, because there had been a solid German block, notwithstanding that the essential railway connecting Poland with the sea ran through this corridor. We had not even felt at liberty to assign the Port of Dantzig itself to Poland. Moreover, he did not contemplate a plebiscite without effective supervision. If any plebiscite took place it would be carefully observed and overlooked, and no plebiscite under coercion would be accepted. In the most friendly way he wished to ask whether if he, himself, stated his reasons publicly and made the proposal he had made this afternoon, that is, that the territory between the line of the crest of the Istrian Peninsula and the line of the Treaty of London should be granted a plebiscite, would M. Orlando feel equally at liberty and justified in publicly stating his objections?

M. ORLANDO said that he first wished to dissipate a misunderstanding. When he had spoken of the intimidation of the Slavs, he had not spoken of anything which was likely to occur before or during a plebiscite. He spoke rather of the fears and apprehensions for the future, which would deter people from voting for Italy. Consequently, a genuine vote would not be obtained. It was not at the moment of the plebiscite that he anticipated constraint but in the future. So far as concerned Poland, whatever the result of the plebiscite, some 1,700,000 Germans would be assigned to Poland. If the whole of the Italian claims were granted and the Austrian figures, notoriously inaccurate as they were, were taken as true, not half this number of aliens would be assigned to Italy. As regards President Wilson's last question, he would naturally try and avoid any public statement, particularly at the present time when attempts were being made to reach a solution, but, if President Wilson should make such a public statement, he would reply as he had replied to-day and would give the same arguments.

PRESIDENT WILSON said that he hoped that before M. Orlando reached a final conclusion, he would consult with his colleagues. He hoped he would remember the difficulty of carrying out the Treaty of London, even if it were correct to. He had joined in creating a machine and method that could not be used for that purpose. He hoped that he would discuss the question again and that he was not tired of trying to find some new course.

M. ORLANDO said that he could reply at once that, whenever conciliation was proposed, he would not refuse. He, therefore, accepted President Wilson's request.

M. CLEMENCEAU said that what struck him was that M. Orlando never made a proposal. From the beginning of these discussions he had never once made any definite proposal. He had made a claim to Fiume. He had applied the principle of self-determination to Fiume. But when he came to discuss Dalmatia he had dropped the principle. There was another contradiction in his method. He had claimed the Treaty of London as regards Dalmatia, but when it came to Fiume he had proposed to break the Treaty of London. Yet another argument was that, as President Wilson said, the Treaty of London was not really a solution. Supposing that France and Great Britain gave Italy the Treaty of London. It would not result in peace, and consequently did not provide a solution. Hence, the only solution put forward was not a solution. Hence, he felt that it was necessary for the methods to be changed. It might be a good plan to have a Committee of four people to examine every suggestion. If a conclusion was not reached, the Council would be the laughing stock of the world, and a position of real danger would be reached. The only solution proposed was one that would put the world in anarchy, and he hoped that when that happened nobody could say it was his fault. He could not agree to a solution that was nothing at all but a continuation of war. Hence, he demanded that the discussion should be continued. At bottom, he was in favour of the maintenance of the Treaty of London. What President Wilson had said about the change of mind of the peoples of the world which had occurred during the war was a very serious consideration. In the earlier parts of the war, people had talked about seizure of territory, but afterwards had come the idea of the liberties of peoples and the building up of new relations. The Italians must recognise this. He was not speaking against the Italian people, but he felt it was time the Italians examined these aspects of the matter, and this was a subject to which he would call his Italian colleagues' attention.

M. ORLANDO said he was quite agreed to a continuation of the discussion.

M. CLEMENCEAU again insisted that M. Orlando never made a proposal. To-day, all he could suggest was the Treaty of London, but this meant anarchy and the continuation of war. He asked M. Orlando to make proposals.

M. ORLANDO undertook to do so.

8. The Articles for inclusion in the Treaties of Peace with Austria and Hungary, approved earlier in the afternoon, were initialled by the Four Heads of Governments.

(Sir Maurice Hankey was instructed to forward them to the Drafting Committee.)

9. The Economic Clauses for insertion in the Treaties of Peace with Austria and Hungary, approved on the 24th inst.,[14] were initialled by the Four Heads of Governments.

(Sir Maurice Hankey was instructed to forward them to the Drafting Committee.)

10. The alterations in the Covenant of the League of Nations, approved at the morning meeting,[15] (addition of Air to Naval and Military Clauses) were initialled by the Four Heads of Governments.

(Sir Maurice Hankey was instructed to forward them to the Drafting Committee.)

APPENDIX I. TO C.F.34
COMMITTEE ON NEW STATES
HUNGARY
DRAFT OF ARTICLES TO BE INSERTED IN THE
TREATY WITH HUNGARY.[16]

Article 1.

Hungary being desirous to conform its institutions to the principles of liberty and justice and to give a sure guarantee to all the in-

---

[14] See the minutes of the Council of Four, May 24, 1919, 11:15 a.m., printed in PPC, VI, 1-14.

[15] For this part of the minutes of the Council of Four of May 26, 1919, 11 a.m., which we did not reproduce, see ibid., p. 25.

[16] The corresponding draft of articles to be inserted in the treaty with Austria does not accompany Hankey's minutes.

habitants of the territories over which it has assumed sovereignty, of its own free will agrees with the other parties hereto to the following articles and recognises them to be obligations of international concern of which the League of Nations has jurisdiction.

Article 2.

Hungary admits and declares to be citizens of Hungary of their own right and without any requirement of special proceedings:

1. All persons who on the 1st August 1914, were habitually resident within the frontiers of Hungary as now established and who were at that date nationals of Austria-Hungary.

2. All persons heretofore born in the said territory except those who have been naturalised in a foreign country other than Austria-Hungary.

Article 3.

Within a period of two years from the coming into force of the present Treaty any such person may opt for citizenship in any other State which consents thereto.

Option by a husband will cover his wife and option by parents will cover their children under 18 years of age.

Persons who have exercised the above right to opt must before the expiration of three years from the coming into force of the present Treaty transfer their place of residence to the State for which they opted.

Article 4.

The persons who have exercised the above right to opt will be entitled to retain their immovable property in the territory of Hungary. They may carry with them their movable property of every description. No export duties or charges may be imposed upon them in connection with the removal of such property.

Article 5.

All persons hereafter born within the frontiers of Hungary as now established who are not born nationals of another State shall *ipso facto* be citizens of Hungary.

Article 6.

Hungary undertakes full and complete protection of the life and liberty of all inhabitants of Hungary without distinction of birth, race, nationality, language, or religion.

All inhabitants of Hungary shall be entitled to the free exercise, whether public or private, of any creed, religion or belief, the practices of which are not inconsistent with public order or public morals.

Article 7.

All citizens of Hungary shall be equal before the law and shall enjoy the same civil and political rights without distinction as to race, language or religion.

Difference of religion, creed or confession shall not prejudice any citizen of Hungary in matters relating to the enjoyment of civil or political rights as for instance admission to public employments, functions and honours, or the exercise of professions and industries.

No restriction shall be imposed on the free use by any citizen of Hungary of any language in private intercourse, in commerce, in religion, in the press or published works or at public meetings.

Notwithstanding any establishment by the Hungarian Government of an official language, reasonable facilities shall be given to Hungarian citizens of other than the official speech for the use of their language, either orally or in writing, before the Courts.

Article 8.

Hungarian citizens who belong to racial, religious or linguistic minorities shall enjoy the same treatment and security in law and in fact as the other citizens of Hungary and in particular shall have an equal right to establish, manage and control at their own expense charitable, religious and social institutions, schools and other educational establishments, with the free use in them of their own language and religion.

Article 9.

The Hungarian Government will provide in the public education establishments of towns and districts in which are resident a considerable proportion of Hungarian citizens of other than Hungarian speech reasonable facilities to assure that instruction shall be given to the children of said Hungarian citizens through the medium of their own language.

In those towns and districts where there is a considerable proportion of Hungarian citizens belonging to racial, religious and linguistic minorities these minorities shall be assured of the equitable share in the enjoyment and application of sums which may be provided for out of public funds by State Department, municipal or other budget, for educational, religious or charitable purposes.

Article 10.

The above provisions regarding public or private instruction in languages other than Hungarian do not preclude the Hungarian Government from making the teaching of Hungarian obligatory.

Article 11.

Hungary agrees that the foregoing obligations shall be embodied in her fundamental law as a bill of rights, with which no law, regulation, or official action shall conflict or interfere, and as against which no law, regulation or official action shall have validity.

Article 12.

The provisions contained in the foregoing articles regarding the protection of racial, religious or linguistic minorities shall be under the protection of the League of Nations, and the consent of the Council of the League of Nations is required for any modifications thereof.

T MS (SDR, RG 256, 180.03401/34, DNA); Mantoux, II, 214-20.

To Norman Hapgood

My dear Hapgood: Paris, 26 May, 1919.

Thank you with all my heart for your note.[1] There are no special suggestions I want to make to you, but I do want to convey my heartfelt good wishes and an expression of my entire confidence that you will need no instructions.

Cordially and sincerely yours,   Woodrow Wilson

TLS (WC,NjP).
  [1] N. Hapgood to WW, May 23, 1919, TLS (WP, DLC). Hapgood had informed Wilson that he was about to leave Paris to assume his new post as American Minister in Copenhagen. He had asked Wilson to transmit to him "either directly or indirectly" any instructions about his new work that Wilson might wish to give him.

To Robert Lansing

My dear Mr. Secretary: Paris, 26 May, 1919.

I would be very much obliged if you would have the enclosed[1] acknowledged in the proper way, and Mr. Paneyko assured that we are giving our most earnest attention to settling the difficulties between Poland and the Ukraine. Please say, also, that I will keep in mind his suggestion about a joint Anglo-American Commission, though it is a little awkward to arrange for such commissions rather than for Inter-Allied bodies including all the principal Powers.

Cordially and faithfully yours,   Woodrow Wilson

CCL (WP, DLC).
  [1] The Editors have been unable to find a communication from Vasil Paneyko that suggests an Anglo-American commission; however, see V. Paneyko to WW, May 26, 1919, TLS (WP, DLC). Also, on May 17, Paneyko had requested an interallied commission to establish the boundaries between Rumania (not Poland) and Ukrainia. V. Paneyko and G. Sydorenko to WW, May 17, 1919, TLS (WP, DLC).

Gilbert Fairchild Close to Vi Kyuin Wellington Koo

My dear Mr. Minister: Paris, 26 May, 1919.

The President asks me to say, in reply to your note of May 23rd,[1] that he will be glad if you will call at his residence, 11 place des Etats Unis, at 2:15 tomorrow, Tuesday afternoon.

Sincerely yours,   [Gilbert F. Close]

CCL (WP, DLC).
  [1] V. K. W. Koo to WW, May 23, 1919, TLS (WP, DLC).

From Robert Lansing, with Enclosure

My dear Mr. President: Paris, May 26th, 1919.

I am transmitting to you herewith a copy of the letter which I have addressed to Mr. Frank P. Walsh after consultation with Colonel House.   Faithfully yours,   Robert Lansing

TLS (WP, DLC).

E N C L O S U R E

Robert Lansing to Francis Patrick Walsh

Sir: Paris, May 24th, 1919.

I have received the letter which you and Messrs. Dunne and Ryan addressed to me on May 16th[1] regarding the issuing of safe-conducts by the British Government to Eamon de Valera, Arthur Griffith and George Noble Count Plunkett, in order that they may proceed from Ireland to France and return and I immediately took steps to acquaint myself with the facts of the case, which transpired before the matter was brought to my attention by your above-mentioned letter.

I am informed that when the question of approaching the British authorities with a view to procuring the safe-conducts in question was first considered every effort was made, in an informal way, to bring you into friendly touch with the British representatives here, although owing to the nature of the case it was not possible to treat the matter officially. The British authorities having consented that you and your colleagues should visit England and Ireland although your passports were only good for France, every facility was given to you to make the journey. Before your return to Paris, however, reports were received of certain utterances made by you and your colleagues during your visit to Ireland.[2] These utterances, whatever they may have been, gave, as I am informed, the deepest offence to those persons with whom you were seeking to deal and consequently it seemed useless to make any further effort in connection with the request which you desired to make. In view of the situation thus created, I regret to inform you that the American representatives feel that any further efforts on their part connected with this matter would be futile and therefore unwise.

I am, Sir   Your obedient servant,   Robert Lansing.

TCL (WP, DLC).
  [1] It is printed as an Enclosure with RL to WW, May 18, 1919.
  [2] See D. Lloyd George to EMH, May 9, 1919, printed as an Enclosure with EMH to WW, May 9, 1919, Vol. 58.

From Robert Lansing

My dear Mr. President: Paris, May 26, 1919.

There has been submitted to me for consideration and reference to you the attached copy of text of resolutions adopted and draft of tentative agreement drawn by the representatives of the banking groups of Great Britain, France, Japan and the United States at a recent meeting held in Paris for the purpose of organizing a new international consortium for Chinese loan business.[1] The Department is ready to approve the matter provided it meets with our approval.

The resolutions show the complete acceptance by all the groups of the principles as laid down by the State Department in July last in proposing the formation of the new consortium. The tentative agreement seems to provide a working arrangement whereby those principles may be put into effect.

I recommend the early approval of the steps so far taken in order that the financial assistance so much needed by China may be made available as soon as possible.

Faithfully yours,   Robert Lansing.

TLS (R. Lansing Papers, DLC).
  [1] The enclosure was Hugh Cleveland to RL, May 23, 1919, TLS, enclosing FLP to RL, May 21, 1919, T telegram, both in the R. Lansing Papers, DLC. The text of the resolutions is printed in *FR 1919*, I, 435-36; that of the draft agreement in *ibid.*, pp. 439-42.

From Louis Marshall

Dear Mr. President: Paris, May 26, 1919.

In my letter of the 23rd inst. the pogroms occurring in Eastern Europe since the armistice were discussed. Permit me now, briefly, to touch upon another and even more alarming phase of the subject affecting those portions of Russia, whose political status is in a state of flux and whose governments have not as yet been recognized. I refer to the Ukraine, to Lithuania, Esthonia, the Lettish provinces and to the larger remnant of the former Russian Empire. Approximately five million Jews live in these regions where they tremble in daily peril of their lives. As a people that has long served as a convenient scapegoat, danger threatens them from whatsoever party that may come into power in these regions. It is an evil inheritance that has sprung from the seed of hatred and political chicanery sown by the former autocracy and bureaucracy and from religious prejudices engendered during mediaeval times, which are certain to prevail among the ignorant when fanned into flame by demagogues seeking a pretext for the concealment of their own misdeeds and inefficiency.

In all these regions there have recently taken place numerous pogroms of the most atrocious kind, whose Jewish victims are said to run into the thousands and whose possessions of large aggregate value have been looted and destroyed. The Bolsheviks and those with whom they are contending for the mastery are equally guilty. The opposing forces seem to vie with each other in their hostility to the Jews, who are viewed by the Bolsheviks as capitalistic and bourgeois, and because some men of Jewish origin are among the Bolshevists, all Jews are indiscriminately denounced by the other parties as Bolsheviks even though their past history belies such a charge.

Those familiar with these lands and with the forces now in operation there, are agreed that unless the Great Powers, as a condition of the official recognition of any new government therein, whatever it be, shall effectively protect the Jewish and other minorities, there will unquestionably result horrors unprecedented in the annals of human atrocities.

The conditions should in the first instance be those that are to be inserted in the treaties between the Principal Allied and Associated Powers and Poland, Roumania, Czecho-Slovakia for the protection of their racial, linguistic and religious minorities individually and collectively.

There should, however, be a further condition couched in the most emphatic terms, which shall bind the new governments to guarantee full and complete protection of life, liberty and property to all inhabitants within their territories, the Jews of necessity being specifically named; which shall require the pledge that no pogroms shall take place within such territories; that any person who shall encourage or incite them by word or act, or who whether in the civil or military service of the State shall fail to take immediate and effective measures to prevent or to suppress them when threatened, shall receive condign punishment; and which shall impose upon the government to be recognized and its successor absolute responsibility for any acts, whether committed by a mob or otherwise, in the nature of a pogrom.

These are minimum requirements, and a government unwilling to accept them, or unable to carry them into effect does not conform with the fundamental conditions of sovereignty.

With these safeguards the Jews of what once was Russia will be enabled to share with their fellow countrymen the duties and responsibilities of citizenship which they will joyfully perform. Without them they will face extermination. They look to you for help in their extremity.   Faithfully yours,   Louis Marshall[1]

TLS (WP, DLC).
    [1] Marshall enclosed with this letter a copy of a telegram from Jacob Henry Schiff and other American Jewish leaders, who had asked Marshall to forward it to Wilson. The telegram informed Wilson that "the greatest demonstration in the history of American Jewry" had taken place in New York on May 21, "when a monster protest was held against pogroms on Jews in Poland and other countries." J. H. Schiff *et al.* to L. Marshall, May 23, 1919, TC telegram (WP, DLC). About the demonstration, see n. 1 to JPT to WW, May 22, 1919.

From Stephen Samuel Wise

[Washington, received 26 May 1919]
    Am joining Taft Lowell and party in League of Nations State conventions trip through country beginning May twenty first to prepare way for acceptance of League Covenant. Find grave uneasiness over omission in published abstracts of anti-religious discrimination clause. Though mindful of difficulties explained by you I still believe it would be immensely valuable to have some message from you making clear that in every separate convention of the Allies with countries such as Poland and Roumania religious and other rights of minorities will be scrupulously safeguarded. Taft shared my feeling and urged above course. A message such as yours to him with permission to publish would answer.   Signed Stephen Wise.

T telegram (WP, DLC).

From Thomas Nelson Page

Personal

My dear Mr. President:　　　　　　　Rome May 26, 1919.

Referring to the matter of which I spoke to you in Paris the other day—the need that I feel of getting home as soon as the situation here shall be sufficiently calm—I am writing to say that since my return here I find this need more than ever exigent, and I should be glad to get away as soon as matters shall have become sufficiently settled for us to feel that my presence here is no longer necessary, and that no public interests will be sacrificed by my going.

My wife[1] has suffered very much from being separated so long from her children,[2] and recent events have worn upon her greatly. I am, therefore, getting her away at the end of this week.

I feel sure that you will understand how reluctant I am to add in any way to your tasks at this time. If it would obviate this, I might be permitted to take my wife home, going on leave myself, as I suggested last winter, and thus give you time to find there some one entirely satisfactory to fill my place.

I feel myself rather worn down, and am conscious that I must have a bit of rest.

Meantime, I think I should be kept advised as to the turn of matters that concern my post here. I feel that the situation here, while obscure, contains elements of peril, not only for the friendship of our two Peoples, but of the Peace itself, but that it can be relieved when a decision is arrived at. I have great confidence in your ability to find eventually a formula in accord with your principles which will be at the same time a basis on which the friendship of our people and the people of Italy can be preserved. Every day, however, adds to the difficulty.

Believe me, my dear Mr. President, with the greatest respect,

Always yours sincerely,　　Thos. Nelson Page

TLS (WP, DLC).
　[1] That is, Florence Lathrop Field Page.
　[2] Minna Field Gibson (Mrs. Algernon Edwyn) Burnaby of Baggrave Hall, Leicester, England; and Florence Field Lindsay. They were Mrs. Page's daughters by her first marriage to Henry Field, brother and former partner of the Chicago department store magnate, Marshall Field.

From Norman Hapgood

Dear Mr. President:　　　　　　　[Paris] May 26, 1919.

I am leaving for England to-morrow morning and thence to Denmark, and wanted to leave with you a few notes about Russia. It is many months now that I have been seeing Russians and Americans of all parties, trying to discern a few facts and it seems to me that several points are really clear.

1. There is only one institution in Russia that is a home growth, very large, and in active operation through the whole revolution; that is the United Co-operative Associations, with a membership of nearly twenty million. They have been working both in town and country in the ordinary way and nobody dares touch them. Mr. Berkenheim,[1] the Vice-President of the United Co-operative Associations, is now in America, asking nothing except the privilege of buying food and necessities and bringing them into any part of Russia. This privilege so far has been denied.

2. It is perfectly obvious that Admiral Kolchak, if backed by France, England and the United States, can bring down the Lenin Government, already vastly weakened by the blockade and the need of constant fighting on many fronts. I think it a great mistake to circulate atrocity stor[i]es about that Government, for I do not believe it is more severe in repressing rebellion than other governments, although it lacks control of some distinctly local elements and acts savagely when frightened by counter-efforts.

3. In deciding to have this Government put down by force it must be remembered that the majority of the leaders of the Social Revolutionaries and the Mencheviks are supporting the Bolsheviks, in spite of their dislike of them, because they resent outside interference. If you put down Lenin's Government, therefore, by sheer force, you leave the leaders of three powerful parties carrying on a constant guerilla warfare against you for an indefinite period, on an issue very difficult to recommend to liberals in our country and elsewhere. It is obvious, I think, that with the right kind of spirit the rule of Bolshevism can be put down without seeming to be an act of external coercion supporting a small and partly reactionary Russian group.

4. Thus tact would consist in treating the Bolsheviks as human beings and to a certain extent in saving their faces. Perhaps the Prinkipo experiment showed that this will not be allowed by their enemies. The principal method of doing it would be to hold a meeting of delegates from all Russia, to draw up a constitution, and recommend all the Russian Governments to accept this step. The Bolsheviks with the Mencheviks and the Social-Revolutionaries supporting them, may well come in if the meeting is called a National Council, *Council* being the exact translation of the word *Soviet*. The expression "Constituant [Constituent] Assembly," however, is a fighting expression which to them means denial of everything in the revolution and I do not think there is any chance

of them accepting this word. One of the guarantees needed would be to supervise the elections, but elections held under the Soviet system, properly supervised, would be as representative as any others, especially if among the conditions were freedom of publication, freedom of discussion and restoration of the Semstovs for a certain period preceding the elections.

I think the Lenin Government would be much more likely to come in if the supervising were done by a group of impartial neutrals, like the Danes, Norwegians and the Dutch. Next best to them (perhaps even better) would be the United States. I do not believe they would accept France and England as impartial.

One group in the Central Soviet Committee wishes to fight on to death. That group has a majority which is overcome by Lenin's personal influence. He wants to find a way of compromising and saving something, at least in principle or appearance, for the Soviet regime. If we can bring Lenin's point of view to triumph over Trotsky's, we may find it possible really to lead Russia to fairly harmonious progress. If, however, we have done nothing but force their parties or their leaders out of power, leaving them desperate, I do not think the outcome would be especially promising.

The object, of course, is to avoid mere support of Kolchak and his largely reactionary following, and to seem genuinely tolerant and universal. In the second case there is at least a possibility of success. In the first case, we make enemies of the whole left wing of the Russian people.   Sincerely yours,   Norman Hapgood

P.S. I am enclosing a copy of the Manchester Guardian.[2]

TLS (WP, DLC).
[1] That is, Alexander Berkenheim.
[2] Editorial page from the *Manchester Guardian*, May 24, 1919, clipping (WP, DLC). Hapgood had marked two editorials, entitled "Conscribing 'Intellect,' " and "Russia and Constantinople," respectively.
The first editorial commented on a news release from Omsk to the effect that Admiral Kolchak had "mobilised the intellectuals." He had issued orders for the conscription of all members of "the learned and artistic professions to serve his cause," which, the editorial sardonically remarked, was apparently "short of prophets and teachers." Kolchak had shown earlier, the editorial continued, that he was not above taking lessons from his enemies, as witnessed by his forcible dissolution of hostile representative assemblies and his elimination of dissenters and critics. However, while such actions were but "the commonplaces of despotism in all ages," Kolchak's latest move was a close copy of a step taken first by the Bolsheviks. Yet, the editorial predicted, just as it had failed with Lenin, Trotsky, and Béla Kun, this "experiment in compulsion of mind" was not likely to be any more successful in Kolchak's case. For, if the intellectuals had refused to work for Kolchak voluntarily, could it not be because they identified him with the old regime? "It is all to the good," the editorial concluded, "that the prospective liberator of Russia should be willing to take lessons even from his enemies, but when he confines his studies to the more tyrannous and futile of their experiments one may be forgiven for doubting his claim to any helpful genius of his own."
The second editorial discussed a recent proposal by certain Russian émigré leaders to give England a temporary mandate over Constantinople and to transfer it to Russia once Kolchak had established a new national government. It was argued, the editorial observed, that, while the Italian clauses of the Treaty of London should be disregarded, its

Russian clauses ought to be carried out. The only two suggestions about the future of Constantinople which the "ordinary Allied public" had so far considered at all viable—the internationalization of the city or an American mandate—had met with strong opposition both in Paris and in Washington. However, Kolchak's recent victories and the possibility of great changes in the government and the policies of Russia had modified the situation. Thus, the editorial concluded, it appeared that a "big bid" was now being made for the promise of the ultimate cession of Constantinople to Russia, which, if successful, would greatly increase the prestige and secure the future of Kolchak's party.

After-Dinner Remarks

[May 26, 1919]

Gentlemen: The honor has been accorded me of making the first speech tonight, and I am very glad to avail myself of that privilege. I want to say that I feel very much at home in this company; though, after all, I suppose no one of us feels thoroughly at home except on the other side of the water. We all feel in a very real sense that we have a common home, because we live in the atmosphere of the same conceptions and, I think, with the same political ambitions and principles.

I am particularly glad to have the opportunity of paying my very cordial respects to Mr. Pessoa. It is very delightful, for one thing, if I may say so, to know that my presidency is not ahead of me, and that his presidency is ahead of him. I wish him every happiness and every success with the greatest earnestness. And yet I cannot, if I may judge by my own experience, expect for him a very great exhilaration in the performance of the duties of his office, because, after all, to be the head of an American state is a task of unrelieved responsibility. American constitutions as a rule put so many duties of the highest sort upon the President, and so much of the responsibility of affairs of state is centered upon him, that his years in office are apt to be years a little weighted with anxiety, a little burdened with the sense of the obligation of speaking for his people, speaking what they really think and endeavoring to accomplish what they really desire.

I suppose no more delicate task is given any man than to interpret the feelings and the purposes of a great people. I know that, if I may speak for myself, the chief anxiety I have had has been to be the true interpreter of a national spirit, expressing no private and peculiar views but trying to express the general spirit of a nation. A nation looks to its President to do that; and I am happy to believe that the guest of the evening, in whose honor this dinner is given, will succeed in expressing not only the feeling of his people, but the new spirit which I am sure has come into Brazil, as it has come into the other American nations.

The comradeship of an evening like this does not consist merely of the sense of neighborhood. We are neighbors. We have always been friends. But that is all old. Something new has happened. I am not sure that I can put it into words, but there has been added to the common principles which have united the Americas time out of mind a feeling that the world at large has accepted those principles, that there has gone a thrill of hope and of expectation throughout the nations of the world which somehow seems to have its source and fountain in the things we always believed in. It is as if the pure waters of the fountains we had always drunk from had now been put to the lips of all peoples, and they have drunk and were refreshed. And it is a delightful thought to believe that these are fountains which sprung up out of the soil of the Americas. I am not, of course, suggesting or believing that political liberty had its birth in the American hemisphere, because of course it did not, but the peculiar expression of it characteristic of the modern time—that broad republicanism, that genuine feeling and practice of democracy that is becoming characteristic of the modern world—did have its origin in America; and the response of the peoples of the world to this new expression is, we may perhaps pride ourselves, a response to an American suggestion.

If that is true, we owe the world a peculiar service. If we originated great practices, we must ourselves be worthy of them. I remember not long ago attending a very interesting meeting which was held in the interest of combining Christian missionary effort throughout the world.[1] I mean eliminating the rivalry between churches and agreeing that Christian missioners should not represent this, that or the other church, but represent the general Christian impulse and principle of the world. I said I was thoroughly in sympathy with the principle, but that I hoped if it was adopted that the inhabitants of the heathen countries would not come to look at us, because we were not ourselves united, but divided; that, while we were asking them to unite, we ourselves did not set the example. My moral from that recollection is this: we, among other friends of liberty, are asking the world to unite in the interest of brotherhood and mutual service and the genuine advancement of individual and corporate liberty throughout the world. Therefore, we must set the example.

I will recall to some of you an effort that I myself made some years ago, soon after I assumed the presidency of the United States, to do that very thing. I was urging the other states of America to unite with the United States in doing something which very closely resembled the formation of the present League of Nations.[2] I was ambitious to have the Americas do the thing first and set the example to the world of what we are now about to realize. I had a double object in it, not only my pride that the Americas should set the example and show the genuineness of their principles, but that the United States should have a new relation to the other Americas.

The United States upon a famous occasion warned the governments of Europe that it would regard it as an unfriendly act if they tried to overturn free institutions in the western hemisphere and substitute their own systems of government which at that time were inimical to those free institutions. But while the United States thus undertook of its own motion to be the champion of America against such aggressions from Europe, it did not give any conclusive assurance that it would never itself be the aggressor. What I wanted to do in the proposals to which I have just referred was to offer to the other American states our own bond that they were safe against us and any illicit ambitions we might entertain, as well as safe, so far as the power of the United States could make them safe, against foreign nations.

Of course, I am sorry that that happy consummation did not come, but, after all, no doubt the impulse was contributed to by us which has now led to a sort of mutual pledge on the part of all the self-governing nations of the world that they will be friends to each other, not only, but that they will take pains to assure each other's safety and independence and territorial integrity.

No greater thing has ever happened in the political world than that, and I am particularly gratified tonight to think of the hours I have had the pleasure of spending with Mr. Pessoa as a member, along with him, of the Commission of the League of Nations which prepared the Covenant which was submitted to the conference. I have felt as I looked down the table and caught his eye that we had the same American mind in regard to the business, and when I made suggestions or used arguments that I felt were characteristically American, I would always catch sympathy in his eyes. When others perhaps did not catch the point at once, he always caught it, because, though we were not bred to the same language literally, we were bred to the same political language and the same political thought, and our ideas were the same.

It is, therefore, with a real sense of communion and of fellowship and of something more than neighborly familiarity that I find myself in this congenial company, and that I take my part with you in paying my tribute and extending my warmest best wishes to the great country of Brazil and to the gentleman who will worthily represent her in her presidential chair.

I ask you to join with me in drinking the health of the President-elect of Brazil.

T MS (WP, DLC).

¹ About this meeting, a "China Dinner" on January 14, 1909, see W. H. Grant to WW, Dec. 19, 1908, Vol. 18, and the news report printed at Jan. 28, 1911, Vol. 22.
² Wilson here referred, of course, to the so-called Pan-American Pact, about which see the Index references in Vol. 39.

To Walker Downer Hines

My dear Mr. Hines: Paris, 26, May, 1919.

I have carefully read your letter of April 24th¹ and May 12th² and am warmly obliged to you for them. They give me a fuller view of the railway question that I had before, and I hope that I shall be in a position, just as soon as I get home, to concert with you some definite advice to Congress.

In unavoidable haste,

Cordially and sincerely yours,   [Woodrow Wilson]

CCL (WP, DLC).
¹ W. D. Hines to WW, April 24, 1919, Vol. 58.
² W. D. Hines to WW, May 12, 1919, TLS (WP, DLC). Hines, who had recently returned from a trip to the West Coast, stated that, in his discussions with railroad experts throughout the country, he had found a growing appreciation of the necessity of a permanent solution of the railroad question. In particular, Hines argued, it was essential to eliminate the problem created by the existence of strong and weak railroads, a situation that could not be remedied by simply returning to the prewar system of private management of the railroads. Thus, Hines repeated his earlier suggestion (see the letter cited in n. 1 above, and n. 2 thereto) of a compulsory consolidation of the railroads. If, instead of compelling consolidations that were in the public interest, the railroads would be merely permitted to consolidate whenever it was in their interest, the country would be strewn with railroad bankruptcies for years to come, "as one weak company after another" would succumb to the unfavorable postwar conditions. Courageous dealing with this problem, Hines emphasized, was indispensable, in order to achieve results conducive to railroad development and public contentment with the situation.
    Hines then continued by discussing again the need for a positive strong assurance of an adequate return on the fair value of railroad property, with the division of any excess profits. However, Hines pointed out, there was doubt among the railroad experts whom he had consulted as to whether this assurance should merely take the form of mandatory rate making, or whether an absolute guarantee by the government should be given on the specific railroad securities. Hines believed that, if a few competitive railroad systems could be created by eliminating the weak companies, a positive statutory rule for rate making, coupled with provisions for the establishment of a general reserve fund out of part of the excess profits, would meet the situation.
    As to the labor problem, Hines observed that he had encountered no clear sentiment about how it should be addressed. His own solution was the establishment of boards of adjustment, composed of an equal number of representatives of labor and management. These bipartisan boards, Hines maintained, would dispose of most labor disputes or would, at least, "greatly diminish the margin of difference" between the workers and management. Moreover, Hines proposed that, in addition to representatives of the government, a representative of labor should be appointed to the boards of directors of the consolidated systems, since such a step would go far toward promoting a common understanding and preventing the outbreak of disturbances.
    In conclusion, Hines mentioned that the so-called Transportation Conference of the United States Chamber of Commerce had studied the railroad question in great detail. However, he believed that, although its recommendations were likely to be progressive and constructive, they would probably fall short of all the essentials, particularly in regard to the compulsory consolidation of the weak and strong railroads.

From Joseph Patrick Tumulty

[The White House, May 26, 1919]

No. 144 Every Republican member of new Foreign Relations Committee openly opposed to treaty.[1] A majority in favor of its amendment. Every Democratic member of the Committee, including Thomas, for treaty and against separation. There is a decided reaction evident against the League, caused, in my opinion, by dissatisfaction of Irish, Jews, Mediterranean[2] Poles, Italians and Germans. Republicans taking full advantage and liable, in order to garner disaffected vote, to make absolute issue against League. Reaction intensified by your absence and lack of publicity from your end and confusion caused by contradictory statements and explanations of "so-called compromises." Simonds' article,[3] appearing in certain American newspapers Sunday, admirable, explaining reasons for Saar Valley and French pact and other controversial matters. There is a vicious drive against League, resembling German propaganda, backed by Irish and Jews. Irish openly opposing; Jews attacking along collateral lines. Could not Lansing or perhaps White—who is a Republican—or yourself inspire publicity or give interview explaining,—officially or unofficially,—the following matters:

1. America's attitude toward publication of terms of the treaty, along the lines of your last cable to me.[4]

2. That the Fourteen Points have not been disregarded.

3. The underlying reasons for French pact, emphasizing the point, as Simonds says, "that French pact is merely an underwriting of the League of Nations during the period necessary for that organization, not merely to get to work, but to become established and recognized by all nations."

I am not at all disturbed by this reaction—it was inevitable. The consummation of your work in the signing of the treaty will clear the air of all these distempers. Your arrival in America, your address to Congress, and some speeches to the country will make those who oppose the League today feel ashamed of themselves.

The New York World had a very good editorial favoring the mandatory of Turkey.[5]   Tumulty.

T telegram (WP, DLC).

[1] Tumulty presumably meant that they were opposed to a treaty that included the Covenant of the League of Nations, to which they all objected to a greater or lesser degree. Senator Lodge, the new chairman of the Senate Foreign Relations Committee, had "packed" that committee with Republican members who were either openly hostile to, or as was Lodge himself, highly critical of the Covenant. The Republican holdovers on the committee were William Edgar Borah of Idaho, Frank Bosworth Brandegee of Connecticut, Albert Bacon Fall of New Mexico, Philander Chase Knox of Pennsylvania, and Porter James McCumber of North Dakota, who at this time supported the League of Nations Covenant with reservations. See the *New York Times*, May 23, 1919. The new Republi-

can members appointed by Lodge were Warren Gamaliel Harding of Ohio and Harry Stewart New of Indiana. For a detailed discussion of the controversy within the Republican party over these appointments, see Stone, *The Irreconcilables*, pp. 97-98.

² "Mediterranean" not in the copy of this telegram in the J. P. Tumulty Papers, DLC.

³ Frank H. Simonds, "The New Alliance as a Guarantee of the League," *New York Tribune*, May 25, 1919. In his long and detailed discussion, Simonds attempted to dispel the notion, apparently prevalent in the United States, that, with the League of Nations as a guarantor of peace, the French security treaty was unnecessary, and that it was, in fact, precisely one of those old alliances which the League was designed to eliminate. To begin with, Simonds argued, the League was presently no more than an association of those nations which had defeated the Central Powers. While it would be augmented in the near future by various neutral countries, it would not be able to perform its intended role until such time as Germany and her former allies would voluntarily join the League and accept its underlying principles. However, Simonds maintained, this could not happen for at least fifteen years. During this period, Germany would be compelled to fulfill the terms of the Versailles Treaty, would have part of her territory occupied, and could not be regarded as anything but a conquered enemy. Moreover, Simonds continued, it was entirely possible that Germany would try to evade her obligations under the treaty, would seek to erect a new alliance composed of Austria, Hungary, Bulgaria, Russia, and any other nations dissatisfied with the outcome of the peace conference, and would again soon be a menace to France and Belgium.

In fact, the peace settlement, which was largely based on the principles of Wilson's Fourteen Points, had left France in a particularly vulnerable position. The French leaders had claimed that only the permanent occupation of the Left Bank of the Rhine and the annexation of the Saar Basin would enable their country to withstand unassisted any possible future German aggression. However, upon Wilson's insistence that permanent peace could only be assured by the creation of a League of Nations founded on a just settlement that precluded territorial annexations, France had reluctantly agreed to abandon those claims. In return, the French leaders had demanded a firm assurance that, if the "Anglo-Saxon experiment" of the League of Nations should fail to preserve peace, France, with an open frontier to Germany, would not have to pay the total cost of a future war and would not again have large parts of her territory invaded before real help arrived.

Thus, Simonds pointed out, it was in order to insure the viability of the League of Nations and to preserve its structure during the crucial postwar period, when Germany and her former allies could not be relied upon to adhere to the principles of the League, that Wilson had committed the United States to guaranteeing, in association with Great Britain, the security of France. If Congress should reject Wilson's proposal and thereby signal to the European powers that the United States had washed its hands of a settlement which it had largely imposed, the League of Nations would "die a swift and violent death." Within the shortest time, a new system of alliances would spring up, and the hopes expressed in the League of Nations would be shattered. Simonds believed, moreover, that this development, in turn, would lead to an unraveling of the peace settlement, since all the various compromises, which were based upon the idea that justice in the settlement would be sustained by the solidarity of the members of the League, would disappear. In fact, the European powers would make a new settlement—a settlement based upon the old necessities and old considerations. It would soon lead to a new war that would not fail again to involve the United States. Simonds concluded:

"Such are the European facts affecting the Anglo-French-American agreement, which is not an alliance in any old-fashioned sense but is in reality no more than guaranteeing the league of nations against dangers which are obvious, so obvious that without the guarantee the league of nations cannot endure."

⁴ WW to JPT, May 24, 1919, T telegram (WP, DLC). This telegram was an almost verbatim copy of the first paragraph of WW to RL, May 24, 1919 (second telegram of that date), printed above.

⁵ "America as a Mandatory," New York *World*, May 24, 1919. In fact, the editorial did not specifically mention Turkey but stated merely that the United States might be "called upon to act as a mandatory for some backward or at present helpless peoples." This prospect, the editorial observed, was "filling many honest men with alarm," and it went on to admit that European envies and intrigues at Paris had tended to transform what would have been a "happy mission" into a "disturbing but unshirkable duty." The mandatories now proposed were to be an alternative to the old imperialistic practice of annexations, and, as such, they conformed to the "enlightened American idea that weak nations should be assisted rather than enslaved or exploited." Moreover, the editorial claimed, as far as the United States was concerned, the only novelty in the recent proposal was the fact that the country would have to assume responsibilities in a different hemisphere. The United States had been a mandatory of the Dominican Republic since 1907; of Nic-

aragua since 1911; it held what amounted to a mandate over Cuba and Panama; and it
was soon going to assume a mandate over the Philippines. Few great nations, the editorial
continued, were so well fitted as the United States for the role of mandatory, and it concluded: "Our motives are not questioned anywhere, and a duty is not to be avoided merely
because it seems disagreeable."

To Jessie Woodrow Wilson Sayre

My dear little Daughter: Paris, May 26, 1919.

Your sweet letter of May fourth[1] was very, very welcome. My heart
is very full of you and the other dear ones, and news of you is just
what I long for.

Things are going with provoking deliberation and slowness here,
and we are beyond measure eager to get back, so that patience becomes more difficult to maintain from day to day. We are well, however. Edith, in attempting to be her own chiropodist, injured her foot
the other day and is in bed for repairs, but is otherwise all right and
I hope will soon be about again.

There is no news to tell of ourselves, but we send hearts full of love
to you all, and are so delighted that the little family is getting on all
right and that you are looking forward with so much pleasure to
being at Martha's Vinyard. I dare not predict when we shall be starting home, but you may be sure it will be on the first day that I can
conscientiously break away.   Lovingly,   Father

TLS (RSB Coll., DLC).
    [1] Jessie W. W. Sayre to WW, May 4, 1919, Vol. 58.

To Helen Woodrow Bones

My dear Helen: Paris, 26 May, 1919.

Thank you for your letter about Fred Yates' death.[1] I had already
learned of his going. I makes me feel very sad and in a sense lonely,
because he had such a vital individuality that his departure seems to
make the world a bit emptier. Of course, Mrs. Yates and Mary will
face the loss with their usual beautiful spirit, but my heart grows
sick for them.

It was sweet of you to write. We think of you very often and with
deepest affection, and are glad to believe from the tone of your letters that you are enjoying your work with the Century Company.

We hope that it is not going to be very long now before we can turn our faces homeward. We are desperately anxious to do so, because we long for the people and the country we love.

In haste,   Affectionately yours,   [Woodrow Wilson]

CCL (WP, DLC).
  [1] Helen W. Bones to WW, May 6, 1919, TLS (WP, DLC).

From the Diary of Dr. Grayson

Tuesday, May 27, 1919.

The President and I after breakfast took a walk around in the neighborhood, and the President, with his usual observing eye, discovered what seemed to be a tiny stream of water trickling down over a hill near the Trocadero. We investigated and found that it was a natural aquarium that extended quite a distance and was filled with various kinds of fish. We looked at it for some little time, and then returned to the house by a roundabout route, which took us through a park where we could see little children basking in the sunlight under the care of their nurses.

At the session of the Big Four this morning the question of what action should be taken in connection with Russia was again taken up. It was decided to send a confidential inquiry to Admiral Koltchak to learn what his intentions were, and especially as to the position he has taken relative to the question of the Constitutional Assembly. The message to Koltchak was in no sense one of recognition of his government, but was merely designed to pave the way for such action should it be deemed wise later on. Lloyd George and Clemenceau continue to urge that Koltchak should be recognized immediately, but the President's position has been and will be that unless he can be assured that the Russian people themselves will determine the nature of the government there will be no recognition of any force in that country at this time. It is very likely that the reply will determine what further action the President will take. As a matter of fact, England is anxious that the Koltchak government should be recognized because she has been promised that all her claims and all her ante-war treaty obligations will be fulfilled. France is anxious that the Koltchak government shall be recognized because she has been assured that the Franco-Russian war debt will be assumed by the Koltchak government. And the Japanese are anxious that Koltchak should be recognized because they have assurances that he is friendly to their aspirations in Siberia.

I made arrangements to have a picture taken of the Big Four. It was taken at the close of the morning session. Lloyd George wanted me to join in the picture, which, of course, I did not do.

Clemenceau said to Lloyd George: "I have a letter for the Big Four from the chairman of the Japanese delegation." Lloyd George said: "What is the letter about?" Clemenceau shrugged his shoulders, and gesticulating with both hands, said: "Oh, it simply says that he loves us but that he doesn't see half enough of us." The Japanese are complaining that they are not given an opportunity to participate in the conference as often as they would like.

Mrs. Wilson is still confined to her bed but is improving and in excellent spirits. The President and I had lunch in her bed room. The President mentioned a number of things that transpired during the morning conference. After lunch I discussed various speakers with the President. Speaking of Daniel Webster, the President said that he never used any superfluous words, and that the President's father, who was a great scholar, used to practice by taking some of Daniel Webster's speeches to see if he could substitute other words to strengthen the speech. But never in his experience could he find one word that he could substitute and improve the meaning of the address.

After lunch the President had a conference with Wellington Koo, and at the conclusion of the conference, the President and I went to St. Cloud for an hour's ride.

The President told me this story: "An American private soldier, in talking to another private soldier said: 'I am taking a girl through the Louvre tomorrow afternoon.' His comrade said to him: 'Have you ever been there?' And he said: 'No.' He said: 'Is she a nice girl?' He replied: 'Yes.' His comrade then said: 'I would advise you to cut it out because there is a lot of rough stuff in there.' "

Lieutenant Colonel Schauffler,[1] of the Army Medical Corps, who was the President's physician when he was Governor of New Jersey, called to see me today. I took him in to see the President for a few minutes. Schauffler told me that he had been a Republican all his life and voted the Republican ticket; that he had helped to elect Frelinghuysen[2] as Senator from New Jersey, but that if he were to meet Frelinghuysen today he would hesitate even to speak to him, because of his un-American attitude towards the President, as well as his stand against the League of Nations.

I have been deeply impressed with the organized campaign of misrepresentation which apparently has set in in the United States while the President is completing his task over here. The United States Senate having very little to do, and with no facts at all before it, has been devoting its time ever since it organized for the special session to open debate on the League of Nations and on the Peace Treaty itself. The lack of efficient Democratic Senators was never so apparent as at the present time. Those men who should be in a position to defend the President's course until such time as he is able fairly and competently to present it to the people have failed to do so. One of the most stupid exhibitions that has yet been shown was the speech of Senator Reed of Missouri in the Senate yesterday. Reed is notoriously opposed to the President—for the reason that the President refused positively to allow Reed to name for office men in Missouri who were notoriously incapable and incompetent. In his criticism Reed appealed to the Southern and Western Democrats to oppose the League of Nations because he said it would put the white race in a minority. This talk is utterly stupid, but it seemed to carry considerable weight, and Senator Hitchcock, who essayed to answer, made it plain that he was not very familiar with the League of Nations covenant. It is very plain that the President has a Herculean task before him when he returns to the United States. The so-called League of Nations Committee, of which former President Taft is the head, has plainly permitted the opposition to carry the fight to them, with the result that they are now on the defensive, although there never was any necessity for this other than the stupidity on the part of certain members. In addition, it is very obvious from three thousand miles away that there is within the Democratic party a very strong minority that is afraid of the President and is hoping that something will happen to him because they want to keep the control of the party within their own hands and are afraid of his fighting methods and his strength with the common people. The Republican party after being the party of protest without policy at last apparently has decided that it must do something to destroy the President's influence with the people. This all adds to making it plain that when the President returns, he will have to go personally before the people, take them into his confidence, and show them just what actually happened over here and what a great task he has performed— one which every American must be proud of when the time comes that he really knows all the facts.

At the afternoon session the Big Four was dissolved and the Council of Ten re-constituted.[3] The reason for this was the absolute inability for the Council of Four to reach an agreement on the terms of reparation which were to be demanded of Austria. It was not a question of money so far as Austria was concerned but rather a question of whether the various new republics which are to be constituted out of the territory that will be taken from the original Hapsburg Monarchy shall pay over pro-rata a share of the war's cost as assessed by the economic experts. The Council of Four could not agree on this, and the Council of Ten did little better. The result was that it was decided to send the Austrian delegates notice that they would be furnished with copies of the proposed treaty on Friday at noon, but that it would not contain the military or economic clauses which would be filled in later on. The selection of Friday at noon somewhat embarrassed the President's plans inasmuch as Friday is Memorial Day, and the President had arranged to speak at two o'clock in the afternoon at a cemetery just outside of Paris. However, it was proposed that the cemetery arrangements could be deferred until after the notification at St. Germain.

The President had dinner in Mrs. Wilson's bed-room and retired early.

[1] William Gray Schauffler, M.D., formerly a physician of Lakewood and Spring Lake, New Jersey, surgeon general of New Jersey from 1911 to 1917, and an aide-de-camp to three Governors of the state. In 1911, Wilson had appointed him to the State Board of Education. After serving as a sanitary inspector with the Thirty-Ninth Division at Camp Beauregard, Louisiana, and in France during the war, Schauffler was at this time an information officer for the Advance General Headquarters in Germany and was attached to the Rhineland High Commission.
[2] That is, Joseph Sherman Frelinghuysen.
[3] Although Hankey's notes of this meeting at 4 p.m. are labeled "C.F.37," this was in fact a meeting of the heads of government with their Foreign Ministers and a number of experts.

To Robert Lansing

My dear Lansing: Paris, 27 May, 1919.

Your suggestion and that of my other colleagues[1] with regard to getting assurances from the governments with which we are cooperating, that no special concessions have been obtained or are in contemplation from the Koltchak government jumps with my own feeling and judgment. But it is a very delicate matter to handle, and I shall have to await a favorable opportunity. I would be interested to know whether any of you have received any intimation of such concessions. I have heard none.

Cordially and faithfully yours,   Woodrow Wilson

TLS (R. Lansing Papers, DLC).
[1] Wilson was replying to RL *et al.* to WW, May 26, 1919, TLS (WP, DLC).

Hankey's Notes of a Meeting of the Council of Four[1]

President Wilson's House,

C.F.35-A.   Paris, May 27, 1919, 11:00 a.m.

1. MR. LLOYD GEORGE stated that General Botha had come to him that morning and had indicated that he was very dissatisfied with the attitude of the Poles in regard to the Polish-Ukranian Armistice. He had asked M. Clemenceau to discuss this along with President Wilson and himself because, to speak quite frankly, he had some reasons to believe that M. Clemenceau was not fully informed as to the attitude taken by the French authorities. He had grounds for the belief that the French Minister in Warsaw[2] had encouraged the Poles in their recent attack on the Ukrainians. A fact which rather confirmed these suspicions was that General Botha reported that he had been unable to secure the attendance of the French representatives at meetings of the Armistice Commission, and this had occurred so frequently that it was difficult to believe that it was not deliberate. Then he quoted General Haller's highly indiscreet speeches, indicating among other things, that Danzig must become Polish. Further, he said that he had that morning received a report to the effect that General Franchet d'Esperey on the 20th May had ordered forces up towards Czernovitz with a view to junction with the Poles, which seemed to indicate an attempt to squeeze out the Ukrainians. Finally, he thought it very curious that the Council had been informed that M. Paderewski was returning to Paris last Friday and they had been put off from day to day and almost from hour to hour with reports that he was expected immediately, whereas in fact he was now in Prague. He was anxious that M. Clemenceau should ascertain whether the agreed telegram had ever been dispatched to General Haller.[3] It was very curious that no reply had been received.

PRESIDENT WILSON recalled the old plan of the so-called sanitary cordon which the Military Authorities had proposed to establish against the Bolsheviks,[4] and which had been rejected. He thought it possible that the Military Authorities were, nevertheless, trying to carry out this plan in fact.

M. CLEMENCEAU expressed incredulity, but promised to make the fullest possible enquiry.

(It was agreed:

1. That Colonel Kisch should attend at the Ministry of War at 2.30 in the afternoon where General Alby[5] and General Mordacq[6] would also be present.

2. That the attached telegram, drafted by President Wilson,[7] the despatch of which had been reserved pending M. Paderewski's return, should be sent at once to Warsaw.

Sir Maurice Hankey was directed to take the necessary action.)

T MS (SDR, RG 256,180.03401/35½, DNA).
    ¹ The complete text of these minutes is printed in *PPC*, VI, 60-62.
    ² Eugène-Léon Pralon.
    ³ For this telegram, which was actually addressed to General Pilsudski, see the minutes of the Council of Four printed at May 21, 1919, 4:15 p.m., and Appendix III thereto.
    ⁴ See the memorandum by Marshal Foch printed at March 27, 1919, and the minutes of the Council of Four, March 27, 1919, 3:30 p.m., both in Vol. 56.
    ⁵ That is, Frederick Hermann Kisch and Henri Marie Camille Edouard Alby.
    ⁶ Jean Jules Henri Mordacq, Clemenceau's principal private secretary at the Ministry of War.
    ⁷ It is printed as an Appendix to the minutes of the Council of Four, May 22, 1919, 6:15 p.m.

Hankey's Notes of a Meeting of the Council of Four[1]

President Wilson's House,
C.F.35.   Paris, May 27, 1919, 11:15 a.m.

1. After discussion with the Members of the Drafting Committee, it was agreed:

1. That the draft Treaty of Peace, omitting the military terms, and the clauses dealing with reparation and debt (since these were a special aspect owing to the break-up of the Austrian Empire into several parts, which necessitates their examination from the point of view of their bearing on the interests and action of the several parts) shall be handed to the Austrian Delegates on Friday, May 30th, at Noon, and that the Drafting Committee shall proceed on this assumption.

2. That, as there was no time to print the Treaty in a final form, it should be handed to the Austrians in proof.

3. That, as there is not sufficient time to print the Articles of the Treaty with the three languages on a single page, the Drafting Committee should have authority to print the clauses in the three languages on separate pages.

4. That the Drafting Committee should devote themselves with the least possible delay to the consideration of the question referred to them on the previous day, namely, as to whether Austria was to be regarded as a new State, or as an old State, the inheritor of the Austro-Hungarian Empire, and should adopt whichever method proved most workable for the drafting of the Treaty.

5. That the draft of the political clauses relating to the territory acquired by Italy from Austria for inclusion in the Austrian Treaty should be circulated at once by the Italian Delegation and considered that afternoon.

6. That Sir Maurice Hankey should arrange with the Secretary-

General for the immediate communication the same afternoon to the Czecho-Slovaks and other new States of the political clauses in the Treaty which concerned them.

7. That the question of guarantees in the Treaty with Austria should be reserved, pending enquiry by M. Orlando to his military advisers.

8. That Sir Maurice Hankey should ascertain whether the Credentials Committee had recognized the full powers of the Austrian Delegates as conferred in the name of German Austria.

2. SIR MAURICE HANKEY, in accordance with instructions, produced in the French and English languages a re-draft of the reply to the Austrian letter of the 24th May,[2] asking that peace negotiations might be opened with the least possible delay.

(The attached letter (Appendix I) was approved, and Sir Maurice Hankey was instructed to arrange with the Secretary-General for its reproduction for M. Clemenceau's signature.

It was agreed that the Austrian Note and the reply should be published together as soon as the reply was dispatched.)

Appendix I to C.F.36.

Your Excellency,   Paris, 27th May, 1919.

I have the honour to acknowledge your letter of the 24th May, asking that Peace Negotiations with Austria may be opened with the least possible delay.

I am asked by the Council of the Principal Allied and Associated Powers to reply that the Draft Treaty of Peace will be ready for presentation to the Austrian Delegation at St. Germain-en-Laye on Friday, May 30th, at Noon.

The following questions, however, must be reserved for further consideration, namely:

1. The size of the military force to be maintained in future by Austria.

2. The question of Reparation and Debt.

These subjects wear a special aspect owing to the break-up of the Austrian Empire into its several parts, which necessitates their examination from the point of view of their bearing on the interests and action of the several parts.

T MS (SDR, RG 256,180.03401/35, DNA).
  [1] The complete text of these minutes is printed in *PPC*, VI, 63-64.
  [2] See n. 4 to the minutes of the Council of Four printed at May 26, 1919, 11 a.m.

Mantoux's Notes of a Meeting of the Council of Four

May 27, 1919, 12 noon.

The members of the Drafting Committee are introduced.

Wilson. The Austrians are showing some impatience. That is why we have decided to separate the parts of the treaty which concern only Austria and which can be ready shortly, from those which involve other states in Central Europe, in particular the clauses relative to armaments and to reparations.

Would we gain any time by having what is ready typed?

James Brown Scott. It will be at least as fast to have it printed.

Wilson. We can give the Austrians the text in proofs, if that is necessary.

Scott. I will observe that there are clauses about which we have not yet received your instructions, notably the economic clauses. Since the articles of the treaty with Germany cannot be transferred without changes to the Austrian treaty, there must be a very careful revision.

Wilson. Mr. Headlam-Morley had said to us that until now we have treated Austria as if she was the heir of the former Austrian state. In asking her to give up certain territories, we are admitting that it is she who possessed them.

Cecil J. B. Hurst. The case of Austria is that of the onion whose skins one successively peels away.

Wilson. In point of fact, Mr. Headlam-Morley presents the case differently; he says that Austria must be treated as a new state. If this is so, then we must establish this state, compel it to recognize the existence and the frontiers of the neighboring states, instead of treating it as if we were dealing with the former Austrian Empire, whom we would ask to cede certain territories.

Scott. It is a rather difficult question. If you consider Austria as a new state, you are not at war with her; as a result, there is no need to sign a peace treaty with her, but a treaty of the same kind as those you can sign with Bohemia and Poland.

Wilson. We have many reasons to proceed in that manner.

Scott. But would that not remove all justification for the articles imposing on Austria, for example, the reduction of her military forces?

Wilson. Our intention is to impose reductions of the same type on other states which are not our enemies.

Scott. It would follow that Austria would have to be admitted to the League of Nations?

Wilson. That is our intention.

Scott. From the point of view which our committee must take, that would lead to a general revision of the draft.

Wilson. That revision is undoubtedly necessary. What kind of delay would result?

Hurst. It will not be very great.

Wilson. It seems to me that we could indicate our position toward Austria in a preamble. We thought that the Drafting Committee, if it does not itself have time to undertake this task, could entrust it to competent persons.

I am told that the economic clauses are based on the old theory of Austria as heir to the Austro-Hungarian Monarchy, whereas the financial clauses are based on the new theory. We must at any rate agree with ourselves. What we are trying to do is to separate Austria from all her old traditions.

Lloyd George. What parts of the treaty are ready now?

Scott. The Covenant of the League of Nations will be inserted verbatim in the Austrian treaty. The questions of frontiers are settled, except for two or three points.

Lloyd George. Those points will be settled today.

Scott. Certain questions raised by Italy are still pending.

Clemenceau. Which ones?

Orlando. They concern the so-called "political" clauses, analogous to those which have been adopted concerning Alsace-Lorraine. We are ready to discuss them.

Lloyd George. We must see these clauses today.

Scott. Almost all the other political clauses are ready. It may be necessary to take a decision about Voralberg.

Lloyd George. Do the Czechs and the other states concerned know about these clauses? They are of the greatest importance to them.

Clemenceau. They must see them.

Lloyd George. I ask that everything necessary be done to obtain their opinion.

Scott. The naval and aerial clauses are ready; the military questions are reserved. We are ready on the question of prisoners of war.

Have the financial questions been reviewed by the heads of government?

Wilson. We will study them this morning.

Scott. The economic clauses are in our hands; we will have to review the wording from the juridical point of view if Austria is considered as a new state; perhaps there may even be grounds for referring the question to the specialists on economic questions.

We have had no indication on the guarantees for execution.

Wilson. You mean an occupation, like the one envisaged for Germany? We foresee nothing of the kind.

Orlando. I ask to consult the military advisers of the Italian government on this point.

Clemenceau. We would be grateful if you did so promptly.

Scott. I hear that some persons object to the term "German Austria." But the credentials of the Austrian plenipotentiaries, which have been received by your representatives, bear this title.

Clemenceau. Who accepted it?

Scott. The Committee on Credentials, M. Cambon.

Wilson. Does the fact that credentials were accepted without observation prevent us from doing anything now?

Scott. No; but it creates a kind of precedent which it is a question of breaking.

Clemenceau. I will see M. Cambon on the subject.

Scott. The question of knowing whether Austria should be treated as a new state requires a very careful study.

Lloyd George. Try to see to it that we are able to transmit the treaty to the Austrian delegates on Thursday.

The Drafting Committee withdraws.

The members of the Financial Commission are introduced.

Wilson. Our Financial Commission was to have heard the observations of the small states of Central Europe on the clauses of the treaty with Austria. I ask Mr. Lamont to report to us what these countries told the commission.

Lamont. They provided us with memoranda and a declaration,[1] in which they protest against all measures which, by placing them on the same footing as the enemy states, would reserve for them the same treatment as for Austria.

M. Beneš has told us that the Czechoslovak Republic is ready to assume its share of the war costs, provided that the word "reparations" be not mentioned. We asked him to provide us with a formula,[2] which we hope to be able to apply to the three other interested nations. That, moreover, would cause the clauses concerning them to be omitted from the treaty with Austria; we shall have to make separate conventions with them.

Lloyd George. M. Beneš said to me: "We cannot be held responsible for a war which we condemn." I pointed out to him that the new states must participate in the costs of the war of liberation. He answered me: "This one is different."

Crespi. We are ready to follow him in this course. We would also wish that the populations in the liberated Italian regions be not treated as enemy populations.

Orlando. These countries did not want to accept responsibility for a war of which they say they are the victims. There is nothing to say to that. I accept that point of view; I accept it particularly regarding the Czechs, who were our effective allies during the war. But if they pay nothing under the heading of reparations, then Trieste should not do so either. As to the contribution to the costs of the war which we will ask from them, Italy has already paid it.

The new states must certainly be granted the satisfaction they ask for.

Lloyd George. The clauses relative to reparations will thus be drafted in this sense, and we shall have to negotiate afterwards with the interested states.

Wilson. The principle accepted is that they participate in the costs of the war to which they owe their independence.

Lloyd George. Apart from that, do we agree on the financial clauses?

Loucheur. Mr. Davis has proposed an amendment to us.

Wilson. It involves giving the Reparation Commission the power to allow exceptions to the principle of the absolute priority of reparation debts. These exceptions could be necessary in order not to ruin the credit of the Austrian state. Are there any objections?

Loucheur. Our only objection would be that the admission of such an amendment could tempt the Germans to request the same advantage.

Wilson. There is a difference between the case of Germany and that of Austria which we will not permit ourselves to minimize.

Loucheur. We have another question. It is that of the railways of southern Austria. It concerns taking measures to safeguard the interests of the bondholders, this network being henceforth divided among several states.

Wilson. We cannot insert a clause favoring a particular enterprise into the treaty.

Lloyd George. If we take this course, this clause will have to extend to all companies.

Orlando. I do not dispute the importance of the question, but undoubtedly you will also find Allied interests in Germany which have to be protected. If we find it just to insert that clause into the treaty with Austria, similar ones will have to be inserted into the treaty with Germany.

Lloyd George. Actually, all legitimate interests are protected by Article 6, which certainly extends to bonds. I would not like to protect by a special measure bondholders whose interests could be linked to speculation.

Loucheur. There is a misunderstanding. We are not requesting special protection for particular interests. But this company will find its network cut into five pieces by the new frontiers. Will it continue to operate? Will it be forced to disappear? Hence the necessity of a stipulation such as the one we propose.

Wilson. Other questions of the same type will arise. It seems to me dangerous to embark upon that course.

Loucheur. If the legitimate interests of which we speak are really protected by Article 6, that is enough for us. But I am not at all certain of it.

Lloyd George. We cannot take the course you propose to us without danger.

The proposal is withdrawn.

Mantoux, II, 228-33.
  [1] For a summary of these documents, see Burnett, *Reparation at the Paris Peace Conference*, I, 296-301 *passim*.
  [2] It is summarized in *ibid.*, p. 301

Hankey's Notes of a Meeting of the Council of Four[1]

C.F.36.   President Wilson's House,
                                        Paris, May 27, 1919, 11:45 a.m.

The Council had before them the Financial Clauses for insertion in the Treaty with Austria.[2]

1. *Mr. Lamont* said that in accordance with the instructions of the Supreme Council the Delegates of the States which had previously formed part of the Austrian Empire had been summoned on the previous day to discuss the question of Reparation. The attitude of all the Delegates had been that they could not bear to be considered as an enemy State or to be classed in the same category as Austria in regard to Reparation. Their declaration had been listened to but no definite answer had been made. After the meeting Dr. Benes had said in conversation that Czecho-Slovakia would be willing to consider favourably a proposal that she should share in the burden of the war provided that this proposal was not put forward in the form of a demand for Reparation. Dr. Benes had been asked to devise a formula which would be satisfactory to him and this formula would in all probability suit all the four new Nations. It would, however, necessitate the making of separate agreements with each of them.

Mr. Lloyd George said that he also had seen Dr. Benes and had gathered that there would be no objection on his part to a contribution towards the expenses of the war which was a war of liberation for Czecho-Slovakia. Indeed there could be no objection to such a proposal seeing that Bohemia is a very rich country and could well afford to make some sacrifice for the sake of its liberty. It was essential that in some form or another these countries should contribute seeing that in Allied countries the burden of war would fall in many cases upon peasantry who were poorer than the inhabitants of liberated countries. But there were good reasons for meeting the wishes of the new States in regard to the precise purpose to be assigned to their contribution.

Signor Crespi said that he accepted the principle especially in view of the fact that Trent[3] and Trieste are also to be treated not as enemy countries but as being in most respects analogous to Alsace and Lorraine.

Signor Orlando said he thought it was quite natural that these States should not wish to be regarded as responsible for the war of which they were the victims. It must be recognized that the Czechs had begun to take the part of the Allies even during the war and that they had made a useful contribution towards victory. He therefore had no objection to make to any proposal which was intended to recognize their special position.

Mr. Lloyd George suggested that as there appeared to be general agreement the Reparation Clauses for Austria should be drafted on this basis and that the experts in charge of them should have full power to negotiate with the component parts of the old Austrian Empire on this principle.

President Wilson suggested that the right phrase to use would be that the new States should be required to make a contribution towards the cost of their own liberation.

2. *President Wilson* said that he was advised that Article 1[4] had the effect of putting a permanent cloud on Austrian credit. He proposed that it should be modified by the insertion at the beginning of the words "subject to such exceptions as the Reparation Commission may make."

M. Loucheur said that the only objection which he would have to this alteration would be that it might perhaps be inopportune to introduce such a modification, seeing that the clause as it stood was similar to the corresponding clause in the German Treaty, and that the text had been already presented to the Germans without any amendment.

President Wilson said that he saw no difficulty in making special arrangements with Austria, and that in fact it was the intention of the Allies to treat Austria differently from Germany.

Mr. Lloyd George said that as a matter of fact the difference amounted to very little because even in the case of Germany certain exceptions had been admitted.

It was agreed that the words "subject to such exceptions as the Reparation Commission may make" should be inserted at the beginning of Clause 1.

3. *M. Loucheur* said that he proposed that a special clause should be inserted to deal with the Compagnie des Chemins de Fer du Sud de l'Autriche. The obligations of this Company in France amounted to 1½ milliards and were in the possession of a vast number of people. The railway system belonging to the Company is to be split up into five separate parts which run through a number of the various new States. The regulation of the affairs of the Company was therefore a very complicated question which could not be settled by the Council, but the view of the French Government was that the Treaty must provide for the making of such a settlement.

President Wilson asked whether this was a Government railway.

M. Clemenceau explained that it was a private company.

President Wilson said that he saw great difficulty in accepting a clause which would make the Allied and Associated Governments a supervising authority in the case of one particular private company. He saw no reason for making special provisions in the case of South-Austrian railways, especially as he was informed that there were at least twenty Inter-national commissions already on which the United States had undertaken to be represented. A great number of similar questions were sure to arise under the Peace Treaties and it was impossible to make special provisions for the settlement of each through international channels. It would be a very serious venture to enter into a control of a single corporation, and in fact the five different groups of the railway would know their interests and arrange their own difficulties a great deal better than any international commission would be likely to do.

Mr. Lloyd George said that he thought the Council should not be asked to interfere in order to safeguard the interests of these particular bond-holders. If private interests were to be safeguarded the principle ought to have been applied all round. In point of fact every legitimate interest is protected by Article 6 of the Financial Clauses which is so drafted as to include bond-holders. The Council could not judge of individual corporations and he would hesitate very much before giving special protection to bond-holders of whom nothing was known and who might very well be speculating.

M. Loucheur said that the French proposal was not intended to obtain special protection for the bond-holders. It was merely intended to provide a solution of a practical problem which was sure to arise. Here is a Company which is going to be split into five different pieces and it is necessary to say how this Company is to function and whether and in what manner it is to be allowed the right of exploiting the five separate parts. If the case is really covered by paragraph 6 of the Treaty the object of the French proposal is gained.

It was agreed that the Financial Clauses should be included in the Treaty with Austria as drafted, subject to the amendment of Clause 1 as proposed by President Wilson. (See paragraph 2 above.)

T MS (SDR, RG 256, 180.03401/36, DNA).
  1 The complete text of these minutes is printed in *PPC*, VI, 65-68.
  2 The text of these draft articles is missing both in SDR, RG 256, DNA, and in WP, DLC.
  3 That is, Trento (Trent).
  4 It stipulated that the first charge upon all the assets and revenues of Austria should be the cost of reparation and all other costs arising under the peace treaty and its supplementary treaties and under the arrangements concluded between Austria and the Allied and Associated Powers during the Armistice. For the final text of this article, see Temperley, *History of the Peace Conference*, V, 235.

Hankey's Notes of a Meeting of the Council of Four[1]

President Wilson's House,
Paris, May 27, 1919, 4:00 p.m.

C.F.36A.

1. M. CLEMENCEAU said that he had made a very full investigation in regard to the various points raised by Mr. Lloyd George at the morning meeting.[2] The first point related to the dispatch to General Pilsudski.

GENERAL MORDACQ said that on May 22nd, M. Clemenceau had given him the dispatch, which he had sent to the Head of the French Mission at Warsaw, with instructions that it was to be given both to General Pilsudski and to General Haller, and that he was to telegraph when he had done this. On the 23rd May, the Head of the French Mission had replied, asking for the dispatch to be repeated. This had been done and an acknowledgement had been asked for. No reply was received on Saturday and so a telegram had been sent asking whether the dispatch had been received. The reply had been that the dispatch could not be deciphered and it turned out that the wrong key had been used for deciphering. The right key to the cipher had then been communicated. On Sunday no reply was received, and a telegram was sent to ask whether the message had been received, deciphered and understood. It was only on Monday, the 26th, that a telegram had been received to say that the dispatch had been deciphered and understood, and the necessary action taken.

M. CLEMENCEAU said he had a telegram which showed that General Henrys said that General Haller had now done the right thing and sent his troops to the German front. He was not satisfied, however, about the treatment of the dispatch.

COLONEL KISCH said that General Henrys said that General Haller's troops had first been sent to the North of Lemberg but now they had been brought back to the German front.

M. CLEMENCEAU said that Mr. Lloyd George's story that the French Minister had supported the employment of General Haller's Army on the Ukrainian front probably had its foundation in the fact that the French Minister presided at a Committee, one of the recommendations of which by a large majority was that the Allied and Associated Powers should not make a reservation about the employment of General Haller's Divisions. General Henrys had said that M. Dmowski wanted the whole matter transferred to Marshal Foch, and this probably was the foundation of the idea that the French were supporting the action of the Poles. Rightly or wrongly the Poles believed that they had the support of Marshal Foch.

MR. LLOYD GEORGE recalled that Marshal Foch had wanted to send General Haller's Army to Poland through Lemberg. He said he was perfectly satisfied now that the matter was in M. Clemenceau's own hands.

T MS (SDR, RG 256, 180.03401/36½, DNA).
¹ The complete text of these minutes is printed in *PPC*, VI, 69-70.
² That is, the meeting of the Council of Four, May 27, 1919, 11 a.m.

Hankey's Notes of a Meeting of the Council of Four[1]

President Wilson's House,
C.F.37.   Paris, May 27, 1919, 4:00 p.m.

1. PRESIDENT WILSON said that the problem the Council was called upon to solve had reference to the frontiers between Austria and Jugo-Slavia in the region of Klagenfurt. He thought the problem could be stated as follows. As far as the so-called Klagenfurt Basin was concerned, it would be found that the economic boundary line ran south of the ethnic line. The ethnic line divided the Basin into two parts, a northern and a southern part. The southern part, although it contained a large number of Slovenes, was indissoluably tied up, economically, with the northern part. Furthermore, the southern part of the Klagenfurt Basin was itself cut off from the country to the south by one of nature's most impressive lines of demarcation, namely, a mountain range, which was far steeper on its southern side than on its northern side, thus constituting a most serious barrier on its southern side.

In his opinion, the question of the delimitation of the Klagenfurt Basin resembled in every respect the case of the Italian boundary line, running down the Istrian Peninsula. In that case, although it was acknowledged that many Slovenes resided on the Italian side of that line, nevertheless, it had been agreed that nature had made that

¹ The complete text of these minutes is printed in *PPC*, VI, 71-77.

the natural boundary line of the Italian Peninsula. A similar situation presented itself here in the Klagenfurt Basin. The Slovene people in the southern part of the Basin, were, economically, intimately connected with the northern people. The question could not, therefore, be considered merely from a political and ethnical point of view. In other words the Council would have to decide whether an unnatural arrangement should be accepted for political expediency, or a natural arrangement, thus disregarding purely political consideration. He, personally, felt very much embarrassed to depart from the principle which he had agreed to follow in the case of the Italian settlement. He certainly had no desire to re-consider the arrangement made with Italy which followed the dictates of nature.

(After some private consultation, between the Heads of Governments, it was decided to adjourn the further consideration of the question.)

2. It was pointed out that the question of Bessarabia had been omitted from the despatch to Admiral Koltchak, and that this would probably cause difficulties with Roumania, when the despatch was eventually published.

(After some discussion, the following addition to the despatch was approved:

"Sixthly, the right of the Peace Conference to determine the future of the Roumanian part of Bessarabia be recognized."

The original Article "Sixthly" to be renumbered "Seventhly."

A copy of the complete despatch is attached in the Appendix.)

3. The Council had before them the attached note (Appendix II)[2] dated May 22, 1919, from the Secretary-General of the Commission on the International Regime of Ports, Waterways, and Railways.

(The Articles for inclusion in the Treaties with Austria and Hungary were approved and initialled by the Four Heads of Governments.

Sir Maurice Hankey was instructed to forward the Articles to the Secretary-General for the information of the Drafting Committee after ascertaining that the experts were unanimous on the subject.)

APPENDIX I

DESPATCH TO ADMIRAL KOLTCHAK.

PARIS, 26th May, 1919.

The Allied and Associated Powers feel that the time has come when it is necessary for them once more to make clear the policy they propose to pursue in regard to Russia.

---

[2] It is printed in *ibid.*, pp. 75-77.

It has always been a cardinal axiom of the Allied and Associated Powers to avoid interference in the internal affairs of Russia. Their original intervention was made for the sole purpose of assisting those elements in Russia which wanted to continue the struggle against German autocracy and to free their country from German rule, and in order to rescue the Czech-Slovaks from the danger of annihilation at the hands of the Bolshevik forces. Since the signature of the Armistice on November 11th, 1918, they have kept forces in various parts of Russia. Munitions and supplies have been sent to assist those associated with them at a very considerable cost. No sooner, however, did the Peace Conference assemble than they endeavoured to bring peace and order to Russia by inviting representatives of all the warring Governments within Russia to meet them in the hope that they might be able to arrange a permanent solution of Russian problems. This proposal and a later offer to relieve the distress among the suffering millions of Russia broke down through the refusal of the Soviet Government to accept the fundamental condition of suspending hostilities while negotiations or the work of relief was proceeding. Some of the Allied and Associated Governments are now being pressed to withdraw their troops and to incur no further expense in Russia on the ground that continued intervention shows no prospect of producing an early settlement. They are prepared, however, to continue their assistance on the lines laid down below, provided they are satisfied that it will really help the Russian people to liberty, self-government, and peace.

The Allied and Associated Governments now wish to declare formally that the object of their policy is to restore peace within Russia by enabling the Russian people to resume control of their own affairs through the instrumentality of a freely elected Constituent Assembly and to restore peace along its frontiers by arranging for the settlement of disputes in regard to the boundaries of the Russian state and its relations with its neighbours through the peaceful arbitration of the League of Nations.

They are convinced by their experiences of the last twelve months that it is not possible to attain these ends by dealing with the Soviet Government in Moscow. They are therefore disposed to assist the Government of Admiral Koltchak and his Associates with munitions, supplies and food, to establish themselves as the governments of all Russia, provided they receive from them definite guarantees that their policy has the same objects in view of the Allied and Associated Powers. With this object they would ask Admiral Koltchak and his Associates whether they will agree to the following as the conditions upon which they accept continued assistance from the Allied and Associated Powers.

In the first place, that, as soon as they reach Moscow they will summon a Constituent Assembly elected by a free, secret and democratic franchise as the Supreme Legislature for Russia to which the Government of Russia must be responsible, or if at that time order is not sufficiently restored they will summon the Constituent Assembly elected in 1917 to sit until such time as new elections are possible.

Secondly, that throughout the areas which they at present control they will permit free elections in the normal course for all local and legally constituted assemblies such as municipalities, Zemtsvos, etc.

Thirdly, that they will countenance no attempt to revive the special privileges of any class or order in Russia. The Allied and Associated Powers have noted with satisfaction the solemn declaration made by Admiral Koltchak and his associates that they have no intention of restoring the former land system. They feel that the principles to be followed in the solution of this and other internal questions must be left to the free decision of the Russian Constituent Assembly; but they wish to be assured that those whom they are prepared to assist stand for the civil and religious liberty of all Russian citizens and will make no attempt to reintroduce the régime which the revolution has destroyed.

Fourthly, that the independence of Finland and Poland be recognised, and that in the event of the frontiers and other relations between Russia and these countries not being settled by agreement, they will be referred to the arbitration of the League of Nations.

Fifthly, that if a solution of the relations between Esthonia, Latvia, Lithuania and the Caucasian and Transcaspian territories and Russia is not speedily reached by agreement the settlement will be made in consultation and co-operation with the League of Nations, and that until such settlement is made the Government of Russia agrees to recognise these territories as autonomous and to confirm the relations which may exist between the *de facto* Governments and the Allied and Associated Governments.

Sixthly, the right of the Peace Conference to determine the future of the Roumanian part of Bessarabia, be recognized.

Seventhly, that as soon as a Government for Russia has been constituted on a democratic basis, Russia should join the League of Nations and co-operate with the other members in the limitation of armaments and of military organisation throughout the world.

Finally, that they abide by the declaration made by Admiral Koltchak on November 27th, 1918, in regard to Russia's national debts.

The Allied and Associated Powers will be glad to learn as soon as possible whether the Government of Admiral Koltchak and his associates are prepared to accept these conditions, and also whether in the event of acceptance they will undertake to form a single government and army command as soon as the military situation makes it possible.   (Sd.).   G. CLEMENCEAU.

D. LLOYD GEORGE.

V. E. ORLANDO.

WOODROW WILSON.

SAIONJI.

T MS (SDR, RG 256, 180.03401/37, DNA).

To Robert Lansing

My dear Lansing: Paris, 27 May, 1919.

I am quite willing to trust to your judgment in this important matter,[1] if you have examined the papers carefully and are satisfied that the right interests are safeguarded.

Cordially and faithfully yours,   Woodrow Wilson

TLS (R. Lansing Papers, DLC).
  [1] Wilson was replying to RL to WW, May 26, 1919 (second letter of that date).

From Robert Lansing and Others

My dear Mr. President: Paris, May 27th, 1919.

Your colleagues on the American Commission feel that as soon as the German Delegation has submitted its reply regarding the Conditions of Peace it would be very desirable to call a meeting of all the Commissioners, Technical Experts and Advisors connected with the American Mission in order that the German proposals might be discussed by the members of the Commission under your guidance.

In the event that you approve of this suggestion we shall be glad to take steps to prepare this meeting at the time and place which you may indicate.   Faithfully yours,   Robert Lansing

Tasker H. Bliss.

Henry White

E. M. House

TLS (WP, DLC).

From Edward Mandell House

Dear Governor: Paris, May 27, 1919.

The reason for the letter of May 27th which Lansing, Bliss and White composed and which I signed is this:

Hoover told me yesterday that for your own protection he strongly hoped that you would do what has been suggested in this letter. I did not go into details with him but I feel sure he was speaking advisedly.

I have no doubt that any view which you would take of the German objections to the Treaty would be the view of every one with whom you would confer. If you do not confer with them, I have a feeling that some of them will be disgruntled and perhaps make trouble.

I told the Commissioners what Hoover had said to me and they proposed the letter. I merely make this explanation so you will understand how it came about.

Affectionately yours,   E. M. House

TLS (WP, DLC).

From Robert Lansing, with Enclosure

My dear Mr. President: Paris, May 27th, 1919

I am enclosing a copy of the telegram which has just been received from Mr. Polk in reply to the message which I sent him urging that Ambassador Morris' report on the Omsk Government be forwarded to the Commission at the earliest possible moment.

Faithfully yours,   Robert Lansing.

TLS (WP, DLC).

E N C L O S U R E

Washington. May 26, 1919

2100. For the Secretary of State.

Your 2242, May 24th. Morris leaving for Siberia end of this week. Could not get away before on account of serious questions pending. His instructions are to report at once. The chances are from what I can gather that the Allies may recognize Omsk Government without waiting for us.   Polk,   Acting.

T telegram (WP, DLC).

Two Letters from Robert Lansing

Dear Mr. President: Paris, Hotel Crillon, May 27, 1919.

I enclose for your information a copy of a memorandum from Dr. S. E. Morison,[1] the American member of the Baltic Commission, requesting an indication of American policy on the Esthonian Question.[2]

Yesterday's telegram from the Council of Four to Admiral Kolchak very largely supplies the answers to the questions raised by Dr. Morison, and answers them substantially in the sense of his first alternative proposal. In other words, the present policy seems to be to leave the final regulation of the status of Esthonia until after the restoration of a stable government in Russia, at which time Esthonia's relations with Russia would be settled, by voluntary agreement between the two countries if possible, or else through the mediation and with the sanction of the League of Nations. If I understand the sense of the telegram to Kolchak aright, such a plan would in no way preclude the Allied and Associated Governments from recognizing the present Esthonian authorities as *de facto*, though I doubt whether it would be legal to make them loans as if they constituted a national government.

The second and third alternatives proposed by Dr. Morison seemed to me clearly imcompatible [incompatible] with the telegram to Admiral Kolchak. It is true, of course, that something approximating the second alternative might be tried: i.e., the Allied and Associated Governments (or the League of Nations), instead of deferring their mediation between Esthonia and Russia until some distant date in the future, might, immediately after the recognition of Kolchak's Government, endeavor to settle the relations between Esthonia and Russia; but I think such action would be premature and that no Russian Government can enter into detailed engagements on this subject before the meeting of the Russian Constituent Assembly.

While the telegram to Kolchak may be taken as substantially settling the question, I hope you may be willing to give Dr. Morison further and more explicit directions.

I am, my dear Mr. President,

Very sincerely yours,   Robert Lansing

[1] That is, Samuel Eliot Morison.
[2] S. E. Morison to RL, May 26, 1919, CCS MS (WP, DLC). Morison began his "resume of the Esthonian question" with a sketch of the country's geographical, ethnic, and historical situation, and he went on to summarize briefly the developments in Estonia during and since the war which had culminated, in April 1919, in the election of a constituent assembly, a declaration of independence, and an appeal to the peace conference for recognition. Although the United States had made no promises to Estonia, Morison said, he believed that its people, who had no territorial ambitions beyond their clearly defined ethnographic frontiers and who had resisted all overtures by both the Germans and the Bolsheviks, seemed entitled to America's "friendly interest and consideration." From an economic point of view, Morison observed, Estonia was probably capable of a "separate national existence," but he pointed out that the country's seaports were "absolutely essential outlets for Russian trade," and that naval control of its coastline appeared essential to Russian safety.

Morison then suggested three possible lines of policy for the United States to adopt on the Estonian question. The first was to recognize Estonia as a *"provisional anti-Bolsh-evist political organization,"* to furnish it with material and moral support as long as there was no recognized Russian government, but to consider its future relations with Russia as an internal Russian question, to be settled between Estonia and whatever Russian government would eventually be recognized. In that case, the Allied and Associated governments could pledge to use their good offices with the future Russian government to have the wishes of the Estonian people respected.

However, Morison argued, this policy, which was advocated by the anti-Bolshevik émigrés of the Russian Political Conference at Paris, was no solution, since it was incompatible with American principles and with "elementary notions of justice." It would amount to encouraging the aspirations of the Estonians as long as their country was useful to the Entente as a bulwark against Bolshevism and then abandoning them to the mercy of Russia. As a result, the Estonians would feel themselves betrayed by the Entente, and they would probably try to secure the best terms they could from the Bolsheviks.

The second option, Morison continued, was to work out a scheme for Estonian autonomy within the Russian state and to require the Russian government, as a condition for recognition, to guarantee this autonomy by treaty. Under this arrangement, Estonia would have a separate legislature that would govern all internal affairs, while Russia would retain control of the Estonian coast, the ports, and the state railways, and would represent Estonia internationally.

The third possibility, Morison suggested, was the recognition of Estonian independence, with such guarantees for Russia to be embodied in a treaty between Estonia and the Russian government recognized by the Allied and Associated governments as the latter might find necessary. These conditions could include Russian control over Estonia's foreign relations, free transit for Russia on the Estonian railways to the principal Baltic ports, Russian naval bases on the Estonian coast, and the assumption by Estonia of a proportionate share of the Russian debt.

In his analysis of these options, Morison argued that there was little practical difference between the latter two schemes, and that either would be a "good basis for a just solution." He believed that the Estonians would be "almost completely satisfied" with the third but would be so dissatisfied with the second option, that they might even conclude a separate peace with the Bolsheviks. On the other hand, the Russian "Democrats" would probably accept the second option, as would Kolchak and his supporters, although the latter would be very dissatisfied with anything but the first option. As to the means of enforcing the respective provisions under the second and third options, Morison pointed out that there was, of course, a greater danger of Russia violating the guarantees to Estonia than vice versa. Moreover, Morison continued, under the third option, Estonia, as an independent nation, could join the League of Nations and could appeal to it for protection; under the second option, all differences between Russia and Estonia would be considered internal Russian affairs, unless some other member of the League agreed to support Estonia's claim. While it was true, Morison concluded, that the third option would sanction a dismemberment of the old Russian Empire, it would still adequately safeguard every real Russian interest in Estonia, which, after all, was entirely non-Russian in race, language, and tradition.

My dear Mr. President: Paris, May 27th, 1919.

I am transmitting herewith a copy of the reply from Mr. Frank P. Walsh,[1] Chairman of the American Commission for Irish Independence, to the letter which I addressed to him on May 24th and which I communicated to you in my note of May 26th.

In the circumstances I am not preparing to answer the points raised by Mr. Walsh in this letter.

                              Faithfully yours,   Robert Lansing.

TLS (WP, DLC).
[1] F. P. Walsh to RL, May 27, 1919, TCL (WP, DLC). In his reply to Lansing's letter of May 24 (printed as an Enclosure with RL to WW, May 26, 1919, first letter of that date),

Walsh took issue with Lansing's statements that the American delegation had made every effort to bring the American Commission on Irish Independence into "friendly touch" with the British representatives in Paris and that "certain utterances" made by Walsh and his associates in Ireland had given the "deepest offense to certain persons" with whom they had been seeking to deal. To begin with, Walsh declared, neither he nor his colleagues had authorized anybody to make any efforts to put them into friendly touch with any British representative, either in Paris or anywhere else. Moreover, Walsh continued, at no time had any member of his commission sought to deal privately or unofficially with anyone regarding the purpose of their mission.

Walsh then repeated a letter which he had written to Polk on March 27, 1919, requesting the issuance of passports for himself, Ryan, and Dunne for the express purpose of visiting France to obtain a hearing at the peace conference for De Valera, Griffith, and Plunkett, and to place before the conference Ireland's claim to self-determination and independence. Upon their arrival in Paris, Walsh and his associates had asked both Wilson and House to obtain from the British government safe conducts from Dublin to Paris for the Irish delegates. Thus, Walsh argued, the implications of Lansing's letter that any person had acted "unofficially, privately, or secretly" was erroneous, and he continued:

"Attempted negotiations on behalf of Ireland in such fashion would not only be violative of our instructions, but obnoxious to the principle, to which we steadfastly adhere with multitudes of our fellow-citizens, that a just and permanent peace can only be secured through open covenants openly arrived at.

"For the verity of the record, which we are anxious to maintain upon this important matter, will you be good enough to give us the names of the persons to whom we gave deep offense by our utterances in Ireland, and with whom you have been informed we 'were seeking to deal,' as well as the name or names of any person or persons who assumed to negotiate or promote any such secret or unofficial dealings upon our behalf.

"We likewise deem it proper to call your attention at this time to the fact that we scrupulously refrained from any public utterances in England, and that our statements to the people of Ireland as to the objects of our mission were in strict conformity with the purposes stated to you in our written application for passports and cherished and advocated by American citizens since the foundation of the American Republic. We are confident that, if your information is correct to the effect that our utterances gave deep offense, such offense was not given to the Irish People or to their duly elected representatives, in whose presence the utterances were made."

Frank Lyon Polk to the American Commissioners

Washington 27 May, 1919.

2106. Japanese Ambassador handed me the following aide memoire on May 24:

"More than six months have elapsed since the provisional government becoming organized at Omsk under the direction of Admiral Kolchak to undertake the restoration order and security in Russia. It has so far borne with admirable tact and determination the most difficult task that has ever fallen upon the lot of any government, while its position seems now to be further strengthened by the recognition reported to have been recently accorded to it as the central authority in Russia by the group at Archangel[1] and Ekaterinburg.[2]

Having regard to the known desire of all the Allies and associated powers, wishes the early reestablishment in Russia of an orderly and efficient government with reasonable promise of stability, and believing it proves official acknowledgement by foreign powers of the International standing of the Omsk government will materially be much to the maintenance of peace, the Japanese government feel the moment is opportune to consider the question of provisional recognition to be extended to the Omsk Government.[3]

The recognition might be made subject to such condition as may be found essential to safeguard the legitimate interest of foreign nations and the government to assume all international obligations and indebtedness undertaken by Russia before the overthrow of Kerensky administration.

In bringing these considerations to the notice of the government to which you are accredited the Japanese Government desire to suggest that the questions might conveniently be discussed among the delegates of the principal Allied and associated foreign powers now assembled at Paris."

Please advise me what reply to make.   Polk.   Acting.

T telegram (WP, DLC).
    [1] That is, the Provisional Government of the Northern Region, headed by Chaikovskii. On April 30, 1919, it had voted unanimously "to recognize officially the supreme and exclusive authority of the present Government of Omsk as the Provisional National Government of all Russia." See D. C. Poole, Jr., to FLP, May 4, 1919, printed in *FR 1919, Russia*, pp. 338-39. For the background of this decision, see Leonid I. Strakhovsky, *Intervention at Archangel: The Story of Allied Intervention and Russian Counter-Revolution in North Russia, 1918-1920* (Princeton, N. J., 1944), pp. 178-83.
    [2] Undoubtedly a garbled decode for Ekaterinodar (now Krasnodar), situated in the Kuban region, which was the headquarters of General Denikin. However, it was not until June 12, 1919, that Denikin, to the surprise of even his closest associates, submitted to Kolchak as "the Supreme Ruler of the Russian Nation and the Supreme Commander of the Russian Armies." See Ammission to FLP, received June 26, 1919, printed in *FR 1919, Russia*, p. 764. See also Dimitry V. Lehovich, *White Against Red: The Life of General Anton Denikin* (New York, 1974), pp. 303-306.
    [3] This sentence *sic*.

From the Diary of Ray Stannard Baker

Tuesday May 27th [1919]

Dr. Borsa[1] of the Milan *Secolo*, a real Italian liberal whom I met in Italy last fall, came to see me to-day. Evidently the Italian leaders are not giving their people the truth about Wilson's position. Orlando declared yesterday to the Four that unless he could get Fiume or make a satisfactory compromise, he would stand on the London treaty. To this Wilson made a strong reply, saying that no nation had any right either by treaty or otherwise, to convey territory without the consent of the people in it. Neither the British nor the French had the right to convey the people of Dalmatia to Italy: all the allied nations had accepted this principle when they signed the armistice with Germany. Orlando doesn't get this point at all & still wants to trade. He reports to his people that Wilson is delaying the settlement because he insists on giving the Jugo-Slaves all of eastern Istria. I asked Borsa to tell me exactly what Orlando (the Italians) would accept. He said they would agree:

1. To make Fiume a free city, but with Italian diplomatic representation abroad.

2. Abandon the hinterland of Dalmatia if they were given Zara & Sebenico & some of the Islands.

He said that Lloyd-George & Clemenceau had declared this to be a fair proposal & hinted that Colonel House also believed it to be reasonable. He said that the obstacle was Wilson who wanted to give eastern Istria to the Jugo-Slavs.

I took a memorandum of this up with me to the President this afternoon & at once got his position. *He will agree to no arrangement which gives any people to Italy without their consent.* He has proposed plebiscites in all the territory covered by the London treaty from the Istrian alps eastward. If the people of eastern Istria decide for Italy then the territory goes to Italy. The same to apply to Dalmatia. Fiume to be a free city. This is very different from giving the territory to Jugo-Slavia. The President said earnestly: "The Italians have got the choice of yielding or of driving the Slavs into the hands of the Germans."

The President was very earnest about this: & wished me to present the situation to the Italian liberals.

The British & French are giving out the report that they (meaning the Four) are prepared to recognise the Russian govt headed by Kolchak if he agrees to certain things. This I have been denying: & today was reenforced by the President's statement to me that there had been no talk of recognising Kolchak. It is a curious thing that such contradictory reports should come out of the Conference of Four men!

¹ Mario Borsa.

To Lord Curzon

My dear Lord Curzon:　　　　　　　　　　　　Paris, 27 May, 1919.

Alas, it is past praying for.¹ I am greatly complimented that your interest should continue to be so lively in my coming to Oxford for the degree by which I should feel so much honored, but it is only too plain to my judgment that I would not be forgiven by the public opinion of my own country if I lingered on my return or went out of my way to receive a personal honor, while Congress is sitting and the whole country is waiting for me to come home and give an account of my stewardship on this side of the water, explaining the many features of the work of the Conference which seem to be very obscure to the view of some men in America.

I have no choice, therefore, but to thank you very heartily again and to say that it will not be possible for me to be in Oxford next month. Please express my regret to all concerned, and believe me,

Cordially and sincerely yours,   [Woodrow Wilson]

CCL (WP, DLC).
[1] Wilson was replying to Lord Curzon to WW, May 23, 1919, ALS (WP, DLC). Curzon was again urging Wilson to come to Oxford on June 25 to receive the honorary degree of Doctor of Laws from Oxford University.

To Joseph Patrick Tumulty

Paris, May 27, 1919.

Please thank Rabbi Stephen S. Wise for his cable[1] and tell him that he may rest assured that the safeguards against religious discrimination which we all have so much at heart will be embodied in the arrangements by which the new states are to be set up.

Woodrow Wilson.

T telegram (WP, DLC).
[1] S. S. Wise to WW, May 26, 1919.

From the Diary of Dr. Grayson

Wednesday, May 28, 1919.

The President arose at his usual hour and after breakfast went for a motor ride prior to the meeting of the Big Four. At this meeting the general questions affecting the Austrian Treaty and also the Adriatic problems were taken up. Baron Sonnino came to the meeting of the Big Four with Premier Orlando, and he endeavored again to secure consideration by the President of the proposal whereby Fiume would be turned over to the Italian government. The President simply declined to consider the matter in any of its aspects, stating emphatically that inasmuch as he considered the Treaty of London a secret program fraught with evil there was no use of trying to work out a solution that would perpetuate the injustice of that document. The entire morning session was devoted to wrangling over the London Treaty.

Orlando, after Sonnino left, stated that he was willing to give Dalmatia to the Jugo-Slavs but he wanted to retain the districts of Zara and Sebenico. Clemenceau at the conference told Orlando and Sonnino that it would be absolutely necessary that the United States participate in any settlement which was eventually agreed upon, and that France and Great Britain, while perfectly willing to carry out the provisions of the Treaty of London, realized the very grave nature of putting through such a problem without the sanction of the United States. As a result of this conference, Orlando later in the day began direct negotiations with the leaders of the Jugo-Slavs.[1]

The President and I lunched with Mrs. Wilson in her bedroom.

At the afternoon session of the Big Four notification was received that the German counter-proposal had been wirelessed broadcast but directed to Washington during the night.[2] This was simply another evidence on the part of the present German government that it had not "learned by experience," as its action in sending out its counter-proposals before they were officially delivered was in utter disregard of all principles of international ethics, and emphasized the boorishness of Erzberger and the men who dominated him, including Count Von Bernstorff, the former Ambassador to the United States. Germany's official reply was a complete effort on her part to evade responsibility for the war; she demanded immediate admission to the League of Nations which had been denied her in the original peace treaty; asked that she be given a mandate over her former colonies, title to which already has passed from her; refused to consent to the trial of the Kaiser or of any of the officers responsible for the inhuman disregard of law during the progress of the war, saying that if they were to be tried they should be tried in the German courts; and declaring that she was willing to make a total indemnity payment of not to exceed $25,000,000,000.

Following the meeting of the Big Four, the President went for a motor ride through the gardens of St. Cloud, and on his return he had dinner with Mrs. Wilson in her apartment. After working for a time in his study, the President retired.

---

[1] Grayson must have been confused or misinformed. There is no evidence that any member of the Italian delegation entered into direct talks with the Yugoslav representatives at this time.

[2] An "unofficial summary" of the "Observations of the German Delegation on the Conditions of Peace" had been released in Berlin as early as May 27, 1919, two days before the note was actually transmitted to Clemenceau. As a result, news about the German counterproposals had reached the United States by May 28, when evening newspapers, such as the New York *Evening Post*, printed an Associated Press report, datelined Berlin, May 27, which outlined the major provisions of the German reply and quoted from it.

In the balance of this paragraph, Grayson summarizes the high points of the counterproposals. Brockdorff-Rantzau's covering letter and a summary of these counterproposals are printed at May 29, 1919. For a detailed discussion, see also Schwabe, *Woodrow Wilson, Revolutionary Germany, and Peacemaking*, pp. 356-62. The Council of Four and others will subsequently discuss the German counterproposals at length.

From the Diary of Colonel House

May 28, 1919.

Tardieu was again my most important caller. He was up last night until one o'clock with the Italians. He came to me at 9.30 to tell how far they had gotten in their discussions. I got in touch with the Pres-

ident over the telephone and afterward went up to see him. I found
Lloyd George already there. After some discussion between us,
George and I went over to his apartment in Rue Nitot and had a conference with Orlando. We then went back to the President. By that
time Clemenceau was with the President and the four of us conferred over Italian matters and the Austrian Treaty.

Clemenceau did not like the Austrians calling themselves "The
German Austrian Republic." Lloyd George insisted that this was the
proper designation. The President sustained him. I took Clemenceau's part and suggested that they be advised to use the name "The
New Austrian Republic." This was tentatively accepted. It was
agreed, however, that Jules Cambon should see the Czecho-Slovaks
and Jugoslavs and ask them whether there was any objection to this
procedure.

We have the Adriatic question whittled down to the vanishing
point. The President is still stubborn and wishes to leave the matter
to the Jugoslavs. Both George and I objected to this and thought the
Jugoslavs should be told that we considered the proposal offered[1] a
fair one and recommend it to them for acceptance. I explained to the
President that there were several nations concerned in the Jugoslav
side of the controversy, and that it was impossible for them to accept
any settlement that was not recommended by the Allies. He finally
yielded.

De Cartier,[2] Paderewski and others made up my list for the day. I
was rushed from the time I got up until bedtime. We went to dinner
with the de Billy's.[3] It was an interesting gathering. Tardieu and I
got together after dinner and talked until we left. He told many
amusing incidents of Clemenceau, George and the President. Tardieu has no great respect for any of them. He longs for the time
when he can use the newspapers as he likes and not be hampered
by being a part of the Government. He is constantly telling me that
the present order of talking statesmen should be superceded by men
of action, and that when we are well rid of them the people will replace them not by their counterparts, but by men who are given to
work rather than talk.

[1] That is, the so-called Tardieu plan, for the text of which see Appendix I to the minutes
of the Council of Four printed at May 28, 1919, 11 a.m.
[2] That is, Emile Ernest, Baron de Cartier de Marchienne.
[3] That is, Edouard and Katherine de Billy.

From the Diary of David Hunter Miller

Wednesday, May 28th [1919]

I had an appointment to ride with Colonel House but he came in very late and we took a short walk together. He said that Tardieu had been up with the Italians until one o'clock in the morning and had another scheme for a settlement which involved the creation of a State. He had been discussing this with the President and Lloyd George and had found the President very hard to move on the matter. He said, however, that they were nearing an agreement and hoped they would reach one. The President had said that the Jugo-Slavs should consent to it but Colonel House said that he had persuaded the President to recede from this position as the Jugo-Slavs could consent to nothing and would have to be told to take it, and the President had agreed.

Miller, *My Diary at the Conference of Paris*, I, 328.

Hankey's Notes of a Meeting of the Council of Four[1]

Mr. Lloyd George's Residence,
C.F.37A.　　　　　　　　　　Paris, May 28, 1919, 11:00 a.m.

1. The Meeting had before them proposals for the settlement of the Italian claims, which had been discussed between Colonel House and M. Tardieu. (Appendix I.)

MR. LLOYD GEORGE apologised for arriving very late to the meeting, and explained that he had been in Conference with President Wilson with a view to reaching a settlement.

M. ORLANDO accepted this explanation.

MR. LLOYD GEORGE said that President Wilson would be glad if M. Orlando would entirely separate the first page from the second page. The President was quite willing to discuss the question of Albania, but it was a new demand, and he could not agree to it right away. He agreed that some mandate was necessary for Albania, but wished the question to be considered as part of the question of mandates. There was no other country that could well take the mandate for Albania. Greece and Serbia were too closely involved in the politics of Albania. Neither France, Great Britain, nor the United States would care for it, and in his own view, Italy would certainly have the first claim. The President did not rule this out, but wanted to reserve it for further consideration. Turning to the first page of the proposals,

---

[1] The complete text of these minutes is printed in *PPC*, VI, 78-81. Wilson was not present at this meeting and was represented by Lloyd George and House.

Mr. Lloyd George said that the President had had two main comments. The first referred to the constitution of the proposed Commission for the administration of Fiume. It was contemplated that
there should be five members, two nominated by Italy, one by
Fiume, one by the Jugo-Slavs, and one by the other Powers. The ultimate effect of this depended on what was meant by Fiume. If
Fiume was taken to refer only to the old town, an Italian would be
chosen, and consequently the whole district would come practically
under Italian administration. The President therefore suggested
that the Commission should be composed of two Italians, one Jugo-
Slav, one elected by the whole state of Fiume, and one by the other
Powers; that is to say, the representative of the Powers would be in
a middle position, and would practically have a casting vote.

Next, as regards the islands. President Wilson commented if all
except Pago were assigned to Italy, it would create great difficulties.
The Jugo-Slavs were violent on the subject of the islands, and would
never agree that all should go to Italy. This was more especially the
case as the island of Veglia was to be assigned to Fiume, although it
was not in the Treaty of London assigned to Italy. On the contrary,
it had been assigned to Croatia, and President Wilson felt that this
made a great difference. He suggested, therefore, that Italy should
name one or two of the islands which were important to her from a
defensive point of view.

COLONEL HOUSE explained that one of the primary motives of
President Wilson was that there should not be to the eastward of Italy a population which was bitterly opposed to her. He did not want
the Jugo-Slav population to have an irredentist movement directed
against Italy.

MR. LLOYD GEORGE asked which of the islands were most important to Italy.

M. ORLANDO said he would examine the matter and referred to
Losina. He said that the islands were largely complementary to Zara
and Sebenico. He would like to examine the question with his naval
experts. In fact, he felt it would be necessary to examine the whole
question with the Italian Delegation, and the sooner he did so the
better. He would give an answer in the afternoon.

MR. LLOYD GEORGE said he would try to sum up the position. As far
as he could judge, President Wilson was anxious to reach an agreement, and was prepared to recommend a reasonable agreement to
the Jugo-Slavs. He considered the assent of the Jugo-Slavs essential. It would make all the difference, however, if President Wilson
was prepared to urge the agreement on the Jugo-Slavs. Then the position would be that the Jugo-Slavs and not the Italians, would be
standing in the way. In his judgement, the great thing was for the

Principal Powers to stand together. If there were any coldness between Italy on the one hand, and France and Great Britain on the other, the position would be a very bad one. He then summed up the proposal as follows:

The State of Fiume to be under the League of Nations, and to consist of a fairly large State, as indicated in the conversations which had taken place the previous evening. The State to be administered by the following: two representatives nominated by Italy, one nominated by the State of Fiume, one nominated by the Jugo-Slavs, and one nominated by the other Great Powers. At the end of 15 years a plebiscite to be held, when the people would decide whether they would remain independent, or become Italian, or become Croatian. Probably they would vote to continue as they were.

The arrangement would be somewhat similar to the Saar Valley settlement and general military protection would be afforded by the League of Nations. The whole of Dalmatia would be left to the Jugo-Slavs.

M. ORLANDO asked if Zara and Sebenico would not stand out. He had thought that these would be assigned to Italy.

MR. LLOYD GEORGE said he did not think President Wilson could possibly agree to this. His idea was that Zara and Sebenico should be free cities under the League of Nations.

M. ORLANDO said that this made a great difference.

COLONEL HOUSE repeated a suggestion made to him by Sir Maurice Hankey, that Zara and Sebenico might be attached to Fiume.

M. ORLANDO did not like this proposal.

MR. LLOYD GEORGE did not think that President Wilson would agree to any proposal that did not leave the sovereignty of Zara and Sebenico under the League of Nations, if not under the Jugo-Slavs. If they were free ports under the League of Nations, they would be just as free to the Jugo-Slavs as to the Italians, (and this was important as they gave access to Dalmatia). The great difficulty appeared to arise in connection with the islands. He urged upon M. Orlando with the utmost insistance that in considering the question of the islands, he should confine himself to as few as possible, and only those necessary for the security of Italy, and that he should choose islands which had a large Italian population. The question of Albania was reserved.

COLONEL HOUSE said that President Wilson's idea had been that a Commission should report in regard to Albania.

M. ORLANDO undertook to consider the general proposal with his colleagues and give an answer at 4.30 in the afternoon.

MR. LLOYD GEORGE handed to M. Orlando a letter which he had

written in reply to a letter he had received a few days before from M. Orlando.

Appendix I to CF-37A.[2]

BASES OF ARRANGEMENT

I. *Fiume and the Istrian Railway.*

Creation of an independent state under the sovereignty of the League of Nations, with the following boundaries:

On the West: From Volosca, the line proposed by the American delegates to a point northwest of San Pietro.

On the North: From the point to Monte Nevoso.

On the East: The line requested in the Italian memorandum, the state to include Veglia.

The government to be by a commission of five members named by the League of Nations (two Italians, one citizen of Fiume, one Jugo-Slav, one from another power).

The *corpus separatum* of Fiume to have municipal autonomy, in accordance with its constitution dating from the time of Maria Theresa.

Fiume a free port. No military service. No other taxes except local levies.

A plebiscite after 15 years.

II. *Dalmatia.*

All of Dalmatia to the Jugo-Slavs, except Zara and Sebenico and their administrative districts.

Neutralization.

III. *The Islands.*

All of the islands of the Treaty of London to Italy, except Pago (Veglia to the Republic of Fiume).

IV. *Albania.*

A mandate for Albania to be given to Italy, from the north frontier as it is at present to a south frontier to be fixed by the Conference.

A railroad to be constructed to Albania with 40% Italian capital, 40% Jugo-Slav, and 20% from other countries.

V. *Region to the North of the Frontier.*

Tarvis to Italy, as well as the region of Bistriza.

VI. *Other Stipulations.*

1. Acceptance of the Italian request concerning the Adriatic fleet (Reparations Commission).

2. The Assling Triangle to Austria, without fortification.

T MS (SDR, RG 256, 180.03401/37¼, DNA).
² Translation from *PPC*, VI, 81.

Hankey's Notes of a Meeting of the Council of Four[1]

President Wilson's House,

C.F.37B.   Paris, May 28, 1919, 11:45 a.m.

COLONEL HOUSE and M. JULES CAMBON were present at the outset.[2]

1. M. CLEMENCEAU said that M. Cambon had received full powers from the Austrian Delegates, which were in the name of German Austria. The question that arose was as to whether they should be accepted for German Austria. His private opinion was that this was not a question to break on, but he thought they ought to be asked to give them in the name of Austria.

PRESIDENT WILSON asked, if, in accepting the full powers, we could not reserve judgement as to whether the designation was a correct one.

M. CAMBON urged that there was only one Austria. There was the Kingdom of Bohemia, the Kingdom of Hungary etc., but Austria was Austria.

MR. LLOYD GEORGE urged that the other nations, constituted out of the former Austro-Hungarian Empire should be consulted.

(It was agreed that M. Jules Cambon should see the representatives in Paris, of the Czecho-Slovaks and Jugo-Slavs, and should report the result on the following morning.)

(M. Cambon then withdrew.)

2. COLONEL HOUSE and MR. LLOYD GEORGE reported the result of their conversation with M. Orlando just before this meeting. A note of this conversation, substantially identical with but slightly fuller than their report, is given in C.F.37.A.

(Colonel House withdrew.)

3. M. CLEMENCEAU read a telegram from General Dupont,[3] reporting preparations in Germany in the event of an Allied advance. He also read another report, according to which Herr Dernberg[4] had told a Member of the French Mission in Berlin that he did not say the Germans would not sign, but if they did sign, the present Government would be replaced by a Socialist Government, which would be unable to carry out the Treaty.

4. M. CLEMENCEAU reported that, as agreed to on the previous day, he had instructed the French Diplomatic Representative at Warsaw that he was to let the Polish Government know that the Four Principal Allied and Associated Powers were unanimous in stopping the

[1] The complete text of these minutes is printed in *PPC*, VI, 82-88.
[2] However, neither Orlando nor Sonnino was present.
[3] That is, Gen. Charles Joseph Dupont, president of the Inter-Allied Commission at Berlin.
[4] That is, Bernhard Jakob Ludwig Dernburg.

advance of the Poles against the Ukrainians, and that they were not supported by the French Government any more than by any other Government. He said he had bad news from that front. He then read a despatch from Bucharest, according to which the Polish offensive had been pushed as far as Stryj, the objective being Stanislau. The Roumanians were pushing north with the same objective. A desperate resistance must be expected on the part of the Ukrainians. If Poland was to receive Galicia, it would be a great scandal and due to the British and French munitions that had been sent there.

(It was agreed that M. Paderewski should be seen at once on the subject. Captain Harmsworth[5] was sent in a motor car to try and bring him before the end of the meeting. Captain Harmsworth, however, had not returned by 1 p.m., when the meeting was adjourned.)

5. PRESIDENT WILSON said he had news that, in spite of the representations that had been made, Italy was still sending troops to Asia-Minor.

MR. LLOYD GEORGE said that, when the question had been discussed at the Council, he had made it quite clear that, if Italy did not withdraw her troops, he would disinterest himself altogether in Italian claims in Asia-Minor. He adhered to this.

M. CLEMENCEAU said that M. Barrère had reported that the trouble in Italy about Smyrna was due to the fact that M. Orlando had never let it be known that he had agreed to the Greek occupation.

MR. LLOYD GEORGE said that the Italians had occupied the zones in Asia-Minor in defiance of the Council.

M. CLEMENCEAU said that he had heard from General Humbert[6] that Fiume had been occupied in the name of the King of Italy, and that all notices, etc., were issued in his name.

6. PRESIDENT WILSON read a letter, dated 27th May, from the Austrian Delegation (Appendix I),[7] asking that General Slatin[8] might be permitted to have direct communication with the Commission concerned with Prisoners of War, with a view to a common and prompt solution being found in regard to these questions.

[5] Capt. Esmond Cecil Harmsworth, Royal Marine Artillery, son of Harold Sidney Harmsworth, Viscount Rothermere, and nephew of Lord Northcliffe. At this time, an aide to Lloyd George.

[6] Gen. Georges Louis Humbert, recently commander of the French Third Army.

[7] K. Renner to G. Clemenceau, May 27, 1919, TCL (SDR, RG 256, 180.03401/37½, DNA). An English translation is printed in *PPC*, VI, 86-87.

[8] Baron Sir Rudolf Carl von Slatin, former British Inspector-General of the Sudan, honorary Major General of the British Army and Lieutenant General in the Egyptian Army. He had spent the war years in his native Austria as head of the prisoner-of-war department of the Austrian Red Cross and had come to Paris as an expert adviser on prisoner-of-war questions to the Austrian delegation. For details of his extraordinary career, see Gordon Brook-Shepherd, *Between Two Flags: The Life of Baron Sir Rudolf von Slatin Pasha, GCVO, KCMG, CB* (London, 1972).

(It was agreed that the Prisoners of War Commission should be authorised to meet General Slatin. Sir Maurice Hankey was instructed to take the necessary action with the Secretary-General.)

7. SIR MAURICE HANKEY read a letter from M. Berthelot with an enclosure from M. Bratiano (Appendix II).[9]

(It was agreed that the following Article, already approved for insertion in the Treaty with Hungary, should be inserted in the Treaty with Austria:

"Roumania accepts and agrees to embody in a Treaty with the Principal Allied and Associated Powers such provisions as may be deemed necessary by the said Powers to protect the interests of inhabitants of Roumania who differ from the majority of the population in race, language, or religion.

"Roumania further accepts and agrees to embody in a Treaty with the said Powers such provisions as they may deem necessary to protect freedom of transit and equitable treatment of the commerce of other Nations."

The above Article was initialled, and Sir Maurice Hankey was instructed to forward it to the Secretary-General for communication to the Drafting Committee.

NOTE. M. Orlando had initialled this Article before the meeting.)

8. SIR MAURICE HANKEY reminded the Council that, on May 20th, they had approved the proposals of the Reparation Commit[t]ee in regard to a request by the Serbian Delegation for one-tenth of the total of the first instalment of reparation demanded from Germany. He had felt some doubt as to how this decision was to be translated into action, and had accordingly referred to Mr. Keynes for advice. Mr. Keynes had replied with a memorandum, from which Sir Maurice Hankey read the following extract:

"Altogether, therefore, Serbia has already had, apart from other loans, a sum of nearly double that proposed in the memorandum as an advance in respect of indemnity receipts. She is also currently receiving money at a monthly rate greater than that recommended. I suggest, therefore, that, in view of these circumstances, no action is needed."

Sir Maurice Hankey asked for instructions as to what action, if any, he should take.

(It was agreed that the question should be referred to a Committee, composed of Mr. Keynes, M. Loucheur and Mr. Norman Davis, who should be asked to consider what executive action

[9] Philippe Joseph Louis Berthelot to M. P. A. Hankey, May 27, 1919, enclosing I. I. C. Brătianu to P. J. L. Berthelot, May 27, 1919, both TCL (SDR, RG 256, 180.03401/37½, DNA). English translations are printed in *PPC*, VI, 87-88.

should be taken, and to make such communications as might be necessary to the Serbians.)

9. MR. LLOYD GEORGE asked if there was any objection to boots, munitions, etc., being sent to Esthonia.

M. CLEMENCEAU said there was none.

10. PRESIDENT WILSON said he had received the draft Articles prepared by the Italian Delegation in regard to the territory of the former Austro-Hungarian Empire to be transferred to Italy, together with some remarks by Mr. Lansing.[10] Among other things, Mr. Lansing had proposed that several of the Articles should be referred to the appropriate Commissions of the Conference. This would involve some delay, so that these clauses could not be handed to the Austrians on Friday.

MR. LLOYD GEORGE said they could be sent subsequently. He insisted strongly that the Czecho-Slovak, Yugo-Slav and Polish Delegations should see these Articles.

(It was agreed:
1. To approve the suggestion of the American Delegation that certain of the Articles should be referred to the appropriate Commissions of the Conference.
2. That the draft Articles should be communicated to the Czecho-Slovak, Yugo-Slav and Polish Delegations, and any other Delegations concerned, for their remarks.

Sir Maurice Hankey was instructed to arrange with the Secretary-General to give effect to this decision.)

11. (It was agreed that a Plenary Conference should be held on May 29th at 3 p.m., to which should be invited the plenipotentiaries of the following States:
1. The Principal Allied and Associated Powers.
2. All States which were at war with Austria-Hungary.
3. The new States formed out of the territory of the former Austro-Hungarian Empire, and all States which are receiving territory from the Austro-Hungarian Empire.

Sir Maurice Hankey was directed to communicate this decision to the Secretary-General.)

11.[sic] SIR MAURICE HANKEY reported that a summary of the Austrian Treaty was being prepared in the British Delegation.

[10] RL to WW, May 28, 1919, TLS (WP, DLC), enclosing "Memorandum," dated May 27, 1919, TMS (SDR, RG 256, 185. 2131/13, DNA). The draft articles, which Wilson had handed to Lansing for his comment on May 27 and which Lansing had returned with his letter of May 28, are missing in both WP, DLC and SDR, RG 256, DNA. However, a revised version, which the Council of Four discussed in its meeting of June 6, 1919, 4 p.m., is printed in PPC, VI, 223-28. For a summary by Wilson of some of Lansing's observations on these articles, see Mantoux's notes of a meeting of the Council of Four, May 28, 1919, 11:45 a.m., printed as the following document.

M. CLEMENCEAU asked that Sir Maurice Hankey would communicate a copy to M. Tardieu, in order that it might be translated into French.

(It was agreed that the summary of the Treaty should be published after communication of the Treaty to the Austrian Delegates.)

12. M. CLEMENCEAU asked how long a time would be given to the Austrian Delegates to give their reply?

MR. LLOYD GEORGE urged the time should be short.

PRESIDENT WILSON thought the same time should be given to the Austrians as had been given to the Germans. The Austrian Delegation had not nearly so many experts with them as the Germans.

13. PRESIDENT WILSON said he had read in the newspapers that 60 of the German Experts had left for Berlin.

M. CLEMENCEAU reported that this was the case. They had accomplished their work and their presence was no longer required.

T MS (SDR, RG 256, 180.03401/37½, DNA).

Mantoux's Notes of a Meeting of the Council of Four

May 28, 1919, 11:45 a.m.

Clemenceau. The credentials of the Austrian plenipotentiaries are drawn up in the name of the "Republic of German Austria." We have not yet given our answer; my intention is not to permit that formula.

Lloyd George. Is it not necessary to ask their opinion from the neighboring states? They can find, on the contrary, that the word "Austria" by itself would seem to transfer to the new state the titles and the claims of the old one.

House. Can we call it "the New Republic of Austria"?

Wilson. What puts us in a quandary is that the Austrians themselves have designated their state under the name of German Austria.

Clemenceau. It remains to be seen whether we will recognize it as such.

Lloyd George. The best thing is to consult the Slavic states and to ask them if they have no objection.

It is decided that instructions will be given in this sense.

House. I was present at the interview between Mr. Lloyd George and M. Orlando; the latter seems inclined to accept a compromise along the lines indicated by M. Tardieu. Fiume would become the center of a small free state, governed by an international commission, of which two members would be Italian. Italy would abandon the entire coast, except for Zara and Sebenico. It remains to be determined which islands should belong to Italy. M. Orlando asked to consult his colleagues.

Lloyd George. In this conversation, I pointed out the opposition of the Yugoslavs to the cession of the islands. I insisted before M. Orlando that he demand only the islands absolutely indispensable and whose population is by majority Italian.

With respect to Zara and Sebenico, M. Orlando demands Italian sovereignty. I said to him: "If these two ports are in the hands of Italy, Dalmatia is deprived of her windows on the sea. If you make them free cities, that is another matter." I made him well understand that there was not the least chance of having either the Yugoslavs or President Wilson accept this compromise if Zara and Sebenico should be Italian.

As for Albania, I believe that that question must be studied without prejudice. There is much to be said in favor of a mandate which could be entrusted to Italy.

House. Mr. Lloyd George forcefully impressed upon M. Orlando that it was not in the interest of Italy to have the Yugoslavs as enemies, with the German population in the Italian Tyrol.

Lloyd George. I wrote a letter to M. Orlando, in order to represent to him clearly the dangers that Italy can run. It is difficult for Italy to claim populations which do not want to be subject to her. An equivalent case cannot be found anywhere in the present negotiations. That is what Italy does not yet admit; but it is necessary that she admit it. What I fear are the conversations between M. Orlando and Baron Sonnino; without being able to take part in them, and in order that our point of view might at least be represented there, I wrote the letter which I just mentioned.

Wilson. Yesterday it was difficult to get a clear view in the question of the frontier between Austria and Yugoslavia, with all those experts around us.

Lloyd George. M. Orlando will be here at 4:30. If we first settle the question between ourselves and Italy, all the rest will become easy.

Wilson. Furthermore, the Italians are continuing to send troops to Asia Minor, despite our warning. What should we do?

Lloyd George. If that continues, I will say that England dissociates herself from all Italian claims in Asia Minor.

Clemenceau. The excitement generated in Italy over the Smyrna affair arises from the fact that M. Orlando never said that he had given his consent to our joint landing.

Wilson. That is not an honest proceeding.

Lloyd George. I believe that, in Asia, the Treaty of London has been torn up by the Italian landings.

Clemenceau. General Humbert, who returns from the Adriatic, informs me that the Italians have taken possession of Fiume in the name of the King of Italy; he saw with his own eyes the trenches and the barbed wire destined for defense against the Yugoslavs.

Wilson. If there must be conflict there in the final analysis, it is better that it take place quickly; that will disturb world peace less.

Clemenceau. It must not be forgotten that we will have enough to do with the Germans in the years to come.

Wilson. We will not have to fight them militarily.

Lloyd George. What do you fear from Germany?

Clemenceau. She will sign the treaty with the firm intention of not executing it. She will overwhelm us with notes and explanations; it will be a perpetual controversy.

I have some interesting news from Germany. A telegram from Berlin indicates that the Germans are preparing for a renewal of hostilities: in the western region, all able-bodied men have been transported to the interior of the territory, the garrisons have been alerted, etc. Another telegram which comes from Haguenin[1] reports a conversation with Scheidemann. The latter says that after the signature, the German government will resign and will be replaced by an Independent Socialist government, incapable of assuring the execution of the treaty, which will compel the Allies to occupy Germany and to administer it themselves.

Regarding Poland, I have a telegram from M. de Saint-Aulaire[2] announcing that the Poles are beginning new offensives in Galicia. The danger is great that the Ukrainians, disappointed by the failure of our intervention, be thrown into the arms of the Bolsheviks.

Wilson. An article must be inserted in the Austrian treaty, imposing on Rumania the same obligations with respect to minorities that we are imposing on the Czechoslovaks and on the Poles; it is a question of Bukovina in particular.

That proposal is adopted.

Hankey. You are aware of a request by the Serbs, who are soliciting financial aid.

The question is referred to Messrs. Keynes and Loucheur.

Wilson. The Italians request the insertion of certain so-called political clauses in the Austrian treaty. These clauses have been examined by Mr. Lansing. One of them stipulates that the period of option in the redeemed territories will be limited to one year. Mr. Lansing asks that we remove Article 31, which would give Italy the right to organize emigration.

Lloyd George. The Italians are making this request in order to divert toward Trieste the commerce of Fiume. This clause, as we have already decided for others, should be communicated to the other interested nationalities.

Wilson. By another article, certain Italian nationals would have the same rights in Austria as the Austrians, without reciprocity. Mr. Lansing proposes to grant them only most-favored-nation treatment.

Several others of these articles must be referred for study to the different competent commissions.

Lloyd George. An abstract of the Austrian treaty will have to be communicated to the Allies. We have prepared one.

Clemenceau. Send it to M. Dutasta, who will have it translated into French. When do you want it to be read to the delegates of the powers?

Lloyd George. Could this reading not take place tomorrow evening? I do not think that all those who were present when we read the summary of the treaty with Germany must be summoned this time. Why should Nicaragua and many others hear the summary of the Austrian treaty?

Wilson. The nations directly involved must be summoned.

Lloyd George. Assuredly: the Czechs, the Yugoslavs, the Rumanians, the Poles must be present.

House. It appears natural to summon all the nations which declared war on Austria-Hungary, as well as the ones which are formed out of the fragments of the Austro-Hungarian Empire.

Lloyd George. We can hold a real conference, in such a way as to allow them to ask questions.

Clemenceau. It is thus settled for tomorrow.

Wilson. On the limitation of military forces, have our experts seen the different governments involved?

Clemenceau. Would the simplest thing not be to set the figure at 30,000 men for Austria, without trying to determine now the effectives allotted to the other states?

Lloyd George. I fear what can happen if these states have armies much superior to that of Austria. I do not have much confidence in Rumania, in Serbia.

Clemenceau. We have the right afterwards to grant more substantial effectives to Austria, if we judge it necessary.

Wilson. It is better to establish a provisional regime as long as the period of uncertainty and disorder continues. It is impossible today, when the east of Europe is in such a critical state, to limit definitively the forces of each state.

Lloyd George. It is these very states which are creating the present difficulties by fighting against one another.

Wilson. Another question raised by Mr. Lansing is that of the Dobrudja, part of which is obviously Bulgarian. When Mr. Lansing spoke of that at the Quai d'Orsay, they replied to him: "We cannot give to an enemy a territory which, before the war, belonged to a friendly power." It is indeed a difficulty; but it is necessary not to violate our principle, which requires that each population be attached to the state that it prefers.

Mantoux, II, 237-41.
[1] Émile Haguenin, Professor of French Literary History at the Friedrich-Wilhelm University in Berlin, 1900-1914; head of the French press bureau in Switzerland during the war; since March 1919 head of a team of French observers in Berlin, there ostensibly to study the problem of food deliveries to Germany. Although the mission had no diplomatic status, its real objective was to persuade the German government and people to accept the peace treaty. See Henning Köhler, *Novemberrevolution und Frankreich: Die französische Deutschlandpolitik, 1918-1919* (Düsseldorf, 1980), pp. 270-94.
[2] Auguste Félix Charles de Beaupoil, Count de Saint-Aulaire, French Minister to Rumania.

Hankey's Notes of a Meeting of the Council of Four[1]

President Wilson's House,
C.F.38.   Paris, May 28, 1919, 4:00 p.m.

1. SIR MAURICE HANKEY read the following letter which he had received from the Chinese delegation:

Sir: May 28th, 1919.

On behalf of the Chinese Delegation I beg to make a formal request for a copy of the Minutes of the proceedings of the Council of Prime Ministers bearing upon the Kiaochow-Shantung question. Since my country is the party most directly concerned in it, I trust that the Council will see their way to comply with my request.

I am Sir,
    Yours truly,

(Sgd)   LOU TSENG-TSIANG.

He had contemplated a reply in the sense that the rule of the Council of the Allied and Associated Powers was not to communicate their Minutes, except to those persons who had been present at a Meeting. A copy of the Minutes of the Meeting at which the Chinese Delegates were present had been forwarded to Mr. Koo on April 23rd.

PRESIDENT WILSON said the letter had been forwarded at his suggestion and he was inclined to think that the Chinese Delegation were entitled to the Minutes for their confidential use.

MR. LLOYD GEORGE pointed out that, in that event, it would be necessary to give the Japanese Delegates a copy of the Minutes of the

Meeting at which the Chinese had been present, and he did not consider this desirable.

SIR MAURICE HANKEY said he had informed the Japanese Delegation that he had no authority to communicate Minutes of Meetings other than those at which their Delegates had been present.

(It was agreed that Sir Maurice Hankey should prepare for the Chinese Delegates a Memorandum based on the Minutes, including the principal undertakings given by the Japanese Delegation.)

2. MR. LLOYD GEORGE described the proposals which he had asked M. Orlando to consider, namely:

A State of Fiume to be created under the League of Nations, to be administered by a Commission composed as follows:

2 members nominated by the Italian Government

1 member nominated by the Jugo-Slavs.

1   "   "   " the State of Fiume.

1   "   "   " the League of Nations.

The nominees of the League of Nations to have a casting vote. At the end of 15 years a Plebiscite to be held. Up to this point he understood that M. Orlando could accept. There were, however, two difficulties, viz: the islands, and the towns of Zara and Sebenico. The Italian Government was prepared to give up its claims to Dalmatia, provided Zara and Sebenico could be ceded to Italy, or, as M. Orlando had suggested earlier, put under an Italian mandate. M. Orlando was also prepared to give up the three largest of the islands in the southern group, the remainder consisting of uninhabited rocks, as well as the island of Pago. M. Orlando urged, however, that the island of Cherso was a continuation of the Istrian Peninsula and should be assigned to Italy. He stated that the majority of the population was Italian, and asked that it should be assigned to Italy. Apparently, however, President Wilson's information on this point was different.

M. CLEMENCEAU asked what would be the official language of Fiume.

MR. LLOYD GEORGE said the State of Fiume would decide that.

PRESIDENT WILSON said that M. Orlando would know that he felt that the Government of the United States had no right to assign territory to anyone: he could only follow the principle on which the rest of the settlement had been based. He was ready to accept the suggestion for a free State of Fiume as the recognised basis of a proposal to Jugo-Slavia, on whose acquiescence the whole settlement must depend. He was willing to ascertain whether a settlement was possible on these lines. He realised how serious an effort M. Orlando had made to give up part of his original claims. Before putting the proposal before the Jugo-Slavs, however, he would like to ask whether he was at liberty to include the attribution of the islands of Veglia and Cherso to the Jugo-Slav State, but not Lussin, which is manifestly Italian in nationality. In the case of Cherso, however, according to an Italian ethnographical map which he produced, only the northern part was Italian. He would like to suggest that the Fiume State should include the eastern slope of the ridge on the peninsula of Istria and include the island of Cherso, but not the island of Lussin, which should be assigned to Italy. The object of this proposal was to put the approaches to Fiume under the control of the State of Fiume. He would also, in making these proposals, like to have in mind that in arranging the Dantzig settlement it had been necessary to guarantee to Poland the utmost freedom of access to the port, and the railway terminals and the railway approaches to the interior. Without such guarantees it would not be a free port, and, this must apply equally to Fiume. If, therefore, he could assume guarantees to the State of Fiume, under the supervision of the Allied and Associated Powers, it would greatly facilitate his conversation.

M. ORLANDO said that he was glad, and it was a comfort to him that President Wilson had recognised the spirit of renunciation by Italy. As regards the freedom of the port of Fiume he could speak unequivocally. He had not the smallest objection to the complete freedom of the port, but, beyond that, he considered it a duty to provide for untrammelled communication with the interior. The territorial arrangements was a more delicate question and all possibility of misunderstanding must be avoided. He had received the document produced by M. Tardieu. He had put all the pressure he could on the Italian Delegation to accept it, but this involved a considerable renunciation for Italy. On its receipt he had telegraphed to Rome. In spite of the difficulty he declared that, for himself he would take the responsibility to accept. But it would be very difficult to persuade his colleagues to accept reductions on this reduction [scale]. He had done his utmost to eliminate as many of the islands as possible. There was no difficulty about surrendering his claim to Lesina, Curzola, and Meleda, which were the only important islands in this group. This was as far as he could go, and he could not make any further reductions on the document presented by M. Tardieu. The islands of Istria were on a somewhat different basis. M. Tardieu's document reserved Zara and Sebenico for Italy. He was willing to give every freedom to those ports and to give an undertaking that no offensive bases should be established there. He would also accept the composition of the Commission for Fiume proposed by President Wilson, namely two nominees for Italy, one for Fiume, one for Jugo-Slavia, and one for the League of Nations. In conclusion he would accept M. Tardieu's document, reserving the second page as he had been requested, with the amendment in regard to the Commission proposed by President Wilson, and with the amendment as regards the relinquishment of the three big islands in the south. He would not say that further renunciations were impossible, but it would be very difficult for him to put them before his colleagues.

PRESIDENT WILSON said that he would do what he could as the friend of both parties to use this proposal as a basis for acceptance, and he would do it in the most friendly possible way.

T MS (SDR, RG 256, 180.03401/38, DNA).
[1] The complete text of these minutes is printed in *PPC*, VI, 89-92.

To the American People

Paris, 28 May, 1919.

Please make public the following message quote My fellow countrymen colon Memorial Day wears this year an added significance and I wish comma if only by a message comma to take part with you in its observation and in expressing the sentiments which it inevitably suggests period In observing the day we commemorate not only the reunion of our own country but also now the liberation of the world from one of the most serious dangers to which free government and the free life of men were ever exposed period We have buried the gallant and now immortal men who died in this great war of liberation with a new sense of consecration period Our thoughts and purpose now are consecrated to the maintenance of the liberty of the world and of the union of its peoples in a single comradeship of liberty and right period It was for this that our men consciously offered their lives period They came to the field of battle with the high spirit and pure heart of crusaders period We must never forget the duty that their sacrifice has laid upon us of fulfilling their hopes and their purpose to the uttermost period This it seems to me is the impressive lesson and the inspiring mandate of the day.

Woodrow Wilson.

CC telegram (WP, DLC).

To Robert Lansing

My dear Mr. Secretary: Paris, 28 May, 1919.

I see very considerable difficulties in regard to this matter.[1] In the first place, the Russian Mission at Washington represents nobody in particular, certainly not the Omsk Government; and in the second

place the Omsk Government has not yet been recognized by anybody. As you know, we are just making inquiries as to its intentions.

I think in any case that this matter should be held off until we get
a reply to the letter we have sent it.

Cordially and faithfully yours,   Woodrow Wilson

TLS (SDR, RG 256, 861.24/13, DNA).
    [1] Wilson was responding to FLP to RL, NDB, and V. C. McCormick, No. 1649, April 19,
1919, T telegram (SDR, RG 256, 861.24/5, DNA). Polk reported that the Russian embassy in Washington had requested that some 68,000 Russian rifles held in storage by
the State Department and as many as practicable of an additional 197,000 Russian rifles
requisitioned by the War Department be shipped to Siberia for the use of the White Russian forces there. The embassy had suggested that the War Department "arrange with
Russian Embassy or with Supreme Commander in Siberia as to guarantee for adequate
remuneration as soon as conditions permit."
    Polk was informed of Wilson's decision in Ammission to FLP, No. 2417, June 4, 1919,
T telegram (SDR, RG 256, 861.24/12, DNA).

Two Letters from Robert Lansing

My dear Mr. President: Paris, May 28, 1919

I have your letter of May 27th, regarding the question of special
concessions from the Kolchak Government and hasten to inform
you that I have not heard of any definite instance where a concession of this nature has been granted.

Allusions to this matter are, however, in the air at present and accordingly it was considered advisable to bring our impressions to
your attention.   Faithfully yours,   Robert Lansing

My dear Mr. President: Paris, May 28, 1919

With reference to my letter dated May 27th, 1919, regarding the
report on the Omsk Government which Ambassador Morris has
been requested to make, I am transmitting to you herewith a copy of
a further message from Mr. Polk[1] stating that in all probability the
report in question will not be received before June 20th.

Faithfully yours,   Robert Lansing

TLS (WP, DLC).
    [1] FLP to RL, No. 2111, May 27, 1919, T telegram (WP, DLC).

From Norman Hapgood

Dear Mr. President: London. W. May 28/19

Since I reached Europe I have talked with a dozen or twenty of
your most influential supporters. I have been almost overwhelmed

by their unanimity and passion. They believe that if faith can exist in the order established at Paris two things are necessary:

1. That the German Counter-proposals be treated seriously.
2. That Russia be handled as patiently as you handled Mexico.

I have marked a few lines in some British papers that point to a tide that may rise high.[1]

With affectionate hope

Sincerely yours   Norman Hapgood

ALS (WP, DLC).
[1] The enclosures are missing.

Frank Lyon Polk to the American Commissioners

Washington, May 28, 1919.

2124. Department's 2070, May 23, 5:00 p.m.[1]

Following telegram received from Peking: "URGENT May 24, 11:00 a.m. STRICTLY CONFIDENTIAL. President Hsu[2] has been informed by Paris Peace Delegation that they may not be able to effect signature with broad reservations. He has sought counsel whether reservation calling merely for the application of international law to questions which may arise concerning the former rights of Germany as reported in my telegram May 14, 8:00 p.m.[3] could be made to stand. I cannot say anything to him as I do not know the situation but if the President or the Department desire to give a helpful hint as to the best solution of the matter it will be conveyed and will be effective without committing anybody." 2124.

Polk   Acting.

T telegram (WP, DLC).
[1] FLP to Ammission, No. 2070, May 23, 1919, T telegram (SDR, RG 256, 185.1158/133, DNA). This telegram repeated a dispatch from Reinsch in Peking of May 5, 1919, in which Reinsch said that he had not been fully informed about the terms of the Shantung settlement with Japan and asked for specific information.
[2] Hsü Shih-ch'ang.
[3] FLP to Ammission, No. 2041, May 21, 1919, T telegram (SDR, RG 256, 185.1158/130, DNA). This telegram repeated a telegram from Reinsch dated May 14, 1919. Reinsch reported that the Chinese cabinet had, on May 14, decided to instruct the Chinese delegates at Paris to sign the peace treaty with a reservation concerning the Shantung settlement.

Henry Churchill King to Gilbert Fairchild Close

My dear Mr. Close: [Paris] 28 May 1919.

I am writing to say, for the information of the President, that the American Section of the Commission on Mandates in Turkey is leaving Paris for Constantinople tomorrow evening, expecting to reach Constantinople not later than June 4th. Mr. Crane has already gone on to Constantinople. If the President has any further instructions, I shall, of course, be glad to receive them tomorrow. Any instructions of any kind after that date for the Commission, can be sent in care of Admiral Bristol at Constantinople.

I am taking the liberty of enclosing a little book which I wrote a little while ago for the soldiers,[1] for it may indicate the spirit, at least, in which I wish to take up this new task to which the President has called me.   Very sincerely yours,   Henry Churchill King.

TLS (WP, DLC).
  [1] Henry Churchill King, *For a New America in a New World* (Paris, 1919).

From the Diary of Ray Stannard Baker

Wednesday May 28 [1919]

Everyone is now asking, 'Will the Germans sign?' Up to noon every day I think they will: after luncheon I am not sure: and just before going to bed I'm persuaded they will not! On the whole, I think they will—with fingers crossed. To-morrow is the last day for the presentation of their demands—

I saw the President as usual this evening. He looked very much worn & the left side of his face twitched sharply, drawing down the under lid of his eye. The strain upon him is very great. Often recently he has had trouble in recalling at the start exactly what the Four did during the earlier part of the day.[1]

The Italian question was hotly discussed. Orlando remaining at Lloyd-George's house. The President is not giving an inch of ground. "The United States does not own any part of the Dalmatian coast," he said to me, "and I have no right to join in conveying it to Italy without the consent of the inhabitants. Neither have France & Great Britain, for that matter. We cannot give away what does not belong to us."

He stands for plebiscites in all the territory covered by the treaty of London—with Fiume a free city under the League of Nations. I asked him if he would recommend plebiscites separately in each island & city:

"They should be by distinguishable political units"

I told the President I thought that this position would be unassailable before the world. The objection that the Italians were making, I said, was that the same principle had not been applied by the decisions in Poland & Bohemia.

"We have applied it everywhere as rigidly as it was possible to do," said the President.

I spoke of the Brenner pass Germans & he said:

"I am sorry for that decision. I was ignorant of the situation when the decision was made."

"Is there not time to change it?"

"I am afraid not: but those Tyrolese Germans are sturdy people—and I have no doubt they will soon be able themselves to change it."

I had up again the subject of American mandatories in Turkey, saying that many of our correspondents were making inquiries as to what our policy was to be.

"I've been giving it a good deal of thought," said the President, "and have not yet made up my mind."

I recalled his statement in his Boston speech in which he referred to our responsibilities in foreign affairs.

"I have not changed my views," he said, "but we must be sure of our ground before we act. That is the reason I am sending a commission to Turkey" (King & Crane)

I told him about Morgenthau's views with which he said he was familiar.

---

[1] The tic was a hemifacial spasm caused by an elongated loop of a blood vessel that compressed the facial nerve at its exit from the brainstem. Often brought on by distress and fatigue, it is common among persons of Wilson's age, usually affects the left side of the face, and is not regarded as a sign of neurological deficit. See Bert E. Park, M.D., *The Impact of Illness on World Leaders* (Philadelphia, 1986), pp. 10-13, and Edwin A. Weinstein, M.D., *Woodrow Wilson: A Medical and Psychological Biography* (Princeton, N. J., 1981), p. 127.

The memory loss noted by Baker was, on the contrary, very significant as a sign that Wilson was again suffering, manifestly, from the dementia occasioned by the cerebrovascular disease, or neurologic illness, that is the subject of the essay and commentaries printed in the Appendix in Vol. 58. It should also be noted that Wilson's handwriting, which had drastically deteriorated in late April and early May 1919 (again, see the Editors' commentary in *ibid.*) and had improved by about May 15, again grossly deteriorated a short time later, and was, on the whole very uncharacteristic of a healthy person through the remainder of the peace conference.

To William McAdoo

My dear Judge McAdoo: Paris, 28 May, 1919.

Your generous letter of May 12th has done me a lot of good. I have moments of deep anxiety over here, not only, but often of deep discouragement also, and such a warm message of confidence and approval acts like a tonic on me, coming from a man whose judgment and character I esteem as I do yours. Thank you with all my heart.

The only thing that mars my pleasure in the letter is the news it contains of your having been knocked down by an automobile and injured. I am thankful that the injury was not serious and I hope with all my heart that by the time this reaches you you will have recovered entirely.

With warm regard,   Sincerely yours,   [Woodrow Wilson]

CCL (WP, DLC).

Gilbert Fairchild Close to William Shepherd Benson, with Enclosures

My dear Admiral Benson: Paris, 28 May, 1919.

I am enclosing herewith the messages which the President would like to have sent to the Secretary of the Navy and also to Lieutenant-Commander Read, expressing the President's congratulations on the successful flight over the ocean.[1] Will you not, in addition to sending the messages enclosed, send also a message to Commander Towers, expressing to him the President's congratulations?

                    Sincerely yours,   [Gilbert F. Close]

CCL (WP, DLC).
  [1] About which, see C. Glass to WW, April 17, 1919, n. 1, Vol. 57.

E N C L O S U R E   I[1]

                    Paris, 28 May, 1919.

Please accept my heartfelt congratulations on the success of your flight and accept for yourself and your comrades the expression of my deep admiration. We are all heartily proud of you. You have won and deserve the distinction of adding still further to the laurels of our country.   Woodrow Wilson.

  [1] Addressed to Albert Cushing Read.

E N C L O S U R E   II[1]

                    Paris, 28 May, 1919.

May I not join with all my heart in the expression of the deep gratification that I am sure all our fellow-countrymen feel in the success of the arrangements made to safeguard the flight of the aeroplanes across the sea? The Navy is warmly to be congratulated for the effective service of the gallant men who carried it through.

                    Woodrow Wilson.

T telegrams (WP, DLC).
  [1] Addressed to Josephus Daniels.

From the Diary of Dr. Grayson

                    Thursday, May 29, 1919.

There was no session of the Big Four today,[1] it having been arranged that the terms of the Austrian Treaty should be communicated to the smaller powers at the Plenary Session during the afternoon. In consequence the President spent a portion of the morning in rest.

The great question uppermost everywhere, not alone in official circles, but voiced by the man in the street, was—"Will the Germans sign?" There was a wide divergence of opinion in the reply to this question. While the strictly official element realized that Germany eventually would have to accept whatever was meted out to her by the Allied and Associated governments, it was very plain that there was in existence in Germany a widespread plan to endeavor to force the Allies to make concessions even though by doing so further hardship would be inflicted upon the country. The Erzberger government in Berlin was working in unison with Brockdorff-Rantzau at Versailles in an effort to drive the Allies into the defensive so far as the treaty was concerned. They were working very carefully and endeavoring to build a back fire both in Great Britain and in the United States. The Socialist element in the United States and in England was declaring that the treaty as originally presented to the Germans was of such a nature that it would make for further wars rather than prevent them, and were utilizing this argument as far as possible to line up public sentiment in the United States to hold the President responsible for the treaty despite the fact that in many respects the document was not of his framing. However, the general opinion was that certain changes must necessarily be made and that when these changes were made, if the Erzberger government did not sign the treaty, another government would be substituted for it in the very near future which actually would do so.

The President again lunched with Mrs. Wilson in her bedroom, and after lunch went for a ride, winding up at the Quai d'Orsay, where a secret Plenary Session had been called, at which it was planned to read the Austrian Treaty to the smaller powers. At the very outset a clash took place. The Roumanian Delegation, backed up by the Serbians, and in fact by all of the smaller powers, with the single exception of Poland, raised bitter objection to that clause in the treaty which was designed to protect religious and political minorities in newly created states by placing them under the jurisdiction of the League of Nations. Roumania boldly challenged the Austrian Treaty, and, in addition, declared that until its delegation had actually read the treaty they would not consent to considering it. Servia, Greece, and Czecho-Slovia concurred in this declaration, with the result that ten minutes after the Plenary Session opened it was adjourned until Saturday.[2] The smaller powers gained a notable victory, not by reason of any merit in their case, but because the President and other members of the Big Four were desirous of conciliating rather than antagonizing.

After the Plenary Session adjourned the President went to the

Crillon Hotel, where he held a conference with the members of the
American Mission, and then went for a motor ride, returning to the
house for dinner with Mrs. Wilson, who still remained in her apartment, her foot being somewhat slow to heal. The President transacted some business in his study before retiring.

[1] Actually, there was a meeting of the Council of Four at 11 a.m.
[2] The minutes of this abortive meeting are printed in *PPC*, III, 391-93.

From the Diary of David Hunter Miller

Thursday, May 29th [1919]

I saw Colonel House in the morning and went out for a drive with
him. He talked about the situation at home and the continuance of
the negotiations about the Italian matter. He said I would have to
take the initiative at Washington as the President would not ask for
help as he never asked anybody for help. I told him that I thought
that with what I supplied Polk and Hitchcock the matter would adjust itself and he agreed. He said that he had been told that Senator
Reed was very crooked. When we came back he showed me a memorandum he had sent the President on unfinished matters,[1] and at
his request I went over it and made certain notes in connection with
treaties with Austria, Hungary, Poland, and Turkey. The memorandum was in six parts, A to F, and I indicated what was for the Conference and what not. I have no copy of these papers.

Miller, *My Diary at the Conference of Paris*, I, 329.
[1] See EMH to WW, May 22, 1919, n. 1.

Hankey's Notes of a Meeting of the Council of Four[1]

President Wilson's House,
C.F.40.   Paris, May 29, 1919, 11:00 a.m.

PRESIDENT WILSON stated that the Heads of Governments had
reached a decision regarding the Southern frontiers of Austria. This
frontier was to be the frontier laid down in the Pact of London of
26th April, 1915, with the addition that the Sexten Valley and Tarvis
should be Italian, and the junction of Villach should be Austrian.

In the Klagenfurt area the red line (see map attached to Report No
2 of Committee on Roumanian and Jugo-Slav Affairs) was to be provisionally the frontier of Austria. In the area between the red and
blue lines there would be a plebiscite within six months of the signing of the Treaty with Austria. The attribution of the area would be

in accordance with the expressed wishes of the population. During the period required for the consultation of the population the area would be administered by an international commission in collaboration with the local Government. In reply to a question by a member of the Delegation he said that the fate of the area round Assling would be decided later in connection with the frontiers of Jugo-Slavia. The remainder of the frontier Eastward, as proposed by the Committee, was adopted.

(It was decided that the experts on Jugo-Slav affairs should meet promptly and draw up a text in accordance with the above decisions, to be sent to the Drafting Committee.)

T MS (SDR, 256, 180.03401/40, DNA).
   [1] The complete text of these minutes is printed in *PPC*, VI, 102.

Count Ulrich Karl Christian von Brockdorff-Rantzau to Georges Clemenceau

TRANSLATION FROM THE GERMAN.

Mr. President,   Versailles, May 29th, 1919.

I have the honour to transmit to you herewith the observations of the German Delegation on the draft Treaty of Peace.[1] We came to Versailles in the expectation of receiving a peace proposal based on the agreed principles. We were firmly resolved to do everything in our power with a view to fulfilling the grave obligations which we had undertaken. We hoped for the peace of justice which had been promised to us. We were aghast when we read in that document the demands made upon us by the victorious violence of our enemies. The more deeply we penetrate[d] into the spirit of this Treaty, the more convinced we became of the impossibility of carrying it out. The exactions of this Treaty are more than the German people can bear.

With a view to the re-establishment of the Polish State we must renounce indisputably German territory, nearly the whole of the province of West Prussia which is preponderantly German, of Pomerania, Danzig which is German to the core; we must let that an-

   [1] "Observations of the German Delegation on the Conditions of Peace," printed in *PPC*, VI, 800-901. This document began with a lengthy preface aimed at showing the unjust and unfair nature of the peace treaty by contrasting it with numerous quotations from the speeches and other public statements of the Allied leaders, especially Wilson, both before and after the Armistice. The main body of the document set forth in great detail the German government's comments on the treaty and its counterproposals to bring about a peace more acceptable to Germany. Brockdorff-Rantzau well summarizes the main points of the document in the above letter. For a discussion of the immediate background of the "Observations," see Schwabe, *Woodrow Wilson, Revolutionary Germany, and Peacemaking*, pp. 356-62.

cient Hanse[2] town be transformed into a free State under Polish suzerainty. We must agree that East Prussia shall be amputated from
the body of the State, condemned to a lingering death, and robbed
of its northern portion including Memel which is purely German.
We must renounce Upper Silesia for the benefit of Poland and
Czecho-Slovakia, although it has been in close political connexion
with Germany for more than 750 years, is instinct with German life
and forms the very foundation of industrial life throughout East Germany.

Preponderantly German circles (*Kreise*) must be ceded to Belgium without sufficient guarantees that the plebiscite, which is only
to take place afterwards, will be independent. The purely German
district of the Saar must be detached from our Empire and the way
must be paved for its subsequent annexation to France, although
we owe her debts in coal only, not in men.

For fifteen years Rhenish territory must be occupied, and after
these fifteen years the Allies have the power to refuse the restoration
of the country; in the interval the Allies can take every measure to
sever the economic and moral links with the mother country and finally to misrepresent the wishes of the indigenous population.

Although the exaction of the cost of the war has been expressly
renounced, yet Germany, thus cut in pieces and weakened, must
declare herself ready in principle to bear all the war expenses of her
enemies, which would exceed many times over the total amount of
German State and private assets. Meanwhile her enemies demand
in excess of the agreed conditions reparation for damage suffered by
their civil population, and in this connexion Germany must also go
bail for her allies. The sum to be paid is to be fixed by our enemies
unilaterally and to admit of subsequent modification and increase.
No limit is fixed save the capacity of the German people for payment, determined not by their standard of life but solely by their capacity to meet the demands of their enemies by their labour. The
German people would thus be condemned to perpetual slave labour.

In spite of these exorbitant demands, the reconstruction of our
economic life is at the same time rendered impossible. We must surrender our merchant fleet. We are to renounce all foreign securities.
We are to hand over to our enemies our property in all German enterprises abroad, even in the countries of our allies. Even after the
conclusion of peace the enemy States are to have the right of confis-
cating all German property. No German trader in their countries will
be protected from these war measures. We must completely renounce our Colonies, and not even German missionaries shall have
the right to follow their calling therein. We must thus renounce the

[2] That is, Hanseatic.

realisation of all our aims in the spheres of politics, economics, and ideas.

Even in internal affairs we are to give up the right of self-determination. The International Reparations Commission receives dictatorial powers over the whole life of our people in economic and cultural matters. Its authority extends far beyond that which the Emperor, the German Federal Council and the Reichstag combined ever possessed within the territory of the Empire. This Commission has unlimited control over the economic life of the State, of communities and of individuals. Further the entire educational and sanitary system depends on it. It can keep the whole German people in mental thraldom. In order to increase the payments due by the thrall, the Commission can hamper measures for the social protection of the German worker.

In other spheres also Germany's sovereignty is abolished. Her chief waterways are subjected to international administration; she must construct in her territory such canals and railways as her enemies wish; she must agree to treaties, the contents of which are unknown to her, to be concluded by her enemies with the new States on the east, even when they concern her own frontiers. The German people is excluded from the League of Nations to which is entrusted all work of common interest to the world.

Thus must a whole people sign the decree for its own proscription, nay, its own death sentence.

Germany knows that she must make sacrifices in order to attain peace. Germany knows that she has, by agreement, undertaken to make these sacrifices and will go in this matter to the utmost limits of her capacity.

1. Germany offers to proceed with her own disarmament in advance of all other peoples, in order to show that she will help to usher in the new era of the peace of Justice. She gives up universal compulsory service and reduces her army to 100,000 men except as regards temporary measures. She even renounces the warships which her enemies are still willing to leave in her hands. She stipulates, however, that she shall be admitted forthwith as a State with equal rights into the League of Nations. She stipulates that a genuine League of Nations shall come into being, embracing all peoples of goodwill, even her enemies of to-day. The League must be inspired by a feeling of responsibility towards mankind and have at its disposal a power to enforce its will sufficiently strong and trusty to protect the frontiers of its members.

2. In territorial questions Germany takes up her position unreservedly on the ground of the Wilson programme. She renounces her sovereign right in Alsace-Lorraine, but wishes a free plebiscite to take place there. She gives up the greater part of the province of

Posen, the districts incontestably Polish in population together with the capital. She is prepared to grant to Poland, under international guarantees, free and secure access to the sea by ceding free ports at Danzig, Königsberg and Memel, by an agreement regulating the navigation of the Vistula and by special railway conventions. Germany is prepared to ensure the supply of coal for the economic needs of France, especially from the Saar region, until such time as the French minds [mines] are once more in working order. The preponderantly Danish districts of Sleswig will be given up to Denmark on the basis of a plebiscite. Germany demands that the right of self-determination shall also be respected where the interests of the Germans in Austria and Bohemia are concerned.

She is ready to subject all her colonies to administration by the community of the League of Nations if she is recognised as its mandatory.

3. Germany is prepared to make payments incumbent on her in accordance with the agreed programme of peace up to a maximum sum of 100 milliards of gold marks,—20 milliards by May 1, 1926, and the balance (80 milliards) in annual payments without interest. These payments should in principle be equal to a fixed percentage of the German Imperial and State revenues. The annual payment shall approximate to the former peace Budget. For the first ten years the annual payment shall not exceed one milliard of gold marks a year. The German taxpayer shall not be *less* heavily burdened than the taxpayer of *the most* heavily burdened State among those represented on the Reparation Commission.

Germany presumes in this connexion that she will not have to make any territorial sacrifices beyond those mentioned above and that she will recover her freedom of economic movement at home and abroad.

4. Germany is prepared to devote her entire economic strength to the service of reconstruction. She wishes to cooperate effectively in the reconstruction of the devastated regions of Belgium and Northern France. To make good the loss in production of the destroyed mines in Northern France, up to 20 million tons of coal will be delivered annually for the first five years and up to 8 million tons for the next five years. Germany will facilitate further deliveries of coal to France, Belgium, Italy and Luxemburg.

Germany is moreover prepared to make considerable deliveries of benzol, coal tar and sulphate of ammonia as well as dye-stuffs and medicines.

5. Finally, Germany offers to put her entire merchant tonnage into a pool of the world's shipping, to place at the disposal of her enemies a part of her freight space as part payment of reparation, and to

build for them for a series of years in German yards an amount of tonnage exceeding their demands.

6. In order to replace the river boats destroyed in Belgium and Northern France, Germany offers river craft from her own resources.

7. Germany thinks that she sees an appropriate method for the prompt fulfilment of her obligation to make reparation, by conceding participation in industrial enterprises, especially in coal mines to ensure deliveries of coal.

8. Germany, in accordance with the desires of the workers of the whole world, wishes to see the workers in all countries free and enjoying equal rights. She wishes to ensure to them in the Treaty of Peace the right to take their own decisive part in the settlement of social policy and social protection.

9. The German Delegation again makes its demand for a neutral enquiry into the responsibility for the war and culpable acts in its conduct. An impartial Commission should have the right to investigate on its own responsibility the archives of all the belligerent countries and all the persons who took an important part in the war.

Nothing short of confidence that the question of guilt will be examined dispassionately can put the peoples lately at war with each other in the proper frame of mind for the formation of the League of Nations.

These are only the most important among the proposals which we have to make. As regards other great sacrifices and also as regards the details, the Delegation refers to the accompanying memorandum and the annex thereto.

The time allowed us for the preparation of this memorandum was so short that it was impossible to treat all the questions exhaustively. A fruitful and illuminating negotiation could only take place by means of oral discussion. This treaty of peace is to be the greatest achievement of its kind in all history. There is no precedent for the conduct of such comprehensive negotiations by an exchange of written notes only. The feeling of the peoples who have made such immense sacrifices makes them demand that their fate should be decided by an open, unreserved exchange of ideas on the principle: "Open covenants of peace openly arrived at, after which there shall be no private international understandings of any kind, but diplomacy shall proceed always frankly and in the public view."[3]

Germany is to put her signature to the Treaty laid before her and to carry it out. Even in her mind, Justice is for her too sacred a thing to allow her to stoop to accept conditions which she cannot under-

[3] That is, the first point of the Fourteen Points.

take to carry out. Treaties of Peace signed by the Great Powers have, it is true, in the history of the last decades again and again proclaimed the right of the stronger. But each of these Treaties of Peace has been a factor in originating and prolonging the world-war. Whenever in this war the victor has spoken to the vanquished, at Brest-Litovsk and Bucharest, his words were but the seeds of future discord. The lofty aims which our adversaries first set before themselves in their conduct of the war, the new era of an assured peace of justice, demand a Treaty instinct with a different spirit. Only the cooperation of all nations, a cooperation of hands and spirits can build up a durable peace. We are under no delusions regarding the strength of the hatred and bitterness which this war has engendered; and yet the forces which are at work for an union of mankind are stronger now than ever they were before. The historic task of the Peace Conference of Versailles is to bring about this union.

Accept, Mr. President, the expression of my distinguished consideration.

Brockdorff Rantzau.

TCL (WP, DLC).

Hankey's Notes of a Meeting of the Council of Four[1]

President Wilson's House,

C.F.41.   Paris, May 29, 1919, 11:00 a.m.

1. The Council had under consideration a letter dated May 28th, 1919, from Mr. Hurst, the British Member of the Drafting Committee, addressed to Sir Maurice Hankey, on the subject of the Language of the Treaty of Peace. (Appendix I.)[2]

(It was agreed that in the event of divergence between the English, French and Italian texts of the Treaty of Peace with Austria, the French text should prevail.) The Drafting Committee was authorised to insert a clause to this effect in the Treaty of Peace. A copy of Mr. Hurst's letter was initialled by the four Heads of States and Sir Maurice Hankey was instructed to communicate it immediately to the Secretary General for the information of the Drafting Committee.)

2. The Council had before them a letter dated May 28th, 1919, from Mr. Hurst to Sir Maurice Hankey, stating that the Drafting Committee had endeavoured to cut out of the Treaty of Peace with Austria, phraseology which definitely committed the Allied and Associated Powers to either view as to the relations which the new

---

[1] The complete text of these minutes is printed in *PPC*, VI, 103-14.
[2] Printed in *ibid.*, p. 111.

Austria bears to the old Austria-Hungary, and for this purpose, they had cut out of Article 297(c) (32 of the Draft Economic Clauses with Austria) the words *"tel qu'il existait au l^{er} Août 1919."* (Appendix II.)[3]

M. ORLANDO said this was not merely a question of drafting, but one of material importance, because it related to damage and who would bear the cost. He suggested that the question should be sent to the Reparations Commission.

PRESIDENT WILSON said that perhaps he had a different idea of the point from M. Orlando. He understood that in the Treaty, Austrian nationals could only be made to pay for damage done by Austria. Consequently, by describing Austria as being the same as she existed on the 1st August, 1914, the field of payment was not really widened. Supposing an English firm suffered by loss in Prague, and this was paid out of Austrian funds in London, this would not be fair. The sum ought to be paid out of the property of Bohemians. It was not fair to impose on an Austria reduced to narrow limits, the cost of damages in other parts of the old Austria-Hungary. It was perfectly fair to link up Hungary, but not Bohemia, and other parts which had ceased to be hostile.

(After some further discussion, it was agreed:

1. To refer the question to the Reparations Commission for remarks.

2. That in the meanwhile, the words *"tel qu'il existait au l^{er} Août 1914"* should retain provisionally in the Treaty of Peace, reserving the right to delete the words after receiving the views of the Reparations Commission.

Sir Maurice Hankey was instructed to communicate these decisions to the Secretary-General for the necessary action.)

3. The Council had before them the following two documents, relating to the Articles previously approved for insertion in the Austrian and Hungarian Treaties, with regard to telegraph and telephone services with the Czecho-Slovak Republic:

1. A letter dated May 26th, addressed by the Secretary-General of the Commission on the International Regime of Ports, Waterways and Railways to the Secretary-General of the Peace Conference, stated that the Technical Committee which drafted the Clause, proposed, in order to make its terms clearer, the following additions to paragraph 2: After the words "to demand new direct line" add "taking as a basis the reduced tariff provided for in Article 23, para. 5 of the International Telegraph Convention (as revised at Lisbon)."

2. A letter addressed by Lord Robert Cecil to Sir Maurice Han-

---

[3] Printed in *ibid.*, pp. 111-12.

key, dealing with the same subject from the point of view of the League of Nations, and suggesting the following alterations:
Paragraph 5,
Omission of the underlined words in the following sentence:
"<u>Whether</u> concerning the conclusion of this Convention, <u>or its interpretation or the interpretation of the present Article</u>."
Addition of a new paragraph 7.
"In case of any dispute between the parties as to the interpretation either of the present Article or of the Convention referred to in paragraph 5, this dispute shall be submitted for decision to the Permanent Court of International Justice to be established by the League of Nations."
Lord Robert Cecil, in his letter, gave the following reasons for these changes:

1. The duties to be performed under paras. 5 and 6 not being of a legal character, could clearly be better performed by a single expert arbitrator backed by the authority of the League, than they could by the International Court.

2. But on the other hand, the interpretation of Treaties like this, which might create specific rights to find any detail, should be done by the International Court. It will exist for such purposes, and especially to deal with matters like this, which, if of minor importance, are extremely contentious.

(Both the above alterations were agreed to, and the Article, as finally approved is contained in Appendix III.[4] This Article was initialled by the four Heads of Governments, and Sir Maurice Hankey was instructed to forward it to the Secretary-General for the information of the Drafting Committee.)

4. M. CLEMENCEAU reported that an advance instalment of the German counter proposals to the Treaty of Peace had been received and was being translated.

MR. LLOYD GEORGE pressed the great urgency of translating and reproducing this rapidly. This could only be done if a large number of translators were set to work, as he was informed that even this advance instalment consisted of 87 printed pages.

Sir Maurice Hankey was instructed to place himself in immediate communication with the Secretary General and with the Secretary of the United States Delegation with a view to as many persons as possible being employed to translate the Treaty.[5]

5. M. ORLANDO reported that the Drafting Committee had received no instructions as to the boundaries between Austria and Italy.

---

[4] Printed in *ibid.*, pp. 112-13.
[5] That is, of course, the German counterproposals.

PRESIDENT WILSON said that according to his recollection it had been understood that the boundary would be that contained in the Treaty of London dated 26th April 1919 [1915], with rectifications giving the Sexten Valley to Italy as well as a certain region in the vicinity of Tarvis.

At this point there was some discussion as to the arrangements to be made in regard to Klagenfurt and President Wilson explained his proposals on a map.

NOTE

At this point the Council adjourned upstairs to meet the Experts for a discussion on the boundaries of Klagenfurt. This discussion is reported as a separate Meeting. On the conclusion of the Meeting, the Experts were left to draw the precise lines of demarcation on a map.

After their return to President Wilson's library, the following resolution was approved and initialled by the four Heads of States:

"The Drafting Committee are instructed to include in the Treaty of Peace with Austria the boundary between Italy and Austria as described in the Treaty of London, dated 26th of April, 1915, with the rectifications shown in the attached map, giving the Sexten Valley to Italy, as well as a certain region in the vicinity of Tarvis.

The Valley of Klagenfurt, including the Town of Klagenfurt, will be disposed of by means of a plebiscite within six months after the signature of the Treaty of Peace with Austria.

The question of the triangle, including Assling, is reserved for the decision of the principal Allied and Associated Powers, and Austria is to accept their decision."

Sir Maurice Hankey was instructed to forward this decision to the Secretary General for the Drafting Committee and to see that the map on which the Experts were working was also forwarded to the Drafting Committee.

6. With reference to C.F.37B.,[6] M. JULES CAMBON made the following report of his interview with the Serbian, Jugo-Slav and Czecho-Slovak Delegations:

"The question of knowing if the powers of the Austrian Delegation ought to be given in the name of the Republic of German Austria, or quite simply of the Republic of Austria, has been put before the Serbian, Jugo-Slav and Czecho-Slovak Delegations.

The Jugo-Slav Delegation is of opinion that the word 'German' ought not to figure in the title of the Austrian Delegation for the reason that the maintenance of this word would tend to encourage the belief that outside the Duchy of Austria there is an Aus-

---

[6] That is, the meeting of the Council of Four printed at May 28, 1919, 11:45 a.m.

tria; but Dalmatia used to form the Duchy and Croatia used to form part of the Kingdom of Hungary.

The Czecho-Slovak Delegation is still more explicit: it would attach great importance to the disappearance of the word 'German.' In fact, if the maintenance of this word seems to lead to the re-attachment of Austria to Germany, a point of view which interests more especially the Czecs, it would create a bond between the Germans residing in Bohemia and those residing in Austria and serve as a pretext for a pro-German division in part of the territories of Czecho-Slovakia.

The two Delegations consulted are of opinion that the term 'German Austria' should be suppressed. On the other hand it is necessary to bear in mind that all the Official Documents of the new Austrian Republic bear this mention of German Austria. It is thus that the law of the 14th March 1919 on the representation of the people has been framed in its Article 8:

'The President of the National Assembly represents the Republic of German Austria in regard to exterior relations, receives and accredits Envoys and ratifies State Treaties etc.'

Consequently the question becomes more extended: the expression 'German Austria' is constitutional and in asking for its suppression one does more than ask for a simple modification in the credentials of the Delegates of the Republic."

MR. LLOYD GEORGE agreed with M. Cambon that the term "German Austria" could not be accepted.

PRESIDENT WILSON also agreed.

The following resolution was approved and initialled by the four Heads of States:

"The Drafting Committee is instructed to provide in the Treaty of Peace with Austria that the Allied and Associated Powers recognise the new State of Austria under the title of the "Republic OF AUSTRIA."

Sir Maurice Hankey was instructed to forward this decision to the Secretary General for the information of the Drafting Committee.

(M. Jules Cambon withdrew.)

7. (NOTE

Sir Maurice Hankey was engaged outside the Council Room during the following discussion.)

Notes sent up as a question of urgency by the Secretary General from MM. Krammarsch and Pasitch,[7] urging the omission from the Treaty with Austria of certain political clauses, including clauses proposed by the Committee on New States, were considered.

[7] That is, Karel Kramář and Nikola Pašić.

(It was agreed to refer these clauses to the Drafting Committee and to give M. Krammarsch and M. Pasitch an opportunity of stating their views at the Plenary Conference in the afternoon. Verbal instructions to this effect were given to the Secretary General's messenger by President Wilson.)

8. M. CLEMENCEAU handed Sir Maurice Hankey, for translation and circulation, two despatches from the French Minister at Warsaw, in regard to General Haller's Army.

9. PRESIDENT WILSON read the following Note prepared for the Council by the Drafting Committee:

Instruction of Supreme Council of 24th May, 1919, for Modification of Text of Articles 102 and 104.

The Drafting Committee has the honour to draw the attention of the Supreme Council to the following observations:

The modification of the text of Articles 102 and 104 of the German Treaty in such a way as to provide for the existence of Dantzig as a free town only after the conclusion of the Treaty with Poland, and the elaboration of the constitution, does not appear to agree with Article 5 of the Instructions of 22nd April (now Article 105 of the German Treaty) according to which "from the coming into force of the present Treaty" the Germans inhabiting Dantzig become "citizens of the free town of Dantzig"—which pre-suppose apparently that the free town of Dantzig will be in existence at that moment.

The terms of the instructions of 22nd April define the purpose of the stipulations in the following terms: "to establish the free city of Dantzig."

Under these circumstances, the Drafting Committee would be grateful if the Supreme Council would confirm the modifications it desires to have made in the Text in question.

For the Drafting Committee.
(Signed)   H. FROMAGEOT.

(It was agreed that the Drafting Committee should receive instructions that the other parts of the Treaty of Peace with Germany should be modified so as to conform with the decision for the modification of Articles 102 and 104 in such a way as to provide for the existence of Dantzig as a free town only after the conclusion of the Treaty with Poland.)

Sir Maurice Hankey was directed to prepare an instruction for the Drafting Committee for the initials of the four Heads of States.

Convention for the occupation of the Rhine Provinces.

Size of the Army of Occupation.

10. SIR MAURICE HANKEY reported that this subject had originally been referred to the Military Representatives at Versailles, who had drawn up a Convention for submission to the Council of the Principal Allied and Associated Powers. On the date when this report was to come forward a letter had been received by Mr. Lloyd George from Lord Robert Cecil asking that the Supreme Economic Council's views might be heard. The Convention had then been remitted for discussion in the first instance between the British Military Representatives and the British representatives on the Supreme Economic Council. A report had now been received which had been agreed to in both cases reluctantly by Lord Robert Cecil and General Thwaites.[8] Sir Maurice Hankey suggested that this revised report should be referred for consideration by the Military Representatives at Versailles together with representatives of the Supreme Economic Council.

PRESIDENT WILSON did not like this procedure as he felt that very large questions of policy were involved. He read a letter he had received from Mr. Noyes, the American delegate on the Inter-Allied Rhineland Commission (Appendix IV).

MR. LLOYD GEORGE said he thought that the whole question of the occupation of the Rhine provinces would have to be re-considered and re-argued. The occupation of Russia by foreign troops had, according to many accounts he had received, created Bolshevism. This had happened both in Archangel and in the Ukraine. It seemed as though troops felt less responsible when in occupation of a foreign country than in their own country. The antagonism of the people was then excited. The army of occupation in this case would have to be maintained at German cost and this would subtract from the fund for reparation. Troops in a foreign country would cost two or three times as much as they would in the home country. Consequently, he took the view that the prolonged occupation of German territory had been agreed to too readily. There would be no danger from Germany for the next fifteen years owing to German exhaustion. After that, however, the danger might re-commence, for in fifteen years Germany would be much stronger than she is now. The Peace Treaty provided that the stronger Germany became the fewer troops would be in occupation of German territory.

M. CLEMENCEAU said he could not agree to a re-consideration of what had been written in the Treaty.

MR. LLOYD GEORGE said that as one of the Powers which had inflicted defeat on Germany he intended to insist on re-consideration of this question and he was entitled to be heard.

[8] That is, Maj. Gen. William Thwaites.

PRESIDENT WILSON said his point of view was that we must insist on the civil life of the people continuing without interference.

M. CLEMENCEAU said he was willing to accept President Wilson's point of view, but he was not willing to have the decision re-considered.

PRESIDENT WILSON suggested that a special Commission composed of persons of political experience should be appointed to re-write the Convention on the lines suggested in Mr. Noyes' letter.

M. ORLANDO said that M. Mantoux reminded him that during the German occupation of France in the war of 1870 they had not participated in any way in the civil occupation.

M. MANTOUX said that they had established garrisons and that was all.

MR. LLOYD GEORGE said that the question of the size of the army of occupation must be considered at the same time. At the present time he had not the slightest idea of what it was to consist.

PRESIDENT WILSON recalled that he had told M. Clemenceau that he could not keep many United States troops on the Rhine, only enough indeed, to show the flag. Mr. Lloyd George had said the same and it had been understood that France was to provide the necessary force on the understanding that it was an international force.

MR. LLOYD GEORGE said that it was, nevertheless, necessary to know what its size would be.

SIR MAURICE HANKEY reported that this question had been referred to the Military Representatives at Versailles, but that General Bliss had first postponed discussing the question until after a conversation between General Pershing and Marshal Foch on May 24th, and had subsequently stated that as no more American troops were being withdrawn for the present, it had no urgency and that in any case he could not discuss it as for the moment it was before the President.

PRESIDENT WILSON said he felt sure that General Bliss would have no objection to a discussion of the strength of the total force, irrespective of the numbers to be supplied by each Power.

MR. LLOYD GEORGE suggested that civilians with political experience ought to be included on this enquiry also.

M. CLEMENCEAU suggested a Commission composed of four civilians and four military men.

PRESIDENT WILSON agreed, and pointed out how closely the two questions were interwoven. If the army were simply concentrated in garrison without interference with the administration, a relatively small force might be fixed, whereas if martial law were imposed and the troops dispersed, a much larger force would be necessary.

MR. LLOYD GEORGE then read a letter which had been sent from the Secretary-General by General Weygand recommending that barracks should be built for the troops required for the occupation of the Rhine provinces and urging that this should be done at German expense.

After some further discussion it was agreed:

1. That a Commission composed of a representative of the United States of America, to be nominated by President Wilson, Lord Robert Cecil for Great Britain, M. Loucheur for France and the Marquis Imperiali for Italy, should be appointed to re-write the draft Convention relating to the occupation of the Rhine provinces on the skeleton plan suggested in the letter from Mr. Noyes, the American delegate on the Inter-Allied Rhineland Commission, to President Wilson, dated May 27th, 1919, namely:

    I. As few troops as possible concentrated in barracks or reserve areas with no "billeting," except possibly for officers.

    II. Complete self-government for the territory with the exceptions below.

    III. A Civil Commission with powers:

        (a) To make regulations or change old ones whenever German law or actions:

            (1) Threaten the carrying out of Treaty terms, or

            (2) Threaten the comfort or security of troops.

        (b) To authorise the Army to take control under martial law either in danger spots or throughout the territory whenever conditions seem to them to make this necessary.

2. That the following Military Representatives should be associated with the above Commission:

    General Bliss for the United States of America
    General Sir Hy. Wilson for Great Britain
    Marshal Foch for France
    General Cavallero for Italy,

    for the purpose of making recommendations as to the total size of the Army of Occupation of the Rhine Provinces without specifying the strength of the force to be maintained by the various nations concerned.

3. That in view of the fact that the German counter provisions are now under consideration the two Commissions should be asked to report at the earliest possible moment.

APPENDIX IV TO C.F.41.

Honorable Woodrow Wilson
  President of the United States of America,
    11, Place des Etats-Unis, Paris.

Dear Sir: Paris, May 27, 1919.

After a month spent in the Rhineland as American Commissioner I feel there is a danger that a disastrous mistake will be made. The "Convention" for the government of these territories, as drafted by the military representatives of the Supreme War Council on May eleventh, is more brutal, I believe, than even its authors desire upon second thought. It provides for unendurable oppression of six million people during a period of years.

This "Convention" is not likely to be adopted without great modification. What alarms me, however, is that none of the revisions of this document which I have seen recognise that its basic principle is bad—that the quartering of an enemy army in a country as its master in time of peace and the billeting of troops on the civil population will insure hatred and ultimate disaster.

I have discussed this matter at length with the American Commanders of the Army of Occupation; men who have seen "military occupation" at close range for six months. These Officers emphatically indorse the above statements. They say that an occupying army, even one with the best of intentions, is guilty of outrages and that mutual irritation, in spite of every effort to the contrary, grows apace. Force and more force must inevitably be the history of such occupation long continued.

Forgetting the apparent ambitions of the French and possibly overlooking political limitations, I have sketched below a plan which seems to me the maximum for military domination in the Rhineland after the signing of peace. Our Army Commanders and others who have studied the subject on the ground agree with this programme:

SKELETON PLAN.

  I. As few troops as possible concentrated in barracks or reserve areas with no "billeting," excepting possibly for officers.
 II. Complete self-government for the territory with the exceptions below.
III. A Civil Commission with powers:
      (a) To make regulations or change old ones whenever German law or actions—
          (1) Threaten the carrying out of Treaty terms, or—
          (2) Threaten the comfort or security of troops.
      (b) To authorize the army to take control under martial law,

either in danger spots or throughout the territory when-
ever conditions seem to them to make this necessary.
Very truly yours,   (Signed) P. B. NOYES.
American Delegate, Inter-Allied
Rhineland Commission.

T MS (SDR, RG 256, 180. 03401/41, DNA).

To Pierrepoint Burt Noyes

My dear Mr. Noyes: Paris, 29 May, 1919.
Thank you sincerely for your letter of yesterday.[1] I find myself in
agreement with you in what you say of the arrangements that ought
to be made with regard to the military occupation of the Rhineland
provinces and am sincerely obliged to you for your helpful letter.
Cordially and sincerely yours,   Woodrow Wilson

TLS (NHC).
[1] Just printed as Appendix IV to the minutes of the Council of Four, May 29, 1919, 11
a.m.

To Robert Lansing

My dear Lansing: Paris, 29 May, 1919
I have the letter[1] signed by yourself, General Bliss, Mr. White, and
House about the desirability of calling a meeting of the Commission-
ers, technical experts, and advisors connected with the American
Mission to discuss the German proposals about to be received, and
am heartily in sympathy with the idea. Indeed, it is just what I my-
self had in mind.
Cordially and sincerely yours,   Woodrow Wilson

TLS (WP, DLC).
[1] RL *et al.* to WW, May 27, 1919.

To Henry Churchill King

My dear Dr. King: Paris, 29 May, 1919.
Here is God-speed. My thoughts will follow you constantly in the
important mission you are undertaking and I am particularly happy

to think of the spirit in which both you and Mr. Crane are acting in this really critical matter.

Thank you for the little book which I shall value.

Cordially and sincerely yours,   [Woodrow Wilson]

CCL (WP, DLC).

From Robert Lansing, with Enclosure

My dear Mr. President: Paris, 29 May 1919.

I am enclosing herewith for your information copy of a memorandum prepared by Mr. W. L. Westerman[n] in regard to certain new demands in Asia Minor made in behalf of Greece by Mr. Venizelos.

Your colleagues on the Commission have given this matter their very careful consideration and recommend it most earnestly to your attention. They are unable to add anything to the statements made by Mr. Westerman, with which they are substantially in agreement.

Faithfully yours,   Robert Lansing

TLS (WP, DLC).

E N C L O S U R E

MEMORANDUM

Prepared by Mr. W. L. Westerman[n], May 28th, 1919.

M. Venizelos has sent a memorandum to President Wilson which has come to our office for analysis.[1] He states that two delegations of the Greek Territorial Commission (these were France and Great-Britain) recommended the assignment to the Greek Kingdom of a coastal portion of Asia Minor. He is now demanding that additional Turkish territory on the north be assigned in sovereignty to Greece, and that the remainder of the area of the Vilayet of Aidin, including the Sandjak of Denizli, be assigned to Greece under the form of a mandate. M. Venizelos' appetite grows with feeding. He has never before, in dealing with the Peace Conference, asked for the Sandjak of Denizli in any form; and he acknowledges that it contains, even by Greek estimates, 197,000 Turks to 7,000 Greeks. Our estimates for Denizli give 247,000 Turks to 4,000 Greeks.

M. Venizelos' argumentation is sophistical:

(1) Since there is no longer any question of preserving an independ-

ent Turkish state, the cultural and economic preponderance of the
Greeks should throw the remainder of the Vilayet of Aidin, including
Denizli Sandjak, under a Greek mandate.
(2) Denizli is the granary of Aidin Vilayet. Its detachment from the
Vilayet of Aidin (Smyrna) will be prejudicial to the interests of the
city of Smyrna.
(3) The irrigation works, which the Greeks have in mind for the
Maeander (Menderez) valley, demand that the upper reaches of the
Maeander in Denizli Sandjak be under Greek control.
Discussion:

This extension of the demands of M. Venizelos corresponds
closely to the territorial price which he set upon the Greek participation in the war on the side of the Entente in the winter of 1914-
15.

The grant of sovereignty over the additional territory in the north
would cut off the Turks absolutely from their one chance of an outlet
on the Aegean, purposely left them, even under the French Recommendation.

The idea that the Greek people are fitted, either economically or
from the standpoint of political morality, for the obligations of mandatory supervision, will not be countenanced by any person who
knows the Near East, and need not be discussed.

We wish to recall to the American Commissioners that our office
has always opposed the Greek claim to territory in Asia Minor. We
still oppose it. The incidents of the Greek occupation of Smyrna on
May 15, carefully excluded from the French papers, are typical of
Greek methods.

Admiral Bristol, under date of May 18, telegraphs: "Greeks,
Smyrna, reported looting Turkish houses, making many arrests, oc-
casional street fights, few killed. Christian population inland apprehensive, Greeks undertook task beyond their power."

The Italian papers reported 400 killed.

T MS (WP, DLC).
    [1] Untitled memorandum dated May 19, 1919, T MS with printed annexes and a map.
It is enclosed with GFC to J. C. Grew, May 21, 1919, TLS (SDR, RG 256, 868.00/138,
DNA). Westermann summarizes its main points well.

From Robert Howard Lord, with Enclosure

My dear Mr. President: [Paris] May 29, 1919.
    Since the Polish-Ukrainian question is so much to the front at
present, I take the liberty of transmitting to you some extracts from
a personal letter which I have just received from Lieut. R. C. Foster,[1]
an observer whom we have had in Poland for the last five months,

and who has just returned from a trip in Eastern Galicia. Lieut. Foster's judgment on the situation may deserve some attention, since in the opinion of all those who have known his work, he has shown himself one of the most capable men we have sent out to Eastern Europe.   Very respectfully,   Robert H. Lord.

TLS (WP, DLC).
¹ Lt. Reginald Candler Foster, member of the American Mission to Poland.

E N C L O S U R E

Warsaw May 25th 1919.

Lt. Col. Farman¹ and I followed the course of the advance south of Lemberg about five days after the first attack began. We started from Chyrow, went to Sambor, Drohobycz, Boryslaw and Strij and in the various towns talked with Ruthenians and Jews as well as Poles. In Sambor we made a tour by automobile of the surrounding villages, Ruthenian and Polish, and in Boryslaw met the Ruthenian and Jewish representatives on the newly elected town council.

The thing that impressed us most was the order and apparent normal condition throughout the district. Fields that had been recently passed over by the two armies were freshly tilled and tilling was going on on every side. It was hardly possible to believe that there had been fighting going on only a few days before. This was due to the fact that the peasants in the Ukrainian army under pressure of the Polish attack simply quit and went back to their farms and judging from those to whom we talked they were perfectly delighted to be through with fighting and get back to work again. They bore no hostile feelings towards the Poles and expressed themselves glad that they had come to establish order again. The Poles on the other hand have shown excellent judgment by demanding no reprisals, showing no hostility towards the Ruthenian peasants that were serving in the Ukrainian army and permitting whatever prisoners they took to return to their farms. The Polish soldiers also showed good discipline and their conduct has been most commendable.

The sum total of our observations is that the Ukrainian Government was most unsatisfactory, that order was not preserved, people being in constant danger of robbery and extortion, that heavy requisitions for food and clothing were made without payment and often without receipt and were directed principally at the Polish population, that all means of transport and communication were hopelessly disorganized, that financial matters were in a desperate state due to the introduction without limit of the new currency which peasant and trades people considered of no value and would not accept and which even the Ukrainian Government would accept only in the payment of taxes. On the other hand the Ukrainian Government forced the exchange of Austrian Crowns at par, this action being directed particularly against the Poles. It was even stated that Ukrainian soldiers would surround people in the market places and search them for Austrian Crowns compelling them to exchange this money for Ukrainian currency. This money question hit the oil concerns of Boryslaw the hardest as their workmen refused to be paid in Ukrainian currency and the Directors were therefore forced to obtain loans of Austrian crowns as their income from sales to the Ukrainian Government was in Ukrainian currency. These Directors told us that they had just reached the limit of their borrowing capacity and in a few weeks would have been forced to close down their plants.

We had opportunities also to verify the reports of outrages to the Poles that have been current here for some time. We talked with Poles who had been deported without reason and submitted to privations and disease and maltreated in a most unpardonable fashion. Several of the cases were most pitiful and it is a marvel to me that the advancing Polish troops have been able to show the restraint they have.

Of course you understand that these conditions that I am describing apply only to the districts that I saw but the evidences of disorganisation and mismanagement, the financial and economic situation, have convinced me that the Ukrainian people are not capable of self-government and during their regime have destroyed rather than constructed and I feel sure that the same conditions exist in the other parts of Galicia still in their hands. Lt. Col. Farman agrees with me in this opinion and he having been in Poland about a week and therefore knowing little of the situation would judge purely by what he saw and heard and could hardly be submitted to the accusation that perhaps some would make of me, namely of being very pro-Polish. Again, too, the relief of the population—Ruthenian, Pole, and Jew—as expressed to us proved their satisfaction at being under Polish rule. They felt that safety and order had again been established and that quiet development could now be expected.

Haller's troops were not used in any way in the advance through this district. It had been planned to use them before it was definitely learned of the promise given to the Entente. They were then immediately withdrawn. The Boryslaw oil fields were not in any way destroyed and there is now stored there about 300,000 tons of crude oil that the Ukrainians never shipped out due to disorganised transportation facilities. Local organisations have not been disturbed by the Poles and local militia formed by them have quickly put a stop to the former unsafe conditions.

Food conditions in the large centers like Boryslaw and Drohobycz were very bad but the Poles are taking immediate steps to ship flour and fats to these people. It is difficult, however, due to the destruction of several of the more important railroad bridges by the retreating Ukrainian forces. These are under repair.

We had sufficient testimony to prove that peasants were forced to serve in the Ukrainian army and the fact that comparatively few prisoners were taken and that we talked with several ex-soldiers working quietly in their fields side by side with Polish peasants gave a pretty good proof that their hearts could hardly have been in the fight.

I don't know what attitude Paris will take towards these last events in this much discussed region but it is hard to understand after what I have seen in the last few days how much faith can be put in the ability of these Ruthenian people to govern themselves and also that this Ukrainian movement was really a national movement. It looks mostly like the scheming of a few ambitious people backed by German and Austrian help. The backbone of the Ukrainian army was clearly stamped "made in Germany" with a touch of Austria and the fact that the Ukrainians accepted this help showed a sympathy that one does not find in these other newly created countries. And yet we treated them on the same basis as the other countries!

Reginald C. Foster.

T MS (WP, DLC).
¹ Elbert Eli Farman, Jr., American Military Attaché in Warsaw since May 14, 1919.

From Tasker Howard Bliss

Dear Mr. President: Paris 29 May, 1919.

You will remember that some time ago the British agreed that the entire military expedition at Archangel and Murmansk should be withdrawn, the movement beginning with the opening of navigation (which is about this time). It is understood that this movement is now proceeding, the Americans being withdrawn first.

A few days ago General Thwaites, representing the British War Office, wrote to me saying that General Ironsides,¹ the Allied commander at Archangel, wanted very much to keep the American Engineer troops until about September 1st, before which time the movement could not be completed.

I submitted the matter to General Pershing and he telegraphed to General Richardson,[2] the American commander at Archangel, for his views. Before General Richardson could have received the telegram he telegraphed to General Pershing on the same general lines. I attach copy of his telegram, dated May 19th, hereto, marked "A."[3] On receipt of General Pershing's telegram, General Richardson sent his second telegram, copy herewith, dated May 24th, marked "B."[4]

General Pershing, who, I believe, has favored the complete withdrawal of this force, has transmitted the telegrams to me without comment.

When General Richardson was recently sent to take command of our forces at Archangel, he had an interview with you before leaving Paris. General Richardson informed me subsequently that you had outlined to him the policy which the United States government was going to follow and which contemplated complete withdrawal of this force; and that the military committees of Congress had been informed to this effect. General Richardson appears to have fallen under the influence of the local British officers and in his telegrams he repeats the arguments which had been often submitted and considered before he went there.

I do not know what is to be the political policy of the United States in Russia; but, even if such policy should involve the use of American troops there, I believe that the present force should be withdrawn because we know from many reports that it has become largely disaffected.[5] I do not believe that it is practicable to form a force of volunteers from that which is now at Archangel, because under the law our drafted troops must be home and mustered out within four months of the date of signature of peace. If any of them remain during the summer they might be unable to get home in time to comply with the law. Moreover, it might easily happen that they would be caught in that northern climate under such conditions as would require them to remain another year. I believe that if we are to continue giving military assistance to the Archangel expedition, it would be better to withdraw our present force and replace it, after our government has determined upon its Russian policy, by a force of regulars to be sent out from the United States.

Therefore, I do not recommend approval of General Richardson's views.

I ask you to note the last sentence in General Richardson's telegram dated May 19th.[6] It indicates, in connection with former reports, that there is a possibility that our troops, and especially our Engineer troops, may be exploited for the benefit of people other than the Russians or the Americans.

Cordially yours,   Tasker H. Bliss.

TLS (WP, DLC).

[1] That is, Brig. Gen. (William) Edmund Ironside.

[2] Brig. Gen. Wilds Preston Richardson, commander of the American forces in North Russia. He had arrived in Archangel on April 17, 1919.

[3] W. P. Richardson to J. J. Pershing, May 19, 1919, T telegram (WP, DLC). Richardson expressed "the hope that all American troops will not be withdrawn from North Russia until the overthrow of the Bolshevik regime in Russia shall have been accomplished, on the ground that this regime was organized as an Ally of Germany to aid in making war upon ourselves and our Allies." "A complete withdrawal at this time," he continued, "would have a very disturbing effect, especially as to the discipline of the new Russian troops and possibly bring further distress and punishment upon many who have been our faithful friends and Allies."

[4] W. P. Richardson to J. J. Pershing, May 23, 1919, T telegram (WP, DLC). Richardson suggested, in response to General Ironside's desire to retain the American engineer battalion, that two companies of fresh American engineer troops be sent to North Russia to replace those returning home. These new men would serve under veteran officers who presumably would volunteer to remain in Russia for "say about four months or until September."

[5] About which, see D. C. Poole, Jr., to W. Phillips, March 31, 1919, FR 1919, Russia, p. 623.

[6] "In what manner are other troops to be sent as replacements or whether the Engineer troops remain or are replaced by others, it would furthermore be wise in my opinion for our government [to] insist upon as definite a pronouncement of policy by our Allies, especially Great Britain, as given by ourselves respecting motives of self-interest or further commercial advantages to the expense of Russia's present helplessness, in order to quiet a growing suspicion and also to prevent the labor of my own Engineer troops being exploited for the benefit of other than the Russian people."

From Thomas Nelson Page

Personal & Confidential.

My dear Mr. President: Rome May 29, 1919.

The press states that the terms of Peace are to be presented immediately to the Austrians, and the mid-day press has a telegram from Paris indicating that a solution is almost arrived at touching the Adriatic question. Please Heaven it may be so, and that it may be a solution which, in this matter as well as in the settlement of other Italian questions, will be such as will enable Italy to feel that her great services to and sacrifices for the Common Cause are appreciated by you and the rest of our people. They have been great— greater than anyone who was not here throughout it all can ever know.

I know that you have a sincere friendship for this great people. I have tried to keep you informed from time to time of what they were undergoing, but no one can know what they underwent who has not been here all the time, and has not has [had] his eyes open to understand the people themselves. I pass over the folly and blindness of the Italian press in these last weeks, and am speaking of Italy as represented by the people, whose most devoted servant the King declared himself the other day to be. I feel that in finding a just solution of the Italian situation, whose justice will take into account what Italy truly is and has truly accomplished in this war, rests the

saving of the friendship which must count for so much in the progress of the world under the new system now being evolved.

I know your great desire to be just, and I know the great responsibilities on you to consider all questions in a broad and liberal spirit
for all concerned. It is for this reason that I am speaking so earnestly
on this matter of not leaving the Italian people under the sense of
having their sentiment for the redemption of their people unappre-
ciated and their sacrifices therefor undervalued. I thought from a report of the geographic boundary experts which I saw when in Paris
that one of the fundamental principles of a possible permanent settlement had, possibly, not been duly considered in arriving at the
conclusion therein set forth—that is the sentiment of the Italian
people touching this matter of irredentism. The present passion of
Italy is for the redemption of the elements of the Italian race who
have been cut off from Italy, and left under foreign subjugation.

I am not speaking of the expansionists or of the wild asserters of
Italian supremacy, but of the people of Italy. Not to meet their deep
feeling in this matter would be to leave that which will rankle long
and leave an irredentist sore whose consequences may be very unhappy.

I somehow feel that you will be able to meet this difficulty and
peril, and will also be able to prove to Italy that you have never been
unmindful of her great part in the Common Cause. Her necessities
are very great, and among these one of the greatest is to be shown
practically the appreciative friendship of yourself as the head of the
American people.

Always, my dear Mr. President,

Your most sincere friend,   Thos. Nelson Page

TLS (WP, DLC).

From the Diary of Colonel House

May 29, 1919.

Loulie and I lunched with Lloyd George. The others present were
his little daughter, Megan,[1] and his son, Major George,[2] and Philip
Kerr. George and I discussed the German objections. That was the
purpose of the luncheon. George always amuses me. I am sure he
does not like me and yet today one would have thought I was his best
friend. He desires to use me because he knows he is to have a fight
with Clemenceau about softening the terms, and he also knows that
public opinion in England demands such softening. I always lead
him one [on] and let him feel that I am innocent of his motives, and
that he apparently succeeds in accomplishing his purposes with me.

I enjoy being with him because he has so much charm and such a fine sense of humor. It is a great pity that some of his qualities cause one to distrust him. . . .

The President, Lansing and White came to Crillon and we had a conference about the Italian question which the President presented to our colleagues as he and I knew it. He suggested that the four of us take the matter up with the Jugoslavs and present the agreement we have reached with the Italians and recommend that they accept it. This meeting is arranged for tomorrow at 10.15.

I brought up our collective desire to have a postponement of the Conference after the German and Austrian Treaties were disposed of. It may be that we will have to write the terms of the Bulgarian and Hungarian Treaties, but after that and the settlement of a few boundaries, we could easily adjourn until the Autumn, and then hold it in Washington to settle what was left.

The President and the other Commissioners were amused when I said that the way to adjourn the Conference to Washington was merely to say that it would adjourn until October first and would be called together at Washington. I told them this was the way Washington was designated for the first meeting of the League of Nations, and the way London was designated for the organization of the League. No one asked me by whose authority I was speaking; and at no meeting of the League was it ever mentioned or questioned. I told Lord Robert Cecil and got him committed, and after—"first meeting of the League of Nations which is to take place in Washington October first." It is very simple if you can carry it through, and it is astonishing how "sheeplike" people are in such matters.

[1] Megan Lloyd George was seventeen at this time.
[2] Either Richard Lloyd George or Gwilym Lloyd George, both of whom had attained the rank of major in the British army.

From the Diary of Ray Stannard Baker

Thursday the 29 [May 1919]

When I went up to the President's house I found the Admiral[1] in bed. . . .

The President explained to me, standing before the big map in his study, the settlement of the southern boundaries of Austria, through the provision for a plebiscite within 6 months in the Klagenfurt basin. This has been a serious bone of contention between Austria & Jugo-Slavia.

He also told me positively that there was no further change in the Italian situation although many French papers are reporting that a settlement has been reached. He is standing like a rock.

He told me also that he had promised to go to Belgium, which will be interesting news up there—

I told him of Louis Marshall's call to-day & of his expressed pleasure with the interview with him (the President) & of his purpose to push hard for the League. Marshall said that all oppressed minorities in the world—religious or political—would be for the League. The Jews in America would be among its most determined supporters.

"All the minorities except the Irish," said the President.

"Yes," I said, "the Irish seem very unhappy. Walsh & Dunne are in my office every day with a new letter or manifesto."

"I don't know how long I shall be able to resist telling them what I think of their miserable mischief-making," said the President, almost savagely. "They can see nothing except their own small interest. They were at first against the League because it contained a reference to the interference of outsiders with the 'domestic affairs' of other nations, thinking that it prevented Irish-Americans from taking part in Irish affairs. Now they are attacking Article X because they assert that it limits the right of revolution. As a matter of fact Article X safeguards the right of revolution by providing that the members of the league shall respect & preserve the integrity of nations only against *external* aggression!"

¹ That is, Dr. Grayson.

To Joseph Patrick Tumulty

Paris, 29 May, 1919.

I would be obliged if you would ascertain from Glass and cable to me the amount of taxes due from me on my salary under the opinion of the Attorney General.   Woodrow Wilson.

T telegram (WP, DLC).

To Robert Bridges

Paris, 29 May, 1919.

I am afraid I cannot get to Princeton by the fourteenth¹ and that I shall miss what would be the greatest possible refreshment to me in meeting the boys then and so I beg that you will give them the most affectionate messages from me and tell them how cheering it is to me always to think of their friendship and of the old days we spent together stop It has been hard work over here but has been lightened all the way through by the thought of the glorious country I was working for which I love more and more every day.

Woodrow Wilson.

T telegram (WP, DLC).
    ¹ Wilson was replying to R. Bridges to WW, May 28, 1919, T telegram (J. P. Tumulty Papers, DLC). It reads as follows: "If you cannot be with us please send message to be read at Fortieth Anniversary Class Dinner on Saturday June fourteenth. Answer."

From the Diary of Dr. Grayson

Friday, May 30, 1919.

The President after breakfast went immediately to his study. There was a brief session of the Big Four during the morning, at which the question of what disposition was to be made of the German counter-proposals was discussed without any action whatever being taken thereon. The session adjourned early because this being Memorial Day the President was scheduled to deliver the leading address here. Following an early lunch the President, Mrs. Wilson and I rode to the Suresnes Cemetery, on the outskirts of Paris, where six thousand American dead are buried, and where some of the notable Americans who succumbed through illness during the war, including Williard D. Straight,¹ were buried. The scene was very beautiful. The regularly arranged graves, each surmounted by a white cross, seemed to cover the whole hillside. The speaker's stand had been arranged so that the beauties of nature stretched far beyond towards the horizon. There was a very large attendance, among the guests being Lord Derby, the British Ambassador to France, and practically all of the American officials. Tardieu represented the France-American Commission at the ceremony, while Field Marshal Foch himself attended as a tribute to the American dead. The weather was very, very warm and a number of women fainted during the services. The President's speech was declared by all who listened to it to be one of his most striking state documents. He fearlessly denounced the old diplomatic atmosphere of bargaining, which he characterized as responsible for the war, and referred to the League of Nations as the legacy of the fallen sons of America. The speech was as follows: . . .

After the President had concluded his address he personally as Commander-in-Chief and as Honorary President of the Boy Scouts of America laid a wreath representing that organization upon one of the graves. The band then played Chopin's Funeral March, swinging into the National Anthem and a verse of the Marseilles. Taps were sounded at the conclusion of the ceremony, and the clear notes of the bugle sounding out through the still air brought tears to nearly every one present.

A very impressive feature of the day's ceremony at the cemetery was when a French lady came across to where the President was standing after he had deposited the wreath in behalf of the Boy Scouts, and addressing him said: "Mr. President, may I be permitted to add these flowers to those which you have just deposited here as a tribute to the American dead, who, in sacrificing their lives, saved the lives of thousands of Frenchmen?" The President nodded, and the woman laid the flowers on the grave, while Field Marshal Foch, stern and hard as he usually is, turned away with tears in his eyes.

The President and Mrs. Wilson upon their return to the temporary White House went for a motor ride in the suburbs, returning just in time for dinner; and after dinner both rested while the President played Canfield in Mrs. Wilson's apartment.

---

¹ Straight had most recently been a liaison officer with the A.E.F. in France. He had died of influenza and pneumonia in Paris on December 1, 1918.

Remarks at Suresnes Cemetery on Memorial Day

May 30, 1919.

Mr. Ambassador, ladies and gentlemen, fellow countrymen: No one with a heart in his breast, no American, no lover of humanity, can stand in the presence of these graves without the most profound emotion. These men who lie here are men of unique breed. Their like has not been seen since the far days of the Crusades. Never before have men crossed the seas to a foreign land to fight for a cause which they did not pretend was peculiarly their own, but knew was the cause of humanity and of mankind. And when they came, they found fit comrades for their courage and their devotion. They found armies of liberty already in the field—men who, though they had gone through three years of fiery trial, seemed only to be just discovering, not for a moment losing, the high temper of the great affair, men seasoned in the bloody service of liberty. Joining hands with these, the men of America gave that greatest of all gifts, the gift of life and the gift of spirit.

It will always be a treasured memory on the part of those who knew and loved these men that the testimony of everybody who saw them in the field of action was of their unflinching courage, their ardor to the point of audacity, their full consciousness of the high cause they had come to serve, and their constant vision of the issue. It is delightful to learn from those who saw these men fight and saw them waiting in the trenches for the summons to the fight that they had a touch of the high spirit of religion, that they knew they were exhibiting a spiritual as well as a physical might, and those of us who know and love America know they were discovering to the whole world the true spirit and devotion of their motherland. It was America who came in the person of these men and who will forever be grateful that she was so represented.

And it is the more delightful to entertain these thoughts because we know that these men, though buried in a foreign, are not buried in an alien soil. They are at home, sleeping with the spirits of those who thought the same thoughts and entertained the same aspirations. The noble women of Suresnes have given evidence of the loving sense with which they received these dead as their own, for they have cared for their graves, they have made it their interest, their loving interest, to see that there was no hour of neglect, and that constantly through all the months that have gone by the mothers at home should know that there were mothers here who remembered and honored their dead.

You have just heard in the beautiful letter from Monsieur Clemenceau[1] what I believe to be the real message of France to us on a day like this, a message of genuine comradeship, a message of genuine sympathy, and I have no doubt that if our British comrades were here, they would speak in the same spirit and in the same language. For the beauty of this war is that it has brought a new partnership and a new comradeship and a new understanding into the field of the effort of the nations.

But it would be no profit to us to eulogize these illustrious dead if we did not take to heart the lesson which they have taught us. They are dead; they have done their utmost to show their devotion to a great cause; and they have left us to see to it that that cause shall not be betrayed, whether in war or in peace. It is our privilege and our high duty to consecrate ourselves afresh on a day like this to the objects for which they fought. It is not necessary that I should rehearse to you what those objects were. These men did not come across the sea merely to defeat Germany and her associated powers in the war. They came to defeat forever the things for which the Central Powers stood, the sort of power they meant to assert in the world, the arrogant, selfish dominance which they meant to establish; and they came, moreover, to see to it that there should never be a war like this again. It is for us, particularly for us who are civilians, to use our proper weapons of counsel and agreement to see to it that there never is such a war again. The nation that should now fling out of this common concord of counsel would betray the human race.

So it is our duty to take and maintain the safeguards which will see to it that the mothers of America and the mothers of France and England and Italy and Belgium and all the other suffering nations should never be called upon for this sacrifice again. This can be done. It must be done. And it will be done. The thing that these men left us, though they did not in their counsels conceive it, is the great instrument which we have just erected in the League of Nations. The League of Nations is the covenant of governments that these men shall not have died in vain. I like to think that the dust of those sons of America who were privileged to be buried in their mother country will mingle with the dust of the men who fought for the preservation of the Union, and that as those men gave their lives in order that America might be united, these men have given their lives in order that the world might be united. Those men gave their lives in order to secure the freedom of a nation. These men have given theirs in order to secure the freedom of mankind; and I look forward to an age when it will be just as impossible to regret the results of their labor as it is now impossible to regret the result of the labor of those who fought for the union of the states. I look for the time when every man who now puts his counsel against the united service of mankind under the League of Nations will be just as ashamed of it as if he now regretted the union of the states.

You are aware, as I am aware, that the airs of an older day are beginning to stir again, that the standards of an old order are trying to assert themselves again. There is here and there an attempt to insert into the counsel of statesmen the old reckonings of selfishness and bargaining and national advantage which were the roots of this war, and any man who counsels these things advocates the renewal of the sacrifice which these men have made; for if this is not the final battle for right, there will be another that will be final. Let these gentlemen not suppose that it is possible for them to accomplish this return to an order of which we are ashamed and that we are ready to forget. They cannot accomplish it. The peoples of the world are awake, and the peoples of the world are in the saddle. Private counsels of statesmen cannot now and cannot hereafter determine the destinies of nations. If we are not the servants of the opinion of mankind, we are of all men the littlest, the most contemptible, the least gifted with vision. If we do not know our age, we cannot accomplish our purpose, and this age is an age which looks forward, not backward; which rejects the standards of national selfishness that once governed the counsels of nations and demands that they shall give way to a new order of things in which the only questions will be: "Is it right?" "Is it just?" "Is it in the interest of mankind?"

This is a challenge that no previous generation ever dared to give ear to. So many things have happened, and they have happened so fast, in the last four years, that I do not think many of us realize what it is that has happened. Think how impossible it would have been to get a body of responsible statesmen seriously to entertain the idea of the organization of a League of Nations four years ago. And think of the change that has taken place! I was told before I came to France that there would be confusion of counsel about this thing, and I found unity of counsel. I was told that there would be opposition, and I found union of action. I found the statesmen with whom I was about to deal united in the idea that we must have a League of Nations, that we could not merely make a peace settlement and then leave it to make itself effectual, but that we must conceive some common organization by which we should give our common faith that this peace would be maintained and the conclusions at which we had arrived should be made as secure as the united counsels of all the great nations that fought against Germany could make them. We have listened to the challenge, and that is the proof that there shall never be a war like this again.

Ladies and gentlemen, we all believe, I hope, that the spirits of these men are not buried with their bodies. Their spirits live. I hope—I believe—that their spirits are present with us at this hour. I hope that I feel the compulsion of their presence. I hope that I realize the significance of their presence. Think, soldiers, of those comrades of yours who are gone. If they were here, what would they say? They would not remember what you are talking about today. They would remember America which they left with their high hope and purpose. They would remember the terrible field of battle. They would remember what they constantly recalled in times of danger, what they had come for and how worthwhile it was to give their lives for it. And they would say, "Forget all the little circumstances of the day. Be ashamed of the jealousies that divide you. We command you in the name of those who, like ourselves, have died to bring the counsels of men together, and we remind you what America said she was born for. She was born, she said, to show mankind the way to liberty. She was born to make this great gift a common gift. She was born to show men the way of experience by which they might realize this gift and maintain it, and we adjure you in the name of all the great traditions of America to make yourselves soldiers now once for all in this common cause, where we need wear no uniform except the uniform of the heart, clothing ourselves with the principles of right and saying to men everywhere, 'You are our brothers, and we invite you into the comradeship of liberty and of peace.'"

Let us go away hearing these unspoken mandates of our dead comrades.

If I may speak a personal word, I beg you to realize the compulsion that I myself feel that I am under. By the Constitution of our great country I was the Commander in Chief of these men. I advised the Congress to declare that a state of war existed. I sent these lads over here to die. Shall I—can I—ever speak a word of counsel which is inconsistent with the assurances I gave them when they came over? It is inconceivable. There is something better, if possible, that a man can give than his life, and that is his living spirit to a service that is not easy, to resist counsels that are hard to resist, to stand against purposes that are difficult to stand against, and to say, "Here stand I, consecrated in spirit to the men who were once my comrades and who are now gone, and who have left me under eternal bonds of fidelity."[2]

T MS (WP, DLC).

[1] Clemenceau's message or letter is missing in WP, DLC. The Editors have found no complete text of it, and only very brief extracts appeared in the newspapers. The *New York Times*, May 31, 1919, printed the following brief quotations:

"Faithful to noble tradition, the living army renders homage to the dead army, and all France has associated itself with this homage."

"France will ever cherish their memories. With America, France will preserve in peace, as an inspiration and example, an undying remembrance of their enthusiasm, discipline, and courage. We see the wreaths on their tombs, and will take care of them as piously and gratefully as the tombs of our own soldiers."

[2] There is a WWT and WWhw outline and a two-page WWT draft of this speech in WP, DLC.

From Edward Mandell House

Dear Governor—   Paris, May 30, 1919.

No one, I think, ever made a greater, nobler speech than yours of today. It will add its share of glory to your name—a name that will gain in lustre through all time.

Your devoted,   E. M. House

ALS (facsimile in WP, DLC).

From Thomas William Lamont, with Enclosure

Austrian Reparation and the Lesser Nations

Dear Mr. President: Paris, May 30, 1919.

The Commission on Austrian Reparation, of which I happen to be the Chairman, has directed me to appear briefly before the Council of Four this morning, if agreeable to you, and lay before you the following situation:

The Council of Four determined some days ago to give the Reparation Commission the power to free the lesser nations from any obligation to pay reparation in connection with the Austrian Treaty, on condition that such lesser nations voluntarily assumed an equitable share of the financial burdens incurred in the war of liberation.

We were accordingly directed to negotiate with these nations, and it is proposed that they enter into an undertaking as evidenced by the attached formula, which was prepared by Lord Sumner. In general, they have expressed a willingness to subscribe to this formula on condition that Italy also subscribes to it, in behalf of those regions which Italy is taking over from the former Austro-Hungarian Empire. Italy objects to this.

It seems to the members of the Commission that Italy's stand is not entirely logical. She was willing to have the Trentino, &c., pay reparation, just as the lesser nations would have paid it, on the theory that they were at one time all a part of the enemy Empires. Accordingly, it does not seem illogical that this same principle should be carried out if we ask these nations to make a voluntary contribution in place of reparation. At any rate, it is very clear that these nations will not sign unless this point is met in some form or other, though I should not think it necessary that Italy should subscribe to exactly the same style of formula.

Crespi will be at the meeting, and the time is so short the matter should be determined promptly.

This is simply to post you beforehand as to the point involved.

With great respect,   Sincerely yours,   T. W. Lamont

P.S. Hoover tells me there will be no meeting before afternoon.

TLS (WP, DLC).

E N C L O S U R E

The Republic of [blank], recognizing how greatly the liberation of its territories from the former Austro-Hungarian monarchies was promoted by the many sacrifices which have been made by the Allied and Associated Powers, desires to assume such equitable share in the burden assumed by those powers in the course of the liberation of [blank] as is proportionate to those sacrifices, and is consistent with its own resources on the one hand, and its immediate situation and necessities on the other.

The Allied and Associated Powers, in turn, are pleased to accept the principle as above stated.

To this end, the said parties desiring to cooperate in the restoration of the countries concerned and in the establishment of security and prosperity by the early conclusion of peace, and considering that the time remaining before the conclusion of peace does not admit of full investigation of the aforesaid matters, with a view to the performance of this promise agree to submit the amount of the said contribution and the time, manner and conditions of its payment to the decision of an independent arbitral commission of three persons, one nominated by the Republic of [blank] another by the Allied and Associated Powers, and the third a lawyer of eminence whom His Majesty, the King of Norway,[1] will be respectfully requested to appoint as Chairman. This commission will hear all material evidence, take account of all just considerations, and decide by a majority as may be fair and right, and such decision shall be final.

T MS (WP, DLC).
  [1] Haakon VII.

From Ignace Jan Paderewski

Sir,   Paris, May 30th. 1919.

As the draft of the territorial clauses is to be presented to the Austrian Delegation before all other parts of the Peace Treaty with Austria, I have the honour to ask you, Sir, to give your kind consideration to the request that we respectfully present in this letter.

Art. 92 of the Peace Treaty with Germany stipulates that all forests, public buildings and other properties of the former Polish State, are to belong to Poland free of all charges and are to be exempted from the consideration of the Commission of Reparation.

After the Partition of Poland, Austria having acted in the same way as Prussia, by appropriating without any payment whatever, the buildings, forests and other properties of the Polish State, it is only just that like Prussia she should now return them.

I have the honour to ask you, Sir, to kindly undertake the necessary steps to insure the insertion in the Peace Treaty with Austria of the text of art. 92 of the Peace Treaty with Germany.

I have the honour to be, Sir,
Your most humble and obedient Servant   I. J. Paderewski

I cheerfully endorse this request   W.W.

TLS (WP, DLC).

Mantoux's Notes of a Meeting of the Council of Four

May 30, 1919, 4 p.m.

Wilson. The fighting between the Slovenes and Austrians in Carinthia seems to be taking a rather serious turn.

Clemenceau. It is necessary to stop the Yugoslavs who are in the process of seizing Klagenfurt.

Furthermore, the Rumanians are advancing and have just taken the place of the French in Arad; this city is in the zone which will eventually be assigned to Rumania, but I feel that the Rumanians should have waited to replace our occupation troops.

I wonder whether the Greeks should not also be asked not to advance far from Smyrna; they have just occupied Magnesia.

Wilson. We decided that they could extend their occupation over the entire *sanjak* of Smyrna and as far as Aidin.

Orlando. Should not a commission composed of Frenchmen, Italians, Englishmen, and Americans be sent to Carinthia in order to interpose themselves between the combatants?

Wilson. Yes, but we can send a warning now to the Yugoslavs.

Orlando. You can communicate with the delegation which is in Paris.

Wilson. We should send them a note to remind them to resort to arms is to challenge the authority of the conference.

Clemenceau. I am ready to sign that letter.

Wilson. Mr. Philip Kerr could be charged with drafting it.

Lloyd George. I am going to ask him to do it immediately.

Reading of a letter from the Grand Vizier,[1] requesting that a Turkish delegation be heard by the conference.

Wilson. We have not yet received an enemy delegation.

Lloyd George. There is no reason to treat the Turks like the Germans. Is there any objection to hearing them?

Wilson. No, but the Bulgarians will ask as much from us.

Lloyd George. Do you see any disadvantage in that?

Wilson. I fear that that might create a difficulty for us with the Rumanians.

Lloyd George. At present, I do not have a settled idea on the Bulgarian question.

Wilson. The Turks will begin by protesting against what we did in Smyrna.

Clemenceau. What difference does that make to us?

Wilson. We must not allow ourselves to become engaged in a discussion.

Orlando. We can always hear them.

Wilson. Yes, but not in the capacity of plenipotentiaries, given the present inadequacy of our preparation. Why not instead make an inquiry on the spot and ask them what points they wish to raise?

Clemenceau. We are consenting to hear them, and that is all.

Lloyd George. Let them say what they wish; that does not present any great danger.

It is decided to draft a note in reply to the letter from the Grand Vizier.

Hankey. The drafting committee refers to you Article 228 of the treaty with Germany. It is one of the articles relative to responsibilities and sanctions. It is a question of knowing if one should retain there the words "by military law." It is pointed out that in Belgium, a certain number of crimes committed by the military are tried by civil courts. The commission proposes to cut out the word "military"; Mr. Lansing, president of the Commission on Responsibilities, is of that opinion.

Wilson. I suppose that military law in different countries is more uniform than civil legislation. By eliminating this word, we risk losing the advantages of a more homogeneous jurisprudence.

Clemenceau. I do not attach any importance to that wording; let the commission do what it wishes.

Orlando. If Belgium sends her accused soldiers before civil courts, even that is part of military law. There is thus no inconvenience in keeping this word.

Clemenceau. Let us allow Mr. Lansing to settle the question.

Lloyd George. We will have to study all the German counterproposals.

Wilson. I handed them over to my experts, in sections, with a view to a complete study. We will have to see to what extent we can take these counterproposals into account.

Lloyd George. I have gathered together those of my colleagues who are in Paris; opinions are rather diverse. I have summoned for Sunday a great meeting in which several ministers, come by express from London, will take part. In the meantime, our experts are beginning a detailed examination of the counterproposals.

Wilson. I will also have a meeting Monday with the American delegation to see whether there is agreement among its members.

Lloyd George. The Germans are advancing certain assertions, notably on the subject of the eastern provinces, which I would like to be able to verify. Perhaps it will be necessary to ask them to transmit their maps to us.

Clemenceau. What is the issue, more specifically?

Lloyd George. Silesia. It seems that the arguments used by the Germans are not without value. They say that this country has not been attached to Poland for more than 700 years.

Wilson. Are you very sure of that? In any case, it is not upon historical grounds that the commission based itself in making its decisions, but upon ethnic considerations.

Lloyd George. The Germans base themselves upon elections in which the majority of the votes, they say, has gone to the German candidates.

From the historical point of view, what is to be remembered is that this country does not have any truly Polish memories. The Commission on Polish Affairs appears to me to have been possessed by a kind of partiality for Poland. I have never seen anything so scandalous as the first draft of its report.

Wilson. You are going too far. In the case of Danzig, you raised an objection to the conclusions of the commission, because it seemed to you that the strategic argument should not take precedence over the ethnographic and linguistic. But the commission, while proposing a different conclusion from your own, provided you with the same facts upon which you based yourself to conclude otherwise, and it did not seek to hide its reasons from you.

Clemenceau. We will have to see.

President Wilson reads the text of a reply to the latest German note on labor legislation.[2]

This text is approved.

Lloyd George. I would like to return to the telegram sent by M. Clemenceau to General Haller. It seems certain to me that the military men directed to transmit our instructions to General Haller have not carried out our orders.

Clemenceau. I have the acknowledgment of receipt of my telegrams.

Lloyd George. I am not speaking of what has taken place these last days but of the instructions which we had given initially; either General Haller is not telling the truth, or Marshal Foch did not let him know, when Polish troops began to leave France, that these troops were only to be used against the Bolsheviks. You recall that

Marshal Foch always had in mind sending his troops to Cracow by way of Lemberg, despite our insistence that they pass through Danzig.

Clemenceau. I will inquire about that.

President Wilson reads aloud a report on the situation in the region of Lemberg.[3] This report is not very favorable to the Ukrainians. The atrocities with which the latter have been reproached are true, and the author of the report is surprised that the Polish army, when advancing into Galacia, acted with such moderation. The Ukrainians do not seem capable of governing themselves.

Lloyd George. The author of this report concludes a bit hastily that the Ukrainians should be turned over to the Poles.

Wilson. At the moment, I am not declaring myself in favor of one or the other. I want to hear what there is to say on both sides.

Lloyd George. From our point of view, what is important is the armistice which we stipulated for them and which they have refused to carry out. Since their resistance has not been followed by any sanction, they continue to defy our injunctions. I fear that sooner or later we will find ourselves dragged into that struggle.

Orlando. In the treaty with Austria, there is a point which remains in suspense, the one concerning punishment for war crimes. The criminals who become citizens of a state other than Austria must be covered by a special article. The Drafting Committee has not yet received any communication on this subject.

Wilson. The difficulty is finding a satisfactory legal formula when it is a question of men who are today citizens of friendly states, participating in the League of Nations.

Orlando. The formula which we propose is simple. It consists of asking each government itself to punish those guilty within its own jurisdiction.

Lloyd George. That seems completely fair.

Clemenceau. I approve this text.

Mantoux, II, 256-260.
  [1] Damad Ferid Paşa.
  [2] Brockdorff-Rantzau's letter of May 22, 1919, and the proposed reply, dated May 28, 1919, are printed in *PPC*, VI, 121-26.
  [3] It is printed as an Enclosure with R. H. Lord to WW, May 29, 1919.

From Jan Christiaan Smuts

Dear President Wilson,   Paris. 30th May, 1919.

Even at the risk of wearying you I venture to address you once more.

The German answer to our draft Peace Terms seems to me to strike the fundamental note which is most dangerous to us, and which we are bound to consider most carefully. They say in effect that we are under solemn obligation to them to make a Wilson Peace, a peace in accordance with your Fourteen Points and other Principles enunciated in 1918. To my mind there is absolutely no doubt that this is so. Subject to the two reservations made by the Allies before the Armistice, we are bound to make a peace within the four corners of your Points and Principles, and any provisions of the Peace Treaty which either go *contrary* to or *beyond* their general scope and intent would constitute a breach of agreement.

This seems to my mind quite clear, and the question of fact remains whether there are any such provisions. If there are, then our position is indeed serious, as I understand it. This war began with a breach of a solemn international undertaking, and it has been one of our most important war aims to vindicate international law and the sanctity of international engagements. If the Allies end the war by following the example of Germany at the beginning, and also confront the world with a "scrap of paper," the discredit on us will be so great that I shudder to think of its ultimate effect on public opinion. We would indeed have done a worse wrong than Germany because of all that has happened since August, 1914, and the fierce light which has been concentrated on this very point.

The question becomes, therefore, most important whether there are important provisions of the Treaty which conflict with or are not covered by, but go beyond, your Points and Principles. I notice a tendency to put the whole responsibility for deciding this question on you, and to say that after all President Wilson agrees to the Treaty and he knows best what the Points and Principles mean. This is most unfair to you, and I think we should all give the gravest consideration to the question whether our Peace Treaty is within the four corners of your Speeches of 1918.

Frankly I do not think this is so, and I think the Germans make out a good case in regard to a number of provisions. All the onesided provisions, which exclude reciprocity or equality, and all the pinpricks, with which the Treaty teems, seem to me to be both against the letter and the spirit of your Points. I cannot find anything in the Points or the Principles which would cover, for instance, the onesided internationalisation of German rivers, and the utterly bad and onesided administration arranged in respect of them. Reparation by way of coal cannot cover the arrangements made in respect of the Saar Basin and its people. I even doubt whether the Occupation of the Rhine for fifteen years could be squared either with the letter or the spirit of your Points and Principles. And there are many other points to which I shall not refer, but which no doubt your Advisers will consider.

There will be a terrible disillusion if the peoples come to think that we are not concluding a Wilson Peace, that we are not keeping our promises to the world or faith with the public. But if in so doing we appear also to break a formal agreement deliberately entered into (as I think we do), we shall be overwhelmed with the gravest discredit, and this Peace may well become an even greater disaster to the world than the war was.

Forgive me for troubling you with this matter, but I believe it goes to the root of our whole case.

Yours very sincerely,   J. C. Smuts.

TLS (WP, DLC).

From Robert Lansing, with Enclosure

My dear Mr. President: Paris, May 30, 1919.

With reference to my letter of May 29th, 1919 and previous correspondence regarding the report on the Omsk Government which Ambassador Morris has been requested to make, I am transmitting herewith a message on the matter which has just been received from Mr. Polk, and I shall be very glad to be informed if you approve of the suggestion that Mr. Morris should not undertake his journey to Omsk until a reply had been received from the communication which has been sent to Kolchak.

Faithfully yours,   Robert Lansing

TLS (WP, DLC).

E N C L O S U R E

Washington. May 29th, 1919.

2139. VERY URGENT.

For the Secretary of State from Polk.

Your 2305, May 28th.[1] I take the liberty of suggesting that in view of the fact it has been decided to support Kolchak under certain conditions would it not be wise to hold Morris in Tokyo pending an answer from Kolchak to communication just sent. There is more than a chance that Kolchak will be afraid for political reasons to abolish the conditions laid down, particularly the recognition of the independence of various parts of the Old Russian Empire and the recognition of the old constituent assembly. If Kolchak should refuse to accept the terms it might be embarrassing for Morris, and an affront to Morris would injure our prestige. It is probable we will have an answer from Kolchak in a short time.   Polk,   Acting.

T telegram (WP, DLC).
    [1] That is, the telegram which embodied the message to Admiral Kolchak printed as Appendix I to the Minutes of the Council of Four, May 27, 1919, 4 p.m. (second meeting).

From Robert Lansing, with Enclosure

My dear Mr. President: Paris, May 30th, 1919.

    I am taking the liberty of calling to your attention the enclosed telegram from Omsk giving the substance of a recent conversation between Kolchak and Consul General Harris.
                        Faithfully yours,   Robert Lansing

TLS (WP, DLC).

E N C L O S U R E

                                Washington, May 29, 1919.

    2126. IMPORTANT For your information, telegram dated May 22 from Peking reading as follows: "Repeated from Omsk. 232, May 21, 1:00 p.m. Had conference with Kolchak today. He laid stress upon the great necessity for economic aid and thought America was in best position to render some. Financial aid also particularly pressing question. He stated that of all the Allies, England had thus far done the most but he hoped America would soon give more assistance. He expressed best sentiments of good will towards America and stated that the anti-American propaganda was not shared by him or his colleagues in the government and that same was now practically over. As concerns the friction in Far East he stated that Government had recalled Ivanoff[1] in order to clear situation who had been succeeded by Horvath.[2] Also stated that Horvath had announced the submission of Semenoff[3] but Department believes Semenoff would cease. On the question of recognition Kolchak said that he was not asking such a step on the part of Allied Governments but was leaving this important matter entirely to their best judgment uninfluenced by any statement from him. Harris.[4] Reinsch." 2126.
                        Polk,   Acting.

T telegram (WP, DLC).
    [1] That is, Gen. Pavel Pavlovich Ivanov-Rinov.
    [2] That is, Gen. Dmitrii Leonidovich Horvat (or Horvath).
    [3] That is, Gen. Grigorii Mikhailovich Semenov.
    [4] That is, Ernest Lloyd Harris, Consul at Omsk.

From Robert Lansing

My dear Mr. President: Paris, May 30, 1919.

In my note to you of April 30th, replying to your inquiry about Montenegro,[1] I referred to the Anglo-American Mission of Investigation, on which we were represented by Colonel Miles, and suggested awaiting his report before taking definite action.

Miles has now returned and has reported to the Commission, and submitted his summary of the situation in Montenegro, of which I enclose a copy.[2]

His conclusions confirm reports from many other sources that the solution of the Montenegrin question, which would best meet the wishes of the people concerned, is the incorporation of this country into Yugo-Slavia under guarantees of autonomy and the protection of local rights.

I am, my dear Mr. President,

Very sincerely yours,   Robert Lansing

TLS (WP, DLC).
[1] RL to WW, April 30, 1919, Vol. 58, and WW to RL, April 26, 1919, CCL (WP, DLC).
[2] S. Miles to J. C. Grew, May 19, 1919, TCL (WP, DLC), printed in *PPC*, XII, 738-40. Miles reported that Montenegro was presently under Serbian military control. He discussed three possible solutions for Montenegro's future. One was to abandon Montenegro to Serbian control, which would be "a political crime." The second—to reconstitute Montenegro as an independent state—would be unsatisfactory, because its barren mountainous country was not economically viable and because there was no possible government for an independent Montenegro except the dynasty of King Nicholas. While it was impossible, without a plebiscite, which Miles considered impracticable, to know what the Montenegrin people really thought of Nicholas, all indications seemed to show that he was "discredited and despised by a majority of his people." Moreover, he was an old man and his sons were "degenerates, utterly unfit to rule." Hence, Miles concluded, as Lansing indicates above, that the third solution—the inclusion of Montenegro into Yugoslavia, under Yugoslav guarantees of autonomy and political rights—was the best possible option.

From the Diary of Edith Benham

May 30, 1919

Today, May 30th, seemed the ending of the week, though it isn't Sunday but Memorial Day. The P. was too busy to go to the church services. I went and sat with the Wallaces in their pew at the big American Church. It was a very impressive service, a military band, and when the clergyman and choir came in they were preceded by one soldier carrying the Cross and another carrying the Flag, and followed by four soldiers, four sailors and four marines. A little French Protestant Clergyman read one of the most beautiful prayers I have ever heard for those who had fallen in the war. It was quite an international affair, with the national hymns of France, Great Britain and the U. S., and a Priest of the Greek Church in gorgeous cloth of gold robes to assist.

The afternoon the services were at the American cemetery at Suresnes where the men who died here after the Chateau Thierry drive when the city was a shambles are buried, with others who died in Paris. Going out the P. was preoccupied and nervous as he always is before a speech. The cemetery is new and bare and brown, but very well kept, and the women of Suresnes have kept flowers on the graves and cared for them, and it will be lovely in time. We could not get out on account of Mrs. W.'s foot, so we watched the P. walk up to the stand and then we drove up behind him and waited in the machine and listened while he made one of the greatest speeches I have ever heard him make. There is no doubt that he is the idol of the little people. I sent out my two boys[1] and Allen.[2] They wanted to go, and I wanted them to have some more ideals to take home and make a part of their lives. I didn't think they would care for it all, but that just shows the big truths aren't meant just for the more educated—they belong to the world. Schindler, who is by no means emotional, told me it was the great day of his life, and he was going to cut out the speech just to inspire him. Next to him, he said, the "little rough-neck motor cycle driver" was crying, and all around the men were too much moved to know if they ought to be still or applaud. As they said, "He is great when he just comes out and stands there." Coming home he, the P., asked if he had said enough about the French. He is the least self-conscious of human beings. After his work was done and he had said what he did about America and the ideals of the League of Nations, he was just quiet, coming home. I told him later in the afternoon what the boys had told me, and their impressions, and he seemed so happy over it, and to know that they, the people, had appreciated the truths he wanted to drive home, and to be carried home.

[1] Her aides, Chief Yeoman Nicholas P. Schindler and Yeoman 1st Class Francis A. Kennedy.
[2] Corporal Allen of the United States Marine Corps, another aide. The Editors have been unable to learn his given names.

From the Diary of Ray Stannard Baker

Memorial Day May 30, 1919

I drove to Suresnes Cemetery this afternoon & heard the President speak. It was the dedication of the first American cemetery on the fields of France & unescapably recalled that other dedication at Gettysburg in 1863 when Lincoln thought he failed. I sat on the platform just below the President, near General Foch. It was a hot, bright day, and dusty in the newly made cemetery. There where thousands of people, mostly our soldiers all about filling the acacia groves on the hillside above, where one looks off so grandly upon the city of Paris.

Well, it was a wonderful speech, so perfectly done, so sure, so musical, so appealing at that hour. Never did an orator have more perfect command of himself, and without palpable effort, either in voice or movement, infuse his audience with his very spirit. He has one of the great assets of art: restraint. So that when his voice rose & thrilled in the high passages in which he invoked the spirit of the dead, or in the last matchless personal confession, it was with incalculable power & grace. I saw tears in the eyes of those around me, & felt them in my own. On the whole I think this is the greatest speech—the greatest in his power over the people who were there— of any I ever heard. . . .

I saw the President afterwards, at the house, & told him something of the impression his speech had made. "I am glad to hear it" he said. "When I speak extemporaneously, I am as uncertain & nervous just after it is over, as I usually am just before."

He told me he had a conference this morning with Orlando, in which Orlando was still trying to trade. "It is curious," he said, "how utterly incapable these Italians are of taking any position on principle & sticking to it. They are forever shifting, trying to trade." The President is standing like a rock. . . .

I saw him lay a wreath on a soldiers grave: and a French woman with tears in her eyes run up to shake his hand & Marshal Foch grip him hard & with emotion that was strongly evident.

I went out for a ride in the Bois with Colonel House this morning: a beautiful spring day. I told him of the blooming acacias and he said, "I was brought up on the odor of locust blossoms." So when we found a fine grove of them, we got out & walked about in it, a real bower of fragrance[.] I never saw trees more heavily loaded with blossoms nor smelt a more overpowering odor. "You are renewing your youth Colonel," I said. "It is Texas again," said he. He told me fully of the happenings of the last few days. Whenever there is trouble the Colonel is called in. There is a grave issue now in the Council of Four over their attitude toward the treaty: whether they shall make substantial changes. Lloyd-George had House to lunch yesterday & told him quite clearly that he favored such changes: that the liberal & labor criticism in England was reaching great strength. He was evidently alarmed. This morning Clemenceau called on the Colonel at the Crillon & had the same problem on his mind. He is sternly against any change whatever in the treaty. He wants to drive it—now that it is finished—straight through[.] Changes, if necessary, can be made later. The Colonel is inclined to agree with him, & thinks that the President will stand nearer to Clemenceau than to L.G. I think so too. (As this Conference has progressed, my regard for Clemenceau has risen—I don't agree with him in the least, but he is a strong, honest, courteous man: while Lloyd-George grows ever shiftier) If changes once begin there will be no end!

The outlook for an early signing either of the German or Austrian treaty is dubious.

An English liberal M.P. said to-day: "Wilson talks like Jesus Christ, but acts like Lloyd-George."

From the Diary of Colonel House

May 30, 1919.

My first caller was Clemenceau. I knew when he sent work [word] that he would like to see me what it was about. He desired to do what Lloyd George did yesterday, that is, commit me to his point of view regarding the German answer to the Treaty. I was able to tell him some interesting facts as to Lloyd George's position, particularly about the letter General Botha has written George[1] and which George carefully failed to reveal to me. This letter almost marks an epoch in British Colonial affairs. Clemenceau thought, and I agreed with him, that he would have more trouble with George than with the President. I told him the President had now begun to appreciate him, Clemenceau, which he did not do when he first arrived in France. Clemenceau replied, "I, too, have learned to appreciate the President, for while he is narrow, yet he travels in the same direction all the time while George travels in every direction, so inconsistent is he from day to day."

Clemenceau declared that he intended to stand firm against any substantial reduction in the terms of the Treaty no matter what the consequences. In my opinion if he does this, he will win. I am not sure that his policy is best. The treaty is not a good one, it is too severe, and notwithstanding the President believes it is well within the Fourteen Points, it is far afield from them. However, the time to have made the Treaty right was when it was being formed and not now. It is a question if one commenced to unravel what has already been done whether it could be stopped. It is also a question as to the effect upon the Germans. I desired from the beginning a fair peace, and one well within the Fourteen Points, and one which could stand the scrutiny of the neutral world and of all time. It is not such a peace, but since the Treaty has been written I question whether it would be well to seriously modify it.

. . . Wallace was another visitor. I did not go to Suresne Cemetery to hear the President. The speech was a masterpiece of it[s] kind. I have written the President what I thought of it. I am quite sincere in believing that the President will rank with the great orators of all time. In truth, I believe that it is as an orator that he excels rather than as a statesman.

The feeling has become fairly general that the President's actions do not square with his speeches. There is a *bon mot* going the round in Paris and London, "Wilson talks like Jesus Christ and acts like Lloyd George." My own feeling is that he is influenced by his constant association with Clemenceau and George. I seldom or never have a chance to talk with him seriously and, for the moment, he is practically out from under my influence. When we meet, it is to settle some pressing problem and not to take inventory of things in general or plan for the fu[tu]re. This is what we used to do. If I could have the President in quiet, I am certain I could get him to square his actions with his words. As a matter of fact, the President does not truly feel as I do, although I have always been able to appeal to his intellectual liberalism.

[1] He meant J. C. Smuts to D. Lloyd George, May 22, 1919.

From the Diary of Vance Criswell McCormick

May 30 (Friday) [1919]

Conference in Davis' room on Austrian Reparation clauses. Loucheur came in, said he had been reading nearly all last night Germans answer and did not like it. Said he thought we should not enter into extended discussion. Said Clemenceau had confidence in Wilson to stick, but was afraid of Lloyd George; afraid he may swing to extreme liberals if it looks popular at home. When I intimated such a contingency to the President some days ago, he said he would not dare.

Bernie[1] and I lunched with Miss Hare.[2] Sorry we could not attend Memorial Day exercises at the United States Cemetery, as the President spoke, but had a Reparation meeting at 3.00 o'clock. Keynes and Lord Sumner, of the British delegation, continued fight over Austrian reparation clauses, Keynes trying to modify them considerably, saying Austria broken and ought to be helped financially. Lord Sumner saying that the present clauses fair and flexible. Committee agreed with Lord Sumner, and Keynes stated he would fight it out before Big Four. Loucheur and Crespi seemed to be getting thick; there is some deal on and I have not discovered it yet.

[1] That is, Bernard M. Baruch.
[2] Unidentified.

From the Diary of Dr. Grayson

Saturday, May 31, 1919.

There was nothing doing in the morning, and after breakfast I persuaded the President to rest as much as possible. He went for a motor ride, I accompanying him. It is remarkable how the President has changed in some respects and how today his viewpoint no longer is a national one but deals with the entire world at large. I have told him what it means to individuals to be able to come in contact with him. Their inability to do so makes them believe that he is cold and does not care about individuals or desire to interest individuals in himself or his projects. I know the impulses of his heart towards his fellowmen and towards people as a whole, who are anxious to meet him and deal personally with him. I know it is entirely a question of diffidence, and not one of indifference, but in the case of the President it has been and is entirely a question of not being able to afford the time to meet people promiscuously or even generally. When once the President actually comes into contact with people generally he enjoys it more than the persons themselves. The President agreed with me in this estimate of his character, which I made to him today.

The President and I lunched with Mrs. Wilson in her room, after which the President went to Quai d'Orsay to attend the secret Plenary Session, at which the Austrian terms were submitted to the smaller nations. It had been expected that these terms would be communicated to the Austrians yesterday, but this was found impossible because of the objections that the smaller nations raised to the approving of the treaty until they had formally approved the terms themselves. This was a disappointment, of course, to the Austrians but they were assured by the Big Four that they would get the treaty not later than Monday.

As soon as the Plenary Session opened the Roumanian delegation again objected to the terms whereby the minorities in the newly created republics were to be safeguarded. The Roumanian Premier[1] characterized this as a complete invasion of the sovereign rights of nations, declaring that if the League of Nations was to be allowed to take any part in the internal affairs of small nations it would mean that the world at large would be ruled entirely by a combination of big powers, and that smaller principalities would be in the position of vassal states. The Premier's denunciation of the clause in the treaty was particularly bitter, and all of the other small nations joined in endorsing his position. The Czecho-Slovaks objected strongly to the proposal that the entire indebtedness of the war chargeable against Austria-Hungary should be pro-rated among the nations that were carved out of the former Hapsburg Monarchy. The controversy was extremely animated, and eventually President Wilson delivered an address which those who heard him said was about the strongest speech he had made since he came to Europe to attend the Peace Conference. He frankly warned the wrangling representatives of the smaller nations that inasmuch as the big powers would be compelled to guarantee the safety of the world in the future it was essential that they mix in the affairs of the small nations. He told the Roumanian Premier that while he was desirous of meeting the views of the small powers as far as possible, yet it was necessary that religious and political minorities who were included in newly created states but who differed in language and custom from the prevailing majority have their rights upheld by an independent organization such as the League of Nations. Servia objected to the Southern[2] boundary, but finally agreed to stand by the decision of the Big Four. Eventually it was decided to withhold the financial and reparation clauses from the Austrian treaty, and then the smaller nations withdrew their protest against the minority provision, accepting the President's promise that this would be changed, if possible, to meet their views, and that the Big Four would confer with the representatives of the small powers before the Austrian treaty was finally signed. It was after six o'clock before the Plenary Session adjourned, and it was then announced that the Austrian treaty would be delivered on Monday, noon, at St. Germain to the Austrian peace delegates.

The various nations were now in possession of the German counter-proposals, and it was apparent that there was a distinct difference of opinion upon the problem of whether the treaty should be revised somewhat in order to meet the more strenuous of the German objections. France, it appears, is in favor of adhering to the original terms of the treaty. The French authorities do not want to change a single word; they want to put it through as it stands. The President's viewpoint is not to recede from any of the principles involved in the treaty regardless of the threatened attitude of the Germans in their counter-proposal. However, the President is willing to make a revision of unimportant parts of the economic and financial sections of the treaty if the Germans can prove that they have better proposals to substitute. The British delegation had changed its attitude during the last few days. Originally, Lloyd George and his associates on the British Peace Commission had fought to force Germany to make every concession possible towards Great Britain. Lloyd George, however, has received a very strong protest from the former followers of Mr. Asquith and the Liberals, who were practically swept out of power at the last general election, and from the extreme labor men. While this protest came from a section that represented less than one-sixth of the total strength of the British Parliament it had been able to influence Lloyd George to such an extent that he sent a call today for the members of the Cabinet to come to Paris, and they all arrived here this evening, dining with Lloyd George in secret at his house. The general feeling was that inasmuch as the Germans seemed determined not to sign, it would be advisable if Great Britain were to advocate conciliation towards Brockdorff-Rantzau, and his associated delegates, by making concessions on the treaty terms at the expense of Poland and possibly of France. The idea as proposed was to grant a plebiscite in Upper Silesia, to make easements in the reparation clauses, to fix a definite figure of $25,000,000,000 as the total that Germany should pay as reparations, and to arrange for the early admission of Germany into the League of Nations. The movement for the changes in the treaty was headed by Lord Milner, Minister of Education Fisher and Alfred Mond.[3] In addition, Generals Botha and Smuts were objecting to that portion of the treaty which provided for the personal punishment of the Kaiser and his associates, they holding that such action would simply stir up further bitter feeling. The whole situation was distinctly and decidedly filled with dynamite.

The President was invited to attend a special performance of *Hello, Paris*, given by the Knights of Columbus Athletic Committee in honor of the competitors in the road race which they had conducted on Memorial Day from Château Thierry to Paris. The Knights had taken up two-thirds of the house and invited the President to be the guest of honor as a tribute to the soldiers. The President gladly accepted. The performance was the usual Parisian speaking type, but there were a number of special attractions which had been arranged, and, in addition, there were several American actors who spoke English. One thing greatly amused the President and gave him a real hearty laugh. A monologue artist ascended a ladder, talking all the while, until finally he reached the topmost rung. Then teetering backward and forward but maintaining his equilibrium, he swung his mandolin around and addressing the audience said: "I will play anything any one here suggests." An enterprising wag called out from the ranks of the American soldiers:

"Well, play us Nearer My God to Thee." The apt application to the
equilibrist, with his head almost in the top sets at the roof of the theatre, convulsed every one, and threw him into such a state of embarrassment that he was forced to say: "I don't know it." This
brought down the house, the President leading the laughter and the
applause.

¹ That is, Ionel (Ion I. C.) Brătianu.
² Actually, the northern boundary.
³ Herbert Albert Laurens Fisher, M.P., historian, President of the Board of Education,
and Sir Alfred Moritz Mond, M.P., industrialist, First Commissioner of Works.

From the Minutes of a Plenary Session of a Meeting of the Inter-Allied Conference on the Preliminaries of Peace[1]

Protocol No. 8   Quai d'Orsay, May 31, 1919, 3:00 p.m.

The Session is opened at 15 o'clock (3 p.m.) under the Presidency
of Mr. Clemenceau, *President.* . . .

The Agenda Paper calls for the communication to the Allied and
Associated Powers of the Conditions of Peace with Austria. . . .[2]

THE PRESIDENT OF THE UNITED STATES, speaking in English,
makes the following speech:

"Mr. President, I should be very sorry to see this meeting adjourn
with permanent impressions such as it is possible may have been
created by some of the remarks that our friends have made. I should
be very sorry to have the impression lodged in your minds that the
Great Powers desire to assume or play any arbitrary *rôle* in these
great matters, or presume, because of any pride of authority, to exercise an undue influence in these matters, and therefore I want to
call your attention to one aspect of these questions which has not
been dwelt upon.

"We are trying to make a peaceful settlement, that is to say, to
eliminate those elements of disturbance, so far as possible, which
may interfere with the peace of the world, and we are trying to make
an equitable distribution of territories according to the race, the ethnographical character of the people inhabiting them.

"And back of that lies this fundamentally important fact that,
when the decisions are made, the Allied and Associated Powers
guarantee to maintain them. It is perfectly evident, upon a moment's reflection, that the chief burden of their maintenance will
fall upon the Great Powers. The chief burden of the war fell upon the
Greater Powers, and, if it had not been for their action, their military

¹ The complete text of these minutes is printed in *PPC*, III, 394-410.
² Here follow the speeches just described by Grayson. They are printed in *ibid.*

action, we would not be here to settle these questions. Therefore, we must not close our eyes to the fact that in the last analysis the military and naval strength of the Great Powers will be the final guarantee of the peace of the world.

"In those circumstances is it unreasonable and unjust that, not as dictators but as friends, the Great Powers should say to their associates: 'We cannot afford to guarantee territorial settlements which we do not believe to be right, and we cannot agree to leave elements of disturbance unremoved, which we believe will disturb the peace of the world?'

"Take the rights of minorities. Nothing, I venture to say, is more likely to disturb the peace of the world than the treatment which might in certain circumstances be meted out to minorities. And therefore, if the Great Powers are to guarantee the peace of the world in any sense, is it unjust that they should be satisfied that the proper and necessary guarantees have been given?

"I beg our friends from Roumania and from Serbia to remember that while Roumania and Serbia are ancient sovereignties the settlements of this Conference are greatly adding to their territories. You cannot in one part of our transactions treat Serbia alone and in all of the other parts treat the Kingdom of the Serbs, Croats, and Slovenes as a different entity, for they are seeking the recognition of this Conference as a single entity, and if this Conference is going to recognize these various Powers as new sovereignties within definite territories, the chief guarantors are entitled to be satisfied that the territorial settlements are of a character to be permanent, and that the guarantees given are of a character to ensure the peace of the world.

"It is not, therefore, the intervention of those who would interfere, but the action of those who would help. I beg that our friends will take that view of it, because I see no escape from that view of it.

"How can a Power like the United States, for example—for I can speak for no other—after signing this Treaty, if it contains elements which they do not believe will be permanent, go three thousand miles away across the sea and report to its people that it has made a settlement of the peace of the world? It cannot do so. And yet there underlies all of these transactions the expectation on the part, for example, of Roumania and of Czecho-Slovakia and of Serbia, that if any covenants of this settlement are not observed, the United States will send her armies and her navies to see that they are observed.

"In those circumstances is it unreasonable that the United States should insist upon being satisfied that the settlements are correct? Mr. Bratiano—and I speak of his suggestions with the utmost respect—suggested that we could not, so to say, invade the sovereignty of Roumania, an ancient sovereignty, and make certain pre-scriptions with regard to the rights of minorities. But I beg him to observe that he is overlooking the fact that he is asking the sanction of the Allied and Associated Powers for great additions of territory which come to Roumania by the common victory of arms, and that, therefore, we are entitled to say: 'If we agree to these additions of territory we have the right to insist upon certain guarantees of peace.'

I beg my friend Mr. Kramar, and my friend Mr. Trumbitch, and my friend Mr. Bratiano, to believe that if we should feel that it is best to leave the words which they have wished to omit in the Treaty, it is not because we want to insist upon unreasonable conditions, but that we want the Treaty to accord to us the right of judgment as to whether these are things which we can afford to guarantee.

"Therefore the impressions with which we should disperse ought to be these, that we are all friends—of course, that goes without say-ing—but that we must all be associates in a common effort, and there can be no frank and earnest association in the common effort unless there is a common agreement as to what the rights and set-tlements are.

"Now, if the agreement is a separate agreement among groups of us, that does not meet the object. If you should adopt the language suggested by the Czecho-Slovakian Delegation and the Serbian Delegation—the Yugo-Slav Delegation—that it should be left to ne-gotiations between the principal Allied and Associated Powers and their several Delegates, that would mean that after this whole Con-ference is adjourned groups of them would determine what is to be the basis of the peace of the world. It seems to me that that would be a most dangerous idea to entertain, and therefore I beg that we may part with a sense, not of interference with each other, but of hearty and friendly co-operation upon the only possible basis of guarantee. Where the great force lies, there must be the sanction of peace. I sometimes wish, in hearing an argument like this, that I were the representative of a small Power, so that what I said might be robbed of any mistaken significance, but I think you will agree with me that the United States has never shown any temper of aggression any-where, and it lies in the heart of the people of the United States, as I am sure it lies in the hearts of the peoples of the other Great Powers, to form a common partnership of right, and to do service to our as-sociates and no kind of disservice." . . .

Printed copy (SDR, RG 256, 180.0201/8, DNA).

Hankey's Notes of a Meeting of the Council of Four[1]

C.F.43.   Quai d'Orsay, May 31, 1919, 5:30 p.m.

1. Attention is drawn to the Acta relating to—
   The proposed Roumanian march on Budapest.
   League of Nations. Drafting Correction to Article 24.
   Omission of an Article on the Assling triangle
   from the draft Treaty of Peace with Austria.
   Invitation to the Grand Vizier of Turkey to come to Paris.
   Carinthia. Cessation of fighting between Austrians and Jugo-
   Slavs.

                    (Appendix I).[2]

2. M. ORLANDO drew attention to the following sentence in the
Preamble of the draft Treaty of Peace with Austria:
   "Whereas, by the free action of the peoples of the former Austro-
   Hungarian Monarchy, this Monarchy has now ceased to exist and
   has been replaced in Austria by a Republican Government, and"
He said that the words underlined would be displeasing to Italian
public opinion, as it would be taken as underrating the Italian Mili-
tary effort.
   (It was agreed to omit the words underlined, as well as the words
   "this Monarchy," and that the clause should read as follows:
   "Whereas, the former Austro-Hungarian Monarchy has now
   ceased to exist and has been replaced in Austria by a Republican
   Government, and")

3. M. ORLANDO also suggested that the clause in the Preamble following the above, in which it was stated that the Czecho-Slovak
State and the Serbo-Croat-Slovene State have been recognised,
should be omitted. He said that Italy had not recognised these
States. He added that he had no knowledge of the instruction to the
Drafting Committee, on which this Preamble was stated to have
been based.
   PRESIDENT WILSON suggested that the clause should begin as fol-
lows:
   "Whereas the majority of the Principal Allied and Associated Pow-
   ers have already recognised etc."
He pointed out that Poland was not included.
   (The Drafting Committee were then sent for, and were intro-
   duced.)
   During the discussion which followed, the Council were re-
minded that the presentation of the full powers of the Croats and
Slovenes to the Germans had been regarded as tantamount to rec-
ognition.

M. ORLANDO then withdrew his objection, and the paragraph was left unchanged.

4. (After some discussion, it was agreed that no alteration should be made in the provisions of the Draft Treaty of Peace with Austria in the clauses relating to Rights of Minorities, as proposed on the same afternoon at the Plenary Conference.)

(M. Jules Cambon entered.)

5. (The attached Article of the Draft Treaty of Peace with Austria, relating to the frontiers between Austria and Czecho-Slovakia, which had been drawn up by the experts under M. Jules Cambon, in consequence of remarks made by the Czecho-Slovak Delegation at the Plenary Conference the same afternoon, was approved and initialled by the four Heads of States.) (Appendix II.)[3]

Sir Maurice Hankey communicated the Article direct to the Drafting Committee.

(M. Jules Cambon withdrew.)

(M. Dutasta was introduced.)

6. M. CLEMENCEAU said he had received a letter from Herr Renner, the Head of the Austrian Delegation, who had asked to talk with him. Subject to the consent of his colleagues, he proposed to reply that it had been agreed that there should be no conversations, but that if Herr Renner liked to send a confidential note, he would undertake to show it only to the four Heads of States.

(This was agreed to.)

(M. Dutasta withdrew.)

7. With reference to C.F.42, Minute 7,[4] SIR MAURICE HANKEY stated that he now had the Articles of the Treaty to which M. Kramarcz's observations referred, and which had not been available on the previous day.

(In view of the discussion at the Plenary Conference that afternoon, it was decided not to discuss the question.)

8. (M. Tardieu entered.)

MR. LLOYD GEORGE read a telegram he had received from General Allenby, indicating that the situation in Syria would be extremely grave unless the Commission of the Peace Conference should come to Syria. (Appendix III.)[5] He said that General Wilson had also received a private letter from General Allenby, dated May 17th, 1919, which fully confirmed the message in the telegram. Hence, he felt that the moment had come to decide whether the Commission was to be sent out. Personally, he would prefer that the Commission should proceed at once. The United States Commissioners had already left for Syria. He himself, did not wish to send out British Commissioners unless the French also sent Commissioners, but in this case, he must inform General Allenby. The situation was so serious that he could not postpone action.

M. CLEMENCEAU said his position was as he had stated a few days before, namely, that he was willing to send French Commissioners as soon as the relief of British troops by French troops was begun. As long as Syria remained entirely in British military occupation, and Mr. Lloyd George's latest proposals held the field it was useless to send French Commissioners. Nevertheless, he would undertake not to send any more French troops against the wishes of the British Government. He was sending some troops to Cilicia, although there was not much object in this from the French point of view, if Cilicia was to go to the United States. As soon as General Allenby would let him know that the replacement of British troops by French could commence, so that the people of Syria knew that they were not exclusively under British force, he would send Commissioners.

MR. LLOYD GEORGE said he had thought it right before taking action, to let his colleagues know exactly what he proposed to do. He would not send Commissioners if the French did not. General Allenby showed clearly that if French troops went to Syria now, there would be very serious trouble. He himself was not in a position to judge of the matter, but General Allenby was a very reliable man, and was the British representative on the spot, and he could not afford to neglect his advice. Mr. Lloyd George then read a copy of the telegram he proposed to send to General Allenby. At M. Clemenceau's request he agreed to alter one passage in order to make it clear that the French were not willing to send Commissioners until the relief of British troops by French troops had been arranged.[6]

M. CLEMENCEAU said he would make no comment beyond asking for the above alteration.

MR. LLOYD GEORGE promised to send M. Clemenceau a copy of General Allenby's despatch.

M. ORLANDO said he would not send Commissioners until the British and French Governments sent them.

9. M. ORLANDO presented several proposed alterations in the Financial Clauses in the Draft Treaty of Peace with Austria which had been signed by the representatives of the four States on the Drafting Committee of the Financial Commission.

PRESIDENT WILSON was reluctant to initial these alterations without having some explanation as to their meaning.

(The question was reserved.)

T MS (SDR, RG 256, 180.03401/43, DNA).
  [1] The complete text of Hankey's notes is printed in *PPC*, VI, 130-37.
  [2] "Council of the Principal Allied and Associated Powers: ACTA," May 30-31, 1919, T MS

(SDR, RG 256, 180.03401/43, DNA), printed in *PPC*, VI, 133-35. This document listed actions taken "between Meetings" on May 30 and 31, 1919. The Rumanians had been ordered not to march on Budapest. The French text of Article 24 of the Covenant was to be amended by the Drafting Committee to make it identical to the English text. The article on the Assling triangle in the Austrian draft peace treaty was to be "suppressed." The Grand Vizier was to be invited to send a delegation to Paris to speak for the Ottoman sovereign, government, and people. Finally, the Yugoslavs were to be urged to cease all hostile operations in Carinthia.

    [3] "FRONTIERES D'AUTRICHE, Article I, 5 avec l'Etat TCHECHO-SLOVAQUE," May 31, 1919, T MS (SDR, RG 256, 180.03401/43, DNA). An English translation is printed in *PPC*, VI, 135-36.

    [4] "7. The Council had before them the remarks of the Drafting Committee on the proposals of M. Kramarz on the Political Clauses for the Czecho-Slovak State. The discussion was adjourned owing to the fact that the Articles of the Treaty to which M. Kramarz' observations referred, were not available." Hankey's minutes of a meeting of the Council of Four, May 30, 1919, 4 p.m., *ibid.*, p. 117.

    [5] "I. Telegram from General Allenby: MEMORANDUM," June 1 [May 30], 1919, T MS (SDR, RG 256, 180.03401/43, DNA), printed in *ibid.*, pp. 136-37.

    [6] "II. Paraphrase of a telegram to General Allenby," May 31, 1919, T MS (SDR, RG 256, 180.03401/43, DNA), printed in *ibid.*, p. 137.

Mantoux's Notes of a Meeting of the Council of Four

May 31, 1919, 5:30 p.m.

Orlando. In the preamble of the treaty with Austria, it is stated that, through the free movement of peoples, the Austro-Hungarian Monarchy has ceased to exist. This wording could displease Italy, where it would be thought that it diminishes the importance of the Italian victory. I propose to write simply that the Monarchy ceased to exist. Moreover, that is all that is important to say in a text of this kind.

Lloyd George. The statement of fact is indeed enough.

Orlando. Further on, I read: "The Allied and Associated Powers have recognized the union of certain parts of that Empire as an independent and allied state, under the name of 'Kingdom of the Serbs, Croats, and Slovenes.' " As a matter of fact, that is not exact, for Italy has not yet recognized that state.

Moreover, it seems to me pointless to mention in that passage the states formed out of the debris of Austria-Hungary. In any case, we would have to cite Poland, whose name I do not see.

Wilson. We wanted to name these states in the preamble, because they are mentioned in the text of the treaty and because we insisted on defining them first in some way.

Orlando. At any rate, Poland is not mentioned.

Lloyd George. From the point of view of the Drafting Committee, there must be a reason for mentioning these states in that place; the best thing is to consult the Drafting Committee on the subject.

Clemenceau. What do we decide on the text relating to minorities, about which we are going to hear Rumania's observations? I propose to leave this text as it is.

Lloyd George. Rumania has no grounds for complaint at the time when we are doubling the extent of her territory.

Clemenceau. It was not the Rumanian soldiers who did it.

Lloyd George. Without us, part of Rumania would have been lost forever.

Clemenceau. Then we will leave the words whose omission M. Bratiano requested: "judged necessary by the Principal Allied and Associated Powers."

Wilson. I believe that these words are necessary, and that we must insist upon our right to intervene in the matter.

The Drafting Committee is introduced.

M. Orlando presents his objections to the preamble of the treaty with Austria.

Fromageot. We have only followed the directions of the Council of Four.

Orlando. Do you see an objection to omitting mention of the states formed out of the territories of the Austro-Hungarian Monarchy?

Fromageot. It is not I who should answer you, for that is a political question.

Wilson. It seems to me necessary to preserve the mention of these states in the preamble, because a certain number of stipulations in the treaty concern them directly. It is true that all of the Allied and Associated Powers have not recognized the Yugoslav state; but can we not write: "Considering that a majority of the said Powers have already recognized. * * * etc.?

Concerning Poland, it is true that she is not mentioned; but Mr. Brown Scott reminds me that we have not yet pronounced on the fate of Galicia.

Orlando. I will observe that the Yugoslav state is not recognized by the majority of the Allied and Associated Powers. In fact, it has only been recognized by the United States.

Clemenceau. If we have not recognized the Yugoslavs, it is out of regard for you. But today they are recognized in fact, since we presented to the German plenipotentiaries their credentials, with the name which they themselves give to their state.

Orlando. I do not know if that is equivalent to recognition.

Clemenceau. We are told that it is. Besides, what does it matter? You will be obliged one day or the other to recognize them also.

The Drafting Committee withdraws.

M. Tardieu is introduced.

Lloyd George. I asked that M. Tardieu be present, because I have already discussed with him the question about which I have to speak to you.

I received a telegram from General Allenby which gives me serious news. According to the Emir Faisal, the rumor in Damascus is that the commission of inquiry will not come to Syria and that a large French army is going to appear, under the command of General Gouraud.[1] A telegram from the Hedjaz says that, if the commission does not make its inquiry, and if Syria is given to France, there will be an uprising of all the Muslim populations, and that responsibility for the blood shed in the resistance of peoples who do not wish to allow themselves to be divided like livestock will fall back on the conference.

General Allenby's commentary on this news from an Arab source is that the situation is very serious and that he personally declines all responsibility. Unless you allow me to reassure Faisal and to tell him that the commission of inquiry is going to Syria, he will raise the Arabs against France and against us. The most immediate danger is for the British troops. We must decide without delay whether or not we are sending the commission, and I must be able to telegraph General Allenby this very day. If France does not think that she can participate in the inquiry, the American commissioners, who have already left, can take charge of it. As for myself, I am ready to leave the affair in their hands. In that case, I shall wire that we are ready to accept their conclusions. The situation is so grave that it is necessary to act without delay.

Clemenceau. My position is very clear. I am ready to send a mission to Syria when I know that the relief of British troops has begun. I do not believe that it is useful to send investigators there to see the population as it could be under the regime of the British occupation.

As for the dispatch of French troops, you know very well that I will not send a single man without being in entire agreement with you. At this very moment, two or three of our batallions are en route to Cilicia, where we no longer have direct interests, because General Allenby requests us to put them there. As soon as the relief has begun, I agree to send our representatives.

Lloyd George. Before acting as I am going to do, I thought it my duty to warn you. General Allenby says that, if we withdraw our troops, there will be immediate danger, and the Emir Faisal says that, if the French make their appearance, the country will revolt. I am going to read you the telegram which I propose to send to General Allenby.

Clemenceau. Its wording concerns only you.

Lloyd George. I insist upon informing you of what I am doing.

Reading of the text of the telegram, which announces the arrival of the commission of inquiry. The American members of that commission are already en route. France has not decided to participate in it.

Clemenceau. It should be added: "before the beginning of the relief." I insist that there be no ambiguity. I have nothing else to say.

Lloyd George. The British commissioners will not be sent to Syria
before those of the French government. I will add that that commission does not have the power to take decisions, but only to prepare a
report which will be submitted to us.

Will Italy send her commissioners to Syria?

Orlando. I will wait for the others.

Wilson. The American commission has already left.

Clemenceau. Mr. Lloyd George has just said that he will not send
anyone to Syria if our representatives do not go there.

Orlando. I will do the same thing as you.

Clemenceau. I will ask you to transmit to me the text of the telegram which you received from General Allenby and the Emir Faisal.

Lloyd George. Very well.

Wilson. I see in the amendments proposed to the treaty with Austria an article on historical properties which are claimed by the different nationalities. What is its scope?

Tardieu. Bohemia, for example, asks that she not be required to
reimburse Austria for the value of the castle of Prague, which is one
of her national properties. Poland likewise requests that her ownership of ancient Polish monuments be recognized, as well as that of
national forests.

Wilson. I do not believe that any of us can oppose that amendment.

Mantoux, II, 261-64.
¹ Gen. Henri Joseph Eugène Gouraud, involved in various French campaigns in Africa
before the war; commander of the French Fourth Army in the Champagne during most
of the war.

To Jan Christiaan Smuts

My dear General Smuts: Paris, 31 May, 1919.

No apologies were needed for your letter of yesterday. I appreciate
the gravity of the situation and thank you for the letter. I am glad to
say that I find my colleagues of the smaller Council quite willing to
re-study some of the conclusions formerly reached, and I hope that
the coming week may be fruitful of at least some important decisions.

Cordially and sincerely yours,   Woodrow Wilson

TLS (J. C. Smuts Papers, National Archives, Praetoria).

To Robert Howard Lord

My dear Professor Lord: Paris, 31 May, 1919.

   Thank you for the extracts from Lieutenant Foster's letter. I took great satisfaction in reading them to my colleagues.

                    Cordially and sincerely yours,   [Woodrow Wilson]

CCL (WP, DLC).

From Ignace Jan Paderewski

Mr. President,   Paris, May 31-st. 1919.

   Reports of various meetings in the United States, in protest at the treatment of the Jews in Poland have reached me.[1] The statements upon which these protests have been made are far from the truth.

   The Polish Government have had the opportunity of repeatedly stating the broad and tolerant views which we profess with regard to the Jewish population. We have proved more than once, that we do not pursue any anti-jewish policy.

   Owing to the war, which has created racial conflicts in all countries, not excluding Poland, some regret[t]able incidents have taken place in certain parts of the country, which, however, were but local transgressions, when compared with the daily massacres of the Jewish population in some parts of Russia. In most cases the provocative attitude of a fraction of the Jewish population was responsible for these incidents in Poland. Numberless articles published in the daily press, also bear a distinctly provocative character, and, whilst exciting public opinion, merely deepen the gulf of mutual resentment. The transgressions which took place in Poland have been severely condemned by the Government and the Nation.

   It would therefore be wronging both the Government and the Nation to give faith to the tendencious rumours which are being spread.

   I appeal to you, Mr. President, to put an end to this unworthy activity, by sending a special mission to Poland, in order to investigate and report on the true state of things, thus dispelling the accusations, under which my country is labouring.[2]

   Polish tradition has at all times been resplendent of the virtue of tolerance, at times, when this virtue was unknown in many other countries. My Nation, therefore, considers of vital necessity that these accusations should be wiped out by the unbiassed testimony of just men.

I have the honour to remain, Mr. President, with the highest regard,

Your obedient, humble servant   I J Paderewski

TLS (SDR, RG 256, 860C.4016/55, DNA).
   [1] See, e.g., JPT to WW, May 22, 1919, n. 1.
   [2] Wilson made two vertical markings along the left side of this paragraph.

Gilbert Fairchild Close to Herbert Clark Hoover, with Enclosure

My dear Mr. Hoover: Paris, 31 May, 1919.

The President has asked me to send to you the enclosed letter from Mr. Norman H. Davis with regard to the gold received from Germany in part payment of food supplies to them and at present stored at Amsterdam and Brussels. You will note that the President has indicated on the letter his approval.

Sincerely yours,   Gilbert F. Close

E N C L O S U R E

From Norman Hezekiah Davis

My dear Mr. President: Paris, May 29, 1919.

Mr. Hoover has received approximately $120,000,000 in gold from Germany in part payment of food supplied to them. This gold is at present stored at Amsterdam and Brussels, and Hoover has not been able to realize the dollars against this gold with which to reimburse himself for the food supplied. This has been due to delay pending negotiations for the conversion by which we hoped to avoid the necessity of shipping this gold to the United States. The delay is, however, very embarrassing to Hoover, because the Grain Corporation and the Commission for Relief in Belgium are having to borrow money in the United States pending liquidation of the gold.

We do not need the gold, and as it may, as you are aware, have a bad political effect for this gold to be shipped to the United States when the European gold reserves are so depleted, I am strongly of the opinion that arrangements should be made to avoid that necessity. We are hopeful of making such arrangements within the next two or three weeks, but in the meantime Hoover does not feel justified in continuing to carry the gold unless he can justify his action by having your sanction. If this does meet your approval, may I ask that you so advise Mr. Hoover?

I am, my dear Mr. President,

Faithfully yours,   Norman H. Davis

Approved   W.W.

TLS (Hoover Archives, CSt-H).

Gilbert Fairchild Close to Francis Patrick Walsh

My dear Mr. Walsh: Paris, 31 May, 1919.

I am writing on behalf of the President to acknowledge receipt of your letter of May 28th with the enclosed telegrams[1] and to say that I am bringing them to the President's attention.

Sincerely yours,   [Gilbert F. Close]

CCL (WP, DLC).
    [1] F. P. Walsh to WW, May 28, 1919, TLS (WP, DLC). Walsh enclosed thirty-one telegrams from individuals and organizations in the United States asking that the case for Irish independence be placed before the peace conference and protesting against Article X of the Covenant of the League of Nations. Some of these can be located in WP, DLC, by consulting the printed index to those papers under "Walsh, F. P." Others have been filed under the names of the individuals or organizations.
    In his covering letter, Walsh suggested that there were four basic reasons why the petitioners objected to Article X. Under it, nations and peoples "claiming age-old territorial integrities of their own" would be "forced under the authority of other nations or even kingdoms, without a hearing." Peoples devoted to the principles of free governments could be forced under the rule of "monarchies or military autocracies." The signatories of the Covenant, including the United States, would be bound under Article X "to prevent the giving of aid by outside advocates of liberty to oppressed nations, which practice has obtained among civilized peoples from time immemorial." Finally, the "powerful signatories," including the United States, might be "compelled to wage war, for the preservation of 'territorial integrity,' no matter how unjust and oppressive in any part of the world."
    Walsh suggested that the following sentence be added to Article X: "Provided, however, that the territorial boundaries of no country at the signing of the Covenant shall be deemed to include any other country or nation, the boundaries of which are natural ones, or clearly defined, inhabited by a homogeneous people, a majority of whom by a vote of its electorate has determined the form of government under which they desire to live, and whose efforts to establish the same and function thereunder are at the time of the signing hereof prevented by an army of occupation or any other form of forcible repression."

From William Shepherd Benson

My dear Mr. President: [Paris] 31 May 1919.

I am sending you herewith, copy of an informal letter from Rear-Admiral Bristol[1] which contains important information relative to the situation in Constantinople and vicinity. There are also enclosed reports from Captain Dayton,[2] commanding U.S.S. ARIZONA, and Dr. MacLachleen, President of one of the colleges at Smyrna;[3] and another from a Turkish source.[4] I have hesitated to forward these reports on account of their length, but if you can take the time to glance over them, I feel sure that the information you will gain will be well worth-while.

I feel so strongly that you have been misinformed or deliberately deceived, that I should especially invite your attention to these reports in order that you may see what the presence of our vessels at Smyrna has really meant.

I shall call on Captain Dayton to inform me whether he or any one made any protest against the outrages committed.

As a sufficient force of Greek soldiers has been landed to control the local situation, and as the continued presence of the ARIZONA will, in my opinion, simply tend to weaken or destroy our prestige in those waters, I respectfully suggest she be withdrawn.

If this meets with your approval, I suggest that she be sent to Constantinople for a short visit in order to show the flag at that place.

Awaiting further instructions, I have the honor to be,

Sincerely yours, W. S. Benson

TLS (WP, DLC).

[1] M. L. Bristol to W. S. Benson, May 20, 1919, TCL (WP, DLC). Bristol declared that the Greek occupation of Smyrna had set off great indignation in all parts of Turkey. He himself had been called upon by "Turks of all classes" and had received "hundreds of telegrams." The Turkish people despised the Greeks, and many had said, "Any nation but Greece" in regard to the occupation of Smyrna. Moreover, American prestige had been seriously damaged by the "apparent participation" of the United States in this occupation through the presence at Smyrna of the battleship *Arizona* and its accompanying destroyers. "It now becomes possible," Bristol said, "for anyone to say that we have joined with European countries in the partition of Turkey." The Turks argued that they had agreed to an Armistice on the basis of Point 12 of the Fourteen Points, and that they had been deceived. "I believe," he continued, "that we should not be drawn into any of the affairs of this part of the world. However, if we must become a mandatory, we should stand out for the whole of Turkey." He asserted that the Greeks were unable to rule any part of Turkey and that the Armenians were unable to govern themselves. Greeks, Armenians, and Turks were "all so mixed together" in Turkey that it would be impossible to create separate protectorates. Hence, it would be unwise for the United States to accept a mandate only over the Armenians.

[2] J. H. Dayton to M. L. Bristol, May 18, 1919, TLS (WP, DLC). Dayton gave a detailed report of the events surrounding the occupation of Smyrna, first by small Allied forces and later by a large force of Greek troops, between May 13 and May 18. Stressing the disorders that followed the landing of the Greeks on May 15, Dayton noted the "unnecessary killing" of numerous Turks, frequent cruelties toward others, and widespread looting and pillaging of Turkish property by both Greek troops and Greek civilians resident in Smyrna.

[3] Alexander MacLachlan to M. L. Bristol, May 18, 1919, TLS (WP, DLC). MacLachlan, president of International College in Smyrna, also gave a detailed account of the occupation of Smyrna. He highlighted the misdeeds of Greek soldiers and civilians.

[4] "STATEMENT REGARDING THE GREEK OCCUPATION OF SMYRNA FROM THE TURKISH MILITARY STANDPOINT," [c. May 18, 1919], T MS (WP, DLC). This account also emphasized Greek misbehavior toward unoffending Turkish soldiers and civilians. MacLachlan wrote on the first page: "From a most reliable source."

Gilbert Fairchild Close to William Shepherd Benson

My dear Admiral Benson: Paris, 31 May, 1919.

The President asks if you will not [be] good enough to acknowledge the attached message from Admiral Bristol[1] and request Admiral Bristol to say to the Ottoman Crown Prince that we have just consented to receive representatives of the Ottoman Empire for an interview here in Paris with regard to the interests of the Turkish people.   Sincerely yours,   [Gilbert F. Close]

CCL (WP, DLC).
    [1] M. L. Bristol to W. S. Benson, [c. May 29, 1919], T telegram (WP, DLC). Bristol reported that the Grand Vizier of Turkey, Damad Ferid Paşa, had asked for information about the "extent of occupation authorized Greeks at Smyrna, and surrounding country." "I earnestly recommend," Bristol continued, "some statement regarding Greek occupations or else occupation of Turkey by the associated military forces."

From Frederic Adrian Delano[1]

My dear Mr. President   Paris—May 31 [1919]
    Permit me to join others in a sincere expression of appreciation for the splendid tribute paid by you to our soldiers who have fallen in the Great War,—and most of all to thank you for what you said, so nobly and in such enduring terms, as to the aims of our Country in this World War.
    I am, my dear Mr. President,
                    Yours respectfully   Frederic A Delano

ALS (WP, DLC).
    [1] Former member of the Federal Reserve Board; at this time a lieutenant colonel in the Engineer Corps involved in the transport of American troops from France to the United States.

From Francis Patrick Walsh and Edward Fitzsimons Dunne

Dear Mr. President: Paris May 31, 1919
    We beg to advise you that, in pursuance of the commission given us by the Irish Race Convention held in the City of Philadelphia on February 22, 1919,[1] and following our letter to you of April 16, 1919,[2] every effort has been made to obtain a hearing for the delegates selected by the people of Ireland to represent them at the Peace Conference. Our information is that the government of Great Britain has definitely denied safe conducts to these representatives, and hence they cannot appear before the Peace Conference or any committee thereof.
    The resolutions and instructions under which we are acting provide that, if opportunity be not given the regularly chosen representatives of Ireland, we should ourselves present her case; her insistence upon her right of self-determination; and to international

recognition of the republican form of government established by her people.

We therefore petition you to use your good offices to secure a hearing for us before the Special Committee of the Four Great Powers, so that we may discharge the duty imposed upon us by our Convention.

In order to avoid misunderstanding we desire to state, and would thank you to convey the information to the other members of your Committee, that we do not hold, or claim to have, any commission or authority from the people of Ireland or their representatives; but desire solely and respectfully to present the resolutions of the American Convention with a brief argument in support thereof.

May we also point out that while the Convention which we represent was unofficial, and while we claim no official authority in the governmental sense, nevertheless, it was a Convention composed of 5,132 delegates, democratically selected, representing every State in the American Union; and the individuals who composed it may fairly be said to have been men and women of all shades of political opinion, of all religious sects, and of practically every trade, profession and avocation which go to make up our National life.

We think it is likewise fair to state that this Convention acted for many millions of our fellow-citizens, who, in this representative way, respectfully urge you to give favorable response to the request of this petition.

We will deeply appreciate it if you will be good enough to give us an early reply to this letter, as the matter of our departure for home is pressing us.

With considerations of our continued great respect and esteem, we are,   Sincerely,   Frank P. Walsh,   Chairman
                                                     E. F. Dunne

TLS (WP, DLC).
  [1] About which, see G. Creel to WW, March 31, 1919, n. 1, Vol. 56.
  [2] F. P. Walsh *et al.* to WW, April 16, 1919, Vol. 57.

Alexander Comstock Kirk to Gilbert Fairchild Close

My dear Mr. Close: Paris, May 31st, 1919.

The attached documents[1] regarding the desire of the Provisional Government of the Republic of Korea to be heard by the Peace Conference have been left at the Hotel Crillon and although they appear to be copies of letters and documents already sent, I am forwarding them to you at the request of our Far Eastern Division.

You will note that one of the documents is addressed directly to the President.[2]   Very sincerely yours,   A. C. Kirk

TLS (WP, DLC).
    [1] Korean Delegation to Peace Conference, THE CLAIM OF THE KOREAN PEOPLE AND NATION FOR LIBERATION FROM JAPAN AND FOR THE RECONSTRUCTION OF KOREA AS AN INDEPENDENT STATE:PETITION and *Memorandum*, both April 1919, printed documents (WP, DLC). Both documents discussed in detail the history of the Japanese annexation of Korea and the reasons why this union should be ended and Korea should again become an independent nation.
    [2] Kim Kyu-sik [John Kiusic Soho Kimm] to WW, May 12, 1919, TCL (WP, DLC). Kim used this covering letter to call Wilson's attention to the documents cited in n. 1 by reiterating several of the more striking arguments for Korean independence that they made.

From the Diary of Colonel House

May 31, 1919.

Following what I said yesterday concerning the President's actions not squaring with his words, he made a speech today at the Plenary Conference in which he said in reply to the Roumanian Prime Minister's pleas for the rights of small nations, that they practically had not rights about certain matters, but that the great powers should determine their course of action because the great powers, in the event of war, would carry the burden, and that they, the great powers, must of necessity lay down the principles of peace. He not only said that, but he wished care taken that the proceedings of the Plenary Conference should not become public. Consider this action with the nobility of his Memorial Day Address of yesterday and one can see why the question is so constantly asked whether his talk means anything at all. His oratory is so great, and he is so convincing that he has been able to sway the multitudes in nearly all lands. But if he is not careful, the feeling of distrust for him will become universal.

. . . The Germans are giving us an example of open diplomacy. They print the Treaty as soon as it is given them, and we are getting in Paris the German edition. It is being sold in Germany and Holland and nearby countries at a ridiculously low price, something like fifty cents a copy. Nevertheless, be it remembered, the United States Senate has never seen the Treaty as a whole, and the President and George have insisted that it shall not be given out. I do not understand the President's position. It is doing him irreparable injury. What news our press obtains is largely from me at our afternoon meetings. They believe, I take it, that I give them this information with the President's sanction, but as a matter of fact, I give it in spite of his disapproval. Now that Hankey sits in with the Council of Four a *proces verbal* is issued. The British Delegation get this, so also do the French, but the President is careful that his American colleagues do not. I have never seen a copy of it. Hankey proposed sending it down to me, but the President vetoed it by saying he was afraid to let it come to the Crillon because there were so many newspaper men around.

The Commissioners held a meeting this morning to determine what to do with the Irish-American Delegation's request for a hearing. The President sat with us for awhile. We determined not to see them officially in the matter about which they desire a hearing, for the reason we do not feel that we have a right to ask a foreign government to permit its own subjects to come to Paris, particularly when this foreign government has representatives here at the Peace Conference. We decided we would see the Irish Americans unofficially and separately. I urged the President to see them and give them a final talk. I thought if he would tell them that if it had not been for their actions while in Ireland, it is probable the British Government would have permitted the so-called "Irish Republic Delegates" to come to Paris.

We had a conference with the Jugoslavs. They brought a refusal to our proposals of yesterday. They called their reply "a concession" but as far as any of us could see, it meant that within three years the whole of the Dalmatian Coast, Istria and the Islands would go to Jugoslavia. They had worked out a careful plan by which after three years and a plebe[s]cite it would be certain to go to them. They did not leave a single loophole for the Italians to win. When I told the President this, he declared they were right. Here is one place he is determined to enforce the Fourteen Points to the limit. His prejudice is coming into full play with the Italians. He cannot do them even scant justice. It is shown every day in directions other than in the Adriatic settlement.

From the Diary of Ray Stannard Baker

Saturday May 31st [1919]

The President made a very important statement of policy to-day at the Secret plenary session, at which the summary of the Austrian treaty was read to the allied powers, preparatory to the presentation of the treaty itself to the Austrians on Monday. The Roumanians, leading the smaller powers, have been more or less in revolt against the benevolent tutelage of the Great Powers. The immediate point at issue was the provision in the treaty for the protection of religious & political minorities (Jews especially) in the smaller states, such protection being guaranteed by the Great Powers. Roumania led the objection to this provision, arguing that it permitted interference by the Great Powers in the internal affairs of the weaker ones. In response the President made a very important speech, in which he set forth clearly for the first time a policy which has been developing from the beginning—that the Great Powers, by virtue of their military & economic strength must necessarily bear the chief burden of maintaining the peace of the world, that if they accepted this responsibility they must assure themselves of the basis upon which it rested. He laid down the principle, "Where the great force lies there must be the sanction of peace"

This, in bold outline, was the position taken by the President, as he told me about it this evening. I urged him to let me put out a verbatim copy of his speech, urging its great importance, but he is not yet ready to do it, though I have a copy at hand.

(Again it appears that the world in future is not to be governed by a democratic society of equal nations, but dominated by a powerful group of great powers with benevolent intentions! Apparently he restores the sanction of force.)

I asked the President what was done at his meeting with the American Commissioners this morning.

"We discussed the Irish question," he said, warning me that nothing was to be made public about it.

He spoke of these "mischief makers," Walsh & Dunne & the trouble they were endeavoring to stir up in America.

"I have one weapon I can use against them—one terrible weapon, which I shall not use unless I am driven to it," he said, "unless it appears that the Irish movement has forgotten to be American in its interest in a foreign controversy."

He paused, and then said,

"I have only to warn our people of the attempt of the Roman Catholic hierarchy to dominate our public opinion, & there is no doubt about what America will do."

He said later:

"I think I will see Walsh & Dunne & tell them exactly what a position they have put themselves in, & that if necessary I shall go home & tell the public how they destroyed their usefulness through their own indiscretion & unwisdom."

He is evidently much disturbed by the rise of Irish-American feeling in America.

From this the discussion shifted to the treaty itself & I could not help saying exactly what I thought: that it was an unworkable treaty. "If the economic clauses are enforced, there is no hope of collecting the reparations. The two clauses are mutually destructive."

"I told Lloyd George & Clemenceau as much when we had it under discussion, but there was no changing them."

I observed that Lloyd-George seemed now inclined to modify the treaty.

"Yes, he is hearing from his own liberals."

I said that the liberals & working groups everywhere in the world were attacking the treaty.

"It has had good support in the United States."

"Yes," I said, "but they do not know what is in it."

"They have had the summary."

"But it gives no such cumulative impression as the reading of the treaty itself."

He asked me if I thought our people were interested in the details

"Not now," I said, "but they will be later. When your enemies in the Senate, Mr. President, begin to attack the League of Nations they will want to examine the basis upon which it rests & what it is they are guaranteeing—& that will mean a close scrutiny of the treaty."

I am afraid I pushed the argument too far, for the President arose & made an end of the conversation. At least I cleared my own mind & expressed my own doubts.

It is plain that at every point the President is thinking of American public opinion.

Charles Seymour to His Family

[Paris] May 31, 1919

I failed to get this off when I meant to, so I will add a postscript. The question of the southern frontiers of Austria, about Klagenfurt, which gave rise to so much trouble has been settled and my point of view, with slight modifications, is accepted by the big Four and will go into the treaty. It is a great satisfaction to me and a personal triumph as I had the French, British, and Italian delegates on the territorial commission opposed to me as well as Johnson.[1] But Wilson backed my point of view and persuaded Lloyd George and Clemenceau. We learned of the decision Thursday morning when several of us were summoned to Wilson's house where the Council of Four were meeting. We sat around in the big room upstairs before the fire-place for half an hour, the Four being down stairs. Then Lloyd George came in and said: "Well we've settled it." Orlando came in with his impassive unexpressionless face and Clemenceau in his grey gloves. Wilson appeared looking very brisk and smiling, and said, "Gentlemen, my colleagues have asked me to tell you of our decision." We went into the next room where the floor was clear and Wilson spread out a big map (made in our office) on the floor and got down on his hands and knees behind it to show what had been done; most of us were also on our hands and knees. I was in the front row and felt someone pushing me, and looked around angrily to find it was Orlando, on *his* hands and knees crawling like a bear towards the map. I gave way and he was soon in the front row. I wish that I could have had a picture of the most important men in the world on their hands and knees over this map. The Italians were not entirely satisfied with the decision and I was interested to see how Wilson parried their objections, very genial but understanding the significance of their points and not yielding. I was also interested that he should be the man of the Four to explain what had been done. More and more the feeling on the inside of the Conference is that he is the biggest man here. Lloyd George is strong by reason of his magnetism and his cleverness, but he lacks background,—is really uneducated. Clemenceau is hampered by his old traditions from which he can never get away. Moreover he feels I think that his chief work is now done, when the frontiers of France are settled and the proportion of French drafts on the indemnities fixed. So he is content in staying in the background. Naturally it has been to his advantage to keep in the background entirely so far as Adriatic questions are concerned. As soon as we had received the decision of the Four we hurried around to the Foreign Office to draft the clauses for the treaty which was to have been handed to the Austrians the next day. We went over again in the afternoon and had a look in at the secret plenary session, which ended a few minutes after it was called, when Bratiano demanded that time be given to the little Powers concerned to look over the treaty. Clemenceau was rather peeved, but it was a reasonable request and had to be granted. So it is likely that the treaty will not get to the Austrians until Monday or Tuesday. In the meantime I have been working over the proofs of the treaty, checking up errors and alterations. The Italians are apt to slip something in at the last moment, have done that, in at least one instance, which might not be noticed. They are slick! . . .

Lots of love, C.

TLI (C. Seymour Papers, CtY).
    [1] That is, Douglas Wilson Johnson.

INDEX

NOTE ON THE INDEX

THE alphabetically arranged analytical table of contents at the front of the volume eliminates duplication, in both contents and index, of references to certain documents, such as letters. Letters are listed in the contents alphabetically by name, and chronologically within each name by page. The subject matter of all letters is, of course, indexed. The Editorial Notes and Wilson's writings are listed in the contents chronologically by page. In addition, the subject matter of both categories is indexed. The index covers all references to books and articles mentioned in text or notes. Footnotes are indexed. Page references to footnotes which place a comma between the page number and "n" cite both text and footnote, thus: "418,n1." On the other hand, absence of the comma indicates reference to the footnote only, thus: "59n1"—the page number denoting where the footnote appears.

The index supplies the fullest known form of names and, for the Wilson and Axson families, relationships as far down as cousins. Persons referred to by nicknames or shortened forms of names can be identified by reference to entries for these forms of the names.

All entries consisting of page numbers only and which refer to concepts, issues and opinions (such as democracy, the tariff, and money trust, leadership, and labor problems), are references to Wilson's speeches and writings. Page references that follow the symbol Δ in such entries refer to the opinions and comments of others who are identified.

Four cumulative contents-index volumes are now in print: Volume 13, which covers Volumes 1-12, Volume 26, which covers Volumes 14-25, Volume 39, which covers Volumes 27-38, and Volume 52, which covers Volumes 40-49 and 51.

INDEX

Academy of Moral and Political Science (Paris): WW's address mentioned, 3; WW's address to, 4-6

A.C.N.P.: *see* American Commission to Negotiate Peace

Adalia, Turkey, 41, 42, 43, 55, 101, 147, 226, 250, 268, 269, 270, 373, 375

Addams, Jane, 117, 189, 450n2

Aden, 88, 102

Adenauer, Konrad, 401n4, 433,n2

Adrianople, 400

Adriatic question, 34, 35, 144, 160, 173-74, 603; Andrews on conditions in Fiume and Trieste, 64-66, 241-42; Page's urgent request to see WW on, 67; Herron on, 68n2; House on, 68, 126, 127, 174, 200-201, 478, 555; D.H. Miller and Cellere discuss, 71-72, 249-50; D.H. Miller's "Definitive Solution," 83,n3; Council of Four on, 85-94, 94-103, 260-61, 502-509, 564-66; WW on, 94-95, 96, 96-97, 329, 339, 552, 574; D.H. Miller meets with Orlando on, 81-84, 125-26,n1, 127; WW tells story of his father's, as comparison to present proposals on, 248, 255; and Italy's insistence on Treaty of London, 478, 479, 480; Lansing on U.S. not withdrawing from peace conference because of, 480-81; R.S. Baker on, 551-52; Tardieu plan, 555,n1, 556-59, 559, 569-71; and issue of islands, 557, 558, 559, 569, 570; and Yugoslavia, 645; *see also* under the names of the specific geographical areas, such as Dalmatia; Fiume

Adriatic Sea: Council of Four on tonnage in, 50-54

aerial warfare: and League of Nations Covenant, 379-80

aeronautics: first transatlantic flight, 576,n1

Afghanistan, 97-98, 326, 337

Aga Khan III (Aga Sultan Sir Mohammed Shah), 87,n4, 97, 98, 207n1

Aharonian, Avetis, 103-104

Aidin (now Aydin), Turkey, 99,n4, 101, 102, 140,n6, 268, 270,n5, 375, 595-96, 613

Aivali, Turkey: *see* Ayvalik, Turkey

Albania, 186, 492, 556, 558, 559, 565

Albrecht-Carrié, René, 61n6, 125n1

Alby, Henri Marie Camille Edouard, 213n2, 324, 354, 531,n5; on Polish-Ukrainian conflict, 323,n4

alcoholic beverages: and taxation, 294

Aldrovandi Marescotti, Luigi, Count of Viano, 213, 257, 435

Alexandretta (now Iskenderun, Turkey), 139, 334, 344

Alexandroupolis, Greece: *see* Dedeagach, Bulgaria

Algeciras, Act of, 498,n2

Alien Property Custodian, 449,n2

Allenby, Sir Edmund Henry Hynman, 139, 345, 369; and Syria, 632, 633, 635-36, 637

Allen, Corporal, 621,n2

Almond, Nina, 60n3

Alsace-Lorraine, 51; Germany on, 581

America as a Mandatory (New York *World*), 524,n5

American Commissioners Plenipotentiary to Negotiate Peace (Wilson, Lansing, Bliss, House, White), 35, 72-74, 286, 286-87, 406, 549, 573; Lansing and R.S. Baker on, 285

American Commission for Irish Independence, 393, 549,n1

American Commission to Negotiate Peace, 237, 317, 349n1, 403n2; and protests from South Tyrol, 348,n1,2; on discussing Germany's proposals under WW's guidance, 546, 546-47; WW agrees to meet with Commissioners on German proposals, 594; and Irish issue, 645, 646

American Jewish Congress, 150

American Jewish Joint Distribution Committee, 411n1

American Jewish Relief Committee, 445

American Relief Administration in Finland, 466n6

Amet, Jean François Charles, 26,n7,27

Anatolia: mandatory issue and, 88, 89, 92, 98, 99, 101, 102, 140, 202, 257, 258, 259, 327, 328, 330, 331, 337, 344, 371; Council of Four on, 142-44,n7; Balfour memorandum on Italy and Turkey in, 208, 209-12; WW on, 335, 340, 345, 374, 375-76

Andrews, Philip: on conditions in Fiume and Trieste, 64-66, 119-20, 241,n1, 241-42

Antalya, Turkey: *see* Adalia

Antwerp, Belgium, 289

Aosta, Duke of (Emanuele Filiberto di Savoia), 64,n3

Arabia, 373

Archangel, Russia, 152; *see also* Russia— Murmansk and Archangel, intervention in

Archiwum Polityczne Ignacego Paderewskiego (Janowska et. al., eds.), 216n5

Argunov, Andrei Aleksandrovich: 156,n4

Arizona, U.S.S., 252, 640,n1, 641

Armenia: and mandate issue, 89, 91, 99, 100, 101, 137, 140, 146, 184, 185, 327, 328, 330, 337, 340, 341, 345, 373, 476, 640n1; WW on suffering in, 103-104; WW on mandates and, 137, 335, 374, 376; Bryce on, 401

Armistice, 135

Armistice Commission, 255-56

arms limitation: Council of Four on, 429-32, 439-40; and Russia, 442; Germany on, 581

Army (U.S.): *see* United States Army

Asia Minor, 45, 91, 102; Italian invasion of, 208-209, 223-25, 225-26, 246, 250-51, 561, 565; Council of Four on mandates or division of, 257-61, 326-36; Clemenceau-Lloyd George conflict over mandatories in, 331-33, 334, 369, 369-70, 370,n1; WW on Lloyd George's proposal on U.S. as mandate for, 335; Lloyd George on U.S. being mandatory for, 336-39; Westermann interview with WW on, 374-76; WW on, 493;

ister to Denmark, 512,n1; T.N. Page on his
resignation, 517

FAMILY AND PERSONAL LIFE

number thirteen, 79; on student days at
Princeton, 40; Seymour on attitudes of,
158-59; maternal ancestors, 190,n3; receives volume and copy of portrait of his an-
cestor Robert Wodrow, 190; rearranges furniture, 245; on summers spent bicycling in
Scotland, 247-48; attributes story to his father, 248, 255; R.S. Baker on literary taste
of, 368; concern over EBW's foot infection,
477; on Fred Yates' death, 526; writes news
to Jessie, 526; unable to attend class reunion at Princeton, 604-605,n1; wishes to
know taxes on his salary, 604; nervous before and after speeches, 621, 622

HEALTH

Senator Gerry on, 124; morning walks, 288-
89, 453; headache, 321; poor vision, 453;
Grayson urges extra rest, 477; memory
lags, 574n1; tired, 574,n1; twitch on left
side of face, 574,n1

OPINIONS AND COMMENTS

There is one thing which does not excite the
jealousy of nations against one another.
That is the distinction of thought, the distinction of literature, the achievement of
the mind. Nations have always cheered one
another in these accomplishments rather
than envied one another, 4; on German
scholarship, 5,n2; my studies in the field of
political science, Sir, have been hardly
more than my efforts as a public man. They
have constituted an attempt to put into the
words of learning the thoughts of a nation,
the attitude of a people towards public affairs, 5; The greatest freedom of speech
was the greatest safety, because if a man is
a fool, the best thing to do is to encourage
him to advertise the fact by speaking, 5; on
Germany's objections to treaty, 12; on Russian situation, 29, 29-30, 31; on medical
specialist versus general practitioner, 79;
on his father as his best teacher, 162; on
German treaty, 187-88; on mandates,
207n1; on Jews and minority rights in Poland, 218, 219, 220, 221; America has a
great and honorable service to perform in
bringing the commercial and industrial undertakings of the world back to their old
scope and swing again, and putting a solid
credit under them. All our legislation
should be friendly to such plans and purposes, 293; has no regrets over not having a
Russian policy, 301-302, 311; I fear being
misquoted, or interviewed: and if I talk
freely, I do not know how to be discreet,
317; against U.S. mandate in Anatolia,

344-45; on women's fashions, 454; on Adriatic question and Treaty of London, 479,
503-506, 507, 552, 574; on Treaty of London as "infamous bargain," 479; It is better
to separate the question of Asia Minor from
the question of the Adriatic. For the peace
of the world, I believe that Italy must remain outside of Asia Minor, 493; the chief
anxiety I have had has been to be the true
interpreter of a national spirit, expressing
no private and particular views but trying to
express the general spirit of a nation, 520;
We, among other friends of liberty, are asking the world to unite in the interest of
brotherhood and mutual service and the
genuine advancement of individual and
corporate liberty throughout the world.
Therefore, we must set the example, 521;
on need to return to U.S. as soon as possible, 552; Our thoughts and purpose now
are consecrated to the maintenance of the
liberty of the world and of the union of its
peoples in a single comradeship of liberty
and right, 571; These men did not come
across the sea merely to defeat Germany
and her associated powers in the war. They
came to defeat forever the things for which
the Central Powers stood, 607; I look for the
time when every man who now puts his
counsel against the united service of mankind under the League of Nations will be
just as ashamed of it as if he now regretted
the union of the states, 608; The League of
Nations is the covenant of governments
that these men shall not have died in vain,
609; There is something better, if possible,
that a man can give than his life, and that is
his living spirit to a service that is not easy,
to resist counsels that are hard to resist, to
stand against purposes that are difficult to
stand against, and to say, "Here stand I,
consecrated in spirit to the men who were
my comrades and who are now gone, and
who have left me under eternal bonds of fidelity," 610; We must not close our eyes to
the fact that in the last analysis the military
and naval strength of the Great Powers will
be the final guarantee of the peace of the
world, 629

RECREATION

plays cards, 3, 48, 369, 420, 606; motor rides,
39-40, 78, 124, 161, 248, 253, 254, 289,
371, 419, 420, 453, 479, 528, 553, 554, 577,
606, 625; visit to Longchamps race track,
124; motor ride through Paris, 186-87; attends theatrical performance given by U.S.
troops, 207; on summers spent bicycling in
Scotland, 247-48; visits Barbizon, 248-49;
early morning walks, 288-89, 321, 370,
453, 527; enjoys watching people, 453-54;
motors to Fontainebleau, 477; attends performance of play, 627-28